HUMAN WORDS

Human Words

THE COMPLEAT UNEXPURGATED, UNCOMPUTERIZED HUMAN WORDBOOK

Containing herein the true unadulterated stories of more than 3,500 unique and remarkably eponymous personalities: saints and sinners, losers and winners, lovers and hate-mongers, murderers and masochists, scoundrels, scalawags and saviors ... that have given their names to the language.

ROBERT HENDRICKSON

CHILTON BOOK COMPANY

PHILADELPHIA   NEW YORK   LONDON

Library of Congress Cataloging in Publication Data

Hendrickson, Robert, 1933–
   Human words.

   Bibliography: p.
   1.   English language—Eponyms—Dictionaries.
I.   Title.
PE1596.H4   423'.1   72-6492
ISBN   0-8019-5697-8

To My Mother and Father

Eunice (from the Greek meaning "happy victory"; "the unfeigned faith that is in thee; which dwelt . . . in thy . . . mother Eunice."—*Second Epistle of St. Paul.*)

Oscar (Anglo-Saxon for "power of godliness," or Celtic for "warrior.")

HUMAN WORDS

garrison finish—to mention just a few unusual examples. Even common fish like *guppies* and *mollies* are named after actual persons; a hangman gave his name to the *derrick;* there was one monarch who had his forename become a synonym for female breasts; great cities honor a horse and a dog; one wily emperor named *five* cities for his mother; and at least six notables saw their names become synonyms for chamber pots or toilets.

Human Words has been designed both for the general reader with a love for words and history and as a reference work that should be of particular value to the student. Practically no historical period has been neglected in the general scheme and every discipline from aeronautics to zoology is covered, the abundant cross references affording a valuable teaching tool. Care has been taken to provide the general outlines of each man's life, including in every case all the important dates, but in this emphasis on accuracy, the "fatufactophile," or lover of nutty facts, has not been forgotten. Where stories are likely apocryphal, they are labeled so, but no good story is omitted merely because it is untrue.

As for the true tales, readers will be pleased or dismayed to learn of the fish dish named after the curly locks of a poet, the lock of a queen's hair that became a comet, the queen with hair between her breasts, the blind monk who put the bubbles in champagne, the prince who may have been Jack the Ripper, the genius who went back to college at seventy-five, the virgins who were buried alive when they didn't remain so, the baseball bat named after a king, the lawyer who bared his voluptuous client's breasts to a jury to prove several points, and the ship's captain who carried his severed ear around in a case and caused a war over it. Then there is the botanist who coined thousands of words still in the dictionaries, the ancestor of the Marquis de Sade who was probably the model for Petrarch's Laura, yarns about Madame Pompadour and most other *les grand horizontals*, the cake that inspired Proust to write his immortal *À la Recherche du Temps Perdu*, and the real mouse that became Mickey Mouse. Note is also made of the reason why George

Washington grew marijuana at Mount Vernon, the man with gall enough to take the title *King of the World*, the gourmet who never spent less than five hundred dollars on his "everyday meals," the real Moby Dick, and the man who invented the & sign. The reader shall additionally be enlightened about how the original Santa Claus got his start by aiding three girls sold to a brothel, as well as the "Sinner's Bible" whose seventh commandment reads "Thou shalt commit adultery," the real Adam's apple tree, the "Essay on Silence" that contained no words, the city named for a boxer, the eponymous anagrams that have become words, and the only human word deriving from the name of a man spelled backwards. Odd flower facts have been given special attention and vendors of words will be surprised and perhaps inspired to know that Edgar Allan Poe received only ten dollars for "The Raven," that the *Atlantic Monthly* paid Mrs. Howe just four dollars for the lyrics to "The Battle Hymn of the Republic," that Ernest Thayer got but five dollars for "Casey at the Bat," and that George Bernard Shaw made only twenty dollars in his first nine years of writing.

Our eponymous personalities are indeed often more fascinating than the words fashioned from them. We meet the three English greats who died after falling off their horses, the legendary soldier who literally perished of a broken heart, the several notables who met their ignominious ends when rocks fell on their heads, and the moneylender-miser who had molten silver poured down his throat. Then there was the very British Lord Raglan, who testily demanded his arm back from the surgeons who had amputated it because it contained the wedding ring his wife had given him; the poet Keats, who wrote his "Ode on a Grecian Urn" after viewing a doubly fake Grecian vase; and that gourmet of gourmets Brillat-Savarin, who carried game and fish around in his pockets until it obtained a high flavor. . . . All people who saw their prenoms or patronyms become synonymous for one thing or another. Probably no greater honor, or indignity, can be accorded a person than having her or his name become a living

INTRODUCTION

Eponym, *n.* (Greek *eponymous,* given as a name, surnamed; *epi,* upon, and *onyma,* a name.)

1. a real or mythical person from whose name the name of a nation, institution, thing, etc., is derived or is said to have been derived.   *Webster's*

As the title indicates, I have tried to make this the most complete book of its kind in English: to include the story of every real person, group of people, or animal endowed with human characteristics whose name has become part of the language. Needless to say, the last hope represented an abysmal ignorance of the number of eponyms that grace or disgrace the pages of our dictionaries. From *Methuselah* to *Mae West,* from *namby-pamby* to *sadism,* these number in the tens of thousands and space alone makes a complete list impossible. Still, I believe I am justified in saying that this is the most comprehensive work of its kind, containing at least ten times as many "human words" as any previous collection. Unlike some scholarly safaris into this wide, wild jungle, I have not included fictional or mythological eponyms except where the fictional character in question is believed to be based on an actual person. Only real people were invited to this orgy of words, all fascinating in one way or another. Aside from that, the only limitations I have imposed are those of importance and interest. Where I know a word is commonly used, I have included it, no matter how prosaic the story behind it; but if a word seemed interesting or unusual enough, it has also been covered, no matter how obscure or how long obsolete. In this way, I believe, the complex relationship between man and language is much more clearly seen and history better served.

No word or phrase has been excised here because it might offend someone's sensibilities. I consider myself no judge of what is or is not obscene (for example, of a pair that did, see *bowdlerize* and *comstockery*) and such self-appointed lobotomizers of language have always reminded me of Vonnegut's dictator who eliminated noses in order to eliminate all odors. And so lovers and hatemongers, murderers and healers, heroes and traitors, pornographers and censors, gourmets and dieters . . . poets, scientists, zoologists, botanists, preachers, politicians, legislators, con men, inventors, destroyers . . . all and more varieties of eponyms vie for space on these pages, their deeds unexpurgated, their lives treated as briefly as possible in trying to capture the essence of the words their names became. Though no incandescent optimist, I can report with pleasure that this study reveals no more than about 10 percent of all eponymous words being derogatory in nature, indicating that good ultimately triumphs—if only because Jung's collective unconscious can bear just so many Hitlers and Torquemadas, or Bluebeards and Jack the Rippers. The extent of our namesakes will probably surprise you, as it did me. Friends suggesting eponyms like Louis Loophole, prominent income tax lawyer, Quentin Quibble, constant reader, and Fred de Foliant, Vietnamese botanist, were surprised to learn that there lived a real lawyer named Shyster (Scheuster, anyway), a labor spy named Albert Fink, and a Joe Dun who hounded debtors. This is not to mention the human counterparts for *billingsgate, bloomers, B.V.D.'s, fanny, hooker, condum, Lady Godiva, Peeping Tom, lush, grog, hootch, booze, Kickapoo joy juice, hooligan, hood, yegg, piker, ritzy, czar, slave, O.K., Uncle Sam, monkey wrench, teddy bear, fudge, pickle, gaga, josh,* and part of the language, and some of these names have lasted as words since centuries before the first dictionaries were written. I hope I have done them all justice, from *A-1* to *Zyrian*.

The obvious debts for a work of this length are so numerous that they must be confined to the bibliography. Especially valuable, however, were the incomparable *Oxford English Dictionary*, H. L. Mencken's *American Language*, and all of the pioneering works of Professor Ernest Weekley and Eric Partridge, who is without question a one man *O.E.D.* On a more personal note, I would like to thank my editor, John Marion, for his kind help and the extensions granted me to do a thorough job. As for my wife, Marilyn, this book is as much hers as mine. In the course of writing it I have uncovered further evidence that her name is a synonym for good, kind, loving and beautiful and all the words appropriate under 897 in *Roget's*.

February 28, 1971
Far Rockaway, N.Y.

A

A-1, A-1 at Lloyd's, Lloyd's of London
A-1, for anything excellent, first class, originated with the expression *A-1 at Lloyd's,* referring to the rating of ships in *Lloyd's Register. Lloyd's of London,* the world-famous insurance association, has insured everything from the first airplane and zaftig Hollywood sex symbols to John Glenn as America's first astronaut, but wrote only marine insurance at its inception. *Lloyd's* takes its name from a coffeehouse operated by Edward Lloyd, the earliest record of whom is in 1688 and who died in 1713. For travelers, Lloyd served as a sort of one-man tourist bureau and there is even evidence that he would fix the press gang who shanghaied men into the naval service—for a price. Virtually nothing else is known about the elusive enterprising Lloyd except that businessmen willing to insure against sea risks congregated at his coffeehouse on Lombard Street and issued marine policies to shipowners. Here *Lloyd's List,* a paper devoted to shipping news, was published in 1734, making it the oldest London newspaper excepting the London *Gazette.* By 1760 the precursor of *Lloyd's Register of Shipping* had been printed and only fifteen years later the phrase *A-1* was used in its pages to denote the highest class of ship, novelist Charles Dickens first applying *A-1* to people and things in 1837. *Lloyd's,* now international in scope, eventually moved to the Royal Exchange and finally to its present $15-million palace on Lime Street. It adopted its name legally when incorporated a century ago, not long before writing the first burglary insurance (1889). *Lloyd's* also wrote the first policy covering loss of profits resulting from fire and pioneered in automobile and workman's compensation insurance. The corporation can issue anything but long-term life insurance. Rather than an insurance company, it is a corporate group of some 300 syndicates composed of about 5,500 strictly supervised individual underwriters, each of whom must deposit large sums—about $35,000—as security against default on the risks each accepts. *Lloyd's* name has been adopted by several foreign shipping companies having no connection with it. Although the group did not write the first marine policy—this dating back to a Florentine policy issued in 1501—its name is synonymous with marine insurance and *Lloyd's* has long pioneered in setting maritime standards and safety measures. *Lloyd's* prime concern is still shipping insurance and it boasts that its agents watch every mile of seacoast throughout the world.

Three million dollars daily in premiums is taken in by *Lloyd's,* an underwriter of the 1880's named Cuthbert Bean having been mainly responsible for the group pioneering beyond marine insurance. Some interesting *Lloyd's* policies and losses in its risky history include:

• A $100,000 "love insurance" policy that provided payment if a certain photographer's model married (she did, but after the policy expired).

• A "happiness policy" that insured against "worry lines" developing on a model's face.

• Losses paid of $3,019,400 after the Lutine Bell rang over the rostrum announcing the *Titanic* disaster; more than $5.6 million on the *Andrea Doria*; $1,463,400 on the San Francisco earthquake; $110 million on Hurricane Carol in 1954.

• $22,400 worth of protection ($74 premium) against "death caused by accident" in the form of a falling sputnik.

• Policies insuring against the chances of having twins, one's golf opponent making a hole in one, war and peace, rained-out church socials, and losing one's lover.

• Betty Grable's legs insured for $250,-000; Jimmy Durante's nose, $140,000; a corporation executive's brain for an undisclosed amount; Flamenco dancer Jose Greco's special trousers insured against splitting at $980 a pair; Fred Astaire's legs for $650,000; Zorina's toes at $25,000 per; Abbott and Costello insured for $250,000 against disagreement over a five-year period; actress Julie Bishop, $25,000 against her gaining four inches around the hips or waist over a seven-year period; and a $250,000 policy on the forty-two-inch bust of an unnamed English actress.

• Risks turned down include a policy insuring the back teeth of an acrobat, who hung from them in her act, and the request by a European gentleman to insure his daughter's virginity.

Aaronical *Aaronic* or *Aaronical*—high priestly, pontifical—has the honor of being the first well-known "human word" in English. It derives from the name of the Biblical Aaron, traditional founder of the Jewish priesthood, who in company with Moses led the Israelites out of Egypt and later became the center of the entire Jewish ritual system—Moses representing Yahweh's secular powers and his brother Aaron his religious counterpart. Aaron is described as God's instrument in the *Exodus* miracles, yet he also made and took part in worship of the golden calf in Moses' absence. In fairness to Aaron it should be pointed out that some Biblical historians believe that *Moses* actually made the first golden calf, convinced that this was the device from under which God wished to be worshipped, and that a later generation turned this into the act of apostasy recounted in *Exodus*, blaming it on his brother.

Aaron Lily, Aaron's Beard, Aaron's Rod Numerous plants are named for the patriarch Aaron. Mention in *Psalms* (133) of "the beard of Aaron" led to *Aaron's beard* becoming the common name of the Rose of Sharon (which in the Bible is really a crocus), ivy-leaved toadflax, meadowsweet, *Aaron's-beard* cactus, and the Jerusalem star, among others, in reference to their beardlike flowers. *Aaron's rod* comes from the sa-cred rod that Aaron placed before the ark in *Numbers* (17:8), a rod which Jehovah caused to bud, blossom and bear ripe almonds. Many tall-stemmed, flowering plants resembling rods, such as mullein, goldenrod and garden orpine, are called *Aaron's rod*, and the term is used in architecture to describe an ornamental moulding entwined with sprouting leaves, a serpent or scrollwork. The *Aaron lily* also honors Aaron, but the name derives from the folk etymology of *arum lily*.

Aaron's Serpent *Aaron's serpent*, a force so powerful as to eliminate all other powers, alludes to the miracle in *Exodus* (8:10–12) when the Lord commanded that Aaron cast down his rod before Pharaoh: "*Then Pharaoh summoned the wise men and the sorcerers; and they also, the magicians of Egypt, did the same by their secret acts. For every man cast down his rod, and they became serpents. But Aaron's rod swallowed up their rods.*"

Linguists have found that the word *tannen* given in the *Exodus* sources really means "reptile," but there is no chance that *Aaron's reptile* will replace *Aaron's serpent* in the language.

Abassi Though of interest only to collectors, the *abassi* is the first of many coins named after famous persons. It is a silver piece worth about twenty-nine cents that was formerly used in Persia and it honors Shah Abas II.

Abigail A lady's maid or servant is sometimes called an *abigail*, which means "source of joy" in Hebrew. Several real Abigails contributed their names to the word. The term originates in the Bible (*Samuel* 25) when Nabal's wife, Abigail, apologizes for her wealthy husband's selfishness in denying David food for his followers—humbly referring to herself as David's "handmaid" six times in the course of eight short chapters. David must have appreciated this, for when Nabal died, he made Abigail one of his wives. The name and occupation were further associated when Francis Beaumont and John Fletcher's *The Scornful Lady*, written about five years after the King James version of the Bible (1611), gave the name Abigail to a spirited "waiting gentlewoman," one of the play's leading characters. *Abigail* was thereafter used by many writers, including Congreve, Swift, Fielding and Smollet, but only came to be spelled without a capital when popularized by the notoriety of Abigail Hill, Queen Anne's lady-in-waiting, 1704–14. Mrs. Masham, as she is better known in history, used her friendship with the queen to curry favors that included an important military appointment for her brother, a peerage for her husband, and the office of keeper of the privy purse for Abigail Hill. Spirited she was, though a servant mostly to herself.

Abram, Abraham Man, Abraham's Bosom *Abram*, or *Abraham man*, a synonym for beggar, can be traced to the parable in *Luke* (16:19–31), where *"the beggar (Lazarus) died and was carried into Abraham's bosom."* But it may derive from the Abraham Ward in England's Bedlam asylum, whose inmates were allowed out on certain days to go begging. *In Abraham's bosom* is an expression for the repose of the happy in death, deriving from the same source. (See also *Beggar; Lazarus*.)

According to Cocker *According to Cocker*, an English proverb similar to the four *According to* entries following, means very accurate or correct, according to the rules. *According to Cocker* could just as well mean "all wrong," however few authorities bother to mention this. The phrase honors Edward Cocker (1631–75), a London engraver who also taught penmanship and arithmetic. Cocker wrote a number of popular books on these subjects, and reputedly authored *Cocker's Arithmetick*, which went through 112 editions, its authority giving rise to the proverb. Then in the late nineteenth century, documented proof was offered showing that Cocker did not write the famous book at all, that it was a forgery of his editor and publisher, so poorly done that it set back rather than advanced the cause of elementary arithmetic. *Arithmetick* was first published in 1678, three years after Cocker died, and this seems to further substantiate the theory that it was designed to cash in on Cocker's name. Even the critic who cried forgery—Augustus de Morgan in his *Arithmetical Books* (1847)—noted that "This same Edward Cocker must have

had great reputation, since a bad book under his name pushed out the good ones."

According to Fowler Many disputes about proper English usage are settled with the words, "according to Fowler. . . ." The authority cited is Henry Watson Fowler (1858–1933), author of *A Dictionary of Modern English Usage* (1926). Fowler, a noted classicist and lexicographer, and his brother F. G. Fowler collaborated on a number of important books, including a one-volume abridgement of the *Oxford English Dictionary* (1911). But *Modern English Usage* is his alone. The book remains a standard reference work, though some of the old schoolmaster's opinions are debatable. Margaret Nicholson's *A Dictionary of American-English Usage*, based on *Fowler*, is its American counterpart.

According to Guinness, Guinness The Guinness family of Ireland has brewed its famous stout since 1820, their registered name synonymous with stout itself for over a century. Arthur Guinness, Son & Co., Ltd. of St. James Gate, Brewery, Dublin, has also published *The Guinness Book of Records* since 1955. Many arguments over a glass of *Guinness* have been settled by this umpire of record performances, which has inspired the contemporary expression, *According to Guinness. . .*

According to Gunter, Gunter's Chain, Gunter's Line, Gunter's Quadrant, Gunter's Scale All the practical inventions listed above, each still in use, were invented by the English mathematician and astronomer Edmund Gunter nearly four centuries ago. Gunter, a Welshman, was professor of astronomy at London's Gresham College from 1619 until his death five years later when only forty-five. In his short life he invented *Gunter's Chain*, the 22-yard-long, 100-link chain used by surveyors in England and the United States; *Gunter's Line*, the forerunner of the modern slide rule; the small portable *Gunter's Quadrant;* and *Gunter's Scale*, commonly used by seamen to solve navigation problems. Gunter, among other accomplishments, introduced the words *cosine* and *cotangent* and discovered the variation of the magnetic compass. His genius inspired the phrase *According to Gunter*, once as familiar in America as *According to Hoyle* is today.

According to Hoyle *A Short Treatise on the Game of Whist* by Englishman Edmond Hoyle, apparently a barrister and minor legal official in Ireland, was published in 1742. This was the first book to systemize the rules of whist and remained the absolute authority for the game until its rules were changed in 1864. The author also wrote *Hoyle's Standard Games*, which extended his range, has been republished hundreds of times, and is available in paperback today. The weight of his authority through these works led to the phrase *According to Hoyle* becoming not only a proverbial synonym for the accuracy of game rules, but an idiom for correctness in general. History tells us little about Hoyle, but he enjoyed his eponymous fame for many years, living until 1769, when he died at ninety-seven or so. Hoyle is responsible for popularizing the term *score* as a record of winning points in games, a relatively recent innovation. "When in doubt, win the trick," is his most memorable phrase.

Which about ends the *According to's* . . . , except that we cannot commit a breach of etiquette and fail to at least mention the contemporary *According to Emily Post* and *According to Amy Vanderbilt*.

Adam's Apple, Shaddock Adam never ate an apple, at least not in the Biblical account of his transgressions, which refers only to unspecified forbidden fruit on the tree in the Garden of Eden. The forbidden fruit of which the Lord said, *"Ye shall not eat of the fruit which is in the midst of the garden, neither shall ye touch it, lest ye die"* (*Genesis* 3:3) was probably an apricot or a pomegranate, and the Moslems—intending no joke— believe it was a banana. Many fruits and vegetables have been called apples. Even in medieval times pomegranates were "apples of Carthage"; tomatoes, "love apple" aphrodisiacs; dates, "finger apples"; and potatoes, "apples of the earth." Similarly, many places have been called the original Garden of Eden. Claims have been made for Persia, Armenia, Chaldea, Basra, and El Mezey near Damascus,

where the waters of the Tege and Barrady divide into four streams that are said to be the four streams of Moses mentioned in *Genesis*. One seventeenth-century Swedish professor even wrote a book to prove that the garden was located in the Land of the Midnight Sun.

At any rate, tradition has it that Adam succumbed to Eve's wiles and ate of an apple from which she took the first bite, that a piece stuck in his throat forming the lump we call the *Adam's Apple*, and that all of us, particularly males, inherited this mark of his "fall." Modern scientific physiology, as opposed to folk anatomy, explains this projection of the neck, most prominent in adolescents, as being anterior thyroid cartilage of the larynx. But pioneer anatomists honored the superstition in the mid-eighteenth century by calling it *pomum Adami* or *Adam's Apple*. They simply could find no other explanation for this evasive lump in the throat that even seemed to move up and down.

In Europe the *shaddock* or pummelo, a thick-skinned grapefruitlike fruit, is often called *Adam's apple*. The *shaddock* is named after English Captain Shaddock, a seventeenth-century voyager who brought its seed from the East Indies to the West Indies, where it was extensively grown thereafter. It has been known in Europe since the twelfth century.

Adam's Apple Tree, Tabernaemontana Coronaria, Nero's Crown Few have heard of this interesting tree, which thrives in subtropical gardens of the United States. The particular tree is popularly named for Adam and the entire genus containing it was named by Linnaeus in honor of German botanist Dr. J. T. Tabernaemontanus (d. 1590), a celebrated Heidelberg botanist and physician who—despite the length of his patronym—also has species in two other plant genera commemorating him. Why the folkname *Adam's Apple tree*? Clearly still another case of a claim on Eden. I quote from the *Encyclopedia of Gardening* (1838) by J. C. Loudon: "The inhabitants of Ceylon say that Paradise was placed in their country . . . They also point out as the tree which bore the forbidden fruit, the *Devi Ladner* or *Tabernaemontana alternifoxlia* (the species name has since been changed to *coronaria*). . . In confirmation of this tradition they refer to the beauty of the fruit, and the fine scent of the flowers, both of which are most tempting. The shape of the fruit gives the idea of a piece having been bitten off; and the inhabitants say it was excellent before Eve ate of it, though it is now poisonous." *T. coronaria*, a five- to eight-foot-high tropical shrub with white fragrant flowers, is also called the East Indian rosebay, crape jasmine, and *Nero's crown* after the Roman emperor—having three eponyms in all.

Adam's Wine or Ale, Adamic, Adamite, I Don't Know Him From Adam, I Wouldn't Know Him From Adam's Off Ox, The Old Adam, The Second Adam For his sins, according to the *Talmud*, Adam was evicted from Paradise after only twelve hours. In addition to the preceding entries, his name is represented by *Adam's wine*, or *ale*, a humorous expression for water; *Adamic*, naked, free like Adam; *Adamite*, a human being or descendant of Adam; *the second Adam*, a Biblical reference to Christ; *the old Adam in us*, a reference to man's disposition to evil; and *I don't know him from Adam. I wouldn't know him from Adam's off ox* is an attempted improvement on the last, referring to the ox in the yoke farthest away from the driver. Neither expression is very accurate. Hardly anyone drives oxen these days, and as more than one humorist has observed, Adam had no navel, wore only a fig-leaf, and shouldn't have been hard to identify at all. Probably the most famous reference to Adam in Western literature is the poem written by Englishman John Ball, a leader of Wat Tyler's insurrection (1381): "*When Adam delved and Eve Span / Who was then the gentleman?*" This doggerel misquoted or adapted from lines by Richard de Hampole Rolle (d. 1349).

Adirondacks The Mohawk Indians contemptuously dubbed a tribe of Canadian Algonquin Indians *Adirondack*, meaning "they eat bark," and the tribe's nickname came to be applied to the mountain region in northeastern New York that these Indians inhabited. The insulting name gives us, literally, "they eat bark" chairs, pack baskets, and even grapes, among many other items characteristic of the *Adirondacks*.

Admirable Crichton, The Like many characters in fiction—witness Don Juan, Hamlet, Madame Bovary, and even Moby Dick—the butler hero of James M. Barrie's play *The Admirable Crichton* (1902) is based on an actual prototype. But no butler was the model for Barrie's resourceful hero, though the historic figure did personify the same admirable qualities as Lord Loam's man. The real Crichton, a son of Scotland's lord advocate, was born in 1560 and while still in his teens was acknowledged the leading mental and physical prodigy of his day. James Crichton earned his Master of Arts degree when only fifteen. By the time he turned twenty he had mastered over a dozen languages, as well as all the sciences, in addition to being a poet and theologian of some note. The fabled prodigy was also said to be handsome—"all-perfect, finish'd to the fingernail," wrote Tennyson—and without peer in his ability as a swordsman. He served with the French Army, then tutored the scions of royalty. Unfortunately, this ideal gentleman proved unwise or human enough to steal the heart of a prince's lady while traveling in Italy. He was, in all probability, assassinated, run through from behind by three masked men in the prince's hire. Another version has it that Crichton met his end at the hands of a pupil in a street quarrel, but in any event he died when only twenty-five or so. The epithet, "Admirable Crichton," first came into use in 1603, but all record of the man's genius might have died had it not been for *Barrie's* genius, Crichton's name now a synonym for the perfect servant. (See also *Peter Pan*.)

Admiral, Admiral Browning, Admiral Butterfly, Admiral Shell, Kentucky Admiral All *admirals*, technically, come from the deserts of Arabia. The word can be traced to the title of Abu-Bekr, who was called *Amir-al-muninin*, Commander of the faithful, before he succeeded Mohammed as Caliph in 632 A.D. The title Amir or Commander became popular soon after, and naval chiefs were designated *Amir-al-ma*, commander of the water, *Amir-al-bahr*, commander of the sea, and even *Amir-al-amara*, commander of commanders. Western seamen who came in contact with the Arabs assumed that *Amir-al* was one word, believing that this was a distinguished title, and by the early thirteenth century officers were calling themselves *amiral*, which merely means "commander of." The *d* was probably added to the word through a common mispronunciation, although one writer has speculated that the resplendent uniform of some forgotten sea lord might have put it there. This theory suggests that *admiral* has nothing to do with the Arabs, deriving from *admire*, which is from the Latin root "to wonder at," the splendid dress of an unknown naval officer having inspired the word. But *admiral* more probably comes from the title of Abu-Bekr, faithful follower of Mahomet. He is also indirectly honored by the *admiral butterfly* and *admiral sea shell*, both as resplendent as that anonymous *admiral's* uniform. *Admiral Browning* is a personified color, slang for human excrement. And H. L. Mencken observed that there has been at least one honorary *Kentucky Admiral*, an *Admiral of the Kentucky River* outranking the whole troop of Kentucky colonels.

Alabama (see *States*)

Alexander For over a century *to alexander* meant to hang someone. Like *lynch* and *debrett* after it, the word derives from the name of a real person. In this case from Sir Jerome Alexander, an Irish judge (1660–74), who mercilessly sent many a man to the gallows, dispensing law but not justice. The word is merely an historical curiosity today.

Alexander, Alexander's Beard, Alexandria, Alexandrian Library Whether the *Alexander* cocktail celebrates Alexander the Great is a matter of dispute, though the conqueror was certainly a drinking man. There is no doubt, however, that ancient *Alexandria* in the Nile delta was founded in 332 B.C. by the king of Macedonia, that the *Alexandrine verse* or line of poetry derives from a French poem written on him, and that even the *Alexandrine rat* or roof rat indirectly comes from his name, via the Egyptian city. Great though he was in war and statecraft, Alexander's personal life was a loss.

Unlucky in love, he bears the dubious distinction of being one of the most celebrated drunks of all time, which may explain his lack of success with the ladies, for, as his tutor Aristotle said, "he had little inclination for amatory pleasures." Alexander could not even triumph in a battle of wits. Freud tells the apocryphal story of a young boy he tried to bait in the streets. Noting the youngster's strong resemblance to him, Alexander asked him if his mother had ever worked in the palace. "No," the boy replied quickly, "but my father did!"

It would be fitting if the *Alexander*, a cocktail made with creme de cacao, gin or brandy and cream, was named for the conqueror. For, excluding the Sicilian ruler Dionysus, he is probably the only king to die from overindulging in drink. One story has it that a six-day drinking bout led to his death, while another claims that his wife, Roxana, persuaded him to plunge intoxicated into an ice-cold pool, causing the conqueror of Persia to die of a high fever at the tender age of thirty-three. Robert Graves, however, points out that Alexander may have died from poisoning after a mushroom orgy rather than a drunken one.

The fabled *continence of Alexander* refers not to the grape but to Alexander's gentlemanly treatment of the women in the family of Darius III after defeating him in battle at Issus in 333 B.C. As for the *Alexandrian Library*, it was founded in *Alexandria* by Ptolemy Soter. It contained 700,000 books, which the Arabs burned to "heat the baths of the city for six months," on the grounds that all knowledge necessary to man can be found in the Koran. Finally, an *Alexander's beard* is no beard at all, the expression observing the fact that the conqueror is customarily pictured beardless. (See also *Bucephalus; Peritas; Philippic*.)

Alice Blue *Alice blue* is one of several colors named for real people. The shade signalizes Alice Roosevelt Longworth, daughter of President Theodore Roosevelt, who favored the pale greenish or grayish-blue. Mrs. Longworth is the witty lady who said of Calvin Coolidge: "He looks as if he had been weaned on a pickle." Another time she observed that the late Thomas E. Dewey, the most prim, proper and straitlaced of presidential candidates, looked like "a bridegroom atop a wedding cake." Princess Alice, as she was called, was born on February 12, 1884, her mother Alice dying from *Bright's disease,* a kidney inflammation, two days after her birth, on the same day that Theodore Roosevelt's mother died of typhoid fever. On February 17, 1906, Alice married Congressman Nicholas Longworth of Ohio in an elegant East Room wedding in the White House. Mrs. Longworth long remained a leader of Washington society, her name and the color *Alice blue* rendered familiar by the tune "Alice Blue Gown" that she inspired. (See also *Eleanor Blue; Isabel; Titian.*)

Alice in Wonderland   For over a century Lewis Carroll's *Alice in Wonderland* (1865) has been the most famous and possibly the most widely read children's book. That there is an *Alice* cult even among adults is witnessed by the numerous works of criticism devoted to the book, which has even been translated into Latin. The model for the fictional *Alice* was Alice Liddell, daughter of Dean Henry George Liddell, noted coauthor of *Liddell & Scott's Greek Lexicon,* still the standard Greek-English Dictionary. Carroll, his real name Charles Lutwidge Dodgson, wrote *Alice* for his friend's daughter, who later became Mrs. Reginald Hargreaves. The author apparently made up the story while on a picnic with Alice and his sisters, actually improvising the classic tale as the group rowed about a lake. Incidentally, Carroll is regarded as the greatest nineteenth-century photographer of children and his best pictures were of Alice Liddell. An *Alice,* in allusion to *Alice in Wonderland,* is sometimes used to refer to a person newly arrived in strange, fantastic surroundings.

Amazon, Amazon Ants, Amazonomachia, Amazon River   Nowadays, especially since the introduction of silicone, any large, nobly proportioned woman might be termed an *amazon,* and oversize chorus girls have even been billed as *glamazons.* The word no longer has much to do with its dictionary definition of strength and aggressiveness, but the original *Amazons,* from the Greek *a* (without) plus *mazos* (breast), were supposedly a tribe of fierce warrior women who cut or burned off their right breasts so as not to impede the drawing of their bows—a far cry from relatively wholesome topless waitresses. Tribe members were all women and any males born from their annual union with a neighboring male tribe were either killed or banished. So at least, according to the legendary tales of Homer, who wrote that these courageous feminists lived in the territory adjoining the Caucasus mountains and credited them with many martial victories, to say nothing of marital victories.

The demibreasted Amazons played an important role in Greek mythology. One of the labors of Hercules was to obtain the girdle of Hippolyta, queen of the *Amazons,* and another *Amazon* queen, Penthesilia, was killed by Achilles when she and her sisters fought against the Greeks in the Trojan War. *Amazonomachia,* in fact, is the word for a battle between Greeks and Amazons, or a representation of this in art. The mythology probably has its basis in fact, but modern scholars believe that the etymology, "without breasts, or deprived of one pap," is false, citing the many examples of Greek art that have been preserved showing *Amazons* with their mammary glands intact. *Amazon* is more generally attributed to either a Persian whose original meaning has been lost, or to a Greek word for the Eastern moon-god *Mazu.*

Breasts or not, *Amazons* have been reported in Africa and South America as well as Greece. The king of Dahomey, in West Africa, led a band of *amazons* against the French as recently as 1894. The great *Amazon River,* which had previously been named Rio Santa Maria de la Mar Dulce by its discoverer, is said to have been rechristened the *Amazon* by the Spanish explorer Francisco de Orellana in 1541 after he was attacked by the Tapuyas tribe in which he believed that women fought alongside the men.

Amazon ants are so named because they are powerful and warlike enough to carry off and enslave the young of another species.

America   Amerigo Vespucci, the Florentine navigator and ship chandler for whom *America* is named, did not discover *America.* Indeed, he may never have made the four voyages to the New World that resulted in the appellation. In the year 1503 Vespucci sent an account of his alleged voyages to his patrons, Italy's notorious ruling Medici family (see *Medicean*). These letters, witty accounts of his adventures, claimed that in 1497 he had discovered a *Mundus Novus* or New World, "a continent more densely peopled and abounding in animals than our Europe or Asia or Africa." Amerigo probably gathered his facts from accounts of the explorations of Columbus, for whom he helped outfit ships, or he may have sailed on voyages led by other explorers that touched upon the continent to which Columbus sailed the ocean blue five years earlier. In any case, the young geographer Martin Waldseemüller was so impressed with Vespucci's account that he included a map of the New World in an appendix to his *Cosmographiae Introductio*, labeling the land *America* and noting in the margin that "Since Americus Vespicius has discovered a fourth part of the world, it should be called, after him, *America*." Waldseemüller's map roughly represented *South America* and when cartographers finally added *North America*, they retained the original name. Spain stubbornly refused to call the New World anything but *Columbia* until the eighteenth century, but to no avail. Columbus today is linguistically credited for his precedency only in story and song (*Columbia The Gem of the Ocean*), while an artful con man is honored by hundreds of words ranging from *American know-how* to *American cheese*. The one copy of the Hauslab-Liechtenstein World Global Map on which Waldseemüller noted Vespucci's name went up for sale at auction in 1950—but there were no takers at the starting price of fifty thousand dollars.

The latest nominee for the "real discoverer" of America is a Bishop Henrikus. There have been many unsubstantiated nominations, but recently decoded messages found on stones uncovered at Popham Beach, Maine, in 1970 indicate that Henrikus or the Vikings may have "discovered" America there in the early twelfth century. The Popham area may have been the real Vinland, one of the three rocks unearthed containing a map with the word "Vnland" etched on it. All three stones describe the trip of a Bishop Henrikus to Vinland, presumably from Greenland, and the date given is "6 October 1123," which would prove that either he or Vikings before him first landed there. Henrikus is mentioned numerous times in Norse sagas and church records. According to some scholars, the recent discovery could be "one of the most important historic breakthroughs in the United States." On the other hand, it could prove to be as fraudulent as Amerigo Vespucci's claim.

Amish, Mennonites The *Amish* people, or any of the strict *Mennonite* groups in Pennsylvania, Ohio, Indiana and Canada, are descended from the followers of Jakob Amman and take their name from the seventeenth-century Swiss *Mennonite* bishop. The *Mennonites* are an evangelical Protestant sect that practices baptism of believers only, restricts marriage to members of the denomination, and is noted for simplicity of living and plain dress. They, in turn, were named for the religious leader Menno Simons (1496–1556). The *Amish* still cling to a rural, simple way of life, but many of the young among them have begun to rebel against seemingly restrictive conventions and yield to the attractions and conveniences of twentieth-century life. Real *Amish* country is still a pleasure to visit, almost like stepping back a century in time, but even such relatively rural areas as Intercourse, Pa. (so named because the area is a crossroads) seem to be falling victim to "progress."

Amp It is often noted that *moron*, as a scientific designation for a feeble-minded person, was the only word ever voted into the language. It was adopted in 1910 by the American Association for the Study of the Feeble Minded from the name of a foolish character in Molière's play *La Princesse d'Elide*. This claim overlooks the fact that the unit of electric current called an *ampere* or *amp* was adopted at the International Electrical Congress held in Paris twenty-nine years earlier. The *ampere*, the unit by which the strength and rate of flow of an electric current can be measured, was named for the brilliant French scientist André

Marie Ampère (1775–1836). His name also gives us such technical terms as *ampere hour, Ampere's law, ampere turn,* and *amperometric titration.*

Ampère's life was a tragic one. When only eighteen he saw his father guillotined during France's Reign of Terror, a shock that rendered him unable to speak or read for over a year. Six years later, he wed a charming young girl, only to see her die a few years after their marriage. These personal tragedies plunged the young man deeper into his work. While teaching at the Collège de France in the early 1800's, he made important discoveries about the nature of electricity and magnetism, and established the law of mechanical action between electric currents, which formed a basis for the study of electrodynamics and is universally considered one of the greatest scientific achievements. He also invented the astatic needle and contributed to the invention of the electric telegraph. Ampère was a haunted, work-obsessed man, so active that he even worked while standing up, his mind constantly laboring to escape the ghosts of the past.

Anadama Bread *Anadama bread,* a Yankee cornmeal recipe, offers one of the most humorous stories connected with an eponymous foodstuff. Tradition has it that a Yankee farmer or fisherman, whose wife Anna was too lazy to cook for him, invented the recipe. On tasting the result of his efforts a neighbor asked him what he called the bread, the crusty Yankee replying, "Anna, damn her!"

Another version claims that the husband was a Yankee sea captain who endearingly referred to his wife as "Anna, damn 'er." Anna's bread was much loved by his crew because it was both delicious and would not spoil on long sea voyages. The captain is said to have written the following epitaph for his wife: "*Anna was a lovely bride, / but Anna, damn 'er, up and died.*"

If you want to try *Anadama bread* use the authentic recipe given in Imogene Wolcott's *The New England Cookbook* (Coward-McCann, 1939). Curse before eating.

Ananias The word *Ananias,* for a liar, refers to the New Testament Ananias (*Acts* 5:1–10), who with his wife, Sapphira, tried to cheat the church at Jerusalem by withholding part of the money he made from a sale of land. Ananias was struck dead after the apostle Peter declared that he had "not lied unto men, but unto God." His wife shared his fate later that day when she maintained his deception and was told of his demise.

Ananias was popularized by President Theodore Roosevelt, who referred to those he suspected of deceit as members of the *Ananias Club,* especially members of the working press who published confidential information they had promised not to reveal. Roosevelt did not coin the phrase, but as H. L. Mencken observed, he popularized or originated scores of expressions, including *walk softly and carry a big stick, to pussyfoot, the strenuous life, one hundred percent American,* and *muckraker,* all of which are still used today. (See also *Teddy Bear.*)

Andrea Ferrara Many Scotsmen will know that an *Andrea Ferrara* is the Scottish broadsword frequently mentioned in Elizabethan literature, and more than a few will proudly claim that the original sword maker was a Scottish drill sergeant named Andrea Ferras or Ferrier. However, it is more likely that the real Andrea Ferrara was a sixteenth-century Italian sword maker who lived in Belluno and whose correct name was *Andrea dei Ferrari,* "Andrew of the armourers." How his swords got to Scotland is something of a mystery; either he was an exile, or, as Sir Walter Scott suggests in the notes on *Waverley,* he was brought over by James IV or V to instruct the Scots in the manufacture of his blades. In any event, he left us with many references in literature to *Andrea Ferraras, Ferraras* and even *Andrews,* all deriving from his name.

Andrew, The *The Andrew* has been British slang for the Royal Navy since at least 1860, and *the Andrew Millar* was used long before that. The expression derives from the name of Andrew Millar or Miller, a notorious press gang leader of Nelson's day, who shanghaied so many men into the navy that his victims thought it belonged to him. The term achieved more currency when a firm headed by an Arthur Millar was later awarded a large contract for supplying the Royal Navy with better rations. A common British catch phrase is, "You shouldn't have joined *Andrew* if you couldn't take a joke."

Ångström, Ångström Crater, Ångström Line A unit of length equal to one ten millionth of an inch is known as an *ångström unit* or *ångström*. It is used primarily to measure wave lengths of light and was named for Anders Jonas Ångström (1814–74), Swedish astronomer and physicist, as was the *Ångström crater* in the moon. Anders Ångström taught physics at Uppsala University, his most important research work undertaken in heat conduction and light, and he is considered one of the founders of spectrum analysis. In 1867 he became the first to examine the spectrum of the aurora borealis, the characteristic bright line in its yellow-green region often called the *Ångström line* in his honor.

Annie Laurie

Her braw is like the snow-drift;
her throat is like the swan;
Her face it is the fairest
That e'er the sun shone on—
And dark blue is her ee;

And for bonnie Annie Laurie
I'd lay me doun and dee. . . .

The lyrics of the famous old song—in the 1835 revision by Lady John Scott above—have lasted for nearly three hundred years, but few are aware that there was a real Annie Laurie. Poet William Douglas sang about his love for the eldest daughter of Sir Robert Laurie of Maxwelton, Scotland, some ten years his junior. Annie, however, wasn't impressed enough, for she married a rival suitor, Alexander Fergusson, in 1709. Douglas, for his part, did not expire of a broken heart, living until 1748 when he died at the age of seventy-six. Annie Laurie (1682–1764) lived on even longer to become the grandmother of still another Alexander Fergusson, who was the hero of yet another song—Robert Burn's "The Whistle."

Annie Oakley Annie Oakley was the stage name of Ohio-born Phoebe Annie Oakley Mozee (1860–1926), star rifle shot with Buffalo Bill's wild west show. Married at sixteen, Annie joined Buffalo Bill when twenty-five and amazed audiences for more than forty years with her expert marksmanship and trick shooting. Annie once broke 942 glass balls thrown into the air with only 1,000 shots. Her most famous trick was to toss a playing card, usually a five of hearts, into the air and shoot holes through all its pips. The riddled card reminded circus performers of their punched meal tickets, which they began to call *Annie Oakleys*, and the name was soon transferred to free railroad and press passes, both of which were customarily punched with a hole in the center. Today all complimentary passes, punched or not, are called *Annie Oakleys*, the expression also used in yacht racing for a ventilated spinnaker or head sail. Annie Oakley was called Little Missy by her employer, Buffalo Bill, and on seeing her amazing skill with a rifle the great chief Sitting Bull dubbed her Little Sure Shot.

Another Richmond in the Field Henry of Richmond, afterwards England's King Henry VII, is honored by this expression, which means that still another, unexpected opponent has shown up to do battle. The phrase is from a speech made by the king in Shakespeare's *Richard III*, though the last line is more famous than the first:

I think there be six Richmonds in the field;
Five have I slain today, instead of him—
A horse! a horse! my kingdom for a horse!

Apache, Apache Dance An *apache* is a Parisian criminal or ruffian and an *apache dance* is a violent dance originated by the Parisian *apaches*. The word in its gangster sense was coined by French newspaper reporter Emile Darsy, who is said to have read of bloodthirsty Apache Indians in the works of American author James Fenimore Cooper and thought that their name would aptly fit denizens of the underworld. The Apache Indians were in reality no better or worse than any group of people. Their name, from a Zuni word meaning enemy, was applied to many nomadic bands of Indians roaming the Southwestern United States. Among their greatest leaders were Cochise and Geronimo. The Apaches called themselves *dené*, an Athabascan word for human being. (See also *Geronimo*.)

Appeal From Philip Drunk To Philip Sober A woman petitioned King Philip of Macedon for justice for her husband and was refused. "I shall appeal against this judgement!" she exclaimed, and Philip—while still in his cups—roared: "Appeal—and to whom will you appeal?" "To Philip sober," the woman replied, and according to Valerius Maximus, who tells the tale, she won her case.

Another saying associated with the powerful Macedonian king is *Philip, Philip, remember thou art mortal*—a phrase supposedly repeated to him each time he gave an audience. Which may account for the woman's success. (See also *Philippic*.)

An Apicius, Apician, Api Apicius might be called the world's first gourmand and *bon vivant* as well as the author of the earliest cookbook. His *De Re Coquinaria*, or *Of Culinary Matters*, has gone through countless editions since first written about fifteen years ago. Some historians claim that Apicius was a rich merchant who collected recipes wherever he traveled, others that his name is a *nom de plume* deriving from *epicure*, but most authorities believe that he was the Roman nobleman Marcus Gavius Apicius, who lived under Tiberius in the first century A.D. Whatever his identity, *an Apicius* still brings to mind a chef and gastronome without peer, one who went to such lengths as spraying his garden lettuce with mead evenings so that it would taste like "green cheesecakes" the next morning, one who concocted *Apician* dishes that remain, in the words of Mark Twain, "as delicious as the less conventional forms of sin." Apicius' death matched his life in elegance. After spending a huge sum—a hundred million sesterces, according to one source—on a fabulous and brilliantly successful banquet, he gave final instructions to his major-domo, retired to his room and either hanged himself or took a lethal dose of poison. He realized that he had only ten million sesterces left—anywhere from one half to one million dollars, depending on the account you read—and that such a paltry sum was not sufficient to support his life style.

At least so tradition has it. Apicius may also figure in the coining of the word *omelette*, as he created a dish of eggs with honey and pepper that he called *ovemele*, which is probably the origin of the word. And the French still call the Red Lady apple *api* after him, honoring the tradition that he first produced this small tasty fruit by grafting.

Aqua Tofana History has known some infamous poisoners, most of them women: Lucretia Borgia; La Voisin; the Marquise de Brinvilliers, so despised that, when she died and her ashes were scattered to the wind, Madame de Sevigne wrote: "All Paris ran the danger of breathing in the atoms of this little woman and thereby becoming infected with the same poisonous desires." All were monsters *par excellence*, but only one so resourceful as to have the poison she used named after her. *Aqua Tofana*, a favorite potion of young wives in seventeenth-century Italy who wanted to get rid of their rich, elderly, or ineffectual husbands, recalls a woman who peddled her deadly home-brew on such a large scale that she has achieved immortality of a kind. Her first name is unknown. Ms. Tofana was either a Greek or Italian lady who died in Naples or Palermo, Sicily, about the year 1690. Apparently, she died a natural death, although five others headed by an old hag named Spara, who had bought her secret formula, were arrested and hanged in 1659. Tofana's poison was a strong, slow-acting, transparent and odorless solution of arsenic which she sold in vials labeled *Manna di S. Nicola di Bari* (the *Manna of St. Nicholas of Bari*), in honor of the miraculous oil that was said to flow from the tomb of the saint. Thus she was also one of the world's first advertising women.

Archimedean Principle, Archimedes' Drill, Pulley, Windlass, The Screw of Archimedes The Greek mathematician and inventor Archimedes, supposedly born at Syracuse in Sicily in 287 B.C., was both the Albert Einstein and Thomas Edison of his day. He devised the *Archimedean drill, pulley*, and *windlass*, and the *screw of Archimedes*, a machine for raising water, among many other inventions. Archimedes, however, thought little of these ingenious contrivances, even declining to leave written records of most of them. He preferred to be remembered for his great work in mathematics, or for his founding of the science of hydrostatics, which his *Archimedean Principle* made possible.

As fate would have it, Archimedes is best remembered for his coining of a word. One day he was asked to determine the amount of silver an allegedly dishonest goldsmith had used for the king's crown, which was supposed to have been made of pure gold. While pondering the solution in his bath, he observed that the quantity of water displaced by a body will equal in bulk the bulk of the immersed body (the *Archimedean Principle*). All he had to do then was to weigh an amount of gold equal in weight to the crown, put crown and gold in separate basins of water, and weigh the overflow to determine how much gold the crown really contained. According to one story, he was so overjoyed with his discovery that he forgot his clothes and ran out into the streets naked, astonishing passersby with his shouts of "*Eureka, eureka!*" (I have found it, I have found it!)

Archimedes is the only mathematician ever to become a legend. His pioneering work in mechanics, for example, is illustrated by his famous saying, "Give me a place to stand and I [will] move the earth." The traditional story of his death offers further evidence of this mythical quality. It seems that Archimedes' giant burning-mirrors or lenses (not to mention his grapnels and improved catapults) held the Roman ships besieging Syracuse at bay for three years by setting them on fire from a distance. When the Romans finally took the town in 212 B.C., strict orders were given that Archimedes should not be harmed. But legend tells us that he was run through by a soldier unaware of his identity, after refusing to follow the man because he was intent upon solving a problem he had etched in the sand. Archimedes was about seventy-five when he died, probably the greatest name in Hellenistic civilization and one of the most remarkable men in all history. His tomb, in accord with his wishes, was marked with a sphere enclosed in a cylinder—for he believed that his discovery of the relation between the surface and volume of a sphere and its circum-scribing cylinder was by far the greatest of all his achievements.

Argyle Socks, Argyle Plaid, God Bless the Duke of Argyle The original pattern for *argyle socks* was the traditional green and white pattern of the Scottish Campbell clan of Argyle or Argyll. The duke of Argyle, head of the clan, was famous among Highlanders for the posts he erected in his pastures to enable his cows to rub their backs and ease the itching caused by insects. Perhaps the posts were only erected to indicate a trail covered with snow, but nevertheless *God bless the Duke of Argyle!* became a common humorous remark whenever a Scotsman scratched himself. The clan found new popularity when mentioned in several of Sir Walter Scott's novels. Not long after, its tartan was adapted by fabric manufacturers as the *argyle plaid*, and socks knitted in such a pattern were called *argyle socks*. Nowadays, *argyle socks* are any two or more bright colors, retaining only the diamond-shaped pattern of the original adaptation.

Aristotelianism A number of words are named after Aristotle (384–322 B.C.), the Greek philosopher who was the pupil of Plato and tutor to Alexander the Great. These include *aristotelianism*, philosophy emphasizing deduction and investigation of concrete, particular things and situations; *Aristotelian logic*, traditional formal logic; *Aristotle's lantern*, a zoological term so called from a reference by Aristotle to a sea urchin that resembled certain lanterns; and the *Aristotelian or dramatic unities*—the necessity for unity of action, time and place in drama. One of the greatest thinkers of all time, Aristotle's habit of giving his lectures in the *peripatos*, or walking place, of the Athenian Lyceum gave his school of philosophy the name Peripatetic, which yielded the English word *peripatetic*, "walking about or carried on while walking about from place to place." Aristotle studied under Plato at his academy, but differed with him in important respects, his school overshadowed by Plato's until medieval times, when many of his doctrines came to be regarded as incontrovertible. The Renaissance was in many respects a revolt against *Aristotelianism*, but the philosopher's reliance upon induction and empirical observation is basic to the modern scientific method. Born in Stagira, the son of a noted physician, Aristotle is sometimes called the Stagirite. (See also *Platonic*.)

Arkansas (see *States*)

Athanasian Wench This eighteenth-century slang term for a promiscuous woman has an amusing origin. It is in allusion to the Ecumenical *Athanasian Creed*, formulated in the fifth century as an exposition of the Nicene Creed promulgated by St. Athanasius (c. 297–373), the saint a much exiled Alexandrian bishop who pioneered in scientific theology and attended the council of Nicaea. *Athanasian wench* comes directly from the *Athanasian Creed*, which is included in the *English Book of Common Prayer*. For the familiar first words of the creed read: "Whosoever desires. . . ."

Attic, Atticism, Atticize, Attic Salt, the Attic Muse *Attic salt*, for pointed wit, and even the *attic* in a house derive from the Greek word *Attikos*, an Athenian, or citizen of Athens. Salt was a common term for wit and the Athenians were noted for their elegant turns of thought. This gave rise to the Roman expression *sal atticus* (*attic salt*); *atticism*, wit and elegance; and *atticize*, to write wittily. *Attic* for the part of a building just below and enclosed by the roof comes to us by a more circuitous route, deriving from the Attic (or Athenian) style of architecture, a feature of which was a decorative wall at the top of buildings. The Athenians had no such storage rooms, but the space behind their decorative walls developed into our *attic* centuries later. Finally, the term, *the Attic Muse*, is often applied to the Athenian historian Xenophon, in reference to his elegant writing.

August, Augustan Age, Caesarea Philippi Augustus Caesar stole a day from February to give *August* thirty-one days —simply because he did not want *July*, named after his great uncle and adopted father, to be longer than his own name-month. History is made of such petty jealousies, but Augustus and Julius Caesar really got along very well; there is no evidence of any generation gap. Born Gaius Octavianus, his mother the daughter of Julius Caesar's sister, Augustus was eventually chosen by the Roman ruler as his heir, adopting the name Caesar. Octavius, as he was commonly known, was only nineteen at the time of his uncle's assassination in 44 B.C. On returning to Rome from Spain, he found that Caesar had secretly adopted him and willed him all his property. It was then that he changed his name and embarked on a celebrated military career that included the conquest of Egypt. In 29 B.C., already immensely popular among the people, he was chosen first emperor of Rome, and two years later the senate bestowed upon him the title *Augustus*, or "imperial majesty." Finally, what was the sixth month of the year (*Sextillus*) before the *Julian calendar* was renamed *Augustus* in his honor—complete with an extra day at his insistence. *August* wasn't chosen because it was his birth month (September), but because it happened to be his "lucky" month of the year—the one in which he first became a consul, reduced Egypt, put an end to civil wars, received the oath of allegiance from his legions at Janiculum, and scored his greatest military triumphs. Octavius Augustus ruled wisely until his death at the age of seventy-five, his reign marked by great progress and a flowering of literature that is today known as the *Augustan age*. The ancient city *Caesarea Philippi*, now Banias, was named for the emperor by its builder Philip the Tetrach. Philip, who managed to honor his own name in the bargain, ably ruled the region east of Galilee; the son of Herod the Great, his wife was Salome, she who danced for the head of John the Baptist. (See also *Caesar*; *July*; *Julian calendar*.)

Aunt May An *Aunt May* is British naval slang for a person generous to sailors. It is aptly named for Mrs. May Hanrahan, the widow of a United States naval captain, who "adopted" sixteen British destroyers during World War II and spent almost a quarter of a million dollars on their crews in the form of presents and comforts. *Aunt May* Hanrahan was received by the queen when she visited England after the war and was piped on board the destroyer *Tartar* while a naval band played on the jetty in her honor.

Austrian Lip The British historian Macaulay wrote that Charles II of Spain, last of the Austrian Hapsburgs, had a jaw so malformed that he couldn't chew his food. Another Hapsburg, Emperor Charles V, possessed a lower jaw that protruded so far beyond his upper jaw that he could not speak an intelligible sentence. This inherited genetic defect is one of the most curious in history, is common to all the Hapsburgs, and can be seen in many of their portraits. It was probably inherited through marriage with the Polish princely family of Jagellon and perpetuated by intermarriage among the Hapsburgs themselves. The term *Austrian lip* describes the deformity far better than "severely protruding lower jaw."

B

Babbitt, Babbitt Soap Congress deemed the invention of *babbitt* or *babbitt metal* so important to the development of the industrial age that it awarded inventor Isaac Babbitt (1799–1862) a twenty-thousand-dollar grant. *Babbitt* is a soft, silver-white alloy of copper, tin and antimony used to reduce friction in machine bearings and was discovered as a result of the inventor's experiments in turning out the first Britannia ware ever produced in America. After the Taunton, Mass., goldsmith successfully manufactured Britannia in 1824, he further experimented with the same three metals and ultimately discovered *babbitt*, which he used to line a patented journal box in 1839. The metal proved far better than any other substance used for reducing friction and is still widely used for machine bearings today. *Babbitt soap*, no longer marketed, also bore the inventor's name. Babbitt, however, was not the prototype for Sinclair Lewis' ambitious, uncultured and smugly satisfied American businessman in his novel of the same name.

Babcock Test Though not as famous as Pasteur, the agricultural chemist, Stephen Moulton Babcock, played an important role in the development of the modern dairy industry. While chief chemist at the Wisconsin Agricultural Experiment Station in 1890, Babcock invented a process for determining the butterfat content of milk. The *Babcock test* makes possible rapid, accurate milk grading and helps farmers develop better dairy herds by enabling them to test milk from their stock. Babcock taught for twenty-five years at the University of Wisconsin, from 1887 to 1913. He died in 1931, aged eighty-eight, the last twenty years of his life spent in research on the nature of matter. (See also *Pasteurize*.)

Babe Ruth No sports records are better known than the legendary Sultan of Swat's 60 home runs in one season, 714 throughout his career, and his "call" of a home run in the 1929 World Series. And when all these records are broken, Babe Ruth's name will still be more famous than his successors'. George Herman Ruth (1895–1948), the poor boy who became the most renowned American athlete of all time, has already become a folk hero, had in fact attained that exalted status while still alive. Some of the little-known stories about the Bambino bear repeating. He began his baseball career, for example, as a catcher, for St. Mary's School in Baltimore, was an outstanding pitcher in the major leagues before switching to the outfield. . . . He once hit a home run that literally went around the world, the ball landing in a freight car. . . . His World Series performance in Chicago was not his first "call" for a home run—he had called his shot on at least one other occasion. He led the major leagues in strikeouts in 1923 with ninety-three, being a strikeout king as well as home run king. One could go on for pages from memory alone. The New York Yankee star, the Homer of Home Runs, has never been equaled for talent or color. His name will remain a synonym for the ultimate in sluggers even after someone has hit 120 homers.

Baby, To Baby The word *baby* does derive from the name of a real person. But not the human *baby*, which comes from the Middle English *baban*, an imitative nursery word in origin. The *baby* referred to is in South African diamond-mining language a sifting machine, *to baby* meaning to sift soil with a *baby* for diamonds. Both expressions honor an American named Babe who invented the machine in about 1880.

Baedeker, Fielding Guide A *Bae-deker* once referred to a specific guide-book published by the German printer and bookseller Karl Baedeker (1801–1859), but the word is now used loosely to mean any travel guide. Baedeker's guides were so authoritative and compre-hensive that they were eventually printed in numerous languages and became al-most a necessity for travelers of the time. Similar to the contemporary *Fielding guides*, named for travel writer Temple Hornaday Fielding (b. 1914), the books covered every aspect of travel, from his-toric questions to cuisine, and started the practice of rating places with one to four stars. *Baedeker* became synonymous for an exhaustive guide, the word adopted in many countries. We even find Chek-hov, great stylist that he was, writing in a letter from rainy Venice: "Here I am alone with my thoughts and my *Bae-deker*."

Bailey Bridge Portable *Bailey bridges*, which were designed to replace bridges destroyed by retreating forces and to carry much heavier loads than military bridges could previously support, were to a large extent responsible for the Allied victory in World War II, particularly in northwestern Europe. They were in-vented by Sir Donald Coleman Bailey (b. 1901), engineer with the British Min-istry of Supply, who was knighted in 1945 for his contribution to the war effort. The versatile truss bridges were first used in 1941 and are still employed throughout the world in flood and dis-aster areas. They are engineering marvels, consisting of some twenty-nine different parts, but made principally of 10-foot-long, 5-foot-wide, prefabricated lattice steel panels weighing six hundred pounds that are held together by steel pins. Bailey bridges, their roadways timber sup-ported by steel stringers, were often erected in two and three tiers. Amaz-ingly strong, capable of supporting up to one hundred tons on spans 30 to 220 feet long, they were of vital help in the rapid advances of Allied troops. A one-hundred-man team could erect a 130-foot span Bailey bridge in one and a half hours in daylight and three hours in total darkness, using very little special equipment. The portable spans were not originally floating pontoon bridges, al-though they were adapted to this use during the war in the form of *floating Baileys*. Pontoon-type bridges, built over vessels, were employed by the Persians for military purposes as early as 537 B.C. and have been used since time imme-morial.

Bakelite Though employed chiefly as an electric insulator, *Bakelite* has many industrial applications, including its use in the manufacture of phonograph rec-ords, machinery, gears, and even buttons, pipe stems and billiard balls. It is a syn-thetic resin or plastic, valuable as a non-conductor of electricity and as a heat re-sistant, and is prepared by the chemical interaction of phenobic substances and aldehydes. *Bakelite* was invented by Leo Hendrik Baekeland (1863–1944), a Flem-ish chemistry teacher who migrated to the United States from Ghent, Bel-gium, in 1889 to manufacture Velox, a photographic paper that he had devel-oped. In 1909 he announced the inven-tion of *Bakelite*, a registered name used by the company he owned for over twenty years.

Balmy *Balmy*, in its sense of silly, foolish, eccentric, is the Americanized version of the British *barmy*, and may derive from the name of St. Bartholo-mew, patron saint of the feeble-minded. Most etymologists, however, trace the word to the old English *barm*, the froth on fermenting beer, which could indeed make one act *balmy*. Still another theory is that the word derives from the Barm-ing lunatic asylum at Kent in England, meaning that a *barmy* or *balmy* person is "one fit only for Barming." This over-looks the fact that the *Oxford English Dictionary* gives the first use of *barmy* as 1535, whereas Barming was established in the early nineteenth century, but it may be that the popularity of the word was enhanced by the asylum. On the other hand, the same could apply to the St. Bartholomew derivation.

Baltimore, Baltimore Clipper, Balti-more Oriole An early dictionary tells us that the *Baltimore oriole* is "so called from the Colors of Or (orange) and Sable in the coat of arms belonging to Lord Baltimore." This oriole is not closely re-lated to the orioles of Europe, belonging to the blackbird and meadowlark rather than the crow family. In fact, many American birds with the same names as European species are in reality birds of a different feather. The American robin, for instance, is really a thrush, and other Old World avian words given new significances include partridge, blackbird, lark, and swallow. But whatever its true species, the *Baltimore Oriole*, definitely takes its name from the Baltimore family, founders of Maryland, the bright colors of the male bird corresponding to the orange and black in their heraldic arms. The city of Baltimore, Md., also honors the barons Baltimore, as do the early nineteenth-century *Baltimore clippers*, more indirectly, the famous ships having been built in the city. The same can be said of baseball's *Baltimore Orioles* and football's *Baltimore Colts*. No particular Lord Baltimore has been singled out for the honor. George Calvert, the first baron Baltimore (c. 1590–1632), prepared the charter for the proposed colony that became Maryland, but died before it could be accepted; the charter was granted to his son Cecilius, but the second baron Baltimore never even visited the province; and the third baron Baltimore, Cecilius' son Charles, governed the province from 1661 to 1684. A Catholic who ruled quite arbitrarily over his predominantly Protestant subjects, Charles returned to England and never came back, leaving little more than the family name behind him.

Bambochades Genre paintings of rural life, especially rustic drinking scenes treated in an exaggerated or comic manner, are called *bambochades* or *bambocciades* after the nickname of Dutch landscape painter Pieter van Laar (c. 1600– c. 1674). Van Laar, or Laer, worked some fifteen years in Italy, where he was nicknamed *Il Bamboccio*, "the cripple." Famous for his landscapes and etchings depicting rustic life—pictures usually in heavy brown tone showing wakes, weddings and other country scenes—the artist was also called *Michael Angelo des Bambochades*. A few of his works, notably *Travelers Leaving the Inn*, hang in the Louvre.

Bang's Disease (see *Brucellosis*)

To Bant, Banting William Banting (1797–1878) might have made a fortune had he published his booklet on dieting a century later in our weight-conscious era. As it turned out, he merely amused Londoners in the mid 1860's, although his name did become a word. Banting was an enormously overweight cabinetmaker and undertaker who couldn't bend to tie his shoelaces and had to walk downstairs backwards to relieve the pressure on his legs. Convinced by his own discomfort, and perhaps from his undertaking activities, that many deaths resulted from overeating, he went on a strict diet, losing forty-six pounds and taking twelve inches off his waist. As so many dieters do, he then wrote a book about his experience, setting forth his method of reducing. *Bantingism* called for a meat diet and abstention from practically everything—beer, butter, sugar, farinaceous foods and even vegetables. Needless to say, it wasn't popular very long, but Londoners humorously took to calling dieting *banting* and to diet *to bant*. Anyway, *banting* didn't hurt Banting, for he lived to the ripe old age of eighty-one before another undertaker got his business.

Barebone's Parliament The historically important *Barebone's Parliament* nominated by Cromwell in 1653 wasn't so called because it was a small body, the skeleton of a real parliament. Rather, the assembly, which first met on July 4th of that year, was derisively nicknamed for one of its members. Praise-God Barebones was his name (or Barebone, or Barbon). Barebones, a famous London preacher, as well as a leather merchant and man of property, was vociferously opposed to the restoration of the Stuarts. Controversial for his Baptist religious views, Praise-God Barebones' preaching attracted large crowds, the meetings frequently disturbed by riots, and one time a mob stormed his house, Barebones barely escaping with his life. The *Barebone's Parliament* passed a number of reforms, including civil marriage, and public registration of births and burials, but was generally unqualified for its task of governing, "more fools than knaves," as someone wrote. Praise-God Barebones, who seems to have taken little part in the debates, long outlived his namesake, dying in 1680, aged about eighty-four. (See also *Cromwell; Oliver's Skull.*)

Barlow Knife Russel Barlow, who has been called "the patron saint of whittlers," invented the *barlow knife* over two hundred years ago and it has been known to Americans under one name or another ever since. The *barlow,* a single-bladed pocket, pen, or jackknife, was the pride, joy, and bartering power of many an American boy, and was mentioned in the works of Mark Twain, Joel Chandler Harris and many other writers. It has also been called the *Russel Barlow knife.*

Barmecide, Barmecide's Feast, Barmecidal *Barmecide* derives from the name of a family of Baghdad princes, one of them immortalized in the "Story of the Barber's Sixth Brother" in the *Arabian Nights.* This rich noble served the beggar Schacabac a succession of imaginary dishes, pretending that the empty golden plates constituted a sumptuous feast. Thus a *Barmecide's feast* is an illusion of plenty, or a meal that leaves much to the imagination, a *Barmecide* is one who offers unreal or disappointing benefits, and *Barmecidal* means providing merely the illusion of plenty. Schacabac, incidentally, got more than a feast for his pains. He wisely went along with the prince, pretending to enjoy every dish, and finally boxed his host's ears while feigning drunkenness from the excellent imaginary wine. Prince Barmecide, amused after he recovered from the attack, ordered a real banquet brought to the table and even invited Schacabac to share in the riches of the castle.

Barnum, Barnumese, Barnumize, Barnum-Like Phineas Taylor Barnum, American impresario and forerunner of all Mike Todds and Sol Huroks of our day, was born in 1810, the son of a storekeeper and farmer. At twelve he was a successful lottery operator, but failed in business, publishing, and lotteries before beginning his career as a showman in 1835. Barnum began by exhibiting Aunt Joice Heth, an aged black woman he fraudulently claimed had been George Washington's nurse. Thousands paid to see the "162-year-old" woman, who wasn't over eighty when she died, illus-trating the saying, probably falsely attributed to him, that "there's a sucker born every minute." The showman soon formed the American Museum in New York, embarking on a career that included exhibitions of the dwarf General Tom Thumb (Charles Stratton), reputedly thirty-one inches tall; singer Jenny Lind, the famous "Swedish Nightingale"; and the first bearded lady—among countless other attractions. Among his many frauds were a sign labeled "To the Egress," implying a mysterious monster but which was actually an exit for emptying his museum and letting more paying customers in; a "genuine preserved mermaid," in reality a monkey's torso expertly sewed to the tail of a fish; dancing turkeys that danced because the floor of their cage was heated; an animal "of a horse's size, a deer's haunches, an elephant's tail, a camel's color, and the curly wool of sheep, with some resemblance to a young buffalo"; a cherry-colored cat (*black* cherry-colored); and Swiss bell ringers who were really British. Barnum opened his circus in Brooklyn in 1871, proceeding to tour the world with the "Greatest Show on Earth." The African elephant, Jumbo, purchased from the London Zoo, was one of the show's stars, as were the famous Siamese Twins, Chang and Eng. Barnum had not only a great flair for showmanship, but was past master or inventor of every method known for fleecing the public, from unscrupulous advertising to inflated attendance figures. "The Prince of Humbugs" became mayor of Bridgeport, Conn., and a member of the state legislature, but his name is rightfuly remembered as a synonym for pretentious ballyhoo and boastful exaggeration, as well as for a great showman. He died in 1891 without ever publically regretting his past, and that he was something of an American folk hero is illustrated by the fact that at least six towns in the United States are named after him. The *Ringling Brothers Barnum and Bailey Circus* also bears his name. (See also *Jenny Haniver; Jenny Lind; Jumbo; Siamese Twins.*)

Bartlett Pear, Seckel Pear The yellow *Bartlett,* grown commercially mostly in Oregon and Washington, where it is less susceptible to blight than in the

East, represents 70 percent of the country's 713,000-ton crop, and is certainly America's most commonly grown pear. It is a soft European-type fruit, in season from July to November, as opposed to earlier hard Asian varieties like the *Seckel*, which is named for the Philadelphia farmer who first grew it in America just after the Revolution. The *Bartlett* was not, in fact, developed by Enoch Bartlett (1779–1860), a merchant in Dorchester, Mass., as is generally believed. Bartlett only promoted the fruit after Captain Thomas Brewer imported the trees from England and grew them on his Roxbury farm. The enterprising Yankee eventually purchased Brewer's farm and distributed the pears under his own name in the early 1800's. They had been long known in Europe as Williams or William Bon Chrétien pears. *Bartletts*, by any name, are one of the most delicious of the over three thousand pear species, and pears have been one of man's favorite fruits from as early as 1000 B.C.

Bartlett's Quotations, Ask John Bartlett Bartlett's *Familiar Quotations* has been a standard American reference work since its publication in 1855. Its compiler, John Bartlett (1820–1905), was born in Plymouth, Mass., and for many years owned the University Book Store in Cambridge. Harvard professors and students made the store a meeting place and Bartlett's encyclopedic knowledge made the phrase "Ask John Bartlett" a customary saying when anyone wanted the source of a quotation, a faith that was justified with the appearance of his book, which has gone through many editions and revisions. In 1863 Bartlett joined Little, Brown & Company and eight years later became a senior partner in that publishing firm. His *Complete Concordance to Shakespeare's Dramatic Works and Poems* is also a standard reference work.

Barter Few, if any, American sport terms derive from the names of great players, no matter how proficient. In baseball a home run is not called a *Babe Ruth*, though we sometimes say *a Ruthian blast*; a hitting streak is not a *DiMaggio*; nor is a strikeout a *Sandy Koufax*. Across the Atlantic this is not the case. *Barter*, for example, is an English cricket term dating back nearly 150 years. It is from the name of Robert Barter, warden at Winchester College from 1832 to 1861, and famed for his half-volley hits. (See also *Babe Ruth*; *Bosey*; *Casey at the Bat*; *Tinker to Evers to Chance*.)

Batiste Fabric One account claims that the popular *batiste fabric* takes its name from the soft linen cloth used in medieval times to wipe holy water off the heads of *baptized* infants. It is more likely that the word derives from one Jean Baptiste, of Cambrai, a thirteenth-century French linen weaver about whom little is known beyond his name. Cambric was at the time already a trade name for a linen manufactured at Cambrai or Kamoric. English merchants needed another word for this new Cambrai product, calling it after the French weaver but misspelling his name. Today *batiste* is no longer only linen material. Sheer cotton *batiste* is used for lingerie, handkerchiefs and children's wear, and sheer rayon, silk and woolen *batistes* are common, too.

Battology, Battologist A stammering man named Battos mentioned in the works of the Greek historian Herodotus, "The Father of History," is responsible for the word *battology*, needless or excessive repetition in speech or writing. The *Oxford English Dictionary* records *battology's* first use in 1603. It was formed by combining the name of the man Herodotus described, *Battos*, with the Greek *logia*—from *logos*, "word." *Battologist* is a term sometimes applied to boring speakers.

Beau Brummell Beau Brummell, born George Bryan Brummell, was more a dandy than a gentleman; it is said that he even refused to tip his hat to ladies, out of fear that he might mess his wig. Brummell's name has indeed been synonymous for a dandy, fop, or fancy dresser for over a century. From his early years at Eton and Oxford the incomparable Beau paid extravagant attention to his dress. There he met the Prince of Wales, later George IV, who became his patron when he left college, commissioning him in his own regiment in 1794. Brummell retired from the service four years later when he inherited a large fortune, and set up a bachelor apartment in Mayfair, where he held sway as London's arbiter of fashion for almost twenty years. Though he showed good taste and originality in dress, he is remembered for his excesses. Beau Brummell often spent a whole day dressing for a royal ball; his gloves were the work of three glovers— one to fashion the hands, another for the fingers, and a third for the thumb; it was his custom to be carried from his room in a sedan chair rather than go out into the dirty streets to hail one. So secure was he in his niche as London's *arbiter elegantiarum* that one tailor wishing to obtain his patronage presented him with a coat the pockets of which were lined with bank notes—this giving rise to the expression "lining the pockets" for bribery or graft.

Extravagance and gambling finally exhausted Beau Brummell's fortune and his sharp tongue provoked a quarrel with his royal patron. Brummell's sharp riposte, "Who's your fat friend?" to an acquaintance walking with the prince finally put an end to the relationship once and for all. In 1816 he fled to France to escape his creditors. Here he spent his last twenty-four years in exile while struggling to survive, imprisoned once for debt and suffering several attacks of paralysis. He died in an asylum for the poor in Caen in 1840, aged sixty-two. He had long before lost all interest in elegant fashion and manners, his dress slovenly and dirty.

Beau Fielding, Beau Hewitt, Beau Nash, Beau D'Orsay George Bryan Brummell is not the only *Beau* in English history. The French word, meaning fine or beautiful, had been used long before him to describe fops and dandies, most of whom achieved fame for a time but are now forgotten. One of the earliest dandies was *Beau Hewitt*, who won a certain immortality as the model for Sir Fopling Flutter, hero of Sir George Etherege's *The Man of Mode* (1676). Then there was *Beau Fielding* (d. 1712), "Handsome Fielding," a favorite of Charles II until he was executed after being convicted of bigamously marrying the regent's former mistress. As for *Beau D'Orsay* (1801–52), he was the successor

to Brummell's mantle, the poet Byron dubbing him *Jeune Cupidon.* (See *D'Orsay Pump.*)

Beau Nash is the only one of these beautiful people comparable to Brummell. Master of Ceremonies at Bath, then England's most fashionable gambling and cultural center, Nash spent much of his long life preening and strutting, riding around in a chariot drawn by six gray stallions and attended by laced lackeys. The "King of Bath" died in 1761, aged eighty-seven, and the town ordered a full-size statue of him erected in the Pump Room between the smaller busts of Newton and Pope. That Beau Nash, too, was remembered for his excesses, and not his many good works, can be seen in Lord Chesterfield's epigram on this statue:

The statue placed these busts between
Gives satire all its strength;
Wisdom and Wit are little seen,
But Folly at full length.

Beaufort Scale The *Beaufort scale,* a means to determine wind velocity, was devised in 1806 by Sir Francis Beaufort (1774–1857), noted surveyor and hydrologist, who later became a rear admiral and served as hydrographer to the British navy from 1829 to 1855. Beaufort's scale consists of numbers from 0 to 12 that indicate the strength of the wind ranging from "light," force 0, to "hurricane," force 12, or in Beaufort's words "that which no canvas could withstand." Wind speeds for these forces are the same on the British and United States version of

BRITISH AND U.S. BEAUFORT SCALE

Beaufort Number	Descriptive Term	Wind Speed
0	light air	less than 1
1	light air	1–3
2	light air	4–7
3	gentle	8–12
4	moderate	13–18
5	fresh	19–24
6	strong	25–31
7	strong	32–38
8	gale	39–46
9	gale	47–54
10	whole gale	55–63
11	whole gale	64–75
12	hurricane	more than 75

the scale, both differing from the international version adopted by most countries in 1874. For example, hurricane force 12 on the international scale means wind speed of more than sixty-five miles per hour, while a hurricane on the British and American scale means wind speed of more than seventy-five miles per hour. Additionally, the U.S. Weather Bureau sometimes extends the scale to gauge wind velocities from 0 to 17.

Béchamel, Béchamel Sauce The Marquis de Béchamel, it is said, made his money financing various fraudulent deals before turning from crookery to cookery, but the French forgave him everything for the sauce he invented. Louis de Béchamel became steward to Louis XIV, the Sun King, as he liked to call himself, whose motto was, "He who eats well works well." While superintendent of the royal kitchens, he created many sublime dishes for the dedicated gourmet king, under whom the now proverbial *Cordon Bleu* school of cookery was established. However, what we call a *béchamel*, a *béchamelle*, or a *Béchamel sauce* today— a cream sauce thickened with flour— bears little resemblance to the original, which was a complicated concoction prepared from egg yolks, cream, and butter blended with an elaborate bouillon made from vegetables, wines, "old hens and old partridges." This may be for the best, though. "Thank goodness," writes the noted chef Raymond Oliver, "[such recipes] are no longer more than pale ghosts of what they were."

As for *Le Roi Soleil*, The Grand Monarch, he lived a full life, shining brightest on epicurean delights until his sunset. Then, alas, the king lost all his teeth and had to resign himself to a diet of moistened breadcrumbs.

Bedouin A *bedouin* has come to mean any wandering person or vagabond, and derives from the French word (*Bedouin*) for the nomadic Arab tribes of the Arabian, Syrian and North African deserts. The French adapted the word from the Arabic *bidwan*, "a dweller in the open lands." The Bedouins of the Arabian desert, about one million in number, are nomadic camel breeders who trade their camels with Persian and Syrian traders for food and other goods.

Living in groups of up to one hundred, they are strongly united through blood relationships, a woman generally marrying her father's brother's son.

Beecher's Bibles *Beecher's Bibles* were Sharp repeater rifles that the Reverend Henry Ward Beecher (1813–87), one of America's most famous and controversial preachers, raised money for at his Brooklyn Heights church in New York and shipped to "Bloody Kansas" in crates labeled "Bibles." Beecher encouraged his parishioners to join the "underground railroad" and even held mock slave auctions at Plymouth Congregational Church in order to illustrate the evils of slavery. The church, still in use, was called "The Church of the Holy Rifles," and is now a national historic shrine. Beecher once wrote that "the Sharp rifle was a truly moral agency . . . [had] more moral power . . . than a hundred Bibles." The great preacher, brother of Harriet Beecher Stowe, was a complex man whose interests ranged from involvement in the antislavery movement to involvement with female members of his congregation. There has never been a balanced biography about Beecher—his biographers all seem to disdain or adore him, which was the way people reacted while he lived.

Beef Stroganoff, Beef Wellington Nineteenth-century Russian diplomat Count Paul Stroganoff has the honor of having the well-known *Beef Stroganoff* named after him. Sold in packaged form today, it is beef sautéed with onions, and cooked in a sauce of consommé, sour cream, mushrooms, mustard and other condiments. *Beef Wellington*, another popular dish, commemorates Arthur Wellesley, first duke of Wellington, for whom a number of words were named (see *Wellington*). *Beef Wellington* combines a choice cut of beef, liver pâté, bacon, brandy and various condiments, all baked in a golden crust of puffed pastry. The elegant dish, once confined to posh restaurants, is now often made at home, thanks to the introduction of frozen pastry dough.

Beggar A *beggar*, as Ernest Weekley pointed out in *The Romance of Words*, is not etymologically one who *begs*, for in the case of *to beg* the verb is evolved from the noun. Many scholars share this opinion. Surprisingly, *beggar* is not of ancient vintage, like "eat" and "drink" and "sleep." The word probably derives from the nickname of the twelfth-century Liége priest, Lambert le Bégue (Lambert the Stammerer), who founded a Belgian lay order devoted to the religious life and chastity as a reaction against the suffering of the Crusades. Little is known about Lambert le Bégue besides the fact that he died in 1177, but his secular order, though it demanded communal living, poverty, and self-denial, was a tolerant and popular one. There were no requirements that his followers take vows or lock themselves in a monastery, and members were allowed to own private property, as well as to leave the order and marry. The nuns of the Béguine order were called *beghinae* in Medieval Latin, and the monks belonging to a male group formed in the Netherlands were similarly called *beghardi*, these Latin formations influenced by the name of their order and by the Old Flemish *beghen*, to pray. But the brotherhood of *beghardi*, or *Beghards*, composed mostly of tradesmen, was very loosely organized, making it easy for thieves and mendicants to pose as members of the poor and ill-clad group. Imposters traveled the Low Countries claiming to be Beghards and asking for alms, the group held in low repute by the end of the thirteenth century—especially because a large number of the Beghards were militant trade unionists who raised havoc wherever they went, and because many other members had become idle, wandering mendicants like their imitators. The old French word *begard*, meaning mendicant, was soon formed from either the Medieval Latin *beghardi*, for Beghards, or from the Middle Dutch *beggaert*, meaning the same thing. *Begard*, in turn, became the Anglo-French *begger*, which was transformed into the Middle English *beggare*, or mendicant, with its verb *beggen* meaning to ask for alms. Eventually we had the English word *beggar* that we use today, the verb *to beg* thus growing out of what the *beggar* did.

Other scholars trace *beggar* to the obscure Old English word *bedecian*, which is only related to a Gothic word meaning

mendicant and is so rare it has been found only once. But even if this is correct, there is no doubt that the Beghards at least reinforced the idea of *beggar* in people's minds. (See also *Bigot*.)

Begonia Michel Bégon (1638–1710) served as a minor navy official at various French ports until a fortunate marriage led to his appointment by Louis XIII as royal commissioner in Santo Domingo, though he wasn't Santo Domingo's governor as is often claimed. Bégon primarily concerned himself with protecting the natives from unscrupulous merchants and attending their medical needs, but the amateur horticulturist ordered a detailed study of the island's plant life, collecting hundreds of specimens. Among these he found the *begonia*, now a common house and garden plant, which he took back to France with him and introduced to European botanists. The *begonia*, however, wasn't named for him until sixty-seven years after his death, when it was first brought to England. Bégon is remembered for his patronage of science and his public spirit. On the opening of his large private library to the public, for example, friends advised him that he would surely lose numerous books. "I had much rather lose my books," he replied, "than seem to distrust an honest man." The *begonia* he discovered is a most valuable garden plant because it prefers the shade, where it flowers freely, is available in a large variety of colors, and can be grown for its foliage as well as its beautiful blooms. The *Begonia* genus contains some one thousand species.

Bel (see *Decibel*)

Belcher Scarf, Ring Jim or Jem Belcher, England's Gentleman Jim Corbett, carried and made popular a large pocket handkerchief, its blue background spotted with large white spots with a small dark blue spot in the center of each. Such handkerchiefs or neckerchiefs, often more descriptively called "bird's eye wipes," were named after the boxer, as was the *Belcher ring*, a huge gold affair set with a large stone that was prominent even on Belcher's massive dukes. Jim Belcher, the most celebrated boxer of his time, lost an eye in 1803, retiring from the ring and owning or operating a pub. He died in 1811, when only thirty years old. Belcher's name, oddly enough, means "fine gentleman" in French. He bore a remarkable resemblance to Napoleon and was in fact billed as the Napoleon of the Ring. (See also *Bendigo*.)

Bellarmine *Bellarmine* is an historical term referring to a glazed stone beer jug designed to ridicule Italian Cardinal Roberto Francesco Romolo Bellarmino (1542–1621). Cardinal Bellarmine, as he is better known, distinguished himself as a Jesuit scholar and was a friend of Galileo, but is usually remembered for his persecution of Protestants in Flanders. The Flemish later retaliated by caricaturing him with the large *bellarmine*, which was designed as a burlesque likeness, having a huge belly and a narrow neck. The controversial cardinal was canonized in 1930.

Ben Day A New York printer named Benjamin Day (1838–1916) invented the Ben Day process of quick mechanical production of stippling, shading or tints on line engravings. *Ben Dayed* means produced by the *Ben Day* photoengraving method. The process, which has been used since about 1879, eliminates the shading of a drawing by hand.

Bendigo The only city ever named for a prizefighter is *Bendigo*, Australia, which has a population of some fifty thousand and is the third largest sheep and cattle market in Australia. *Bendigo*, the site of a famous gold strike in 1851, honors the ring name of English pugilist William Thompson (1811–1889), as does the *bendigo* fur cap popular in the late nineteenth century. Thompson was born the same year that Fighting Jim Belcher died. He may have been one of triplets nicknamed Shadrach, Meschach and *Abednego*, or his nickname could have stemmed from his evangelical pursuits, but, in any event, in 1835 he signed his first ring challenge Abed-Nego of Nottingham, and used the nickname Bendigo for the remainder of his career—until he gave up fighting to become a full-time evangelist. *Bendigo*, Australia, had some second thoughts about its eponymous name, changing it to Sandhurst in 1871, but reverted back to the old appellation in 1891, two years after Thompson's death.

Benedick, Benedict A *benedick* is strictly a sworn bachelor entrapped in marriage, while a *benedict* refers to a bachelor of marriageable age. The former term derives from the name of the character Benedick in Shakespeare's *Much Ado About Nothing* and the latter honors St. Benedict (d. 543), founder of the Benedictine order and great advocate of celibacy. *Benedict* originally meant a perennial bachelor sworn to celibacy and it is probably for this reason that Shakespeare adopted and adapted the name—for its amusing contrast to his Benedick, the young lord who vows at the beginning of *Much Ado About Nothing* to forever remain a bachelor and is finally talked into marriage. Shakespeare may have borrowed his idea from Thomas Kyd's *The Spanish Tragedy*, and the Latin *Benedictus*, the blessed, probably also influenced his choice of the name. Although there is a distinction between the two words, they are used interchangeably today, meaning not a bachelor anymore, but a newly married man who had been a bachelor for a long time. *Benedict*, as in "a happy *benedict*," is the usual spelling. (See also *Benedictine*.)

Benedict Arnold *Quisling* and a few others have endured, but most traitors were not even bad enough to be good enough to be included in the dictionaries. Or else we just want to forget them. *Benedict Arnold* is an exception. The term has been used for over two hundred years in America, and is still a common one. Every schoolboy knows the story of how General Benedict Arnold plotted to deliver the garrison at West Point to Major John André, how the plot failed with André's capture and Arnold fled to the British army. Less familiar are the facts that Arnold was a brilliant soldier and that his treason was provoked by shabby treatment at the hands of superiors several times during the course of the Revolutionary War. Historians have generally agreed that these provocations did not nearly justify his actions, however, vindicating the use of his name. Benedict Arnold lived his last years, for all intents and purposes, as a man without a country, anathema to Americans and scorned by the British. He died a broken man in London on June 14, 1801, only sixty years old. (See also *Bolo; Laval; Lord Haw Haw; Petain; Quisling; Tokyo Rose.*)

Benedictine, Benedictines Many famous drinks—champagne, coffee, Chianti, mocha, Scotch, Seltzer, and Vichy water—are named after places, but the celebrated liqueur *Benedictine* is named for a famous religious brotherhood. The particular monk who concocted the drink was one Don Bernado Vincelli, a man whom the medieval archbishop of Rouen declared as important to humanity as any saint for his inspiration. *Benedictine,* one of the oldest liquors in the world, was first made at the *Bénédictine* monastery at Fécamp, France, in about 1510. Called *Bénédictine* in honor of the order, its makers dedicated it "to the greater glory of God." Though the monastery was destroyed during the French Revolution, monks managed to save the secret formula and fifty years later a Frenchman named Le Grand began manufacturing *Benedictine,* his distillery still standing on the site of the abbey. Le Grand labeled each bottle D.O.M., which are the initials of the order and stand for *Deo optimo maximo,* "for the most good and great God."

St. Benedict, founder of western monasticism about 530 A.D., at Naples, was a rather austere man to have a liqueur named after him, even indirectly. He lived as a hermit for many years and imposed intense industry and strict celibacy on his followers. (See also *Benedick; Dom Perignon.*)

Benny, Benjamin Today a *benny* is usually American slang for any amphetamine tablet, especially *Benzedrine,* a trademarked name, but it also signifies both a pawnbroker, and an overcoat. A pawnbroker became a *benny* because he often makes loans on overcoats, which are sometimes called *bennies* or *benjies,* a shortened form for *benjamins.* The *benjamin,* at first a certain tight-fitting style of overcoat and then any overcoat at all, probably derives from the Biblical Benjamin, in humorous reference to his brother Joseph's coat of many colors (*Genesis* 37:3). But some scholars claim that the *benjamin* was created by a mid-nineteenth-century London tailor of that name, the Biblical tale rendering the term

popular, and Mencken suggests that *benny* for an overcoat may have derived from the Romany *bengru,* a waistcoat. *Benny* is also slang for a *derby.*

Berenice's Hair, Coma Berenices, Varnish, Vernis Martin *Berenice's hair* is the lock of a woman's hair that became a constellation. It was made famous by the five surviving lines of the poem *The Lock of Berenice* by the Greek poet Callimachus and the poem is said to be based on a true story.

Berenice was married to Ptolemy III, king of Egypt, and when he invaded Syria in 246 B.C. to avenge the murder of his sister, she dedicated a lock of her hair to the gods as an offering for his safe return. The hair mysteriously disappeared, but the court astronomer, Conon of Samos, perhaps to assuage her, pretended to discover that it had been carried to heaven and transformed into a constellation of the northern hemisphere, which has been known ever since as *Coma Berenices.* A coma is the hazy envelope around a comet, and the word comet itself derives from the Greek and Latin words for hair, alluding to a fancied resemblance between the tails of comets and hair blowing in the wind. Ptolemy returned from the wars safely, but soon after his death in 221 B.C. the fabled Berenice was murdered at the instigation of her son.

Later the Greeks named the town of *Berenike* in Libya for Berenice. Here a paint industry thrived and one new coating was called *Berenice,* its color said to resemble the amber hair of the queen. Called *bernix* in Medieval Latin, the Italians corrupted the paint's name to *vernice,* which became *vernis* in French and *varnish* in English—the chances being that the floor underneath your feet has something of the color of Berenice's hair. *Vernis martin,* or *Martin varnish,* a finish for furniture, is twice eponymous, being named for the brothers Martin, eighteenth-century French craftsmen who invented it in imitation of Chinese lacquer.

Alexander Pope's famous "The Rape of the Lock" was also based on a true incident involving a piece of hair. The English poet wrote the mock-heroic poem when one Lord Petre snipped off a lock belonging to a Miss Arabella, this resulting in a quarrel between the two families. Ultimately the poet only made the feud worse. (See also *Charles' Wain; Halley's Comet.*)

Bertillon System The first modern scientific method for identifying criminals was the *Bertillion system*, devised by Alphonse Bertillion (1853–1914), French anthropologist and pioneer criminologist. Bertillion developed *Bertillionage*, as the system is also called, when he headed the criminal identification bureau in the Seine prefecture and described it in his book *La Photographie judiciare.* Adopted by France in 1888, the revolutionary method relied on anthropometry—the classification of skeletal and other body measurements, plus the color of hair, eyes, etc., for purposes of comparison. Fingerprints were a late addition to these *Bertillion measurements* and soon supplanted the system itself. The term is still used, though, to describe fingerprints and all anthropometric measurements. Bertillion, who came from a distinguished family of anthropologists, is remembered for his role in the Dreyfus case, where he appeared as an expert handwriting witness for the prosecution.

Bessemer Converter, Bessemer Process, Bessemer Steel We might almost as fairly call the *Bessemer process* the *Kelly process.* This revolutionary method for converting pig or cast iron to steel is named after Englishman Henry Bessemer (1813–1898), but it was discovered almost concurrently by American inventor William Kelly (1811–88). Bessemer, the son of a French artist, was already a respected metallurgist and the inventor of a machine used to reduce gold and bronze to powder when he began experimenting to produce better and cheaper iron for cannon during the Crimean war. He started his work about the year 1854, being granted his first patent a year later, and in 1856 discovered the basic principle involved in his process, which he described in his paper, "The Manufacture of Iron Without Fuel." Bessemer's secret was the removal of carbon and other impurities from pig iron by melting it in his *Bessemer converter* and forcing a blast of air through the molten metal. The *Bessemer process,* much improved today, produced far better steel more cheaply and faster than ever before, tripling English steel production within a few years after its introduction.

American William Kelly, on the other hand, discovered purely by accident the same process Bessemer had developed through painstaking research. Kelly had been the master of an iron furnace in Eddyville, Ky., when he noticed that an air blast blowing directly on uncovered molten metal raised its temperature greatly by oxidation. When Bessemer patented his discovery in the United States in 1857, Kelly convinced the patent office of the priority of his claim. He established an iron works near Detroit in 1864, but another American began to use Bessemer's patents the following year at Troy, N.Y. A long court battle ensued that was finally settled by a consolidation of the rival companies, Kelly retiring and Bessemer's claim never challenged again. The Englishman was knighted for his discovery in 1879.

Bibb Lettuce An amateur gardener named John B. Bibb developed *Bibb lettuce* in his backyard garden in Frankfort, Ky., about 1850 and the variety has been an American favorite ever since. *Bibb* is the most famous and best of what are called butterhead lettuces, having a tight small head of a dark green color and a wonderful flavor. Because the variety is inclined to bolt in hot weather, a *summer Bibb* is now offered by nurserymen for the home garden. Several kinds of lettuce are named after their developers, including *blackseeded Simpson,* a loose-leaf variety. The vegetable can be traced back to ancient India and Central Asia, but takes its name from the Latin word *lac,* meaning milk, the Romans favoring lettuce for its milky juice and calling it *lactuce. Bibb* is not often found in the market, the most popular sellers in the United States being Iceberg lettuce, a heading variety, and loose-leaf Boston lettuce.

Bibles Named After People Numerous editions of the Bible have been named for their translators or patrons, the most famous being the *King James* or *Authorized Version,* which was prepared by a group of British scholars working at the command of King James I from 1604 to 1611. James commissioned this version mainly because other Bibles of the time had marginal notes questioning the divine right of kings. *Coverdale's Bible, Cranmer's Bible, Cromwell's Bible, Matthew's Bible, Matthew Parker's Bible, Taverner's Bible, Tyndale's Bible,* and *Wycliffe's Bible* are all famous in history. *Coverdale's Bible* is sometimes known as The Bug Bible because it reads "Thou shalt not need to be afraid for any bugs by night" in a passage from *Psalms*, using "bugs" instead of "terror" in the sentence. Other amusing instances of printer's errors occur in The Wicked Bible (1805), where the seventh commandment reads "Thou shalt commit adultery"; the Unrighteous Bible, which says that "the unrighteous shall inherit the Kingdom of God"; and The Sin On Bible, which in the book of *John* reads "sin on more" instead of "sin no more." There is even a vegetarian Bible and one with no references to sex. (See also *Gutenberg; Jefferson.*)

Big Ben *Big Ben* is not the huge clock in London's Parliament tower, though it is often given this name. The words really describe the huge, deep-toned bell in St. Stephen's Tower which strikes the hours over the British Houses of Parliament. *Big Ben,* cast from 1856 to 1858, weighs 13½ tons, more than twice the weight of the 6½-ton bell in Philadelphia's Independence Hall. The great bell's first stroke, not the last, marks the hour, four smaller bells in the tower striking the quarter hours on the famed Westminster Chimes. The tower clock, 329 feet high, was designed by lawyer and architect Edmund Grimthorpe (1816–1905) and named St. Stephen's Tower. This was to be the name of the bell, too, but newspapers took to calling it after Sir Benjamin Hall, Chief Commissioner of Works at the time, and the sobriquet stuck. *Big Ben,* though a notable achievement in bell founding, is far from being the world's largest bell. Moscow's Tsar Kolokol, a broken and unused giant weighing about 180 tons, is called the King of Bells, while another Moscow bell of 128 tons is the largest in use. *Big Ben* is not even the greatest bell cast in England, an honor belonging to the 18¼-ton specimen in New York's Riverside Church, the largest bell that has ever been tuned.

Big Bertha On close examination, *Big Bertha,* the famous cannon that shelled Paris during World War I is not so complimentary to the woman for whom it was named. *Big Bertha* is a translation of *die dicke Bertha,* "the fat Bertha," a nickname the Germans had for their 42 cm. howitzers. They had in mind portly Frau Bertha Krupp von Bohlen und Halbach, whose husband owned the giant Krupp steel and munitions plant at Essen, it being mistakenly believed that the howitzers were manufactured by Krupp, whereas they were actually made at the Skoda works in Austria-Hungary. The *Big Bertha* aimed at Paris, an even larger gun with a range of 76 miles, began bombarding the city on March 23, 1918, firing every third day for 140 days and killing 256 people in all. On Good Friday of that year alone its shells killed or wounded 156 worshippers in the church of St. Gervais. It was at this time that journalists resurrected the term from the German and began applying it specifically to the Paris gun. Bertha Krupp von Bohlen und Halbach died in 1957, aged seventy-one.

Bignonia A widely distributed woody flowering vine, the *bignonia* is sometimes confused with the *begonia,* and the names of the men the two plants honor are often confused as well. The species are not related, and Abbé John Paul Bignon, court librarian to Louis XIV, did not discover the beautiful *bignonia* vine bearing his name. The *bignonia* was named by the French botanist Tournefort about 1700 in honor of the abbé, who had never ventured from Europe. Bignon's name is also found in the plant family *Bignoniaceae,* comprising 100 genera and over 750 species, as well as in the genus *Bignonia,* which contains the *bignonia vine.* The plant is popularly called the trumpet flower or cross vine. (See *Begonia.*)

Bigot The legend that the word *bigot* was born when the Norman lord Rollo refused to kiss the royal foot of Charles the Simple as an act of homage, shouting indignantly, "*Ne, se, bi got*" (No, by God!), is an amusing old story but probably no more than that. It is unlikely that *bigot* arose because this phrase of Rollo's was applied thereafter to any obstinate person. But some scholars do suspect that *bigot* stems from the Teutonic oath *bi got,* suggesting that it may have been bestowed as a nickname upon the Normans, who were apparently obstinately or intolerantly devoted to their own religion. The Normans were so intolerant that for centuries they called an Englishman a *godon* or "*God damn it!*"

Another suggestion is that *bigot* derives from the Spanish *bigote,* whiskers, which may have come to mean a fiery fellow or zealot. Whatever the case, the formation of *bigot* was almost certainly influenced by the fanatical behavior or reputation of members of both the Beguttae Order of St. Augustine and the Beguine religious order, the last named after the priest Lambert de Bégue. (See *Beggar.*) Interestingly, Bigot was included in Camden's English collection of surnames published in 1605. But then, so were Devil, Loophole and Gallows.

Billies and Charlies Collectors will pay premium prices for genuine *Billies and Charlies,* even though they are fake historical objects. William (Billy) Smith and Charles (Charlie) Eaton manufactured such bogus medieval articles from 1847 to 1858, planting them around London and then "discovering" them in excavations. The spurious objects were made, quite ingeniously, from lead or an alloy of lead and copper.

Billingsgate, Billingsgate Pheasant *Billingsgate,* coarse and abusive language, is language similar to that used by the fishwives in the Billingsgate fish market along the Thames in London. The area was named for whoever built the gate below the London bridge leading to the old walled city. But who built Billing's Gate is a matter of controversy. Some historians credit a Mr. Billings (or Billin, or Belin), a builder or famous burgher who owned property thereabouts; others suggest that Billing's Gate was named for an ancient tribe called Billings, or for one Belen (Belinus), a legendary monarch, citing a 1658 map that ascribes it to "Belen, ye 23rd Brittish Kinge." In any case, the real eponym would be glad not to have his name definitively associated with the vile rhetoric of the viragoes who sold fish by his gate.

Billingsgate pheasant is a humorous expression for the common red herring.

Billy Wells (see *Jack Johnson*)

Binet-Simon Tests The first intelligence tests were developed by Alfred Binet (1857–1911), a French psychologist who directed the laboratory of psychology and physiology at the Sorbonne, in conjunction with psychologist Theodore Simon. The initial tests, later extended in age, determined the intelligence quotient of children three to twelve, each subject asked questions adapted to the intelligence of a normal child of his age. The *Binet-Simon tests* have been revised many times since their invention in 1905. Intelligence quotient or I.Q. on such tests is merely a ratio, expressed as a percentage, of a person's mental age to his actual age, his mental age being the age for which he scores 100 percent on all the questions. The score 150 is generally accepted as genius and below 70 classified as mental deficiency. The highest score ever recorded is the 200 achieved by a London girl, Somerset Hughes, in 1960 when she was five years old, but historical researches put the figure for John Stuart Mill, who learned Greek at the age of three, at "over 200."

Bing Cherry *Bing cherries* are popular dark red, nearly black fruit of the Bigarreau or firm, crisp-fleshed group. The tree was developed in 1875 by a Chinese named Bing in Oregon, where over a quarter of the country's sweet cherry crop is grown. Other cherry varieties named after their developers include the *Luelling,* for the man who founded Oregon's cherry industry in 1847, the *Lambert* and the *Schmidt.* Countless varieties honor famous people, such as the *Napoleon,* the *Royal Ann,* and the *Governor Wood,* though none is named for George Washington. Surprisingly, sour cherries outnumber sweets two to one in the United States, probably because they are easier to grow and are more in demand for cooking and canning. Cherries were probably first cultivated in China over four thousand years ago, so Bing was carrying on a great ethnic tradition.

Birrelism, Birreligion Both the charm and unobtrusive scholarship displayed by Augustine Birrell (1850–1933) in his *Obiter Dicta* and other works led to the formation of the word *birrellism* for shrewd cursory comments on humankind and life in general. Birrell, a barrister elected to Parliament in 1889, became president of the national board of education and chief secretary for Ireland (1907–16). He is noted for Birrell's Educational Bill of 1906 and the founding of the Roman Catholic National University of Ireland. It has been observed that Birrell's good-humored detachment and gently ironic view of life, the same qualities that enhanced his writing, were responsible for his downfall politically as a result of the Easter Rebellion in Ireland. *Birreligion* indicated the political import of his educational bill.

Bishop Another murderer whose name became a word. Unlike *burke*, which it resembles, the expression *to bishop* is used only historically today, although the words arose at about the same time and for essentially the same reason. *To bishop* is to murder by drowning. It is named for a Mr. Bishop, who in 1831 so murdered a little boy in Bethnal Green, England, in order to sell the child's body to surgeons for dissection, the murderer probably influenced by the earlier work of Burke and Hare.

A second Bishop claiming eponymous infamy is the otherwise unknown man responsible for the term *to bishop* or *bishoping*, meaning to file down the teeth of a horse to make him appear young for resale. (See also *Aqua Tofano; Bluebeard; Burke; Borgia; Crippen; Jack the Ripper; Thugs.*)

The Bishop Hath Put His Foot In It This old proverb led to the common expression, *Now you've put your foot in it*. Bishop is, of course, usually an honorific, but the original proverb, used when soup was scorched, may have arisen because of the reputation a certain bishop or various bishops had for burning heretics. An alternate explanation is that the saying arose when an anonymous cook stood at the window watching a procession headed by a noted bishop and blamed him for the port soup she burned.

Blackguard Most etymologists believe that the original *blackguards* were the medieval kitchen servants of the rich, who were humorously referred to as such in allusion to their appearance and the black pots and pans they guarded when the household retinue moved from place to place. The modern meaning of *blackguard*, a low contemptible person, is said to derive from the characteristics of these "rough and worthless" knaves. Somehow the theory doesn't sound convincing. Perhaps, as has been suggested, the word derives from some actual band of soldiers wearing black uniforms whose low, vicious crimes are lost to history.

Black Maria A police van or paddy wagon is often called a *Black Maria*. The traditional story is that the word honors one Maria Lee, a fearsome black woman who owned a Boston boardinghouse, but the full tale is seldom told. Maria Lee, at first a teamster, supposedly became an American heroine in 1798 when she delivered swivel guns to outfit the first little cutters Alexander Hamilton had ordered built to protect merchant ships on the high seas. Maria guided her team over muddy Philadelphia back roads to the waterfront. It is said that she was ambushed by smugglers who tried to steal the cannon, but she demolished the band of them and got the cannon to the cutter *Scammel* on time.

Later, in the early 1800's, Maria opened her boardinghouse for sailors, the best mannered place on the waterfront because even hardened criminals feared her awesome strength. The giant woman once rescued a policeman being attacked and aided the police so frequently that the saying "Send for the Black Maria" became common whenever there was trouble with an offender. Fiery Maria sometimes helped escort prisoners to jail, and when the first British police horse vans were introduced in 1838 they may have been christened in her honor.

The tradition is largely unsupported for lack of evidence. Critics point out that the first van itself was *black* and that *Maria* could have come from numerous sources, but no better source has been offered.

Blanket There may have been a Thomas Blanket of Bristol, England, who made *blankets*, setting up "the first loom for their manufacture in 1340." But the word *blanket* comes from the Old French *blankette*, originally a white wool cloth used for clothing and exclusively the *blanket* we know today by the mid fourteenth century. This is not to say that Thomas Blanket couldn't have adopted the name *blanket* for his product and made the word more popular.

Blighia Sapida, Captain Bligh A *Captain Bligh*, commemorating the captain of *Mutiny on the Bounty* fame, is still used to describe a cruel, cold-hearted taskmaster. Captain William Bligh is also remembered by the ackee fruit, which looks and tastes like scrambled eggs when properly prepared, but can be poisonous when over- or under-ripe. The ackee tree's botanical name is *Blighia sapida*, after the man who introduced it along with breadfruit. Bligh was called "Breadfruit Bligh" for his discovery of that fruit's virtues and was in fact bringing specimens of the breadfruit tree from Tahiti to the West Indies in 1789 when his mutinous crew foiled his plans. The lesson of *Bounty* apparently taught him little or nothing, for his harsh methods and terrible temper aroused a second mutiny, the Rum Rebellion, while he served as governor of New South Wales. Bligh, a brave and able officer, retired from the navy a vice admiral. He died in 1817, aged sixty-three.

Blind Pigs Saloons serving illegal liquor during prohibition were called *blind pigs*. The name comes from the nickname of a band of soldiers called the Public Guard serving in Richmond, Va., about 1858. Their militia hats had the initials P.G. on them, the sobriquet arising because "P.G. is a pig without an *i*, and a pig without an *eye* is a blind pig."

Blondin *Blondin* was the stage name of one of the greatest tightrope walkers of all time, the Frenchman Jean François Gravelet (1824–1897). The inimitable Blondin, whose name became a synonym for a star acrobat or tightrope walker, began his career at a mere five years of age and performed many great feats thereafter. The first man to cross Niagara Falls on a tightrope, on June 30, 1859, he later made the crossing while pushing a wheelbarrow, twirling an umbrella, and with

another man on his back. The rope was 1,100 feet long, only three inches thick, and was suspended 160 feet above the falls.

Bloomers *Bloomers* were once as controversial as hot pants, the miniskirt, or the braless look have been since, though not in the sense that we now use the word. Newspapers, magazines, and orators railed against *bloomers*. Preachers banned women wearing them from church, threatening excommunication and pointing out that the Bible forbids a woman donning anything that pertains to a man (*Deuteronomy* 22:5). For *bloomers* were originally billowing Turkish pantaloons, bound with elastic around the ankles and covered by a short skirt and a loose-fitting tunic. They were designed and first worn in about 1850 by Mrs. Elizabeth Smith Miller, daughter of the wealthy abolitionist, Gerrit Smith, but feminist Amelia Jenks Bloomer (1818 –1894) defended the masculine pantaloons with the same vehemence as their detractors and it is her name that they immortalize.

Mrs. Bloomer was at first involved in the temperance crusade to a greater degree than the women's rights movements, her small magazine *The Lily* being the house organ of the Seneca Falls Ladies' Temperance Society. However, she had always been something of a feminist, supporting Susan B. Anthony and even insisting the word "obey" be omitted from the marriage vows when she wed Dexter C. Bloomer in 1840. Amelia learned of the outfit her name would later adorn from suffragist Elizabeth Cady Stanton, their inventor's cousin. She wrote about the costume in *The Lily*, describing it as "sanitary attire" in an 1851 issue. Soon she was wearing it and promoting it on lecture platforms across the country, probably for the first time publicly in July, 1851, at a gala ball she held in Lowell, Mass. Mrs. Bloomer insisted, quite logically, that fashionable hoopskirts were both cumbersome and unsanitary, picking up dust and mud on the then largely unpaved streets, and reminded her religious critics that *Genesis* made no distinction between the fig leaves of Adam and Eve. She even inspired a troop of *Bloomer girls* to sail to England, where they were generally met with laughter or indignation, yet she always denied that she invented or first wore *bloomers* and protested against the costume being called by her name. Nevertheless, her proselytising, and the fact that the pantaloons "bloomed out" so, made the appellation stick in the public's mind.

When the Civil War erupted, Amelia Jenks Bloomer forgot *bloomers* and turned her attention to the Union cause. Her life is the subject of several biographies and *Bloomer Girl* (1944), a Broadway musical comedy. The *bloomers* named after her were worn up until the turn of the century, especially during the bicycling craze of the 1890's, but they never succeeded as a fashion, primarily because they were such an ugly costume. They did survive as a name, now usually humorous, for women's underpants, which their first detractors would hardly object to ladies wearing at all. (See also *Knickers; Pants.*)

Blucher Boots This half boot has evolved into today's basic, low-cut men's shoe. Originally laced low boots or high shoes, *bluchers* were named for Gebhard Leberecht von Blucher (1742–1819), a Prussian field marshal who fought with Wellington against Napoleon at Waterloo. Field Marshal von Blucher did not design but sponsored the boots in 1810, considering them better footwear for his troops. Another word commemorating him was the British slang expression *Blucher*, for a cab allowed to take passengers to London station only after all others had been hired—in allusion to the fact that the old man had arrived at Waterloo too late to be of much help.

Bluebeard According to local tradition in Brittany, the real *Bluebeard*, who murdered six of his seven wives, was the Frenchman General Gilles de Retz, the Marquis de Laval, a monster burnt at the stake for his crimes in 1440. This sadistic creature was made famous by Charles Perrault's story *Barbe Bleue* (Blue Beard), in which the murderer's last wife discovers the bodies of her husband's victims in a secret, locked room and is saved from death herself by her brother's arrival in the nick of time. *Bluebeard* has come to mean a man who murders women he has married, and a number of contemporary

wife killers, including the Frenchman Landau, have been called The Modern Bluebeard. Perrault's story was published in his *Contes du Temps* (1697), which contains "Sleeping Beauty," "Red Riding Hood," "Puss In Boots," "Cinderella," and many of the most famous fairy tales, collected from various sources.

Bluenose, Blue Laws, Blue Movies The lumbermen and fishermen of northern New England may have been puritanical, but it is not for this reason that they were the first people to be called *bluenoses*. The word simply referred to the color of their noses, a color induced by their long exposure to cold weather. Only later was the term used, possibly in describing inhabitants of Boston's Back Bay area, as a synonym for a person of rigid puritanic habits. *Bluenose* is also used to describe Nova Scotians, probably deriving here from the name of a Nova Scotian potato.

Blue laws has nothing to do with either of the above derivations. This synonym for Never on Sunday moral laws, may derive from a nonexistent Connecticut "blue book" rumored to contain fanatical laws. The Reverend Samuel Peters, an American Tory who returned to England, spread the rumor out of personal revenge. He claimed that the fictitious blue-bound book contained laws such as one making it illegal for a man to kiss his wife on the Sabbath.

The word *blue* for obscene, as in *blue movies*, is still more difficult to trace. It may be from the customary blue dress of harlots in the early nineteenth century, or from a series of off-color French books called *La Bibliothèque Bleue*.

Bluestockings "A bluestocking," said Rousseau, "is a woman who will remain a spinster as long as there are sensible men on earth." Undoubtedly male chauvinism, especially when we look at the word's origins. The original *bluestockings* were a group headed by a Mrs. Elizabeth Montagu (her first name is variously given, and "Montagu" is often spelt with an "e") that first met in her London home and the homes of friends about 1750. Their purpose was to replace idle evenings of chatter with a literary salon based on Parisian models, and they hoped to attract the era's leading intellectuals.

The club members dressed simply as a reaction against the sumptuous evening clothes of the time. These eggheads were soon held in contempt by "proper" society and a noted wit dubbed them The Bluestocking Club, or *bluestockings,* for the blue-colored hose that one *male* member wore in place of gentlemen's black silk hose. For no good reason, a *bluestocking* came to mean an intellectual or affectedly literary, dowdy woman, although the group probably did have a few such members. The appellation seems all the more unfair when one considers that only a Mr. Benjamin Stillingfleet wore the homely blue-gray tradesman's stockings responsible for the club's name. Ironically, the word *bluestocking* really derives from a man.

Blurb Blurb is neither a strictly human nor fictional human word, but is too good not to include. It was invented by humorist Gelett Burgess with the publication of his *Are You a Bromide?* in 1907. Burgess' publisher, B. W. Huebish, tells the story: "It is the custom of publishers to present copies of a conspicuous current book to booksellers attending the annual dinner of their trade association, and as this little book was in its heyday when the meeting took place I gave it to 500 guests. These copies were differentiated from the regular edition by the addition of a comic bookplate drawn by the author and by a special jacket which he devised. It was the common practice to print the picture of a damsel—languishing, heroic, or coquettish . . . on the jacket of every novel, so Burgess lifted from a Lydia Pinkham or tooth-powder advertisement the portrait of a sickly sweet young woman, painted in some gleaming teeth, and otherwise enhanced her pulchritude, and placed her in the center of the jacket. His accompanying text was some nonsense about 'Miss Belinda *Blurb,*' and thus the term supplied a real need and became a fixture in our language."

Other notable invented words, aside from those deriving from fictional characters, include: Lewis Carroll's *chortle; debunk,* invented by American novelist William Woodward; *googol,* a number followed by one hundred zeroes, coined by the nephew of American mathematician Edward Kasner; *ecdysiast,* a stripteaser, invented by H. L. Mencken; *heebie-jeebies* and *hotsy-totsy,* coined by American cartoonist Billy De Beck; *pandemonium,* Milton; *panjandrum,* English dramatist Samuel Foote; *nihilism,* Turgenev; *quark,* James Joyce; *runcible,* Edward Lear; *Shangri-la* James Hilton; *spoof,* after a game invented by British comedian A. Roberts; *teetotal,* British abstainer R. Turner; and *Utopian,* Sir Thomas More.

Mr. Burgess' book is also responsible for the word *bromide,* describing a tiresome person. He is the author of the famous "Purple Cow":

I never saw a Purple Cow,
  I never hope to see one;
But I can tell you anyhow,
  I'd rather see than be one!

And:

Ah, yes! I wrote the "Purple Cow"—
  I'm sorry now, I wrote it!
But I can tell you anyhow,
  I'll kill you if you quote it!

Bob, Joey A *bob* is a British slang word for a shilling familiar to all English-speaking peoples. It has been suggested that the word may come from the name of Sir Robert (Bob) Walpole (1676–1745). Robert Orford, the first earl of Walpole, was intimately connected with money in his posts as army paymaster, first commissioner of the treasury, chancellor of the exchequer, and finally as England's prime minister. In fact, his administration in the last capacity had been based on two major principles: freedom from wars abroad and *sound finance at home.* The only trouble is that the word *bob* isn't recorded until about 1810, some sixty-five years after Walpole's death. The *Oxford English Dictionary* lists the derivation as unknown, but then numerous public officials have given their names to units of money. These include Joseph Hume, British Member of Parliament, for whom the *Joey* fourpence piece was named.

Bobadil Ben Jonson's play *Every Man in his Humor* (1598) gave us the character Captain Bobadill, an old soldier who gravely boasts of his conquests and is proved as vain and cowardly as he is boastful. From the old soldier's name we have the word *bobadil*, a braggart who pretends to great prowess, but Jonson patterned his character on Boabdil, a late fifteenth-century Moorish king of Granada. King Boabdil was noted for the same characteristics as the fictional captain.

Bobby, Peelers, Robert *Bobby* is probably the most familiar of our myriad and sundry eponymous words, despite the fact that *copper* or *cop* is more often used today to describe an English policeman. The well-known word honors Sir Robert Peel, British Home Secretary (1828–30), when the *Metropolitan Police Act* remodeled London's police force. Peel, whose wealthy father bought him his seat in Parliament, as was customary in those days, first won fame as chief secretary for Ireland, where he was nicknamed Orange Peel for his support of the Protestant "orangemen." It was at this time that he established the Irish constabulary under *The Peace Preservation Act* (1814), his policemen soon called "Peel's Bloody Gang" and then *peelers*. *Peelers* remained the name for both Irish and London police for many years, *bobby* and *robert* not being recorded in print until about 1851.

Peel became Britain's prime minister first in 1834 and again in 1841, his many reforms including the abolition of capital punishment for petty crimes and the *Catholic Emancipation Bill*, which permitted Catholics to sit in Parliament. He lost office in 1849, his fruitful career cut short when he died in a freak accident a year later. Like two other English eponyms—Lord Cardigan and Soapy Sam Wilberforce—he died after being thrown from his horse, only a day after making a speech indicating his desire to return to public life.

Bodelian Library England's *Bodelian Library* at Oxford, among the greatest in the world, honors its founder Sir Thomas Bodley (1545–1613), who devoted nearly twenty years of his life to developing the library. The *Bodelian* is entitled under the national *Copyright Act* to receive on demand a copy of every book published in the United Kingdom. Thomas Bodley, a Protestant exile who returned to England from Geneva when Elizabeth as-

cended the throne, served in Parliament and as a diplomat in several European countries before retiring from public life in 1596. He began to restore the old Oxford library two years later and left most of his fortune to it as an endowment.

Boeotian, Boeotian Ears One of the many words dishonoring a whole people, *Boeotian* means ignorant, dull and lacking in refinement. It recalls the inhabitants of Boetia, a farming district in ancient Greece, whom the urbane Athenians (see *attic*) found thick and stupid, with no understanding of art or literature. More knowledgeable Greeks, including Pindar and Horace, noted that the region produced Pindar and Plutarch as well as country bumpkins. As for *Boeotian ears*, they are ears unable to appreciate good music or poetry.

Bogus "The word *bogus*," according to the Boston *Courier* in 1857, "is a corruption of the name Borghese, a man who, twenty years ago, did a tremendous business in supplying the Great West of America with counterfeit bills on fictitious banks. The western people came to shortening the name Borghese to *bogus*, and his bills were universally styled 'bogus currency.'" This story may not be *bogus*, for the *Dictionary of Americanisms* gives the first use of *bogus* as 1838, about the time Mr. Borghese was said to be operating.

Another source claims this word for fake or spurious can be traced to May, 1827, when the Painsville, O., *Telegraph* ran a story about the arrest of a gang of counterfeiters who were turning out coins so perfect that the reporter compared them to the work of some bogeyman. A similar version says the word is related to the name of a device called a bogus, used for making counterfeit coins in the same state in the same year, connecting this machine with "tantrabogus," an old Vermont term for bogeyman. But still others suggest a direct passage from *boghus*, a gypsy word for a counterfeit coin, or from *baggasse*, a similar French expression. *Webster's*, wisely, gives the derivation as "uncertain."

Bohemian, Bohunk, Honkie, Hunkie *Bohemian* was first used as a synonym for gypsy during the middle ages, people mistakenly believing that the gypsy tribes came from or entered the West via the ancient kingdom of Bohemia, which is now a province of Czechoslovakia. Actually, the gypsies were wandering tribes from the Caucasus, of Hindu origin. *Bohemian* initially meant an aimless vagabond, but became synonymous with a poor writer or artist with French novelist Henri Murger's stories in *Scènes de la Vie de Bohème* (1848), his book the basis for Puccini's opera *La Bohème*. The English novelist William Makepeace Thackeray made the word a synonym for a *nonconformist* artist in *Vanity Fair* (1848) when he wrote of his headstrong heroine Becky Sharp: "She was of a wild, roving nature, inherited from father and mother, who were both Bohemians by taste and circumstances." Since then quarters throughout the world housing the avant-garde, such as the Left Bank in Paris and New York's Greenwich and East Village, have been labeled *Bohemias* and their inhabitants *bohemians*.

Bohunk, a low expression for a Polish or Hungarian-American that arose at the turn of the century, is probably a blend of *Bohemian* and *Hungarian*, while *honkie*, a derisive Negro term for a white, most likely stems from *bohunk*, or *hunkie*—black workers in the Chicago meatpacking plants either mistaking their Polish co-workers for Hungarian *hunkies* or deriving the expression from the former word. (See also *Gypsy*.)

Bolivia, Boliviano, Bolívar Commemorative of Simón Bolívar (1783–1830), the legendary South American revolutionary, soldier and statesman, are the *bolivar* monetary unit of Venezuela and the *boliviano* of Bolivia. Simón Bolívar, the Liberator, led Venezuela's revolution against Spain and founded Greater Colombia (then a union consisting of Venezuela, Ecuador and New Granada, the present-day Colombia). He is one of the few men in history to have a country named after him in his lifetime and probably the only one to create and give that same country its constitution. *Bolivia*, or Upper Peru as it was then known, was first named *Republica Bolivar* in the great soldier and statesman's honor. Azacucho, Peru, was the scene of the decisive victory in 1824 that finally ended Spanish domination in the New World. Bolívar became president of Greater Colombia, and the most powerful man in South America, but like many great leaders was bitterly hated while he ruled. On the famous September Night, September 24, 1828, he barely escaped assassination by jumping from a high window and hiding. Resigning the presidency early in 1830, he died eight months later of tuberculosis, a bitter, disillusioned man. "We have ploughed the sea," he once said. Only after his death was the Liberator's greatness recognized and today he is the most revered of South American heroes. *Bolívar* is also a state in Venezuela, Caracas his birthplace.

Bolo Paul Bolo, a French traitor popularly known as Bolo Pasha, faced a firing squad in 1917, having been convicted of treason the previous year. A *bolo*, though now generally an historical term, saw extensive use during World War I in describing a traitor, fifth columnist, or spy, someone working underground for Germany. Bolo's treason consisted principally of spreading pacifist propaganda financed by the Germans. (See also *Benedict Arnold*; *Laval*; *Lord Haw Haw*; *Petain*; *Quisling*; *Tokyo Rose*.)

Bolshevik, Bolshie Synonymous today for an agitator or radical reformer, *bolshevik* originally signified the left wing of the Russian Social Democratic Party, the designation evolving from a party conference in 1902 when the majority (*Bolsheviki*), as opposed to the minority (*Mensheviki*), accepted the views of Nikolai Lenin. The vote was close (25-23) and behind the tactical issues involved lay great differences—such as the minority belief that revolution in Russia should be gradual in contrast to Lenin's insistence that there be an immediate overthrow of the Czarist regime. In 1917 the Bolsheviks again gained a majority in the Socialist party congress, though not in Russia itself, and simultaneously overthrew the existing Russian government. Ironically, it was Lenin's view that the *Bolsheviks* (the majority party) should be composed of a small select minority rather than the masses.

Bolshie, for an agitator, is simply a corruption of *bolshevik*. (See also *Marxism; Molotov Cocktail; Leninism; Stakhanovite; Stalinism.*)

Bonaparte's Gull, Zenadia Bird *Bonaparte's gull*, one of only two black-headed species in the United States, was described scientifically for the first time in Prince Charles Lucien Bonaparte's *American Ornithology*. Bonaparte, Napoleon's nephew, resided in this country from 1824 to 1833. The gull bearing the naturalist's name breeds hundreds of miles from the sea, becoming a sea bird in winter, and inland bird watchers consider it a harbinger of spring. *Zenadia*, the scientific designation for several species of wild doves and pigeons, is named for Bonaparte's wife, Princess Zénaïde. (See also *Franklin's gull.*)

Booze, Boozer Every *boozer* or *boozehound* in America is related to E. G. or E. S. Booze of either Philadelphia or Kentucky, *circa* 1840. Mr. Booze was a distiller who sold his *booze* under his own name, the whiskey often flowing from bottles made in the shape of log cabins. The relationship is a tenuous one, though, *booze*, probably having its roots in the Middle English verb *bousen*, to drink deeply, which comes from an earlier German word. But the English use *booze* only for beer and ale and there is no doubt that the labels on our Mr. Booze's bottles influenced the American use of the word for hard liquor and strengthened its general use. Today *booze* most often signifies cheap, even rot-gut whiskey. Those log cabin bottles, incidentally, cashed in on the United States presidential campaign of 1840, when Tippecanoe and Tyler, too, General William Henry Harrison and John Tyler, ran against Van, Van The Used Up Man, President Martin Van Buren (see *O.K.*). General Harrison and cohorts reminded the voters a thousand times that he had been born in a log cabin, a fact which the bottles commemorated, and Mr. Booze's *booze* probably tasted good to the Whigs, if not the Democrats. Anyway, Harrison did so well with the ploy that Daniel Webster publicly regretted that he hadn't been born in a log cabin.

Borgia, Nepotism Whether any Borgia was ever a poisoner is a matter of dispute, but Lucrezia and Cesare Borgia, children of Pope Alexander VI (1431–1503), were reputed to indulge in such activities. Tradition has it that the Borgias employed some secret deadly poison to eliminate their enemies. Historians have never been able to substantiate this, but *a glass of wine with the Borgias* has long been proverbial for a great but risky honor, and *a Borgia* is still a synonym for a poisoner. (See also *Aqua Tofana.*)

There is no doubt that the Borgias were murderers, the family generally a pretty unsavory lot. They are also responsible for the word *nepotism*, this directly from the Latin *nepos*, "a descendant, especially a nephew," coined when Pope Alexander VI filled important church offices with his relations. Among the many family appointments Rodrigo Borgia made were the installing of his son Cesare as an archbishop when the boy was only sixteen, and the bestowing of a cardinal's hat on his young nephew, Giovanni.

As for the proverbial *to dine with the Borgias*, Sir Max Beerbohm had this to say in his *Hosts and Guests*: "I maintain that though you would often in the fifteenth century have heard the snobbish Roman say, in a would-be off-hand tone, 'I am dining with the Borgias to-night,' no Roman was ever able to say, 'I dined last night with the Borgias.' "

Bosey A *bosey* is a cricketing term familiar to Australians but not much used any more in England, where it originated. The term honors the English bowler, B. J. T. Bosanquet, who popularized the technique known elsewhere as the *googly* when he toured Australia in 1903–04. The *googly* is, according to the *Oxford English Dictionary*, "an off-break ball bowled with leg-break action." There is no popularly known technique in American baseball, basketball or football named after its player-inventor, so B. J. T. Bosanquet is somewhat unique in the world of sports. (See also *Barter.*)

Boswell, Boswellize "I have a notion," Somerset Maugham once observed, "that it is pleasanter to read Boswell's record of the conversations than it ever was to listen to Dr. Johnson." A *Boswell*, for the ultimate in biographers, honors James Boswell (1740–95), whose *The Life of Samuel Johnson* (1791) is the prototype of biographies. Boswell, born in Scotland, met Dr. Johnson only after numerous rebuffs but became both friend and admirer of the great English biographer and man of letters. Over a relatively short period, he recorded in detail Johnson's words and activities. "That Boswell was a vain, intemperate man of dubious morals is of no matter to history," writes one biographer. "He shines in the reflected glory of his great portrait."

To *boswellize* means to write biography in the same detailed, intimate and faithful manner as Boswell did. "Bozzy," as he was called, once wrote the following poem about himself, said to be remarkable for its self-perception:

Boswell is pleasant and gay,
For frolic by nature designed;
He heedlessly rattles away
When company is to his mind.
"This maxim," he says, "you may see,
We never can have corn without
chaff";
So not a bent sixpence cares he,
Whether with him or at him you
laugh.

(See also *Johnsonese.*)

Bougainvillaea, Bougainville The largest island in the Solomon group, two Pacific straits, and a brilliantly flowering South American vine are all named after the French navigator and adventurer Louis Antoine de Bougainville (1729–1811). Bougainville commanded a French expedition around the world in 1766–69, discovering the Solomon Islands. Naturalists in his party named the woody climbing vine family, of which there are about a dozen known species, *Bougainvillaea* in his honor. Bougainville helped popularize Rousseau's theories on the morality of man in his natural state, especially as concerns sexual freedom. He fought for America during the Revolution and in his later years Napoleon I made him a senator, count of the empire and member of the Legion of Honor. The plant named after him is often cultivated in greenhouses, can be raised outside in the southern parts of the United States, and is regarded as the handsomest of tropical vines.

Boulangism, Boulangerite General Georges Ernest Jean Marie Boulanger (1837–91) won the admiration of all France for his exploits during the Franco-Prussian war. That he was a handsome man who looked impressive astride a horse in parades didn't hurt his image, either. In 1886 Boulanger was made minister of war and insisted that he was the man to retrieve the lost glories of France with doctrines of militarism and reprisal against Germany. For a short time a wave of political frenzy called *Boulangism* swept over France, but the movement came to nothing, the general in reality no Napoleon and his backers largely reactionary elements. Boulanger eventually went into exile, ending his life in Brussels as a suicide.

Boulangerite, a sulfide of antimony and lead, bears no relation to the general, having been named for a nineteenth-century French mineralogist of the same name.

Bourbon *Bourbon whiskey* takes its name from Bourbon County, in Kentucky, home of the first still that produced it. But the word *Bourbon* for a political reactionary derives from France's Bourbon kings, a dynasty that reigned over two hundred years, beginning in 1589, and of whom it was said that they "forgot nothing and learned nothing." *The Dictionary of Americanisms* gives its first use for a political diehard as 1876.

Bovaric, Madame Bovary Gustave Flaubert and his publisher were charged with "immorality" when his great novel *Madame Bovary* appeared in magazine form in 1856, but both were acquitted and the book was published a year later. The fictional Madame Bovary is based in part on Louise Colet (1810–76), a French poet and novelist with whom Flaubert carried on an affair for some nine years, beginning in 1846. The real Madame Bovary lived in Paris with her husband, Hippolyte Colet, and her affair with Flaubert was the author's only serious *liaison*. It is hard to see where Flaubert could have gained his amazing insights into feminine psychology except by his intimate observations of this woman.

Louise Colet's story is told in her novel *Lui: roman contemporain* (1859). A *Madame Bovary* has come to mean a woman with an inflated, glamorized opinion of herself. *Bovarism*, a rare word which should have greater currency, means, to quote Aldous Huxley, "the power granted to man to conceive himself as other than he is," *bovaric* and *bovarize* deriving from it. Whether Louise Colet shared these qualities with Madame Bovary is debatable, but her name is linked with the words.

Bowdlerize
"If any word or expression is of such a nature that the first impression it excites is an impression of obscenity, that word ought not to be spoken nor written or printed; and, if printed, it ought to be erased." Dr. Thomas Bowdler

His inability to stand the sight of human blood and suffering forced Dr. Thomas Bowdler to abandon his medical practice in London, but this weakness apparently did not apply where vendors of words were concerned. Bowdler so thoroughly purged both Shakespeare and Gibbon that they would have screamed in pain from the bloodletting had they been alive; to *bowdlerize* becoming a synonym for to radically expurgate or prudishly censor in the process.

Thomas Bowdler, the most renowned of self-appointed literary censors, was born at Ashley, near Bath, England, on July 11, 1754. After he retired from medicine, a considerable inheritance enabled him to travel about Europe, writing accounts of the Grand Tour that seem to have offended or pleased no one. Though he came from a religious family, Bowdler never earned the "Reverend Doctor" title often applied to him and his early years are conspicuous for the lack of any real accomplishments, unless one counts membership in organizations like the "Society for the Suppression of Vice." Only when he was middle aged did he retire to the Isle of Wight and begin to sharpen his rusty scalpel on the Bard of Avon's bones. His *Family Shakespeare* was finally published in 1818. In justifying this ten-volume edition, Bowdler ex-

plained on the title page that "nothing is added to the text; but those expressions are omitted which cannot with propriety be read aloud in a family," adding later that he had also expunged "Whatever is unfit to be read by a gentleman in a company of ladies." What this really meant was that Bowdler had completely altered the characters of Hamlet, Macbeth, Falstaff, and others, and totally eliminated "objectionable" characters like Doll Tearsheet. Strangely enough, the poet Swinburne, who saw his own works *bowdlerized* by others, applauded the doctor many years later, writing that "no man ever did better service to Shakespeare than the man who made it possible to put him into the hands of intelligent and imaginative children."

Few writers then or now would agree with Swinburne, though *The Family Shakespeare* was a best seller and won some critical acclaim. Bowdler went on to expurgate Edward Gibbon's *The History of the Decline and Fall of the Roman Empire*, castrating that masterpiece by removing "all passages of an irreligious or immoral tendency." He firmly believed that both Shakespeare and Gibbon would have "desired nothing more ardently" than his literary vandalism and would probably have turned his scalpel to other great authors if death had not excised him in 1825. About ten years later Bowdler's name was first used as a verb, the official definition then "to expurgate by omitting or modifying words or passages considered indelicate or offensive." Today the word more often means prudish, arbitrary, ridiculous censorship. Bowdler himself has been described as "the quivering moralist who is certain in his soul that others will be contaminated by what he himself reads with impunity."

Bowie Knife One writer defines the *bowie knife* (pronounced *boo-ie*) as "the principal instrument of nonsurgical phlebotomy in the American Southwest." Sad to say, this lethal instrument was not invented by the legendary Colonel James Bowie (1799–1836), friend of Davy Crockett and hero at the Alamo. According to testimony by a daughter of Rezin Pleasant Bowie, the colonel's older brother, it was her father who invented the knife in about 1827, though Jim Bowie did make it famous in a duel that year at Natchez, Miss., in which six men were killed and fifteen wounded. The common long-bladed hunting knife was originally made at Rezin Bowie's direction by a Louisiana blacksmith, who ground a large file to razor sharpness and attached a guard between the blade and handle to protect the user's hand. After he killed one man with it in the Natchez duel, Colonel Bowie is said to have sent his knife to a Philadelphia blacksmith, who marketed copies of it under his name. Its double-edged blade was ten to fifteen inches long, and curved to a point. Once called an "Arkansas toothpick," it was even carried by some congressmen.

The two Bowies, along with their brother John, began their careers as slave-runners in the 1820's, smuggling slaves into Louisiana in cahoots with the pirate Jean Lafitte, who reigned supreme on Galveston Island. James became a leader of settlers and a colonel of the Texas army in the revolution against Mexico. He was butchered on his sickbed at the fall of the Alamo, his brother Rezin dying five years later. The *Bowie* or *Toothpick State* used to be a nickname for Arkansas, and *Bowie Racetrack* in Maryland honors another branch of the family.

Bowler, Billycock The same hat by different names, each probably named for a different person. Its shape can be traced back to the helmets worn by the ancient Greeks, but the *billycock*, a round, soft felt hat with a wide brim, most likely first graced the head of William Coke, a rich British landowner, in 1850. It is said to have been designed at "Billy" Coke's request by a hatter named Beaulieu because Mr. Coke's tall riding hat was frequently parted from his head by tree branches when he rode to the hounds. There is little doubt about the origin of *billycock*, then, and *bowler* may derive from the hatter, M. Beaulieu. The only trouble is that some authorities credit a London hatter named William Bowler, quoting a newspaper item tracing his "invention" to 1868. Still others say *bowler* is simply named for the hat's "bowl shape" or from the fact that it is round, stiff brimmed and can be bowled along. (See also *Derby*.)

Boycott Captain Charles Cunningham Boycott (1832–97) is famous for but one thing in his life—his name, which has become the most international of eponymous words and was probably the quickest to be adopted into any language. Boycott, a rather stubborn British soldier turned farmer, had been hired to manage the Earl of Erne's estates at Lough Mask House in Connaught, County Mayo, Ireland. Absentee landlords like the earl owned most land in Ireland at the time, and were evicting poverty-stricken tenant farmers who could not pay their rents—due primarily to numerous crop failures which culminated in the disastrous 1880–81 famine. The fiery Irish leader, Charles Stewart Parnell, a member of Parliament, had already formed his National Land League, agitating for land reform by these "English usurpers." In September, 1880, Parnell addressed tenants near Connaught, advocating that anyone working a farm from which a man had been evicted, or any landlord refusing to accept his new, reduced rent scales, should be ostracized "by isolating him . . . as if he were a leper of old . . . by leaving him strictly alone. . . ." When, in a test case, Captain Boycott harshly refused to accept more reasonable lower rents, and tried to evict one farmer, Boycott's tenants went Parnell one better. Although he had merely acted on Lord Erne's orders, Boycott was not merely given the silent treatment. His workers and servants were forced to leave him; organized marauders destroyed his property; his fences were torn down and cattle driven into his fields; he was refused service in all local stores; his mail went undelivered; he was jeered in the streets, hung in effigy, and his life was repeatedly threatened. Eventually, Ulster Orangemen laborers, guarded by nine hundred British soldiers, gathered his crops, but Boycott had to be spirited out of Connaught when they left, he and his wife fleeing to England the following year. Sons of the old sod continued to make life miserable for many landlord-agents in this way, the British Parliament finally passing a land reform bill in 1881. Yet so successful had been the famous "excommunication" against Captain Boycott that it was commonly called a *Boycott* in the newspapers within two months, the word printed without a capital within six years. Not even the new Crimes Act of 1887 could effectively deal with these far from nonviolent *boycotts*. Captain Boycott, who did little, lived to see his name immortalized as a synonym for refusal to deal with a person or business firm, not only in English but in French, German, Dutch, Russian and a number of Asiatic languages as well. This despite the fact that his stubborn "no" was the only word he ever uttered considered interesting enough to record.

Boysenberry Americans have always been pie makers without peer, thanks to sugar resources close by, an abundance of native fruit, and a willingness to experiment. The blackberry, long regarded as a nuisance and called a bramble or brambleberry in England, is a case in point. Many varieties of blackberries have been developed here, long before anyone paid attention to the family *Rubus* in Europe. Among them is the *Boysenberry*, a prolific, trailing variety that is a cross between the blackberry, raspberry and *Loganberry*, another eponymous berry. The *Boysenberry*, a dark wine-red fruit that tastes something like a raspberry, was developed by California botanist Rudolf Boysen in the early 1900's. Single plants commonly produce two quarts of the large ¾-inch-round, 1½-inch-long fruit. (See also *Loganberry; Youngberry*.)

Braille When only three years old, Louis Braille was blinded by an awl driven into his eye while playing in his father's leather-working shop. Total blindness extended to both eyes, but young Louis attended the village school in Coupvray outside Paris, where he learned his alphabet by feeling twigs in the shape of letters, and then the *Institution Nationale des Jeunes Aveugles*, where he learned to read from three huge four-hundred-pound books engraved with large embossed letters. This last method had been invented by Valentin Haüy, Father and Apostle of the Blind, the Institute's founder, but it could not be

easily written by the blind and was thus inadequate. At about the time that Louis Braille was made a junior instructor at the Institute, French army officer Captain Charles Barbier introduced his "night writing," a system of twelve raised dots and dashes which fingers could "read," enabling brief orders like one dot for advance, or two dots for retreat to be written with a simple instrument and understood in total darkness. Barbier demonstrated his invention at the Institute and it fired young Braille's imagination. When only fifteen he began work on the system that bears his name.

Young Braille soon improved the *Barbier letter*, which occupied an area too long to be covered by a child's fingertip, and by 1829 he had published his type. His simpler system of raised print writing was based on a "cell" consisting of just six raised dots, three high and two wide. Sixty-two combinations were possible within this "cell," allowing for all the letters in the French alphabet and all the necessary punctuation, the letter W later being added at the request of an Englishman. *Braille* could easily be written with a stylus and guide slate, and led to such inventions as *braille* typewriters, slide rulers, and watches. Louis Braille, highly regarded as an organist and composer in his own right, also invented a *braille* musical notation, but *braille* was not officially adopted at the Institute where he taught, until 1854, two years after his death. Tradition has it that a blind organist performing at a fashionable salon told her audience that she owed everything to Louis Braille, who had died unheralded of tuberculosis in 1852 when only forty-two years old, and that her touching story finally led to universal recognition of his system.

Today, a more sophisticated, refined *braille* is taught to the blind. Beginners learn *Braille A*, much like the original, while advanced students learn *Braille B*, which is a more complicated code, its dot patterns standing for whole words and phrases. Unfortunately, however, one survey has revealed that only 15 percent of the blind feel comfortable with *braille*. The search for a still better system goes on.

Brain Trust The group of experts forming the first *brain trust* were the advisers around Franklin Delano Roosevelt while he prepared presidential campaign speeches at Hyde Park, N.Y. in 1932. The *brain trust* consisted of Columbia University professors Adolf A. Berle, Jr., Raymond Moley, and Rexford G. Tugwell. The expression was coined by *New York Times* reporter James M. Kieran when he learned that they were in residence. Kieran originally called the group the *brains trust* in his *Times'* dispatches, but other reporters and headline writers soon eliminated the cumbersome *s*. By the time Roosevelt became president, *brain trust* was commonly being used for his larger group of supposedly nonpolitical experts. The phrase had been previously employed in sarcastic reference to the first American general staff, in 1901, not at all in the same sense. *Prime the pump, economic royalist, good neighbor policy, court packing, isolationist,* and *underprivileged* were among many other terms introduced under F.D.R.

Bramley's Seedling *Bramley's seedling* is a delicious English apple, notable not only because it was discovered by a butcher named Bramley of Southwell, Nottinghamshire, in his garden, but because it is a "sport" or mutation. Most mutations, or changes in genes, occur in seedlings, but the *Bramley* was the result of a bud mutation, a variation in which only part of a plant is affected. Thus the first *Bramley*, as well as the first Golden Delicious apple, and the first New Dawn Rose, among others, developed on one branch of a plant bearing an entirely different race. The Boston fern, which originated in a shipment of ferns sent from Philadelphia to Boston in 1894, is another well-known mutation, but the most famous bud sport is the nectarine. The first nectarine, or smooth-skinned peach, occurred on a peach tree well over two thousand years ago, and nectarines are still often found on peach trees, and vice versa, where there has been no cross-pollination. Sometimes one side of the fruit is a peach and the other a nectarine. No one knows what causes these bud mutations, but they do occur. So start looking in the garden—you may become rich and eponymous.

Brevoortia Ida-Maia The floral firecracker, as this plant is popularly called, shows how oddly things sometimes get their names. Ida May, the daughter of a nineteenth-century California stagecoach driver, had noticed the bulbous plant many times in her travels and pointed it out to Alphonso Wood, a naturalist always interested in collecting botanical specimens. Wood named the single plant, a member of the lily family, *Brevoortia Ida-Maia*, its prenom in honor of his fellow American naturalist J. C. Brevoort, and its patronym in gratitude to the observant little girl who had brought the scarlet-flowered perennial to his attention.

Briareus of Languages Briareus was a mythological giant with fifty heads and one hundred hands, but the phrase *Briareus of languages* first honored Cardinal Giuseppe Caspar Mezzofanti (1774–1849), chief keeper of the Vatican library. The term is used to describe an accomplished linguist, having been invented by the English poet, Byron, who called the cardinal "a walking polyglot; a monster of languages; a Briareus of parts of speech." Mezzofanti, we are told, learned Latin and Greek fluently while listening to an old priest giving lessons to students next door to the shop where he had been an apprentice to a carpenter. He eventually mastered thirty-nine languages, from Albanian to Wallachian, speaking these as well as he did his native tongue. All in all, he could speak sixty languages and seventy-two dialects fluently and could translate 114 languages. Among these were such exotics as *Bimbarra, Geez, Koordish, Tonkinese,* and *Chippewa*. A modern *Briareus of languages* is Charles Berlitz of the famous school, who can get by in some thirty tongues. No one speaks all the world's languages, which number from twenty-eight hundred to five thousand, depending on whose estimate you accept, and which include such far-out dialects as *Kookie, Saliva, Watty-Watty, Yairy-Yairy,* and *Zaza*.

Bright's Disease and Other Maladies One of the scores of maladies named for medical researchers is *Bright's disease*, after English Dr. Richard Bright (1789–1858), whose findings determined the nature of the kidney affliction. Other eponymous words in the same morbid category include *Basedow's disease*, a swelling of the thyroid gland, for German Dr. Karl von Basedow (1799–1854); *Hodgkin's*, a disease of the lymphatic glands, after English Dr. Thomas Hodgkin (1798–1866); *Lindau's*, a brain disease, for Arvid Lindau, a Swedish pathologist; *Paget's*, a disease of the breast, after Sir James Paget (1814–99); *Pott's*, a tuberculosis infection, after English surgeon Percivall Pott (1714–88); *Riggs pyorrhea*, for American dentist John M. Riggs (1810–85); *Jacksonian epilepsy*, after English Dr. John Hughlings Jackson (1835–1911); and *Vincent's infection*, trench mouth, for French Dr. Jean Hyacinthe Vincent (1862–1950). All go by far longer medical names.

Brillat-Savarin *"The destiny of nations depends on the manner wherein they take their food." "A dessert course without cheese is like a beautiful woman with one eye." "Animals feed: man eats; only a man of wit knows how to dine."* Anthelme Brillat-Savarin, author of these and many other well-known aphorisms on *la cuisine*, was seventy when he published his *Physiologie du Goût* (Physiology of Taste) in 1825, his celebrated book thirty years in the making. He was to die the following year but not before he had given the world the most trenchant discussion of food and its effects on trenchermen ever written. The greatest of French bon vivants had been born, appropriately enough, in the town of Belley —"Belley is its name and Belley is its nature," wrote Michael Stein over a century later. He became the town's mayor after the French Revolution but had to emigrate to America during the Reign of Terror, living in Connecticut for a few years. Portly and gregarious, the sage of Belley remained a bachelor all his life— perhaps too devoted to food and women ever to marry, possibly because he loved his cousin, the society beauty Madame Récamier. A lawyer who wrote on political economy and law, and penned a few licentious tales as well, he is remembered above all for his Bible of gastronomy. "Tell me what you eat and I will tell you what you are," he once declared, and the gastronomic tests in his book have been acclaimed as small masterpieces of psychological insight almost as brilliant as his discussions of food.

Though he was something of an eccentric—he often carried dead birds around in his pockets until they became "high" enough for cooking—Brillat-Savarin's reputation has not suffered for his eccentricities, his name long synonymous with supreme authority on cooking. The greatest of gourmets also has the *savarin*, a yeast cake soaked in a rum or kirsch-flavored syrup, named for him, and there are countless restaurants and a coffee using the last half of his hyphenated name, as well as two classic garnishes, both made in part with truffles, the most éclat of gourmet foods.

Brillat was actually Anthelme's real name—he took on the hypen and *Savarin* when his great aunt left him her entire fortune on the condition that he add her name to his, Mademoiselle Savarin wanting a little immortality and getting more than she bargained for. Love of food seemed to run in the Brillat family. Anthelme's youngest sister, Pierrette, for instance, died at the dinner table. She was almost one hundred and her last words are among the most unusual in history: "And now, girl, bring me the dessert." *Physiologie du Goût*, incidentally, had to be printed at the author's expense. And when Brillat-Savarin's brother later sold the rights to a publisher, he got only $120—after throwing in a genuine Stradivarius as well!

Brinell Hardness, Machine, Number, Scale A *Brinell machine* or *tester* determines the hardness of a metal, especially steel, by forcing a hard steel or tungsten carbide ball into it under a fixed hydraulic pressure. By dividing the force applied by the indenter into the surface area of the indentation made, the metal's *Brinell number* is obtained, this indicating its relative *Brinell hardness* on the *Brinell scale*. The machine and method were devised by the Swedish engineer, Johann August Brinell (1849–1925), who first demonstrated his famous invention at the Paris International Exposition of 1900.

Brocard, Brocard's Circle and Ellipse
Brocard was the French name for Bur-
chard, an eleventh-century bishop of
Worms. Bishop Brocard published a collection of canons, *Regulae Ecclesiastecae*,
celebrated for its short, sententious sentences, and a *brocard* soon came to mean
both a brief maxim or proverb in philosophy or law, and a pointed jibe or biting
speech.

Brocard's circle and *Brocard's ellipse*
are mathematical terms named for French
mathematician Henri Brocard (1845–
1922).

Broderick Johnny (The Boffer) Broderick is still remembered as a tough New
York City cop who relied on his fists as
much as his police revolver. Known as the
world's toughest cop, Detective Broderick
worked the Broadway beat, often dealing
out punishment with his fists on the spot
—so often that *to broderick* became a
synonym for *to clobber*. Broderick once
flattened the hoodlum Jack (Legs) Diamond, and he knocked out and captured
Francis (Two-Gun) Crowley before Crowley could find the courage to shoot. Another time he battered two men molest-
ing a woman, throwing them through a
plate glass window and then arresting
them for malicious destruction of property. In fact, Bellevue Hospital used
him as an exhibit to show how much
punishment the human hand could take.
Broderick, an image of sartorial splendor,
was used as a bodyguard by many celeb-
rities, including Franklin Roosevelt and
Jack Dempsey. Dempsey confessed that
the detective was the only man he
wouldn't care to fight outside the ring.
This graduate of New York's gashouse
district was immortalized by Damon
Runyon as Johnny Brannigan and played
by Edward G. Robinson in *Bullets or
Ballots*. By the time he retired in 1947,
after twenty-five years on the force, Broderick had won eight medals for heroism.
Broadway gamblers once gave 9–5 odds
that he would be killed on any given day,
but he died in his bed in 1966, seventy-
two years old.

Brodie, Do a Brodie On July 23,
1886, Steve Brodie reputedly made his
famous leap from the Manhattan side of
the Brooklyn Bridge to win a $200 bet.
Some say the young man, twenty-three at

the time, never jumped at all; however,
The New York Times reported the next
morning that he eluded guards on the
bridge, climbed to the lowest chord and
plummeted 135 feet into the water below, where friends were waiting to retrieve him in a rowboat. Brodie was arrested for endangering his life and reprimanded by a judge, but his barroom bet
resulted in *to do a Brodie* or *pull a Brodie*
becoming proverbial for "to take a
chance." In 1888 "the man who wouldn't
take a dare" made still another fabulous
leap, this time winning $500 by jumping
212 feet from a railroad bridge in Pough-
keepsie, New York. Brodie later became
a successful saloon keeper, never changing
his story, though others claimed that he
had really pushed a dummy from the
bridge.

It is said that the intrepid Brodie once
angered fighter Jim Corbett's father by
predicting that John L. Sullivan would
knock out his son. "So you're the fellow
who jumped over the Brooklyn Bridge,"
the elder Corbett said when the two met
for the first time. "No, I jumped *off* of
it," Brodie corrected him. "Oh," replied
Corbett, "I thought you jumped *over* it.
Any damn fool could jump off it."

A number of higher leaps than Brodie's
have been recorded. Professional divers
regularly plunge 126 feet from La Que-
brada Cliff in Acapulco, Mexico, and in
September, 1941, Cornelia Van Ireland,
twenty-two, "impulsively" jumped off the
Golden Gate Bridge and lived—she
leaped 238 feet, hitting the water at 70
m.p.h. Only a few years ago a man leaped
off the George Washington Bridge, from
250 feet up, and then swam 200 yards to
shore. These figures pale beside the record of the Russian pilot, I. M. Chissov.
In January, 1942, Lieutenant Chissov
bailed out from his plane, his parachute
failed to open, and he lived after falling
22,000 feet into a snow-covered ravine.

**Bronx, Bronx Cheer, Bronx Cocktail,
Bronx River** The *Bronx*, one of New
York City's five boroughs, takes its name
from Jonas Bronck, a Dane who first
settled the area for the Dutch West India
Company in 1641. Points of interest in
the celebrated borough are the *Bronx zoo*
and botanic gardens, the Edgar Allan
Poe cottage, and the Yankee Stadium

"the house that Ruth built," where the *Bronx cheer*, another name for the razz or raspberry, probably arose in the 1920's —this "cheer" a sound of contempt made by vibrating the tongue between the lips. The *Bronx River* runs from Westchester County through the *Bronx* and into the East River. The *Bronx cocktail* was named in honor of the borough, or invented there in about 1919.

Brother Jonathan At about the same time that *Uncle Sam* became a nickname for America and her people the sobriquet *Brother Jonathan* was also being used. It, too, may come from the name of an historical figure: Jonathan Trumbull (1710–85), the governor of Connecticut, who was a trusted friend and advisor of George Washington. The unsupported story is that General Washington, greatly perplexed because he needed ammunition and none of his council of officers could offer a practical solution to his problem, announced, "We must consult Brother Jonathan." Trumbull came up with an answer and the phrase *to consult Brother Jonathan* became proverbial. *Brother Jonathan*, meaning an American, first appeared in print in 1816. It has been pointed out, however, that Jonathan was a very common American name at the time, and that the British had used the term in allusion to the Puritans as early as the seventeenth century. The appellation may even have originated in the Biblical story of David's lamentation for Jonathan (II *Samuel* 1:26). If *Brother Jonathan* does honor Jonathan Trumbull, it is one of the few national names deriving from the name of an actual person, the English *John Bull* and the French *Nicholas Frog* being fictional sobriquets.

Brougham

"Education makes people easy to lead, but difficult to drive; easy to govern but impossible to drive."

Lord Henry Brougham

The *brougham*, a four-wheeled carriage for two or four passengers, honors Henry Peter Brougham, Baron Brougham and Vaux (1778–1868). This name for a one-horse carriage with an open driver's seat and a closed, low-slung passenger cab behind also designated the first tall electric automobiles, as well as an early gasoline-powered limousine with the driver's seat unenclosed. The amazing Lord Brougham, born in Edinburgh, Scotland, was among the most versatile of men—a noted lawyer, orator, politician, statesman, scientist, writer, publisher, advocate of the abolition of slavery, reformer, and one of the great wits of his day. As Whig leader of the House of Commons, he inspired many reforms, and his great speech as Lord Chancellor in the House of Lords led to eventual passage of the historic Reform Bill of 1831. Brougham's most famous court case was his successful defense of Queen Caroline in the House of Lords against the charges of adultery brought by her husband, the regent and later King George IV. He established that many of the prosecution's witnesses were bribed and in collusion with one another, his memorable final speech rewritten seventeen times. The bulbous-nosed, almost grotesque Renaissance man became internationally known in his long lifetime, the French in fact asking this Englishman to run for their national assembly in 1848. The *brougham* was named after Lord Brougham in about 1850, his design for the "garden chair on wheels" similar to the old "growler" horse cab. In his later years the many-faceted genius built a cottage in Cannes. His presence there was directly responsible for the town's great vogue as an international resort.

Browning Rifle The *Browning automatic rifle* or BAR of World War II fame was invented by John M. Browning (1854–1926) of Ogden, Utah, who designed many famous weapons. The BAR, an air-cooled weapon capable of firing 200–350 rounds per minute, was generally assigned one to a squad. It is said that none of the prolific Browning's designs ever failed. These included the light and heavy Browning machine guns, the calibre .45 pistol, the calibre .50 machine gun, the 37mm. aircraft gun, and a number of shotguns and repeating rifles. Browning took out his first patent in 1879, on a breech-loading, single-shot rifle that the Winchester Arms Company purchased. After his entry into the military field, the U.S. Army relied almost exclusively on his automatic weapons.

Brucellosis, Bang's Disease These are the same names for what is probably the most diversely named disease—it is also called undulant fever, Malta fever, Gibraltar fever, rock fever, Mediterranean fever and goat fever. Its cause, an infectious bacteria called *Brucella*, was discovered in 1887 when Scottish physician Sir David Bruce (1855–1931) performed an autopsy on a patient who had died of the illness on the island of Malta. Later, Danish veterinarians Bernhard L. F. Bang and V. Stribolt isolated a second strain of *Brucella* and in 1895 found that it caused a disease in cattle, which was called *Bang's disease* in that scientist's honor. *Bang's disease*, this name still used for the cattle infection, is thought to have been responsible for the epizootic disease or storms of abortions which commonly occurred in American and European cattle herds in the early nineteenth century. Scientifically speaking, all diseases caused by *Brucella* bacteria are termed *brucellosis*. The disease affects not only cattle and goats, but swine, chickens, dogs, cats, wild deer and bison as well. It is usually contracted by humans from contact with infected animals or by ingesting infected milk, and is sometimes fatal. No complete cure is known for infected animals and incidence of the disease is said to be on the rise throughout the world.

Brucine Another poison named for a real person, but this time not for someone who used it for nefarious purposes. *Brucine* is a bitter, poisonous vegetable alkaloid found in seeds of various *Strychnos* species, especially *nux vomica*. It resembles strychnine, though it isn't as powerful and it is rapidly eliminated from the body. *Brucine*, used in the denaturing of alcohol, was named for the apparently innocent Scottish traveler and explorer, James Bruce (1730–94), who merely discovered it. (See also *Aqua Tofano; Borgia*)

Brumby In Australia a wild horse is often called a *brumby* or *brumbie*. The word possibly derives from the name of Major William Brumby, an early nineteenth-century settler from England whose family still lives in Australia. Major Brumby was a noted breeder of horses, but much of his stock escaped and ran wild. *Brumby* may come, however, from the Aborigine *booramby*, wild.

Brutus Marcus Junius Brutus (c. 85–42 B.C.) was, of course, the principal assassin of Julius Caesar and *a Brutus* is often applied to any treacherous person, especially a former friend. *Et tu Brute,* Caesar's last words when he glimpsed his friend, is among the most familiar of quotations. History holds two opinions of Brutus. One claims that he conspired with Cassius to save the republic from Caesar's tyranny. The other suggests that his reputation as a moneylender and his friendship with the self-seeking Cassius prove that his motives were far more crass. Two years after he took part in Caesar's assassination, Brutus committed suicide, following a battle at Philippi that the republicans lost to Mark Antony and Octavian (later Augustus Caesar). A *brutus*, without the capital, is both a rough, cropped wig and a bronze variety of chrysanthemum.

Bucephala, Bucephalus I know of no other city named for a horse, although ancient *Peritas* may have been named for a dog. Alexander the Great is said to be responsible for both christenings, at a time when he was powerful enough to name the world after a mite. Bucephalus was Alexander's favorite Thracian charger, a spirited steed, legend tells us, that only he could ride and which would kneel down to take up his master. The fiery, unmanageable stallion had been offered for sale to Alexander's father, Philip, when the conqueror was a boy. Only Alexander was able to control the giant horse and Philip presented Bucephalus to his heir, saying with parental pride, "My son, Macedonia is too small for you; seek out a larger empire, worthier of you." Alexander took him at his word and then some. He alone rode Bucephalus in all his eastern campaigns and "the ox, or bull-headed one" is said to have died of wounds or heart strain after swimming the Jhelum river and then carrying his master in full armour through a day's hard fighting. The emperor named the ancient city of *Bucephala* in northern India in his horse's honor, perhaps even building it as the fabled charger's mausoleum, its site identified by a mound outside the modern Jhelum. The name

Bucephalus probably refers to the horse's bull-like courage rather than a bull-shaped head and is today applied to any high-spirited steed.

Buckhorse If you gave him a few shillings, the English fighter, John Smith, who went by the ring name of Buckhorse, would let you punch him on the side of the head as hard as you could. The well-known boxer found his nickname becoming slang for a punch or a blow beginning about 1850; that is, if he saw anything but stars after a while.

Buddhism Buddha, "the Enlightened One" was the title given to Prince Siddhartha (c. 563–c. 485), the Hindu prince who founded *Buddhism* in the sixth century B.C. It had been prophesied on his conception that the prince would renounce the world upon seeing a sick man, an old man and a corpse, which human misery he saw while riding through the royal park one day when he was twenty-nine years old. Prince Siddhartha left his wife and child, and after six years of solitude and contemplation, when he devoted himself to the severest asceticism, living on seeds, grass and even dung, he emerged as the Buddha, preaching a religion based on salvation by suffering. Existence, he proclaimed, was evil, and desire was the cause of sorrow. *Nirvana*, the absorption into the supreme spirit, was the reward obtained by the suppression of desire. Gautama Buddha (Gautama is from his clan name and he is called Sakyamuni Buddha from his tribal name) spent all his life as a wanderer, preaching his doctrine from the time he attained enlightenment under a Bo tree at Buddh Gaya in northern India, until his death forty-five years later. Buddha, or the Enlightened, derives from the Sanskrit *Bodhati*, "he awakens." It is estimated that *Buddhism* has about 140 million followers today.

Buffalo Bill Colonel William Frederick Cody (1846–1917), the peerless horseman and sharpshooter who became the original *Buffalo Bill*, earned his nickname as a market hunter for buffalo (bison) hides and as a contractor supplying buffalo meat to workers building the Union Pacific railroad in 1867. To his glory then, and shame now, he killed 4,280 buffalo in one year, mostly for their hides and tongues, cutting the American herd in half. It is hard to separate truth from fiction in Cody's life, his fame owing much to the dime novels that made him a celebrity in the late nineteenth century. *Buffalo Bill* was a herder, a Pony Express rider, a scout and cavalryman for the U.S. Army in the Civil War, and an Indian fighter who is said to have killed the Cheyenne chief, Yellowhand, singlehandedly. He was a member of the Nebraska state legislature. His Wild West Show, which he organized in 1883, toured the United States and Europe, bringing him great personal fame, yet financial problems caused this legendary American hero to die in poverty and relative obscurity. Today his name conjures up visions of "sportsmen" picking off buffalo from the platforms of trains, abundant buffalo meat rotting on the plains, and the destruction of the great herds that once swept the plains. Thanks to early conservationists some twenty thousand American bison survive today, all protected on government ranges.

Bugger The expression "he's just a little bugger" is innocuous enough in America, meaning chap or fellow, but to an Englishman it might suggest that the little chap in question was a sodomite—in fact, use of the word in print was actionable in England until 1934. For *bugger* derives, down a tortuous path, from the Medieval Latin *Bulgarus*, meaning both a Bulgarian and a sodomite. *Bugger* first referred to a Bulgarian and then to the Bulgarian Albigenses or Bulgarian heretics, an eleventh century religious sect whose monks and nuns were believed, rightly or wrongly, to practice sodomy. Some historians claim that the charge of sodomy against these heretic dissenters was a libel invented with the approval of the Church to discredit them. They had already been banished from Bulgaria, were living in the south of France, and the trumped-up story caused the French to oust or exterminate them, too. An interesting literary note on the word: when Dylan Thomas wrote his radio play, *Under Milk Wood*, the staid B.B.C. assumed that the fictional village Llareggub therein was authentically Welsh—until someone spelled it backward, after the play was already aired, and realized the poet's bawdy joke.

Bulldozer The earth-moving bulldozer takes its name from a band of political terrorists. After the Civil War, a group of Louisiana vigilantes, who brutally prevented freed slaves from voting as they pleased, were termed "bulldozers," the word first printed in an 1876 newspaper account of their activities. It is not certain whether they were whites forcing blacks to vote Democratic, Republican Negroes forcing their brothers not to vote Democratic, or groups of both. Neither is the exact origin of their name clear—it probably came from *bull-dose*, to mete out "a dose of the bull" with the long heavy bullwhip often made from the animal's penis. *Bulldozer* was soon used for a revolver and to describe anyone resembling the original terrorist bullies. Later the huge earth-moving machine, which brutally pushes everything in its path aside, became a natural candidate for the designation. Few people realize that when someone is called a *bulldozer* today he is being named not for the machine, but for the vigilantes so much like him. (See also *Derrick; Monkey-wrench*.)

Bunsen Burner, Bunsenite Robert Wilhelm Bunsen (1811–99) invented the *Bunsen burner* that is standard equipment in every chemistry laboratory. This laboratory burner, which mixes gas with air to produce a hot smokeless flame, wasn't the only scientific contribution the German chemist made. He discovered with Gustav Kirchhoff the elements cesium and rubidium, and shared with Henry Roscoe the discovery of the reciprocity law, doing much original work in spectrum analysis. The Heidelberg professor also has *bunsenite*, a nickel monoxide, named in his honor.

Burbank, Burbank Plum, Burbank Potato There has been muted controversy over whether the plant breeder Luther Burbank (1849–1926) was a "plant wizard" or something of a failure. Burbank was born in Lancaster, Mass., and there developed the *Burbank potato*, his most important achievement, while just a boy experimenting with seeds in his mother's garden. At twenty-six he moved to Santa Rosa, Cal., using the $150 he made from the sale of his potato to pay for the journey. It was in Santa Rosa, his "chosen spot of the earth," that he bred almost all the varieties of fruit, vegetables and ornamentals for which he became famous. These included at least sixty-six new tree fruits, twelve new bush fruits, seven tree nuts, and nine vegetables, of which a number, notably the *Burbank plum*, bear his name. However, according to Dr. W. L. Howard (University of California Agricultural Experiment Station Bulletin, 1945), only a few of the several hundred varieties developed by Burbank have stood the test of time. Nor was Burbank the first American plant breeder— Thomas Jefferson, George Washington Carver, and Charles Hovey, originator of the *Hovey strawberry*, came long before him. Yet he undoubtedly deserves his place in history for the contributions that he did make and the example he set for others. Burbank was strongly influenced by Darwin's *Variations of Animals and Plants under Domestication*. His credo can be summed up in his statement "I shall be contented if, because of me, there shall be better fruits and fairer flowers." The city of *Burbank* in southern California is named for the horticulturist. He lies buried on his home grounds in Santa Rosa under his favorite tree, a deodar, the "divine tree of the gods," which was sent to him from the Himalayas, and his tools still stand in the greenhouse nearby.

Burgoynade "Gentleman Johnny" Burgoyne hardly deserved his eponymous fate. General John Burgoyne (1722–92), an accomplished dramatist as well as a soldier, commanded the British forces that came down from Canada to capture New York's Fort Ticonderoga during the Revolutionary War. It was his intention to join with Howe's army farther downstate, but due to a delay on Howe's part, excellent American tactics, and enemy forces three times the strength of his own, he was forced to surrender after the battle of Saratoga. English Tories condemned him for his defeat, liberals berated him for his alleged use of savage Indians, and his name in the form of *burgoynade* came to mean the capture of a notable person, particularly a general or high-ranking officer. The cultivated Burgoyne figures in Shaw's *The Devil's Disciple* and Kenneth Robert's *Rabble in Arms* as well as in the dictionaries and history books.

Buridan's Ass The well-known philosophical sophism called *Buridan's ass* should really be called *Buridan's dog*. The dilemma, illustrating the will's indecisiveness when confronted with two equal choices, is usually presented in this way: "If a hungry ass were placed exactly between two haystacks in every respect equal, it would starve to death, because there would be no motive why it should go to one rather than to the other." But the French scholastic philosopher Jean Buridan (c. 1295–c. 1366) made the observation of a dog, not an ass, dying of hunger between two equal amounts of food in a commentary he wrote on Aristotle's *De Caelo*. Buridan was rector of the University of Paris in 1328 and 1340. Other myths about him, as false as *Buridan's ass*, insist that he founded Vienna University and was the lover of Joan of Navarre or Margaret of Burgundy, queens of France. (See also *Occam's Razor*.)

Burke The best-known of eponymous murderers and among the most unwise, William Burke (1792–1829), was an Irish laborer who emigrated to Scotland in 1817. There he eventually opened a used clothing store in Edinburgh and, far more importantly, rented a room from William Hare, a fellow Irishman and owner of a boardinghouse catering to vagrants and elderly pensioners. This was the era of the body snatchers or resurrectionists, those moonlighting grave-robbers who supplied anatomists with bodies for dissection. Body snatchers were subject to heavy fines and deportation, but if they left the corpse's clothing behind, they could not be convicted of robbery or any serious offense. Cadavers were much in demand at the time, no questions asked, for only the relatively few bodies of men executed for murder were then legally available for the dissection table and anatomy was first coming into its own as a science.

It was in 1827 that Burke and his partner embarked upon their career. One of Hare's lodgers—an old man named Donald—had died owing him four pounds, and the landlord convinced Burke that

they had stumbled upon an easy source of income. Ripping the cover off the coffin in which parish authorities had sealed Donald, the pair hid his body in a bed and filled the coffin with tanner's bark, resealing it and later selling the cadaver for seven pounds ten shillings to Dr. Robert Knox, who ran an anatomy school in Surgeon's Square. Burke and Hare soon expanded their operation. Another boarder lingered too long at death's door and they helped him through, smothering the man with a pillow and selling his body to Knox for ten pounds. Hare and his wife, and Burke and his mistress, Helen McDougal, proceeded to dispatch from fourteen to twenty-eight more unfortunates in similar fashion, receiving up to fourteen pounds for each body. They were careful to smother their victims, leaving no marks of violence, so that it would appear that they were merely graverobbers. Whenever the boardinghouse supply ran low, they lured victims there, usually choosing old hags, drunks and prostitutes, whom they often plied with drink. If a candidate offered too much resistance for a pillow, Burke would pin him down while Hare smothered him, holding his hands over the victim's nose and mouth.

But the murderers got careless. First, they killed Mary Paterson, a voluptuous eighteen-year-old, so free with her body that it was quickly recognized by Knox's young medical students, who even preserved it before dissection as a perfect example of female pulchritude. Then they did in "Daft Jamie" Wilson, a familiar, good-natured imbecile who made his living running errands on the streets of Edinburgh. Finally, the suspicions of neighbors aroused, police caught them with the body of a missing woman named Mary Dougherty. Hare turned state's evidence at the ensuing trial, which began on Christmas Eve, he and his wife freed, and Helen McDougal was discharged for lack of evidence. Burke for some reason foolishly refused to give state's evidence. He was convicted and hanged a month later on January 28, 1829, before a crowd of some thirty thousand. The word the murderer contributed to the language was even heard as he stood on the scaffold in the Grassmarket, spectators exhorting the executioner with cries of "Burke him, Burke him!" (i.e., don't hang but smother or strangle him to death). The crowd wanted to *burke* Hare, too, despite his immunity, but the real brains behind the operation escaped them and is believed to have died of natural causes many years later in England where he lived under an assumed name. Throughout the trial Hare's wife had sat in court holding their baby in an attempt to win sympathy, even though the child suffered from whooping cough. Burke, who signed a post-trial confession admitting to some sixteen murders, was himself dissected at Edinburgh University Medical School following his hanging, his remains viewed by tens of thousands, and for all anyone knows his skeleton might still be propped up in the corner of some classroom there. As for Dr. Knox, the crowd turned against him after the execution, threatening to destroy his school, and only police protection saved his life. Despite his protestations of innocence, he was ostracized and eventually forced to leave town.

William Burke was not the first person to murder for cadavers, or even to murder for this motive by suffocation; two female nurses, Helen Torrence and Jean Valdig, had been hanged for this crime in 1752. But with all the publicity Burke's name came to literally signify the act and figuratively to mean "stifle or hush up" in any manner, the usage perhaps strengthened a half-century later by the Fenian murder of Thomas Henry Burke, undersecretary for Ireland. It is a little ironic that Burke's name, in the form of *to burke, burke*, and *burking*, should be so remembered, for Hare probably did more of the actual suffocating, his confederate's greater strength needed to hold their victims down. Burke and Hare are thought to be the inspiration for Robert Louis Stevenson's *The Body Snatchers*. As a result of their Hare "anatomy murders," existing dissection laws were modified, making it easier for anatomists to obtain bodies without resorting to illegal means. (See also *Bishop*.)

Burke's Peerage Like *Debrett* before it, *Burke's Peerage* has often been called the "studbook" of the British aristocracy. Originally published in 1826, it was fully titled A *Genealogical and Heraldic History of the Peerage and Baronetage of the United Kingdom*, and has been issued annually since 1847. The famous reference book, the first alphabetical guide to the British aristocracy, was the inspiration of John Burke (1787–1848), an English genealogist whose family hailed from Tipperary. Burke's son Sir John Bernard, a genealogist and barrister, assisted him in the compilation, and began its annual re-editing. John Burke also published *Burke's Landed Gentry* (1833–38), another work well known by those interested in tracing lost ancestors.

Busby A *busby*, once a large eighteenth-century bushy wig, is now the name for the plumed fur cap comprising part of the full-dress uniform of the British Hussars and Royal Home Artillery. It has long been thought to derive from the name of the noted schoolmaster and disciplinarian, Dr. Richard Busby (1606–95). Dr. Busby, headmaster of Westminster school, had among his pupils such greats as Dryden, Locke and Prior, and once boasted that he at one time or another birched sixteen of the bishops then in office with his "little rod." As far as is known, however, the good doctor did not wear a frizzled wig. Perhaps his hair naturally stood on end, suggesting the wig when it came into vogue, or possibly there was another Busby thus far unknown to history.

Buttinsky *Buttinsky*, slang for one who interrupts conversations or intrudes in matters not concerning him, is widely used today, the prejudice that inspired the word having long been forgotten. *Buttinsky* was formed at the end of the last century as a pun on Russian and Polish names ending in *sky*. It is now used just as often to describe *buttinskies* among those who slurred the newly arrived immigrants.

B.V.D's, Beeveedees Men's underwear as well as women's (see *Bloomers*) has its eponymous heroes. Anyone found stripped down to his B.V.D.'s might make conversation from his perhaps embarrassing condition by advising onlookers that B.V.D.'s derives from the initials of the three men (Bradley, Voorhees and

Day) who founded the company in 1876. B.V.D. is a trademark and cannot be legally used to describe the product of any other company, though it is often used, unlawfully, as a generic term for underwear. *Beeveedees* is a variant spelling that is recorded in print as early as 1915.

Byerly Turk, Darley Arabian, Godolphin Barb These are the three eponymous oriental horses from whom, without exception, all modern thoroughbred racehorses descend through the male line. *Byerly Turk*, first of the founding fathers, was the charger of English Captain Bylerly at the Battle of the Boyne (1690). Little is known about him except that he was a Turkish stallion purchased abroad a few years before. *Darley Arabian*, most celebrated of the three sires, was sent from Syria to Richard Darley of Yorkshire by his son Thomas in 1704; he was a certified Arabian stallion. *Godolphin Barb* or *Arabian*, called "the mysterious Frenchman," was brought to England from France in 1730 by Edward Coke and later sold or given to the earl of Godolphin. Much of the history of these horses remains a blank, but it can safely be said that every thoroughbred that races anywhere throughout the world is descended from one of the three.

Byronic George Gordon, Lord Byron (1788–1824), contributed to the creation of the *Byronic* hero with deeds as much as words. Byron's slight lameness, his good looks (which were likened to the Apollo Belvedere), his myriad and often sensational romantic entanglements, his wanderings on the Continent and his devotion to the cause of Greek freedom, were among many factors that made the English poet the perfect model for the wildly romantic yet dispairing and melancholy heroes of his poems. Byron's poetry was the most popular of his day, at home and especially abroad, despite its criticism on what today might be considered ridiculous moral grounds. No English poet but Shakespeare had greater influence on European literature and all Byron's major works, such as *Childe Harold's Pilgrimage* and *Don Juan*, have stood the test of time. The poet was haunted in his lifetime by the charge that he committed incest with his half-sister, Mrs. Augusta Leigh. His tempestuous life, the panache and bravura of this poet: "His eyes the open portals of the sun—thing's of light and for light," in Coleridge's words; "The only man to whom I could apply the word beautiful," according to another contemporary, were more romantic than any of his poems. Byron died in Missolonghi, Greece, of malarial fever when only thirty-five. His heart is buried there, where he had sought a soldier's grave in the name of Greek freedom. His body lies buried in England in a small village church, the authorities having refused his burial in the Poet's Corner of Westminster Abbey.

C

Cabal This word for a group of conspirators has for many years been popularly regarded as the most famous acronym in English. Tradition has it that the word was formed from the initials of certain members of King Charles II's infamous ministry in the years 1667–73. Clifford, Ashley (Shaftesbury), Buckingham, Arlington and Lauderdale were only five among a number of Charles's ministers who plotted often diametrically opposed secret intrigues. They rarely met all together, although they did constitute the Privy Council foreign committee, two or three of the group generally meeting with other ministers to conspire. The infamous five did, however, secretly sign the Treaty of Alliance with France in 1672, without Parliament's approval, forcing the nation into war with Holland. After this shameful episode, their enemies were quick to point out that their initials formed the word *cabal*, but this does not say that *cabal* originated with the acrostic ministry. *Cabal*, for a society of intriguers, had previously been introduced into English from the Latin *cabbala*, which derives, in turn, from the Hebrew *qubbalah*. The *qubbalah* were doctrines said to be originally received from Moses, enabling their possessors to unlock secrets of magical power. During the Middle Ages, the secret meetings of *cabbala* groups claiming knowledge of such doctrines gave rise to the English word *cabal*. *Cabal* did, however, take on a new political significance and popularity in English with the machinations of Clifford and the others. The historian Macaulay writes, for example, that "These ministers were called the Cabal, and they soon made the appellation so infamous that it has never since their time been used except as a term of reproach."

Cadillac The *Cadillac*, which is of course a trade name, has long been to ex-

pensive automobiles what the *Ford* has been to low-priced cars. Ironically, the Detroit Automobile Company, formed by Henry Ford in 1899, was the forerunner of the Cadillac Company, Cadillac later being absorbed by General Motors. The *Cadillac*, in the United States and elsewhere, has become a symbol of success to some, signifies vulgar pretension to others, and is a synonym for an expensive car to all. It bears the name of Antoine de la Mothe Cadillac (1658–1730), a minor nobleman and French colonial governor who, in 1701, founded Detroit as an important post for French control of the fur trade. Cadillac also established a trading post in what is now *Cadillac*, Mich., on *Lake Cadillac*. Unlike the car bearing his name, the Frenchman seems to have been popular with no one. Neither Indians nor settlers could get along with him at Fort Pontchartrain (present-day Detroit) and his later governorship of the vast Louisiana Territory (1711–16) met with similar hostility. Cadillac, recalled to France, died in his native Gascony.

Cadmean Letters, Cadmean Victory Myth is often a reflection of fact, and the sixteen letters of the old Greek alphabet said to be introduced to the Boetians by the mythological hero Cadmus from Phoenicia really do derive from Phoenician script. It is uncertain whether there was an actual Cadmus, a prototype for the hero who introduced the *Cadmean letters*. A *Cadmean victory* refers to the same mythological warrior. It derives from the story that Cadmus killed a dragon and sowed the dragon's teeth. Armed warriors sprang up and he set them fighting by throwing a stone among them, only five surviving and these becoming the ancestors of the noble family of Thebes. A *Cadmean victory*, in remembrance of these five surviving stalwarts, became proverbial for a victory achieved where the victors can hardly be distinguished from the vanquished, which is often the case with victory. (See also *Boetian; Pyrrhic Victory*.)

Cadogan Hair Style, Cadogan Teapot Perhaps the only man whose coiffure ever inspired a ladies' hair style was William Cadogan, the first earl of Cadogan. Lord Cadogan (1675–1726) was a British soldier, famous for his intrepid leadership under Marlborough of "Cadogan's Horse" cavalry. He later became commander in chief of the British army. A well-known portrait of Cadogan pictured his hair knotted in the back by a ribbon. This *cadogan style* was aped by eighteenth-century males, including many American founding fathers, and became popular among ladies, too, when it was introduced by the Duchesse de Bourbon at the French court. The *Cadogan teapot*, a lidless teapot that is filled through the bottom, in imitation of an inverted Chinese winepot, may also be named for Cadogan, though no one knows why.

Caesar, Caesarea, Caesarian, Caesarism, Caesarist, Caesarize, Caesaropapism, Render Therefore Unto Caesar More than a score of expressions commemorate Gaius Julius Caesar or his descendants, most of these covered under separate entries. The great Roman soldier and statesman, whose name is responsible for more words in our language than any other, was probably born in 102 B.C., though the traditional date is two years earlier. After crossing the Rubicon in early 49 B.C., conquering Italy and defeating Pompey in Greece, Caesar returned to Rome where he became dictator. He was assassinated during the Ides of March, on March 15, 44 B.C. Historical estimates of Caesar range from one extreme to the other, but the life of this commanding genius, who in Shakespeare's words bestrode "the narrow world like a colossus," is well known to many. His military genius, his address to Rome after he defeated Pharnaces at Zela in 47 B.C., "*Veni, vidi, vici*" (I came, I saw, I conquered) is folklore in many countries. His fascination for Cleopatra, their son Caesarion, later put to death by order of Augustus is also a familiar story. Most words deriving from his name reflect Caesar's great power. *Caesaria* was an ancient seaport in Israel, the Roman capital of Palestine. *Caesarian* or *Caesarean* means pertaining to Caesar or the Caesars. Three other terms, *Caesarism* (imperialism), *Caesarist* (imperialist), and *Caesarize* (imperialize), commemorate the first Caesar's adopted son and successor, Augustus, referring to the imperialist government the first Roman emperor instituted. *Caesaropapism* is the possession of supreme authority over both church and state by one person. Of the many proverbs that recall the great Roman's name the most famous is probably *Render therefore unto Caesar the things which are Caesar's, and to God the things that are God's*, which is, of course, the familiar Biblical injunction (*Matthew* 22:21) from Jesus to the Pharisees. (See also *Caesar cipher; Caesarian section; Caesar's mushroom; Caesar's Wife; Czar; Jersey; Julian Calendar; July; Kaiser; New Jersey; Sherry*.)

Caesar Cipher In his secret communications Julius Caesar would simply write down the third letter following the one he meant (thus in English today the letter A would be D and the word *dog* would be *GRJ*). Though this simple cipher or substitution code was used long before him, cryptologists still call it the *Caesar cipher*. His successor, Augustus Caesar, made the process even simpler, merely substituting the letter immediately following the one he meant, which enabled him to write in code as quickly as he could in normal letters.

Caesarian Section According to popular belief, the first of the Caesars was brought into the world by the *Caesarian section* operation named in his honor. Julius Caesar probably *wasn't* extracted from his mother's womb by this section or cutting through of the abdomen walls, but the operation was commonly practiced on dead mothers in early times. Caesar, whose mother Julia lived many years after his death, probably has his name confused with the operation because it was mandatory under the *lex Cesare*, the codified Roman law of the time, just as it had been under the *lex regia* before this. Roman law prescribed that every woman dying in advanced pregnancy should be so treated. The first

Caesarian on a *live* woman was performed about the year 1500 and deaths resulting from the operation were over 50 percent well into the nineteenth century, the process still a hazardous one. Probably the most famous scene in literature involving a *Caesarian* is the death of Catherine Barkley after the operation in Ernest Hemingway's *A Farewell To Arms.*

Caesar's Mushroom *Amanita caesaria* or *Caesar's mushroom*, honoring Julius Caesar, happens to be one species of the deadly *Amanita* genus that is edible, but more than a few "experts" have been poisoned thinking that they had distinguished this delicacy from its deadly relatives. Every summer brings a score of deaths from mushroom poisoning, which has plagued man since the earliest times. Hippocrates referred to cases of mushroom poisoning, and Horace warned the ancients to beware of all fungi, no matter how appetizing the appearance. One of the first recorded cases of mushroom poisoning occurred in the family of the Greek poet, Euripides, who lost his wife, two sons and a daughter when they partook of a deadly *Amanita* species. Pope Clement VII, the Emperor Jovian, Emperor Charles VI, Czar Alexander, the wife of Czar Alexis, and the Emperor Claudius (uncle of his wife Agrippina, who poisoned his boleti) are among other historical figures who lost their lives in the same way. Many species of *Amanita* are lethal even when eaten in minuscule amounts and the *Amanita verna*, the Destroying Angel, is easily confused with several edible species.

Caesar's Wife Must Be Above Suspicion According to Plutarch and Suetonius, Julius Caesar divorced his second wife, Pompeia, not because he believed her guilty of bedding down with Clodius, as rumor had it, but because he held that *Caesar's wife* must be clear of even the suspicion of wrongdoing. It is hard to believe that even Caesar would have been so vain as to take the word of any crank with a grudge against poor Pompeia. There was probably little love lost between the couple, Caesar's pronouncement constituting an easy way to get rid of his spouse.

Cain, Cain-Colored, Curse of Cain, Mark of Cain, Raising Cain Cain, first-born child of Adam and Eve, and the first Biblical murderer, slew his brother Abel, and lied to the Lord that he did not know his whereabouts ("I know not: Am I my brother's keeper?"). He was condemned to be "a fugitive and a vagabond . . . in the earth." It was forbidden to kill him because of the *mark of Cain* the Lord set upon him, and the *curse of Cain* refers to the legend that he was never to die or reach home again. *Raising Cain*, or to cause much trouble or a loud disturbance, is a synonym for "to raise the devil," for whom *Cain* was an early euphemism. Why Cain's hair (or Judas Iscariot's) is traditionally represented as reddish-yellow or *Cain-colored* remains a mystery. Cain and Judas were usually depicted with such hair and beards in ancient tapestries, but not necessarily because their acts suggested murder or the shedding of blood.

Calamity Jane Martha Jane Burke (c. 1852–1903) won the nickname *Calamity Jane* because her fast, deadly guns threatened and dealt "calamity" to anyone taking liberties with her. Her sobriquet was long a synonym for a female desperado. Although Calamity Jane dressed in men's clothing and early photographs depict her as a sorry sight, Wild Bill Hickok was rumored to have been her lover. She is buried near him on Boot Hill, Deadwood, S.D. An accomplished horsewoman and famous shot, she nevertheless died a natural death, not in a gunfight as has been suggested. (See also *Deadman's Hand.*) Lucky in battle, Calamity was not so fortunate in love— at least her nuptial partners weren't. Eleven of the lady's twelve husbands died before their time due to her intemperate actions.

Calvinism, Calvinist The system of theological thought called *Calvinism* was founded by French Protestant reformer John Calvin or Cauvin (1509–64). *Calvinist* beliefs, found much modified today in Presbyterian and Reformed churches, were formulated as the Five Points in 1618. These are, briefly: (1) Original Sin, man's natural inability to exercise free will since Adam's fall; (2) Predestination; (3) Irresistible grace; (4)

Perseverance of the saints or elect; and (5) Particular redemption. *Calvinism* has overwhelmingly been regarded as a bleak, forbidding theology, and it is hard to believe that Calvin was a young man in his twenties when he set down much of his philosophy in his *Institutes of the Christian Religion*. *Calvinists* considered dancing and music sinful, dressed ultraconservatively and rarely even ate to enjoy themselves. Yet the system's insistence on personal, individual salvation, as well as other tenets, has done great good. *Calvinism* was much in evidence in early New England, though not to the extent that some commentators have suggested.

Camellia One of the most beautiful flowering plants, the evergreen *camellia* is named for George Joseph Kamel (1661–1706), a Moravian Jesuit missionary and amateur botanist who wrote extensive accounts of the shrub, which he found in the Philippine Islands in the late seventeenth century. Kamel, who called himself Camellus, the Latinized form of his name, operated a pharmacy for the poor in Manila, planting a herb garden to supply it. He published reports of the plants he grew and observed in the Royal Society of London's *Philosophical Transactions*. Some authorities say that Kamel sent the first specimens of the shiny-leaved *camellia* back to Europe. In any event, he was the first to describe the shrub, a relative of the tea plant, the great Swedish botanist Linnaeus reading his accounts in *Transactions* and naming the plant *camellia* after him. *Camellias* are used extensively as garden shrubs in southern areas of the United States and England. Their wax-like, long-lasting flowers are white, red or pink.

Camel's Hair Brush Camel's hair paintbrushes are not made from camel's hair, as is generally believed, but from the hair taken from a squirrel species inhabiting cold areas like Siberia and the Tatar Autonomous Soviet Socialist Republic. One explanation for the misnomer is that a German artist named Kemel was the first to use brushes made from the hair of squirrel tails and that *camel's hair* is simply a corruption of "Kemel's hair." This may be so, but there is little evidence to substantiate the theory.

Cannibal, Caliban, Caribbean Sea When Columbus encountered the Caribs upon landing in the Lesser Antilles, these natives gave him their name as *Canibales*. This word was merely a dialectic form of *Caribes* and these people were Caribs themselves, but the Spanish thereafter called the whole Carib tribe *Canibales*. Because some of these fierce, bold warriors ate human flesh, their name was being used within a century in Europe as a synonym for man-eaters, *cannibalism* being substituted for the classical "anthropophagy." The word was probably also influenced by the Spanish word *canino*, meaning canine or voracious. Columbus, incidentally, thought that he had landed in Asia and that the *Canibales*, as his Caribs called themselves, were subjects of the Great Khan or Can, another doubtful but possible influence on the word's formation.

The Caribs of the South American coast were far more adventurous and warlike than those of the larger islands like Cuba, and it is from these expert mariners—they were one of the few New World peoples to use sails—that the *Caribbean Sea* takes its name. In fact, at the time of Columbus, the natives in the Lesser Antilles spoke two separate languages, the men one and the women another. This situation had developed when fierce South American Caribs invaded the islands some years before, butchering and eating all the relatively peaceful Arawak male inhabitants and claiming their women. In retaliation, the women devised a separate "female language" based on Arawak, refusing to speak *Carib* and maintaining silence in the presence of all males, a revenge that they practiced for generations afterward.

Another word derived from the Caribs or Canibales is Shakespeare's Caliban—Prospero's half-human slave in *The Tempest*, and hence any bestial, degraded man. *Caliban* was probably formed either by metathesis from the Spanish *canibal* or as a variant of *Cariban*, a Carib.

Cant *Cant*, for a whining manner of speech or pious hypocritical talk, surely derives from the Latin *cantare*, to sing or chant. Yet some evidence indicates that the word's meaning may have been influenced by the unpopularity of a Scottish preacher named Andrew Cant (1590–1663). In fact, the *Spectator* tried to trace *cant* to the Reverend Cant in an article written in 1711, observing that he talked "in the pulpit in such a dialect that it's said he was understood by none but his own Congregation, and not by all of them." However, the word was used long before the Aberdeen preacher was born and Cant was reputedly "one of the most bold and resolute men of his day." The former chaplain to the Scottish army (1640) once preached such staunch Royalist sentiments before a group of English officers that those supporters of Cromwell advanced on the pulpit with drawn swords. One writer reports, "The intrepid minister opened his breast and said, 'Here is the man who uttered these sentiments,' urging them to strike him if they dared." That hardly sounds like hypocrisy, but there is no doubt that both Andrew Cant and his brother Alexander were zealous leaders of the Scottish Covenanters, supporting among other principles the reformation of religion in England. Another source notes that they were indeed bigoted and hypocritical, persecuting religious opponents ferociously while praying for their souls at the same time. Most dictionaries do not recognize the connection between the preacher's name and *cant*—the usual explanation being that the word evolved from the Latin *cantare*, in reference to the whining speech of beggars. But there seems to be enough evidence to indicate that Reverend Andrew Cant's unpopularity at least strengthened the word's meaning.

Capuchin, Capuchin Monkey, Capuchin Pigeon The order of Capuchin monks, established in 1520, came into being when Franciscan friar Matteo di Bassi insisted that the habit worn by the Franciscans wasn't the one that St. Francis had worn. He stubbornly fashioned himself a sharp-pointed pyramidal hood (*capuche*), let his beard grow and went barefoot, the Pope granting him permission eight years later to wear this costume and form a separate order which would preach to the poor. The new offshoot of Franciscans came to be named for the headdress its monks still wear, and it wasn't long before a woman's combined cloak and hood was dubbed a *capuchin* after the monks' cowl. The word in its latter meaning was used frequently and is even recorded in a bawdy Scottish ballad: "As Molly Lee came down the street, / Her capuchin did flee; / She coost a look behind her / To see her negligee."

The tropical *Capuchin monkey* and *Capuchin pigeon* are also named for the Capuchins' costume, the monkey's black hair and appearance resembling their monastic cowl, and the pigeon having a hoodlike tuft of black feathers. Today the Capuchins have some two hundred missionary stations throughout the world and are known as the poorest of all orders.

Carbine The *carbine*, a short, light rifle, probably takes its name from the Medieval Latin *Calabrinus*, meaning a Calabrian. Calabria in southern Italy was noted for its light horsemen or skirmishers, the first such weapons having been either used or manufactured there. *Carabins*, as the weapons were called in sixteenth-century England, were originally "large pistols . . . having barrels 3 ft. long." They were much shorter and less cumbersome than muskets, however, and were employed by light cavalry troops. By the early seventeenth century *carbine* was being spelled in its present form, although it took many years for the weapon to develop into the short, light rifle that we know today.

Cardigan "It is magnificent but it is not war," was Marechal Bosquet's memorable remark on the charge of the Light Brigade, famous in history and Tennyson's poem of the same name. The charge at Balaclava during the Crimean War was led by James Thomas Brudenell (1797–1868), the seventh earl of Cardigan. Cardigan, a foolish, vain, violent-tempered man, somewhat redeemed himself by his great personal courage. He had been forced to purchase the command of his famous 11th Light Dragoons for forty thousand pounds, after being relieved of a previous post for his irrational behavior —having in less than two years made over seven hundred arrests and held more than one hundred court-martials. The charge of the Light Brigade in the Crimea (October 25, 1854) probably resulted as a misinterpretation of orders. In any event, Cardigan, sword flashing, an image of sartorial splendor in his cherry-color and royal blue uniform, miraculously rode through Russian guns on both flanks and in front of him, walking back with his horse Ronald to tell the tale—although he left two-thirds of his cavalry dead on the battlefield behind him. Brave as he was, he probably wouldn't have come back at all if an aristocratic Russian friend hadn't recognized him and ordered him captured alive, but Cardigan eluded his pursuers. The then major general became England's hero of the hour. That is, until survivors returned to tell the whole story of the "charge into the Valley of Death," embellishing the tale with such true accounts as how the Noble Yachtsman had lived aboard a friend's palatial yacht while they endured the cold and mud.

Cardigan's troops were the most precisely drilled and splendidly dressed of British soldiers, their commander invariably surpassing them in the last respect. The knitted woolen vest he wore to protect himself against the Crimean winter was named in his honor during his fleeting moments of fame, but today the *cardigan* is a collarless, three-button sweater or jacket with a round or V-neck, bearing little resemblance to the original. Lord Cardigan eventually attained the rank of lieutenant general. Like eponymous heroes Sir Robert Peel (see *Bobby*) and *Soapy Sam* Wilberforce, he died after a fall from his horse.

Carême "The king of cooks and the cook of kings" was born in Paris on June 8, 1784, in his own words one of twenty-five children "of one of the poorest families in France." Marc-Antoine Carême worked from the time he was seven as a kitchen scullion. In his teens he was accepted as an apprentice chef and after much study under many masters went on to found *La Grande Cuisine Française*, classic French cooking as we still know it today. Carême's creations reflected his considerable artistic abilities, his pastries often looking more like sculpture than food, and his supreme taste and meticulous standards illustrated in his many books, as well as his forty-eight course

dinners, made the French cuisine sovereign throughout Europe. Among other notables, Carême cooked for Talleyrand, the future George IV of England, Czar Alexander I, Lord Castlereagh, Baron Rothschild, the world's richest man, and France's Louis XVIII, who granted him the right to call himself "Carême of Paris." But his motto was "One master: Talleyrand. One mistress: Cooking." He was always faithful to his first benefactor and as a result is the one noted chef in history who was also a spy, relaying information from all over Europe he overheard at important dinner tables to the French minister of foreign affairs. Carême's word was law to all chefs worthy of the name in what was probably the world's most extraordinary culinary period; monarch of the entire culinary empire, his name is today synonymous for a great chef. He died on January 12, 1833, while sampling a *quenelle* of sole prepared by a student in his cooking school. "These are good," he is supposed to have murmured critically, "but prepared too hastily. You must shake the saucepan lightly—see, like this. . . ." These were his last words for, as he lifted the saucepan, he collapsed and fell to the floor dead. Someone wrote that he had died "burnt out by the flame of his genius and the heat of his ovens."

Carnegie, Carnegiea The largest cactus in the world, *Carnegiea gigantea*, or the saguaro, takes its botanical name from one of the world's richest and kindest men, Andrew Carnegie (1835–1919). A *Carnegiea* specimen found near Madrona, N. Mex., in 1950 had candelabra-like branches rising to fifty-three feet. The species had been named for Carnegie a half century before in gratitude for his help in financing Tucson's former Desert Laboratory. Carnegie, whose family emigrated to America from Scotland when he was a youth, rose from rags to riches, starting as a bobbin boy in a cotton factory at $1.20 a week and becoming a multimillionaire with his Carnegie Steel Company, which was merged with the United States Steel Corporation when he retired in 1901 to live on his estate in Scotland. Carnegie believed that it was a disgrace to die rich and he became one of the greatest individual philanthropists in history, his benefactions totaling about $350 million. Numerous schools, foundations and research institutions are named for him, including: the *Carnegie Corporation of New York*; Pittsburgh's *Carnegie Hero Fund Commission*; *Carnegie Institute of Pittsburgh*; *Carnegie Institute of Washington*; New York's *Carnegie Foundation for the Advancement of Teaching*; *The Carnegie Endowment for International Peace*; the *Carnegie Trust for the Universities of Scotland*; and the *Carnegie United Kingdom Trust*. While he lived, Carnegie greatly aided Tuskegee Institute under Booker T. Washington, worked for spelling reform, built some twenty-five hundred libraries, and established large pension funds for both his former employees and American college professors, among philanthropies which have literally filled one book. His philosophy was summed up in his essay, "The Gospel of Wealth": "This, then, is held to be the duty of the man of wealth: to set an example of modest unostentatious living, shunning display or extravagance; to provide moderately for the wants of those dependent on him; and, after doing so, to consider all surplus revenues which come to him simply as trust funds, which he is called upon to administer. . . . The man of wealth thus becoming the mere trustee and agent for his poorer brethren."

Carry Nation Any intemperate temperance agitator. Carry Nation (1846–1911), convinced that she was divinely appointed to bring about the downfall of the saloon, embarked upon her career in Kansas in 1899, chopping her way through the United States and Europe with her "hatchetings" or "hatchetations." Her temperance lectures were not as interesting as her spectacular destruction of saloon interiors with her trusty axe, but the title of her autobiography, *The Use and Need of the Life of Carry A. Nation* (1904), is a classic. Carry, poor girl, had an unhappy childhood and her first marriage to the intemperate Dr. Charles Gloyd—Nation being her second husband's name—would have driven anyone else to drink. Yet the much ridiculed schoolteacher seemed to believe that she was made for martyrdom; she even enjoyed her frequent stays in jail.

Cartesian *Cartesian* refers to the philosophy of René Descartes (1596–1650) and his followers, deriving from *Cartesius*, the Latinized form of his name. The French philosopher was an eminent mathematician who based the starting point of his philosophy on the famous phrase *Cogito, ergo sum* (I think, therefore I am). His influence on science, philosophy and literature has been immense, for he was among the first to rely on the rule of reason, rejecting all philosophical tradition. *Cartesian* also means "the explanation of philosophical problems by mathematics." Descartes spent much of his life in Holland, dying in Sweden, where he had been invited by Queen Christiana. His major work is *Discours de la Méthode* (1637). I remember reading somewhere that Descartes was fascinated all his life by women with a squint, which means absolutely nothing but might be of encouragement to some readers.

Caruso, Sauce Caruso, A Touch of Caruso The greatest of tenors, Enrico Caruso (1873–1921), was no slouch as a gourmand, either. His *Sauce Caruso*, a marinara sauce with chicken livers and sautéed mushrooms added, is a noble topping indeed for spaghetti. Caruso was born in Naples, Italy, of a poor family and had little musical training except in singing the sensuous Neapolitan ballads of his city. He first came into prominence with his appearance in Puccini's *La Bohème* in 1898, this performance in Milan the beginning of a career never matched by an opera singer for riches and adulation, his performances and recordings carrying his "celestial golden voice" around the world. From 1903 on Caruso was the leading tenor at New York's Metropolitan Opera House. A lighthearted man of boyish charm, he was something of a cutup. When he pinched a girl's derrière in a Paris park, the resulting publicity gave rise to the nautical expression *a touch of Caruso*, meaning the turn of a ship's engines astern. Caruso's great vocal range and power have never been equaled. His was a tragic death. He ruptured a blood vessel while singing in 1920 and died the following year. (See also *Chicken Tetrazzini*; *Melba*.)

Caryatid *Caryatids* are draped or partially clothed female figures used in place of columns or pillars as supports, especially in Greek or Roman architecture. The statues did not adorn any ancient Playboy Club but were used to support temple entablatures. They take their name from the maidens of *Caryae* (Latin for *Karyai*), a town in Laconia, Greece. The Karyatids, or maidens of Karyai, danced in temples at the festival of Artemis and occasionally assumed the poses represented in the statues. Some accounts say that their figures were first used by the Greeks in place of columns as a reminder of their disgrace—for the Karyatids had supported the Persians at the battle of Thermopylae (480 B.C.). Numerous examples of *caryatids* survive, one in the British Museum. *Atlantes*, their male counterparts, take their name from the legendary Atlas.

Casanova Giovanni Jacopo Casanova de Seingalt's famous memoirs run to some 1,500,000 words, and only take us through his forty-ninth year. It is said that his autobiography should be trusted in the main outline as a picture of the eighteenth century, but not in the details, yet it seems relatively tame today and the details are not as licentious or racy as they once appeared. It is often forgotten that the Italian adventurer was a man of many talents: in turn, journalist, raconteur, soldier, gambler, gastronome, preacher, abbe, philosopher, violinist, alchemist, businessman, diplomat, spy, and so on. Perhaps his guiding philosophy is expressed in a little quoted passage found midway in the *Memoirs*: ". . . . The instants that man is compelled to give up to misfortune or to suffering are so many moments stolen from his life; but he doubles his existence when he has the talent of multiplying his pleasures, no matter of what nature they may be." So Casanova lived his life, from age sixteen, when expelled from a seminary in his native Venice for immoral conduct, to his death in Bohemia, where he served as a librarian for Count von Waldstein, at Dux Castle, in 1798, aged seventy-three. His elegant wit made him the welcome guest of giants like Voltaire and Frederick the Great, but he was never more than a *homme à bonnes fortunes*. Casanova is of course best remembered as a great lover, his name equaled only by *Don Juan's* as a synonym for a promiscuous womanizer. Women, as he said, were his cuisine, and he knew or invented every trick to lure them to his banquet-bed— from ploys like his "oyster game" (he would convince a likely prospect that they should eat oysters from one another's tongues) to poetry, music and exaggerated accounts of his prowess in every sphere. The fabled lover is the typical example of the neurotic great seducer whose need to please is the very breath of life, yet he was a sensualist and a gentleman, a combination rare.

Casey at the Bat

Oh! somewhere in this favored land the sun is shining bright,
The band is playing somewhere, and somewhere hearts are light;
And somewhere men are laughing, and somewhere children shout,
But there is no joy in Mudville—mighty Casey has struck out.

This mock-heroic poem by Ernest Laurence Thayer (1863–1940) was first published in the San Francisco *Examiner* on June 3, 1888, and *Casey at the Bat* has been popular ever since. Its initial popularity was due as much to the actor De Wolf Hopper, who included the thirteen-stanza poem in his repertory, as it was to the poet, a former editor of the *Harvard Lampoon*. Everyone knows that there was no joy in Mudville when the mighty Casey struck out, but few are aware that Thayer patterned his fabled slugger on a real player, Daniel Maurice Casey, who was still posing for newspaper photographers fifty years after the poem's initial publication. Dan Casey, a native of Binghamton, New York, holds no records worthy of recording—not even as a strike-out king. He was a pitcher and an outfielder for Detroit and Philadelphia, his career overshadowed by the exploits of his elder brother, Dennis, an outfielder for Baltimore and New York. Casey died in 1943, when he was seventy-eight, in Washington, D.C. As for Thayer, he was paid only five dollars for his poem, which De Wolf Hopper recited over five thousand times. But then Poe, legend has it, received only ten dollars for *The Raven* and *The Atlantic Monthly* paid Mrs. Howe four dollars for the lyrics to "The

Battle Hymn of the Republic." Whitman printed *Leaves of Grass* himself. (See also *Bosey; Babe Ruth; Tinker.*)

Casey Jones Engineer John Luther Jones, who died in a wreck of the Chicago and New Orleans Limited on March 18, 1900, probably inspired the perennially popular folk ballad, *Casey Jones.* The song's authorship is unknown and it may have been adapted from a ballad about a Negro railroad fireman. Casey Jones' story was dramatized in Robert Ardrey's *Casey Jones* (1938). There are numerous versions of both music and lyrics, the folk song based on the tradition that "there's many a man killed on the railroad and laid in his lonesome grave."

Castilloa Elastica This tree species—commonly called the ule or Mexican rubber tree—is not by any means the most important source of rubber today, but is an historical curiosity, having yielded the heavy black rubber balls Columbus was amazed to see natives playing with on his second voyage to South America—the first recorded observation of rubber by a European. The tree *C. elastica* is a species of the *Castilloa* genus, of the mulberry family, and is named for Spanish botanist Juan Castillo y López. Like Columbus, later explorers were astounded by the resilient balls made from the tree's vegetable gum, remarking that they rebounded so much that they "seemed alive," but rubber wasn't brought into commercial use in Europe until three centuries after its discovery. The tree *Hevea brasiliensis*, yielding high-grade Para, is by far the most important rubber source today. *Castilloa elastica*, however, still yields a good quality Caucho rubber, the large tree particularly valuable when Para rubber is high priced.

Catawba Grapes A light reddish variety of grape grown in the eastern United States, the Catawba was developed by John Adlum in his vineyard near Georgetown in 1820, its dominant parent the Northern fox grape. It was named three years later for the Catawba Indians of the Carolinas, or for the *Catawba River*, which takes its name from the Indian tribe. The *Catawba*, long a traditional favorite, contains some vinifera blood and is one of the best grapes for white wines.

By 1860, nine tenths of all grapes grown east of the Rockies were *Catawbas*, but they were thereafter replaced by the Concord, perfected in 1850, as the leading American variety.

Catchpenny The folk etymology is that *catchpenny* arose in 1824 when London printer James Catnach sold, at one penny apiece, "the last speech" by the murderer of a merchant named Weare. The sheet sold so well, the story goes, that Catnach decided to capitalize on the murder again. He printed another penny paper headlined WE ARE ALIVE AGAIN, but ran the first two words close together so that the headline looked like WEARE ALIVE AGAIN. Gulled buyers of this Catnach penny paper, it is said, punned on his name after discovering the cheap trick, referring to his paper as *catchpenny*, which soon came to mean any low-priced fraudulent item. The fault in this ingenious story lies in the fact that *catchpenny* was used in the same sense, "any flimflam that might catch a penny," as early as 1759, sixty-five years before the Catnach ploy. James Catnach (1792–1841) was a real person, however; he did a thriving business selling historically valuable "dying speeches of . . ." and "topic of the moment songs" from his Seven Dials printing works in London. His "Catnach paper" undoubtedly gave the word *catchpenny* greater currency.

Catherine Wheel The Christian martyr, St. Catherine of Alexandria, is said to have confessed her faith to Roman Emperor Maximinus and rebuked him for the worship of false gods. Maximinus ordered her broken on the wheel, *after she converted his wife and the Roman general who escorted her to prison,* but the spiked wheel was shattered to pieces by her touch. This virgin of royal descent was then put to death by the axe and tradition has it that her body was carried by angels to Mt. Sinai, where Justinian I built a famous monastery in her honor. St. Catherine is known as the patron saint of wheelwrights and mechanics, her name day November 25. The *Catherine wheel*, fireworks in the shape of a wheel rotated by the explosions; the circular, spoked *Catherine wheel window*; and to turn *Catherine* *wheels*, lateral somersaults, all derive from her name. St. Catherine's existence is generally admitted, but modern Catholic scholars accept very little of her traditional story.

Catiline, Catilinarian Catiline's conspiracy (64 B.C.) gives us the term *Catiline* for a conspirator or plotter against the government. Lucius Sergius Catiline (c. 108–62 B.C.), already guilty of at least one murder and extortion, had plotted with other nobles to kill the consuls, plunder the treasury and set Rome on fire, but Cicero's eloquent *Catilinarian oration* alerted the public, foiling the conspirators. Catiline, sentenced to death, attempted to escape but was defeated in battle by Antonius and slain near Pistoria. Catiline represented himself as a democrat who would cancel all debts and outlaw all wealthy citizens. Ironically, Julius Caesar, the victim of assassins himself twenty years later, was probably a party to the planned assassinations.

Catlinite A clay-stone of pale grayish-red to dark red color, *catlinite* honors American painter and writer George Catlin (1796–1872). Early used by American Indians for making pipes, it is commonly called pipe-rock. Catlin, a self-taught artist, is remembered for his primitive but authentic paintings of Indian life. An impresario, too, he displayed troupes of Indians in the East and Europe long before Buffalo Bill or Barnum.

Cattleya, Cattleya Fly, Cattley Guava This most popular of florist's orchids has nothing to do with cattle, having been named for William Cattley (d. 1832), English amateur botanist and botany patron. The *Cattleya* genus includes some forty species, though over three hundred hybridized forms are known. *Cattleya labiata*, with its two hundred or so named varieties, is the most commonly cultivated orchid in America—the showy magenta-purple-lipped, yellow-throated "florist's orchid." To most people it is *the* orchid, although the enormous orchid family contains perhaps five hundred genera and fifteen thousand species. The *Cattleyea fly*, and the *Cattley guava*, a subtropical fruit, also commemorate the English plant lover.

Caucasian When the German anthropologist Johann Blumenbach divided mankind into the *Caucasian, Mongolian, Ethiopian, American* and *Malayan* races in 1795, he chose a skull from the Caucasus, in what is now the Soviet Union, as the perfect type in his collection. He also claimed that the Caucasus area was the home of the hypothetical race known as "Indo-Europeans," to whom many languages can be traced. Blumenbach's theories proved unscientific and tinged with racism. In *Webster's* the word he coined is now given "in default of a better" and as "one of the main ethnic divisions of the human race: (including) the Mediterranean, Alpine and Nordic subdivisions, and is loosely called the white race." *Caucasian* also refers to the people of the Caucasus, their languages and their culture.

Cayuse A small horse bred by the Cayuse Indians of Oregon and Washington gave the name *cayuse* to all Indian ponies, the word also meaning a horse of little value. The Cayuse were of Waiilatpuan linguistic stock. In 1847, blaming whites for a smallpox outbreak, they attacked and killed fourteen missionaries near the present city of Walla Walla, Washington. They were subdued and put on a reservation in 1855. No full-blooded Cayuse survives today. In early times the word was often spelt *kiyuse*. "Twice our kiyuse broke nearly out of the harnass. . . . The kiyuse is never properly tamed," one pioneer-author observed.

Cecil's Fast Now chiefly an historical term, a *Cecil's fast* is simply a fish dinner. William Cecil, Lord Burghley (1520–98), long-time chief minister to England's Queen Elizabeth, is responsible for the phrase. Cecil, hoping to restore the fish trade, introduced a bill calling for the eating of fish on certain days of the week and all such meals were named for him.

Celsius The centigrade thermometer is often called the *Celsius thermometer* in honor of the eminent Swedish astronomer who invented the *Celsius scale*. Anders Celsius (1701–44) first suggested his improvement of the Fahrenheit scale before the Swedish Academy of Sciences in 1742, proposing the more obvious gradation between 0 and 100. Today the mercury thermometer patterned on this theometric scale is widely used in Europe for meteorological and all other temperatures. Celsius also founded the observatory at Uppsala, where he was a professor, and made and collected many observations of the aurora borealis. Boiling water is 212° on the Fahrenheit scale and 100° on the Celsius or *centigrade scale*; freezing water is 0° centigrade and 32° Fahrenheit. Centigrade temperatures can be converted to Fahrenheit by multiplying the centigrade reading by 1.8 and adding 32 to the result. (See also *Fahrenheit*.)

Chapel, Chaplain St. Martin of Tours converted to Christianity when a young pagan soldier in the Roman army under Constantine. According to Butler's *Lives of the Saints*, "In a very hard winter, during a severe frost, he met at the gate of the city a poor man almost naked, begging alms of them that passed by. Martin, seeing those that went before take no notice of this miserable creature . . . had nothing but his clothes. So drawing his sword, he cut his cloak into two pieces, gave one to the beggar and wrapped himself in the other half." That night Martin saw a vision of Christ "dressed in that half of the garment he had given away" and decided to enter into the religious life. He eventually became bishop of Tours and was credited with many cures and miracles. After his death, in about 400 A.D., Martin became patron saint of the Frankish kings, who preserved the remaining half of his cloak, or *cappella*, as a relic. It was enshrined in a chest in a special sanctuary, which also came to be known as a *cappella*, and the soldiers who watched over it, or carried it into battle and from place to place, were called *cappellani*. These two words, in French *chapelle* and *chapelain*, are the source of the English *chapel* and *chaplain*, the former deriving initially from St. Martin's cape and the latter from the soldiers who guarded it in its sanctuary.

Charlatan *Charlatan* can be traced to the Italian *ciarlatano*, for a quack, but a notorious quack dentist may have helped it along. A. M. Latan, it is said, was a nineteenth-century Frenchman who dressed in a long-robed exotic costume and often toured Paris in a magnificent dispensary car, a horn player heralding his approach. Spectators would cry out "*Voila le char de Latan*" (There is Latan's car), the words *le char de latan* popularizing *charlatan*. Most likely Latan was an assumed name, chosen to accompany his *char*, but the mischievous Frenchman probably strengthened the meaning of a word that had been used in English since the early seventeenth century.

Charles' Wain Much legend surrounds Charlemagne, Charles the Great (742–814 A.D.), king of the Franks and founder of the Holy Roman Empire. Charlemagne is said to have been eight feet tall and so strong that he could bend three horseshoes together. He had four wives and five mistresses who between them presented him with fifty children. Charles the Great was also associated, probably erroneously, with the legendary King Arthur. The constellation now better known as the Big Dipper, the Plough, Ursa Major, or the Great Bear was at that time called *Arthur's Wain* because it resembled a wain or wagon of old, the stars in the handle of the Dipper being the wagon's shaft. Since there was a legendary association between Charles the Great and King Arthur, the star-cluster called *Arthur's Wain* eventually became known as *Charles' Wain*, too. (See also *Berenice's Hair*.)

Charley, Charlie, Charlies Long before English policemen were dubbed *bobbies*, London nightwatchmen were called *Charleys*, or *Charlies*. The obsolete designation is believed to derive from the name of Charles I, who extended and improved the London night watch in order to curb street offenses in 1640, or from his son the lascivious Charles II. Charles I, beheaded by Cromwell in 1649, also wore a short, triangular beard called a *Charlie* that is now known as a *Van Dyke*. The slang *charlies* for a woman's shapely breasts, one etymologist suggests, derives from "the opulent charms displayed by the mistresses of Charles II"—*charlies* probably originally *charlie's* because they were playthings "belonging" to the king. The word in this sense is a contradiction in terms, for the proper name "Charles" means "man." (See also *Bobby*; *Charley Horse*.)

Charley Horse Did this term for a muscular leg cramp arise from a lame horse named Charley that pulled a roller across the infield in the Chicago White Sox ball park in the 1890's? There probably was such a horse, but the expression had been printed several years before his working days, in 1888, to describe a ballplayer's stiffness or lameness. Another ingenious derivation traces *Charley horse* to the constables or *Charleys* of seventeenth-century England. This term for local police survived in the United States through the nineteenth century and because aching legs, as well as flat feet, were an occupational disease among *Charleys*, ballplayers suffering such maladies were compared with the coppers and said to be "weary for riding Charley's horse." Both theories, however, are speculations and the term's origin remains unknown. (See also *Charleys*.)

Charley More "Charley More—the fair (or square) thing" was the legend on the huge tavern sign of a Maltese publican about 1840. His name became synonymous with fair or straight dealing, *Charley More* long a British naval term for one who is honest and upright.

Charley Noble Another British navy term dating from the nineteenth century. Commander, captain, or ship's cook Charles Noble (c. 1840) demanded that the cowl of the copper funnel of his galley stove always be kept brightly polished. Up until about 1900 galley funnels were called *Charley Nobles* in his honor. Or so the old story goes.

Charlie Chaplin, Chaplinesque, Charlie Chaplin Moustache The great film comedian, born in England on April 16, 1889, began his career in London vaudeville, going to Hollywood in 1910, where Mack Sennett eventually hired him to make movies with the Keystone Comedy Company. Of his many famous pictures, *The Goldrush* is considered his masterpiece. Chaplin's brilliant creation of the wistful tramp that he consistently played resulted in a number of familiar words, including *Chaplinesque*, *Charlie Chaplin walk*, and the toothbrush *Charlie Chaplin moustache*. Now a resident of Switzerland, he is still active producing, writing, directing and acting in his own films.

Charlotte Russe, Apple Charlotte Carême, the greatest chef of his day, created a lavish pastry which he called the *Apple Charlotte* after England's Princess Charlotte, George IV's only daughter. The master chef apparently could not forget Charlotte, for while serving Czar Alexander in Russia, he created a jellied custard set in a crown of ladyfingers that he named the *Charlotte Russe* in her honor. Carême's creations were so valued that it is said that they were stolen from the table at the court of George IV—not to be relished at home, but to be sold in the market at high prices. (See also *Carême*.)

Charterhouse *Charterhouse*, the venerable London public school and hospital, was, in the fourteenth century, the site of a religious house of the Carthusian monks. When one Thomas Sutton died in 1611, he endowed a hospital, chapel and school on this property, which had come into his possession that same year. All three institutions were called *Charterhouse*, as was the Carthusian monastery before them, the word deriving from the early English spelling (Chartrouse) of the French *maison Chartreuse*, "Carthusian house." The school moved to Surrey in 1872, but the hospital, or almshouse, still stands on its old site. Many of the *Charterhouse* buildings were destroyed in World War II. (See also *Chartreuse*.)

Chartreuse Liqueur A cordial that takes its name from a monastery of the Carthusian monks. La Grande Chartreuse, the mother house of the Carthusian order, was founded by St. Bruno of Cologne in 1084 near Grenoble, France, the monastery taking its name from nearby Carthusua, after which the Carthusians had been named. Early in the seventeenth century the Maréchel d'Estrées gave the monks a recipe for a liqueur made from fragrant herbs and brandy; the Carthusians called the liqueur *Chartreuse*. They began to manufacture and sell it on a large scale only when they returned to La Grande Chartreuse after their expulsion during the French revolution, using the revenues to rebuild and maintain their devastated monastery. Le

Chartreux, as the French call the Carthusians, were again expelled from France in 1903, their distillery and trademark being sold and an imitation *Chartreuse* marketed by a commercial firm. Cognoscenti hold that only the liqueur made by the monks is worthy of the name, claiming that *Chartreuse* owes its distinctive flavor to the still secret formula that employs angelica root and other herbs of the Grenoble region. The Carthusians were allowed to return to Grenoble in 1938, and now sell their liqueur under the *Les Pères Chartreux* trademark. The best *Chartreuse* is a pale apple-green, hence the color *chartreuse*. (See also *Benedictine, Charterhouse, Dom Perignon*.)

Chateaubriand One old story tells us that Brillat-Savarin dined in Paris with the Vicomte François René Chateaubriand on the night that an anonymous restaurant proprietor invented *steak Chateaubriand* in his honor. The occasion, according to this version, was the publication of the French romantic's *La Génie du Christianisme* and the succulent tenderloin was encased between two flank steaks, symbolizing Christ and the thieves. The outer steaks, seared black, were discarded, leaving the tenderloin rare and juicy. More likely, *steak Chateaubriand* was invented and named by the novelist's chef, Montmirel, and served for the first time at the French embassy in London. Vicomte Chateaubriand (1768–1848) advocated the return of France to Christianity after the French revolution. Temperamentally opposed to all government—he once wrote a pamphlet so critical of Napoleon that he slept with it under his pillow and had his wife hide it under her dress during the day—he nevertheless turned his attention to politics in later years, becoming ambassador to Berlin and London under Louis XVIII. Chateaubriand had left France for America during the Revolution, "exploring" the wilderness along the Ohio and Mississippi rivers, and had also been wounded fighting with the Royalists against the Republican army during his seven-year exile. Few men of his time led more exciting, eventful lives. Vanity, of course, was not one of his weak points. "He thinks himself deaf,"

Talleyrand once said of him in his old age, "because he no longer hears himself talked of." But the writer remained consistent to the end, even having his mistress with him on the night that he died. The steak commemorating Chateaubriand is often served with a *Béarnaise* sauce, surrounded with potatoes, mushrooms and other vegetables. The meat itself is a thick cut of tenderloin from the middle of the filet mignon.

Chauffeur The first *chauffeurs* were members of a band of brigands. *Jean l'Écorcheur* (Jack the Scorcher) was a bandit leader whose gang took advantage of the chaos created by the French revolution to terrorize the French countryside in the late eighteenth century. Jack and his henchmen would force their way into homes and demand that all hidden valuables be surrendered, tying up those householders who refused and roasting their bare feet in the fire until they capitulated. Jack's men came to be known as *chauffeurs*, firemen, their nickname deriving from the French *chauffer*, to heat or stoke. Long after its application to Jack the Scorcher and his *chauffeurs*, the word was logically applied to steamship stokers, locomotive firemen and, finally, to the stokers required to tend early steam-powered automobiles. These stokers often operated someone else's car and the word was retained when *chauffeurs* no longer needed to be firemen in addition to drivers.

Chauvinism Jingoism, spread-eagleism, the German *Hurrapatriotismus*—excessive nationalism or superpatriotism by any name is known in many languages as *chauvinism*. Nicolas Chauvin of Rochefort, a French soldier of the First Republic and Empire under Napoleon, is responsible for the word. A veteran trooper, Chauvin was wounded seventeen times while serving with La Grande Armée. Retired when he was so scarred that he could fight no more, he received a medal, a ceremonial saber and a pension of two hundred francs (about 40 dollars) a year as compensation for his wounds. Instead of growing bitter, Chauvin turned in the opposite direction, for after all his sacrifices had to mean something. Chauvin became an idolator of the Little Corporal; even after Waterloo and

Napoleon's exile, he spoke of little but the infallibility of his hero and the glory of France. The veteran became a laughingstock in his village for his excessive zeal on behalf of a lost imperial cause, his lack of common sense, and his mad demonstrations of loyalty and patriotism. He would have escaped national attention, however, if the dramatists Charles and Jean Cogniard had not known of him and used him as a character in their comedy *La Cocarde tricolore* (1831), epitomizing him with the line "Je suis français, je suis Chauvin" (I am French, I am Chauvin). The play truthfully represented Chauvin as an almost idolatrous worshipper of Napoleon and was followed by numerous comedies by other authors caricaturing the old soldier—these including Scribe's *Le Soldat Laboureur*, Charet's *Conscrit Chauvin*, and Bayard and Dumanoir's *Les Aides de camps*. As a result the French word *chauvinisme*, our chauvinism, became synonymous with fanatical, unreasoning patriotism and all that such blind, bellicose worship of national prowess implies.

Chesterfield Overcoat, Couch, Chesterfieldian *Chesterfieldian* usually means writings on dress and manners, referring to Philip Dormer Stanhope, the fourth earl of Chesterfield (1694–1773), whose posthumous *Letters to His Son* and *Letters to His Godson* are models of their kind. Lord Chesterfield, whose last words were "Give Dayrolles [a visitor] a chair," did not intend his letters for publication. Dr. Johnson described them as teaching "the morals of a whore and the manners of a dancing master"—but then the Great Cham was hardly an unprejudiced judge, Chesterfield having neglected the plan for his great *English Dictionary*, which resulted in Johnson's famous letter rejecting his support when it was finished. The witty *Letters* of the statesman and diplomat were meant to be filled with worldly knowledge and thus reflected the morality of the age.

Johnson's famous put-down of Chesterfield came when the latter wrote favorable reviews of Johnson's *Dictionary* after refusing to support the author while he was working on it. "Is not a patron, my lord," he wrote, "one who looks with unconcern on a man struggling for life in the water, and when he has reached ground encumbers him with help?" Johnson also said of Chesterfield, on another occasion: "This man I thought had been a lord among wits; but I find, he is only a wit among lords." Yet Chesterfield did have a great wit. One time, for example, an enemy pushed him off the pavement saying, "I never give the wall to a scoundrel." Replied Chesterfield, tipping his hat, "Sir, I always do."

The large overstuffed *chesterfield couch* and the man's velvet-collared overcoat with concealed buttons called a *chesterfield* were introduced in the nineteenth century. Both may have been named in honor of Philip Stanhope, but it is more likely that they commemorate a later earl of Chesterfield, who may even have invented them. Just which earl no one seems to know.

Chicken à la King *Chicken à la King*, diced pieces of chicken in a sherry-cream sauce, is now available canned, frozen and even in army mess halls, a long way from the éclat tables where it was served in the late nineteenth century. The dish was invented for no king, as is popularly believed, yet it's hard to pinpoint just who *chicken à la King* does honor. Some say New Yorker Foxhall Keene, self-proclaimed "world's greatest amateur athlete," suggested the concoction to Delmonico's chef. Of the numerous stories surrounding its creation the most reliable seems to be that of the famous Claridge's Hotel in London. Claridge's claimed that the dish was invented by its chef to honor J. R. Keene, whose horse had won the Grand Prix in 1881. Perhaps J. R. passed on the recipe to his son, the peerless Foxhall. At any rate, the Keenes did not hold public interest long enough and the *Keene* in *Chicken à la Keene* eventually became *King*.

Chicken Tetrazzini Luisa Tetrazzini, the Italian-born diva whose role of Lucia di Lammermoor made her famous to opera lovers throughout the world early in this century, counted this dish as her favorite. *Chicken Tetrazzini* is diced chicken in cream sauce flavored with sherry and baked in a casserole with thin spaghetti, cheese and mushrooms. According to those who saw her, Madame Tetrazzini shared a problem common to most opera stars, looking as if she had dined many times on the highly caloric dish. The coloratura soprano made her debut in Florence in 1895 and ended her concert career in 1931 after starring in Spain, Portugal, Russia, England, America and many other countries. She died in 1941, aged sixty-nine. (See also *Caruso; Melba.*)

Childe Ballad American ballads are generally classified in three groups: *Childe ballads,* broadside ballads and native American ballads. *Childe ballads* are not about children but 305 early songs were collected by Harvard English professor Francis James Childe (1825–96) in the late nineteenth century. Of Childe's *English and Scottish Popular Ballads,* half the songs were brought to America by English settlers; they are considered the best of American ballads, all still sung today in one form or another. Often these songs underwent great transformations through the years. The old favorite "On Top of Old Smoky," for example, was much more powerful and said something quite different in its original version as "The Waggoners' Lad," as is witnessed by the following two stanzas:

So hard is the fortune of poor womankind.
They are always controlled and always confined.

Controlled by their parents till they are made wives,
Then slaves to their husbands the rest of their lives.

Women today are singing the same tune *and* the same words.

Chinook, Chinook Salmon, Chinook State, Chinook Wind *Chinook,* an important pidgin language, enabled eighteenth to nineteenth-century American farmers and traders, French trappers, and even visiting Russian seal hunters to converse with Indians in the Pacific Northwest. *Chinook* jargon was used for more than one hundred years. Named for the Chinook Indians, who had large settlements along the Columbia River, this lingua franca combined various Chinook dialects, other Indian languages, English, French and probably Russian.

Chinook wind, so called by early settlers because it blew from the direction of the Chinook Indian camps, designates a dry wind blowing from the west or north over the Rocky Mountains—warm in winter and cool in summer—while a *wet Chinook* is a warm, moist wind blowing from sea to land in Washington and Oregon. The Chinooks decreased in number until there were only about three hundred of them on reservations in 1950. Washington is sometimes called the *Chinook State* in their honor, and the *Chinook salmon* is also named for them. Chinook words adopted into English include *potlatch,* a giving of gifts, *high muck-a-muck,* and *cayuse.*

Chippendale The elegant, exquisitely carved, and always well-made furniture designed and manufactured by Thomas Chippendale (c. 1718–79). Thomas Chippendale worked primarily in Louis XV, Chinese, and Gothic styles, sometimes combining them without incongruous results. He set up his factory in London in 1749, later publishing *The Gentleman and Cabinet Maker's Directory* (1754), in which he illustrated some 160 designs. Somehow Chippendale almost invariably managed to combine comfort, grace and solidity in his wide variety of furniture, which is highly valued today. Because so many of his designs were slavishly copied during the latter half of the eighteenth century, it has always been difficult to identify his work, dealers sometimes using the term *Chippendale* as the label for a large variety of mahogany furniture in his style. After Chippendale died, his son Thomas II (d. 1822?) carried on the family business, complicating the identification problem even more.

Chisholm Trail In the spring of 1866 Jesse Chisholm (c. 1806–68), a half-breed Cherokee Indian trader and government agent, drove his wagon loaded with buffalo hides through the Oklahoma territory to Wichita, Kans. The wheels cut deep into the prairie, providing rut marks for a route that was to become the most important and famous of all western cattle trails, extending from San Antonio, Tex., to Abilene and other Kansas railheads. The trail was used for more than twenty years after the Civil War, 450,000 Texas longhorns having been driven up it in 1872 alone. Remnants of the trail, celebrated in folklore and cowboy ballads like "The Old Chisholm Trail," still remain along the Santa Fe Railroad line.

Chow The *chow* or *chow chow,* a medium-size, generally red, black or brown nonsporting dog of Chinese breed, may derive its name from *chow,* a pidgin word for food, or from *chow-chow,* the Chinese mixed fruit preserve. Another theory, which seems more plausible, is that it is simply from the Chinese *Chou,* this being the name of the ancient Chinese race that formed the Chou Dynasty, which ruled from about 1122 to 256 B.C., bringing China's first "golden age." The *chow* is noted for its sturdy build, large head, and deep-set eyes. Probably originally bred in northern China, it can be traced back as early as 150 B.C.

Choctaw *Choctaw,* a fancy step in ice-skating, and southern slang for unintelligible speech, is from the Choctaw Indian tribe of southern Mississippi. The Choctaws, named from the Spanish *chato* (flattened), for their practice of flattening the heads of male infants, fought against the British during the American Revolution and aided the United States in later years against the Creeks. They ceded their lands to the government in 1832, the majority moving to reservations in what is now Oklahoma. The Choctaws, one of the Five Civilized Tribes, are also one of the few Indian tribes surviving the white man, their numbers—about twenty thousand—remaining substantially intact.

Christian The first usage of *Christians* for followers of Christ is recorded in the Bible, *Acts* 11:25–26: "So Barnabus went to Tarsus to look for Saul; and when he had found him, he brought him to Antioch. For a whole year they met with the church, and taught a large company of people; and in Antioch the disciples were for the first time called Christians." The word *Christ* is from the Greek *Christos,* "the Anointed one."

Christmas *Christmas* simply means *Christ's mass.* The Christian holiday celebrates Christ's birth, but there are no trustworthy records of the real date— August 28, May 20, April 19 or 20, November 17, and March 28 having all been suggested by scholars as more accurate than December 25. In the north *Christmas* was originally a pagan feast celebrating the winter solstice, a time when ancient peoples built great bonfires to give the winter sun god strength and receive him. The early church fathers wisely chose the day of the winter solstice as a date to celebrate Christ's birth, the return of light becoming associated with the hope of the world in the birth of the savior. Over five centuries later, in 601, Pope Gregory I gave Christian missionaries instructions to appropriate pagan feasts and adapt them to Christian usage, this allowing converts to retain old customs. *Christmas,* which had been solely observed by religious services, by the Middle Ages became both a reverent and joyous holiday, marked by feasting, the giving of presents, mistletoe, the Yule log, the Christmas tree and other ancient pagan customs that we still observe today. The word *Christmas* itself derives directly from the Catholic midnight mass held to celebrate the birthday of Christ as early as the sixth century. Christmas celebrations were forbidden in England in 1644 when the Puritans came into power, as a reaction against wild revels that distorted the day's real meaning. Some even tried to substitute *Christtide* for *Christmas,* to abolish the reminder of the outlawed Catholic mass, but both attempts were of course doomed to failure. The Puritan reaction, which served a purpose, is akin to the feeling of many Christians today about the commercialization of *Christmas,* and the distortion of the true spirit of Christ's birthday.

Christy Minstrels Folk music fans may be surprised to learn that the name of the popular Christy Minstrel group honors an early American songwriter and that the term *Christy minstrels* is a synonym for Negro minstrel-type groups. Edwin Christy (1815–62) popularized his songs through his blackface troupe, which toured America and England and was widely imitated up until the beginning of this century. Christy wasn't the first to perform in blackface, but his group brought the minstrel show to perfection. His name had such great drawing power that it was assumed by the man who took over the troupe when he retired.

Churchillian Often accompanying elegant oratory or prose, great wit and statesmanship, and even a large cigar, this familiar adjective commemorates British Prime Minister Sir Winston Leonard Spencer Churchill (1874–1965). "On the 30th of November at Blenheim Palace, the Lady Randolph Churchill, prematurely, of a son," read the one line in the London *Times* announcing his birth, but Churchill's life was to fill volumes. Soldier, journalist, writer and statesman, his brilliant public career included service as home secretary, first lord of the Admiralty, secretary of state for war, and chancellor of the exchequer. But all his life, he felt, was merely a preparation for his crucial premiership during World War II. Some have gone so far as to say that England would not have survived the Blitz of 1940–41 without his leadership. Great *Churchillian* words and phrases include the much quoted, "I have nothing to offer but blood, toil, tears and sweat"; "Never in the field of human conflict was so much owed by so many to so few"; "The soft underbelly of the Axis"; the "iron curtain"; and his words on the fall of France: "Let us therefore brace ourselves to our duties, and so bear ourselves that, if the British Empire and its Commonwealth last for a thousand years, men will still say: *'This was their finest hour!'*" On April 9, 1963, Winston Churchill was paid the unique honor of being proclaimed a citizen of the United States. President Kennedy's *Churchillian* official proclamation read as follows: "In the dark days and darker nights when Britain stood alone—and most men save Englishmen despaired of England's life —he mobilized the English language and sent it into battle. The incandescent quality of his words illuminated the courage of his countrymen. Given unlimited powers by his fellow citizens, he was ever vigilant to protect their rights. Indifferent himself to danger, he wept over the sorrow of others. A child of the House of Commons, he became in time its father. Accustomed to the hardship of battle, he has no distaste for pleasure. By adding his name to our rolls, we mean

to honor him—but his acceptance honors us far more. For no statement or proclamation can enrich his name—the name Sir Winston Churchill is already legend."

Churrigueresque This man's name itself is elaborate, suggesting the style it represents. Extravagant overornate architecture, especially that of seventeenth and eighteenth-century Spain, is called *churrigueresque* after Spanish architect and sculptor José Churriguera (1650–1725). Churriguera, a native of Salamanca, was an architect of the baroque school whose important works include the great catafalque for Queen Maria Louisa (1688), the palace of Don Juan de Goyeneche, and a portal of the Church of Santo Gayetano. Spanish baroque, with its free lines and vast profusion of detailed ornament, is named for him because he and his two sons were the most successful practitioners of this Renaissance form. *Churrigueresque* strongly influenced the Spanish colonial style in the southwestern part of this country and Mexico.

Cicero, Cicerone, Ciceronian If you travel in Italy, any guide you hire will be called a *cicerone*, these guides often being well versed about the places of interest and objects they point out. The Italians turned to the name of Marcus Tullius Cicero (100–43 B.C.) for this word because the eloquent statesman, orator and writer epitomized the knowledge and style they expected of their *cicerones*. The word has come to mean a guide in any country. The story, from Plutarch, is that Cicero got his name from the Latin *cicer* (a wart) due to the "flat excrescence on the tip of his nose."

Cicero is also honored by *Ciceronian*, pertaining to his clear, forceful and melodious oratorial or prose style, and *Cicero*, a unit of print similar to a pica.

Cinchona About 1639 the Condesa Ana de Chinchón, wife of the Conde de Chinchón (c. 1590–1647), Spanish viceroy of Peru, was stricken with a persistent tropical fever. After European doctors failed to restore her health, she was cured by the powdered bark of a native evergreen tree that Peruvian Indians brought to her. The Condesa and her husband collected the dried bark, which contains quinine, and sent it back to

Spain. There the miracle bark was at first called "Countess bark" or "Peruvian bark," but when Linnaeus named the genus of trees and shrubs yielding it in the Condesa's honor, he misspelled her name. What should have been the *Chinchona tree* became known to history as the *Cinchona tree*. Today the native South American *Cinchona* is widely grown throughout the world, notably in Java and India. The *quinine* extracted from its bark derives from *quinaquina*, its Peruvian Indian name.

Circassian *Circassian beauty* refers to the legendary charms of the Circassian women, inhabitants of a region in the northeast Caucasus once known as Circassia. Circassian fathers often sold their beautiful, voluptuous daughters to Turkish merchants for the harems of Eastern monarchs. No degradation was implied, the women considering their sale an honor. The Circassians had a number of unusual customs: any young man who purchased a bride was required to come with friends, fully armed, and carry her off from her father's house; a younger brother had to rise from his seat whenever an elder brother entered the room and remain silent whenever he spoke; a murderer could escape punishment by rearing the newborn child of his victim until its education was completed; and any man pursued by enemies had sanctuary after he touched the hand of a woman, so long as he remained under her roof. Russia finally subjugated these proud, warlike Moslems in 1864, many of them migrating to Turkish territory. Today Circassia forms the state of Kuban in the U.S.S.R.

Cities Named After People Thousands of cities around the world honor famous people in their names. Following is a brief list of American towns, and several islands, similarly named:

Albuquerque, New Mexico—founded by and named for the duke of Alburquerque, viceroy of New Spain in 1706, the first *r* later dropped.

Baltimore, Maryland—see *Baltimore Oriole*.

Buffalo, New York—named after a local creek that had been named for an Indian who had once lived on its banks.

Charleston, South Carolina—English settlers called the community Charles Town after King Charles II in 1680.

Charlotte, North Carolina—named after Queen Charlotte, wife of England's George III.

Cleveland, Ohio—laid out in 1796 by General Moses Cleaveland and later named for him, the general an ancestor of President Grover Cleveland.

Columbus, Ohio—for Christopher Columbus (see *Columbus*).

Dallas, Texas—in 1841 Tennessee trader John Neely Bryan built the first house on the town's site and three years later named the village he founded there for his friend George Mifflin Dallas, later vice-president under Polk.

Denver, Colorado—for James W. Denver, governor of the Kansas Territory in 1858, eastern Colorado being part of his jurisdiction.

Houston, Texas—founded in 1836 and named in honor of Samuel Houston, hero of the Texas war for independence from Mexico.

Jacksonville, Florida—see *Jacksonian*.

Louisville, Kentucky—see *Louisville Slugger*.

Nantucket—there is an old tale, probably untrue, that an old man owned the island groups off Massachusetts. To his favorite daughter he gave his most productive island, *Martha's Vineyard*; to his next he gave the islands closest to home, *Elizabeth's Islands*; and to his last daughter, Nan, he just offered what remained, and *Nan-tuck-it*.

New Orleans—founded in 1718 by Le sieur de Bienville and named for Philippe II, duke of Orléans.

New York City—see New York.

Omaha, Nebraska—named for a local tribe of Indians known as "they who go upstream or against the current."

Orlando, Florida—originally named for its first settler, Aaron Jernigan, the city was rechristened Orlando in 1857 in memory of Orlando Reeves, a soldier who had been killed in a skirmish with the Indians.

Pittsburgh, Pennsylvania—the French Fort Duquesne fell to the British in the eighteenth century and they named it Fort Pitt in honor of William Pitt, then prime minister of England. The city's name derived from the fort's.

St. Louis, Missouri—chosen as the site for a trading post in 1763 and named for Louis IX, the patron saint of France.

Seattle, Washington—named in 1853, two years after it was founded as a lumber settlement, for a chief of the Duwamish and Suquamish Indians.

(See also *Nations; Pancake, Pa.;* and *States.*)

Clarkia, Lewis and Clark Expedition, Lewisia Captain William Clark (1770–1838) is best known for his leadership with Meriwether Lewis of the *Lewis and Clark Expedition* to find an overland route to the Pacific, their party being the first to cross the Continent within the limits of the United States. But the army officer and veteran Indian fighter had an avid interest in natural history, describing many plants in his journals of the 1803–07 expedition. The showy *Clarkia* genus, native to California, was named in his honor. These hardy annual flowers, available in several showy colors, have been popular for many years in American gardens. Clark, the youngest brother of the famous frontier military leader, George Rogers Clark, was appointed superintendent of Indian affairs when his expedition returned.

Clark's partner Captain Meriwether Lewis has *Lewisia*, a genus of twelve species of low-growing perennial flowers widely grown in the rock garden, named in his honor. Lewis, who had been Thomas Jefferson's secretary, was appointed governor of the Louisiana Territory after the expedition. He died suddenly in 1809, only thirty-five years old, his death shrouded in mystery. He had been traveling to Washington to prepare the expedition journals when he died alone in an inn near Nashville, Tenn. Suicide, or more probably murder, has been suggested as causing his death.

Cleopatra Cleopatra was only thirty-eight when she died in 30 B.C., but in her short life she became one of the great romantic heroines of all time, her name is still synonymous with feminine allurement and charm. When seventeen the Queen of the Nile had married her younger brother, as was the custom, leading a revolt against Ptolemy XIII when he deprived her of her royal authority. Inducing Julius Caesar to fight a war to place her on the throne, she became his mistress, living openly in Rome with him after she poisoned her second younger sibling-husband. Caesar's assassination marked her return to Egypt with their son Caesarion. There, in 41 B.C., Mark Antony fell under her spell, gave up his wife for her, and she became his mistress, hoping that he would restore her former powers. However, Octavian (later Emperor Augustus) declared war on them, vowing to destroy the two lovers, and defeated Antony at Alexandria. Cleopatra coldly accepted Octavian's proposal to assassinate Antony and persuaded him to commit suicide so that "they might die together." Antony took his life by falling on his sword, believing that Cleopatra had already done so, but "the serpent of the old Nile" was unable to win over Octavian, despite her treachery. She ended her own life by putting an asp to her breast. Her three sons by Antony were allowed to live but Caesarion was put to death soon after.

Cleopatra's Needles *Cleopatra's Needles* is a misnomer. The two originally pink obelisks—one 68½ feet tall standing on the Thames embankment, and the other 69½ feet tall in New York's Central Park—really have nothing at all to do with the Queen of the Nile. Hieroglyphics on the needles show that Pharaoh Thotmes III erected them centuries before Cleopatra. Originally raised at Heliopolis in 1475 B.C., the obelisks were moved to Alexandria under Augustus in about 14 B.C., where they adorned the Caesareum. In 1878 and 1880 respectively Ismail Pasha made gifts of them to England and the United States, and it is said that they have suffered more from erosion in their present locations over the last ninety-odd years than they did over thousands of years in Egypt. The formerly rose-red syenite granite obelisks were probably named for Cleopatra because they stood outside the Caesareum honoring her dictator lover.

Cleopatra's Nose "If the nose of Cleopatra had been shorter the whole face of the earth would have been changed," wrote the French philosopher Blaise Pascal (1623–62) in his famous *Pensées*. His proverbial observation refers to the effects of Cleopatra's charms on

Caesar and Mark Antony, but a different nose length, at least a moderately different one, would probably have made little difference to history. For Cleopatra's allure did not depend on her physical beauty; most sources, in fact, indicate that she wasn't a beautiful woman at all. What she was was an accomplished artful lover, and the "salad days" that Shakespeare has her admit to—when she was young and loved unskillfully, like a salad, green and cold—were distant memories long before she had married at seventeen.

Cleopatra's Pearl Cleopatra and Mark Antony were always doing things for each other. Legend has it that she once filled a room ankle high with rose petals so that he would not hear his footsteps when he walked, and that he was so pleased with the dinner a chef prepared for Cleopatra that he made the cook the gift of a city all his own. *Cleopatra's pearl* concerns a sumptuous banquet Cleopatra gave to Antony. Her lover, the story tells us, expressed astonishment at the costly meal, and she promptly removed a pearl earring, dropped it in a cup of vinegar and let it dissolve, saying "My draft to Antony (the cost of this banquet) shall far exceed it." Vinegar would not dissolve a pearl, however, and anything strong enough wouldn't have conveniently been on Cleopatra's table. Unless the wileful woman planted it there —in which case it is just as possible that she used a fake pearl. Sir Thomas Gresham is said to have repeated this episode with Queen Elizabeth, grinding a precious fifteen thousand-pound stone to dust, mixing it in his glass of wine and drinking to the Virgin Queen's health.

Clerihew

Sir Humphry Davy
Abominated gravy.
He lived in the odium
Of having discovered sodium.

This was the first *clerihew* written by Edmund Clerihew Bentley (1875–1956). The English detective story writer composed it while only a schoolboy, according to his schoolmate G. K. Chesterton, "when he sat listening to a chemical exposition, with his rather bored air and a blank sheet of blotting paper before him." Bentley, one of the few men to have a word honoring his middle name, could in Chesterton's words "write clear and unadulterated nonsense with . . . serious simplicity." He went on to Oxford, but ignored his quatrains until he began working as a journalist, which also apparently bored him, thus his second effort:

Sir Christopher Wren
Said "I'm going to dine with some men.
If anybody calls
Say I'm designing St. Paul's."

There followed a series of comic verses that Bentley eventually published in book form as *Clerihews*, such as:

Alfred de Musset
Used to call his cat Pusset.
His accent was affected.
That was to be expected.

Chesterton called his friend's a "severe and stately form of Free Verse." The satirical often biographical verse has seldom been imitated and will perhaps be remembered longer than the writer's *Trent's Last Case*, which introduced the realistic hero, Philip Trent, to the detective novel. Bentley's favorite *clerihew*:

It was a weakness of Voltaire's
To forget to say his prayers,
And which, to his shame,
He never overcame.

Clipper Ship While the origin of the *clipper* in *clipper ship* is not definitely known, it may be yet another word that we owe to Cleopatra. The first authentic *clipper ship* was the *Ann McKim*, built in Baltimore in 1832, but an early French ship of the type was christened *Cleopatra-cum-Antonio*, this name, some scholars say, shortened in usage to *Clipster* and then to *Clipper*, the last becoming the designation for all ships of its class. Other authorities contend that rude *clippers* were being built before the War of 1812 and were known as *Baltimore clippers* because they literally clipped the surface of the sea; another source holds that the expression "going at a clip" resulted in the word; and still other investigators claim that *clipper* is an invention of the poet Burns or Shelley. But the French developed the principle for this type ship in the eighteenth century, long before even the *Baltimore clippers*, and as the *Cleopatra-cum-Antonio* dates from that period, the Cleopatra theory has much to say for it. The long narrow *clipper ship*, with its "cloud of sails," revolutionized sea travel, sailing at up to eighteen knots as it cleaved the waves carrying commerce to the far corners of the world. Among famous *clippers* were the *Cutty Sark*—which once covered 363 miles in a day's travel—the *Flying Cloud*, the *Sea Witch*, the *Witch of the Waves*, and the *Nightingale*. The age of this last and fastest of the great sailing vessels ended when the prosaic steamship began to forge past it. *Clipper ship* was later applied to transoceanic flying boats, the famed *Flying Clippers*. (See also *Cleopatra*.)

Cocktail The *cocktail party* can be traced back as far as ancient Athens, where you could drop by your neighbor's early in the evening with your own goatskin of wine and be treated to a variety of "provocatives to drinking" that included caviar, oysters, shrimp, cheese, and even marinated octopus and roasted grasshoppers. There are well over fifty theories as to the word *cocktail's* origin, H. L. Mencken alone presenting seven plausible ones in his *American Language*. These include a derivation from the French *coquetier*, an egg cup, in which the drink was supposedly first served in 1800; from *coquetel*, a mixed drink of the French Revolution period; from the English *cock-ale* fed to fighting cocks; from *cock-tailings*, the last of several liquors mixed together; and from a toast to that cock which after a cockfight had the most feathers left in its tail. Just as reliable as any of these guesses is the old folktale that Aztec King Axolotl VIII's daughter *Octel* or *Xochitl* concocted the first *cocktail*; or, in another version, that an Aztec noble sent his emperor a drink made of cactus juice by his daughter, the emperor enjoying it so that he married the girl and called the drink by her name—again *Octel* or *Xochitl*. According to this story, General Scott's soldiers are supposed to have brought the drink back to America centuries later. Suffice it to say that the origin of the word, first printed in 1806, is really unknown. Mencken, who knew that the real value of a *cocktail* was not

in its etymology, once hired a mathematician to figure out how many different cocktails could be fashioned from the stock of a first-class bar. The answer was 17,864,392,788.

Codger An *old codger* is generally a nuisance or an eccentric old man, but can also be a term of affection akin to "old chap" or "old fellow." No dictionary honors the derivation, but both definitions may have been strengthened by the existence of a club called The Ancient Society of Cogers formed in London in the 1860's. The Cogers came onto the scene half a century after *codger* was first used in its whimsical sense, but they were well known, all prominent writers and artists. The debating club derived its name from the word "cognitation" and these thinking men, "ancient" at least by title, met at the Barley Mow Tavern on Fleet Street (the tavern now named The Cogers in their honor, though they moved to the Cock Tavern in 1921). *Codger* probably comes from the Scottish *cadger*, for a wandering peddler or beggar, but it is not hard to imagine the *Cogers'* influence on the word. "Ancient . . . Cogers" could easily have become *old codgers*, meant either affectionately or derisively.

Cologne A perfume that almost takes its name from a woman. The Roman emperor Claudius established a colony in what was then Oppidum Ubiorum in 50 A.D., renaming the place *Colonia Agrippina* (colony of Agrippina) after his wife, Nero's mother, who had been born there. This cumbersome name was later modified by the French to *Cologne*, the beautiful German cathedral city that we know today. When centuries later a resident Italian chemist, Johann Maria Farina, invented a perfume made with alcohol and aromatic citrus oils, it was named *Eau de Cologne* or *Cologne water* for the city where he had settled in 1709. *Agrippina* had been lost over the years and only a fragment of her *Colonia* remained, but the perfume was unknowingly and obliquely named for her.

Colt When Samuel Colt (1814–62) ran away to sea from his home in Hartford, Conn., at sixteen, he spent his lonely nights on deck whittling a wooden model of the *Colt revolver* that was to make him famous. Young Colt had several metal models made of his gun upon arriving home and patented his invention, forming the Patent Arms Manufacturing Company in Paterson, N.J. to manufacture the weapon. The *Colt* was used in the Seminole War (1837) and the war between Texas and Mexico, but neither the revolving-cylinder breech pistol nor its rifle counterpart caught on, Patent Arms failing in 1842. Samuel Colt turned to other pursuits for the moment, inventing a submarine mine and the first underwater telegraph cable, until an unexpected U.S. Army order for one thousand pistols during the Mexican War put him back in business again. He built his armory into the largest in the world, his use of interchangeable parts and the production line making him one of the richest men in America. As for the *Colt*, the first pistol that could be effectively employed by a man on horseback, it played a more important part in the conquest of the West than any other weapon, the famed "sixshooter" becoming so popular that its name became a generic term for revolver.

Columbia, Columbium, Columbus America was unjustly named for someone else, but Columbus did win fame on the globe as the name for *Colombia*, South America, the U.S. *District of Columbia*, and a number of towns and cities. *Columbus* itself has for centuries meant an intrepid discoverer or explorer; *Columbus Day* (Oct. 12) commemorates the discovery of America; and *Columbia* is the feminine symbol for America from which the element *columbium* is named.

Christopher Columbus — Cristoforo Colombo in his native Italian and Christóbal Colon in Spanish—discovered America in 1492; a familiar story that needs no repeating here. He came ashore in the Bahamas on an island he named San Salvador and which is now called Cat or Watling Island. A sailor named Rodrigo de Triana first sighted the New World. It is often forgotten that Columbus actually made *four* voyages, all in futilely seeking a new route to Asia—discovering Jamaica on his second, South America on his third, and Central America on his last expedition. The explorer might not have happened upon

America had he held the course he took on leaving the Canary Islands during his first voyage; he switched his course on the insistence of Martin Alonso Pinzon, the pilot who commanded *Pinta*. Columbus never did find a route to the Far East, though he believed that he had landed in Asia. The great admiral of the ocean died neglected and almost forgotten in 1506, when only fifty-seven years old. His descendants can be traced through the female line to the Larreatigui family, which still retains his titles of admiral and duke of Veragua.

Columbus' Egg Washington Irving told this proverbial tale in his *History of . . . Christopher Columbus*. It relates a classic squelch supposedly made by Columbus at a banquet given by Cardinal Mendoza shortly after the explorer had returned from his first voyage: "A shallow courtier present, impatient of the honors paid to Columbus, abruptly asked him whether he thought that in case he had not discovered the Indies, there were not other men in Spain who would have been capable of the enterprise. To this Columbus made no immediate reply, but taking an egg, invited the company to make it stand on end. Every one attempted it, but in vain. Whereupon he struck it upon the table so as to break the end and left it standing on the broken part; illustrating in this simple manner that when he had once shown the way to the New World nothing was easier than to follow it." Although Irving had the tale on good authority, it may really apply to an earlier historical figure, an Italian architect named Brunelleschi.

Comptonia Henry Compton, Bishop of London, was a collector of rare and exotic plants. The prelate, an antipapal leader during the Revolution of 1688, had many admirers in England, even after his death in 1713 at the ripe old age of eighty-one. One of these was the great naturalist Sir Joseph Banks, who traveled to Newfoundland and Labrador in 1766 to collect native plants and accompanied Captain Cook on his first voyage two years later for the same purpose. Banks expressed his admiration for the plant-loving divine by naming the *comptonia bush* (*Comptonia peregrina*) after him. The *comptonia* is a single shrub, sometimes called sweet bush or sweet fern. Native to eastern North America, it is highly aromatic, with fernlike leaves and green, rather inconspicuous flowers.

Comstockery About 160 *tons* of books, stereotyped plates, magazines and pictures were destroyed by Anthony Comstock (1844–1915), founder of the New York Society for the Suppression of Vice, in his long career as a self-appointed crusader against immorality in literature. Comstock, who inspired Boston's Watch and Ward Society, headed a YMCA campaign against obscene literature in 1873, the same year in which he came to national prominence by founding his society and securing federal passage of the so-called *Comstock Laws* to exclude objectionable matter from the mails. Appointed special agent of the Post Office Department and chief special agent for the society, he is said to have arrested three thousand persons over a forty-odd year career, destroying some fifty tons of books alone that he deemed obscene. The *Comstock Postal Act*, in Mencken's words, "greatly stimulated the search for euphemisms," pregnant being translated as "enceinte," syphilis and gonorrhea as "social diseases," and so on. Comstock had the power of an inquisitor, *comstockery* becoming a synonym for narrow-minded, bigoted and self-righteous moral censorship. The crusader particularly objected to Shaw's play, *Mrs. Warren's Profession*, and Shaw coined the word making good clean fun of his name.

Comstock Lode, Comstocker A Nevada sheepherder and prospector named Henry Tompkins Paige Comstock first laid claim to the Comstock lode that bears his name in 1859. Old Pancake, as he was known, had taken possession of a cabin belonging to Ethan and Hosea Grosh, who had discovered the lode but had died tragically before filing their claim. Finding their records, Comstock did so, but he later sold all his rights for a pittance. The Virginia City mine became the world's richest known silver deposit, producing twenty to thirty million dollars annually at its peak and making great fortunes for many a "silver king." Virginia City mushroomed to forty thousand inhabitants and anyone associated with the mines, hopeful prospector or millionaire, was called a *Comstocker*. The town became a center of fabulous wealth and luxury, and here Samuel Clemens first adopted the pen name Mark Twain as an editor of *The Territorial Enterprise* (1862). By 1898, the *Comstock Lode* was virtually abandoned, due to wasteful mining methods and the demonetization of silver.

Condum This most unlikely of eponymous words derives from either of two real persons. Proksch in his *Prevention of Venereal Diseases* traces *condum* to a London doctor in the court of Charles II named Dr. Conton and insists that the contraceptives should thus be called "contons." Dr. Conton's invention is said to have been made from lamb intestines, dried and well oiled to make them soft and pliable. They immediately became popular and Casanova is on record as buying a dozen, though he called them "English caps." It was only in 1826, Proksch claims, that a papal bull by Leo XIII damned Conton's discovery, "because it hindered the arrangement of providence." Dr. Conton probably did improve upon the *condum*, but an equally reliable source traces the word derivation to a Colonel Condum of Britain's Royal Guards. This authority notes that the colonel devised the "French letter" early in the mid-seventeenth century to protect his troops from the French. (The French, *chauvinistic*, too, called *condums* "English letters.") In 1667 three English courtiers—Rochester, Roscommon and Dorset—even wrote a pamphlet entitled *A Panegyric Upon Condum* extolling their countryman's invention. It is interesting to note that both Dr. Conton and Colonel Condum were associated with Charles II, a notoriously lascivious monarch (see *Charlies*), and that the word was first printed in 1665. But the use of sheep intestines for contraceptives has long been practiced in the Middle East and probably neither of our possible eponymous heroes really first "invented" the *condum*. Another theory worth investigating—considering the synonym "French letter"—might be the word's possible derivation from the town of Condom in Germany, "a fortress of considerable strength" that was taken by the English during the Hundred Years' War.

Conestoga Wagons, Stogy The heavy, covered, broad-wheeled *Conestoga wagons* that carried American pioneers westward, crossing many a waving "sea of grass" like "prairie schooners," were named for the Conestoga Valley in Pennsylvania, where they were first made in about 1750. But, as Mencken points out, *Conestoga Valley* derives in turn from the name of a long-extinct band of Iroquois Indians. So little has been done for the Indian that we should honor him where we can.

The wagons, pulled by their six-horse teams, also supplied the West with manufactured goods and brought back raw materials, some carrying up to eight tons of freight. *Stogy*, any cheap cigar today, was coined by the *Conestoga* teamsters—either after the *Conestoga Valley tobacco* that they rolled into thin unbound cigars for their long trips, or after the wagons themselves.

Confucian, Confucianism, Confucius Say When Confucius was appointed minister of crime in ancient Chung-tu, we are told, there soon was no crime. The sage of China's ethical teachings, based primarily on his "golden rule"— "What you do not like when done to yourself do not do to others"—influenced his country's development in many spheres and played a great part in shaping the character of her people. Born in 551 B.C., the philosopher came from a poor but noble family, *Confucius* being the Latinized form of his clan name K'ung (Kung), K'ung Fu-tze (Kung Fut-se), "the philosopher or master K'ung." After an early career as a teacher, he held a number of government positions, gathering around him what amounted finally to three thousand disciples who helped spread his largely secular teachings. Though he left no writings but one poorly regarded book, his wise and essentially conservative maxims have been widely quoted throughout the world. *Confucianism* is a philosophy of ethics and politics rather than a religion, Confucius himself learning many of his principles to restore a less chaotic social order from his study of the ancient books. Positive evidence of the philosopher's life is meager, and a great number of the popular *Confucius say* maxims attributed to him are nonsense, not even coming from collections made by his pupils. Confucius died in 479 B.C., his burial place outside the city of K'iuh-fow (Kufow) still is a place of homage. In this cemetery a number of disciples built huts, the site of one now marked by a small house. A number of followers mourned their master's death in these huts for three years, his favorite disciple Tze-kung remaining by his grave for twice that length of time. The Kung clan, which makes its home in a nearby city, became a sacred caste after Confucius died and today numbers some fifty thousand or more descendants.

Cook's Tour *Cook's Tour* has become synonymous for a humorous excursion as well as a travel tour. *Cook's tours* of the trenches were given to visiting brass as early as World War I and the words are now used to describe even the tour of a fertilizer factory. The expression is from the name of Thomas Cook (1808–92), the English travel agent who founded the venerable Thomas Cook & Son travel agency in 1841. Cook, a former village missionary and woodturner, began his career in that year when he persuaded the Midland Railway to run the first publicly advertised excursion train in English history, charging the passengers a shilling a head for their journey to a temperance convention. In 1856 he launched the first grand tour of Europe. *Cook's tour* became a byword for an excellently organized tour of places, and the firm proved so reliable that the British government employed it to convey General Gordon to the Sudan in 1884, entrusting Gordon's relief force of eighteen thousand men to the firm as well. The 130-year-old travel agency still has offices in London, New York, and other parts of the world.

Coolie The *Oxford English Dictionary* traces the derivation of *coolie*, an unskilled Asian laborer, to *Kuli* or *Koli*, the name of an aboriginal tribe of Guzerat, a province in India. Others claim the word is from the Urdu *Kūlī* or the Tamil *kūli*, both meaning "hireling," but most authorities accept the *O.E.D.* theory. *Coolie* labor emigration came about mainly as a result of the outlawing of slavery in British colonies in 1834. Cheap labor was needed and obtained primarily from India and China in the form of natives hired under five-year contracts that were enforceable by prison terms. Conditions were often intolerable for these *coolies*, of whom the *Kulis* were apparently among the first, their home on the northern Indian coast making it easy to recruit them. *Coolie ships* were often as inhuman as African slave ships, many thousands dying on the long voyages. Chinese *coolies* were instrumental in building the United States transcontinental railroad and in 1904 Britain hired fifty thousand to work the Transvaal gold mines. The term is now applied to any cheap labor, usually in a jocular or derisive sense.

Copernican, Copernican Theory Early in the sixteenth century the *Copernican theory* established that all the planets, including the earth, revolve in orbits around the sun, in opposition to the older *Ptolemic theory* that the sun and planets move around the earth. It immortalizes Copernicus (1473–1543), the Latinized form of the surname of Mikolaj Koppernigk, whose work revolutionized astronomy, changing man's entire outlook on the universe and influencing a profound change on the inner man as well. The great astronomer, born in Prussian Poland, made his living as a physician and canon of the cathedral of Frauenburg. He completed his theory as early as 1530, when he circulated in manuscript a brief popular account of it, but *De Revolutionibus Orbium Coelestium* wasn't published until thirteen years later, when he lay on his deathbed. Though the work was dedicated to Pope Paul III, it was placed on the index of forbidden books. *Copernican* also means revolutionary, in reference to the new system's impact on the world.

Corduroy Plebian cotton forms the basis for the rough ribbed cloth we know as *corduroy* today, but the fabric was once woven from regal silk. The word had generally been thought to derive from the French *corde du Roi* (cord of the King), no one venturing to say which Gallic king first wore the material. But no such word has ever been used by the French, *velours a côtes* being their name for corduroy. Thus it has been suggested that the fabric had its origins in England, the *Oxford English Dictionary* pointing out that an 1807 French list of cloths used the English words "king's cordes." The surname Corderey or Corderoy is one possibility, from its first manufacturer's name, or it may be that some enterprising merchant, relying on snob appeal in advertising, christened the product "cord of the king," using the French *corde du Roi* for even greater distinction. The word was first used for a cloth in 1787. Some forty years later it was applied to the rude *corduroy roads* in America built of logs laid crosswise over swampy ground.

Cossack, Cossack Post The Cossacks, quartered in eleven communities throughout the country, were four million strong before the revolution in Russia. In return for certain privileges their men were all required to give military service for twenty years, from age eighteen. These cruel, fearless fighters and expert horsemen, constituting an elite Russian cavalry, were used by the czars to suppress revolution and were much feared by the people. A *Cossack* is still often used to describe a brutal or brave warrior. The Cossacks were descended from serfs who had fled their masters in the fifteenth to seventeenth century and settled on the border steppes, their name coming from the Russian *Kayaki*, wanderers. In World War II they were used as cavalry by the Soviet Union. A *Cossack post* is a small outpost commanded by a noncommissioned officer, and a *cossack* is a Cossack pony.

Couéism *"Every day, in every way, I am getting better and better."* The bow-legged man who repeated this famous psychotherapeutic formula too often and became merely knock-kneed is a myth, but Émile Coué (1857–1926) is not. The French pharmacist and hypnotist turned psychotherapist established a free clinic in Nancy in 1910. Here he put into practice his system of therapeutics, based primarily on his theory that, by means of autosuggestion, ideas which cause illness may be eliminated from the will. This power of the imagination over the will was best expressed in his formula and Coué claimed to have effected organic changes. He lectured widely abroad and his healing methods became well known in the United States and England during the 1920's.

Coulomb, Coulomb's Law, Coulometer Charles Augustin de Coulomb (1736–1806), a French military engineer who became a physicist when bad health forced his retirement from the army, did much work on electricity and magnetism. He designed his torsion balance for measuring the force of magnetic and electric attraction in 1777, while still an army engineer, but didn't publish his findings until about ten years later, finding that Michel had invented the same system independently. Bearing his name are *Coulomb's law* of magnetism, the *coulomb*, a unit for measuring the quantity of an electrical current, and the *coulometer*, which is more often called a *voltameter*.

Coventrate, Coventry Blue, Send To Coventry, To Coventry The historic city of Coventry in England may have been built near and taken its name from *Cofa's tree*, in which case the otherwise anonymous Cofa family name is remembered in at least three words or phrases. The most common of these would be boycotting a person by refusing to associate or have dealings with him, which is called *sending him to Coventry*. This phrase is of uncertain origin, arising either because Royalist prisoners were sent to the staunchly Puritan town during the Great Rebellion, or due to the fact that Coventry was at one time so antimilitary that any soldier posted there found himself cut off from all social intercourse, townspeople even refusing to talk to the troops.

The Germans with their devastating *Baedeker raids* laid waste to much of Coventry in World War II, destroying seventy thousand homes, all but the great spire of the fourteenth-century Cathedral of St. Michael, the tenth-century Ford hospital, and many other historic sites, which led to the term *to coventrate*—to attempt to bomb a city out of existence. *Coventry blue*, an historical term for a blue thread made at Coventry in the sixteenth and seventeenth century ("as true as Coventry blue"), is a proverbial expression. *To Coventry*, another historical expression, doesn't pertain to the town. Meaning "to mutilate," the word arose when, in 1670, supporters of Charles II waylaid Sir John Coventry and slit his nose as punishment for his criticism of the monarch's dissolute private life. Parliament as a result passed a law against mutilation called the *Coventry Act*. (See also *Boycott; Lady Godiva; Peeping Tom*.)

Coxey's Army Over his long life—he died in 1951, aged ninety-seven—Jacob Sechler Coxey lived through everything from the Civil War to the atomic bomb. His Coxey's Army was one of the first and best remembered groups to march on Washington, D.C., to demand change of some kind; the appellation *a Coxey's Army* is still used to describe such groups. Coxey's followers were a band of unemployed workers who presented Congress with a "petition in boots" the year following the Panic of 1893. It was their leader's plan to have Congress authorize money for public construction, which would provide employment, an idea to be implemented during the great depression in the 1930's. But his highly publicized march from Massillon, O., on Easter Sunday failed to accomplish its purpose. The 100 men who started never swelled to 100,000 as he had predicted and only about 500 reached Washington on May Day to protest their situation. "The Commonweal of Christ" came to an anticlimactic end when its leaders were arrested for walking on the Capitol lawn. Coxey led another march through The City of Magnificent Distances in 1914 and agitated during the depression. This quixotic character was a perennial candidate for public office, and was elected mayor of Massillon, 1931–33. He wrote three books on monetary problems, which fascinated him so that he named one of his sons Legal Tender.

Crapper Possibly the most ignominious fate recorded by any eponymous person is that of poor Thomas Crapper, whose name is about as close as anyone would normally want to get to the fourth most expurgated word in the English language. Crapper, an Englishman, developed the modern toilet bowl, which U.S. soldiers in World War I saw and used everywhere, bringing the name home with them to America. The story of his life, of "the power behind the throne," has recently been published here under the title *Flushed with Pride*. It is apparently not a put-on. As a reviewer wrote: "Although the book has the ring of a classic hoax, the author presents ample evidence that his man not only lived but made a lasting contribution to mankind's comfort."

Crapper's name, of course, is only a lucky or unlucky coincidence. It does not give us the word *crap*, from the Dutch, *Krappe*, scraps, which through the ages has been applied to offal or excrement. *Crap* is now most often used metaphorically to mean nonsense or lying, as in "That's a lot of crap." In fact, the long unprintable *crap* is now a euphemism for the other four-letter word. So it goes. (See also *Fontange*; *Furphy*; *Oliver's skull*; *Sacheverell*; and *Twiss* for more examples of the same.)

Craps Dice have been found in ancient Egyptian tombs and in the ruins of Babylon, but the game as we know it today, often called *craps*, dates to the early nineteenth century and may owe its origin to a Frenchman. Johnny Crapaud was the sobriquet of French gambler Bernard Marigny, who introduced dice to New Orleans in about 1800, the nickname being slang for any Frenchman and owing to the belief that three *crapauds* or toads were the ancient arms of France. High-roller Marigny became associated with the game, which was named *Johnny Crapaud's game* after his nickname, this eventually shortened to *craps*. It is said that Marigny even named the present Burgundy Street "Craps Street" in honor of his favorite pastime.

That is one story, anyway. In *Sucker's Progress* (1938), Herbert Asbury tells us that dice is simply a form of the old game of hazard. *Crabs* or *craps* was the lowest throw in that game as played in France, Asbury says, and the French *craps* was adopted when dice came to New Orleans in 1840. Other speculations include vague associations with *crabapple*, and with *crapaud*. *Craps* is still the lowest—or highest—roll in the game, a point of two (snake eyes) or twelve (boxcars) that loses on one's first shot with the dice.

Crassus A *Crassus* describes a rich man of unbounded avarice and ambition. Marcus Licinius Crassus (c. 115–53 B.C.), Roman "real estate dealer," military leader, and statesman, personified these qualities. It is said that crafty Crassus made his fortune by forming his own fire fighting company and forcing the sale of houses on fire by letting them burn until he could buy cheap—holding off his fire brigade until the sale was consummated. Other ploys of his included buying confiscated property at nominal prices from those outlawed by Sulla, under whom he served, by slave trafficking, and usury. By such means he became the richest man in Rome and a force to be reckoned with in the corrupt politics of the day. Crassus suppressed the slave uprising of Spartacus in 71 B.C. and was elected consul with Pompey the following year, both men joining with Caesar in forming Rome's First Triumvirate ten years later. In this last capacity Crassus encouraged the infamous *Cataline conspiracy*. Finally, his ambitions outran his ability. Lusting for military glory, he launched a campaign against the Parthians in Syria. However, his army was routed by Parthian archers at Carrhae in one of the most notable examples of military stupidity in history (see Charles Fair's *From The Jaws of Victory*, 1971). Crassus was captured by the Parthians and put to death; one story has it that they poured molten silver down his throat.

Cravat The modern *cravat*, another word for necktie, was originally a huge colorful linen or muslin scarf edged with lace and worn knotted loosely around the neck. The scarves were introduced into France by mercenaries enlisted in the royal Croatian regiment during the Thirty Years' War (1618–48). French men and women, impressed by such sartorial splendor, adopted the scarves, tying them with long flowing ends and calling them *cravats* after the French word (*Cravate*) for a Croatian. Croatia, part of Austria at the time, is now a republic of Yugoslavia.

Crêpe Suzette When or where *crêpe suzettes* were invented in France is a mystery, but the dessert pancake must have been named for someone's favorite Susy, *Suzette* being the French diminutive for the proper name Suzanne. The thin, rolled pancakes, or *crêpes*, are generally heated in an orange-flavored liqueur sauce and flambéed at the table, making the blazing dessert one of the more spectacular glories of the French cuisine.

Cretin During the Middle Ages, many deformed idiots suffering from the thyroid condition we know as myxedema (possibly due to a lack of iodine in the drinking water) lived in the Alpine regions. The Swiss called these unfortunates *Chretiens*, Christians, because the word distinguished human beings like these people from brutes and they believed such childlike innocents were incapable of actual sin. The kindly word *Chretien* went into French as *cretin*, meaning idiot, which became our pejorative *cretin*.

Crillon "The bravest of the brave," as he was called by Henry IV, is still remembered more than four centuries after his birth, the famed *Crillon Hotel* in Paris named in his honor. Louis Balbis de Berton de Crillon (1541 or 1543–1615) was a French soldier who joined the army when only fourteen, distinguished himself in many battles, was wounded numerous times, and became one of the greatest captains of the sixteenth century. It is said that in his old age Crillon was listening to the story of the crucifixion in church one day and unable to bear the outrages Christ suffered any longer, leaped to his feet, drawing his sword and crying out, "Where were you then Crillon?"

Crippen *Crippen* is often the nickname of any man wild and unkempt in appearance, but is more common for a doctor-murderer, of which there have unfortunately been too many. Dr. Hawley Harvey Crippen, English murderer, killed his wife Cora and was hanged for his crime on November 23, 1910. Captain Kendall of *The Montrose* transmitted a message on July 22 of that year leading to Crippen's capture, making the murderer the first to be caught by wireless telegraph. Dr. Crippen, born in Michigan in 1861, received his medical education in London and settled there in 1896 with his shrewish wife, who had previously appeared unsuccessfully in opera

and on the music hall stage as Belle Elmore. Crippen fell in love with his secretary and on New Year's Eve, 1910, poisoned his wife, dissected the body and after destroying what he could by fire, interred the remains in the cellar. He and Ethel le Neve eventually fled England, but Captain Kendall recognized them from their pictures and wired Scotland Yard to come aboard.

Crispin A word often found in literature for a shoemaker, but rarely used in everyday speech. *Crispin* commemorates the legendary brothers Crispin and Crispinian, patron saints of shoemakers and all leather workers, noble Romans who left Rome for Gaul in 303 A.D. to preach Christianity, supporting themselves by their craft. They made many converts and survived several attempts by Emperor Maximian to put them to death, but were finally beheaded about 286. The martyrs also have *St. Crispin's lance*, humorous for a shoemaker's awl, named after them. *St. Crispin's Day* is October 25.

Crisscross Crisscross sounds like a mere reduplication of sounds similar to zigzag, or ding-dong, but when we call a series of crossing lines *crisscross* we are really saying *Christ-cross*, the cross of Christ. In the old sixteenth-century hornbook primer—originally one vellum sheet slotted into a wainscot board frame and protected by a thin transparent front covering of horn—only the alphabet, a few numbers, a little spelling and the Lord's Prayer were taught. Most teachers at the time were trained for the ministry and so there was a close connection between education and religion. Thus the alphabet printed on the sheet's top line was preceded by a small cross that was referred to as the *Christ-cross* or *Christ's cross*. Soon the alphabet row came to be called *Christ-cross* row, this eventually becoming *crisscross* row due to the reduplicative tendency of tongues, or because the word was pronounced slurred like *Christmas* or *Christian*. Eventually *crisscross* alone was applied to any pattern of crossing lines similar to the cross at the beginning of *crisscross* row. Generations of English and American children learned their letters from hornbooks. Their frames were shaped like Ping-Pong paddles and a cord on the handle enabled youngsters to attach the books to their belts when not in use.

Croesus When we say, as the ancient Greeks did, that a man is *as rich as Croesus*, we are using the name of the last King of Lydia (560–546 B.C.). As a result of his conquests and trade, King Croesus was regarded by the Greeks as the wealthiest man on earth, his riches proverbial even at that time. Croesus probably minted the first gold and silver coins. Although he had subjugated the Ionian cities of Asia Minor, he was friendly to the Greeks, making spectacular offerings to their oracles. According to a legendary story told by Herodotus, the Athenian Solon once advised Croesus that no man could be deemed happy, despite his riches, until he finished his life happily. Later, after Croesus had been defeated by Cyrus the Great and condemned to be burned alive, he cried out Solon's name three times from the pile. Cyrus, moved by his explanation and perhaps reflecting on his own fate, spared his captive's life and they became great friends. The tale, however, is chronologically impossible and only one of a number of legends concerning this very real Midas.

Cromwell, A Cromwellian His name was once pronounced "Crumwell," hence the historic Royalist toast, "God send this crumb well down!" Royalists had every reason to wish this brilliant military leader and forceful statesman no good. A devout Puritan and member of Parliament who vigorously supported the Roundheads, Oliver Cromwell (1599–1658) eventually led his new model army to victory over Charles I's forces in battle, had the king executed in 1649, and abolished the kingship. In 1653 he became England's Lord Protector, rejecting the offer of the crown but accepting what was an undisguised dictatorship. He who had established the Commonwealth and began his career as an opponent of absolutism had become an absolutist himself. Cromwell died a natural death, naming his ineffectual son, Richard, as Lord Protector on his deathbed. He was buried in Westminster Abbey, but when the Royalists regained power in 1660, his body was exhumed, hanged from a gallows and beheaded. Such was their revenge on the man who had said of Charles I: "I tell you we will cut off his head with the crown upon it." (See also *Oliver's Skull.*)

Cullinan Diamond Most famous of the precious stones bearing someone's name is the 3,106 metric carat (over 1¼ lbs.) diamond found in South Africa's Premier Mine in 1905. The stone, the largest diamond ever unearthed, was named after the mine's discoverer—director, Sir Thomas Major Cullinan. Presented to England's King Edward VII in 1907, it was cut into a number of specimens worth collectively over a million pounds. The Star of Africa made from it is at 530.2 metric carats the largest cut diamond in the world.

Curie, Curie Point, Curium Several words honor the husband and wife co-discoverers of radium, whose work laid the foundation for much later research in nuclear physics. The *Curie point*—the temperature at which the magnetic properties of a substance change—had been named for Pierre Curie (1859–1906) before he married Marja Sklodowska in 1895. He and Madame Curie, who came from Poland to study at the Sorbonne, worked together to extract from pitchblende the twin radioactive elements polonium and radium in 1898, the former being named for Mme. Curie's native country. But it took them four years of incredible labor to extract one gram of radium salts from over eight tons of pitchblende, enough to prove that radium was a new radioactive substance. The Curies refused to patent their discovery or accept any profit whatsoever from it. In 1903 they and Henri Becquerel were jointly awarded the Nobel Prize in physics, for the discovery of radioactivity. Pierre Curie was killed in a street accident three years later and Marie took over his chair of physics at the Sorbonne, becoming the first woman to teach at any French university. In 1911 she became the first person to be awarded the Nobel Prize twice, this time in chemistry for the discovery and isolation of radium. Madame Curie died in 1934, aged sixty-seven.

These geniuses also produced daughter Irène Curie Joliot, who, in 1935, shared with her husband the Nobel Prize for chemistry, and Eve Curie, who wrote the acclaimed *Madame Curie,* a biography of her mother (1937), which has since been translated into some twenty-five languages. Marie Curie's name has become more widely known than her husband's; it was she who first suspected the presence of new elements in pitchblende, and she was a pioneer woman scientist as well. But the *curie* or *curiegram*—a unit of measurement for radioactivity—was named for *both* scientists in 1910, as was the radioactive element *curium* when discovered by Glenn Seaborg and his co-workers at the University of California in 1945.

Mme. Curie hated publicity and would not even take time out from her work to give autographs. One time an autograph hound sent her a check for twenty-five dollars, figuring that the check would come back endorsed with her signature. He received the following letter from her secretary: "Madame Curie has asked me to thank you most kindly for your check, which, however, she is not going to cash. It so happens that she is an autograph collector and therefore will add your signature to her collection."

Curlicism Publisher Edmund Curll (1675–1747) spent an hour in the pillory for his publication of the obscene *Memories of John Ker of Kersland* in 1728. He was also fined or imprisoned for publishing the indecent *The Nun In Her Smock,* a book on flagellation, and other works. For such indiscretions, which have redeeming social value today, the word *curlicism,* literary indecency, was coined. Alexander Pope, who claimed Curll had published an unauthorized edition of his letters, lampooned the publisher in the *Dunciad,* mentioning "Curll's chaste press" and describing him as a "fly in amber." He is also preserved in Swift's poem, "The Death of Dr. Swift." An excellent, appropriately titled biography is Ralph Strauss' *The Unspeakable Curll* (1927). Probably the wittiest and most accurate comment on the publisher was contemporary John Arbuthnot's remark that his biographies were "one of the new terrors of death."

Curzon Line The *Curzon line* now separating Russia and Poland was suggested in 1919 by the British Conserva-

tive politician, statesman and writer George Nathaniel Curzon, first Marquess of Kedleston (1859–1925). Lord Curzon, secretary for foreign affairs at the time, served in many capacities for the British government. As Viceroy of India from 1899 to 1905 and Chancellor of Oxford University from 1907 to 1915, he became noted for his aloof regal manner, which was the butt of many jokes. Behind the facade was a witty, modest, friendly man whose sheer willpower overcame serious physical weakness (a curvature of the spine). Curzon failed in his ambition to become the British prime minister in 1923, Stanley Baldwin chosen over him. It is said that he died of overwork. The *Curzon line,* marking Poland's eastern frontier and violated by her before World War II, was confirmed at Yalta in 1945. The diplomat wasn't at all like the rhyme composed about him at Balliol College in the late 1870's: *My name is George Nathaniel Curzon, / I am a most superior person.*

Cut a Dido *To cut a dido,* or play a prank, though an almost obsolete expression, may be the origin of the phrase *cutting up.* The original cutup could be Dido, the legendary princess who founded and became Queen of Carthage. The daughter of a Tyrian king, Dido married her uncle and upon his murder by her brother Pygmalion sailed to the African coast with his treasure. There she purchased land from a native chieftain, with the provision that all the ground she could cover with an oxhide would be hers. She then cut the hide into thin strips long enough to enclose a space which became the fort of Carthage. In a later myth, Virgil's *The Aeneid,* Dido is the lover of Aeneas and commits suicide upon her own funeral pyre when he abandons her at the command of Jupiter. It's a shame to spoil a good story, but the legend of Dido probably arose because the fortress protecting Carthage was named *Bozra. Bozra* meant "hill city" in Phoenician, but "oxhide" in Greek and most likely the tale was fabricated by some ancient Greek seeking to explain a fort named Oxhide.

Cynic Disciples of the Greek philosopher Antisthenes (b. c. 440 B.C.), especially his later followers like Diogenes, were nicknamed *kunikos* (cynikos), "dog-like" or "snarlers," for their insolent, currish manners. Antisthenes and his pupils believed that independent virtue formed the sole basis for happiness, scorning freedom, honor, art, learning, health, riches—life itself. Insolently self-righteous, this small but influential band of ascetics derided all social customs, even sleeping in kennellike quarters. Due to their churlishness and rude manners, we probably have our word *cynic*, meaning a surly, sarcastic person who believes that only selfishness motivates human behavior. It is possible, however, that this nickname was only a coincidence and that *cynic* derives from *Cynosarges* (white dog), the Greek gymnasium outside Athens where Antisthenes taught, or perhaps each word contributed to the other. (The gymnasium was supposedly named for a white dog that carried off part of a victim being offered to the gods.) But the *Cynics* outraged public standards of decency with their animal-like philosophy and behavior. They lived without family, society or religion, even adopting a dog as their common badge or symbol. The fact that Diogenes, a later *Cynic*, was nicknamed "the dog" may have also contributed to the coining.

Cyrano de Bergerac The most famous proboscis in history. Anyone with a prodigious nose is likely to be called a *Cyrano de Bergerac* after the eponymous hero of Edmond Rostand's play of the same name (1897). Rostand's hero was based on the very real Savinien Cyrano de Bergerac (1619–55), who had a nose as long as his fictional counterpart's and whose exploits were even more remarkable. The historical Cyrano was a brave soldier, great lover, and eloquent influ-

ential writer of comedies and tragedies. His works are said to have inspired Molière, and Swift's *Gulliver's Travels*. This swaggering swordsman fought countless duels with those foolish enough to insult or even mention his nose, and his duel singlehandedly against one hundred enemies while serving as an officer in the Guards is a well-documented fact. Cyrano's exploits became legend long before Rostand fictionalized him. Surprisingly, he did not perish on the wrong end of a sword. Cyrano died as a result of a wound caused by a falling beam or stone while staying at the home of a friend.

Czar, Tsar, Tsarina, Tsarevitch, Tsarevna When Julius Caesar died, his proper name was adopted by the Roman emperors, beginning with Augustus, and retained until the fall of the Holy Roman Empire. The title later came to be adopted by various European countries with minor changes in spelling. *Czar* or *Tsar* can be traced to the old Slavic word *cesare*, deriving from "Caesar" and introduced into Russia in the fifteenth century as a title. The word, first spelled *Tsesar*, was applied to all Russian rulers after Ivan the Terrible assumed it officially to describe his rule as king of Poland. The Russian *Tsar* was considered to be appointed by God as head of church and state, his authority unlimited by laws of any kind; his wife was called the *Tsarina*, his son the *Tsarevitch*, and his daughter the *Tsarevna*. Today, *czar* is often used for any tyrannical despot with absolute power, a *czarist* anyone who believes in such a system of government. Spelling of the word varies in both British and American dictionaries—neither form accepted by all authorities in either country. (See also *Caesar*.)

D

Dago, Dago Red An offensive word that may derive from the name of a saint. H. L. Mencken traces this disparaging term to 1832, when it was used in Louisiana to describe a Spaniard, not an Italian. But *dago* is a corruption of the very common Spanish name *Diego*, or alludes to St. Diego, Spain's patron saint, or both. *Diego* was used in Elizabethan times for a "swarthy" Spanish or Portuguese seaman. As recently as the beginning of this century the word also meant the Italian language, and a professor or student of Italian. The pejorative term is not heard as often today as its derivative *dago red*, any cheap wine, which is sometimes used by Italian-Americans themselves. *Dago* may also come from "day come, day go," a term reputedly used by early Italian laborers in expressing their patient philosophy. Far more offensive is *wop*, which arose toward the end of the last century. This ugly word comes from a relatively innocuous one, the Neapolitan *guappo*, a term used by immigrant laborers signifying a showy, pretentious person. Similarly, the offensive *guinea* may have originally referred to Italian laborers working for the equivalent of a guinea a day.

Saint James the Greater, called Santiago in Spain, was one of the Twelve Disciples, the brother of St. John. Numerous places are named for him, including Santiago, Chile; San Diego, California; and the Court of St. James, formerly the royal residence in London.

Daguerreotypes His wife often complained of the "malodorous vapors" pervading their house, but Louis Jacques Mandé Daguerre (1787–1851) persisted in his experiments and in collaboration with Joseph Nicéphore Niepce (d. 1833) succeeded in inventing the first permanent photographic process that really worked. Daguerre had originally been an inland revenue officer, then a scene painter for the opera. In 1822 he and artist C. M. Bouton invented the diorama, an exhibition of translucent scenic views painted on both sides of each canvas, heightened by changing lights, and displayed in a circular room where the floor revolved slowly past each scene. Four years later Daguerre met Niepce, who since 1814 had been experimenting with photographic systems. The two men worked together to develop the héliographie process, producing the first *permanent* picture made from sunlight upon plates, paper or glass, but Daguerre did not perfect his more refined *daguerreotype* process until after his friend's death. In 1839 he was awarded the French Legion of Honor for this milestone in photographic science, and both his process—roughly a photograph produced on a silver plate treated with iodine vapors—and the pictures obtained from it were named in his honor. *Daguerreotype* is actually a combination of *Daguerre* and the Greek *tupos*, impress. Englishman W. H. Fox Talbot improved on the invention in 1839 and the word *photography* was coined from his *photo*genic drawing process and the Niepce-Daguerre *héliographie* system.

Dahlia Over fourteen thousand named varieties of *dahlias* have been cultivated and crossed from the single plant that the German naturalist, Baron Alexander von Humboldt, discovered in Mexico in 1789. Sent to Spain in that year, the specimen was named there by the head of Madrid's Botanic Garden, Professor Cavanilles. But Cavanilles named the plant for a fellow professor, ignoring Humboldt. Thus the entire *Dahlia* genus honors Swedish botanist and pupil of Linnaeus, Anders Dahl (1751–89), who had died at about the time the flower was discovered. The first single-flowered *dahlia* bore little resemblance to the giant colorful double-flowered species so important in gardens today. There was, incidentally, a time in the nineteenth century when *dahlia* roots were touted as an excellent substitute for potatoes. They were easy to grow and unsusceptible to blight, said their advocates, but unfortunately no one seemed to like the way they tasted.

Dallia, Dall Sheep Both a tasty fish and a familiar sheep honor scientist William Healey Dall (1845–1927). *Ovis dalli*, the *Dall sheep* or *Dall's sheep*, is the white-haired wild mountain sheep of northwestern America named for the Boston naturalist. Dall, who became an authority on marine life for the Smithsonian Institution, first recorded the large curved-horned sheep while exploring the West for zoological specimens. A pupil of the great Louis Agassiz at Harvard, Dall later wrote one of the first books on Alaska's immense resources. The edible blackfish of Alaska called the *Dallia*, a species of the genus *Dalliidae*, does honor to his pioneer work in the territory.

Daltonism, Dalton's Law So determined was scientist John Dalton (1766–1844) to solve the mystery of color blindness that he willed his eyes for study after his· death. His pioneering paper, "Extraordinary Facts Relating to the Vision of Colours" (1794), is the earliest account of the problem, based on observations of himself, his brother and other similarly afflicted persons. As a result of his descriptions, *daltonism* became a synonym for color blindness, especially the inability to distinguish between the colors red and green. One of the great pioneers in science, the industrious Dalton also kept a meteorological diary in which he entered 200,000 observations over fifty-seven years. This diary both resulted in a remarkable book on weather conditions (*Meteorological Observations and Essays* (1793), and contained the germs of his atomic theory, Dalton's major scientific contribution and the basis of modern chemistry. Born of a poor family in Manchester, England, John Dalton had only an elementary education, being for the most part self-taught. The brilliant scientist, teacher and writer was elected to the Royal Society in 1822 and awarded a medal for his atomic theory three years later. *Dalton's Law* is the law of partial pressures, which he formulated in 1803.

Damiens' Bed of Steel The most horrible public execution in history was that of Robert François Damiens (1715–1757), the madman who made an attempt on the life of France's King Louis XV, inflicting a slight knife wound on the monarch. Thousands turned out to witness this "spectacle," many even applauding the prisoner's agonies. In the morning Damiens had been put on the rack and wounded deeply with glowing forceps, molten lead, boiling oil, pitch and sulfur poured into his many open wounds. Later he was chained to a heated iron bed, or by some accounts to a low wooden platform, his hand held in a sulfurous fire, and chunks of flesh ripped from his body, molten lead and oil again poured in the open wounds. His screams never ceased and the stench pervaded the entire court. Finally, Damiens' limbs were ripped off one by one in the Place de Grève by four wild horses that had to be increased to six to accomplish their purpose. The execution lasted until almost nine that night and the pathetic creature stayed alive through all of it. It is said that his rump still twitched at the end, that his black hair had turned completely white before his remains were burnt at the stake. "Such was the end," wrote the Duke de Croy, an eyewitness, "of that poor unfortunate who it may well be believed—suffered the greatest tortures that a human being has ever been called upon to endure." Only the execution of François Ravaillac, the murderer of France's Henry IV in 1610, rivals that of Damiens' for barbaric, sadistic cruelty. *Damiens' Bed of Steel* has become a symbol for such barbarity as well as the name of the instrument of torture.

Damon and Pythias (Phinotias) Two ancient Greeks of the early fourth century whose names became proverbial and synonymous for devoted friends. In the Greek version of the legend Phinotias (Pythias) was condemned to death by the tyrant Dionysus. Damon offered himself as a hostage so that his friend could make a last visit home. True to his word, Phinotias returned, but Damon insisted that his own head be put on the block, so impressing the monarch that he freed both philosophers and begged to be allowed to join their brotherhood. The phrase should therefore be Phinotias and Damon, but when Richard Edwards wrote his play Damon and Pythias in 1564, he turned the tale around, using the corruption Pythias instead of Phinotias, and it was from this source that the story became popular.

Daniel Boone "A good gun, a good horse, and a good wife," in that order, were the ingredients for Daniel Boone's prescription for happiness. The American pioneer's name has long been synonymous with such terms as the greatest of frontiersmen, an intrepid explorer or hunter, and a resourceful backwoodsman. Boone's accomplishments have been exaggerated in popular accounts, but there is no doubt that his explorations "opened the way to millions of his fellow men." Born near Reading, Pennsylvania, the great folk hero moved to North Carolina with his Quaker family in his early years. After serving under British General Braddock as a wagoner, he explored Florida, and fought as a lieutenant colonel of militia during the American Revolution, among many other activities. But his major contribution was the blazing of the famous Wilderness Road, which he and a band of thirty men forged in March, 1775, to found Boonesboro on the Kentucky River. Daniel and his wife, Rebecca, figure in more frontier lore than any other pioneers and he has been commemorated in numerous place names. Boone was eighty-six when he died in 1820, a legend in his own time.

Darbies Darbies is a British expression for handcuffs, but the word, oddly enough, derives from the name of a usurer. It seems that a shrewd sixteenth-century lawyer and moneylender named Derby drew up an ironclad bond which left no loopholes for debtors to escape through. This contract, used extensively by usurers, came to be called "father Derbie's bands." Because they were also impossible to "unlock," it wasn't long before all manacles were known as derbies, too, the word often pronounced darbies. Darbies is first recorded in 1576, no other plausible explanation having been offered for its derivation except "unknown."

Darby and Joan

Old Darby, with Joan by his side,
  You're often regarded with wonder:
He's dropsical, she is sore-eyed,
  Yet they're never happy asunder.

This verse was printed in the Gentlemen's Magazine in 1735 under the title "The Joys of Love Never Forgot: a song." Its anonymous author may have been poet Henry Woodfall, the ballad, in a number of stanzas, praising Darby and Joan, whose names have come to stand for any mutually affectionate and contented old married couple. The poet, if he did write the verses, probably patterned his pair on John and Joan Darby who lived in Bartholomew Close, London. Woodfall had served an apprenticeship under John Darby, the printer and his wife having been widely known for their good works and faithfulness to each other.

Darlingtonia When an insect enters the pitcher-shaped leaves of the curious California pitcher plant, Darlingtonia, it is trapped by down-pointing hairs which allow it to crawl in but not out, then drowned in liquid from the leaves, and, according to some scientists, ultimately is eaten or digested by the plant. Not a particularly wholesome thing to have named after one, but the single specie's scientific name honors William Darlington (1782–1863), an American botanist who wrote several biographies of famous botanists and authored American Weeds and Useful Plants (1859). The naming was done by a fellow botanist, John Torrey, there being no record of bad feelings between the two men. Darlingtonia is sometimes sold as Chrysamphora californica and is not the only insectivorous plant. These include the famous Venus's-flytrap, bladderwort, sundew, butterwort, and pitcher plants belonging to the genus Sarracenia, all varying in the ways they capture their prey.

D'Artagnan Memoirs attributed to Charles de Batz-Castelmore d'Artagnan (c. 1623–1673) were used by the novelist Alexander Dumas père in his fictional series beginning with *The Three Mus-keteers*. In real life Gascon d'Artagnan did serve in the king's musketeers, but he wasn't a *comte*, as he called himself, claiming the title without right. About all that can be verified about the man is that he captained the contingent that arrested the powerful French superinten-dent of finances Nicolas Fouquet in 1661, became a brigadier general nine years later, and was fatally wounded at the siege of Maastricht. Yet d'Artagnan will always be remembered for the heroic adventures Dumas and his collaborator Maquet adapted or created from his story.

Darwinian "A hairy quadruped, fur-nished with a tail and pointed ears, prob-ably arboreal in habits." So Charles Rob-ert Darwin (1809–82) described our com-mon ancestor in *The Descent of Man* (1871), which didn't sound at all like Adam and Eve. The epochal theory of evolution was formulated by Darwin in his *On The Origin of the Species by Means of Natural Selection* (1859), *The Descent of Man* and other works. Evi-dence gathered during a five-year cruise to South America and the Galapagos Islands as a naturalist aboard the *Beagle* (1831–36) enabled Darwin to confirm or-ganic evolution, and to propose his the-ory of natural selection, explaining it twenty years later. Darwin deduced that all species descended from a few primal ancestors and that favorable variations within a species better enabled it to sur-vive—the survival of the fittest, as Her-bert Spencer called the process. Special development and natural selection, he explained, not special creations, accounted for the diversity of species on earth. The *Darwinian theory* is widely known and accepted today, but provoked a storm of controversy in the nineteenth century in both religious and scientific circles. Dar-win, a retiring genius and something of a hypochondriac, left the defense of his work to the brilliant Thomas Huxley, who gloried in his crusading role. His discovery came when the world was ripe for it, Alfred Russel Wallace, in fact, arriving at the same conclusions inde-pendently and almost concurrently. But the massive documentation and brilliant arguments Darwin provided succeeded in making the theory scientifically accept-able. The first edition of his *Origin of the Species*—1,250 copies—sold out on the day it was printed, his theory, of course, profoundly changing the world. Darwin, in his *Life and Letters* (1887), attributed his success to "the love of sci-ence, unbounded patience in long reflect-ing over any subject, industry in observ-ing and collecting facts, and a fair share of invention as well as of common sense." He further wrote: "I have steadily en-deavoured to keep my mind free so as to give up any hypothesis, however much beloved . . . as soon as the facts are shown to be opposed to it." The great English naturalist was the grandson of Erasmus Darwin, scientist and poet, and Josiah Wedgwood, the famous potter, *Darwinian*, in fact, used to describe the poetic style of Erasmus a generation be-fore Charles Darwin formulated his the-ory. It is enlightening to note in the age of astrology that Darwin and the world were nearly the victims of another fad—physiognomy. Darwin had a snub nose and Captain Fitzhugh of the *Beagle*, a devotee of the "science," almost didn't hire him as the ship's naturalist because a snub nose was supposed to indicate a lack of energy and determination.

Davenport In America a *davenport* generally means a large, often convertible, sofa, while in England it is a small desk or escritoire. The British meaning came first and nobody is sure where the word derives from. *Webster's* attributes it to its original nineteenth-century manufac-turer, another source to "a Captain Dav-enport who first commissioned it," and a third to "some now forgotten crafts-man." The word for a desk was first recorded in 1853 and most likely honors an English furniture maker of c. 1820–40. The sofa, which came later, may have been devised by another manufacturer of the same name.

Davis Cup, Wightman Cup While still an undergraduate at Harvard in 1900, American statesman and sports-man Dwight Filley Davis (1879–1945) donated a silver cup to be presented as a national trophy to that country win-ning an international championship con-test in lawn tennis. From the beginning, teams were composed of four amateur players and all *Davis Cup* ties consisted of four singles and one doubles match. The first *Davis Cup* winner was the United States, Great Britain winning the title in 1903. Davis, an outstanding player himself, held many high-level government positions, including secretary of war (1925–29) and governor general of the Philippines (1929–32).

Mrs. George Wightman, the former Helen Hotchkiss, donated the *Wightman Cup* for competition between teams of women players from the United States and Britain in 1923, the first contest held at Forest Hills. Mrs. Wightman had been the American national singles champion from 1909 through 1911.

Davy Crockett David (Davy) Crockett, as the song goes, was "a son of the wild frontier" from his earliest years. Born in 1786 in Limestone, Tenn., Davy was hired out to a passing cattle driver by his Irish immigrant father when only twelve, wandering the frontier until he turned fifteen before finally returning home. He became a colonel in the Tennessee militia under Andrew Jackson, during the Creek War, and after serving as a justice of the peace and state legislator, acted on a humorous suggestion that he run for Congress in 1827. Much to his surprise, he won the election. Crockett served two terms in Congress, and was noted in Washington for his backwoods dress and shrewd native humor, though many of the comments often attributed to him are largely apocryphal. His motto was "Be sure you are right, then go ahead." When defeated for reelection in 1835—mainly because he opposed Jacksonian banking and Indian policies—he moved to Texas, where he joined the Texas war for independence from Mexico. On March 6, 1836, Colonel Crockett was killed with the defenders of the Alamo. The folk hero's famous autobiography, *A Narrative of the Life of David Crockett of the State of Tennessee* (1834), was probably dictated, but is written in his robust style, complete with many examples of the tall tale.

Davy Jones' Locker No one has fathomed the origins of this phrase. The original Davy Jones may have been the sixteenth-century owner of an English pub, commemorated in the ballad, "Jones

Ale is Newe," who stored his ale in a mysterious locker for some reason much feared by seamen. On the other hand, *Jones* could be a corruption of *Jonah*, the Biblical character swallowed by a whale, and *Davy* the Anglicization of the West Indian word *duppy* or *duffy*, meaning a malevolent ghost or devil. A third explanation proposes *Jonah* as above for *Jones*, but derives *Davy* from *St. David*, the patron saint of Wales often invoked by Welsh sailors. Jonah was indeed considered bad luck to the sailors aboard the vessel on which he was trying to flee God's wrath, and probably has something to do with the origin of the phrase. In any case, the words *Davy Jones* have been current at least since Tobias Smollet wrote *The Adventures of Peregrine Pickle* in 1751:

" '. . . I'll be damned if it was not *Davy Jones himself. I know him by his saucer eyes, his three rows of teeth, and tail, and the blue smoke that came out of his nostrils. . . .' This same Davy Jones, according to the mythology of sailors, is the fiend that presides over all the evil spirits of the deep, and is often seen in various shapes, perching among the rigging on the eve of hurricanes, ship wrecks, and other disasters to which seafaring life is exposed, warning the devoted wretch of death and woe."*

For over two centuries *gone to Davy Jones' Locker* has been used by seamen to indicate death, especially death by drowning, *locker* probably coming from an ordinary seaman's chest. But complicating the matter further is the fact that the phrase was first recorded by Captain Francis Grose in his *Dictionary of the Vulgar Tongue* (1785) as *David Jones' Locker*, which lends more support to the Welsh patron saint theory. (See also *Jonah*.)

Davy Lamp, Davy Medal, Davite Sir Humphry Davy, who "abominated gravy" (see *clerihew*), invented the *Davy lamp* and has the mineral ore *davite* named in his honor. The great English chemist (1778–1829) invented the safety lamp for miners in 1816; largely outmoded today, it is a flame enclosed in a fine-meshed wire cage that prevents high heat from escaping and has saved thousands of lives that would have been lost due to the igniting of explosive gasses. Like Madame Curie, the largely self-educated genius refused to take out a patent for his discovery. Among his myriad scientific achievements were: his electrical theory of chemical affinity, said to be one hundred years before its time; the discovery of the anesthetic effect of "laughing gas"; the isolation of the alkali metals potassium and sodium; the isolation of calcium, barium, strontium, magnesium and boron; and the discovery that chlorine is an element. Davy was presented with an expensive dinner service of silver by grateful coal mine owners for his invention of the *Davy lamp.* In his will he decreed that it be melted down and sold, interest from the proceeds to be used to establish the *Davy Medal* of the Royal Society, "given annually for the most important discovery in chemistry anywhere made in Europe or Anglo-America."

Deadman's Hand The dead man was Wild Bill Hickok and the poker hand aces and eights. James Butler "Wild Bill" Hickok (1837–76) had come to Deadwood, Dakota Territory, in the last years of his life to make a stake for the bride he had just taken. But lawless elements, fearing his appointment as town marshal, hired gunman Jack McCall to assassinate him, giving McCall three hundred dollars and all the cheap whiskey he needed for courage. Wild Bill was playing cards in the No. 10 saloon (his back to the open door for only the second time in his long history of gun-fighting) when McCall sneaked in and shot him in the back of the head. Hickok's last hand held aces and eights, which has ever since been known as the *deadman's hand.* He is buried in Mt. Moriah cemetery just outside a reconstructed Deadwood. McCall, freed by a packed miners' court, was later convicted by a federal court, his plea of "double jeopardy" disregarded on the ground that the miners' court had no jurisdiction. He was later hanged for his crime. (See also *Calamity Jane.*)

Deadwood Dick *Deadwood Dick* became proverbial through many late nineteenth-century dime novels, especially those written by Edward L. Wheeler, and long stood for a fearless Indian scout and outlaw fighter. The prototype for Wheeler's westerns was Richard W. Clarke (1845–1930), who had been nicknamed *Deadwood Dick* long before his fictional exploits. Clarke, an Englishman attracted to the Black Hills by the gold diggings, won fame as both an Indian fighter and an express guard for gold shipped from the mines in and around Deadwood, S.D. Many of the *Deadwood Dick* myths have been debunked, but he was certainly a real character. Clarke lies in a mountain grave near Deadwood.

Debrett's Peerage Another guide to the British aristocracy. *Debrett's Peerage* was published in 1802 as a *Peerage of England, Scotland, and Ireland,* making it the first compilation of its kind. Its publisher, John Debrett, who died twenty years later, also published a *Baronetage of England* (1808). In England "to be in Debrett" means "to be of noble birth." (See also *Burke's Peerage,* a more familiar term to Americans.)

Decibel "Watson, come here; I want you." These were the undramatic words spoken by inventor Alexander Graham Bell to his lab assistant on March 10, 1876, the first complete sentence conveyed over the telephone. Bell was a Scottish immigrant who in 1871 came to the United States, where he lectured to teachers of the deaf on his father's visible speech method and opened his own school of vocal physiology in Boston. In the course of work on his harmonic telegraph, he invented the first practical telephone, an idea he had conceived as early as 1865. Later inventions included the photophone, the first practical phonograph record, the audiometer, and a telephonic probe for locating bullets in the human body. The *Bell Telephone Company* was formed in July, 1877. The inventor, who married a deaf girl and remained interested in his original work all his life, also generously supported aviation pioneers, founded *Science,* the official publication of the American Association for the Advancement of Science, and was president of the National Geographic Society and a regent of the Smithsonian Institution. He died in 1922, aged seventy-five. The words *bel,* a unit for measuring the loudness of electrical signals, and *decibel,* one tenth of a *bel,* derive from the inventor's name. *Decibel* is more commonly used in this age of noise pollution as a unit for measuring the volume of sound—one *decibel* being the faintest sound the human ear can detect.

Delaware "There is no place in the world," Robert Louis Stevenson observed, "where nomenclature is so rich, poetical, humorous and picturesque as the United States of America. . . . The names of the states themselves form a chorus of sweet and most romantic vocables: Delaware, Ohio, Indiana, Florida, Dakota, Iowa, Wyoming, Minnesota and the Carolinas: there are few poems with a nobler music for the ear: a songful, tuneful land." Mencken, quoting the English author, points out that the map of this country is indeed "besprinkled with place names from at least half a hundred languages, living and dead." Of the eight classes he lists as their sources "surnames" comes first. *Delaware* falls into this category, being the first alphabetically of American states that take their names from the names of individuals. The Diamond State commemorates English soldier Thomas West, Baron De la Warr (1577–1618), who in 1609 was appointed the first governor of Virginia by the Virginia company. *Delaware Bay* was named for Lord De la Warr by Sir Samuel Argall, who discovered it when the governor sent him on an expedition to locate supplies for the starving settlers at Jamestown, both *Delaware* and the *Delaware Indians* deriving their names from this body of water. De la Warr had been appointed governor of Virginia for life, but died on his second trip from England to the colony and was buried at sea.

Delilah A *Delilah*, from the name of the Biblical courtesan, signifies both a temptress and a seductive wife or mistress who turns to treachery. Delilah in the Biblical story (*Judges* 16:4–20) had been bribed by the Philistines to learn the source of Samson's strength. Samson lied to her three times, but on her fourth attempt she learned that his power lay in his long hair, had his head shaved while he slept upon her knees, and betrayed him to his enemies. Little is told of Delilah except that she was "a woman in the valley of Sorek." After she collects "eleven hundred pieces of silver" for her haircutting treachery, she is heard from no more. (See also *Samson*.)

Demijohn The shape of a portly lady is suggested by the *demijohn*, which is narrow at the neck and round in the body. For this reason some etymologists trace the word, first recorded in 1769, to the French *Dame Jeanne*, Lady Jane, theorizing that the large glass bottle was named for some forgotten French housewife whose bulging figure it resembled, or for such portly women in general. The theory that *demijohn* is a corruption of *Damaghan*, a Persian town where glassware was manufactured, is not generally accepted. A *demijohn* generally holds five gallons and is usually encased in wickerwork. (See also *Bellarmine*.)

Demosthenes, Demosthenic There are legends that the great Greek orator Demosthenes was a stammerer, that he could not pronounce the letter *p*, and that he overcame his impediments by practicing with pebbles in his mouth against the sound of the surf, or by declaiming as he ran uphill. According to still another tradition, Demosthenes also mastered language by copying Thucydides' direct and graphic *History of the Peloponnesian War* eight times. Whatever the truth of these stories—and there is little doubt that Demosthenes did have some speech defect as a boy—the Greek statesman ranks as the greatest orator of all time, surpassing even Cicero, who patterned himself on the Athenian. Demosthenes (c. 383–322 B.C.) is particularly noted for his denunciations of Philip of Macedonia (see *Philippics*), which roused his countrymen to the danger of the subjugation of Greece. The word *Demosthenic* refers to his oratory and also means eloquent, patriotic speech, for his two most constant themes were the greatness of Athens and the need to preserve her tradition. As a young man Demosthenes is said to have studied law and rhetoric in order to recover property embezzled by his guardians. All his speeches were models of logic, sincerity, intensity and felicity, his style always justified by his theme and free of rhetorical embellishment. His greatest speech, outside of the *Philippics*, was probably "On the Crown," a successful defense of his right to wear a crown awarded for services to Athens. Demosthenes committed suicide after the defeat of the confederate Greeks. The Macedonian general Antipater had demanded his surrender. Trapped by Antipater's emissaries in the sanctuary of the temple of Poseidon on Calauria, he drew his cloak over his head and sucked poison from a pen with which he was pretending to write a last letter. He stumbled from the temple, his last words: "But I, O gracious Poseidon, quit thy temple while I still live; Antipater and his Macedonians have done what they could to pollute it." An orator till the very end.

Derby, English Derby, Kentucky Derby *Derby* is the American name for a version of the dome-shaped, felt hat that the English call a bowler. The man it honors also has the *English Derby* at Epsom Downs and the *Kentucky Derby* named for him. The twelfth earl of Derby, Edward Stanley (d. 1834), came from a family that traced its origins to William the Conqueror. He had a great interest in horse racing and little in his wife—a mutual feeling—devoting most of his time to the improvement of the breed. Races had long been held at Epsom Downs, but in 1780 the earl started a series of annual contests for three-year-olds, these named in his honor both because he suggested them and was such a convivial host each season at The Oaks, a house near the course that had belonged to his uncle General "Johnny" Burgoyne (see *burgoynade*). The *Derby* became so popular that almost a century later, in 1875, the *Kentucky Derby* adopted part of its name.

After the Civil War, American spectators at the "Blue Ribbon of the Turf" noticed that English sportsmen often wore odd-shaped bowler hats. A few were brought back home, where it is said that a Connecticut manufacturer made a stiff felt, narrow-brimmed version that an unknown New York store clerk sold as "hats like the English wear at the Derby." In any event, the *derby* became not only the American term for bowler, but the most popular headwear for men up until the 1920's. The name is also commemorated by *The Brown Derby*, a famous Hollywood restaurant built in the shape of a hat, and *Derby dog*, British slang for an irritating interruption, in allusion to "that inevitable dog which so often appears on the course just before the race." (See also *Billycock*.)

Derrick, Dick, Dirk A professional hangman gave his name to the large crane for lifting and placing heavy objects that we call a *derrick*. Godfrey Derrick, or Derick, a convicted rapist, had been pardoned by Robert, Earl of Essex, his commander in a military expedition, when he agreed to become executioner at famous Tyburn Prison just outside London. The young and handsome Essex, long a favorite of Queen Elizabeth, was condemned for treason and sentenced to be executed at Tyburn in 1601. By an odd twist of fate, Derrick became his executioner, although as a headsman, for nobles were not required to suffer the indignities of hanging. The story is recorded in the old English ballad *Essex's Good Night:*

Derrick, thou knowes't at Cales [Calais]
  I saved
Thy life lost for a rape there done. . . .
But now thou seest myself is come
By chance into thy hands I light;
Strike out thy blow, that I may know
Thou Essex loved at his good-night.

Despite the lord's instructions, Derrick botched the job on the block, hacking at least three times at Essex's neck before he severed his head. Essex's admirers were so incensed that guards had to be called to Derrick's rescue. From then on he is heard of primarily as a hangman, probably responsible for over three thousand executions in his long service as public executioner, which extended into the reign of James I. His name was most likely applied to the gallows itself and then to the crane which the gallows resembled, though the comparison may have been between his and the crane's great strength or stature, or, doubtfully, because he fashioned an improved gallows with a hoisting device that was the prototype for a kind of rude crane.

At any rate, we find Derrick's name proverbial by 1608. "He rides circuit with the devil, and Derrick must be his host, and Tyborne the inn at which will light," wrote Thomas Dekker in *Bellman of London* that year. Among the dreaded hangman's victims were many sneak thieves and picklocks, who often carried short daggers. These came to be called *dirks* after Derrick, which is a Dutch name identified with Dietrich, Theodoric and Dirk. This, anyway, is one explanation, *dirk* first recorded at the time of the hangman's tenure. *Derrick* no longer means a gibbet, is still used for the modern motorized crane, and in underworld slang means a shoplifter. Partridge even suggests that *dick*, a common slang term for penis, comes from the hangman's name, as indeed it could, through the word *dirk*.

Godfrey Derrick was at least an improvement on earlier hangmen, some of whom were so inept that friends or relatives were permitted to pull on a victim's dangling body to end his suffering—which gruesome practice may be the origin of the humorous expression *you're pulling my leg*.

Derringer *Derringers* are of course the little but deadly, large-bored guns so often concealed in the sleeves of gamblers and the bosoms of dance-hall girls in Westerns, and which in real life have been the choice of a large variety of villains, including assassin John Wilkes Booth. The pistol, often carried in pairs, is named for Philadelphia gunsmith Henry Deringer, who invented it in 1835. Posterity cheated Deringer a bit, though, for the stubby gun came to be spelled with a double *r*. Deringer, who started his career selling squirrel rifles to Delaware river boatmen in exchange for lumber, had a prosperous business before his invention, but the little box-lock pistols made his one of America's largest armories. He alone is said to have fashioned ten thousand of them in his long lifetime—he lived to be eighty-two—however, many imitations were made of his gun. One of these was a European make signed *Derringer*, the spelling that somehow became accepted. The original model had a 1½-inch barrel and .4 bore, but today any small pistol of a large calibre is called a *derringer*.

Dewar Flask, Thermos The *Dewar flask*, the original thermos bottle, is named for its inventor, Sir James Dewar (1842–1923), a Scottish chemist and physicist who devised the vacuum-jacketed vessel in 1892 for the storage of liquid gasses at low temperatures. The first experimenter to liquify hydrogen and to produce liquid oxygen in quantity, Dewar invented the explosive cordite with Sir Frederick Abel. His great manual dexterity—developed when he made violins as a hobby after a childhood accident—is said to have been largely responsible for his various inventions. Much honored in his lifetime, he taught for many years at London's Royal Institution.

The *thermos* takes its name from the company that adapted Dewar's invention commercially. Originally a trademark, the word is now spelled without a capital in most dictionaries.

Dewey Decimal System The father of American library science, Melvil Dewey (1851–1931), first proposed his famous *Dewey Decimal system* in 1876 while serving as acting librarian at Amherst College. It is now used by some 85 percent of all libraries. The classification scheme, invented when he was in his early twenties, divides the entire field of knowledge into nine main classes (from 000 to 999), a second set of numbers following a decimal point indicating the special subject of a book within its main class. A man of fantastic energy and originality, Dewey later became chief librarian at Columbia College (1883–88), where he founded, in 1887, the first American school of library science. As director of the New York State Library (1889–1906), he reorganized the state library, making it one of the most efficient in the nation, and originated the system of traveling libraries. Dewey also helped found the American Library Association, the New York State Library Association, and the *Library Journal*. He crusaded for simplified spelling and use of the metric system, among many other causes.

Dewitt *To dewitt*, or brutally lynch, is chiefly an historical expression today. The brothers DeWitt—Jan (b. 1625) and Cornelius (b. 1623)—were Dutch statesmen opposed to the war policies of their monarch when the French invaded the Netherlands in 1672. Jan DeWitt, King William III's major opponent, and a wise, eloquent statesman, was arrested that same year and tortured in the Gevangenpoort at the Hague. When his brother Cornelius came to visit him in jail, an incensed *chauvinistic* mob gathered and broke into the prison, hacking the two men to pieces and hanging their limbs and parts on lamp posts. For many years after *to dewitt* meant to perform such grisly lynchings or mob murders, one of the few such verbs in English deriving from someone's name. (See also *Alexander; Lynch.*)

Dickens, Dickensian The expression *what the dickens* has nothing to do with author Charles Dickens' name, as is often believed, *the dickens* in this case probably being an old euphemism for *devil*. *Dickensian* is another, greater story. As a noun *Dickensian* refers to the novelist Charles John Huffam Dickens (1812–70) and his works, while as an adjective it describes the energy and living presence of his characters, the tremendous vitality and richness of the world he created. Dickens did exaggerate his characters, but no one before or after has been able to exaggerate just like him. The people he created in his fourteen novels and many shorter works are better known universally than those of any English author save Shakespeare. Micawber, Pickwick, David Copperfield, Steerforth, Oliver Twist, Scrooge, Tiny Tim, Sarah Gamp, Uriah Heep, Gradgrind, the Artful Dodger, Fagin, Little Nell—and so many others—have become words in themselves as well as names, stepping out of the books that contained them. Dickens, the son of an improvident government clerk —elements of him are found in both Micawber and Dorrit—had to go to work in a blacking factory at the age of twelve when his father was imprisoned for debt. He had little formal schooling and, after being apprenticed to a lawyer, served as a parliamentary reporter for newspapers. Following the success of *Sketches by Boz* (his penname) and *Pickwick Papers* in 1836, his fame was assured, and books like *Oliver Twist*, the semiautobiographical *David Copperfield*, and *Hard Times*, with their descriptions of the brutality of industrial society, made him one of the world's most influential novelists. Dickens toured America twice, his unflattering *American Notes* the result of his first visit. His more complex works such as *Bleak House, Great Expectations, Our Mutual Friend, Little Dorrit* and *Hard Times* have been acclaimed by critics as Dickens' greatest novels, but his early books, *A Tale of Two Cities* and his Christmas stories have remained just as popular over the years. *A Christmas Carol*, as G. K. Chesterton pointed out, did much to revive the true spirit of Christmas throughout the world. Dickens died suddenly and prematurely at the age of fifty-eight, probably of overwork, but his wildly comic, grotesque, and tearfully pathetic characters lived on. As Chesterton wrote in his brilliant essay on the novelist, "There can be no question of the importance of Dickens as a human event in history . . . a naked flame of mere natural genius, breaking out in a man without culture, without tradition, without help from historic religions or philosophies or from the great foreign schools; and revealing a light that never was on sea or land, if only in the long fantastic shadows that it threw from common things." Dickens' grave is in the poets' corner of Westminster Abbey.

Dick Test Like the more famous Curies, Drs. George Frederick and Gladys H. Dick form a famous husband-and-wife scientific team. In 1923 they isolated the streptococcus causing scarlet fever. The following year the Dicks devised the test used to determine an individual's susceptibility to the disease and developed a serum providing immunity. In the *Dick test* scarlet fever toxins are injected into the arm; if the individual is not immune, the skin reddens around the injection. George Frederick Dick (b. 1881) was professor of clinical medicine at Rush Medical College when he and his wife made their discoveries. He served as chairman of the department of medicine at the University of Chicago Medical School from 1933 to 1945.

Diehard Colonel William Inglis commanded the famous British 57th Foot at the battle of Albuera on May 16, 1811. His regiment, part of a thin line of 1,800 redcoats, occupied an important strategic position in the small Spanish village, and had been pinned down by a deadly French fire. "Die hard! Fifty-seventh!

Die hard!" Inglis cried out from where he lay wounded. His men responded. Of 579 troops 438 were killed or wounded, and the 57th passed into legend as the *Die Hards*. This nickname was later used to describe ultraconservative political groups or individuals refusing to change with the times. The British won at Albuera, the battle generally considered a mistake strategically but providing inspiration that aided Wellington in future battles against superior French forces. Inglis, later knighted and made a general, died in 1835, at the age of seventy-one. (See also *Doctrinaire*.)

Diesel Dr. Rudolf Diesel, the German mechanical engineer who invented the heavy-duty internal combustion engine bearing his name, didn't live to see his invention's numerous applications. Diesel developed the oil engine in 1892–97 at the Krupp factory in Essen (see *Big Bertha*), spending the rest of his life perfecting it and manufacturing *diesel engines* at a factory he founded in Augsburg. At the time of his death the diesel's use was relatively limited, but today it is employed in locomotives, ships, generators, trucks, submarines and much heavy-power equipment like power shovels. Diesel became rich and famous as a result of his invention—he received one million gold marks alone from the manufacturer who bought the North American rights to his patents. Yet his death in 1913, when only fifty-five, is still shrouded in mystery. Diesel may have fallen overboard while crossing the English Channel on a mail steamer the night of September thirtieth, but his hat and overcoat were found by the rail, suggesting suicide. His body, later recovered, was buried at sea.

Dine With Duke Humphrey It was popularly believed in days of yore that Humphrey, Duke of Gloucester (1391–1447), a man noted for his hospitality, was buried in London's old St. Paul's Cathedral. For many years after his death those poor who remained in the cathedral during dinner hours, or those debtors afraid to leave the sanctuary for fear of imprisonment, were said to be *dining with Duke Humphrey*. Although the good duke had actually been buried at St. Albans, the expression *to dine with Duke Humphrey* remained linked with St. Paul's and came to mean to go without any dinner at all. It is now solely a literary expression, often found in the novels of Dickens and other great English authors.

Diogenes, Diogenes Crab, Diogenes Cup, Diogenic He is said to have walked the streets of Athens with a lantern in broad daylight searching for an honest man, thus expressing his contempt for his generation. His home was a narrow, open earthenware tub which he trundled about with him. On seeing a child drinking from cupped hands, he threw away his only worldly possession, a wooden bowl. On being asked by Alexander the Great if the emperor could oblige him in any way, he replied, "Yes, by standing out of my sunshine." More lore surrounds Diogenes of Sinope (c. 412–323 B.C.), a relatively minor philosopher, than many a more deserving thinker. Diogenes the Cynic held that the virtuous life was the simple life and advocated a return to such ways; the lack of all pleasure, self-control, and even pain and hunger, he considered essential to achieving goodness. The Greeks nicknamed him "dog" for what they considered his shameful ways (see *Cynic*), but Diogenes considered himself a governor of men; in fact, he once told pirates who had captured him that he would like to be sold to a man who needed a master. Diogenes died on the same day as Alexander the Great, who had said, admiringly, "If I were not Alexander, I would be Diogenes." Today a *Diogenes* or a *diogenic* person is a cynical, churlish, but independent one, while a West Indian hermit crab bears the philosopher's name because it lives in empty shells reminiscent of his tub.

Dioscorea While many genera and species of flowers and fruits are named for people, the yam is the only major vegetable, excluding vegetable varieties, to take even its scientific name from a real person. The yam's botanical name is *Dioscorea Batatas*, the genus, containing many species, named by Linnaeus for Pedanius Dioscorides, or, more correctly, Dioscurides, a first-century Greek physician and an early father of botany. A surgeon in Nero's Roman army, Dioscorides gathered information about six hundred medicinal plants and other remedies of the period, which he recorded in his *De Materia Medica*, translated in 1934 as the *Greek Herbal of Dioscorides*. Dioscorides' work remained standard for centuries and he is considered to be the first man to establish medical botany as an applied science. *Dioscorea Batatas*, the yam, is often incorrectly called a sweet potato, to which it is no relation, despite the similarity in taste. The vine, its tubers two to three feet below the ground, is primarily grown in the South.

Disneyan Among Walt Disney's thirty-nine awards from the Academy of Motion Picture Sciences, and his more than eight hundred awards and decorations for his work from other sources, there is one that honors him "for creating a new art form in which good was spread throughout the world." It is on this creation that his fame rests secure. Walter Elias Disney (1901–66) did not invent the animated cartoon but brought it to perfection and created characters that have become a permanent part of American folklore (see *Mickey Mouse*). His many full-length animated motion pictures (*Snow White and the Seven Dwarfs, Bambi, Fantasia, Dumbo, Pinocchio, Cinderella, Alice in Wonderland, Robin Hood, Peter Pan*, and so on) set a standard for all others. Disney's Mickey Mouse film, *Steamboat Willie*, was the first animated sound cartoon and he is credited with the invention of the storyboard and other innovative cartoon techniques. On another less creative level, the artist has been invidiously called "the Henry Ford of the entertainment industry" for his *Disneyland* in California and the *Disney World* recently launched in Florida. But the *Disneyan* world populated by Mickey Mouse, Donald Duck, Pluto, Goofy, Oswald Rabbit, et al., will not soon disappear; it constitutes an American art form, perhaps marked the beginning of a nonlinear culture. Like Henry Ford—and Disney films were his favorites—Disney's was a typical American success story: humble beginnings (although the family traces its origins to England's noble D'Isney clan), hard work and hardships of every description—the story is a com-

mon one. Even the success marred by crass commercialism in later years is not unfamiliar. Yet the genius—which more often springs from the much maligned American lower middle class than critics are willing to admit—triumphs in the end. Disney's characters remain, in the words of British artist David Low, "the most significant figures in graphic art since Leonardo."

A Dives Dives is not named in current versions of the Bible, but he is the rich man mentioned in the parable told by Jesus in *Luke* 16:19–31 and his name has become proverbial for a wealthy, often insensitive person. The Biblical story follows:

"There was a rich man, who was clothed in purple and fine linen and who feasted sumptuously every day. And at his gate lay a poor man named Lazarus, full of sores, who desired to be fed from the rich man's table; moreover the dogs came and licked his sores. The poor man died and was carried by the angels to Abraham's bosom. The rich man also died and was buried; and in Hades, being in torment, he lifted up his eyes, and saw Abraham far off and Lazarus in his bosom. And he called out, 'Father Abraham, have mercy upon me, and send Lazarus to dip the end of his finger in water and cool my tongue; for I am in anguish in this flame.' But Abraham said, 'Son, remember that you in your lifetime received your good things, and Lazarus in like manner evil things; but now he is comforted here, and you are in anguish. . . .'"

Dives then asks that someone be sent up to warn his brothers so they might repent, but is told that if they "do not hear Moses and the prophets, neither will they be convinced if some one should rise from the dead."

Dixie, Dixieland It sounds incredible, but the first *Dixieland* or *Dixie* may have been in New York City. Some etymologists lean to the following derivation of the word given by the Charlestown *Courier* of June 11, 1885: "When slavery existed in New York, one Dixie owned a large tract of land on Manhattan Island, and a large number of slaves. The increase of the slaves and of the abolition sentiment caused an emigration of the slaves to more thorough and secure slave sections, and the Negroes who were thus sent off (many being born there) naturally looked back to their old houses, where they had lived in clover, with feelings of regret, as they could not imagine any place like Dixie's. Hence it became synonymous with an ideal location combining ease, comfort, and material happiness of every description." Although no slave "lived in clover," the explanation seems somewhat less doubtful than other theories about Dixie—that it derives from the eighteenth-century *Mason-Dixon line*, or that the word comes from the French-Creole word *dix*, meaning ten, which was prominently printed on the back of ten-dollar notes issued by a New Orleans bank before the Civil War. According to the latter theory, the banknotes were issued in prosperous times and circulated so freely that Louisiana and then all the southern states became known as *the land of Dixies*, the association between good times, money and the South making *Dixieland* a favorite expression of Southerners. But this demands as much stretching as any other theory, leaving some unanswered questions as well (how did *Dixes* become *Dixies?*), and such eminent word detectives as Eric Partridge and Dr. Percy Scholes support the Mr. Dixie derivation, noting that the South was often called *Dixie's Land*. At any rate, there can be no doubt that minstrel and songwriter Daniel D. Emmett popularized the word with his "Away Down South in Dixie" (1859), later adopted as the favorite marching song of the Confederacy. And Emmett composed "Dixie" on his violin "while looking out on the cold dreary streets of New York City and wishing he were in Dixie. . . ." (See also *Mason-Dixon Line*.)

Doberman Pinscher Louis Dobermann, a German breeder of Apolda in Thuringia probably helped develop the ferocious, medium-sized guard dog we know as the *Doberman pinscher*. The *Dobermans* were originally bred from *pinscher* hunting dogs to be used as herders for livestock. About all that is known about the breed is that it was developed by Dobermann in about 1890, its origins before that being a mystery. The short-haired fearless dog is generally black or rust in color, proud of bearing, and the male stands twenty-four to twenty-seven inches, weighing sixty to seventy-five pounds. *Dobermans* are used extensively by the military and as guards for department stores and other commercial establishments. Their ferocity is fabled and there are tales of them holding onto a gunman's arm after being shot to death. There have been several cases reported of poorly trained *Dobermans* turning on and killing their owners.

Doctrinaire This word for a pedantic theorist is taken from the nickname of Pierre Paul Royer-Collard (1763–1845), whose political party, in turn named the "Doctrinaires" in his honor, made it their business "to preach a doctrine and an orthodoxy." Royer-Collard's party arose in France in 1815 after the second restoration of Louis XVIII. Moderate royalists, he and his colleagues desired a king who would govern liberally, accepting the results of the French Revolution, and were noted for the rigidity of their arguments. Unattuned to political realities, the "Doctrinaires" were destroyed by a reactionary Charles X in 1830. Before being applied as a nickname to Royer-Collard the word had been the popular name for a religious order founded in 1592. Today *doctrinaire* is used contemptuously to describe an inflexible theorist as distinguished from one who tries to accomplish something within the existing political system.

Doily His first name is unknown and his surname may have been Doily, Doiley, Doyley, or Doyly, but it is probable that a London linen draper sold and perhaps invented the first *doily* napkins. Eustace Budgell, a cousin of British essayist Joseph Addison, uses the former spelling in the January 24, 1712 number of *The Spectator*, noting, "The famous Doily is still fresh in everyone's memory, who raised a Fortune by finding out Materials for such Stuffs as might at once be cheap and genteel . . . (a) frugal method of gratifying our pride. . . ." But Dryden mentions "*doyley* petticoats" and Steele writes of his "*doiley* suit." At any rate, in his shop on the Strand, some "hungry and ingenious" man with a similarly spelled name, possibly a French refugee, sold both a popular, lightweight woolen fabric called *Doily cloth* for summer clothing (now obsolete) and a fringed, ornamental lace table napkin originally intended for use when serving desserts. These embroidered or crocheted cloths were first known as *Doily napkins*, then *doilies*, and were eventually used as decorative mats to protect furniture surfaces from scratches made by glasses or bowls. Mr. Doily is also briefly noted in history as a great hunter of natural curiosities, such as the pair of old "buffalo" horns he displayed in his shop. It is possible that he was one of two brothers.

Everyone seems eager to accept the Mr. Doily origin for *doily*, but one courageous researcher points out that a certain d'Oily family, years before, was presented the manor of Fish Hill for giving the king "a tablecloth of three shillings in price."

Dollar "The almighty dollar," despite the sarcastic intent of Washington Irving's 1836 phrase, seemingly can at least be traced to a saint. Three Saint Joachims vie for the title, but the most likely one is the canonized St. Joachim, the father of the Blessed Virgin, for whom the small mining town Sankt (Saint) Joachimsthal in what was once Bohemia had been named. It happened that the town and valley, or *thal*, belonged to a vast estate owned by the Counts of Schlick, who in 1519 began minting their own one-ounce coins (equivalent to a gold gulden) from a rich silver mine on their property. These coins, with a picture of St. Joachim on the face, were at first called *Joachimsthalers* (of the valley of Joachim). But the cumbersome name was soon shortened to *thalers*, this pronounced *dahlers* in Northern German dialect and *dalers* in both Dutch and Danish.

The popular *thaler*, a standard coin, became the German monetary unit, which it remained, in fact, until replaced by the mark in 1873. The name eventually got to England as *daller*, and by the end of the seventeenth century *dollar* was the accepted form. By this time the *dollar's* origins were forgotten and the English thought it meant any foreign coin, applying the word to the much-used Spanish *pesos duros*, or "pieces of eight," so called because they were worth eight *reales* and had large figure 8s on

the faces. These *pesos* or *dollars* were familiar in America by the time of the Revolution and even before the newly formed United States adopted the French decimal monetary system, in 1785, it had been "resolved that the money unit of the U.S.A. be one *dollar* (Spanish)"—a complete break with England. The first American *dollars* were coined in 1792, provisions made for a *silver dollar*, smaller silver coins, and $2.50, $5 and $10 gold coins. It was at this time that the *dollar* became a monetary unit rather than a small silver coin. Values would change in later years— "greenback" *dollars* as we know them today would be first used during the Civil War, the United States would go on the gold standard—and few would remember the *dollar's* origins in silver and saints.

As for $—the *dollar sign*—it probably didn't derive from the figure 8 on the Spanish "pieces of eight"—the usual explanation—most likely being modified from the seemingly twisted Pillars of Hercules stamped with a scroll around them, or other old Spanish and Mexican *pesos*. The $ may, however, result from a combination of the two symbols, or be a corruption of the Spanish *Ps*, the contraction for *peso*. Which all goes to prove that money can have its roots in saintliness, heroism and a number of admirable qualities.

Dom Pérignon The man who put the bubbles in champagne and after whom *Moët et Chandon* named its most famous vintage some years ago. Dom Pierre Pérignon (1638–1715) was a blind man who renounced the world when only fifteen and joined the Benedictine order. Cellarmaster of the monastery near Épernay, France, his fantastic sense of taste and smell enabled him to experiment in improving the wines he attended. Dom Perignon eventually found that corks tightly drawn in his bottles would not be forced out like rags and yet would retain naturally expanding gasses, allowing for the so-called second fermentation in the bottle that is essential for any true sparkling champagne. The story is unproved, but it certainly rates a toast, if only as an excuse for another glass.

Champagne is strictly only sparkling

wine produced from grapes grown in the ancient French province of Champagne as defined by French law; it must be fermented in the bottle, not in huge pressure tanks, and varies from *brut*, the driest, to *doux* champagnes with up to 4 percent sugar content. "The wine of wines," "the wine of love," "the wine of gods," "the devil's wine," is the most celebrated of all festive drinks. Beauties have bathed in it and drunk it from slippers; Madame Pompadour called it "the only wine that leaves a woman beautiful after drinking it," and today Marlene Dietrich has a clause in her movie contract giving her the right to unlimited bubbly at any time she so desires. Once Confederate General Beauregard, to celebrate the first Battle of Bull Run, gave a party where champagne was piped into the fountain in his courtyard and flowed all night. As for the champion champagne drinker of all time, he appears to be a Monsieur Willy Jourdan, who drank over forty thousand bottles in his ninety-four years—better than a bottle a day from the time he was weaned. (See also *Benedictine*; *Chartreuse*.)

Don Juan Of the names most frequently applied to libertines and lovers—*Casanova*, *Don Juan*, *Cyrano*, *Valentino*, *Romeo* and *Lothario*—only the last is completely fictional. *Don Juan*, though immortalized in Byron's incomplete cantos, Mozart's *Don Giovanni*, and the myths and literature of many countries, is supposedly based on the fourteenth-century Spanish nobleman Don Juan Tenorio. That this original Don Juan had 2,594 mistresses, according to the valet's figures in Mozart's opera, is doubtful if not impossible, but the aristocratic libertine's conquests were legion. His last was the daughter of Seville's commandant. While attempting to ravish young Doña Anna, the legendary lover was surprised by her father, whom he dispatched in a duel. But local Franciscan monks decided that this was one debauchery too many and lured Don Juan to their monastery, where he was killed with his boots on. The monks, to conceal their crime, claimed that he had been carried off to hell by a statue of the commandant on the grounds and thus the legend of *Don Juan* had its basis in fact. Another version of the story, however, says that Don Juan Tenorio mockingly invited the commandant's tombstone statue to a feast he had prepared honoring his own victory, whereupon the statue dragged him down to hell. The first dramatization of the story was *El Burlador de Sevilla* (*The Deceiver of Seville*), by Tirso de Molina, the pseudonym of Gabriel Telley (c. 1571–1648). Since then Don Juan has inspired many pens of authors, including Molière, Corneille, Mérimée, Dumas père, Balzac, de Musset, Flaubert, Rostand, Shaw, and even von Sacher-Masoch (see *Masochism*). The result has often been a Don Juan bearing little resemblance to Commandant Ulloa's murderer. Zorrilla's *Don Juan Tenorio* is usually performed in major Spanish cities during the first week of November, and is regarded as a national work, despite its debt to Dumas. Scholars have pointed out that similar stories are the subject of myths in many countries and that the Spanish version even contains elements of the French myth of Robert the Devil. In other words, *Don Juan* was always a universal type, as he is today.

Donner Party, Donner Pass, Donner Lake The scene of one of the most gruesome tragedies in western history is named for the two Donner families who were part of a California-bound wagon train of emigrants that set out across the plains from Illinois in 1846. The *Donner Party*, beset by great hardships, paused to recoup their strength at what is now *Donner Lake* in eastern California's Sierra Nevada mountains, only to be trapped by early snows that October. All passes were blocked deep with snow and every attempt to get out failed. Forty of the eighty-seven members of the party, which included thirty-nine children, starved to death during the winter, and the survivors, driven mad by hunger, resorted to cannibalism before expeditions from the Sacramento Valley rescued them in April. The *Donner Party*'s gruesome yet heroic adventures have figured in much native literature. California's *Donner State Historic Monument* commemorates the event, the *Donner Pass* today traversed by U.S. Highway 40.

Don't Hurry, Hopkins A Mr. Hopkins, late of Kentucky, once returned a promissory note to a creditor along with instructions that "The said Hopkins is not to be hurried in paying the above." Since that day in the middle of the last century, it is claimed, said Hopkins has been remembered by the admonition *Don't hurry, Hopkins,* an ironic reproof to deadbeats late in paying their bills or persons slow in anything else. But the phrase was used in England almost a century before with just the opposite humorous meaning, implying "don't be too hasty." In this sense it derived from a Mr. Hopkins, or Hopkin, "that came to jail over night, and was hanged the next morning."

Dorothy Perkins' Rose Ranking with Peace and Crimson Glory as the best known of American roses, the *Dorothy Perkins* is a pink rambler introduced by the famous Jackson & Perkins Nursery of Newark, N.Y., in 1901. It is a small, cluster-flowering type and though ramblers have bowed in popularity to larger-flowered varieties, remains a sentimental favorite much mentioned in literature. The rose was named for the wife of the firm's co-owner.

D'Orsay Pump, Dossy, Quai D'Orsay The last of the dandies, Count d'Orsay, Alfred Guillaume Gabriel (1801–52), designed the innovative *D'Orsay pump* that became the model for women's footwear. Like his contemporary Beau Brummel, d'Orsay, the son of a distinguished French general, was an *arbiter elegantarium* of English society, and the slang term *dossy,* for elegant or smart, may also derive from his name. The man's shoe he devised in 1838 fit more snugly than any pump before it, due to its lowcut sides and V-shaped top, and was soon adopted by women. D'Orsay, an ex-French soldier who came to London in 1821, won fame as a painter, sculptor, diarist and wit, being "the most perfect gentleman of his day." An exceptionally handsome man of great taste and talent, he counted fencing, riding, shooting and even boxing among his many interests. His strange relationship with the Earl and Countess of Blessington—a ménage peculiar enough to be mentioned frequently in Lord Byron's correspondence—led to his marriage to their fifteen-year-old daughter Harriet. While he and his young wife almost immediately separated, d'Orsay remained part of the fashionable Blessington literary and artistic circle until he went bankrupt in 1849. Then, again like Brummel before him, this supreme dandy had to flee to France to escape his creditors. He died in relative poverty, ironically only a few days after he had been appointed state director of fine arts by Louis Napoleon, whom he had befriended in London before the French *coup d'état.* Named for d'Orsay's famous father is the *Quai d'Orsay*—that quay along the south bank of the Seine in Paris which has become synonymous for the French Foreign Office, Department of Foreign Affairs and other government offices located there. (See also *Beau Brummel; Beau Fielding; Downing Street.*)

Doubting Thomas History's first *doubting Thomas* was a saint, one of the twelve apostles. His story is found in *John* 20:24–29. St. Thomas, called the Twin, the meaning of his name in Aramaic, doubted the resurrection of Christ: *"Now Thomas, one of the twelve . . . was not with them when Jesus came. So the other disciples told him, 'We have seen the Lord.' But he said to them, 'Unless I see in his hands the print of the nails, and place my fingers in the mark of the nails, and place my hand in his side, I will not believe.' Eight days later . . . Jesus came and stood among them, and . . . said to Thomas, 'Put your finger here, and see my hands; and put out your hand, and place it in my side; do not be faithless, but believing.' Thomas answered him, 'My Lord and my God!' Jesus said to him, 'Have you believed because you have seen me? Blessed are those who have not seen and yet believe.'"* Thomas also questions or doubts Christ in an earlier passage, *John* 14:5. He figures in a number of legends. Later, when he was no longer a doubter, tradition says that he went on a mission to India. There a king gave him a large sum to build a magnificent palace and he spent it on food for the poor, "erecting a superb palace in heaven." He thus became the patron saint of masons and architects.

Douglas Fir Only the giant sequoias and redwoods of California among North

American trees exceed the *Douglas fir* in height and massiveness. The coniferous evergreens grow to heights of three hundred feet and twelve feet in diameter, yielding more lumber than any other American species. The *Douglas fir* or *Douglas spruce*, as it is sometimes called, was named for its discoverer David Douglas (1798–1834), who came here from Scotland in 1823 to study American plants and collect specimens for the Royal Horticultural Society. The former gardener at Glasgow's botanical gardens collected more than two hundred plants and seeds then unknown in Europe. His eleven-year journal became historically valuable because he was one of the first travelers in the Pacific northwest. The *Douglas fir*, which he first observed in 1825, is botanically of the pine family, and yields a hard strong wood of great commercial importance, its thick bark used in tanning. Douglas died one of the strangest of deaths; in 1834 he extended his travels to the Hawaiian Islands where he was killed by a wild bull. (See also *Sequoia*.)

Downing Street, Downing College, A George Downing Like its French counterpart, the Quai d'Orsay, England's 10 *Downing Street* is another famous diplomatic address deriving from a family name. *Downing Street* is used figuratively to mean the British foreign office or government in power, No. 10 Downing Street having been the official residence of almost all British prime ministers since George II gave the house to Sir Robert Walpole for that purpose in 1735. The street in London, which also contains the British foreign and colonial offices, is named for soldier and diplomat Sir George Downing (c. 1624–84). Downing, a nephew of Massachusetts' governor John Winthrop, was graduated in the first class at Harvard, but returned to England where he performed the difficult trick of serving under both Cromwell and then Charles II. A talented but selfish man, his character is said to have been "marked by treachery, servitude, and ingratitude." In his own time *a George Downing* was proverbial for a false man who betrayed his trust. *Downing College,* Cambridge, derived its name later from his generous grandson, but *Downing*

Street was on the king's property and named for the statesman during Charles II's reign. The facade of No. 10 Downing is the same as it was in 1735. Who's at No. 11? The Chancellor of the Exchequer. The government whip's office is at No. 12. (See also *d'Orsay Pump*.)

Draconian, Draconic "The Draconian Code is written in blood," one Greek orator declared, and Plutarch observed that under Draco's code "for nearly all crimes there is the penalty of death." They referred to the severe laws —now largely lost—codified and promulgated by the Athenian legislator Draco about 621 B.C. Draco was the first to collect Athens' unwritten laws, but his assignment wasn't to modify them and he is therefore not really responsible for their proverbial harshness. The written *Draconian Code* proved valuable because it substituted public justice for vendettas and made it impossible for magistrates to side openly with the nobility. Its severity may have been exaggerated by future generations. Draco's laws, except for those dealing with homicide, were abolished or ameliorated by the wise *Solon* thirty years later, but they were so harsh or thought to be so harsh, that the word *Draconian* remains a synonym for "severe" and *Draconian laws* still means any code of laws or set of rules calling for ironhanded punishment of their violators.

Dr. Fell, Fell Types

I do not love thee, Dr. Fell,
The reason why I cannot tell;
But this alone I know full well,
I do not love thee, Dr. Fell.

Dr. John Fell's classes at Oxford must have been something to see. The English divine (1625–1686) was quite a permissive teacher for his day, initiating many educational reforms and even allowing classroom debates, which often ended in fistfights. Fell, dean of Christ Church, Oxford, and bishop of Oxford, is also noted for the *Fell types* he collected for the university press and for the extensive building program he began at the university. Yet his name is used to describe someone disliked for no apparent reason. He owes his unjust fate to Thomas Brown (1663–1704), once his student at Christ Church and later an author and translator. Dean Fell had threatened to expel Brown for some offense if he could not translate a couplet of Martial. The resulting jingle above bore little resemblance to the thirty-third epigram, but Dr. Fell, to his credit, good-naturedly accepted the paraphrase. As for Tom Brown, he never wrote anything else that was remembered.

Dr. Livingstone, I Presume! The phrase is still used in a humorous sense, as it was several generations ago. It recalls, of course, the very British greeting of journalist Sir Henry Morton Stanley when after a long, arduous journey—only 700 miles in 236 days—he found the ailing Scottish missionary-explorer David Livingstone on the island of Ujiji in the heart of Africa. The star reporter had completed one of the greatest manhunts of all time. Deserted by his bearers, plagued by disease and warring tribes, he was probably too tired and overwhelmed to think of anything else to say. Stanley (1841–1904) had been sent to Africa by the New York *Herald* to locate the famous explorer, Livingstone, feared dead or swallowed up by the Dark Continent. Born John Rowlands in Denbigh, Wales, Stanley assumed the name of his adoptive father when he emigrated to America as a youth. He later became a noted explorer in his own right. Dr. Livingstone died, aged sixty, a year after the reporter left him in 1873. His body was shipped back to England and buried in Westminster Abbey. Should you happen by chance to jet to Ujiji next weekend, you can visit the house where Livingstone lived. You'll know it by the brass spikes adorning the ornately carved door, which are there to discourage not tourists but inquisitive elephants.

Drummond Light Anyone in the limelight is—or was—in the *Drummond light*. Thomas Drummond (1797–1840) invented this first limelight, utilizing calcium oxide, or lime, which had been isolated by Sir Humphry Davy in 1808 and gives off an intense white light when heated. Royal Engineer Drummond, a Scottish inventor, devised his light as an aid in murky weather while assisting in a land survey of Great Britain, and later adopted it for use in lighthouses. He became secretary of state for Ireland in 1835, noted as an able administrator who told absentee Irish landlords that "property has its duties as well as its rights." The incandescent *Drummond light* wasn't perfected as a spotlight for the stage until after his death. It has long been replaced by arc and kleig lights, but the phrase *in the limelight* still survives. (See also *Kleig Lights*.)

Drury Lane Theatre This long-famous street and theater in London get their name from the Drury House, which once stood just south of the present lane. The house was built by English statesman and soldier Sir William Drury (1527–1579) during the reign of Henry VIII. There have been four Drury Lane theaters, including the present, the first originally a cockpit that was converted into a theater under James I. All of the great English actors, from Booth and Garrick on, have performed at one or another *Drury Lane*.

Du Barry, A Among famous French mistresses only La Pompadour is better known than the Comtesse Du Barry, Marie Jeanne Bécu. Born the illegitimate daughter of a tax collector, Marie became, while still in her teens, a Parisian courtesan and the lover of Jean Du Barry, who conveniently married her off to his brother. Comte Du Barry, a gambler, used his mistress as bait for dupes in his various operations and in 1769 succeeded in installing the seductive beauty as Louis XV's official mistress. Madame Du Barry wasn't as ambitious as the king's first mistress, Mme Pompadour, but until his death five years later exercised great control over Louis, dictating many of his decisions and preferences. The king built her a great mansion at Luciennes, presented her with much jewelry, and even awarded her the *Cordon Bleu* for her culinary accomplishments. Du Barry spent her life, aside from minor political intrigues, in buying clothes, furnishing her apartments, planning great parties and making herself attractive for her royal lover. After he died, however, she was forced to retire on a pension, and when the French Revolution came she found it necessary to journey to England to sell her jewels. On her return the Revolutionary Tribunal accused her of conspiracy with the British and condemned her to death. She was guillotined in 1793, only forty-seven when her pretty head dropped in the basket. (See also *Fontange; Maintenon; Pompadour*.)

Dukes Both favored derivations indicate that the slang term *dukes*, for fists, has something to do with the duke of York (1763–1820). Frederick Augustus, the second son of England's George III, was duke of York and Albany, as well as earl of Ulster, yet stood little chance of becoming king. As commander-in-chief of the army he experienced disaster after disaster in the field; nevertheless he remained popular among his subjects. Frederick had once dueled with the future duke of Richmond on the Wimbledon Common, which associated his name with fighting, and being an ardent sportsman, he was often seen at the racetrack and prize ring. Perhaps this led boxers to nickname their fists "Dukes of York," the phrase finally shortened to *dukes*. Or else "Duke of Yorks," Cockney riming slang for "forks," was associated with fingers, then hands, and finally fists or *dukes*—with the duke of York somewhere in mind.

Another ingenious explanation has it that noses were called *Dukes* because the duke of Wellington's nose was big—fists therefore dubbed *Duke busters*, which finally became *dukes*. As for Frederick Augustus, he ended his career in disgrace. In 1809 he was relieved of his command and tried before the House of Commons for taking bribes. It developed that his mistress had been taking the bribes with his permission, but that he had received no money himself. Though he was acquitted and reappointed commander in chief, he had to pension off Mary Ann Clarke, fearing that she would publish his letters. (For another eponymous Duke of York see *New York*.)

Dun "Send Dun after him," creditors would say when a person was slow to pay his debts. According to the traditional story, they referred to Joe Dun, a London bailiff during the reign of Henry VIII, who had proved himself particularly efficient in collecting from defaulting debtors. Other authorities trace *dun* to various words meaning noise, din, or thundering noise, sometimes connecting this with the drum that town criers pounded when they shouted out the names of debtors. The drum theory sounds good. As anyone who has been *dunned* knows, *dunning* is not so much characterized by noise, or thundering noise, as it is by *repetitive* noise.

Duncan Phyfe Style Duncan Phyfe's famous furniture workshop stood on the site of the present Hudson Terminal building in New York City. The Scottish-born master craftsman had come to New York in 1783 at the age of fifteen, apprenticed himself to an Albany cabinet-maker, and moved to Manhattan nine years later, opening his own shop and changing his name from Fife to Phyfe. Soon he opened the store on Fulton Street (then Partitution Street) that became famous the world over. Duncan Phyfe and Sons employed more than one hundred artisans at its height of popularity, but the master craftsman's best work was done in the early period up until 1820, when he evolved his own style, using Sheraton, Hepplewhite and the Adam brothers as models. This work has become known as the *Duncan Phyfe style*, characterized by excellent proportions, graceful, curving lines and beautifully carved ornamentation. Phyfe's craftsmanship was so well known that the unlettered West Indian natives who cut trees for his mahogany chairs and tables learned to call particularly fine logs *Duncan Phyfe logs* and mark them "D.P." to be put aside for his order. Phyfe is also responsible for many innovative furniture designs, such as extension tables. He retired in 1847 and died seven years later, eighty-six years old.

Dunce Ironically, one of the most brilliant scholars and philosophers of the Middle Ages is the source for the word *dunce*. Little is known about John Duns Scotus outside of his new theology. He was probably born in 1265, in Scotland, most likely died while still a young man, aged forty-three or so, and his middle name is presumably a place name, either from the village of Duns, Scotland, Dunse in Berwickshire, or Dunston in Northcumberland. The "Subtle Doctor," as he was called, apparently taught at Oxford and the University of Paris, but again there is no hard evidence available. Duns Scotus did found a school of philosophy that attracted numerous followers. A Franciscan, he successfully opposed the teachings of St. Thomas Aquinas and the Dominicans, challenging the harmony of faith and reason, and insisted on the doctrine of the Immaculate Conception, for which he was known as the Marian Doctor. After his death—tradition has it that he died in Cologne, buried alive—Duns Scotus remained a great influence on scholastic thought. His works were studied in all the great universities throughout Europe and his followers, called Scotists, reigned supreme. However, these same *Dunsmen* sabotaged his reputation some two hundred years later. During the Renaissance, blindly resistant to change, "the old barking curs" raged from the pulpit against the new learning, being scorned and ridiculed as hairsplitters and stupid obstructionists. *Dunsmen* became *dunses* and finally *dunces*, "blockheads incapable of learning or scholarship." Exactly the opposite of the precise learned mind of the man who started it all.

Dutch, Dutch Courage, Dutch Treat, Dutch Uncle The Dutch people have been so offended by the English language over the past three centuries that in 1934 their government ordered its officials to drop the word *Dutch* and use Netherlands instead whenever possible. But the stratagem didn't succeed in stopping the dike. *Dutch* remains what one dictionary calls "an epithet of inferiority." In both England and America a torrent of verbal abuse has descended upon the Dutch. Perhaps there is some good to be found in these Dutch pejoratives, for neither in England nor America are there relatively many Dutch around to be personally hurt by these national slurs, which may spare other groups. But the metaphors have been carried to ridiculous lengths. H. L. Mencken points out, for example, that Italian laborers were once derisively termed "Dutch daubs from Italy." It all began with the bitter hostilities between England and Holland in the seventeenth century, when the Dutch colonial empire threatened to usurp Britain's own. Two major wars were fought over this naval and trade rivalry and a flood of invective was loosed upon the Dutch that has barely subsided over the years. To complicate matters, the name *Dutchman*, from the German *Deutsch*, has been applied to Germanic peoples (i.e., the Pennsylvania Dutch), such contacts and two World Wars adding still more derogatory expressions to the list. Below is a short dictionary of abusive terms using the word. Though it runs to some one hundred expressions, surely a complete list would more than double this amount. All of these terms but a few are derogatory. If only in the subtlest way, each makes the Dutch either cheap, cowardly, stubborn, deceitful, or worse, all a far cry from the traditional picture of Hans Brinker, bright tulips and gently turning windmills:

Double-Dutch—double talk; gibberish; also an American play-language.

Dutch Act—suicide, probably referring to a supposed German morbidity, rather than a cheap Dutch way to end it all.

Dutch Anchor—something important left behind, from the story of the Dutch captain who wrecked his ship because he left the anchor home.

Dutch Auction—an auction starting off with inflated prices.

Dutch Bargain—one clinched over liquor; a one-sided bargain.

Dutch Bond—an economical brickwork bond of alternate courses of stretchers and headers.

Dutch Brig—cells on board a ship.

Dutch Build—a thickly built person.

Dutch by Injection—an Englishman living with a Dutch woman.

Dutch Cap—a prophylactic or pessary.

Dutch Cheese—cottage cheese; a baldheaded person.

Dutch Clinker—a long, narrow, hard yellowish brick made in Holland.

Dutch Clover—white clover, *Trifolium repens.*

Dutch Comfort—consolation—"Thank God it wasn't any worse."

Dutch Concert—a great uproar; everyone playing a different tune.

Dutch Courage—courage inspired by booze, the Dutch once said to be heavy drinkers. "*The Dutch their wine and all their brandy lose, / Disarmed of that from which their courage flows—*" Edmund Walles, 1665.

Dutch Cupboard—a buffet with open upper shelves.

Dutch Defense—a surrender, no defense at all.

Dutch Door—a two-section door that opens at the top or bottom.

Dutch Feast—one where the host gets drunk before his guests.

Dutch Foot—a furniture foot.

Dutch Gold—an originally Dutch alloy of copper and zinc used for cheap imitation gold leaf.

Dutch Kiss—sexually intimate kissing.

Dutch Lap—an economical shingling method.

Dutch Luck—undeserved luck.

Dutch Lunch—an individual portion of cold cuts; probably an American expression referring to the Pennsylvania Dutch.

Dutchman—a hard lump in brown sugar.

Dutchman's Breeches—the popular plant *Dicentra Cucullaria*, the flowers resembling baggy breeches; patches of blue in a stormy sky, in allusion to patches on a Dutchman's trousers, or because there is just enough blue to make a cheap pair of pants for a Dutchman.

Dutchman's Drink—the last one in the bottle.

Dutchman's Headache—drunkenness.

Dutchman's Land or Cape—illusory land on the horizon.

Dutchman's Log—a piece of wood used in an economical navigation method, the practical method itself.

Dutchman's Pipe—a climbing vine, *Aristolochia Sipho*, whose calyx resembles a tobacco pipe.

Dutch Medley—everyone playing a different tune.

Dutch Nightingale—a frog.

Dutch Oven—economical heavy kettle or brick oven.

Dutch Palate—a coarse, unrefined palate.

Dutch Pennants—untidy ropes hanging from aloft on a ship.

Dutch Pink—blood.

Dutch Praise—condemnation.

Dutch Pump—a nautical punishment.

Dutch Reckoning—pure guesswork, or a lump account that would be cheaper if itemized.

Dutch Red—a highly smoked herring.

Dutch Route—American slang for *Dutch Act* above.

Dutch Straight—a poker hand.

Dutch Treat—a meal or entertainment where each pays his own way.

Dutch Two Hundred—a bowling score of 200 made with alternate strikes and spares.

Dutch Uncle—an unsparingly frank and critical person, an Americanism probably referring to the Germans.

Dutch Wife—the pillow of an Englishman in the tropics who takes no native mistress; or a framework used in beds to support the legs.

High Dutch—high German.

His Dutch Is Up—he's angry.

I'm a Dutchman If I Do—Never! From the days when *Dutchman* was synonymous with everything false.

In Dutch—in trouble; in jail; this may refer to the early New York Dutch but probably refers to the Germans.

It's All Dutch to Me—it's all Greek to me, an American expression.

Low Dutch—low German.

My Old Dutch—my wife, but possibly from the word *duchess*.

Pennsylvania Dutch—German emigrants in Pa.; their language.

That Beats the Dutch—to beat the devil, deriving from an American song of the Revolution.

To Dutch—to harden or clean by placing in hot sand.

To Dutch—to run away, desert.

Duxelles Sauce A *duxelles* today is a purée of mushrooms and onions, the tasty sauce once made from a much more elaborate recipe. It was named for the Marquis d'Uxelles, employer of the too often ignored chef, François Pierre de la Varenne. La Varenne's *Le Cuisinier François* (1651) is a landmark of the French cuisine and his rare pastry book *Le Pastissier François* has been called the most expensive cookbook in the world. The chef is said to have been trained by those Florentine cooks brought to France by Marie de Médicis, second wife of Henry IV. It is often claimed that these Italians taught the French the art of cooking, but La Varenne's cuisine was much more delicate and imaginative than that of his masters; and if any one man can be called the founder of French cuisine he deserves the honor. La Varenne did not name the *duxelles* after his employer; this was done at a later date when it became customary to honor a man's name in a recipe. He called his creation *Champignons à l'Olivier*. The pioneering chef's cookbook was the first to index recipes alphabetically. According to one authority, "*Le Cuisinier François* seemingly at a stroke . . . altered the cookery standards which had prevailed in France and the rest of Europe . . . since medieval days."

E

Eddyism *Eddyism*, a synonym for Christian Science, honors its founder Mary Baker Eddy (1821–1910). Though she lived until nearly ninety, Mrs. Eddy was plagued all her life by illness and unhappiness. Married three times, her first marriage was ended by her husband's death and the second by divorce. A serious street accident in 1866 turned her to the Bible. The story in *Matthew* of Jesus healing the paralyzed man brought her the spiritual enlightenment she attributed to her discovery of Christian Science. "The Bible was my textbook," she once wrote. "It answered my questions as to how I was healed; but the Scriptures had to me a new meaning . . . I apprehended for the first time . . . Jesus' teaching and demonstration, and the Principle and rule of spiritual Science and metaphysical healing—in a word, Christian Science." Before this, however, Mrs. Eddy had been treated by Phinias P. Quimby, a faith healer of Portland, Me., and his influence may be reflected in her work. An indefatigable worker, she remained the leader of the movement until her death. In 1908 she established the famous international newspaper, *The Christian Science Monitor*.

Edgar The *Edgar* is a small bust of Edgar Allan Poe presented annually to the best writers of detective stories by the Mystery Writers of America. *Edgars* are awarded in several categories, such as best novel and best short story. Poe himself once won a prize for his "The Gold Bug" (1843), the code in the story developing from his interest in cryptography. Though he did invent the detective story in his "The Murders in the Rue Morgue," "The Purloined Letter," and "The Mystery of Marie Roget," the writer is best remembered for his poetry and horror tales. His story is well known —how this son of itinerant actors quar-

reled with his foster father, joined the army, and was expelled from West Point; his marriage to his thirteen-year-old cousin Virginia Clemm and her death years later in their Fordham cottage, where they were so poor that she stroked their tortoise-shell cat to keep warm; his love affairs and his alcoholism. Poe published his first book of poems, *Tamerlane and Other Poems*, anonymously at his own expense. Among his greatest stories are "The Fall of the House of Usher," "The Black Cat," "The Pit and the Pendulum," and "The Tell-Tale Heart"; his best poems include "To Helen," "Israfel," "Ulalume," and "Annabel Lee." But Poe's genius was never tangibly rewarded in his lifetime. "To coin one's brain into silver," he once wrote, "is to my thinking, the hardest job in the world." He had his best year when he edited the *Southern Literary Messenger*, for eight hundred dollars. His "The Raven" was one of the few poems recognized as a work of genius when it appeared, but this apparently did him no good, for legend has it that it was a year and a half before he pried loose his ten dollars from the New York *Mirror*. After his wife's death, Poe claimed that he lived with only "intervals of horrible sanity." He died at forty, perhaps addicted to drugs, spent his last days stumbling into Baltimore polling places and casting ballots for drinks. "Three-fifths genius and two-fifths sheer fudge," was Lowell's facile opinion of Poe, but Yeats declared him "always and for all lands a great lyric poet."

Edison, Edison Effect When Thomas Alva Edison died in 1931, aged eighty-four, the New York *Times* devoted four and a half full pages to his obituary, calling him the greatest benefactor of humanity in modern times. His name is a synonym for inventor and his over thirteen hundred United States and foreign patents establish him as probably the world's greatest genius in the practical application of scientific principles. Born in Milan, O., but reared in Port Huron, Mich., Edison was interested in science since childhood, so curious, in fact, that he once fed another boy a large dose of Seidlitz powders to see if the gas generated would enable him to fly. He had less than three months of formal schooling, was educated by his schoolteacher mother, and at twelve became a newspaper boy on the Grand Trunk Railway, his hearing having been impaired at that time by a cuff on the ear from a railroad conductor. Edison's first successful invention was an improved stock ticker, which he proceeded to manufacture. He then devoted his full time to the "invention business." The Wizard of Menlo Park—where one of his first shops was located—soon had a new laboratory in West Orange, N.J., where he could "build anything from a lady's watch to a locomotive." A list of only his most noted inventions is still almost unbelievable. These included assisting in the invention of the typewriter; invention of the carbon telephone transmitter; the first commercially practical electric light; an entire complex system, complete with many inventions, for the distribution of electricity for light and power, which resulted in the first central electric light power plant in the world in New York City; an electric automobile; the first full-sized electric motor; electric railway signals; station-to-station wireless telegraphy; an efficient alkaline storage battery; the magnetic ore separator; paraffin paper; an improved Portland cement; the dictaphone; a mimeograph machine; the phonograph; the fluoroscope; and a motion picture machine called the kinetoscope, from which developed the modern motion picture. Many of his inventions spawned giant modern industries—the electric light, his telephone transmitter, the phonograph and the motion picture camera being only four such discoveries. Ironically, the *Edison effect*, one of the few discoveries named for him, was not exploited by the inventor. It is the principle of the radio vacuum tube that made radio and television possible. The *Edison base* of light sockets also bears the immortal inventor's name, as does a town in central New Jersey. One of his five children, Charles Edison, served as that state's governor.

Eggs Benedict Oscar of the Waldorf once confirmed the story that *Eggs Benedict* were invented by a man suffering from a hangover. It seems that early one morning in 1894, Samuel Benedict, a prominent New York socialite, tread softly into the old Waldorf-Astoria Hotel after a night of partying—his head hurt that much. But he had what he thought was the perfect cure for his splitting headache—a breakfast of poached eggs served on buttered toast and topped with bacon and hollandaise sauce. Oscar, the maître d'hôtel, thought this combination excellent, but substituted an English muffin for the toast and ham for the bacon, naming the dish in Benedict's honor. Whether the cure worked or not isn't recorded, and another version of the tale claims that the dish was created between Oscar and New Yorker Mrs. Le Grand Benedict.

Eiffel Tower At the time it was erected in the Champ-de-Mars for the Paris Universal Exposition of 1889, the *Eiffel Tower*, standing 984.25 feet high, ranked as the world's tallest structure. The structual iron tower had been designed by French engineer Alexandre Gustave Eiffel (1832–1923), the earliest and foremost builder of iron structures in France and a pioneer in the science of aerodynamics with his *The Resistance of Air* (1913). The tower, with three platforms at different heights reached by stairs and elevators, has since become as much a symbol of France as the fleur-de-lis. The interior structure of the Statue of Liberty, presented to the United States by France in 1884, and a symbol of America, was also designed by Eiffel, although the statue itself was created by F. A. Bartholdi. The Chrysler Building ended the *Eiffel Tower's* reign as the world's tallest structure in 1929. It was topped by the Empire State Building in 1931, and today, aside from several television towers, the title is held by New York's World Trade Center—110 stories and 1,353 feet high.

Einstein, Einsteinium Albert Einstein (1879–1955) was unquestionably one of the greatest thinkers of all time, and *an Einstein* is still widely used as a synonym for a genius. *Einsteinium*, a man-made radioactive element, was named for the physicist in 1953 by its American discoverer Albert Ghiorso, who formed it in the laboratory after it had been detected among the debris of the first H-Bomb explosion the year before. Einstein's genius wasn't apparent in his early years. Born in Ulm, Germany, he had been regarded as a dullard and even "slow, perhaps retarded" in his first years at school there. The same opinion may have been shared by his parents, for he did not learn to walk until a relatively late age, nor begin to talk until he was past three. The backward boy, always something of a loner and mystic, developed an interest in mathematics in his youth, however, and slowly began to assert himself. Einstein was graduated from the Polytechnic Institute of Zurich and took employment with the Swiss Patent Office, devoting all his spare time to pure science. In 1905, at twenty-six, his genius suddenly, inexplicably, burst into full bloom with three discoveries in theoretical physics that included his revolutionary theory of relativity, which reshaped the modern world. He was awarded the Nobel Prize in 1921 —but not specifically for his theory, which few understood at the time. Stripped of his German citizenship by the Nazis in 1934 because of his Jewish origin, Einstein became an American citizen, appointed as a member of the Institute for Advanced Study at Princeton, N.J. Ironically, his famous $E = mc^2$ formula, energy equals mass times the square of the speed of light, came to be practically applied in the first atomic bomb. For, though his letter to President Roosevelt led to this country's development of the weapon, Einstein had been a lifelong humanitarian and pacifist, only fears of Nazi world dominion causing him to write his appeal. He protested the bombing of Hiroshima and in his remaining years crusaded for the abolition of atomic weapons. It is probable that no other scientist, not even Copernicus, or Newton, or Darwin, so profoundly revolutionized scientific thought.

Eisenhower Jacket One of the most popular presidents in American history, Dwight David Eisenhower (1890–1969) was elected to a second term in office in 1956 by the largest vote ever given to a presidential candidate. Graduated from West Point in 1915, the Texas-born soldier later became General Douglas MacArthur's aide in the Philippines. "General Ike," or "Ike," as he was known to G.I.s, was appointed commander of all Allied armies in World War II, noted for his success as both a strategist and a diplomat who fashioned his command into a smoothly functioning machine. At this time the *Eisenhower jacket*, a waist-length woolen jacket once worn as part of the service uniform, was named in his honor. Eisenhower probably could have been elected to a third term as president, but he was the first president to be limited to two terms by the 22nd Constitutional Amendment. After leaving the presidency, he retired to his Gettysburg farm to write his memoirs. Eisenhower's great decency manifested itself in everything he did. Though he was criticized as being too moderate and prosaic, his ideas were often liberal, progressive ones. When Senator McCarthy charged that the U.S. Information Agency had communist books in its European libraries, for example, Eisenhower counseled students at Dartmouth: "Don't join the bookburners. . . . Don't be afraid to go to the library and read every book."

Elberta Peach The most widely sold of American peaches was probably imported from Shanghai in 1850, but more than one source records a story that at least shows more imagination. According to this tale, Samuel Rumph of Marshallville, Ga., supposedly received peach-tree buddings from a friend in Delaware, planted them, and eventually harvested a good crop. His wife Elberta accidentally dropped a few pits from these peaches into her sewing basket and when their grandson wanted to start an orchard ten years later, she dug them out and asked her husband to plant them. By 1870 trees from the pits were flourishing, and by an accidental cross-pollination a new golden variety resulted, which Samuel named for his spouse. *Elbertas*, anyway, have been celebrated since the middle nineteenth century, although the great pomologist U. P. Hedrick considered them "scarcely edible by those who know good peaches." They are good shippers, however, and attractive, which is why 90 percent of store peaches are *Elbertas*.

Eleanor Blue Like *Alice blue*, this color is named for a Roosevelt, in this case Anna Eleanor Roosevelt (1884–1962), whose dresses popularized the dark blue shade while she was "first lady of the world." Eleanor Roosevelt married her distant cousin, Franklin Delano Roosevelt, in 1905, two weeks after her uncle, Theodore Roosevelt, had been inaugurated as president. When F.D.R. was stricken with polio, she encouraged him to overcome his handicap and return to politics. He became the only man ever to be elected to the presidency four times, breaking the two-term tradition, and from 1933 to 1945, when he died, Eleanor was by far the most active first lady in American history. Among many activities, she wrote the syndicated newspaper column "My Day" and traveled extensively abroad on good-will missions. Outspoken on all important issues, she remained active even after her husband's death, serving as a delegate to the U.N. general assembly and chairman of the U.N. Commission on Human Rights. Orphaned at ten and starved for love and affection in her childhood, Mrs. Roosevelt nevertheless became one of the most compassionate human beings of modern times, always an enemy of prejudice and poverty despite her aristocratic origins. Recent biographies have revealed that the Roosevelts' personal life wasn't a happy one but, if this is the case, it further emphasizes the woman's great courage. *Eleanor and Franklin*, a new biography by Joseph P. Lash, is an excellent account of F.D.R. and his wife, especially of Eleanor Roosevelt's adaptation to responsibility.

Elizabethan Age The era when Queen Elizabeth of England reigned (1558–1603) was a vital one in which great accomplishments were achieved in literature, poetry, drama, architecture, exploration, commerce and many other areas. Elizabethan is used as an adjective to both describe the Elizabethan spirit—adventurous, vivid, eloquent, artistically brilliant, and generous, among numerous admirable qualities—and to describe its counterparts today. Shakespeare, Edmund Spenser, Francis Bacon, Francis Drake and Walter Raleigh were only a few of the giant figures produced in the forty-five-year period that Elizabeth ruled. Though "Good Queen Bess" was certainly vain, capricious and jealous—she had put to death, for example, her cousin Mary Queen of Scots, and her favorite, the Earl of Essex—her personal courage and sense of responsibility made the last of the Tudors one of England's greatest rulers and probably the greatest queen in history. The only daughter of Henry VIII and his second wife Anne Boleyn, beheaded for alleged adultery, Elizabeth was an intelligent, well-educated woman whose court became the center of England's cultural life as it had never been before and has never been since. The Virgin Queen's reign would not be surpassed. "There will never be a queen," she once told parliament, "sit in my seat with more zeal to my country and care to my subjects. And though you have had and may have princes more mighty and wise sitting in this seat, yet you never had or shall have any that will be more careful and loving." She died in 1603, having lived a Biblical three score and ten.

Elmer, Warren Many given names derive from the last names of famous persons. *Elmer*, which has come upon bad times recently, is the most surprising of them. *Elmer* was even more popular than Washington as a given name during the Revolution. Its origins have long been forgotten by most, but *Elmer* originally honored the brothers Ebenezer and Jonathan Elmer, Revolutionary War patriots from New Jersey—"pamphleteers, organizers of Revolutionary militia, surgeons and officers in command of troops throughout the Revolution, members of Congress and fierce debators of a hundred stirring issues of their times." Furthermore, said the same New York *Herald Tribune* editorial on January 18, 1935: "The name Elmer . . . has such an honorable geneology that it is time for America's countless Elmers to know it and stand up for it."

Another little-known name deriving

from a patronym is *Warren*, for Joseph Warren, one of the first heroes of the Revolution. Familiar ones are legion, ranging from *Washingtons* to the *Delanos* named for Franklin Delano Roosevelt (whose given name derives from Benjamin Franklin), and the *Nixons* that are doubtless being named today. (See also *Howard*.)

Empress Eugénie Hat A number of fashions that held sway in the nineteenth century commemorate the French Empress Eugénie, wife of Napoleon III. This beautiful, elegant and charming woman, the undisputed leader of French fashion which led the world then as now, was especially celebrated for her smart hats. She sometimes wore five different specimens in a day, one of her favorites, a small model with the brim turned up on the side and often decorated with ostrich plumes, named the *Empress Eugénie* in her honor. Born Eugénie Marie de Montijo de Guzmān, the empress was the daughter of a Spanish grandee and a Scottish noblewoman. Prince Louis Napoleon at first offered to make her his mistress, but she intrigued to become his wife and prevailed. Their marriage was celebrated in 1853 at Notre Dame. "The Spanish Woman" seemed too conservative in politics to be popular with the French at the time, but strongly influenced Napoleon, often efficiently governing the Empire as regent in his absence. When the Second Empire fell in 1871, she fled to England with her husband, where she died almost half a century later in 1920, ninety-four years old and a legend in her time.

English The word *english*—roughly spin on a ball in billiards or baseball—doesn't stem from any derogatory American reference to the affectedness or tricky ways of Englishmen, as has often been proposed. It was probably suggested by *body English*, the way the body gestures when words cannot be found to express an action. The English call *english* "side." A number of words are prefaced by the adjective *English*, including *English ivy*, *English muffin*, *English saddle*, *English sparrow*, *English type*, and *English walnut*. The English language itself has replaced French as the world's second language. Native to some 270 million people, it is used as an official language in over thirty other nations, is the common language of many crafts, trades, and sciences, and more educated persons speak it than any other tongue.

Epicure, Epicurean "The fountain and root of every good is the pleasure of the stomach," is a quotation attributed to Epicures by the Greek writer Athenaeus five centuries after the philosopher's death. Nothing could be further from the spirit of Epicures. The Greek philosopher (341–270 B.C.) did not teach that mere sensual pleasure is man's reason for being. He argued, rather, that while pleasure constitutes the happiness of life, pleasure means peace of mind and freedom from want and pain, which can be achieved only through noble thoughts, self-control, and moderation. Though this generous, brave man regarded virtue as having no value in itself, the real harm in his philosophy lay in the fact that it was an escapist one—permitting, for example, no marriage, children, or participation in public life. Later students of his garden school in Athens—which lasted over two hundred years—distorted his teachings completely, using them as an excuse for selfish hedonism and heedless indulgence. Seizing upon his idea of pleasure, they magnified it so that an epicure became one entirely devoted to gluttony, debauchery, and every wanton sensual pleasure imaginable. It took centuries before the word acquired its present meaning of gourmet or connoisseur, one with refined tastes and knowledge of food and drink, and even today's *epicure* is still far removed from the simple serene philosophy of Epicures. "But while every pleasure is in itself good," the sage once wrote, "not all pleasures are to be chosen, since certain pleasures are produced by means which entail annoyances many times greater. . . . Moreover . . . it is not possible to live pleasantly without living wisely and well and righteously."

Erlenmeyer Flask Emil Erlenmeyer put his name in mothballs for posterity when he devised the first formula for naphthalene, used in making them. The German organic chemist also invented the cone-shaped, flat-bottomed *Erlenmeyer flask* made from thin glass and commonly used in chemistry laboratories. Erlenmeyer, who taught at Heidelberg, conducted many important experiments in his long, fruitful career. He died in 1909, aged eighty-four.

Esau's Mess of Pottage There are two versions of the proverbial story in the Bible. In one (*Genesis* 25:27–34) Esau sells his birthright to his twin brother Jacob for a mess of red pottage, while in the other (*Genesis* 27) Jacob conspires with his mother Rebekah to cheat his older twin out of his paternal blessing. Historians believe that the stories symbolize conflicts between the *Edomites*, led by the eponymous Edom or Esau, and the Israel tribe headed by Jacob. The *Edomites* were probably wandering hunters, as represented by Esau in both stories, and the Israelites more civilized pastoral nomads. The phrase is generally used today without Esau's name. Incidentally, the "mess" was most likely tempting. Arabians still prepare lentils in what is thought to be a similar way, blending onions and rice with them and simmering the concoction in sesame seed oil—a delectable dish, we are told.

Escoffier Sauce, Escoffier Garnish If one man had to be chosen to epitomize modern gastronomy it would have to be Auguste Escoffier (1847?–1935). Escoffier, made a member of the French Legion of Honor in 1920, was renowned as chef and restaurateur, operating, with Cesar Ritz, the Ritz in Paris, London's Savoy and the Grand Hotel in Monte Carlo. Author of a number of books on the art of cooking, he invented both the basic sauce and the chopped, carmelized almond topping for *peach melba* that bear his name. (See also *Melba; Ritzy*.)

Esperanto Over the past seven centuries scores of artificial universal languages have been invented. The French philosopher Descartes devised one in 1629; there is another called Sobresol based on the notes of the musical scale; and a third, Timerio, is written solely in numerals (i.e., 1-80-17—"I love you."). *Esperanto* is far better known than any such invention. It takes its name from the pseudonym chosen by its inventor, Lazarus Zamenhof, when he wrote his first book on the subject, *Linguo Internacia de la Doktoro Esperanto*. Dr.

Lazarus Ludwig Zamenhof (1859–1917), the "Doctor Hopeful" of the title, was a Warsaw oculist who believed that a world language would promote peace and understanding. He launched his system in 1887 and today the movement has some eight million supporters, from half a million to a million people capable of speaking *Esperanto* fluently. Advocates claim that the language—based primarily on words common to the major tongues, with a Latin-type grammar—is much easier to learn than any other and can be mastered in a relatively short time. Esperanto is now taught in over 750 schools in 40 countries around the world, has textbooks for study in 54 languages, has been used in more than 8,600 books, and is the subject of some 145 periodicals.

Essenes, Essenian, Essenic According to unsubstantiated traditions, both Jesus and John the Baptist were originally Essenes, the sect a group of pre-Christian Jews that emphasized ascetic self-discipline, communal property, ceremonial purity, and baptism. The Essenes dressed in white, strictly obeyed the Sabbath, ate no meat and drank only water. They led a monastic life, shunning marriage and wealth, and similarly ascetic persons are sometimes called *Essenes* or *Essenic* today. Little accurate historical information is available about the Essenes, but since the discovery of the Dead Sea Scrolls in Qumran, thought to be the *Essenian* homeland, there has been renewed interest in the group.

Euclidian The Greek mathematician Euclid's *Elements*, written in the third century B.C., was a collection of theorems and problems that formed the basis for geometry. So famous were Euclid's mathematical works—the *Elements* alone consisted of thirteen "books"—that they completely overshadowed his life, almost nothing known about the man himself. The mathematician probably received his training from pupils of Plato in Athens and it is certain that he founded a school in Alexandria about 306 B.C. Euclid is said to have told Ptolemy that "there is no royal road to geometry" when the ruler asked if there wasn't an easier way to learn it. Much of his *Elements* owes a great debt to the work of earlier mathematicians, but its logical structure is Euclid's alone. Geometry is still classified as *Euclidian* or *non-Euclidian*, the former word used derivatively to describe any "lucid and orderly exposition of geometrical evidence."

Euhemeristic *Euhemeristic* is an adjective applied to attempts to interpret myths, especially primitive religious myths, on an historical basis. The Greek writer Euhemerus is responsible for the word, it being this mythmaker's theory that the gods popularly worshipped in the fourth century B.C. had all originally been kings and heroes. In his philosophical romance *Sacred History* Euhemerus depicted the gods thus, insisting that they had merely been deified by their subjects or admirers. The writer claimed that he had discovered an inscribed gold pillar in a temple on an island in the Indian Ocean confirming his theory. The island is doubtless imaginary and Euhemerus probably derived his theory from the Phoenicians or some other oriental people before him.

Eupatorium (see *Mithridatize*)

Even Steven Contrary to some accounts, there was never a gentleman named Steven who matched his wife blow for blow. The term apparently stems from a far less equitable character in Jonathan Swift's *Journal to Stella* (1713): " 'Now we are even.' quoth Steven, when he gave his wife six blows to one." Stella was Swift's name for Esther Johnson, the *Journal* letters to her describing his daily life in London. Their relationship was a complicated one. Swift, fourteen years his Stella's senior, taught her to read and write, loved her all his life and when he died was buried beside her, but the two lovers probably never married.

F

Fabian Tactics, Fabian Planning Such delaying tactics are named after Quintus Fabius Maximus, the Roman dictator who over a ten-year period defeated Hannibal's superior Carthaginian army. His strategy was to avoid open engagements and employ his troops only in harassing raids and skirmishes in the hills, where Hannibal's cavalry was ineffective. Marches, countermarches and other hit and run tactics were among the "masterly inactivities" devised by this cool, unemotional man to gradually erode Hannibal's forces, despite the objections of the subjects who had elected him dictator. After his victory in the Second Punic War, in 209 B.C., he earned the agnomen, or official nickname, of "Cunctator," the "slow-goer" or "delayer," for his wariness. George Washington was called the *American Fabius* for his similar strategy during the Revolutionary War, and the sixteenth-century military leader, the Duc de Montmorency, is known historically as the *French Fabius*. England's socialist *Fabian Society*, founded in 1884, adopted Fabius Cunctator's name upon rejecting Marxist revolutionary theory and decided to accomplish "the reorganization of society" without violence, "by stealing inches, not by grasping leagues," this giving the word a new, political significance. *Fabian policy* is thus patient, long-range planning. Famous *Fabians* included Sidney and Beatrix Potter Webb, H. G. Wells, George Bernard Shaw and Annie Besant. The organization joined in founding the British Labor Party in 1900; it no longer functions as a major political agency, but remains a research institution.

Fahrenheit In the form of the letter F., following temperatures, this inventor's name has become the shortest and one of the most widely used human words. In 1714 Gabriel Daniel Fahren-heit perfected and manufactured the first practical mercury-in-glass thermometer, and invented the scale for measuring temperature that is named after him. Galileo had developed a faulty air-thermoscope long before this, and there were numerous contact thermometers employing alcohol starting from 1654, but Fahrenheit's was the first fairly precise instrument of its kind. Even at that, his theometric scale has had to be revised since he invented it—his thermometer being inaccurate enough for him to regard 96° as the temperature of a healthy man. Today only two of his fixed reference points—32° and 212°, the freezing and boiling points of water under standard atmospheric pressure—are still used on the *Fahrenheit scale*. The inventor, a German born in Danzig, Poland, lived most of his life in Holland and England after being orphaned at fifteen. Failing at the merchant's career for which his father had trained him, he turned to the study of physics, becoming before he was twenty a manufacturer of meteorological instruments—of which he invented a good number, including an improved hygrometer. Fahrenheit was elected to Britain's Royal Society before his death in 1736 when only fifty years old. Thermometers in the United States and England still use his scale, the centigrade scale being standard in most countries. (See also *Celsius Scale*; *Reaumur Scale*.)

Fanny This euphemism may be an unknown personification, the diminutive of the feminine name Frances, or it may have a more objectionable history than the word it replaces. For Partridge suggests that the euphemism for the euphemism "backside" comes from the eponymous heroine of John Cleland's hardly euphemistic novel *Fanny Hill* (1749). The term in this sense is originally an

American one, however, probably deriving from the English slang use of Cleland's *Fanny* for "the female pudenda." Or else Americans were reading *Fanny Hill* long before it was legally permissible to do so. Cleland's classic of brothel life, which he wrote to escape debtor's prison, has already been made into a movie, has had vast sales in paperback, and, judging by recent examples, may indeed finally prove euphemistic for its genre. Another etymologist feels that *fanny* may come from the obsolete expression "fancy vulva"; still another source traces the word to a pun on "fundament" (which became "fun," then "fan," then *fanny*), and *Webster's* derives it from "the fanciful euphemism 'Aunt Fanny' for the buttocks." *Fanny*, the mildest of words today, was in 1929 included in a list of expressions that the Keith booking office forbid vaudevillians to use.

Fanny Adams, Fannys, Sweet Fanny Adams, Harriet Lane The British nautical term for stew, hash or tinned mutton is among the most gory of eponymous words. Fanny Adams had been murdered and mutilated in 1812, her body cut into pieces and thrown into the river Wey at Alton in Hampshire. Her murderer, one Fred Baker, was publicly hanged in Winchester. Young Fanny's name, given wide currency, was adopted by sailors to indicate a particularly distasteful meal. Fanny Adams had been disposed of in a kettle, making the term even more apt, and in fact, when kettles came into use in the navy they were dubbed *Fannys* from the tins before them. There is no doubt that Fanny Adams is the basis for the military expression *Sweet Fanny Adams*, meaning something worthless, or nothing at all. Another similar merchant marine term is *Harriet Lane*, for Australian canned meat, because it supposedly resembled the chopped up body of this girl, murdered by a man named Wainwright in about 1875.

Fanny Heath Raspberry, Lloyd George Raspberry Raspberries have not been cultivated for nearly as long as fruits like apples, peaches and pears. Called a brambleberry and considered a nuisance in England, it was not until about 1830 that the delicate, delicious fruit began to be developed in America. The *Fanny Heath* variety is a tribute to a determined pioneer woman who emigrated to North Dakota in 1881. This young bride had been told that she could never grow anything on the barren alkaline soil surrounding her house, but forty years later her homestead was an Eden of flowers, fruits and vegetables. After her death in 1931, the black raspberry she developed was named in her honor. A red raspberry variety honoring a famous person is the *Lloyd George*, named after British Prime Minister David Lloyd George (1863–1945), who led Britain to victory in World War I and dominated British politics in the first quarter of this century.

Farad, Faraday Born into extreme poverty, he had virtually no formal education and is said to have possessed a very poor memory, yet Michael Faraday (1791–1867) became probably the world's greatest experimental genius in the physical sciences. Apprenticed to a bookbinder from an early age, Faraday applied for a job as Sir Humphry Davy's laboratory assistant in 1813, carefully preparing, illustrating and binding notes from the great scientist's chemistry lectures and sending them to him along with his request. Davy trained him well. As both a physicist and chemist Faraday became one of the immortals of science —discovering the principle of the electric motor, developing the first dynamo, formulating the laws of electrolysis, producing the first stainless steel, and discovering benzene and butylene, among many other brilliant accomplishments. His discovery of electromagnetic induction alone provided the basis for our modern electrified world and produced his "field concept," which in turn was the basis a century later of Einstein's revolutionary theory of relativity. In 1824 Faraday was elected to the Royal Society, but later refused its presidency, just as he refused knighthood and many other honors offered him. The following year he became director of the laboratory of the Royal Institution, where he had begun his career as Davy's assistant. The *farad* named for the scientist is an electromagnetic unit, while a *faraday* is a unit of electricity used in electrolysis. Faraday invented the electrical terms "anode" and "cathode." (See also *Davy Lamp*.)

Faro *Faro*, which is now a card game principally played in gambling houses, derives its name from an Egyptian pharaoh, but, so far as we know, from no particular king except the king of spades. The game came to England from France or Italy and little more is known about it than that. The French version was named *pharaon* (pharaoh), this altered to *faro* as it grew popular among the English. It is assumed that at a certain stage in the game's history a likeness of one of the ruling Egyptian pharaohs appeared on either all the cards, or, more likely, on the king of spades. No one has ventured to guess just who the pharaoh might be.

The term "tinhorn gambler" is related to *faro*. A tinhorn gambler in the early West was one who played chuck-a-luck rather than the royal game, rolling his dice from a tin can that came to be associated with his cheapness.

Father Damien *Father Damien*, the religious name of Joseph De Veuster (1840–1889), is often used to describe a selfless, heroic man of God. Damien de Veuster, a Belgian Catholic missionary of the Society of the Sacred Heart of Jesus and Mary, was sent to the Hawaiian Islands in 1863 to replace his ailing brother, and was ordained as a priest the following year. He volunteered to be the first resident chaplain for the leper colony on Molokai ten years later. For many years the courageous priest labored almost single-handedly to improve the condition of the seven hundred lepers there, contracting leprosy himself but remaining in the colony among his people until he died. In 1936 Father Damien's body was removed from Molokai for burial in Belgium.

Father Mathew A Capuchin priest and Irish social worker, Father Mathew took a pledge of total abstinence in 1838 and through his campaigning in Ireland, England and America, gained a tremendous following, coming to be known as "the Apostle of Temperance." His name became proverbial for a temperance reformer, his good work rewarded by a pension Queen Victoria bestowed upon him.

Father Mathew was sixty-six when he died in 1856.

Feijoa The delicious guava, *Feijoa sellowiana*, is native to South America and grown in Florida and California for its highly esteemed white-fleshed fruit. The small tree was introduced into southern Europe in 1890, the genus *Feijoa* named for Spanish naturalist J. da Silva Feijo. *Feijoa*, of the myrtle family, is a small genus noted only for the pineapple guava, which is often called *feijoa*, without a capital. Closely related to the true guava, its fruit is used widely for jam and jelly. The oblong fruit, about two inches long and a dull green marked with crimson, has a delicate pineapple flavor, literally melting in the mouth.

Fermium, Fermi Statistics *Fermium*, like *einsteinium*, is an artificially produced radioactive element first detected by American physicist Albert Ghiorso in the debris of the first H-bomb explosion. Element 100 was named for Enrico Fermi (1901–54), "the father of the atomic bomb," the year after his death. Professor Fermi, Italian-born, left Italy in 1938 to receive the Nobel Prize for his theory of radioactive substances known as Fermi statistics. Opposed to Mussolini's anti-Semitic policies, he did not return, emigrating to America and becoming a citizen of the United States. Fermi directed the scientific team that produced the historic self-sustained nuclear chain reaction at the University of Chicago in 1942, and worked on the development of the atomic bomb at Los Alamos, N.M.

Ferris Wheel Not even Little Egypt, the first belly dancer to perform in America, outdrew the *Ferris wheel* introduced at the World's Columbian Exposition held in Chicago in 1893. The ride was the work of George Washington Gale Ferris (1859–96), a Galesburg, Ill. railroad and bridge engineer. A giant steel structure weighing over 1,200 tons, the first *Ferris wheel* stood 140 feet high and measured 250 feet in diameter, 36 cars at its rims capable of carrying 1,440 riders. The chief wonder of the "World's Fair" had been built on the tension spoke principle, the large power-driven vertical wheel revolving on a stationary axis and rotating between two pyramids.

So great was the wheel's success that imitations soon became standard at all amusement parks worthy of the name. The recent long-distance *Ferris wheel* champion is Californian Richard Ford, aged thirty—he rode a *Ferris wheel* twenty days and twenty nights, sixteen hours and thirty minutes at San Francisco Playland Park. (The nonstop *seesaw record* is 124 hours, set in Gardenia, California in April, 1971—and don't forget that on July 19, 1969, an Oklahoma woman threw a two-pound rolling pin 138 feet and 11 inches to set the world's longest rolling pin throw record.)

Fiacre St. Fiacre can be invoked as both the protector of greenthumbs and cabdrivers. The name of the patron saint of Brie, France, was first applied to the small horse-drawn cabs called *fiacres* in about 1648, when a M. Sauvage hired out the hackneys from a stand at the Hôtel de St. Fiacre in Paris. This was not a hotel in the modern sense, but a great town house of the nobility in the rue Saint Martin, so-called because an image of St. Fiacre hung outside it. Sauvage, who apparently wasn't an innkeeper, as the *Oxford English Dictionary* makes him, rented his cabs for about five sous per hour (the hackneys, in fact, were originally named *carrosses à cinq sous*), and both the carriages and their bad-tempered drivers came to be called *fiacres* after the hotel where he did business.

St. Fiacre was an Irish prince christened Fiachra or Fiachrach (Fr. *Fiacre*) who founded a seventh-century monastery at the modern Breuil, near Paris, about 670. This land, which the clever monk barely turned up with his staff instead of a plough when the Bishop of Meaux granted him "as much land as he could turn up in a day," eventually grew into the village of St. Fiacre. It is said that the Irish saint restored many people to mental health by hard work in his gardens, a principle that has its counterparts in modern psychology. It is his fate to be invoked for perhaps the most unpleasant assortment of diseases that any saint is responsible for—including diarrhea, venereal diseases and even warts on the knees of horses. The saint died in 670 when about seventy years old. His remains are in the Cathedral of Meaux, France, and his day, appropriate for the harvest, is August 30.

Filbert, Gilbert Filbert About the only connection between the Frankish St. Filbert and filbert nuts is that the saint's feast day falls on August 22, the height of the nut harvesting season. This was enough reason, however, for Norman gatherers to name the nuts *philberts* in his honor. St. Philibert, his name Filuberht in Old High German, was a Benedictine who founded the Abbey of Jumieges in 684. What Americans call *filberts* after him are actually hazel nuts. *Filberts* are confined botanically to two European nut varieties—about 250 million pounds of them bearing the saint's name each year.

A *Gilbert Filbert* was British slang for a very fashionable man about town early in this century, deriving from the popular song "Gilbert, the Filbert, Colonel of the Nuts," and *cracked in the filbert* meant eccentric or crazy.

Fink, Ratfink, Mike Fink The original *fink*, or *ratfink* for that matter, may have been either a Pinkerton man or a cop named Albert Fink who worked for southern United States railroads. Mencken prefers the former explanation, tracing the term to the 1892 Homestead steel strike when Pinkerton men or "Pinks" were hired as strikebreakers, these brutal "Pinks" becoming *finks* in time, the word synonymous with the earlier "scab" or the British "blackleg." *Finks* and "scissorbills" were anathema to the early labor movement—scissorbills workers adamantly opposed to unions—but just the former word survived and is now used to describe not only a strikebreaker, but any treacherous contemptible person or police informer.

Mr. Albert Fink could just as well have inspired the term in similar fashion. The German-born Fink, according to a reliable source, long headed a staff of detectives with the Louisville and Nashville Railroad and then switched to the New York Trunk Line Association in about 1875. He was not involved in railroad labor disputes but his operatives probably policed rates charged on the lines and some of them were likely planted spies who came to be known as *Finks*. This gives the word more a management than labor flavor, but it is possible that *fink* gained currency in this way before being adopted by union men. It is at least as plausible as the transformation of "Pinks" to *finks*.

Webster's believes that *fink* is "perhaps from the name of a notorious American strikebreaker," while *Random House* suggests the German or Yiddish slang word *finch*, "a student who does not belong to a club." There are many theories. Mike Fink, as has been claimed, is not responsible for the derivation. He was a real American frontier hero (ca. 1770–1822), a river boatman and Indian fighter whose tall tales contributed greatly to the American folklore of exaggeration, a fact witnessed by the eleven or more different accounts of his death.

The town of Fink, Tex., according to one news item, will adopt any person bearing the name Funk or Zink as an honorary citizen—but apparently doesn't want to be associated with anyone named Fink.

Flash, Flashy This word is used to describe flashy dressers, among many showy, ostentatious things, and may not derive from "a sudden flame" or "lightning" as one would suppose. We may owe the expression to the nineteenth-century Flash men from outside the village of Flash in England's Derbyshire. These squatters, like gypsies, traveled from fair to fair in the district, doing no good, their slang dialect called *Flash talk* and their distinctive clothing making them quite conspicuous. The term *flashy* could well have been applied to anyone like them, though no investigator has yet offered complete proof of this. Similarly, the British word for underworld lingo, *flash*, may be from *Flash talk*, a *flash man*, a thief, and *flash notes*, counterfeit bills, deriving in the same way.

Fletcherize The author of *Glutton or Epicure* (1899) advocated cutting out regular meals and eating only when really hungry, consuming only very small amounts of food at one time, and chewing each tiny mouthful vigorously and thoroughly before swallowing. Horace Fletcher (1849–1919), a Lawrence, Mass., businessman turned nutritionist, believed that this regimen—which he had followed from the time he went on a diet

and lost sixty-five pounds at age forty—would promote better digestion and health as excellent as his own. *Fletcherism*, described more fully in a later book of that name, swept the country; thousands attended Fletcher's lectures and followed his instructions to the letter. As a result of the health fad, the word *Fletcherize*, to masticate food thoroughly—at least thirty-two chews to the bite—became a common expression that still remains in the dictionaries. Fletcher had really borrowed his idea of thirty-two chews to the bite from British Prime Minister Gladstone, who "made it a rule to give every tooth of mine a chance," and who claimed he owed much of his success in life to this rule. Slogans like "Nature will castigate those who don't masticate" won Fletcher many famous converts, including John D. Rockefeller, Thomas Edison, William James, and the West Point cadets. Philosopher James, however, had to give up Fletcherism after only three months. "It nearly killed me," he wrote later.

Fontange Through the ages woman's hair has been tortured into shapes of full sails, bird nests with fledglings in them, and even windmills, but no style has ever topped the *fontange* created by Louis XIV's beautiful red-haired mistress. In the brief time that they were lovers "The Sun King" made Marie Angélique de Scorraille de Roussilles duchesse de Fontanges, a territory in France. She died all too soon in 1681, when only twenty, but a year before her death the lovely young woman introduced what was probably the most extravagant, expensive hairdress in the history of coiffures. Called a *fontange* after her, this pile of style rose to heights of two feet and more above the wearer's head, including feathers, bows and a large assortment of jeweled ornaments in the gummed-linen circular bands that held them in place. So great a nuisance did *fontanges* become that Louis XIV had to issue a royal decree abolishing them in 1699. To the Duchesse's further shame, the hairdress was dubbed a "commode" in England, and *fontange* itself was adopted as a polite word for a commode, the piece of furniture having come into use in the late seventeenth century and serving as a toilet among other uses. (See also *Crapper; Furphy; Oliver's Skull; Sacheverell; Twiss*.)

Ford John Dillinger, the first "public enemy number one," once wrote Henry Ford extolling the performance of his car as a getaway vehicle. Which shows just how widespread was the *Ford's* really incalculable influence on society, beneficial or disastrous. Henry Ford's motor cars, though not the first invented, put America and the world on wheels for better or worse, his assembly-line, mass-production methods marked the beginning of modern industry, and his "Five Dollar Day" heralded a new era for labor. Ford (1863–1947), born on a farm near Detroit, Mich., founded the Ford Motor Company in 1903. First came his two-cylinder *Model A* and then, in 1909, the immortal *Model T*, the Tin Lizzie, the flivver, America's monument to love, available in any color so long as it was black. Fifteen million of these cars were built over almost twenty years—a record that lasted until the Volkswagen broke it in 1972—and any cheap, dependable car became known as a *ford*. The word is seldom uncapitalized anymore, but *Ford* still remains a symbol of American mechanical ingenuity. Though he was often controversial and foolish in his public life, no one has ever doubted the inventor's genius. He is honored today by both the motor company bearing his name and the philanthropic *Ford Foundation*. (See also *Cadillac*.)

Forsythia These handsome yellow-flowered shrubs, their bloom the first obvious sign of Spring in many places, were named for William Forsyth (1737–1804), a Scottish gardener and horticulturist who became superintendent of the royal gardens at St. James and Kensington in London. Forsyth introduced many unusual ornamental plants to England and may have personally brought the *forsythia* from China. The inventor of a plaster that stimulates new growth in dying diseased trees, he received formal thanks from Parliament for this contribution. The *Forsythia* genus is especially valuable to gardeners because it is easy to propagate, virtually carefree and does well in partial shade.

Fortunella *Fortunella*, or the kumquat, is the only genus of well-known fruit trees to be named for a living person, and no more deserving eponym could be found than Robert Fortune (1813–1880), Scottish botanist and traveler. Few men have equaled Fortune as a plant hunter. The author of *Three Years' Wanderings in the Northern Provinces of China* (1847) and other botanical books began traveling in the Orient for the Royal Horticultural Society in 1842. A former employee in the Society's English gardens, his express orders were to collect flora and he brought many beautiful plants back to Europe, including the kumquat, tree peonies, the Japanese anemone and a number of chrysanthemums. Fortune also introduced the tea plant into India for the East India Company, founding its cultivation there. The tallest species of *Fortunella* is only ten feet high, the smallest a bush of about three feet, and the kumquat fruit is orange-like but smaller, having three to seven cells or sections as opposed to eight to fifteen in the orange. The kumquat, which is eaten fresh or preserved, has been crossed with other citrus fruits into a number of strange hybrids like the citrangequat and limequat.

Fourdrinier The brothers Fourdrinier, Henry and Sealy, invented the *fourdrinier* machine that makes most of the paper we use. In 1807 they patented the first practical machine for converting wood-pulp into paper, but labored thirty years in perfecting it, aided only by a partial grant from Parliament. The English papermakers revolutionized the industry with their *fourdrinier*, which is today a huge automatic machine working on the same basic principle but bearing little resemblance to the original.

Fourierism *Fourierism*, or utopian socialism, has inspired at least forty-one experimental communities around the world at one time or another, all of them failures. Developed and introduced by François Marie Charles Fourier (1772–1837), a French merchant reacting against his commercial background, the system advocates dividing the world into phalanxes of 1,620 people or 400 families. Each phalanx would live in a common building, or phalanstery, with separate apartments. One common language, a federal world government and the encouragement of talent and industry were among other features of this very elaborate scheme, its ultimate goal being a systematic agricultural society. Fourier made a number of converts in France and wasn't dismayed when the only community established in his lifetime failed. His disciples later brought his doctrine to America, where several *Fourier communities* were established, none of them remaining today. *Fourierism* was not a communistic plan, as it did not discard capitalism altogether; its intent was rather to destroy the artificial restraints put upon man by civilization.

Franc "John the Good" (1319–64), King John II of France, is responsible for this French unit of currency. Captured by the British after the battle of Poitiers, he was freed in 1360 so that he could return to France and raise a ransom of three million gold crowns. This John failed to do, but in so trying he ordered a new gold coin struck that was equivalent in value to the livre. He was pictured on horseback upon the coin's face, the Latin legend beneath his effigy reading, *Johannes Dei gracia Francorum rex*, "John, by the grace of God, King of the Franks." It is from this coin, and a similar one honoring his successor Charles V, that the word *franc*, derived. John, though he debased the currency, proved to be a man of honor. He returned to England when one of the hostages held for him escaped, and died there in captivity.

France, Frank, Frankincense, Franking Privilege, Frankfurter Late in the sixth century the warlike Francs conquered Gaul, giving their name to *France* and the *French*. The Gauls had named these Germanic tribes after the Latin *Franci*, the name the Romans bestowed upon the fearless warriors for the "javelins" they carried. Soon *Franc* itself, *Frank* in English, came to mean "free"— for the barbaric tribes reduced the Gauls to virtual slavery and were the only truly free nobles in the land. This meaning eventually led to such English words as *franking privilege*, free use of the public mails, but the Frank influence does not end there. Similarly, our *frank* for

straightforward, or candid, derives from the Franks' blunt integrity in dealing with others—they were so powerful that there was no need for subterfuge; and *frankincense*, an incense of "pure or high quality," refers to what they at least considered their racially pure origins. Finally, *frankfurter*, or *frank*, can also be traced to this people, for it was in Frankfurt, Germany, that these "hot dog" sausages (New York's "tube steaks") were first made centuries after the city was so named because it was "the ford of the Franks," the place from which they set out on their raids.

Frangipane, Frangipani The Marquis Frangipani, a major general under Louis XIV, is said to have invented the pastry cake filled with cream, sugar and almonds called *frangipane* or *frangipani*. The name is also applied to the fragrant but ugly *Plumeria rubra* tree or shrub, and to a perfume either prepared from or imitating the odor of its flowers. The perfume is usually associated with the name of its otherwise unknown inventor —possibly a Frangipani relative or the marquis himself. Its sweet, cloying odor is not often associated with the young and innocent in fiction. An alternate suggestion is that both pastry and perfume may have been introduced by an earlier member of the Italian Frangipani family, a relative who came to France with Catherine de Médicis a century before the marquis. Considering Catherine's many contributions to French cooking, this is not unlikely.

Franklin Conductor, Franklin Spectacles, Franklin Stove, Franklin Tree Benjamin Franklin (1706–1790), one of the broadest and most creative minds of his time—statesman, scientist, writer, printer and inventor—devised the *Franklin stove*, a great improvement over its predecessors, in 1743. This portable, coal-burning iron fireplace had a pipe connecting it to the chimney, producing heat cheaply and relatively efficiently. Franklin's other inventions include *Franklin's bifocals*, and his famous experiment with a kite during a thunderstorm in 1762 led to his development of the *Franklin lightning rod*. Every branch of science held his interest, but Franklin's contributions to mankind did not end here. Among many civic achievements, he founded America's first circulating library, set up Philadelphia's first fire company, established what is now the University of Pennsylvania, organized the American Philosophical Society, wrote and published *Poor Richard's Almanack* —which sold ten thousand copies a year —and published the Pennsylvania *Gazette*, its circulation the largest in America. His career as a patriot and statesman is well known. This brilliant, practical, witty and always human man has been called "the first American." The ornamental *Franklinia* or *Franklin tree* (*Gordonia altamaha*) is also named in his honor. The species has an unusual history—introduced into cultivation in 1770, it has never been found again in its wild state.

Franklin's Gull *Franklin's gull*, the only bird ever to have a monument erected to it, is intimately connected with English and American history. The black-headed gull was named in honor of Sir John Franklin (1786–1847), the English explorer who died in discovering the North-West passage that so many other mariners had striven to find. The story of his expedition and his wife's later attempts to find him is one of the most interesting in maritime history. But *Franklin's gull* (*Laridae pipixcan*), which has the same upland-breeding and seashore-wintering habits as the *Bonaparte gull*, is even more prominent in American folklore. In 1848 an invasion of grasshoppers threatened starvation for the Mormon settlers near the Great Salt Lake and it was checked only by the appearance of flocks of *Franklin's gulls* that devoured the crickets and saved the crops after all other means had failed. The Sea Gull Monument, on Temple Square in Salt Lake City, is dedicated to the species, "in grateful remembrance of the mercy of God to the Mormon pioneers."

Freesia There is some question about the naming of this fragrant and beautiful genus of South African herbs. Containing three species but scores of horticultural forms, *freesias* grow from a bulblike corm, belonging to the iris family and bearing typically white or yellow flowers at the end of their stems. They are generally raised in greenhouses and are a popular florist's flower. Some authorities, including *Webster's Biographical Dictionary*, say the genus was named for E. M. Fries (1794–1878), a Swedish botanist; others cite F. H. T. Freese, a pupil of Professor Klatt, the christener of the genus.

French The prejudice that anything French is wicked, sexual and decadent has let Frenchmen in for more than their fair share of abuse in English. Many such expressions date back to 1730–1820, the height of Anglo-French enmity, but some are current and others go back even further. *French leave* and *French disease* are covered in entries following. For *French letter* or *French cap* see *condum*—the French changed this to *capote anglaise* soon after the English coined it, changed it to *capote allemande* during World War I and then changed it back again when the English stubbornly refused to say *German cap*. At one time *French by injection*, like its Dutch counterpart, meant any English woman living with a Frenchman. *French kiss*, for the lingual "soul kiss"; *French fare*, overelaborate politeness; *French postcards*, "dirty" prints; and *pardon my French* for "excuse my strong language" are all familiar expressions. By no means are such phrases confined to English, either. In Prussia, for example, lice are called *Franzosen*.

The French, however, have done their share of international name-calling, too. Their word for a louse is *espagnol* (Spanish), for a flea *espagnole* (Spanish woman), and for a creditor they once said *un Anglaise* (an Englishman). The French phrase for a dirty trick is *a Chinese trick*, their red tape is *chinoiserie*, their expression for our *that's Greek to me* is *that's Hebrew to me*, our *Dutch courage* is their *German happiness*, and our *Dutch treat* is their *going Swiss*. As recently as the early sixties they introduced *la vice anglaise* as a synonym for homosexuality.

On the whole English reflects admiration for the French exceeding any animosity. There are some one hundred words prefixed with *French* and most recognize French expertise. Among the most common would be *French cuffs*, *French heel*, *French twist*, *French clean-*

ing, *French roof, French doors* and *windows, French telephone, French harp, French horn, French cuisine, French dressing, French endive, French bread, French ice cream, French pancake, French pastry, French toast, French fried,* and *French fries.* Many, of course, acknowledge the great French culinary expertise.

French Disease, The One still hears this term, which was coined nearly five centuries ago, to describe syphilis when it first appeared on a large scale in Europe. The French were widely associated with anything sexual and at the time were England's most detested enemies. When in 1496 an Italian gentleman wrote that "the French disease is a new plague . . . contracted by lying together," the English quickly adopted the phrase. The *French disease* has had many similar synonyms since. Syphilis has been *a Frenchman, French pox, French marbles, the French sickness, the French goods,* and *French gout. French crown* was long baldness produced from *the French sickness,* to be *Frenchified* meant to be venereally infected, and a *French pig* was a venereal sore. *French measles* was still another name for syphilis but also a synonym for *German measles,* possibly because Dr. DeBergen, a French physician, made certain discoveries concerning the disease in 1752.

Other nations joined in falsely damning the French for syphilis. The Germans, too, called it the *French disease* and in Italy it was *mala de Franzos* or *Morbus Gallicus.* As for the French, they made do with *the Italian malady.* To put the matter in perspective it must be noted that among mainland Greeks syphilis was the *Corinthian disease,* and that the English often called it the *Spanish gout.* It has been blamed on nearly every country and continent, always by residents of other countries and continents. (See also *Syphilis.*)

French Leave The French are noted for their politeness—witness the preceding expression *French fare,* overelaborate manners. Which makes it all the more clear that the pejorative *French leave* was invidiously coined. In eighteenth-century French society it was the custom to depart from a dinner or ball without formally bidding the hostess or guests goodbye. Such a surreptitious departure was dubbed *a French leave* by the decorous English, but the voluble French always pinned the custom on their self-conscious cousins, calling it *taking English leave, s'en aller* (or *filer*) *à l'anglaise. French leave* is also widely used for a soldier who has gone A.W.O.L. or "over the hill." In all cases it means someone who has slipped out before his absence is noticed.

Freudian, Freudian Slip No other contemporary thinker has influenced twentieth-century intellectual thought more profoundly than Dr. Sigmund Freud (1856–1939), the founder of psychoanalysis. His *Freudian theories,* though often modified and even discarded over the years, emphasize the importance of the unconscious, infantile sexuality and the role of sexuality in the development of neuroses, while *Freudian methods,* such as free-association, are methods for treating mental disorders. A *Freudian slip* is popularly a slip of the tongue revealing a repressed subconscious thought or desire. The Austrian physician and psychoanalyst met with extreme hostility when he published *The Interpretation of Dreams* in 1900, but his views increasingly became accepted. He founded the International Congress of Psychoanalysis seven years later, gathering around him such giants as Adler and Jung, the group pioneering many psychological concepts. Freud practiced in Vienna until 1938, when he fled Nazi anti-Semitism to London, where he died the following year. Some of his disciples broke with him over the years to form new groups, but all acknowledged their great debt to the master.

Froebelism, Froebal Teaching Methods That young children should be taught according to their natural instincts, by stimulating and creating interest, is an accepted view today in educational circles. But when Friedrich Wilhelm August Froebel (1782–1852) put such ideas into practice in the world's first kindergarten (children's garden), which he founded in Blankenburg, Germany, in 1837, his *Froebal teaching methods* met with wide disapproval. The German schoolmaster, and former forester, nevertheless remained convinced that preschool education was essential, devoting his life to establishing kindergartens and training teachers for them. Pleasant surroundings, self-activity, the use of play, the study of nature and the importance of the family were stressed in these schools. Froebel's *The Education of Man* (1826) set forth his views, which were strongly influenced by an unhappy childhood both at home and in school. He died without realizing the impact his methods would have on education, his death in fact hastened by a state decree forbidding the establishment of kindergartens in Prussia.

Fuchsia, Fuchsian Group, Fuchsin *Fuchsia*, a vivid bluish or purplish red, takes its name from the ornamental *fuchsia* shrubs that honor German physician and botanist Leonhard Fuchs (1501–66). These principally Mexican and South American shrubs, which are of the evening primrose family and can have purple, red, yellow or white flowers, were named for Fuchs in 1703 by the French botanist Charles Plumier. Dr. Fuchs was noted for his treatment of the "English sweating sickness," a plague that had spread to Europe. He became professor of medicine at the University of Tubingen in 1535, remaining there until his death over three decades later. His herbal *De historia stirpium* (1530) was widely known, this compendium of medicinal and edible plants probably the main reason why the genus *Fuchsia* was named in his honor. The genus contains some 100 species, the *fuchsia* shrubs only one of its many widely cultivated plants.

Fuchsin or *fuchsine* is a purplish-red analine dye, and *Fuchsian group* is a mathematical term that derives from the name of I. L. Fuchs (1833–1902), an eminent German mathematician.

Fudge "There was, sir, in our time one Captain Fudge, commander of a merchantman, who upon his return from a voyage, how ill-fraught soever his ship was, always brought home a good cargo of lies, so much that now aboard ship the sailors, when they hear a great lie told, cry out, 'You fudge it.' " So wrote Isaac D'Israeli, father of the British prime minister, on the derivation of *fudge*, for lies or nonsense, in his *Curiosities of Literature* (1791). A notorious liar

named Captain Fudge, his nickname "Lying Fudge," did live in seventeenth-century England, and it is just possible that the word derives from this source. Several etymologists concede that *fudge* has something to do with the perfidious captain, probably in combination with the German word *futsch*, no good. Where *fudge* candy comes from no one seems to know.

Führer, Fuehrer, Hitler, Schicklgruber Before Adolf Hitler preached his doctrines of the "master race" and The Thousand Year Reich *Führer* was simply a German word for leader. But Nazi blood purges, millions dead in gas chambers and concentration camps, towns like Lidice wiped off the map, broken treaties, militarism and planned world conquest made both his name and title symbols for terror, horror and evil, synonyms for a mad tyrant or megalomaniac. *Der Führer* was the title Hitler chose when he combined the offices of president and chancellor in 1934. His is undoubtedly the most familiar true horror tale in all history, yet he would never have believed himself anything but a kind and gentle man. His favorite books were the children's stories of Karl Mays about hunters and trappers, a thirty-volume set of which he kept by his bedside. (Which fits in well with Erich Fromm's estimate of him as a necrophilic aggression-prone character, "attracted to all that is dead, sick, unalive, or purely mechanical . . . [who] hates and wants to destroy life.") Hitler is said to have committed suicide in his Berlin bunker in 1945, aged fifty-six, but legends persist that he still lives, which indeed he does, if only symbolically. *Schicklgruber* is another word often used to describe someone like him, but contrary to widespread belief, it was not his legal name—Hitler's father, Alois, an illegitimate child, bore his mother's name, Schicklgruber, for a time, but changed it to Hitler, his father's name, before Adolf was born. A *Hitler* or *Mr.* or *Mrs. Hitler* is a blustering, domineering person.

Furphy A latrine rumor, or any rumor or baseless report, is in Australian military slang called a *furphy* and honors, or dishonors, one of three possible candidates. One theory proposes the firm of Furphy & Co., whose name appeared on World War I latrine buckets supplied to the Australian forces. Another nominates that contractor Furphy who supplied rubbish carts to Melbourne army camps about 1915. The third candidate is Australian writer Joseph Furphy (1843–1913), who wrote many tall tales under the pen name "Tom Collins." The expression *furphy king,* for a soldier in the habit of circulating rumors, seems to favor the first theory—the *furphy king* on his throne and all that. (See also *Crapper; Fontange; Oliver's Skull; Sacheverell; Twiss.*)

G

Gadolinite, Gadolinium In 1794 Finnish chemist Johann Gadolin analyzed a black mineral found in rare-earth elements at Ytterly, near Stockholm, Sweden. The mineral, from which he extracted the oxide yttria, was named *gadolinite* in his honor eight years later. Gadolin (1760–1852) also has the metallic chemical element *gadolinium* to commemorate him. It was discovered in 1880 by the Swiss chemist J. C. G. de Marignac, being one of several elements extracted from *gadolinite*. Marignac did not name the new element for Gadolin until six years after his discovery.

Gainsborough Hat Paintings have inspired a number of fashions (see *Cadogan hair style*), but no artist has been more influential than English portrait painter and landscapist Thomas Gainsborough in this regard. The *Gainsborough* is a wide-brimmed, large hat, turned up at the side, similar to those included in many of his portraits. Gainsborough (1727–88) did not invent the plumed velvet or taffeta hat, but painted it so well that it has been revived several times by designers, as have a number of the gracious fashions he depicted.

Ga-Ga, Gaga Someone cuckoo, off his rocker, mentally unbalanced. It has been suggested that *gaga* is of French origin, the word from the French artist Paul Gauguin, who gave up banking to become a painter at the age of thirty-five, having experienced considerable mental anguish toward the end of his life. The word seems inappropriate, however, to express Gauguin's tortured genius, and would be a cruel and stupid coining, if true. Alternatives are the theories that *gaga* derives from the French *gâteux*, "an old man feeble-minded and no longer able to control his body," or that it is in imitation of an idiot's laugh. The Gauguin explanation may be right, for the phrase was originally artist's slang, but according to the *gâteux* theory, *gaga* originated in the theatrical world about 1875, eight years before Gauguin (1848–1903) became a painter. The word is usually pronounced *gah-gah* in America and *gag-a* by the British.

Gallup Poll The best known, though not the first or only public opinion poll —originated by Dr. George Horace Gallup (b. 1901) a professor of journalism at Northwestern University. Gallup developed his technique about 1933, basing it on carefully phrased questions and scientifically selected samples, and became prominent nationally on predicting the outcome of the 1936 American presidential election, when many other pollsters failed. His poll, operating both at home and abroad, has proved remarkably accurate, but is far from infallible. In the 1948 national elections, for example, Gallup chose the late Governor Thomas E. Dewey over incumbent President Truman.

Galvanic, Galvanism, Galvanize The word enshrines Luigi Galvani (1737–98), a brilliant physiologist at Italy's University of Bologna—although *galvinism* originally proved something less than brilliant. Galvani's experiments began in about 1771. No one knows if his observant wife Lucia pointed out the first *galvanic* reaction, or if the professor had been preparing frog legs for her dinner— the tale has numerous versions—but one evening Galvani did notice that the skinned leg of a frog he was dissecting twitched when he touched it with a scalpel. After experimenting for about twenty years, Galvani wrote a paper concluding that the reaction had been produced by "animal electricity." Actually, the original frog's leg had twitched because his scalpel had touched the brass conductor of a nearby electrical machine, the charged knife shocking its muscles involuntarily "into life" with a current of electricity. Alessandro Volta (see *Volt*) quickly pointed out that the contact of two different metals really produced the electricity, but controversy raged between his and Galvani's supporters for years. This led to widespread research in the development of electricity, many investigators using the metallic arc made of two dissimilar metals that Galvani had invented in his years of experimentation. "Animal electricity" or the "life force" proved nonexistent—though everything from slaughtered animals to decapitated criminals were made to twitch—but despite his monumental mistake, Galvani's name was lionized in numerous scientific terms indicating the use of direct current. Technically, we speak of *galvanizing* by shocking with an electric current, or *galvanizing* metal by giving it a protective zinc coating, while *galvanic* refers to electricity produced by chemical action. Yet the words have much broader nontechnical meanings when they imply arousal or stimulation. As when we say someone is *galvanized* into action by a *galvanic* happening—shocked into an excited response like Galvani's frog.

Garand Rifle (M-1) Canadian-born John Cantius Garand invented the semiautomatic *Garand*, which works on the principle of expanding gas, while employed as a civilian ordnance engineer at the U.S. Armory in Springfield, Mass. in the early 1930's. The famous M-1 was adopted in 1936 as the official U.S. Army rifle. The .30-calibre 8-shot, clip-loading weapon proved to be a great improvement on the old standard Springfield, firing up to four times as many shots at 100 rounds per minute, and contributed greatly to the Allied victory in World War II. Garand has never been paid a cent in royalties for his invention, never earning more than twelve thousand dollars a year in his thirty-four-year service with the U.S. Ordnance Corps. At eighty-three, he is alive and well, scraping along on a meager pension in Springfield and, understandably, feeling neglected. "I guess they think I'm dead," he has recently been quoted as saying. "I don't think I want too much. I would like to be able to take the wife around

the country and put my grandson through college." Although the Garand provoked criticism because its range of about two hundred yards equaled less than half that of the Springfield, it had far less recoil, making it an ideal weapon for the average soldier, and delivered much greater fire power. Long range wasn't necessary by this time, anyway, mortars having taken over this function in modern warfare, and in those few cases where it was required, such as in sniping, the army continued to use the Springfield.

Gardenia "Mr. Miller has called it Basteria. But if you will please to follow my advice, I would call it Gardenia, from our worthy friend Dr. Alexander Garden of S. Carolina."

"If Dr. Garden will send me a *new* genus, I shall be truly happy to name it after him, Gardenia."

These quotations from an exchange of letters between a friend of Linnaeus and the great botanist himself, 1757–58, reveal the politicking that is sometimes involved even in naming something. Linnaeus did honor his promise to their mutual friend and two years later dedicated a newly discovered tropical shrub to Garden, even though the amateur botanist did not discover the beautiful, sweet-smelling *gardenia*. Dr. Alexander Garden (c. 1730–91), a Scottish-American physician, resided in Charleston, S.C., where he practiced medicine and also devoted much of his time to collecting plant and animal specimens, discovering the Congo eel and a number of snakes and herbs. Garden carried on an extensive correspondence with Linnaeus and many other European naturalists, probably as much out of loneliness as for intellectual stimulation. An ardent Tory, he returned to England during the Revolutionary War, resuming his practice in London and becoming vice-president of the Royal Society. Dr. Garden was by all accounts a difficult, headstrong man. When his granddaughter was named Gardenia Garden in his honor, he still refused to see her. After all, her father had fought against the British!

Garibaldi Shirt, Garibaldi Fish In the crowning achievement of his eventful life, Giuseppe Garibaldi, commanding his one thousand Redshirt volunteers, conquered Sicily, crossed back to the Italian mainland and expelled King Francis II from Naples. One year later, in 1861, Italy was united under King Emmanuel and Garibaldi became an international hero. Both a woman's loose, high-necked blouse with full sleeves—similar to those worn by his followers—and a currant biscuit were named for him, as well as an edible, brilliant orange fish (*Hypsypopa rubicundus*) discovered off the southern California coast by Italian-American fishermen. The red woolen shirts that inspired the women's fashion were presented to Garibaldi by the Uruguay government while he was in Montevideo raising his Italian legion. They had been dumped on the market because a war with Argentina prevented their export and the government had purchased them cheaply. The Italian patriot and soldier, one of the founders of modern Italy and a legend in his own lifetime, was later elected to Parliament. He died in 1882, seventy-nine years old.

Garrison Finish, Jockey "Snapper" Garrison held Montana back from the rest of the pack until they came into the homestretch. Then, at the last possible moment, standing high in the stirrups and bending low over the horse's mane in his famous "Yankee seat," he whipped his mount toward the finish line, moving up with a rush and winning the 1882 Suburban by a nose. It was this race that made jockey Edward H. Garrison an American turf hero and added his name to the language. Garrison used his new technique many times over his long career, winning most of his races in the last furlong, and the *Garrison finish* became so well known that it was applied to any close horse race, finally becoming synonymous with all winning last-minute efforts—in sports, politics or whatever. The inventive Garrison, who died in 1931, is all but forgotten, his wins just another statistic in the record books, but his name and "Yankee seat" are enthroned in the language.

Jockey is also from an eponym—or numerous eponyms. Jock or Jockey were first the common nicknames for all horse dealers in England, the transition from a horse trader to a professional rider a natural one.

Gasconade *Gasconade*, extravagant boasting or swashbuckling braggadocio, represents in language the Gascon inhabitants of Gascony, France, a region and former province near the Spanish border. Gascons have traditionally been regarded as flamboyantly boastful, a poor people except in their bravery and bragging. One old story tells of a Gascon being asked how he liked the great Louvre in Paris. "Pretty well," the braggart replied, "it reminds me of the back part of my father's stables." D'Artagnan in Dumas' *The Three Musketeers* is from Gascony, and the model of a Gascon.

Gat, Gatling Gun The *Gatling gun* won fame as the best of some eleven mostly eponymous Civil War machine guns (i.e., the *Ripley*; the *Ager* "Coffee Mill"; the *Claxon*; the *Gorgas*; and the *Williams*, which, when used by the Confederates on May 3, 1862, became the first machine gun to be fired in warfare). Designed by Doctor Richard Jordan Gatling (1818–1903), a North Carolina physician and inventor, the *Gatling* was perfected by 1862 but adopted by Union forces too late to be used in more than a few battles. Mounted on wheels, it had a cluster of 5–10 barrels that revolved around a central shaft, the gunner, by turning a handcrank, controlling the rate of fire at up to 350 rounds per minute. Despite the weapon's late introduction, the *Gatling's* effective range of two thousand yards had a strong psychological effect upon the Confederacy; adopted by many nations after the Civil War, it remained in use until about 1900. Although the weapon is only of historical importance today, as the precursor of the modern machine gun, another word deriving from it has wide currency. *Gat*, a slang term for a small gun, apparently arose as a humorous exaggeration. By 1880, however, fictional characters were talking of having *gatlins* under their coats and it wasn't long before *gatlin* or *gatling* was shortened to *gat*. One authority derives *gat* from *cattling up*, meaning "to rob itinerant workers at pistol point," but the accepted theory gives the dubious distinction to Dr. Gatling. The word is rarely used seriously anymore, though often heard in humorous conversations probably not unlike those that resulted in its coining a century ago.

Gauss Known as "the prince of mathematicians," and possibly the greatest mathematical genius of all time, Karl Friedrich Gauss (1777–1855) was a German prodigy who when only ten discovered independently how to sum up complex arithmetic series. He did much important work in his field before turning twenty-one, including a proof of the fundamental theorem of algebra, but did not confine himself to mathematics. Of his many important contributions in topology, physics and astronomy—he headed the Gottingen Observatory—one of the most valuable is his founding of the mathematical theory of electricity. Thus the *gauss*, a unit of intensity of the magnetic field, pays honor to his name.

Geiger Counter The *Geiger counter* is sometimes called the *Geiger-Müller counter*, for both German physicist Hans Geiger (1882–1945) and the scientist who helped him improve upon it in 1927. Actually, it might better be named the *Geiger-Rutherford-Müller counter*, because the British physicist Ernest Rutherford had invented the device, with Geiger, fifteen years earlier. The clicking electronic counter, owned by many hopeful prospectors today and widely used as a detecting device for nuclear radiation, is employed in medicine to locate malignancies. Geiger designed other types of counters as well. His father, Abraham, was a noted rabbi and student of the Orient.

Gentian Among the loveliest of wild flowers, the *fringed gentian* has been immortalized by Bryant and other poets, and the large *Gentiana* genus to which it belongs, containing some four hundred species, provides us with many valued alpine plants for the rock garden. *Gentians* take their name from the powerful monarch Gentius, who reigned as king of Illyria, an ancient seaport on the Adriatic, about 180–167 B.C. Gentius is said to be the first to experience the medicinal values of *gentians*, Pliny and Dioscorides writing that he discovered or noticed this. Since early times the roots and rhizome of the European *yellow gentian* (*Gentiana lutea*) have been used as a means of dilating wounds, as a bitter

tonic and counter-poison, and has been employed in curing diseases. Certain alcoholic beverages are made from the plant, too. The beautiful flowers, predominantly blue, despite *Gentians lutea*, are generally found at high altitudes. Difficult to cultivate, they are nevertheless extensively grown in the home garden. *Gentianaceae*, the *Gentian* family, consisting of eight hundred species and thirty genera, also bears the Illyrian king's name.

Georgette Whether she invented it or not isn't known, but the finespun fabric *georgette* renders honor to Madame Georgette de la Plante, a celebrated Parisian dressmaker and modiste of the late nineteenth century. The formerly trademarked sheer silk crepe is used primarily for blouses and gowns. It is sometimes called *Georgette crepe*.

Georgia, Georgian *Georgia* is named for George II of England (1683–1760). Discovered by Hernando de Soto in 1540, it became the last of the thirteen original colonies, established in 1732 when a British charter was granted for the establishment of "the Colony of Georgia in America." George II, a methodical man who "took the greatest pleasure in counting his money piece by piece, and . . . never forgot a date," wasn't a particularly popular monarch. Historians, straining for something interesting to say about him, seem only to be able to tell us that he was the last British sovereign to command an army in the field—at the battle of Dettingen (June 27, 1743) in the War of the Austrian Succession.

Georgian refers to art and literature in the reign of England's *George V*, particularly the period 1919–25.

German Measles, German Shepherd, German Silver During both World Wars anything *German* was anathema to her enemies. As Mencken points out, *Bismarck herring* became *Eisenhower herring*, sauerkraut, "liberty cabbage," and "German measles" even became "liberty measles." *German measles*, or rubella, is a milder virus disease than measles, though particularly dangerous to the offspring of pregnant women who are exposed to it, and the *German* may be spurious in that sense, but it could be so named because it was first identified by

Dr. Friedrich Hoffmann, a German physician, in 1740. Similarly, *German silver* was initially made at Hildburghausen, Germany, although the fact that it is a silvery alloy, a *fake* silver compound of copper, nickel and zinc, may have influenced its name. In peacetime the Germans have generally been spared the embarrassments of other groups in English, but see *Dutch* for some exceptions. *German comb*, the four fingers and thumb, is an expression invented by the fastidious French. More typical of words using the national adjective is the now ubiquitous *German shepherd* guard dog, which is properly an Alsatian. There are far more of them around than there are burglars and muggers.

Geronimo *Geronimo!* has been the battle cry of paratroopers leaping from their planes since World War II, when the 82nd Airborne adopted it at Fort Bragg, N.C. Some say the slogan was inspired by a popular movie featuring the Indian warrior Geronimo shown near the paratrooper training base at Bragg, others that it arose at Fort Sill, Okla., where, at Medicine Bluffs, Geronimo is said to have made a daring leap on horseback in order to escape his U.S. cavalry pursuers. According to the latter story, Geronimo cried out his name as he jumped to freedom down a steep cliff and into a river below. In protecting his people's land against white settlers, the nineteenth-century Chiricahua Apache leader and prophet terrorized the American Southwest and northern Mexico with cunning, brutal raids. Captured for the last time in 1886, he died under military confinement at Fort Sill in 1909, well over seventy years old. During his many years of captivity, Geronimo became a member of the Dutch Reformed Church and dictated his autobiography to a white writer.

Gerrymander Above editor Benjamin Russell's desk in the offices of the *Centinel*, a Massachusetts Federalist newspaper, hung the serpentine-shaped map of a new Essex County senatorial district that began at Salisbury and included Amesbury, Haverhill, Methuen, Andover, Middleton, Danvers, Lynnfield, Salem, Marblehead, Lynn and Chelsea. This political monster was part of a general reshaping of voting districts that the Democratic-Republican controlled state legislature had enacted with the approval of incumbent Governor Elbridge Gerry. The arbitrary redistricting would have happily enabled the Jeffersonians to concentrate Federalist power in a few districts and remain in the majority after the then yearly gubernatorial elections of 1812, and was of course opposed by all Federalists, a fairly common practice of the times. So when the celebrated painter Gilbert Stuart visited the *Centinel* offices one day before the elections, editor Russell indignantly pointed to the monstrous map on the wall, inspiring Stuart to take a crayon and add head, wings and claws to the already lizard-like district. "That will do for a salamander," the artist said when he finished. "A *Gerry*-mander, you mean," Mr. Russell replied, and a name for the political creature was born.

Many copies of the Stuart map, titled The Gerrymander, were distributed, helping to offset the Gerry-approved manipulation of voting districts and foiling him in his bid for a third term. His name immediately became a new noun for an old political practice, *gerrymander* coming into use as a verb within a year. Rewarded for his party loyalty with the Jeffersonian party's nomination for vice-president the same year that he lost the governorship, Gerry was elected with and served under Madison until his death in office. Elbridge Gerry (1744–1814) wasn't ever extremely popular with the American people—he had refused to sign the Constitution, objecting to taxation, and had been roundly condemned as a Jacobite for his role in the infamous XYZ affair. But he might have been remembered for his patriotic service before and after the Revolution, his signing of the Declaration of Independence, or even his courageous support of the War of 1812. That his name became just another term for political deception and chicanery is only tempered by the fact that the word and name are no longer pronounced exactly alike—Gerry's name pronounced with a hard g and the word pronounced "jerrymander."

Gestapo *Gestapo* is a contraction formed from *Gehheime Staatspolizei*, the Nazi secret state police agency that was formally declared a criminal organization at the Nuremberg trials. Founded in 1933 by Hermann Goering, it came under Heinrich Himmler's control as part of the S.S. the following year. The group's ruthless methods of capture, torture and extermination, the fact that it was responsible for all concentration camps, and its exemption from any control by the courts made it the symbol for brutal, sadistic repression that it is today.

Gibberish Both Dr. Johnson and Grose thought that *gibberish*, meaning nonsense or words without meaning, derived from the name of Geber, an eleventh-century Arabian chemist who wrote his formulas in seemingly unintelligible jargon and anagrams in order to avoid the death penalty for sorcery. Today many authorities speculate that the word is imitative of the sound of nonsense, at most only influenced by Geber's name. Jabir ibn Hayyan (*Jabir* is the Arabic for *Geber*) was actually an eighth-century alchemist, apparently a prolific writer though scholars tell us he could not have written the two thousand books attributed to him. Little is known of Geber except that he was respected enough for many medieval scientists to cite him as an authority, and for one fourteenth-century Spanish alchemist to go so far as to adopt his name. *Gibberish*, once also "a secret disguised language," does not derive from the verb *gibber*, which it preceded in use, and apparently has no roots in "gypsy jabber," as has been stated. *Jabber, gabble, giggle* and *gurgle* are some other imitative or echoic words.

Gibbon Is this long-armed ape really named after a man? Possibly, if it's true that the naming was the practical joke of an eminent naturalist. Several respected etymologists believe that this is the case. Apparently the French naturalist Buffon first named the Indian ape in his *Natural History* (1749). The witty Buffon may have been aware that the tombs of the English Gybbon family in Kent, "dating from about 1700, are surmounted by an ape's head, the family crest." A less inspired derivation suggests that *gibbon* comes from an Indian dialect, but there is no abundant evidence for either theory.

Gibraltar, Rock of Gibraltar *Rock of Gibraltar* signifies any impregnable stronghold. *Gibraltar* was anciently called Calpë, forming the renowned "Pillars of Hercules" with Abyla on the opposite coast, but when the Saracen conqueror Tarik captured it from Spain and built a castle there in 710 A.D., it was named *Jebel el Tarik*, the mountain of Tarik, in his honor. *Gibraltar* is simply an English corruption of the longer name. The island, a rocky promontory on Spain's southern coast, acquired a further reputation for impregnability when the British captured it in 1704, made the island a fort and naval base, and successfully repelled several invasions in future years. *Gibraltar* remains in British hands today; despite recent demonstrations for its return to Spain, the British consider "the Rock" a symbol of power and have not been willing to relinquish it. Strategically important because it commands the only entrance to the Mediterranean from the west, the island is honeycombed with natural and man-made caves used by the military. It is also an important tourist center, a major attraction being the Barbary apes that live there.

Gibson Cocktail, Gibson Girl A bartender at the New York Players Club is supposed to have run out of olives and garnished artist Charles Dana Gibson's martini with a pearl onion instead, giving us the *gibson cocktail*. Gibson was no stranger to such honors. The popular American artist's *Gibson girls* appeared on the covers of national magazines in the period 1896 to about 1920 as frequently as Norman Rockwell's work has in recent times. His pen-and-ink drawings typically depicted slender, waspwaisted beauties clad in sweeping skirts, shirtwaists and large hats. The well-bred *Gibson girls*, widely imitated, were the ideals of young men and women alike up until about the end of World War I, when their vogue ended, but their creator remained active until his death in 1944, aged seventy-seven. Gibson also illustrated a great number of popular novels, and his series *The Education of Mr. Pipp* (1899) became the basis for a play of the same name.

Gibus A *gibus* is the folding opera hat invented by Parisian hatmaker Antoine Gibus in 1837. This cloth top hat with collapsible crown proved ideal for gentlemen attending the opera, who could fold it flat and put it out of the way, the patented gimmick making a considerable fortune for its inventor and his heirs. By now almost a relic of the past, the *gibus* is rarely used today.

Gideon Bible In 1910 one very proper Bostonian sought an injunction to prevent the *Gideon Society* from distributing the Bible—"on the ground that it is an obscene and immoral publication." But not even crackpots have deterred the organization of traveling salesmen from their goal of placing a *Gideon Bible* in every hotel room and Pullman car in America. The *Gideon Society*, formally the Christian Commercial Young Men's Association of America, was founded in Boscobel, Wis., in 1899 and is now based in Chicago. Its name derives from that of the Biblical Gideon, a judge of Israel who became a warrior and ingeniously delivered Israel from the Midianites, giving his country forty years of peace (*Judges* 6:11–7:25).

Gilbert Physician to Queen Elizabeth I, and author of the first scientific book published in England, William Gilbert, or Gylberde (c. 1544–1603) was the most distinguished scientist of his day. His work on magnetism—he was the first European to accurately describe the behavior of magnets and the earth's magnetism—led to the *gilbert*, a unit of magnetic force being named in his honor. Gilbert first used the terms "electricity," "electrical force" and "magnetic pole" in English, and introduced the *Copernican theory* to his countrymen.

Gilbert & Sullivan, Gilbertian These two terms are used to describe lighthearted fanciful wit similar to that characterizing the many comic operas by Sir William Schwenck Gilbert (1836–1911) and Sir Arthur Seymour Sullivan (1842–1900). Notable examples are *The Mikado* (1885), *The Pirates of Penzance* (1879) and *H.M.S. Pinafore* (1878). Gilbert, the librettist, and Sullivan, the composer, collaborated for twenty-five years before a quarrel ended a perfect partnership peerlessly combining social satire with grand opera. Sullivan is also known as the author of many songs and hymns, including "Onward, Christian Soldiers." Gilbert died a hero's death, dying of heart failure while trying to save a drowning girl. He was seventy-five years old at the time.

Gimlet A "healthy" cocktail invented by a naval officer. Anyway, it was a lot healthier than drinking gin neat, which is exactly why Sir T. O. Gimlette devised the *gimlet* that commemorates him. Gimlette, a British naval surgeon from 1879–1917, believed that drinking gin straight harmed the health and impaired the efficiency of naval officers, so he introduced a cocktail that diluted the gin with lime juice. Today the *gimlet* is made with gin or vodka, sweetened lime juice and sometimes soda water.

Gin Rickey *Rickeys* can be made of any liquor, carbonated water and lime juice, but the most famous drink in the family is the *gin rickey*, invented in about 1895 and named after "a distinguished Washington guzzler of the period," according to H. L. Mencken. Just which Washington Colonel Rickey was so honored is a matter of dispute, however. Several theories have been recorded by Mencken in his *American Language, Supplement I*, and other sources, but none is generally accepted.

Gladstone Bag At least one writer claims that English statesman and orator William Ewart Gladstone (1809–98) never carried the *Gladstone bag* named after him. Neither did the four-time prime minister *invent* the light, hinged leather bag, but he did do much traveling in his long public career and the flexible bag was made with the convenience of travelers in mind. Gladstone's name was given to certain cheap clarets—*Gladstone wines*—because he lowered the customs duty on French wines while Chancellor of the Exchequer in 1860, and a two-seated, four-wheeled carriage also paid him honor. Gladstone has been rated as the most inspiring and among the five greatest British prime ministers, but his private life sometimes provoked comment. Until he was well past seventy-five, for example, he made it his habit to walk the streets of London nights trying to persuade prostitutes to convert to a different way of life. When the prime minister left office for the last time, he was eighty-five years old. Over his long public career he had had his differences with many notable figures. "He speaks to me as if I were a public meeting," Queen Victoria once complained, but his major political opponent was his arch rival Disraeli. One time Disraeli offered a definition of the difference between a misfortune and a calamity. "If Gladstone fell into the Thames, it would be a misfortune," he explained. "But if someone dragged him out again, it would be a calamity." (See also *Fletcherize*.)

Goethian, Goethite, Gothite, Faust, Faustian It is sometimes forgotten that Johann Wolfgang von Goethe (1749–1832) won fame as a scientist as well as a poet and writer. The creator of *Faust*, which ranks with *Hamlet* and Dante's *Divine Comedy* as an unparalleled achievement of the poetic mind, completed many researches into natural science. His *Theory of Colors* (1810) and *Metamorphosis of Plants* (1817–24) were the results of but two such investigations. For this reason the iron-bearing *goethite* or *gothite* minerals are named in his honor. *Goethian*, intellectual yet humane and sympathetic, refers to the writer's life and work. "In our younger days," Goethe once wrote, "we were sure we could build palaces for mankind. With experience we learn that the most we can do is clean up their dung hills." His Faust is based in part on a real person, Dr. Johann Faust (c. 1480–c. 1538), a German magician and astrologer who was believed to have sold his soul to the devil. The Faust legend inspired Goethe as it did Marlowe before him.

Goldwynism "Include me out," "In two words: im-possible," and "We have passed a lot of water since this" (for "a lot of water has passed under the bridge") are but three legendary *Goldwynisms*. An American film pioneer, Samuel Goldwyn has long been considered a modern "Mr. Malaprop," unrivaled for his fractured English. Goldwyn, born in Warsaw, Poland, on August 27, 1882, founded Goldwyn Pictures Corporation, which became part of Metro-Goldwyn-Mayer in 1924, and later turned independent producer. His films include *Dodsworth, Wuthering Heights, The Little Foxes, Pride of the Yankees, The*

Best Years of Our Lives, and *Porgy and Bess.* In declining health in recent years, the producer lives in Beverly Hills. In 1971 the Medal of Freedom was presented to him by President Nixon for "proving that clean movies could be good box office."

Goliath, David and Goliath The original Goliath stood between 9 ft. 9 inches and 11 ft. 3 inches tall, depending on how you value the "6 cubits and a span" given as his height in the Bible. Nevertheless, the stripling David slew him with a stone from his sling (*I Samuel* 49–51) and defeated the Philistines. A *Goliath* has since meant a giant or someone of great strength, while a *David and Goliath* contest is one between a great and a small man. Not to take anything away from David, Goliath was a stripling compared to the giant Og (16 ft. 2½ inches) and other Biblical big men. All such claims, however, are most likely based on our ignorance of ancient measurement units. The tallest man in history, of whom accurate records were kept, was American Robert Pershing Wadlow, born in 1918. He died when only twenty-two, weighing 491 pounds and measuring 8 ft. 10.3 inches. The title of tallest giantess goes to Marianne Wehde, who grew to 8 ft. 4 inches before she died in Berlin in 1883, aged seventeen.

Gongorism It is only fair to say that the arrows that were transferred into "flying asps" and the birds that became "feathered zithers" were part of a larger plan. Luis de Góngora y Argote (1561–1627) wrote in a twisted, torturous style in his later years, his syntax deliberately distorted, in order to highlight words and create an unreal world. But he inspired many imitators, who inspired many critics, and unfortunately, his name is now a synonym for a deliberately obscure, meaningless, and affected ornamental style. The Spanish poet after whom *gongorism* is named is essentially a lyric poet in his early years; his work was much admired by Cervantes, though no poem of his was published in his lifetime. Readers have discovered that his baroque *gongorisms*, a great influence on modern poetry, are far from meaningless, as difficult as the long poems like *Soledades* are to read. Gongora, who adopted his mother's name, was a priest as well as a poet and dramatist. Toward the end of his life he turned back from cultivated obscurity to a simple, unaffected style. (See also *Guevarism*.)

Good Samaritan The story is told by Christ in *Luke* 10:30–35: "*A man was going down from Jerusalem to Jericho, and he fell among robbers, who stripped and beat him, and departed, leaving him half dead. Now by chance a priest was going down that road; and when he saw him he passed by on the other side. So likewise a Levite . . . passed by on the other side. But a Samaritan, as he journeyed, came to where he was; and when he saw him, he had compassion, and went to him and bound up his wounds, pouring on oil and wine; then he set him on his own beast and brought him to an inn; and took care of him. And the next day he took out two denarii (about forty cents) and gave them to the innkeeper, saying, 'Take care of him; and whatever more you spend, I will repay you when I come back.'*" This *good Samaritan* remains nameless in the Bible. We only know that he lived in the district of ancient Palestine called Samaria, northern kingdom of the Hebrews. But over the centuries the anonymous man has remained a symbol for a kind, helpful, philanthropic person, one who does good with no thought of personal gain. The *Samaritans* are also a religious community who claim that they are descendants of the ten tribes of Israel and that their religion contains the true undiluted teachings of Moses. Formerly inhabiting Samaria in Palestine, they are now represented by a few families living in Jordan. These *Samaritans*, who broke with the Jews in about 458 B.C., observe the Torah even more scrupulously than orthodox Jews. As in Biblical times, they celebrate Passover with the killing of lambs.

Gordian Knot When we say someone cut the *Gordian knot*, we mean that he solved a baffling problem by a single bold and incisive act. The saying remembers the workman Gordius of old, who was chosen king of Phrygia when he fulfilled an oracle's prophecy that the first man to approach the temple of Jupiter driving a wagon would rule the land. King Gordius dedicated his wagon to

the god and tied it to a temple beam with a knot of cornel bark so cunning that another oracle declared that whosoever should untie it would become lord of all Asia. Enter Alexander the Great, whose hopes lie in that direction. "Well then it is thus I perform the task," the conqueror says, without hesitation, and cuts the knot in twain with his sword. The whole story is improbable, scholars tell us, although Gordium, the capital of ancient Phrygia, had been named for Gordius, the father of King Midas. But a *Gordian knot* remains an intricate problem and *gordian* has even been used as a verb for "to tie in knots" and as an adjective. "*She was a gordian shape of dazzling hue, / Vermillion-spotted, gold and green and blue. . . .*" John Keats, referring to a serpent, in his poem "Lamia."

Gordon Setter In contrast to the red-coated Irish setter, bred at about the same time, the *Gordon setter* is a brilliant black and tan in color. The breed originated in Scotland, partially developed by Alexander, the second duke of Gordon (1743–1847), a Scottish breeder and sportsman who also served in the House of Lords and wrote a number of folk ballads. The long-haired Irish and *Gordon setters*, extensively used by sportsmen for game pointing, both descend from the English setter developed some three centuries before them.

Gothic After overthrowing Rome in the fifth century, the Gothic tribesmen, an east German people, dominated much of Europe for the next three hundred years. Not much is known of them, and their architecture was certainly not *gothic*, but Renaissance architects bestowed their names on all buildings characteristic of the Middle Ages, considering such structures crude and barbaric, suitable for the Goths. The twelfth- to sixteenth-century building style, characterized by the pointed arch, as well as *Gothic art*, *Gothic type* and myriad other things, were therefore named for a people who had nothing to do with them at all.

Grable-bodied Seamen Movie actress Betty Grable, her "million dollar legs" insured by Lloyds of London, was the pin-up girl par excellence during World War II. British sailors used the term

Grable-bodied seamen to describe long-stemmed lovelies in the Wrens (Women's Royal Naval Service) who fit the description. Miss Grable, born in St. Louis, Mo., in 1916, was formerly married to bandleader Harry James. She has made few recent films.

Graham Bread, Graham Crackers
Young Presbyterian minister Sylvester Graham (1794–1851) became so ardent a temperance advocate that he not only traveled far and wide to lecture on the demon rum, but invented a vegetable diet which he was sure would be a cure for those suffering from the evils of drink. Graham soon extended his mission to include changing America's sinful eating habits. Meats and fats, he said, led to sexual excesses and mustard and catsup could cause insanity, but Graham mainly urged the substitution of homemade unsifted whole wheat flour for white bread. From 1830 on *Graham boardinghouses, Graham Societies* and *Graham food stores* sprang up throughout the land, these opposed, often violently, by bakers, butchers and people who simply liked meat and white bread. Graham was driven off many a platform. Great thinkers took sides in the great war against white bread, Lowell, for example, writing that "I am becoming more and more inclined to Grahamism every day," and pitch battles were often fought between Graham's followers and mobs of disbelievers. Among his followers were Bronson Alcott, father of the author of *Little Women;* Joseph Smith, founder of the Mormon church; and Amelia Jenks Bloomer of *bloomers* fame. When all controversy ended, it developed that the seemingly eccentric reformer had been right in a few respects. Modern science has affirmed his belief that refining flour robs it of vitamins and minerals, and most of his regimen, including vegetables and fruits in the diet, fresh air while sleeping, moderate eating, and abundant exercise, is now widely accepted. His memorials are the *Graham flour, Graham bread* and *Graham crackers* that his followers ate and dedicated to him.

Gramont's Memory The name is often spelled "Grammont" due to its misspelling in the *Mémoires de la vie du comte de Grammont.* A *Gramont's mem-* ory, a convenient one, derives from a tale told about the count and Lady Elizabeth Hamilton. While visiting England in 1663, the sharp-tongued Gramont is said to have grossly insulted and refused to apologize to La Belle Hamilton, whose brothers followed him as he prepared to leave the country, drew their swords, and asked if he hadn't forgotten something. "True, true," he replied, unruffled. "I promised to marry your sister." This he did. In fact, it would be expected, judging from the French courtier's life. Only the year before his marriage, Philibert, Comte de Gramont had been exiled from Paris for attempting to rival King Louis XIV in a love affair. The French diplomat's memoirs, a masterpiece of their kind, vividly describe the licentious court of England's Charles II. They were written by Gramont's brother-in-law, Anthony Hamilton, from materials supplied by the count. So sharp-tongued was Philibert that one writer describes the immense feeling of relief expressed by the French court when, in 1707, it was announced that he had died. Even at eighty-seven he was still a threat to anyone who crossed him.

Grangerize Reverend James Granger (1723–76) himself clipped some fourteen thousand engraved portraits from other books to use as possible illustrations for his *Biographical History of England.* . . . Some of the books he pillaged were rare ones, and to make matters worse, he suggested in his preface that private collections like his might prove valuable someday. This resulted in a fad called *Grangerizing,* or extra-illustration, thousands of people mutilating fine books and stuffing pictures and other material into Granger's. Editions following the 1769 *Biographical History . . . adapted to a Methodical Catalogue of Engraved British Heads* provided blank pages for the insertion of these extra illustrations; the book eventually increased to six volumes from its original two. Sets of Granger illustrated with up to three thousand engravings were compiled and so many early English books were ravaged that *to grangerize* came to mean the mutilation that remains the bane of librarians today.

Great Dane Although this dog may have originally been Danish, the origin of the name *great Dane* is unknown. The strong, graceful working breed was developed in sixteenth-century Germany to hunt boars and probably has Irish wolfhound and English mastiff blood. Over the ages it has been called by many names, until, in 1880, German breeders officially adopted *great Dane*. Among the largest of modern breeds, the dog's smooth coat may be harlequin, fawn, steel-blue, black or brindle. Adult males measure 30 inches or more at the shoulder, weighing up to 140 pounds. The *great Dane*, relatively easy to train, is commonly employed for sentry and guard duty, though it is increasingly becoming a house dog. Dogs resembling the breed have been recorded in ancient Egypt, China, Greece, and first-century England.

Great Scott! Old Fuss-and-Feathers, General Winfield Scott (1786–1866), may be honored in this exclamation. At any rate, the term hasn't been traced before his day, the story being that the hero of the Mexican War lent his name to it during his campaign as Whig candidate for president in 1852. Scott, a brigadier general at twenty-eight, was known for his swagger, one version claims, his opponents jeeringly calling him "Great Scott." Scottophiles insist that these words were really an expression of admiration for the hero's great dignity. Finally, the anti-General Scott school contends that the term is just a euphemism for "Great God!" a play on the German *Gott*.

Greek, Grecian The Greeks are the subject of many proverbs still heard. *Beware of Greeks bearing gifts* dates to a line in Virgil, "I fear the Greeks especially when they bring gifts," and refers to the fabled wooden horse containing soldiers that the Greeks gave to the Trojans. *Greek trust* was to the Romans no trust at all; and *when Greek meets Greek then comes the tug of war* commemorates the resistance of the ancient Greek cities to the Macedonian Kings Philip and Alexander the Great. Putting something off *until the Greek calends* is to never do it, for the Greeks, unlike the Romans, had no term like *calends* for the first days of their months. *To play the Greek* is to live a luxurious life, while the modern term *when Greek meets*

Greek, they open a restaurant at least admits that Greeks are enterprising.

Terms commemorating this people include *Greek fire*, an incendiary of obscure composition that ignited upon contact with water, probably invented by the Byzantine Greeks during the Middle Ages; *Greek letter fraternity* or *sorority*; *it's all Greek to me*; and the slang term *Greek* for a gambler. *Grecian* is found in *Grecian bend*, a posture bent forward from the waist much affected in the late nineteenth century, and the straightlined *Grecian profile*, among other expressions. To many, *Grecian* itself is the term "for all civilized and subtle thoughts and feelings," the *Grecians* "swelling o'er with arts," as Shakespeare wrote. (See also *Gringo*.)

Greenacre The rope broke when they hanged James Greenacre at Newgate prison in 1837. But little sympathy was shown for the murderer, who had hacked up his victim and buried sections of the lady in various parts of London. Stevedores, in fact, promptly adopted the killer's name to indicate the falling of cargo. Whenever rope slings broke while goods were being loaded or unloaded, the cry *Greenacre!* went up along the docks.

Greengage Plum, Reine-Claude *Greengage plums* are actually yellow with a tinge of green. The renowned plum, which has two eponymous names, was brought from Italy to France about 1500, where it was named and is still called the *Reine-Claude* after Claudia, *la bonne reine*, queen to Francis I from their marriage in 1514 until his death. About 1725 Sir William Gage, an amateur botanist, imported a number of plum trees from a monastery in France, all of which were labeled except the *Reine-Claude*. A gardener at Hengrave Hall in Suffolk named the unknown variety *Green Gage* in honor of his employer and the *Reine-Claude* has been the *greengage* in England ever since. The *blue* and *purple gage* were developed from their illustrious ancestor on the fertile grounds of Gage's estate, probably much to the delight of his eight children.

Gregg System *Gregg* is the most widely used shorthand writing in the world and by far the most popular in the United States. Not the first of shorthand systems by any means (see *Tironian notes, Pitman*), it was invented by John Robert Gregg (1864–1948), an Irishman who explained *Gregg* in *The Phonetic Handwriting* (1888) and emigrated to America to introduce it here. "Light-Line Phonography" is an improvement on the earlier phonetic *Pitman* in that it is based on the same smooth, forward slant as ordinary script and is thus much easier to write. Being phonetic like its predecessor, it can be adapted to any spoken language.

Gregorian Calendar, Chant, Epoch, Telescope While an improvement on its predecessors, the inaccurate *Julian calendar* resulted in the calendar year gradually losing on the actual solar year, or the time it takes the earth to travel around the sun. By the sixteenth century, for example, the first day of spring came on March 11 instead of March 21. As this interfered with seasonal church celebrations, Pope Gregory XIII introduced a modified calendar in 1582, decreeing that the day after October 4 in that year would be October 15, making up for the lost days in this way and assuring that they would not be lost again by ruling that century years would no longer be leap years unless divisible by 400. Pope Gregory probably did not devise the "New Style" calendar, but it was named in his honor. Immediately accepted in Catholic countries, the *Gregorian calendar* wasn't adopted in England or America until 1752—when the calendar gained twelve days on sun but people missed their birthdays on those twelve days. Imperfect itself, it is nevertheless used today throughout most of the world.

The *Gregorian Epoch* is the day on which the *Gregorian calendar* commenced. *Gregorian chant* and *Gregorian telescope* have nothing to do with Pope Gregory XIII. The medieval church music was introduced by Pope Gregory I, Gregory the Great (d. 604), and the first reflecting telescope invented by Scotch mathematician James Gregory (1638–75). (See also *Julian Calendar*.)

Gregorian Tree A synonym for the gallows. Obsolete in speech, though not in literature, since the early nineteenth century, the expression derives from the names of two or more hangmen. Gregory Brandon, royal executioner in the time of England's James I, was succeeded by his son Richard, often called "Young Gregory," who beheaded Charles I in 1649. The Two Gregories, like Derrick before and Jack Ketch after them, became so widely associated with the gallows over half a century that their name was applied to it. There may have been a third executioner named Gregory to reinforce the meaning, but Gregory Brandon is remembered as the hangman granted a coat of arms for his gruesomely efficient work on the scaffold. He must have been just as proficient with the sword, too, for noblemen were generally spared hanging, neck stretching being considered an affront to their dignity. Even today there is discrimination of sorts as regards execution in England. A lord not only has the right to be tried before a jury of lords—if sentenced to die he can demand a silk rope rather than one of common hemp.

Gresham's Law The tendency of bad money to drive good money out of circulation is known as *Gresham's Law*, but it was formulated as an economic principle long before Sir Thomas Gresham (c. 1519–1579). Gresham, a London merchant and founder of what is now the Royal Exchange, noted that the more valuable of two equivalent coins would be hoarded, but Copernicus and others had already made similar observations. Unaware that he had not even formulated the principle, the economist H. D. MacLeod named the law for Gresham in 1857. The British businessman is also commemorated by the expression *to sup with Sir Thomas Gresham*, to go dinnerless, the Royal Exchange that he built having been a common resting place for those without enough money for a meal. For the story of Gresham's famous diamond see *Cleopatra's pearl*.

Gringo

Green grow the rashes O
The happiest hours that ere I spent
Were spent among the lasses O.

It seems doubtful that these tender lyrics by Bobby Burns were sung by battle-hardened American soldiers in the Mexican War. But the song's first two words are commonly believed to be the origin of the contemptuous name *gringo* that the Mexicans bestowed upon the Americans. Most scholars disagree and trace the term to the Spanish *gringo*, "gibberish," which is a corruption of the Spanish word *Griego*, a "Greek." *Gringo*, by this theory, would be related to the old saying "It's all Greek to me," indicating that Yankees were strange and unfamiliar in their ways.

But we haven't exhausted all the conjectures by any means. Mencken puts his trust in "a slang term for foreigners who spoke bad Spanish," and another etymologist claims "green coat" as the base for *gringo*. Major Samuel Ringgold, dreaded by Mexican forces during the Mexican War, is a third possibility. Ringgold's name, pronounced with a trilled *r* and without the last two letters, as it normally would be by a Mexican, might yet prove the correct source for the word. The brilliant strategist was killed at the Battle of Palo Alto in 1846. An army post in Texas is named after him, as are several places in the southwestern part of the United States.

Grog, Grog Blossom, Groggery, Groggy, Mount Vernon *Mount Vernon* was named after Vice Admiral Sir Edward Vernon by George Washington's half-brother Laurence, who served under "Old Grog" when he led six little ships to the West Indies and captured heavily fortified Portobello during the War of Jenkins' Ear (1739). This action made Vernon England's hero of the hour, Parliament voting him formal thanks and street pageants being held on his birthday to celebrate his humbling of the Spaniards. But the arrogant former war hawk M.P. never won popularity with his men. Old Grog had been nicknamed for the impressive grogram cloak he wore on deck in all kinds of weather, the coarse taffeta material symbolizing his tough and irascible nature. Then, in August, 1740, the stern disciplinarian issued an order that made his name a malediction. In order to curb drunken brawling aboard ships in his command, and to save money, he declared that all rum rations would henceforth be diluted with water. Incensed old sea dogs cursed Vernon roundly, for half a pint of rum mixed with a quart of water seemed weak stuff indeed to anyone on a raw rum liquid diet. Furthermore, the rationed bilge was divided into two issues, served six hours apart. His men soon defiantly dubbed the adulterated rum *Grog*, using the nickname they had bestowed upon the admiral. Vernon's order served its purpose and "three water rum" became the official ration for all enlisted personnel in the Royal Navy, but *grog* quickly took on the wider meaning of any cheap, diluted drink. Low taverns were christened *grog shops* in England and *groggeries* in America, and facial blemishes or pimples resulting from overindulgence in any kind of rotgut were jokingly called *grog blossoms*. Eventually, *grog* came to mean liquor itself, diluted or not, and it was either a little stronger *grog* or a lot of the weaker concoction that made one unsteady on one's feet and resulted in the pugilistic and now general *groggy*. Admiral Vernon, of course, never imagined that he would be remembered for anything but Portobello. Old Grog continued to serve in his usual belligerent eccentric way. But he went too far. In 1746 he was dismissed from the Royal Navy for writing pamphlets attacking the Admiralty. He died in 1757, aged seventy-three. (See also *Booze*; *Hootch*; *Jenkins' Ear*.)

Guevarism, Euphuism Spanish writer and moralist Antonio de Guevara (c. 1480–1545) has been regarded as the father of *euphuism*, for which his name is equivalent. But *euphuism*, an ornate artificial writing or speaking style characterized by alliteration, eloquence and high-flown phrases, was coined more than a century after his death. *Euphuism* takes its name from *Euphues: the Anatomy of Wit* (1579) by John Lyly, who displayed such a style in his book in an attempt to "soften" the English language, Euphues being the name of the main character in his romance. Guevara may have been among Lyly's inspirations, for the Spanish author's *The Golden Book of Marcus Aurelius* (1535) and other works were early translated into English. (See also *Gongorism*.)

Guido's Scale, Aretinian Syllables The work of Italian musician and singing teacher Guido d'Arezzo (c. 990–1050) forms the basis of the modern system of musical notation. This inspired genius devised the *Guido scale* or *Aretinian syllables* that sing praises to him in about 1040. The names he gave to the musical notes of the scale are still used today in modified form (*do, re, mi, fa, sol, la*). The Benedictine monk based them on six lines of an old Latin hymn to St. John the Baptist, which happened to form the scale—the lines being:

UT *queant laxis*
RESo*nare fibris*
MIr*a gestorum*
FA*muli tuorum*
SOLv*e polluti*
LA*bir reatum*
Sancte Joannes!

Over the years the final syllable *ti* was added to the scale and two centuries ago the syllable *do* replaced *ut* in English. Solfeggio is the English word, taken from the Italian, to describe the musical exercise sung with *Guido's scale*. Guido claimed that by his method a pupil could learn to sing in five months instead of ten years and he reputedly taught Pope John XIX the art in a relatively short time.

Guillotine, Louisette Dr. Joseph Ignace Guillotine (1738–1814) did not invent the *guillotine*, did not die by the *guillotine*, and all his life futilely tried to detach his name from the height reducer. The confusion began on October 10, 1789, when the eminent Parisian physician, a member of the National Assembly during the French Revolution, suggested that a "merciful" beheading device replace the clumsy sword and degrading rope then used by French executioners. Guillotine may have studied similar instruments abroad and definitely knew they existed, for the infamous "Maiden" had been used even in France during the Middle Ages and was still widely employed throughout Europe. In his speech to the French chamber Guillotine contended that hanging brought disgrace upon a criminal's family, that beheading probably felt better, being quicker and less painful at least, and that there wasn't any equality in a nobleman being dispatched by the sword while a commoner legally had to swing by a rope for his crimes. His ideas, especially the

last, gradually took hold in egalitarian France, and two years later the Assembly adopted decapitation as the legal means of execution for "every person condemned to death." The specific machine accepted for the purpose was designed by Dr. Antoine Louis, secretary of the Academy of Medicine, and constructed by a German named Tobias Schmidt, who even supplied a leather bag to hold the severed heads. For some 329 francs, inclusive, the first *Louisette* or *Louison*, as it came to be called, was erected on the Place de Grève, and on April 22, 1792, the head of a notorious highwayman named Peletier became the first to plop into its basket. But Dr. Guillotine remained in the public's mind for his eloquent speech and one of many popular songs about the new machine claimed that he had invented it. Not much time passed before *La Louisette* lost out to *La machine Guillotine, Madame Guillotine* and then *guillotine* itself.

The legend that Dr. Guillotine was hoist with his own petard springs from several circumstances. For one, its real designer, Dr. Louis, lost his inventive head to the *guillotine* during the Reign of Terror—as did thousands of victims, including of course the mechanically inclined Louis XVI, who is said to have recommended its oblique cutting edge as a refinement to the inventor. Secondly, Dr. Guillotine was indeed *condemned* to die for protecting friends suspected by Robespierre, only escaping execution by the narrowest of margins when Robespierre himself was *guillotined*. Finally, a Dr. J. B. V. Guillotine of Lyons had been so executed during the Terror, his name, of course, confused with the more prominent doctor's. Many wanted to think that Guillotine became the victim of his own Frankenstein monster, like Hugues Aubriot, the designer of the Bastille and the first man to be imprisoned in it, but the good doctor lived on. He lived to see Napoleon suppress the Revolution and saw the method he advocated become a symbol of needless and brutal slaughter rather than humanitarianism. But he died a full twenty-two years after the machine was introduced—in his own bed, peacefully, of a carbuncle on his shoulder. After his death, his children petitioned the French government to change the name of the *guillotine,* but won only permission to change their own names.

Gun, Gun Moll The Scandinavian female name *Gunhildr* most likely won favor among missile throwers in the Middle Ages because its components, *gunnr* and *hildr,* meant war and battle in Icelandic. There is a possibility, however, that some forgotten soldier may have named a specific ballista *Gunhildr* for his wife or sweetheart, the name gaining currency in this way. Whatever the case, we find *Gunhildr* used before 1309 in England, where it was shortened to *gunne,* and then *gun,* the last designation transferred to firearms upon the invention of the cannon. The list of weapons at Windsor Castle in 1330 mentions a "large ballista called Lady Gunhilda," a mechanical catapult used to hurl huge stones and balls of fire at enemy troops. This particular ballista, its name derived from the Scandinavian, must have been around for a number of years and may even have been the particular *Gunhilda* abbreviated to *gunne* some years before.

Gun does not derive from the echo of its sound, as has been stated. Many obvious expressions stem from the word, including *give it the gun,* originally an aviation term for throw open the throttle of an airplane. *Gun moll* may come from an entirely different source. Mencken suggests that the *gun* in the term is from the Yiddish *ganov,* a thief. A *gun moll* in the 1920's was a female pickpocket, these professionals reformed or transformed only when newspaper reporters mistakenly took to calling any racketeer's girl a *gun moll.*

Guppy, Guppy Submarine By far the best known and most popular of home aquarium fish is the *guppy* or rainbow fish (*Lebistes reticulatus*), also called the millions fish. *Guppies* take their name from R. J. L. Guppy of Trinidad who presented the British Museum with specimens of the species in the late nineteenth century. Since then many handsome exotic types have been developed. In courtship the smaller males (1 inch long) are particularly interesting, fanning out their colorful tails to attract the females. *Guppies* bear their young live, giving birth to from an average of 50 to as many as 185 babies at a time and bearing offspring every four weeks. Abundant in South America, the fish devours mosquito larvae and so helps to prevent malaria. It has also proved useful in genetic experiments.

The streamlined *guppy submarine* developed toward the end of World War II is named for the *guppy,* but its name is also an acronym, the first four letters standing for "greater underwater propulsion power." The *guppy* was twice as fast as any old-style sub. (See also *Molly.*)

Gutenberg Bible, Mazarin Bible The first printed Bible, long thought to be the first book to be printed from movable type in the Western world, is named for Johannes Gutenberg (c. 1398–1468), the German printer generally believed to be the inventor of movable type. Few great men of relatively modern times have left such meager records of their lives as Gutenberg. No likeness exists of him and his life is veiled in obscurity. Gutenberg may have adopted his mother's maiden name, for his father's surname appears to have been Gensfleisch. It is known that the goldsmith Johann Fust loaned the printer money to establish his press at Mainz, which Gutenberg lost to him in 1455 when he failed to repay the loan. But no book extant bears Gutenberg's name as its printer and though he is still regarded as a likely candidate, he may not have invented printing in the West or even printed the *Gutenberg Bible* (1450). The Bible is certainly not the first book to be printed in Europe, Gutenberg himself printing several small works before it. As for movable type, it had been used in Korea before its uncertain European invention. Whoever printed the *Gutenberg Bible* produced a beautiful work complete with colored initials and illumination by hand. It is often called the *Mazarin Bible* because the first copy to come to attention was found in the library of Cardinal Mazarin in 1760.

Guy American expressions often vary greatly in meaning from their identical British cousins. The slang expression to "knock up" a woman, for example, means only to knock on her door in England, but if a Britisher were to say "I'll knock you up," to an American lady the most charitable response he'd get in most circles would be a slightly incredulous look. Similarly, "a regular guy" to many Englishmen means "a thoroughly grotesque person," not "a decent chap" at all. The difference is not as pronounced as in the past, but the American meaning still has a strange ring to British ears. For the English *guy* owes its origin to the grotesque effigies of Guy Fawkes, a leader of the infamous Gunpowder Plot, that are carried through the streets of England and burnt in bonfires on November 5, *Guy Fawkes Day*. The Gunpowder Plot, a plan to blow up King James I and the entire Parliament when he was expected to open that body on November 5, 1605, blew up itself when Francis Tresham, one of the conspirators, anonymously warned his brother-in-law, Lord Monteagle, not to appear at the opening session. This set off an investigation that revealed thirty-six barrels of gunpowder concealed under coal and kindling in a storeroom the conspirators had rented directly beneath the House of Lords. The intrepid Guy Fawkes, all ready to ignite the powder, instead found himself arrested on the eve of November 4. Fawkes, born in 1570, was an English soldier noted for his bravery; a convert to Catholicism, he zealously opposed the anti-Catholic laws that he and his co-conspirators were protesting.

Only two of the gunpowder plotters escaped. Guy Fawkes and six others were executed the following year, the remainder of the cabal either killed when captured or imprisoned. Beginning in 1606, November 5 was celebrated as *Guy Fawkes Day* in England, a holiday similar to our Halloween on which children build ridiculous effigies of Fawkes clad in rags and go door to door begging for "a penny for the guy." The grotesque effigies, sometimes stuffed with fireworks, are paraded through the streets and burned in bonfires that evening. From these ragged, odd-looking effigies of Fawkes, and other people held in derision, came the word *guy*, any person resembling the ludicrous dummies, especially in dress. All of the festivities through the years probably mellowed the meaning of the word to include both good and bad *guys*. But only in America, far removed from the Gunpowder Plot in distance as well as time, is *guys* widely used for any "chaps" or "fellows," no ridicule intended. In England to this day a *guy* remains a ridiculous-looking person.

The verb *to guy*, to tease or make fun of someone, has an obvious connection with *Guy Fawkes Day*, but is first recorded in print in 1872 by Mark Twain. *Guy wire*, used to steady or brace things, is just a shortened form of guide wire, deriving from *guie*, an old French word for to guide. It has been suggested, but not proved, that this last *guy*, also an early English synonym for a guide or leader of men, may be the real source of our decent chap or good *guy*—leaving Guy Fawkes to his original infamy.

Gyp, Gyp-artist, Gitano When the Gypsies first appeared in England in the early sixteenth century, it was assumed that they came from Egypt and they were labeled *'gypcians*. In the course of their wanderings these nomads had sojourned in Egypt, but they originally hailed from India, as their language indicates. *Gypcians* they became in England, though, where they were reputed to be great cheats, pickpockets, and thieves. Soon their erroneous name was shortened again to *gypsy*, which became the source for *to gyp* or cheat. *Gyp-artists*, swindlers, came much later, as did *gitano*, a trickster, from the Spanish word for *gypsy*, and the American expression *gyp* for a bitch or female dog.

So almost everyone believes but the Gypsies, who call themselves *Romany people*, anyway. The *Oxford English Dictionary*, however, does not dishonor their name, tracing *gyp* to *gee-up*, which meant "to treat roughly" in some localities of England. Another attempt that saves face for the *gypsy* is the *gippo* theory. A *gippo*, later shortened to *gyp*, was a short seventeenth-century jacket worn by valets to undergraduates at Oxford. The word, it is said, was eventually applied to the servants themselves, who were often known as cheats and thieves. *Gippo* bears no relation at all to the *gypsies*, deriving from an Arabian mantle called the *Jubbah*, or *jibbah*, as it was first called in the West.

H

Halley's Comet *Halley's comet*, the first comet whose return was accurately predicted, was observed by English astronomer Edmund Halley in 1692, when he correctly estimated its reappearance in 1758, sixteen years after his death as it turned out. Halley based his calculations on Newton's theory; a long-time friend of the great scientist, he had paid for the initial printing of Newton's *Principia*, collaborating on the section dealing with comets. Over his eighty-six-year lifetime Halley made a number of important discoveries, which resulted in his appointment as astronomer royal in 1720. The comet that blazons his name across the sky last appeared in 1910. (See also *Berenice's Hair*.)

Hamiltonian, Hamiltonianism American founding father and statesman Alexander Hamilton (1757–1804), in his essentially conservative political philosophy, advocated a strong central government and protective tariffs. A *Hamiltonian* is one who supports this doctrine of *Hamiltonianism*, the word loosely describing a level-headed political conservative. Hamilton's *Federalist* essays were largely responsible for the ratification of the Constitution by the critical states. Secretary of the Treasury under Washington, he became known as a brilliant financier and able politician distrustful of mobocracy. "The Little Lion" was plagued all his life by controversy about his illegitimate birth. Even though a Federalist, he refused to support "that cold-blooded Cataline" Burr in the congressional presidential run-off against Jefferson. This fostered bitterness that resulted in Hamilton's death in the famous duel three years later.

Hansard What the *Congressional Record* is to the United States Congress, the *Hansard* is to the British Houses of Parliament. A *Hansard* is the official printed report of proceedings in Parliament, the name in honor of Luke Hansard (1752–1828) and his family after him, private printers who published the reports from 1774 until 1889. Today the proceedings are recorded by the government, but the reports still bear the printing firm's name.

Hansom If Joseph Aloysius Hansom invented the *Hansom cab*, once the most popular of horse-drawn carriages—"the gondolas of London," as Disraeli called them—he certainly gained nothing from his invention. Most authorities vouch for Hansom, but one source claims that Edward Bird invented the vehicle, presenting the idea gratis to his brother-in-law, Edward Welch, a partner in Hansom's Birmingham architectural firm. Hansom (1803–82) was an English architect specializing in churches and public buildings. He did patent the cab—possibly as Bird's Patent Safety Cab—but the financial arrangement he made upon selling his patent rights proved disastrous. Promised ten thousand pounds, Hansom received, according to conflicting accounts, either nothing or a mere three hundred pounds for his patent. *Hansom cabs*, however, made millions for their manufacturers. The low, two-wheeled covered carriage, with the driver's seat above it in the back, was noted for its maneuverability and safety features as well as its privacy and unobstructed view for passengers. Soon after its appearance, in 1834, it became the most popular cab in London and around the world. The last Hansom disappeared from London in 1944 but a few are still available for hire in New York's Central Park.

Harlot Arlette or Herleva, the attractive daughter of the tanner Falbert of Falaise was kneeling naked, washing her clothes, when Robert le Diable, duke of Normandy, came cantering through his duchy. The result: William the Conqueror, known also in history as the Bastard, and the word *harlot*. It's a shame that this traditional story is not true. Robert may have been something of a devil and Arlette *was* William's mother, but *harlot* had been born long before their illegitimate offspring. The word first meant a person of low birth and was applied to both men and women. It has had a large variety of meanings since deriving, probably, from the old German *hari*, army, and *lot*, loiterer, "an army loafer or camp follower." This does not rule out the very remote possibility of some other Arlette by name and nature influencing the word's formation.

Harvard, Harvard Beets, Harvard Chair Perhaps the unknown chef who invented *Harvard beets* noticed that their deep red color resembled the crimson jerseys of the then vaunted *Harvard* football team. At any rate, the dish is named for the university. It is made from sliced beets cooked in sugar, cornstarch, vinegar and water. The *Harvard chair*, a seventeenth-century three-legged armchair, also bears the university's name. *Harvard*, the first institution of higher learning in North America, honors John Harvard (1607–38), an English minister who lived for a time in Charlestown, Mass. A 400-pound grant from the colony general court in 1636 established the "schoale or colledge" but Harvard's legacy of half his estate, 780 pounds, and his library of more than four hundred books greatly aided the fledgling institution. The town of Cambridge, Mass., where Harvard is located, pays honor to Cambridge University in England. (See also *Yale*.)

Haussmannization *Haussmannization* is frequently heard today in connection with the blight and plight of cities around the world. To *Haussmannize* means to remodel a city along beautiful lines and celebrates Baron Georges Eugène Haussmann (1809–91), who administered a facelifting to Paris, starting in the middle of the nineteenth century. While Prefect of Paris, Haussmann completely remodeled the city. He laid out the Bois de Boulogne and other parks, constructed new streets and widened old ones, instituted a new water supply and sewer sys-

tem, created wide, open spaces and vistas, and built new bridges, railroad stations, and numerous public buildings. These and many other improvements required expenses and loans which resulted in a public debt of hundreds of millions and eventually led to Haussmann's dismissal in 1870, seventeen years after he had begun his scheme. Interestingly, Haussmann was trained not as an architect but as a financier. The *Boulevard Haussmann* also bears his name.

Havelock "General Havelock is not in fashion, but all the same we believe that he will do well," wrote an observer in her diary. "No doubt he is fussy and tiresome, but his little old stiff figure looks as active and fit for use as if he were made of steel." An accurate thumbnail sketch. Sir Henry Havelock (1795–1857) was rarely in fashion—it took him twenty-three years to be promoted to captain, for example—but this most British of British soldiers did eventually do well. Havelock, an evangelist as well as a soldier, served over thirty-four years with the British Army in India, taking only one leave home in all that time. Known as "the Saint" to his men for his habit of trying to convert everyone under his command to temperance and moderate ways, he was indeed among the fussiest and most tiresome of men. But as to his military ability and bravery there is no doubt. Havelock led his troops to many victories during the Sepoy Rebellion (1857) and is remembered for his recapture of Cawnpore and his stand at Lucknow until reinforcements arrived. The general died of dysentery brought on by the arduous Lucknow defense. The *havelock* that he had devised for his "Ironsides" brigade wasn't his invention, similar helmet coverings having been used since the Crusades. This trademark of the French Foreign Legion in films was fashioned of white linen, hanging halfway down the back and protecting the neck from the sun.

Hayism "Acidosis," Dr. William Howard Hay advised in his book *Health Via Food* (1933), causes almost all bodily ills. Therefore, since proteins need acid for their digesting and carbohydrates require alkaline, such foods should not be eaten in combination—no milk with your potatoes or vice versa—for "no human stomach can be expected to be acid and alkaline at the same time." Hays ignored the fact that most foods contain mixtures of proteins and carbohydrates. Like most food fads (see *Fletcherism, Graham*), his regimen had its loyal, even fanatical followers. *Hayism*, incidentally, recommended frequent fasting—which is said to cause acidity or acidosis.

Hays Code, Office Long the moral code of the American film industry, the *Hays Code* commemorates Will Harrison Hays (1879–1954). "Czar" of the movies, Hays served as first president of the Motion Picture Producers and Distributors of America from 1922 to 1945. A former chairman of the Republican National Committee and postmaster general under Harding, he helped formulate the so-called *Hays Code* in 1934 and zealously administered it from what was dubbed the *Hays Office.*

Heaviside Layer, Kennelly-Heaviside Layer Increasing deafness forced Oliver Heaviside (1850–1925) to retire from his post with the British Great Northern Telegraph Company when he was only twenty-four. The mathematical physicist and electrician devoted the remainder of his long life to theoretical investigations into electricity. In 1902 he suggested that a conducting layer of ionized gas exists in the upper atmosphere which conducts, reflects and refracts radio waves. This *Heaviside layer*, about sixty miles above us, reflects radio waves back to earth, and enables reception around the globe. Because Edison's former assistant Arthur Edwin Kennelly (1861–1939) postulated the same theory shortly before the British scientist, the stratum is also called the *Kennelly-Heaviside* layer. Today it is more generally known as the ionosphere.

A Hector, To Hector Why did Hector, Troy's mightiest, bravest defender in Homer's *Iliad*, become a blustering, domineering bully? His name, symbolic for a gallant warrior in early English literature, today means not only a bully, but to bully, torment or treat insolently. The change seems to have taken place toward the end of the seventeenth century when a gang of young bullies, who considered themselves paragons of valiant courage,

adopted the honorable name "Hectors." This ruffian band insulted passers-by, broke windows and became notorious for their bullying, terrorizing the streets of London. It is probably from their name that *hector* and *to hector* derive, rather than from that of the exalted magnanimous Hector, noble in victory and defeat. Some scholars point out, however, that Hector was represented in medieval drama as boastful and domineering, possibly from the notion that any hero is swashbuckling and blustering. There also might be some connection with "heckle."

Heisman Trophy The *Heisman Memorial Trophy* has been called the ultima Thule for undergraduate football players, being awarded annually since 1935 to the best of their breed in the country. It is named for John W. Heisman, former Georgia Tech coach. Called "Shut the Gates of Mercy" Heisman, the coach was a great mentor, though not noted for being a gentleman on the playing field. On one occasion he allowed his team to rack up an incredible 220 points on an opponent. Notable *Heisman Trophy* winners include Tom Harmon of Michigan (1940), Paul Hornung of Notre Dame (1956), and O. J. Simpson of Southern California (1968). Jay Berwanger of Chicago won the initial award in 1935.

Helot The original *helots*, slaves or serfs, were inhabitants of the town of Helos in Laconia enslaved by the Spartans in ancient times. The Spartans actually ranked their *helots* midway between citizens and slaves, but certainly treated them like flunkeys. As an object lesson to Spartan youth that drunkenness is evil, *helots* were often forced to drink more than they could handle and then exhibited in the public square. (See also *Laconic*.)

Henry Scientist Joseph Henry's career constitutes a series of famous firsts and foremosts. The U.S. Weather Bureau was created as a result of his meteorological work while first director of the Smithsonian Institution, and Henry was the first "weatherman" to make forecasts from collected scientific data. Not only a brilliant administrator, who initially planned the Smithsonian's scope and activities, Henry has been acknowledged as the leading physicist of his day. His researches on sound gave America the best fog signaling service among maritime nations, he stimulated geologic and geographical exploration, and his influence on the character of science, especially concerning the free publication of scientific results, was exceeded by no contemporary. Before becoming secretary of the Smithsonian in 1846, Henry taught physics at Princeton, where he built the first electromagnetic motor (1829), and devised the first practical telegraph (1830–31). It is not for the theory of electromagnetic induction that the *henry*, the measurement unit of induction, is named in his honor. This theory is credited to the English scientist Faraday, although Henry's experiments may have preceded his, and it is for his theory of producing induced current (1832) that the International Congress of Electricians gave the American's name to the standard electrical unit in 1893. The contributions mentioned here constitute only a fraction of Henry's work. The scientist, incidentally, started off as something of a dropout, leaving school at thirteen to become an apprentice to a watchmaker, and resuming his education three years later. He died in 1878, aged eighty-one.

Henry Rifle, Martini-Henry Rifle The *Henry rifle* has been called the grandfather of repeating arms. Invented by Benjamin Tyler Henry (1821–98), one of the Henry family of gunsmiths, the weapon was tested under fire by Union forces in the Civil War. The breech-loading, lever-action rifle never became popular as a military weapon but saw some use on the frontier and is featured in many a western. Henry may also have worked on the *Martini-Henry* rifle adopted by the British army in 1889. This was basically an improvement on the *Martini* invented by Swiss mechanical engineer Frédéric de Martini (1832–97), but another Henry, a Scottish gunsmith, possibly deserves the credit for it.

Hepplewhite Style Nothing is known about the British furniture designer George Hepplewhite except that he operated a fashionable cabinetmaking shop in the parish of St. Gile's, Cripplegate, London, died in 1786, and willed his business to his wife Alice. But his furniture was widely imitated in England and the

United States, resulting in a style often eloquent and graceful, and often little more than ugly. It has been assumed that the original *Hepplewhite styles* were delicate and soundly constructed. The cabinetmaker invented or popularized the shield-back chair; the "spider leg" for chairs, tables and sideboards; and was among the first to inlay much of his furniture with exotic woods. Hepplewhite's small pieces, such as inlaid knife boxes, fire screens and tea caddies, are highly valued by collectors. His *The Cabinet-Maker and Upholsterer's Guide*, published by his wife in 1788, inspired the host of imitators at home and abroad.

Herd's Grass (see *Timothy grass*)

Hessian As an American epithet *Hessian* can be traced back to the Revolutionary War, when the British employed thirty thousand Hessian mercenaries and their name, justly or not, came to mean any boorish, uncouth person of low moral character. The Hessians came from the former Grand Duchy of Hesse in Germany. Their name is also found in the high-tasseled *Hessian boots* fashionable in early nineteenth-century England; *Hessian cloth*, a strong coarse jute or hemp cloth originally made in Hesse; *Hessian* for any mercenary; and the *Hessian fly* so destructive to wheat, which was erroneously believed to have been brought to America by the Hessian soldiers.

Highbinder A *highbinder* can be a swindler and cheat, especially a confidence man, or a gangster or rowdy. The word, first used in its latter meaning, derives from a gang of ruffians called the Highbinders that plagued New York City about 1806. Later their name was applied (in the lower case) to members of American-Chinese secret societies believed to be employed in blackmail and assassination.

Hippocratic Oath

You do solemnly swear, each man by whatever he holds most sacred, that you will be loyal to the profession of medicine and just and generous to its members; that you will lead your lives and practice your art in uprightness and honor, that into whatsoever house you shall enter, it shall be for the good of the sick to the utmost of your power, you holding your-

selves far aloof from wrong, from corruption, from the tempting of others to vice; that you will exercise your art solely for the cure of your patients and will give no drug, perform no operation, for a criminal purpose, even if solicited, far less suggest it; that whatsoever you shall see or hear of the lives of men which is not fitting to be spoken, you will keep inviolably secret. These things you do swear. Let each man bow the head in sign of acquiescence. And now, if you will be true to this, your oath, may prosperity and good repute be ever yours; the opposite if you shall prove yourself forsworn.

This is one abridged form of the *Hippocratic Oath* still administered upon graduation to medical school students. The longer original version, outdated in many respects, begins with an invocation to the gods: "I swear by Apollo the physician. . . ." All forms of the oath memorialize Hippocrates (c. 460–377 B.C.), "The Father of Medicine," but not a line of it was written by the Greek physician and surgeon, it being rather the body of Greek medical thought and practice of his day. The words do, however, represent Hippocrates' ideals. Believed to have been born on the island of Cos off the coast of Asia Minor, the son of a physician who claimed descent from the Greek god of medicine, Hippocrates apparently studied medicine with his father and philosophy under the famed Democritus. He separated medicine from superstition, his acute observations used in medical teaching for centuries. Some of the physician's writings still survive, the chief of these his *Aphorisms* (i.e., "The life so short, the craft so long to learn"). Two portions of the old *Hippocratic oath* no longer sworn include: "I will not give to a woman a pessary to cause abortion"; and "(I will) hold my teacher in this art equal to my own parents . . . make him partner in my livelihood . . . when he is in need of money . . . share mine with him." Hippocrates was at least 85 when he died and some estimates give his age at death as 110.

Hitchcock *Hitchcock chairs* were so well made that they have become collectors' items even though they were originally mass produced. In 1818 Lambert H. Hitchcock (1795–1852) established a factory in Barkhamsted, Conn., where some one hundred employees turned out his product. *Hitchcock chairs* came in a variety of designs and sizes, but were characterized by strong legs, curved-top backs and seats (initially rush bottomed) that were wider in the front than the back. The chair maker won such renown that Barkhamsted renamed itself Hitchcocksville in his honor, although the town changed its name again to Riverton in 1866. The sturdy chairs, all identified by Hitchcock's signature stenciled on the back edge of the seat, include the first rocking chair designed and made as such —i.e., not made by just adding rockers to a regular chair.

Hitchcock Ending An often ironic, surprise ending characteristic of the fifty-three films, plenteous television plays, short-story anthologies and magazine stories directed, sponsored, collected and published by Alfred Joseph Hitchcock. Hitchcock's films have received high critical praise as well as a great popular following. The English director, born in London in 1899, began his career as a scenario writer, becoming an art director and production manager before embarking on directing films in 1925. His many suspenseful melodramas, object of a cult for their brilliant camera technique, include *The Lodger, Blackmail, The 39 Steps, The Lady Vanishes, Rebecca, Suspicion, Foreign Correspondent, Shadow of a Doubt, Lifeboat, Spellbound, Rope, Strangers on a Train, North by Northwest, Psycho,* and *The Birds.* Hitchcock now lives in the United States, where he has made the majority of his most recent movies. He appears in brief walk-on roles in all or many of his films.

Hitler (see *Führer*)

Hobsonize *To kiss,* from the only person in history whose name the dictionaries immortalize in this way. Lieutenant Richmond Pearson Hobson (1870–1937) won fame during the Spanish-American War, stepping into the national limelight when he tried to sink the collier *Merrimac* and block Santiago harbor. No matter that Hobson and his seven men failed on that morning of June 3, 1898—a Spanish shell hit the steering gear and their ship sank in a broad part of the channel where it couldn't prevent Admiral Cervara's squadron from leaving. Other tactics were employed, the entire Spanish fleet destroyed at the battle of Santiago a month later. Hobson, a handsome Annapolis graduate—known there as "The Parson" for his religious fervor—became a hero for leading the daring early morning mission. The young naval engineer was honored with parades and dinners wherever he went when he returned to the United States in August 1898. His good looks and popularity led to his name becoming a verb meaning *to kiss*, women often flinging their arms around him and showering him with kisses when he appeared in public. "Kissing-bug Hobson," as he was called, resigned from the navy and ran for Congress back home in Alabama, a state that later gave us another osculatory politician, Governor "Kissin' Jim" Folsom. At any rate, the hero got himself easily elected, serving from 1907–15. Hobson adopted the prohibition cause and advocated naval expansion in years to come, lecturing around the country. Though *hobsonize* is an obsolete expression today, it remains in historical dictionaries as one of the most curious of linguistic curiosities.

Hobson-Jobson The substitution of native English words, unrelated in meaning, for foreign ones, especially oriental expressions, is called *Hobson-Jobsonism*. Hobson and Jobson were applied to the Moslem processional chant "Ya Hassan! Ya Hussein!" by British soldiers in nineteenth-century India because these traditional English surnames sounded something like the repeated exclamations of the parading Mohammedans. (Hodge was originally the first of the English names, but it became Hobson by reduplication). The Hassan and Hussein of the chant are the grandsons of Mohammed, their names still honored at the festival of Muharram. The term *Hobson-Jobson* for a kind of pidgin language was popularized with the publication of a book of the same name by the English Sanskrit scholar Arthur Coke Burnell in 1886.

Hobson's Choice When you rented a horse from Thomas Hobson, you rented the horse nearest the livery stable door, the one best rested, no matter what your preference or how many horses were available. In this way, Richard Steele wrote one hundred years after Hobson's death, in an article in *The Spectator* (No. 509): "Every customer was alike well served according to his chance, and every horse ridden with the same justice." A *Hobson's choice* is therefore no choice at all, a take it or leave it proposition. It is amazing how this proverb has lasted for over three centuries, deriving as it does from the name of an obscure English carrier and innkeeper. Thomas Hobson, who drove his stage from Cambridge to London sixty miles away, kept some forty horses on the side to rent to students at Cambridge University. A humane man, who realized that "the scholars rid hard," he put his mounts on a strict rotation basis so that the best and most often chosen horses would not be ruined. Hard-headed Hobson probably became celebrated because he didn't placate the young Cambridge aristocrats like most fellow tradesmen. He died in 1631, aged eighty-six, his death said to be caused by idleness resulting from lack of business brought on by the black plague then ravaging London. Much has been made of the fact that an English merchant, living in Japan, used "Hodgson's choice" fourteen years before Hobson's death, but Hobson's name may have already been familiar at that time, "Hodgson" simply a misspelling or mispronunciation. In any case, almost everyone accepts the familiar derivation. Besides being the subject of Steele's essay, Hobson is immortalized by two punning epitaphs penned by his contemporary, John Milton. Wrote Milton, in part of one epitaph:

Ease was his chief disease; and to judge right,
He died for heaviness that his cart went light;
His leisure told him that his time was come,
And lack of load made his life burdensome. . . .

Hocus-Pocus, Hoax, Hocus, Hokey Pokey, Hokum, Okus "I will speake of one man . . ." wrote Thomas Ady in *A Candle in the Dark* (1656), "that went about in King James his time . . . who called himself, The Kings Majesties most excellent Hocus Pocus, and so was called, because that at the playing of every trick, he used to say, *Hocus Pocus, tontus talontus, vade celeriter jubio*, a dark composure of words, to blinde the eyes of the beholders, to make his trick pass the more currantly without discovery." Whether this juggler's assumed name became the basis for our *hocus-pocus*, deception or trickery, no one really knows. Ochus Bochus, "a wizard and demon of Northern Mythology," or "a seventeenth century magician," whose identity has been established in neither case, has also been nominated. Neither is there proof positive that *hocus-pocus* is a blasphemous Scandinavian corruption of the first words of the consecration in the Catholic Mass, *Hoc est corpus* (filii), "This is the body [of the Son of God]." Many scholars lean to this last theory, pointing out that *hokus-pokus-fileokus* is still unwittingly used in Norway and Sweden, just as *hocus-pocus-dominocus* (for *hoc est corpus Domini*, "this is the body of the Lord") is an expression common in children's play in America. (I remember the possibly euphemistic *hocus-pocus-minniocus*.) Perhaps the word does originally come from the perversion of the sacramental blessing, reinforced by the nickname that the ancient juggler assumed from his diverting pseudo-Latin patter, and further strengthened by the names of other successful jugglers and magicians named after him. We do know that many Tudor conjurors famous for their legerdemain were called Hocus Pocus or Hokas Pocas after their predecessor and that Master Hocus Pocus became a symbol of illusion and deceit. From *hocus-pocus* came, in all probability, the words hoax, a trick—*hoax* is merely *hocus* said quickly—and *hokum*, which is a blend of *hocus-pocus* and *bunkum* or *bunk*. Sometimes *hokey-pokey* is used as a synonym for *hocus-pocus*, the *hokey-pokey man*, the ice-cream vendor of yore, perhaps earning the name because customers never knew what went into his cheap product. *Hokee-pokee* was used to describe ceremonial Indian dances in the past and *hocus* is a verb meaning to cheat or tamper with,

especially to drug someone's drink. Finally, *okus* is pickpocket slang for a wallet, probably deriving from *poke*, for a wallet, and the *hocus-pocus* involved in lifting one. All possibly thanks to a magician who named himself for his babbling mock Latin or double-talk.

Hogarthian Uncompromisingly realistic in style, his name came to indicate the same, but English painter William Hogarth (1697–1764) wasn't above fantastic flights of the imagination. Once when an ugly client refused to pay for a realistically ugly portrait, Hogarth threatened to add a tail and other appendages to his likeness and dedicate it to "Mr. Hare the famous wild-beast man." His client paid on condition that the portrait be destroyed. Hogarth's great ability as a painter was overshadowed by his consummate skill as a caricaturist, which he used in his engravings to expose the hypocrisy and degeneration of English society. Among his numerous satiric works the most celebrated are *The Rake's Progress*, the *Marriage à la Mode* series, *Gin Lane* and *Four Stages of Cruelty*. These are noted for their frank humor and realistic attention to detail. It has been said that Hogarth, despite his great skills, was less a painter than an author, "a humorist and satirist upon canvas." Yet he was capable of painting masterpieces like the *Shrimp Girl* and *Captain Coram*.

Homeric, Homeric Laughter Some authorities doubt that there ever was a poet Homer, pointing out that his name means "one who puts together" and ascribing his work to a number of authors. But modern scholars tend to support the traditional story that the author of the *Iliad* and the *Odyssey* was the blind Greek Homer, who lived in the ninth century B.C. and wandered from city to city reciting his epic poems. Homer's life is a blank historically, but his name and works have left us a number of words. *Homeric laughter* is the hearty, lusty laughter of the gods in the greatest of epic poems, and *Homeric* itself is used to denote the majestic qualities of Homer's poetry, or poetry similar to it. *Homer sometimes nods* advises that in long written works, even Homer's, a drowsy interval or two is permissible, and that the best of us can make mistakes. (See also *Hector; Nestor; Stentorian.*)

Hooch, Hootch The American soldiers who first occupied Alaska in 1867 were forbidden any liquor, but the long Alaskan nights were cold. Lacking women, crude firewater apparently made do, a brew made in their own rude stills from yeast, flour, sugar or molasses. This *booze* has been blamed on a local Indian tribe called the *Hoochen* by slightly *chauvinistic* or *groggy* etymologists, but these Alaskan natives only happened to live nearby—they were in reality the *Hutsnuwu*, Tlingit Indians, a name easy to mispronounce, and probably had no part in brewing the potent *hoochino* that the soldiers named after them. The brew's name remained *hoochino* or *hoochinoo* until the Klondike gold rush in 1897, when more of it was needed more often, in a hurry, and it was shortened to *hooch*. Being firewater, *hooch* was splendidly accurate to describe the bathtub concoctions made during Prohibition, which wasn't called The Grand Experiment, however, for this reason. The name caught on and is still with us, though more in a comic sense for all liquor. *Hootch* is a variant spelling.

A *hooch* to those among U.N. troops in Korea, 1951–1954, was a temporary shelter, but there the word derives from the Japanese *uchi*, house. The *hootchy-kootchy*, though *hooch* can make you dance that way, probably comes from the English dialect words *hotch*, to shake, and *couch* (cootch) *out*, to protrude. It is the Turkish belly dance that many of us, as the old joke observes, "have no stomach for."

Hood, Hoodlum Robin Hood, a good guy really, has nothing to do with *hood* or *hoodlum*. But take your choice again; it's another word that stumps the experts. *Hoodlum* is first recorded in 1871. Bartlett tells us on hearsay evidence that a San Francisco reporter exposed a street gang at that time and changed its leader's name from Muldoon to Noodlum because he feared reprisals. The Irishman's name became *Hoodlum*, and soon a synonym for a cheap gangster, when the paper's compositor mistook the reporter's handwritten *N* for an *H*. Variation number two on this tale has

the Irish leader's name spelled backward, but associated with *Hooligan* and receiving the *H* that way. Variation number three suggests that this scourge of the Barbary Coast was so feared by the crusading newsman that he spelt the name *Hoodlum* all the way.

But there are multifarious versions, aside from the varations. One, unlikely, is that *hoodlum* comes from the gang cry *huddle 'em*. Another, very unlikely, has the word deriving from the pidgin English *hood lahnt*, "very lazy mandarin," in some vague reference to the many Chinese in San Francisco. In addition to the Chinese, the Spanish and Germans have also been called upon to take the Hibernians off the hook. Some authorities claim that the derogatory word is of Spanish origin, explaining no further, and the latest theory, which Mencken supports, suggests that *hoodlum* comes from the Bavarian dialect term *hodalump*, meaning a small-time gangster. There were numerous German-Americans in the San Francisco area at the time and for this reason a mispronunciation of *hodalump* for *hoodlum* has its loyal defenders. However, the *hoodlums* I know pronounce the word like *mood*, not *hood*, the way the double *o* is pronounced in Muldoon. Adding this to the prominence of the Irish in early cutthroat American gangs, which make modern youth gangs seem almost like gentlemen's clubs, the number of gang names which have become words (see *Highbinder*), and derivations like *hooligan* and *burke*, I would opt for the mighty Muldoon theory, or as one respected scholar puts it, "a perverted back-spelling of Muldoon." It is said that San Francisco newspaper readers soon identified the real Muldoon with Hoodlum. Whether Muldoon did, and what happened to the reporter if he did, is not recorded.

Despite its similarities, *hoodwink* does not derive from *hoodlum* or *hood*. It stems from a practice of sixteenth-century thieves, who often pulled the hoods or cowls their victims wore down over their eyes to blind or *hoodwink* them while they were being robbed.

Hooker One explanation for this word is that U.S. Civil War General Joseph Hooker, a fiery, opinionated man, didn't believe that his men should dissipate their energies in the Washington, D.C., red-light district, putting the area strictly off limits. His troops, it seems, counterattacked by dubbing all prostitutes *hookers*, a revenge that has lasted far longer than the memory of "Fighting Joe's" military exploits. These were considerable. West Point graduate Hooker first came to notice during the Peninsular campaign when he earned his sobriquet. He criticized and supplanted General Burnside of *sideburns* fame as commander in chief of the Army of the Potomac, but angrily resigned that position when General Sherman failed to give him command of the Army of the Tennessee. Later, however, Hooker fought valiantly under Sherman. The tempestuous, thrice-wounded general died in Garden City, L.I., in 1879, aged sixty-five.

Some writers trace *hooker* to the way a prostitute "hooked" prospective customers by linking arms with them; but why, then, is the word not in common use until about 1865? Bartlett (1859) does derive the word from "a resident of Corlear's Hook," in reference to the large number of sailors and women of the night in the old area of New York City, but there is little evidence, aside from the earlier date, to support his claim. It seems likely that General Joe's formations at least had something to do with *hooker's* formation.

Hooligan A proper name is the origin for this word for a violent roughneck, a fact conclusively established when British etymologist Eric Partridge brought to light Clarence Rook's *Hooligan Nights* (1899) in his *Dictionary of Slang*. Excerpts from Rook's sociologically valuable work follow: "There was, but a few years ago, a man called Patrick Hooligan, who walked to and fro among his fellow men, robbing them and occasionally bashing them. . . . It is . . . certain that he lived in Irish Court, that he was employed as a chucker-out (bouncer) at various resorts in the neighborhood. Moreover, he could do more than his share of tea-leafing (stealing) . . . being handy with his fingers. . . . Finally, one day he had a difference with a constable, put his light out. . . . He was . . . given a lifer. But he had not been in

gaol long before he had to go into hispital, where he died. . . . The man must have had a forceful personality . . . a fascination, which elevated him into a type. It was doubtless the combination of skill and strength, a certain exuberance of lawlessness, an utter absence of scruple in his dealings, which marked him out as a leader among men. . . . He left a great tradition. . . . He established a cult."

This man called Hooligan made the Lamb and Flag pub in the Southwark section of London his headquarters, attracting a gang of followers around him. The entire rowdy Hooligan family, the nucleus of his gang—their real name was probably Houlihan—"enlivened the drab monotony of Southwark," as another observer put it. The entry "Hooligan gang" is found on many police blotters in the late 1890's, and the gang's brawling even inspired a popular music hall song of the time. It is all but certain then that Pat Hooligan and his unruly family, gave us the first example of *hooliganism*, not "the Hooley Gang, a name given by the police in Islington to a gang of young roughs led by one Hooley." Ironically, *hooligan* has also been used as a synonym for a prison guard or screw or hack.

Hoover, J. Edgar Hoover, Hooverize, Hooverville, Hoover Apron, Hoover Cart, Hoover Commission, Hoover Dam Before Herbert Clark Hoover (1874–1964) became the thirty-first president of the United States, he had a distinguished career as an engineer and administrator, popularizing scientific management among businessmen and inspiring the building of the Colorado River Boulder (now *Hoover*) Dam, for example. Hoover first came to national attention as the head of various European relief agencies and U.S. Food Administrator during World War I. In the latter capacity he met the food crisis by ending farm hoarding of crops, curbing speculation, and urging Americans to live by "the gospel of the clean plate" and to institute "wheatless and meatless" days. It was only a few days after these suggestions that the term *to Hooverize* began to appear in newspapers around the country and housewives soon adopted the phrase when discussing ways to stretch food. *Hoover apron*, a dress for women similar to coveralls, also came into use at this time. Later, when Hoover was president during the Great Depression, more than a few derogatory terms bearing his name were invented. The *Hoover cart* was a southern mule-drawn wagon made from the rear axle and chassis of a discarded automobile, and a *Hooverville*, a collection of shacks housing the unemployed at the margins of cities throughout the country. Hoover continued his long public career after serving as president. *Hoover Commissions* under both Truman and Eisenhower studied the reorganization of the executive branch of government and suggested many improvements which were later adopted into law.

A *J. Edgar Hoover* is common for a top lawman, heroic to some, despotic to others, and is of course for J(ohn) Edgar Hoover, born 1895, died 1972, director of the Federal Bureau of Investigation since 1924. Hoover has been subject to much apparently justified criticism lately, but there is no denying that he built the F.B.I. into a model organization of law enforcement. The F.B.I., by the way, was founded by Charles Bonaparte, grandnephew of Napoleon, under Theodore Roosevelt.

Still another eponymous Hoover headed the company that built the machine now famous as a synonym for an electric vacuum cleaner, though the term *hoover* is not heard as frequently recently as in the past.

Horatio Alger Story Horatio Alger (1834–99) wrote 120 novels and countless articles and stories in his thirty years as an author, making him one of the most prolific American writers. Today his books for children, such as *Luck and Pluck* and *The Making of a Man*, all filled with poor but honest characters who struggled to get ahead against overwhelming odds and invariably became rich and famous, are of interest to virtually no one but historians. But dull and unimaginative, filled with preachments though his pages might be, Alger's books served a real need in his time. The most popular author of his day, his philosophy of hard work and clean living strongly influenced three generations of Americans.

Unfortunately, Alger never came close to fulfilling his ambition to become a great novelist. According to Herbert R. Mayes in his biography, "Each book bound him closer to the mediocrity he sought to avoid. Each book made it less possible for him to accomplish the ambition of his life." Toward the end Alger began to shed the puritanical attitudes that shackled his spirit. In *The Paris Diaries of Horatio Alger* we find him recording such sentiments as: "I was a fool to have waited so long. It is not nearly so vile as I had thought." Humorous and yet tragic. Alger died that same year in Paris and our only lasting memory of him is the phrase *an Horatio Alger story* as a synonym for a rags to riches success, something the author never really achieved.

Hore-Belisha, Belisha Beacon These black-and-white striped posts topped with yellow globes honor Lord Leslie Hore-Belisha, British Minister of Transport, 1934–37, who introduced them to indicate pedestrian crossings. A colorful, controversial figure, Hore-Belisha instituted a campaign to halt "mass murder" on the highways and the beacons were a warning to drivers that pedestrians had the right-of-way at approaching intersections. Not overly modest, Lord Leslie seems to have named the lights after himself. The British statesman, born in 1895, fought in World War I as a major, was a member of Parliament, and served as head of the British War Office at the beginning of World War II. The beacons are often called *Hore-Belishas*.

Hosackia Few people know that New York's Rockefeller Center was once the site of the famous Elgin Gardens, one of the first botanic gardens in America. The Elgin Gardens were established by Dr. David Hosack (1769–1835) who subsequently deeded them to Columbia University, now the landlord of Radio City. Hosack, a professor at Columbia, is remembered as the physician who attended Alexander Hamilton after his fatal duel with Aaron Burr. He served on the first faculty of Columbia's College of Physicians and Surgeons, and helped found Bellevue Hospital, as well as founding and serving as first president of the now defunct Rutgers Medical College. Hosack wrote a number of medical and botanical books, including a biography of Casper Wistar (see *wisteria*). *Hosackia*, a genus of over fifty species of perennial herbs of the pea family, is named for him. Its most cultivated species is *H. gracilis*, witch's teeth, a rock garden plant about twelve inches high with pretty rose-pink flowers borne in small umbels.

Hottentot *Hottentot* can be gibberish, or a contemptuous word to describe a stupid, depraved person. Sometimes used as an ugly slang word for a black person, it is the name the Boers gave to the South African Khoi-Khoin tribe, closely allied to the Bushmen. The Dutch and other Europeans, imposing their own values on another civilization, have long called this pastoral people "small and stupid," hence the word's latter meaning. The Khoi-Khoin dialect is full of harsh, staccato clicks and clacks and kissing sounds, unique in that it is spoken by breathing in rather than out. These noises made by the tongue (similar to the way we would say "tsk-tsk") sounded like so much stammering or clucking to Dutch ears. The Boers therefore named the people after what the language sounded like to them, calling them Hottentots from the Dutch *hateren en tateren*, to stammer and stutter. It wasn't long before *hottentot* was applied to any gibberish at all. The *Hottentots*, the first natives to come in contact with the Dutch settlers of the Cape of Good Hope, lost most of their land and number less than twenty thousand today. These people, constantly parodied in Western literature and drama, thought much better of themselves than their detractors. Their name *Khoi-Khoin* means "men among men."

Houdini, Pull a Houdini Someone who *pulls a Houdini* performs an amazing disappearing act or escape, and *a Houdini* is anyone with seemingly magical powers in any field. The expressions lionize Eric or Ehrich Weiss (1875–1926), an American magician who adopted the stage name Harry Houdini. Houdini named himself after Jean Eugene Robert Houdin (1805–71), a celebrated French magician noted for the fact that he did not at-

tribute his feats to supernatural powers. Harry Houdini became world famous for his escapes from "impossible traps" like locks, handcuffs, and straightjackets while suspended high in the air, or chained in chests submerged under water —all tricks, it is said, that can be explained today. A magician's magician who invented many magic tricks, he exposed numerous spiritualists and other fraudulent performers. Houdini wrote a number of books and left his extensive magic library to the Library of Congress, where there is now a Houdini Room. The supreme magician has become the object of almost cultlike worship among fellow necromancers. Once he claimed that if anyone could break the shackles of death and contact the living from the grave, he could. Since his death—"He was fifty-two when he died, his life like a deck of cards"—followers have periodically held seances where he is buried in Glendale, L.I., in Machpelah Cemetery, a granite bust of the magician staring down at them. He has inspired a *Houdini Hall of Fame* at Niagara Falls, N.Y., and a worldwide research committee has recently been formed to determine whether the "Handcuff King" was really born in Budapest, Hungary, on March 24, 1874, or in Appleton, Wis., on April 6, 1874.

Howard This surname has an odd history. General Oliver Otis Howard (1830–1909) served as commissioner of the Freedmen's Bureau after the Civil War (1865–74), his liberal policies making him the favorite hero of freed slaves. So many chose his name for their own that one authority estimates that more than one third of all *Howards* in the United States are blacks. General Howard, a hero who had lost his right arm at Fair Oaks, took part in some of the bloodiest campaigns of the Civil War. Devoted to the cause of Negro betterment, he helped found *Howard University* and Lincoln Memorial University in Ohio, and his work in the Freedmen's Bureau prevented many more blacks and whites from starving than, in fact, did perish. He is also noted for his part in several Indian campaigns. Howard's negotiations with Chief Joseph led to his biography of the Nez Percé leader in 1881. (See also *Elmer*.)

Hun After the Great Wall of China was built to contain them, the warlike nomadic tribe called the Huns thrust westward to Europe, where under Attila the Hun European Russia, Hungary, Poland and Germany were tributary to them. The Hun's ethnic origins are unknown and there were at least four peoples bearing the name, but Attila, "the scourge of God," and his tribe destroyed the Burgundian German kingdom in 437 and occupied a large part of Germany. However, the use of *Hun* for a German did not occur until 1900, when the Kaiser himself lovingly applied it to German soldiers leaving to fight in China. The name stuck because their behavior in the Orient proved "hunnish" and headline writers gladly adopted the nickname during World War I. In World War II *Heinie*, *Kraut* and *Gerry* were substituted by the British for Hun, but none of these terms were much used in America, *Nazi* taking their place.

Hung Higher Than Gilderoy's Kite Among his many crimes—he proudly boasted that these included robbing old Cardinal Richelieu in the presence of the king, and picking Cromwell's pocket—the handsome highwayman Patrick MacGregor happened to have hanged a judge. This clearly constituted a mistake, for the judge who sentenced this Robin Hood after his capture by a London detective and his conviction in 1636 was a *hanging judge* who didn't want to become a *hanged* judge. He sentenced Gilderoy, as MacGregor was nicknamed for his red hair ("Gillie roy," a red-haired lad) to be hung far higher than his four confederates. Such was the custom of the times—the greater the crime, the higher the gallows—but MacGregor's gallows stretched a full thirty feet into the Edinburgh sky. They indeed "hung him high *aboon* the rest," as the old ballad goes, and left him hanging there as a warning for weeks. No kite, or body, had ever been hung higher than Gilderoy's, it was said by the thousands who saw him, *to be hung higher than Gilderoy's kite* signifying the most severe punishment possible from that sad June day on.

Husky Any man called *husky*, stocky and muscular, is actually being compared to a sled dog—specifically, to a *husky*, or Eskimo dog, a strong breed capable of pulling great loads and covering sixty miles a day. *Husky* is used loosely for any arctic dog, but the breed is a recognized one. An unusual animal that yelps or howls like a wolf, although not closely related to the wolf, the *husky* normally feeds on fish and sleeps without shelter in the snow. Its name is a corruption of either the Tinneh Indian *uskimi*, an Eskimo; *Esky*, English slang for Eskimo; or the word *Eskimo* itself. Early explorers in the far north named the dog after the natives who bred it, and the dog's name was later applied to trappers who exhibited the breed's vigor, endurance and stocky build.

Eskimo itself is an Algonkian word meaning "eaters of raw flesh." The Eskimos do not recognize it. They proudly call themselves *Innuit*, "*the* people," or "the human beings."

I

Illinois This central "Prairie State" is named for the Illinois Indians, as the French called the confederation of six Indian tribes in the area. Frenchmen were the first Europeans to enter Illinois territory in 1673. They changed the Indian name *Hileni* or *Ileni*, meaning "man," to *Illin*, adding their *ois* plural. Since the Indian plural is *uk*, *Illinois* might be *Illinuk* today if they hadn't done so. The Illinois group is almost extinct today, numbering between two and three hundred, compared to an estimated eight thousand in the seventeenth century. (See also *States*.)

Immelmann A word still familiar to flyers and aviation buffs, *immelmann* honors a World War I ace. German pilot Max Immelmann devised this aerial maneuver in which a pursued flyer pulls up and comes over in a sharp turn that puts him on the offensive at his pursuer's tail. Immelmann was only twenty-six when he was shot down and killed in combat in 1916.

Imperial Beard Louis Napoleon (1808–73), nephew of Napoleon Bonaparte, staged a coup d'état in 1851 that made him emperor the following year. As Napoleon III the despot reigned until his empire was overthrown twenty years later and he retired to England. While emperor, Napoleon sported a small, pointed tuft of hair under the lower lip that was named an *imperial beard* in his honor. (See also *Napoleon*.)

Indian The *Dictionary of Americanisms* alone lists some two hundred terms prefixed with *Indian*, other sources bringing the total to nearly double this. Indian compounds include: *Indian barn*—a hole in the ground covered with bark and dirt; *Indian clubs*—a bottle-shaped exercise club named for the Indian weapon; *Indian corn*—maize, so called to avoid confusion with the "corn" grain (wheat) grown in England; *Indian devil*—the wolverine or the cougar; *Indian drug* or *weed*—tobacco, the term originally referring to West Indian tobacco; *Indian file*—the way Indian bands traveled through the forests over narrow trails; *Indian-giver*—to take back a gift, as Indians were supposed to do when they didn't get an equally valuable one in return; *Indian grass*—any of a number of wild grasses; *Indian paintbrush*—the bright orange-pink wildflower; *Indian pudding*—a baked dessert invented by colonial housewives; *Indian razor*—a pair of clam shells with which Indians pulled out their hair; *Indian sign*—to put a jinx on someone, a magic art in which the Indians and the "witches" Cotton Mather drowned were supposed to be proficient; *Indian summer*—mild, warm weather in late October and early November (of unknown origin but perhaps so named because it is false, as so many settlers thought the Indians were); and *Indian turnip*—the jack-in-the-pulpit flower, whose tuber is burningly pungent when eaten raw.

Indian was even used as a synonym for bogus or false. Indeed, most of these terms—*honest Injun* is a probable exception—impugn the Indian's honesty or intelligence, as if he had not suffered enough from the very beginning. But our ancestors, generally considered Indians bloodthirsty savages—"the only good Indian is a dead Indian"—and lumped these diverse peoples all together. There is also much confusion between the Indians of India and the American Indian, stemming from the fact that Columbus believed he had reached the western outskirts of the East Indies on landing in the Bahamas and named the islands the West Indies, calling the natives *Indians*. To avoid confusion, the British invented the term *Red Indian*, but the word *Amer-*

inds used by ethnologists is less insulting. *India ink,* by the way, didn't come from either India or the *Amerinds.* It was originally made in China and should be called Chinese ink.

Indiana (see *States*)

International Name-Calling Such ragging or name-calling, often the pot calling the kettle black, has always been common among nations. To the ancient Romans, for example, *Punic faith* was treachery, but there is no need to look to the past. Today, to the Romanians, inept statesmanship is *Bulgarian diplomacy.* A dirty trick in Spain is a *Basque trick,* in Holland a *German trick.* Sloppy management in Germany is *Polish economy.* A *German joke* in Spain is no joke at all, while the American *that's Greek to me* is *that's Spanish to me* in Germany, *that's Chinese to me* in Russia, and *a Turkish sermon* in Poland. Often these designations are humorous, but they can be vicious references to race and religion, true obscenities which have nothing directly to do with sex at all.

Intransigent *Los Intransigentes* was the nickname of a Spanish political party that tried to introduce a form of communism into Spain in 1873, five years after Queen Isabella II had been deposed and the country was rulerless. This splinter group, the left wing of a party favoring a republic, called themselves "the volunteers of liberty" but they were dubbed *Intransigentes (in* the Latin for "not" and *transigo* Latin for "to come to an agreement") because they stubbornly refused to compromise in any way with other political viewpoints. A dictator outlawed the party the following year, and in 1875 Isabella's son Alfonso restored the monarchy, but *Los Intransigentes* lived on. Their name quickly came into English as *Intransigeant* and then *intransigent,* meaning any unyielding, inflexible person or doctrine. (See also *Doctrinaire.*)

Iowa (see *States*)

Irish No one would think that anyone could best those with "the gift of tongues" when it came to the English language. But the Irish have been done more harm than ever they inflicted. In fact, many expressions bearing their name seem too good to have been coined by anyone but an Irishman himself, as indeed some undoubtedly were. The English began this verbal war on the Hibernians with expressions like *Irish mail,* a sack of potatoes; *Irish draperies,* cobwebs; *Irish lantern,* the moon; *Irish wedding,* the emptying of a cesspool; *Irish hurricane,* a flat sea; *Irish battleship,* a barge; *Irish bull,* any obvious contradiction in terms; and *Irish blunder,* which Swift defined as "to take the noise of brass for thunder." But when the Irish emigrated to America, the other immigrants, old and new, did worse by them, appropriating some ancient expressions and adding some new ones. *Irish evidence* here was perjury; an *Irish beauty,* a girl with two black eyes; an *Irish diamond,* a rock; an *Irish spoon,* a spade; an *Irish apple,* a potato; an *Irish bouquet,* a brickbat; an *Irish promotion,* a demotion; an *Irish dividend,* an assessment; *Irish confetti,* bricks; and an *Irishman's dinner,* a fast. It all was enough for them to *get their Irish up,* which they occasionally did, though it didn't hurt as much as the common *No Irish Need Apply* signs.

Somehow all the favorable coinings didn't help matters much. These include *Irish daisy, Irish potato, Irish moss, Irish setter, Irish stew, Irish terrier, Irish wolfhound* and, of course, *Irish whiskey* and *Irish coffee*—this last hot coffee and whiskey sweetened and topped with cream. There are many more so honorable, all remembered long after the others were just old jokes at which the Irish finally could afford to laugh.

Isabel, Isabelline Traditionally, this lady's soiled underwear gives her name to the brownish-yellow or grayish color *isabel.* The full story is rarely told. Archduchess Isabella of Austria was the daughter of Spain's Philip II and his fourth wife, Anne of Austria, daughter of Austrian ruler Maximilian II. In 1598 King Philip married Isabella to Austrian Archduke Albert, and as part of a plan to reconquer the United Provinces, handed over the whole of the Netherlands to the newly married couple as a sovereign state. Philip died that same year, but his war continued, which is where Isabella's underwear makes its contribution to history. Supposedly, Isabella vowed never to remove her underwear, even for washing, until husband Albert took the city of Ostend by siege. But Ostend's Flemish defenders had little sympathy for either Isabella or Albert. They held out for three years, playing a glorious role in the Dutch struggle for independence. Ostend was in ruins and forty thousand Spanish lives had been lost before the Belgian port city surrendered in 1604.

After three years Isabella's underwear certainly must have been *isabelline*, and she might have worn it even longer, for we are told that Albert did not win Ostend at all. General Ambrogio Spinola captured the city. Perhaps this led to jokes about why Albert and Isabella had no children, but, at any rate, the couple ruled wisely after a twelve-year truce was effected in 1609, the war resuming again at the truce's expiration.

Albert died in 1621 and Isabella thirteen years later. Some authorities, such as the *Oxford English Dictionary*, flatly reject the dirty underwear hypothesis, while others, like *Webster's*, admit it with a cautious "it is said," and with still others that washes well. Often a similar tale is told about Isabella of Castille and the siege of Granada, "linen" being used in all versions as a euphemism for underwear. The Isabella and Albert affair was first recorded in Isaac D'Israeli's *Curiousities of Literature* (1791). That Albert did not capture Ostend and that a July, 1600, list describes one of England's Queen Elizabeth's gowns as an "Isabella-colour satten" doesn't necessarily make the story false. Isabella could have made her vow earlier, perhaps while Albert was attacking Nieuport or another city, and it may be that Queen Elizabeth's gown was a different color entirely. In any event, the soiled dun color is associated forever with a queen who let her underwear become "of a dingy hue," a brownish-yellow with a shade of red.

Ishmael "Call me Ishmael," begins Melville's *Moby Dick*, this probably the most familiar opening sentence in American literature. An *Ishmael* is an outcast, which is one reason why Melville gave the name to his narrator. Ishmael was the son of Abraham and Hagar, he and his mother banished to the wilderness by Sarah, where an angel predicted that he

would forever be at odds with society (*Genesis* 21:9–21). The Moslems, however, do not share this Biblical tradition, considering Ishmael their progenitor.

Italian There has been much controversy recently about the use of the word *Mafia*, which recalls prohibition days in Chicago when *Italian* was used so frequently in describing gunmen that newspapers bowed to Italian objections and, ironically, began to use *Sicilian* instead. In reality, Italians have been abused as much as any group in the country, but the adjective *Italian* is attached to few derogatory expressions. Aside from the *Italian malady* (see *French disease*), an ancient synonym for syphilis used no more, it is hard to think of even one popular expression defaming the name. *Italian aster, Italian clover, Italian cypress, Italian greyhound, Italian honeysuckle*—all innocent terms describing innocuous things. Compared with groups like the Dutch and Irish, the Italians have indeed fared well, linguistically. Sometimes home gardeners curse *Italian ryegrass*, not realizing that it is an annual grass that won't come up the next year, but that's about the extent of *Italian's* infamy. (See also *Dago; Italian Hand*.)

Italian Hand, Italic Type, Italicize *Italic type*, in which the preceding two words are printed, was invented about 1500 by the noted Italian printer Aldus Manutius, the Latin name of Teobaldo Mannucci. There is a tradition that the printer modeled his invention on the fine *Italian hand* of the poet Petrarch, but the *Italian hand*, a beautiful, cursive style, had been widely used for copying manuscripts since its development by scholars in the twelfth century. In fact, it was so well known that *a fine Italian hand* had already become a synonym for the scheming *Machiavellian* politics or assassination by stiletto for which Italian nobles were notorious. Manutius, also a classical scholar, had his type cast by Francesco Griffi of Bologna and in 1501 first used it to publish an edition of Virgil, dedicating the book to his native Italy. Because of that Aldine Press dedication, the new slanting style—the first type that wasn't upright—came to be known as *Italicus*, which means Italian or Italic. Today words are *italicized* in print mainly to give them emphasis, and to indicate titles and foreign language words. This is *not* the case in the King James or Authorized Version of the Bible, however, a fact which creates confusion for many people. Words *italicized* in the Bible should not be emphasized in reading, for they merely indicate that the original translators, who considered the text sacred, arbitrarily supplied a word not existing in the text in order to make its meaning clearer.

J

Jack Horner *"He put in his thumb and pulled out a plum / And said, 'What a good boy am I!'"* The Jack Horner of the above nursery rhyme is supposed to have been, in reality, steward to the abbot of Glastonbury at the time that the monasteries were being dissolved in England. Jack somehow obtained deeds to the Manor of Mells in the area, either by subterfuge, or, as the popular story states, when he found the papers hidden in a pie he was delivering from the abbot to Henry VIII. By this account, he lifted the crust, put in his thumb, and pulled out the "plum," becoming owner of the property himself. This may be the only nursery rhyme based on fact. In any event, the real Jack Horner's descendants have owned the manor for generations.

Jackanapes Applied to any pretentious upstart who apes his betters, the word *jackanapes* probably comes from the nickname of William de la Pole, Duke of Suffolk. Jack was a common name for a tame male ape in England at the time (attached to the word like it was to jackrabbit, jackass, etc.) and Suffolk's coat of arms bore the clog and chain of a trained monkey. When, in 1550, the duke was arrested and beheaded at sea off Dover for alleged treason against Henry VI, he was derisively styled "the Ape-clogge" and later won the nickname Jack Napes or Jackanapes. Perhaps the ending means "of Naples," from where apes were brought to England in the early fifteenth century, but there is little doubt that the word earned its popularity and present meaning through Suffolk's nickname, which was even recorded in a satirical song of the day. There have been other theories, such as one relating to the "Jack o' nails" face card in a fourteenth-century Saracen card game, but the weight of evidence falls on the unfortunate Duke of Suffolk

as surely as the axe fell upon his neck. Suffolk, incidentally, may have been the victim of a frameup by the duke of York.

Jack Johnson, Billy Wells John Arthur (Jack) Johnson, his memory recently revived by the play, *The Great White Hope,* loudly proclaimed that he reigned as the first black world heavyweight champion in 1908 when he KO'd Englishman Tommy Burns—though his title claim was disputed and not settled until he demolished Jim Jeffries, the original "great white hope," in 1910. Johnson held the title until 1915, when giant Jess Willard knocked him out in twenty-six rounds at Havana, Cuba. The American fighter had often been called the "Big Smoke" in the United States, "smoke" being common slang at the time for Negro. For this reason, and because he was so powerful a man, the German 5.9 howitzer, its shell, and its shell burst were named after him. A formidable weapon, whose shells emitted thick black smoke upon exploding, the *Jack Johnson* saw action against the allies during World War I, when Johnson's name was prominent in the news for his fights and love affairs. Johnson, in fact, had fled to Europe in 1913 after being convicted of violating the Mann Act, unjustly or not. The great boxer died in 1946, aged sixty-eight.

British heavyweight "Bombardier" Billy Wells is another fighter of the era who gave his name to the war effort, a *Billy Wells* meaning any big gun or shell during World War I.

Jack Ketch "Do not hack me as you did my Lord Russell!" were James, Duke of Monmouth's arch last words as he looked up from the block at his executioner. But Jack Ketch, his name even then the nickname for a hangman or executioner, butchered him as badly or worse than he had William, Lord Russell, two years before in 1683. For thirteen pence a victim executioners were supposed to hang commoners and behead royalty efficiently, but Ketch was notorious as a clumsy, barbaric bungler who had taken several strokes to sever Russell's head, after he moved slightly while the axe was falling. John Ketch, appointed public hangman in 1663, is first mentioned in a broadside titled *The Plotters Ballad, being Jack Ketch's incomparable Receipt for the Cure of Traytorous Recusants and Wholesome Physick for a Popish Contagion* (1672). He later apologized for his clumsiness, explaining that Russell did not "dispose himself as was most suitable," and that he had been disturbed while taking aim. No one believed him, though, and his name became a mark of execration. At least one ballad dishonored him. "There stands Jack Kitch, the son of a Bitch," went one contemporary rhyme. After he died in 1686 this government or common executioner's name was even used for the bungling executioner in the Punchinello or Punch and Judy show imported from Italy. Of all hangmen his name would be remembered longest, given, as Macaulay wrote, "to all who have succeeded him in his odious office." (See also *Derrick; Gregorian tree*.)

Jackknife The ubiquitous American *jackknife*, which dates back in use to the early eighteenth century, may be based on the earlier Scottish *jocktelig* and that clasp knife possibly takes its name from that of its original maker, a Frenchman named Jacques de Liege. A respected Scottish historian traced the word to this source in 1776, but modern scholars have been unable to confirm his derivation. The word has long been used as a synonym for "to double up," as the body does in a *jackknife dive*, in allusion to the way the knife's big blade folds into the handle.

Jack Robinson *As quick as you can say Jack Robinson* has no connection with Jackie Robinson, the first black major league baseball player, though he was quick enough to beat out many a bunt and steal many a base. Notable attempts have been made to trace this eighteenth-century British phrase, all unsuccessful. One popular explanation, first advanced by Grose, is that the saying has its origin in the habit a certain Jack Robinson had of paying extraordinarily quick visits to his friends, the gentleman leaving even before his name could be announced. But *Jack Robinson* was probably used in the phrase simply because it is a very common name in England and is easy to pronounce.

Jackson, Jacksonian Democracy, Jacksonism *Jacksonism* is the term for the political principles and policies advocated by Andrew Jackson, seventh president of the United States, and his followers. Old Hickory, so called because he was as tough as hickory wood, commanded troops in the War of 1812. Elected to the presidency in 1829, General Jackson served two terms, espousing a widespread *Jacksonian democracy* while vigorously opposing nullification and the national Bank of the United States. His famous "Kitchen Cabinet," the first of its kind, was simply a group of intimate advisers, and by adopting the "spoils system," the granting of political jobs and favors to loyal supporters, he established a well-knit Democratic Party but intensified evils that were not removed until the Civil Service system came into being half a century later. A man of the people with little education, Andy Jackson enjoyed enormous popularity with the electorate, famed for his bravery and exploits as an Indian fighter. Yet he became the first president against whom an assassination attempt was made, miraculously escaping injury when two pistols—carried by Richard Lawrence, a deranged housepainter—failed to fire at point-blank range, the odds against this happening estimated at over 100,000 to 1. *Jackson boots, hats, jackets* and *trousers* were all named after The Hero, who died in 1845, aged seventy-eight. Today almost one hundred places in the nation bear his name. *Jackson Day*, January 8, is a legal holiday in Louisiana, celebrating his victory at the Battle of New Orleans in 1815.

Jackson did not invent the "spoils system" or even the name for it. The name arose from a speech Senator W. L. Marcy made in 1832 defending the appointment of a minister to England, when he used the phrase "to the victors belong the spoils."

Jackstraw A worthless person, a man of straw. Jack Straw was the name or nickname of a leader of the Peasants Revolt, Wat Tyler's rebellion of 1381. This revolt against English king Richard II mainly protested restrictions on pay increases to laborers and repudiated higher poll taxes. Richard agreed to the peasants' demands, but the revolt was suppressed and his promises unfulfilled when Tyler was slain by the mayor of London at a meeting held between the two men. In the original march on London to petition the king Tyler and his followers burned and wrecked much property, incurring the wrath of many. The protester called Jack Straw must have been particularly hated, for his name soon took its present meaning.

Jack the Ripper Testimony recently revealed indicates that the legendary *Ripper* may have been Albert Victor Christian Edward, Duke of Clarence and Avondale, Queen Victoria's grandson and heir to the throne of England. After eighty-two years, *Jack the Ripper's* name remains the most familiar of all murderers' and no other single criminal has been so exhaustively examined in literature and on stage and screen. The Ripper murdered and disemboweled at least five and possibly nine or more prostitutes and gin-soaked whores in London's East End in 1888, in one of the most gruesome, gory series of crimes in British or any other history. "Saucy Jack" was never captured in the foggy night streets of Whitechapel or Spitalfields, his pseudonym derived from his signature on the bizarre, mocking notes he reputedly sent to the police. (Sept. 30th: "Double event this time. Number one squealed a bit—could not finish straight off—had no time to get the ears for police.") "Bloody Jack" was described as a man of medium height who wore a deerstalker (cap), sported a small mustache and "talked like a gentleman." For almost a century writers have speculated on the *Ripper's* real identity, naming literally hundreds of suspects, including even Prime Minister Gladstone, but no one ever considered the Duke of Clarence, who was first in line for the throne eventually occupied by his younger brother King George V. Then, in November, 1970, the eminent British surgeon Thomas E. A. Stowell published an article in the *Criminologist*, a small British magazine, claiming that he could name the murderer. "His grandmother, who outlived him, was very much the stern Victorian matriarch, widely and deeply respected," wrote Stowell at ninety-three. "His father, to whose title he was heir, was a gay cosmopolitan and did much to improve the status of England internationally. His mother was an unusually beautiful woman with a gracious personal charm and was greatly beloved by all who knew her." Among much other evidence, the surgeon said his suspect had contracted syphilis just after his sixteenth birthday while carousing ashore on a cruise to the West Indies and inferred that he died of syphilis of the brain. (The Duke of Clarence did travel to the West Indies and informed speculation has it that he did die of syphilis, not of pneumonia as was claimed officially.) Stowell's information apparently came in great part from his close friend, Caroline Acland, daughter of the royal physician Sir William Gull, by whom, he said, the aristocratic *Ripper* had been treated. Stowell never revealed his suspect's name, using only the letter S, but London's *Sunday Times*, in commenting on his article, said only the Duke of Clarence, heir to the British Crown, could be the man. "All the points of Mr. Stowell's odd story fit this man," the *Times* noted. "He did die young, he was ill, he was almost certainly affected mentally by his illness." Many others agreed, although Buckingham Palace, of course, denied the story, releasing rather insufficient evidence to the contrary through informal sources. The controversy will doubtless rage forever—for Stowell's royal suspect was also shamelessly shielded by Scotland Yard, which led to at least one more needless murder. But Stowell's theory is by far the best ever offered concerning the *Ripper's* identity; the facts seem to fit down to the deerstalker Clarence was noted for wearing. "I have great admiration for the royal family—and for the family of the young man I suspect—(but) I am not going to exclude anybody," Stowell later said in refusing to support or deny the idea that the Duke of Clarence was the murderer. "All I will say is that the Ripper was not Queen Victoria or His Holiness the Pope." Said the B.B.C.: "The Duke of Clarence was a keen deerstalker and familiar with disemboweling stags. He was linked to the murders by the royal doctor, Sir William Gull, who was . . . another Jack the Ripper suspect known to prowl around the East End." Unfortunately, surgeon Stowell died two weeks after he wrote his article and his son burned his dossier of evidence, the *Ripper* again shrouded in a little more of the fog in which he so much liked to operate. Which is, after all, perhaps best for such a story.

Jacobin During the French Revolution the *Société des Jacobins*, a radical club or society active beginning in 1789, was responsible for many extreme measures, including the bloody Reign of Terror in which thousands were killed. Though it began as a liberal organization, its name in the form of *Jacobin* came to mean any extreme political radical, as it does today. The Jacobins, only three thousand strong, managed to control the French Revolution until their leader Robespierre's death in 1794, when it went underground. Five years later the group was finally suppressed.

Jacob's Ladder, Jacob's Stone *Jacob's ladder* takes its name from the ladder seen by the patriarch Jacob in a vision: "*And he dreamed that there was a ladder set up on the earth, and the top of it reached to heaven; and behold, the angels of God were ascending and descending on it. And behold, the LORD stood above it. . . .*" (Genesis 28:12–13) The ladder symbolized the hopes of Jacob for his descendants. It can today be an herb or flower formed like a ladder; a steep flight of steps up a cliff or a winding path up a mountain; a burglar's ladder; and, more familiarly, a ship's wooden runged ladder primarily used to let people ascend from or descend to smaller boats alongside. The English also use *Jacob's ladder* or *ladders* as slang expressions for runs in women's stockings.

The stone upon which Jacob rested his head while dreaming is called *Jacob's stone*. Tradition has it that the Coronation Stone brought to England from Scotland is this stone. Kings of Scotland had been crowned on the stone and the Scotch believe that wherever it rests will reign one of the royal family of Scotland.

Jacquard Loom Silk workers in Lyons bitterly opposed the *Jacquard loom* when it was introduced in 1801 at the Paris Industrial Exhibition, and its inventor was hated in every French mill town because the new machine put thousands out of work. But the revolutionary loom proved so efficient that within eleven years there were eleven thousand in use throughout France. This first automated machine (controlled by punched cards) could weave patterns in many fabrics. Napoleon quickly purchased the loom for the state and declared it public property, rewarding Joseph Marie Jacquard (1752–1834), a former Lyons' weaver, with a three-thousand-franc yearly pension and a royalty on each machine sold. Jacquard improved on his creation in 1806, adapting several features of a similar invention by Jacques de Vaucanson. Although he had not foreseen the widespread unemployment caused by the loom, his belief that it would greatly increase output was more than justified. The *Jacquard loom* revolutionized the textile industry, creating a new era in manufacturing. Today a statue of Jacquard stands in Lyons.

Jaegers, Dr. Dentons *Jaegers* can be any of several rapacious sea birds, but in England they are also woolen underwear. The underwear is named for Dr. Gustav Jaeger, whose Dr. Jaeger's Sanitary Woolen System Co. Ltd. manufactured and marketed the various undergarments he designed, beginning about 1890. Americans are familiar with the term through *The Bishop's Jaegers* (1932), a novel by Thorne Smith, creator of the inhibited banker Cosmo Topper and his ectoplasmic friends. In the United States *Dr. Dentons*, one-piece pajamas for children, are similarly named.

Jamie Duff A professional mourner. There is a story that this Scottish nickname for a mourner at a funeral comes from the name of one James Duff, an odd character who attended many funerals in the mid-nineteenth century because "he enjoyed the ride in the mourning coach." More likely the term is from the name of an old firm that supplied mourners for a price.

Janissary A collective bodyguard or household guard is called a *janissary* after the Sultan of Turkey's *veni-tsheri*, or "new army," originally recruited by the Sultan Orchan in his reign from 1329–59. To strengthen the then feeble military, Orchan at first ordered every fifth Christian youth to be surrendered by his parents to the service of the sultan, given instruction in Mohammedanism, and specially trained in the arts of warfare. The *yeni-tshari*, the word corrupted into the English *janissary* in the process of passing through several languages, became the flower of the newly independent kingdom's standing army. Its reputation for courage and discipline was highly respected and the fur-capped corps received many privileges, making compulsory recruitment soon no longer necessary. But by the nineteenth century the "new army" numbered some 135,000 and had begun actively defying the government. In 1826 specially trained Moslem troops were employed to abolish them, a brutal massacre that year resulting in the death of almost every *janissary*.

Jay Hawk, Jayhawker This word for a Kansan may come from the nickname of a "Doc" Jennison, who led a regiment of Kansas Free State men in the years preceding the Civil War. It is said that abolitionist Jennison, "a frolicson immigrant from New York State," was called Gay Yorker, the name naturally applied to his band. Even the proslavers, at least Quantrill's raiders, were eventually called *Jayhawkers* in Kansas, as were all residents of the *Jayhawk State*. The transformation from Gay Yorker to *Jayhawker* does seem unlikely, though, and can at best be regarded as doubtful. Since *Jayhawker* was also nineteenth-century slang for a bandit, I would say that the word has something to do with the quarrelsome, thieving blue jay and the warlike hawk. Or perhaps there really was a rapacious jay hawk bird, as someone has suggested but nobody has ever confirmed.

Jazz Enough men to form a good *jazz* group are credited with lending their names to the word. One popular choice is a dancing slave on a plantation near New Orleans, in about 1825—*Jasper* reputedly was often stirred into a fast step by cries of "Come on, Jazz." Another is

Mr. *Razz*, a band conductor in New Orleans in 1904. Charles or *Chaz* Washington, "an eminent ragtime drummer of Vicksburg, Miss., c. 1895," is a third candidate. A variation on the first and last choices seems to be Charles Alexander, who "down in Vicksburg around 1910, became world famous through the song asking everyone to 'come on and hear Alexander's Ragtime Band.' Alexander's first name was Charles, always abbreviated Chas. and pronounced Chazz; at the hot moments they called, 'Come on, Jazz!', whence the *jazz* music."

Few scholars accept any of these etymologies, but no better theory has been offered. Attempts to trace the word *jazz* to an African word meaning hurry have failed, and it is doubtful that it derives from either the *chasse* dance step; the Arab *Jazib*, one who allures; the African *jaiza*, the sound of distant drums; or the Hindu *jazba*, ardent desire. It can only be said with certainty that the music was originated by Negroes on plantations in the South, the word used by them since prerevolutionary days, long before *jazz* came to New Orleans. To complicate matters further, *jazz* was first a verb for sexual intercourse, as it still is today in slang.

Jefferson Bible, Jeffersonian The *Jefferson Bible*, or *Jefferson's Bible*, is a collection of Jesus' teaching compiled from the New Testament by Thomas Jefferson and published at various times under his name. The author of the Declaration of Independence, founding father, and third president of the United States, led an almost incredibly active life. His interests included aeronautics, agriculture, architecture, botany, cuisine, education, ethnology, geography, geology, government, invention, linguistics, literature, mathematics, medicine, music, philosophy, zoology . . . and he made outstanding contributions in all these and many more fields. His first term as president is noted for the Louisiana Purchase, but history best remembers Jefferson for his idealistic championship of democracy and *Jeffersonian* has become homologous with democratic. On retiring to Monticello in 1809, the former president maintained his interest in public affairs, his humanitarianism and lofty ideals always an example for Americans. Jefferson was eighty-three when he died on July 4, 1826—the fiftieth anniversary of the Declaration of Independence and the same day on which his friend and fellow patriot John Adams died. Some forty-four towns and counties bear his name.

Jenkins' Ear, The War of Jenkins' Ear

The Spanish own they did a waggish thing,
Who cropped our ears and sent them to the King.
                                    —Alexander Pope

Master mariner Robert Jenkins brought one of his ears back to London in a leather case, claiming that Spanish coast guards at Havana boarded his brig, the *Rebecca*, which had been peacefully trading in the West Indies, rifled her, and that their commander had lopped off the ear as a further humiliation. Jenkins presented his case and encased ear to the king, but no action was taken until seven years later, in 1738, when he brought the matter before Parliament. "I commended my soul to God and my cause to my country," Jenkins told a House committee and passed his ear around for all to examine, though it must have deteriorated some by then. Parliament, all ears for once, listened intently to his story and the press magnified it so that some readers thought *both* his ears had been cut off. Public opinion was outraged, the government decided, despite Prime Minister Walpole's objections, that this was one cutting Spanish insult too many, and Jenkins' ear became the major cause of the war between England and Spain that led to the War of the Austrian Succession. The immediate war, in 1739, was popularly called *The War of Jenkins' Ear* and remains so in the history books, definitely the oddest named of all conflicts and the only one ever caused by a sensory organ. Admiral Vernon of *grog* fame later put down the Spaniards at Portobello and master mariner Jenkins was given command of another ship in the East India Company's service, eventually becoming a company supervisor at St. Helena.

Jenny Haniver During idle hours at sea, sailors would sometimes shape and carve out strange mummies from dried skates, rays or mantas they had caught, manipulating these sea creatures so that they looked half human. Back in port gullible collectors often purchased these "mermaids," "dragons" and other fantastic creations, believing them to be real. This provided the seamen with an extra source of income and the incentive to continue their artistic endeavors. For three hundred years, beginning in the thirteenth century, sailors turned out such *Jenny Hanivers*, many specimens lasting for six hundred years and more, but no one can say for sure why they were so named. Perhaps the surname is a corruption of Antwerp, a bustling seaport of the time, but it is just as possible that some anonymous sailor bestowed the name of a real woman on the lifelike mummies. P. T. Barnum helped launch his career with a *Jenny Haniver* he claimed was a mermaid captured in the "Fejee" islands, sending it on tour around the country. Actually, it was a monkey's torso sewed to the head of a fish. But then Barnum claimed that "there should be poetic license in mermaids." (See also *Barnum*.)

Jenny Lind One of the less sensational P. T. Barnum attractions was Jenny Lind. The incomparable showman brought his "Swedish Nightingale" to America in 1850 for a concert tour, the golden-voiced operatic soprano giving ninety-five concerts in nineteen cities and grossing some $712,000—over half a million being Barnum's share. Jenny Lind, at the height of her powers, became the most famous singer of her time, due in large part to Barnum's hoopla. Her name and nickname are only rarely heard today, but were once commonly used to describe a gifted singer, and many fashions of the day, including a carriage, were named after her. There were rumors that Barnum and the singer were romantically involved, but she married composer Otto Goldschmidt in 1852, the couple later living in England. She died in 1887, aged sixty-seven. (See also *Barnum*.)

Jeremiad A lengthy tale of woe or complaint that takes its name from Jeremiah, the major Hebrew prophet of the Old Testament *Lamentations* and *Jeremiah*. Jeremiah's long and sorrowful complaints were a protest against the sins of his countrymen and their captivity, his tirades and dire prophecies rarely equaled in history. Strangely enough, Jeremiah, who lived in the sixth century B.C., is thought to be the author of several of the *Psalms*.

Jeroboam, Jorum, Rehoboam Jeroboam reigned as the first of the kings of Israel, "a mighty man of valor," who "did sin and make Israel to sin" (I *Kings* 14:16). Which may be why the oversized wine bottle, holding from eight to twelve quarts, was named after him by some scholarly wit at the beginning of the nineteenth century. The bottle is certainly "mighty" enough, anyway, and its contents can surely cause "sin." The *rehoboam*, two *jeroboams*, is named after Solomon's son and successor Rehoboam, who was at least wise enough to carry on his father's marital policies. Rehoboam had eighteen wives, plus sixty concubines, and probably needed many *rehoboams*. *Jeroboam* also describes the large bowl or goblet better known as the *jorum*, the latter name in allusion to another Biblical king, who brought King David "vessels of silver, and vessels of gold, and vessels of brass" (II *Samuel* 8:10).

Jerry-Built No one has come up with the first name of the Mr. Jerry or the Jerry Bros. of Liverpool whose cheap, flimsy constructions may have inspired the word *jerry-built*. No matter, these firms have more imposing competitors, in the past as well as the present. *Jerry-built* may be connected with the trembling, crumbling walls of Jericho; the prophet Jeremiah (see *Jeremiad*), because he foretold decay; the word *jelly*, symbolizing the instability of such structures; or the Gypsy word *gerry* for "excrement." Another theory suggests a corruption of *jerry-mast*, a name sailors and ship builders gave to makeshift wooden masts midway through the last century. Jerry-masts or rigs derive their name from the French *jour*, a day, indicating their temporary nature.

Jersey, Jersey Cow, Jersey Cream Close-fitting knitted sweaters and shirts, or similar women's garments, are called *jerseys* because they were first made from *Jersey cloth*, machine-woven fabrics of wool, nylon, etc., manufactured on *Jersey*, the largest of England's Channel Islands.

The island was named for the Caesars, having been called *Caesaria* when the Romans ruled over it, *Jersey* simply a corruption of *Caesaria*. In the eighth century B.C., *ey*, the suffix of the word *Jersey*, meant an island, so therefore *Jersey* is "the island of Caesar," or "Caesar's island." Little evidence of the Roman occupation remains in *Jersey* or any of the islands in the English Channel. The Romans added the islands to their empire after the Gauls had ruled there and, except for coins showing that their money circulated for over five hundred years, the only evidence of their occupation is traces of Roman buildings found in Alderney.

The *Jersey* is also a breed of cattle, raised on *Jersey* and noted for yielding milk with a high butterfat content. *Jersey cream* is the famous cream that comes from the famous cow. (See also *Caesar*; *New Jersey*.)

Jesse James Jesse Woodson James became a kind of American Robin Hood in his own brief lifetime. A member of the Confederate Quantrill gang in his youth, he and his brother Frank later led the most notorious band of robbers in this country's history. The gang's daring bank and train robberies caused many deaths, but James was regarded as a hero by a public that hated foreclosing banks and greedy railroads. In 1882, changing his name to Thomas Howard, Jesse went into hiding at St. Joseph, Mo. There, six months later, Robert Ford, "the dirty little coward that shot Mr. Howard," killed him for a reward. Jesse James was only thirty-five when he died. He is still a demihero, commemorated in a popular ballad, folk tales, novels and at least one play. Besides its obvious meaning, a *Jesse James* is a truckman's name for a police magistrate and has been applied by baseball players to umpires.

Jezebel, Jehu, Jumping Jehoshaphat Jezebel "painted her eyes, and adorned her head, and looked out the window" when Jehu entered Jezreel. But Jehu, not to be tempted, promptly cried out "Throw her down," and appropriately enough, three eunuchs responded. Jezebel's defenestration was complemented with her body being trampled by horses and eaten by dogs in one of the bloodiest of vengeful Old Testament passages (II Kings 9:30–37). What had she done? The wicked ways of this worshipper of Baal were said to have brought evil upon the Kingdom of Israel. So much so that *Jezebel* is still used figuratively for "a woman who flaunts loose morals," "a harridan," "a shameless bitch," or "a bold-faced prostitute." Jezebel was the wanton wife of the wicked King Ahab and daughter of the King of Tyre. When the dogs were done with the Phoenician princess, all that remained was "the skull, and the feet and the palms of her hands," fulfilling Elijah's prophecy that no one would be able to say of her corpse, "This is Jezebel."

Jehu is an old expression for an intrepid coachman. The son of Jehoshaphat (of *Jumping Jehoshaphat!* fame) "rode in a chariot" when he went to war, the Bible tells us, a hot rodder that "driveth furiously."

Jim Crow An emancipated Negro named Jim Crow did emigrate from Richmond to London early in the nineteenth century, acquiring "quite a fortune," according to the *Negro Yearbook*, 1925–26, but no one has established that his name has anything to do with repressive *Jim Crow* laws. The term more likely originated with a song introduced by blackface minstrel Thomas D. Rice about 1828. "Jim Crow," sung and danced by Rice in the United States and England, has as its introduction:

Come, listen all you gals and boys,
I'se just from Tucky hoe;
I'm goin' to sing a little song,
My name's Jim Crow.

The chorus ran:

First on de heel tap, den on de toe,
Ebery time I wheel about I jump Jim
    Crow.
Wheel about and turn about and do jis
    so,
And ebery time I wheel about I jump Jim
    Crow.

Rice is said to have patterned his song and dance on that of an old Kentucky field hand he had observed. His routine became so familiar that a few years later an antislavery book was titled *The History of Jim Crow* and it is from such uses of *Jim Crow* to signify "Negro" that the discriminatory laws and practices take their name, though the first such laws were not enacted until 1875. *Jim Crow cars*, banned legally in 1956 in interstate traffic, were special railway cars set aside for use by blacks only, and *Jim Crow* also meant deception or double-dealing up until the beginning of this century.

Job's Comforter, Jobation, Patience of Job, Job's Tears, Job's Turkey His stock all stolen, his servants slain, his sons and daughter killed, his body afflicted "with loathsome sores from the sole of his foot to the crown of his head"—not exactly Mr. Lucky, yet, "In all this Job did not sin or charge God with wrong." Job's misfortunes and his patience with these afflictions by which Satan is said to have tested him are paralleled nowhere else in the Bible. The *Book of Job* in the Old Testament is one of the world's greatest writings, questioning the existence of justice and moral order in the universe, its magnificent poetry more than ever appropriate today. Many phrases from it (". . . the skin of my teeth"; "Naked I came from my mothers womb, and naked I shall return"; "The Lord gave, and the Lord hath taken away . . .") are proverbial in English. While *the patience of Job* refers to great patience indeed, a *Job's comforter* is someone who in meaning to comfort you adds to your sorrows, especially by advising that you brought your misfortunes upon yourself—"Miserable comforters are ye all," Job told the three friends who came to console him in his misery. *Jobation* is for the scolding lectures Job's friends delivered to him, and *poor as Job's turkey* is a humorous American expression coined in the early nineteenth century and used to describe someone even poorer than Job. All turned out well for Job in the end: ". . . and the Lord gave Job twice as much as he had before. . . . He had also seven sons and three daughters. . . . And Job died, an old man, and full of days."

Job's tears is a tall, annual grass native to Asia whose small, terminal flowers develop into dirty-white bead-like structures. The grass has long been cultivated for adlay, the nourishing kernel within the tears.

Joe Louis, Brown Bomber Joe Louis, perhaps the greatest of all heavyweight fighters, came to be nicknamed the *Brown Bomber* for his blockbusting right and the color of his skin. Joe Louis Barrow, born on May 13, 1914, in Lafayette, Ala., was the son of a sharecropper who died when Joe was four. The family moved to Detroit where Joe helped support them when only sixteen by taking odd jobs that included work as a sparring partner in a local gym. This led to a boxing career that finally saw him take the heavyweight title from Jim Braddock in 1937. He defended his title more than any other champion in ring history and only Jack Dempsey outpolled him in the Associated Press survey of 1950 in which sports writers picked the best boxers of the century. Louis lost three times in a career interrupted by service in World War II, once to Max Schmeling, whom he knocked out in a rematch, before he became champion, and then to Rocky Marciano and Ezzard Charles, after he had retired as undefeated heavyweight champion but was attempting a comeback. His ring record included sixty-four K.O.'s, eight decisions and one win by default. A *Joe Louis* is synonymous for the utmost in a fighter, a heavyweight without peer.

Joe Miller Joe Miller doesn't deserve to have his name associated with "any stale jest." The English comic actor Joseph or Josias Miller (1684–1738), a favorite at Drury Lane Theatre in his day, probably told very few jokes, and, being illiterate, he could not have written the book that made the expression *a Joe Miller* popular. Miller played minor comic parts such as the first gravedigger in Hamlet. *Joe Miller's Jest-Book*, or *The Wit's Vade Mecum* was written and published the year after he died by a certain John Mottley, who had no permission to use Miller's name and only included three jests of Miller's in the entire collection of poor puns and dull witticisms. Being the only jokebook extant, however, Mottley's collection went through many editions that were widely imitated and quoted. All the hoary jests in a dozen or more *Joe Miller Joke Books* were so often repeated that people would cry out *a Joe Miller* on hearing one, the term soon becoming a synonym for any time-worn joke that was no longer funny.

Joe-Pye Weed A weed, according to the old saying, is only an uncultivated flower. Sometimes even more. The *Joe-Pye weed*, for instance, may have been named for an Indian medicine man of that name because he "cured typhus fever with it, by copious perspiration." The tall, common plant, with clusters of pinkish or purple flowers, might well be the only weed dedicated to a real person. Records from 1787 reveal the existence of a Joseph Pye, or Shauqueathquat, who was possibly a descendent of the original Salem, Mass. healer, but the colonial Joe Pye has not yet been unveiled. Typhus wasn't known by that name when Joe Pye practiced, but he could have cured a similar fever, or the botanist who traced the weed to him in 1828 may simply have chosen the wrong, parachronistic word.

Joey An infant of one year when he made his debut at London's Drury Lane Theatre, the actor Joseph Grimaldi (1779–1837) performed almost half a century in England. Starting as a dancer, he became internationally famous as the first of modern clowns, a great pantomimist so well known and beloved that *Joey* for a circus clown was coined by American circus performers in his honor. Grimaldi, the London-born son of an Italian actor, had no equal in pantomime; his much-acclaimed portrayal of a clown in *Mother Goose* has been revived many times. The first *Joey's* memoirs (1838) were edited by Charles Dickens, and his son Joseph Grimaldi (d. 1863) succeeded him on the London stage.

Another Joseph honored by a *Joey* is British politician Joseph Hume (1777–1855), who, in 1835, recommended the coining of the fourpenny piece that paid regard to him.

John Dory, St. Peter's Cock The European *John Dory* or *St. Peter's cock* (*Zeus faber*), a flattened, highly-valued food fish, had its religious name long before its humorous one. *John Dory* is most likely a jocular designation for some real or imaginary person, perhaps from the name of John Dory, a notorious privateer active in the sixteenth century, and the subject of a popular song of the time. Like the haddock, which also has a dark black spot on each side, the golden yellow *John Dory* has the reputation of being the fish from which the apostle Peter extracted money. In France, it still bears the name *St. Peter's cock*, its oval spots said to be finger marks left when Peter held the fish to take the coin from its mouth. The only reference to the story in the Bible is in *Matthew* 17:27, when Jesus tells Peter how to raise money for the tax collectors: ". . . not to give offense to them, go to the sea and cast a hook, and take the first fish that comes up, and when you open its mouth you will find a shekel. . . ."

John Hancock, John Henry That he was a vain man may explain his imposing handwriting, or he may have wanted King George to be able to read it, as the old story goes. In any event, if John Hancock had done nothing else, he would be remembered for his big, bold, belligerent signature, the first on the Declaration of Independence, writ "so big no Britisher would have to use his spectacles to read it." "King John" Hancock (1737–93), also known as the King of Smugglers, was a Revolutionary patriot who led local merchants in protesting the Stamp Act, heading as he did the largest mercantile firm in Boston. Immensely popular in his own lifetime, he became a major general of militia, a member and president of the Continental Congress and except for one term, was elected annually as governor of Massachusetts from 1780 until his death. His name, as everyone knows, is commonly used to mean a signature or as a synonym for name itself. It is interesting to note that John Hancock was the only signer to attach his signature to the Declaration of Independence on July 4, 1776. July 2 should, strictly speaking, be Independence Day— July the Second—for it was on that date that the Congress voted for independence, the July Fourth document merely being a revision of the first draft voted upon. Most of the other delegates signed their names to the Declaration on August 2, the last signer, Thomas McKean of Delaware, who was among the absentees on that day, being given permission to affix his signature five years later in 1781.

John Henry, another term for a signature, arose in the American west as cowboy slang. There is probably no connection here with the black folk hero John Henry, who outdrove a steam drill with his hammer, the phrase remaining "of unknown origin."

Johnnycake, Kickapoo Joy Juice "New England corn pone" is what someone has called this flat corn bread that was once cooked on a board or griddle over an open fire. New England is still famous for it and and *Johnnycake Hill* in New Bedford, Mass., home of the Seamen's Bethel so vividly described in *Moby Dick*, is named for the corn bread. Mencken, who is usually correct in such matters, traces *Johnnycake* to *Shawnee cakes* made by the Shawnee Indians, who even in colonial times were long familiar with corn and its many uses in cooking. Not all scholars agree, leaving the word's origins doubtful. One popular theory holds that *Johnnycake* is a corruption of *journeycake*. The corn bread lasted much longer than breads baked with soft wheat flour, small hard cakes of it often carried by travelers and hunters in their saddlebags along with such staples as pemmican—dried meat patties made of venison flavored with tart bog cranberries. However, *johnnycake* is recorded before *journeycake* in the form of *Jonikin*, "thin, wafer-like sheets, toasted on a board . . . eaten at breakfast with butter," these baked by New England housewives in the early eighteenth century. In fact, *jonikin*, usually spelled *Johnnikin*, is still used on the eastern shore of Maryland for the thin griddle cake. *Webster's*, who first advanced the *journeycake* theory, now cites the Shawnee derivation. The word probably progressed from *Shawnee* to *jonnikin* and *johnnycake*, and then to *journeycake*.

The Shawnee are an Algonquin tribe related to the Sauk, Fox, and Kickapoo— the Kickapoos lionized by the alliterative *Kickapoo joy juice*, humorous for any cheap liquor. Formerly resident in Pennsylvania and Ohio, they now live in Oklahoma.

John O'Groat's House *From John O'Groat's (house) to the Land's End is* a colloquial expression for from one end of Britain to the other. The house in question once stood on the northeastern coast of Scotland, having been built by John de Groat, who came with his two brothers from Holland in about 1500 and purchased property there. The brothers' descendants eventually grew to eight families and quarrels began over the matter of precedency when they met each year at John O'Groat's. Old John solved this problem neatly by building an eight-sided room with a door to each side and an eight-sided table, so that each family would be at the "head of the table." A small green knoll in the vicinity of Duncansby Head is said to be the site of the house. It is not the northernmost point of Scotland as is often claimed.

Johnsonese, Johnsonian Dr. Johnson, as the great English writer and man of letters Samuel Johnson is usually called, remains most famous for his monumental *Dictionary* published in 1755 and the immortal *Life of Samuel Johnson* written by James Boswell, generally considered the greatest English biography. A man of enormous energies who would have done even more were it not for the debilitating scrofula and often dire poverty that plagued him all his days, Johnson was revered as a moralist and a brilliant conversationalist. His *Dictionary* was the first to introduce examples of word usages by prominent authors. Along with his *Lives of the English Poets*, brilliant but essentially one-sided appraisals, it is still read today. Anecdotes about Johnson abound, but appropriate here is his reply to the lady who asked him why in his dictionary he defined *pastern* (part of a horse's foot) as the *knee* of a horse —"Sheer ignorance, Madam!" he explained. The two words that do Johnson honor reveal opposite sides of the Great Cham. *Johnsonian* refers to the good common sense reflected in his writings and conversation, while *Johnsonese* remembers the rambling polysyllabic style into which he would often slip—the very opposite of pithy *Johnsonian* phraseology. Partridge notes a third term honoring Johnson in his *Dictionary of Slang*: "*Doctor Johnson*, the *membrum virile*: literary: ca 1790–1880. Perhaps because there was no one that Dr. Johnson was

not prepared to stand up to." An observation worthy of London's influential "Literary Club" which Dr. Johnson helped found in 1764. Johnson died in 1784, aged seventy-three. Boswell's biography gives us the essence of the Great Cham, but Macaulay's famous short essay is also excellent on the spirit of the man and the times. (See also *Boswell; Chesterfield*.)

A Jonah Jonah sailed to Tarshish instead of preaching against the evils of Nineveh as the Lord bade him. But the Lord sent a mighty storm to punish him for fleeing, so "that the ship was like to be broken," the frightened sailors aboard deciding that he was an evil influence, a loser, real bad luck. "And they said . . . Come, and let us cast lots, that we may know for whose cause this evil is upon us. So they cast lots, and the lot fell upon Jonah" (*Jonah* 1:7). After they jettisoned Jonah, calm returned to the seas, but Jonah, of course, was swallowed by a whale and after three days and nights "vomited out upon dry land," whereupon he did what he was supposed to do in the first place. A *Jonah* still means a bringer of bad luck that spoils the plans of others, the phrase so popular that it has even become a verb, as in "Don't *jonah* me!" (See also *Davy Jones Locker*.)

Jonathan Apple The *Jonathan apple*, named after Jonathan Hasbrouck, an American judge who died in 1846, is fifth in order of commercial importance in America. It is a late fall-ripening apple, bright red and often yellow-striped, its round fruit mildly acid and the trees bearing it very prolific. The *Jonathan*, grown mainly in the northwest, is but one of numerous apple varieties commending their growers or other notables. The *Gravenstein, Grimes Golden, McCoom,* and *Stayman* are only a few others that come to mind. (See also *Bramley's Seedling; Micah Rood's Apples; McIntosh*.)

Joseph Coat "Now Joseph was handsome and good looking. And after a time his master's wife cast her eyes upon Joseph, and said, 'Lie with me.'" Joseph refused but Potiphar's wife persisted. ". . . One day, when he went into the house to do his work and none of the men of the house was there in the house, she caught him by his garment, saying 'Lie with me.' " Again Joseph abstained, this time fleeing from her and leaving his upper coat limp in her hand. Mrs. Potiphar proceeded to frame Joseph for attempted rape and her husband, captain of the Pharaoh's guard, had him flung into prison, though all went well with our hero "because the Lord was with him." It is from this story recorded in *Genesis* 30, and the "coat of many colors" which Joseph's father made him, that the woman's long riding coat called the *joseph* derives. The name was probably applied by the eighteenth-century tailor who designed the short riding coat, later being given to the woman's long coat and a cloaklike one worn by men.

Josh Henry Wheeler Shaw (1818–85) wrote his deliberately misspelled crackerbox philosophy under the pen name Josh Billings. He employed "dialect, ridiculous spellings, deformed grammar, monstrous logic, puns, malapropisms . . . and anticlimax," becoming one of the most popular literary comedians of his time. Shaw's many humorous newspaper columns and books, beginning with *Josh Billings, His Sayings* (1865), may have something to do with our word for "to kid" or "fool around." The expression was used in a similar sense about eighteen years before the humorist began writing in 1863, but his salty aphorisms probably strengthened its meaning and gave the term wider currency. Despite many theories the origin of *josh* remains unknown, *Webster's* and a number of dictionaries suggesting that the word is a merging of *joke* and *bosh*.

Joule Though he made his living as the owner of a large brewery, James Prescott Joule (1818–89) had devoted himself to scientific research since inventing an electromagnetic engine as a youth. In 1840 the English physicist formulated *Joule's Law* of conservation of energy, the first law of thermodynamics. That same year he was the first to determine the mechanical equivalent of heat and the heat equivalents of electrical energy, the unit of work or energy called the *joule* later named for the measurements he made. Only twenty-two when he had these valuable discoveries to his credit, Joule went on to perform other important researches, becoming one of the first to broach the kinetic theory of gasses.

Judas, Judas Goat, Judas Kiss, Judas Slit, Judas Tree On Easter Eve in Corfu the people still throw crockery into the streets in enacting their traditional imaginary stoning of Judas Iscariot. Thousands of years have passed and Christ's betrayer remains the most infamous traitor of all times, his name recorded in many expressions:

Judas or *Judas Iscariot*: any treacherous person who turns against a friend for some reward, as Judas did for thirty pieces of silver.

Judas kiss: outward courtesy clothing deceit, alluding to the way Judas identified Jesus to the high priests in the Garden of Gethsemane.

Judas tree: any of the several *circis* species, whose purple flowers suggest dark blood and upon which, tradition says, the traitor hanged himself after his act of betrayal.

Judas goat: the stockyard goat that leads unsuspecting animals to slaughter.

Judas slit or *hole*: the peephole in a prison door through which guards can look and check on prisoners.

Judas' blood money is said to have gone to buy a potter's field called *Aceldama*. According to the Biblical story, the twelfth apostle and treasurer of Christ's disciples was tempted by Satan and motivated by avarice, although one theory holds that Judas' real object had been to compel Jesus to display his Messianic power in saving Himself. (See also *Cain-color*.)

Jug, Juggins, Jughead, Silly Juggins Ernest Benzon, a wealthy playboy, was dubbed "Jubilee Juggins" because he foolishly squandered his entire fortune—a quarter of a million pounds—within two years after beginning to bet at the track during Queen Victoria's Jubilee in 1887. One source claims that the nickname "Silly Juggins" also attached itself to him, and perhaps we do refer to young Jubilee when we use that term. *Juggins*, however, was synonymous with simpleton long before Jubilee Juggins. Possibly it is a rhyming variation of *muggins*, which derives from an unknown personal name and means the same. Or *juggins* may be a diminutive of *Jug*, a sixteenth-century pet name for Judith, Jane or Joan. Jugs, Judiths, Janes or Joans were often maid-servants or barmaids at the time and most servants of the day were considered dull and stupid, at least by their masters. The word *jug*, for a pitcher, could also come from these maid-servant Jugs, who often handled them, but the Greek word *keramos*, potter's earth, is another possibility. Most authorities regard these etymologies as not being capable of proof, yet it is likely that all of these words—and thus *jughead*—make fun of a personal name. *Jug*, in fact, may have arisen from some squat Joan or Jug's resemblance to a drinking vessel of similar shape. (See also *Bellarmine*.)

Jukes and Kallikaks, The Their names happen to be fictitious, but the Jukes and the Kallikaks are real families whose histories showed early twentieth-century sociologists that heredity, rather than environment, was the cause of feeble-mindedness and the poverty and crime often resulting from it. The Jukes were a New York family given their pseudonym by Richard L. Dugdale, a prison sociologist who traced the clan back several generations after finding its members in various state prisons. Tracing the family to a backwoodsman named Max, who had married two of his own sisters, Dugsdale uncovered a fantastic record of criminal activity, disease and poverty. Of the 709 descendants on whom he obtained precise information, he established that 140 Jukes had been in prison, 280 had been paupers, and that the Jukes family in seventy-five years had cost New York State $1,308,000. The Kallikaks, another real though pseudonymous family, were studied in New Jersey and revealed the same pattern of a high incidence of crime, disease and delinquency, the two names soon linked together by writers on the subject. *Kallikak* combines the Greek *kallos*, beauty, and *kakos*, ugly, bad.

Julian Calendar, Julian Day, Julian Era You can clip precious time from your age if you emigrate to Addis Ababa, the capital of Ethiopia, where the *Julian calendar* is still used locally. The "slow" Julian calendar, instituted by Gaius Julius Caesar and honoring his middle name, was corrected and replaced by the *Gregorian calendar* in 1582, although it con- tinued to be used in England until the middle sixteenth century, when it was proclaimed, in 1752, that Wednesday, September 2, would be followed by Thursday, September 14. Inaccurate, but a great reform at the time, the *Julian calendar* had been introduced in 46 B.C. It established the year as 365¼ days, every fourth or leap year having 366 days to allow for the odd quarter days. Caesar's calendar divided the months into the number of days they presently contain, except for *August*, which Augustus Caesar insisted have thirty-one days when it was later named in his honor, not wanting Julius' *July* to contain more days than his month. The *Julian day* also pertains to Julius Caesar. It is a chronological reckoning used by astronomers enabling every day since the beginning of the *Julian era* (fixed at January 1, 4713 B.C.) to be numbered consecutively, thus avoiding complications due to months and years of unequal length. The *Julian day* was devised by Joseph Scaliger in the same year as the *Gregorian calendar*. (See also *August; Caesar; Gregorian calendar; July*.)

Julienne One celebrated word sleuth seems to feel sure that *julienne*, when applied to a clear soup garnished with vegetables cut into thin strips, comes from the French *potage à la julienne*, the name "bestowed by the chef of the Comte de Julienne." The *Oxford English Dictionary* is not so sure, citing "the French Jules or Julien, personal name," and another big dictionary, sweeping male chauvinism aside, gives us "French, special use of Julienne woman's name." *Webster's* brings our French male chef to America, without a master, and has *julienne* "named after Julien, a French caterer of Boston," as do several American writers on the cuisine. While the controversy simmers, people will go on enjoying the soup, and all kinds of foods cut into *julienne strips*.

July Before Caesar introduced the *Julian calendar*, *July* was *Quintilis*, the fifth month of the year, which had thirty-six days on the old Alban calendar. The birth month of Gaius Julius Caesar, Mark Antony suggested that it be named *Julius* or *July* in his honor when the *Julian calendar* was introduced, the name coming into use after Caesar's assassination in 44 B.C. The Anglo-Saxon names for the seventh month had been *Heg-monath*, "hay month," *Maed-monath*, "mead-month," in reference to the meadows then being in bloom, and *Lida aeftevr*, "the second mild month." *July* was first spelled "Julie" in English, rhyming with "truly" and "newly" in poems. No one has been able to account for the change in spelling or pronunciation. (See also *August; Caesar; Gregorian calendar; Julian Calendar.*)

Jumbo

JUMBO THE ONLY MASTODON ON EARTH . . . THE GENTLE AND HISTORIC LORD OF BEASTS . . . THE TOWERING MONARCH OF HIS MIGHTY RACE . . . THE PRODIGIOUS PET OF BOTH ENGLAND AND AMERICA . . . STEADILY GROWING IN TREMENDOUS HEIGHT AND WEIGHT . . . JUMBO, THE UNIVERSAL SYNONYM FOR STUPENDOUS THINGS. . . .

All in one handbill. Thus P. T. Barnum, in his subdued fashion, advertised the only elephant we know of whose name did become "the universal synonym for stupendous things." Barnum had purchased the fabled elephant from the London Zoological Garden in 1881 for "The Barnum and Bailey Greatest Show on Earth." Jumbo, captured by a hunting party in 1869, was one of the largest elephants ever seen in West Africa, the natives naming the 6½-ton beast from the Swahili *jumbo*, meaning chief. He had become a great favorite in the London Zoo, giving rides to thousands of children, and his sale to the American showman caused quite an uproar. Not that this deterred Barnum. When his agent excitedly cabled that Jumbo was lying in a London Street blocking traffic, Barnum replied, "Let him lie as long as he likes. Great advertisement." Within six weeks the incomparable P. T. had reaped $336,000 from his $30,000 investment. But he did make Jumbo's name a synonym for huge throughout America and the world. Billing the animal as a star attraction in his circus, he even persuaded Philadelphia merchants to call a shade of cloth *Jumbo gray*. Within a year after his purchase the

elephant's name had become a household word. When Jumbo was accidentally killed in an Ontario railroad yard in 1885, Barnum cried and much of the world wept with him. (See also *Barnum.*)

June The murderers of Julius Caesar, himself honored by *July*, belonged to the Junius clan or gens for which *June* is probably named. But the month commemorates their illustrious ancestor, Lucius Junius Brutus, who in 510 B.C. drove the last of the Tarquin kings from Rome. Most scholars believe that this first consul of Rome decreed that his name be so honored, while others say that *June* derives from the moon goddess Juno, the protectress of women and marriage, whose festival fell at that time of the year, or that it was dedicated to the *juniores*, Rome's young people. These last reasons at least reinforced the name's popularity and helped make *June* the favorite month for weddings from earliest Rome to the present, although a long-standing taboo against May marriages also made eager young couples wait until *June*. May, the month for elders, was considered unlucky for marriages because both the festival of Bona Dea, the goddess of chastity, and the festival of the unhappy dead fell in that month. *June*, the month of the summer solstice, had its last day added by Caesar. Before the *Julian calendar* reform it had been the fourth month of the year.

Jungian *Jungian psychology* differs from *Freudian* essentially in that it believes that the libido or energy derives not from sexual instinct, but from the will to live. Carl Gustav Jung (1875–1961), an early disciple of Freud, broke with the master over what he considered an excessive emphasis on sex as a cause of neurotic disorders and a regulator of human conduct. He became a world-renowned figure, postulating the existence of two unconscious influences on the mind—the personal unconscious, containing an individual's own experience, and the collective or racial unconscious, holding the accumulated memories of generations past. The Swiss psychiatrist divided mankind into introverts and extroverts, using those or similar terms for the first time. Among many other innovations, he invented the word-association test.

K

Kaiser Like *Czar*, *Kaiser* too derives from the surname of Gaius Julius Caesar, being merely the German word for *Caesar*. *Kaiser* was the title of the emperor of the Holy Roman Empire and the emperors of Germany and Austria. The word has less of a stigma attached to it than *Czar*, meaning a king, monarch, or emperor. Another title for a ruler often attributed to Caesar is Shah. Shah, however, actually derives from a Russian word meaning dominion. (See also *Caesar; Czar*.)

Kansas (see *States*)

Keeping Up with the Joneses There was no real Jones family, but the comic-strip artist who created the expression lived in a community where some people did and still do try to *keep up with the Joneses*. Arthur R. ("Pop") Momand resided in Cedarhurst on New York's Long Island, when he and his wife "lived far beyond our means in our endeavor to keep up with the well-to-do class which then lived in Cedarhurst." Momand was wise enough to quit the scene and move to New York, where he rented a cheap apartment and eventually created his once immensely popular *Keeping Up with the Joneses* comic strip, launched in 1913. The title of the strip, based on Momand's experience in Cedarhurst, gave currency to the phrase. As for the name, he first "thought of calling it, *Keeping Up with the Smiths*, but finally decided on *Keeping Up with the Joneses* as being more euphonious."

Kelvinator, Kelvin Scale Barely ten years old when he entered Glasgow University, William Thompson was appointed a full professor of natural philosophy there when only twenty-two. The Scottish mathematician and physicist early became one of the greatest scientists of his or any other era and toward the end of his career was created first Baron Kelvin of Larga. In his long lifetime Lord Kelvin made fundamental theoretical contributions in numerous scientific fields including thermodynamics, electricity, solar radiation and cosmology. He also personally supervised the laying of the transatlantic cable in 1866, initiated the determination of electrical standards, and invented many useful instruments—among them the modern compass, a deep-sea sounding apparatus, an electric bridge, a standard balance, the mirror galvanometer, the siphon recorder, and a variety of instruments for electrical engineers. As a teacher few could surpass him, one writer noting: "Extreme modesty . . . was combined with the utmost kindliness in Lord Kelvin's bearing to the most elementary student. . . . The progress of physical discovery during the last half of the nineteenth century was perhaps as much due to the kindly encouragement which he gave to his students . . . as to his own researches and invention; and it would be difficult to speak of his influence as a teacher in stronger terms than this." This great, good, and kind man invented the absolute or *Kelvin temperature scale*, which has the advantage of expressing any temperature in a positive number, and the British *Kelvinator* or refrigerator was named in his honor in 1914 when theories he had advanced made the appliance possible. Lord Kelvin retired from Glasgow University after teaching there half a century, but three years later formally matriculated as a student in order to maintain his connection with the university—this making him, at seventy-five, the oldest if not the only genius ever to go back to school. He died in 1907, aged eighty-three, still a student and still learning.

Kibitzer German card players of the sixteenth century found meddlesome onlookers just as annoying as card players do today. The constant gratuitous "advice" of these chatterers reminded them of the *Kiebitz,* the lap wing or plover, whose shrill cries frightened game away from approaching hunters. Thus all *kibitzers* are named for this troublesome bird, our pewit. The word, deriving from the German *kiebitzen,* to look on at cards, has been extended to include anyone who offers unsolicited, unnecessary, uncalled for advice in any sphere of human endeavor.

Kike One respected authority offers the surprising theory that this vulgar offensive term of hostility and contempt, often used by anti-Semites, offends not only persons of Jewish descent and religion but the Italians and Irish as well. The *Random House Dictionary of the English Language* suggests that it is "apparently modeled on *hike,* Italian, itself modeled on *Mike,* Irishman, short for Michael." In other words, the deliberately disparaging term painfully illustrates the transfer of prejudice from one newly arrived immigrant group to the next. This view runs counter to the prevailing theory, however. Mencken and others, including *Webster's,* believe that the word "derived from the ki or ky endings of the surnames of many Slavic Jews." Neither theory seems capable of absolute proof.

Kilroy Was Here Hundreds of suggestions have been made as to the identity of the original Kilroy. The phrase *Kilroy was here* first appeared on walls and every surface capable of absorbing it during World War II and is still seen today in the remotest corners of the globe, either freshly inscribed or a relic of older, if not better, days. Other names like *Clem* and *J. B. King* have been substituted, but only *Kilroy* endures, so much so that *a Kilroy* is now "someone who travels a great deal." The most popular theory seems to be that the first man to use the phrase was an inspector Kilroy in a Massachusetts shipyard who chalked the words on equipment to indicate that it had his O.K. From Quincy the phrase traveled on crates all over the world, copied by soldiers, sailors and airmen wherever it went. If this is the case, Mr. Kilroy has probably been quoted

more often than Mr. Shakespeare. The *Kilroy* graffito is treated, along with thousands of wall writings, in Robert Reisner's excellent *Graffiti,* in which the author quotes one graffitologist who insists that *Kilroy* represents an Oedipal fantasy, combining "kill" with "roi," the French word for "king." In any (psychological) case, *Kilroy Was Here* reigns supreme on walls everywhere, from the ruins in Pompeii where *Figulus Loves Ida* to the New York City subways where *Franz Kafka Is a Kvetch, Sarah Lee Is a Diabetic* and hundreds of schizophrenics have urged us to *Support Mental Health.*

King Bomba A *King Bomba* is an expression very rarely used today, but might well be revived. The original King Bomba was Ferdinand II (1810–1859) of Naples who reigned from 1830 to 1859. At one point in his reactionary reign the treacherous monarch held forty thousand political prisoners. He was called *King Bomba* for his ruthless bombardment of Sicilian cities in 1848, in which much damage was done, many atrocities committed, and many innocent people hurt. Since then *King Bombas,* whatever their motives, have been all too common.

King Cole The "merry old soul" of nursery rhyme fame is in British tradition a king of the third century. The monarch is mentioned in *Historia Regum Britannica* (1508) by Geoffrey of Monmouth, who says nothing about him calling for his pipe, bowl or fiddlers three, and whose veracity, in fact, has been questioned. Old King Cole may also have been the grandfather of the Emperor Constantine. The city of Colechester doesn't derive from his name, as is often stated, probably being named from the Latin *colonia.* (See also *Jack Horner.*)

Kings Among the specific kings enthroned in words and phrases are the following:

King Charles' Spaniel: for England's Charles II, who favored this black-and-tan-coated English toy spaniel.

King George's War: waged by England and her colonies against France in North America (1744–48) and named after the reigning British monarch.

King James Bible: the authorized version of the Bible, completed in 1611 by scholars appointed by England's James I.

King Philip's War: six hundred New England colonists were killed and twenty-five towns destroyed in this bloody conflict led by Philip, son of Massasoit, who in 1775 headed an Indian confederacy to drive settlers from native hunting lands.

King William's War: here England, her American colonies, and her Indian allies fought against France and her Indian allies; the war, named after the English King, began in 1689 and ended in a stalemate in 1697.

A host of additional candidates, often referring to no particular king, includes:

King's English: educated or correct English speech, the way a king would or should use English; the expression became popular shortly before Shakespeare's time.

King's Evil: scrofula. This constitutional disorder of a tubercular nature, characterized by swelling of the lymphatic glands in the neck, was believed to be capable of cure by the royal touch. France's Louis IX is thought to be the first king to employ the practice, which soon spread to England, where Macaulay records that Charles II touched 92,107 persons during his reign. The practice ended with Queen Anne, Dr. Johnson being one of the last persons to be "touched" in 1712.

King's Weather: warm, sunny and mild weather, weather fit for a king that seemed to greet George V—George the Well-Beloved—wherever he traveled abroad.

The King of the World: someone actually had the gall to take this title: Khorrum Shah, Mongol emperor of Dahli from 1628–1658.

King Tut Egyptian King Tutankhamen's tomb was discovered in 1922 by George E. S. M. Herbert, earl of Carnarvon and Howard Carter in the valley of the tombs of the kings at Karnak. Tutankhamen, heretic king of the XVIII dynasty in the fourteenth century B.C., lay swathed in a gold sarcaphogus surrounded by a fortune in jewels, furniture and other relics that threw much light on Egyptian history. His difficult name was condensed to *King Tut* and his immense wealth caught the public's imagination. *Don't act like King Tut* or *he thinks he's King Tut* became expressions applicable to any person pretending to be much more than he was, acting as if the world should pay him homage as it did King Tutankhamen.

Kinkaider American Congressman Moses Kinkaid (1854–1922) saw his *Kinkaid Act* granting homesteads to Nebraska settlers passed into law in 1904. The homesteaders who settled these 640-acre grants under the provisions of the act were called *Kinkaiders* by the newspapers of the day and his name passed from the pages of the *Congressional Record* to the dictionaries.

Kinsey Report Dr. Kinsey's *Sexual Behavior in the Human Male* (1948) and *Sexual Behavior in the Human Female* (1953) were popularly labeled the *Kinsey Report.* Alfred C. Kinsey (1894–1956) aroused great controversy on publishing these and other works, but his researches gradually became accepted in America, virtually effecting a sexual revolution. Kinsey's reputation as an eminent professor of zoology at the University of Indiana, and his detached, scientific manner, enabled him to accomplish so much in a field where scholars long feared to tread. His colleagues today carry on his work at the university.

Kit-Cat Though pastry cook Christopher (Kit) Catt—or Kat, or Catling—created little but mutton pies, he nevertheless travels in the company of Titians of the art world. Kit Catt's mutton delights were called *kit-cats* and some leading Whigs of the early eighteenth century enjoyed them so much that they formed a club on his pastry shop premises in London. However, when Sir Godfrey Kneller was commissioned to paint forty-two portraits of the *Kit-Cat Club's* prominent members, who included Steele, Addison, Congreve and Walpole, a problem soon presented itself. The rooms were so low in height that Kneller had to restrict his portraits to three-quarter size, each canvas measuring exactly 28 by 36 inches. Such canvasses were called *kit-cats* after the club where they hung and the term is still used for any portrait of these dimensions representing less than half the length of the sitter but including the hands. The site of the original Kit-

Cat Club is now occupied by the Law Courts in London and Kneller's paintings are in the National Portrait Gallery.

Klieg Eyes, Klieg Light Hollywood movie stars adopted the dark glasses that became their trademark because of the intense *klieg light* introduced to stage and studio early in this century. These bright incandescent lights, rich in ultraviolet rays, caused a form of conjunctivitis marked by burning of the eyeballs, redness, tearing and photophobia that was common to all who worked under the arcs. In order to conceal and protect their *klieg eyes*, the stars and lesser galaxies took to wearing "shades," and have traditionally done so ever since. The *klieg light* was the invention of the German-born brothers Kliegl, John H. (1869–1959) and Anton T. (1872–1927), who emigrated to the United States and in 1897 established the firm of Kliegl Brothers, pioneering in the development of lighting equipment and scenic effects for the stage and early motion pictures. The light they invented was first called the *Kliegl light*, which proved too difficult to pronounce, their real name modified like those of many of the actors who worked under them. (See also *Drummond Light*.)

Knickers, Father Knickerbocker The prominent Knickerbocker family settled near Albany, N.Y., about 1674. Among its prosperous descendants was the wealthy Harman Knickerbocker (b. 1779), the great-great-grandson and namesake of the family founder, who became known as "the prince of Schaghticoke" for his great manor along the Schaghticoke River. So when author Washington Irving burlesqued a pompous guide book of the day with his two-volume *A History of New York from the Beginning of the World to the End of the Dutch Dynasty* (1809), he decided to capitalize on the old familiar name, choosing the pseudonym Diedrich Knickerbocker. Irving could not have concocted a better pen name in satirizing the stodgy Dutch burghers than this thinly veiled alias for the well-known Dutch "prince," although the first great book of comic literature written by an American was also a satire on Jeffersonian democracy, pedantry and literary classics. Soon his humorous work became known as *Knickerbocker's His-*tory of New York, but it wasn't until English caricaturist George Cruikshank illustrated a later edition in the 1850's that the Knickerbocker family name was bestowed on the loose-fitting, blousy knee breeches still worn today. In that English edition Cruikshank depicted the alleged author and his fellow Dutch burghers wearing voluminous breeches buckled just below the knee. His drawings of this style that the early Dutch had worn were widely copied for boys' knee pants, baggy golf trousers (plus fours) four inches longer, and even silk bloomers for women—all dubbed *knickerbockers* after the family Irving had immortalized. Eventually, the name for *knickerbocker trousers* was shortened to *knickers* and *knicks* in England. The style is no longer worn by schoolboys but was revived recently as a fashion for women.

As a result of Irving's work *Father Knickerbocker* also became a synonym for New York City. There is a theory that the writer coined *Knickerbocker* from the Dutch words *knickers*, a clay marble, and *bocker*, a baker—the origin of the family patronym—but it is much more likely that he used the real name of Harman Knickerbocker and his well-known clan.

Know-Nothing The first political *know-nothings* to be labeled *Know-Nothings* were members of a secret society named the Order of the Star Spangled Banner, organized in New York in 1849. Pledged to complete silence, the group's stock reply to outsiders trying to obtain information about their order was "I know nothing about it." Later, when they merged with other groups into the national American Party in 1856, their reply is said to have been "I know nothing in our principles contrary to the Constitution." A strange statement for a party that was anti-Catholic, whose members were pledged to vote only for native Americans, and which supported a twenty-five-year residency requirement for citizenship, among other reactionary principles. Some of their antichurch principles, such as nonsupport of parochial schools, were generally accepted and the *Know-Nothings* achieved considerable success in local elections, but they lost the national elections as the American Party in 1856, even with ex-president

Millard Fillmore as their presidential candidate. After that the road was downhill; they were heard of no more as a power after 1860 except for their name, which is often used as a synonym for any reactionary political group or individual that knows nothing and appeals to base emotions. (See also *Doctrinaire; Intransigent; Jacobin*.)

Kreutzer Beethoven dedicated his famous violin sonata (op. 47) to violinist and fellow-composer Rodolphe Kreutzer in 1803 and it has since been universally known as the *Kreutzer Sonata*. The musician, a Frenchman of German extraction, was professor of violin at the Paris Conservatoire and conductor at Vienna's Imperial Theater. A prolific composer with some forty operas, numerous concertos and sonatas, and forty unsurpassed études for the violin to his credit, Kreutzer died in 1831, aged sixty-five. Tolstoy's novella, *The Kreutzer Sonata* (1890), takes its title from the Beethoven work.

Kriss Kringle This synonym for Santa Claus is still occasionally heard in America and, in fact, originated here. The expression stemmed from a misunderstanding of the German *Christkindlein*, which really means "the Child in the Manger," or "the little Christ child." It arose in about 1830 and was spelled *Krisskring'l* before taking its present form. (See also *Santa Claus*.)

L

Labanotation Perhaps in some future 1984 a form of *labanotation* will be used by "Big Brother" and computer to chart tomorrow's movements for the omniverse —such would at least be the theme for a good science-fiction story. This little-known word—oddly no major dictionary defines it—describes an important notation system that amounts to a graphic shorthand for dance, enabling a choreographer to delineate every possible movement of the human body individually or in ensemble. Introduced by its creator Rudolph Laban in his book *Kinetographie Laban* (1928), *labanotation* was the first practical method capable of scoring the various complex movements and positions of an entire ballet or musical comedy. Unlike the old numbered-footprint plans familiar to us all, the Laban system amounts to a complete break with tradition. It dispenses entirely with the musical five-line horizontal staff, using a three-line vertical staff that is divided in the center. Code symbols on each side of the line indicate foot and leg movements, while symbols in parallel columns outside the lines pertain to all other body gestures. Every slight movement from toe to head can be noted, as well as their direction, timing and force, and by grouping together the staffs for individual dancers an entire work can be "orchestrated."

Laban did for the dance what Guido d'Arezzo did for musical notation almost a thousand years before him (see *Guido scale*). Prior to his system dancers had to rely on their memories of performers who had appeared in classical ballets, but now almost exact revivals can be given and ballet composers can finally adequately copyright their creations. Born in Pressburg (Bratslavia) on December 15, 1879, the German dance teacher and choreographer had a great influence on modern dance, with Mary Wigman and Kurt Jooss among his pupils. Rejecting nineteenth-century traditionalism, he tried to express industrialized urban life in his work, even experimenting with group improvisations, using masses of German factory workers after World War I. Laban wrote many books, including *Effort* (1947), with F. C. Lawrence, and *Principles of Dance and Movement Notation* (1956). He died in London on July 1, 1958.

Laconic "If we enter Laconia, we will raze it to the ground," an Athenian herald (or Philip of Macedonia) is said to have announced to the Laconians.

"If," was the reply he received from the sententious Spartan magistrates. The Lacadaemonians were all supposed to be so parsimonious with words, and were noted in the ancient world not only for their stoic Spartan lifestlye but also for their short, brusque and pithy way of speaking and writing, which was appropriate for their outward lack of emotion. Not only in Sparta, the capital, but throughout the country youths were taught modesty and conciseness of speech, taught so well that the word *laconic* comes to us by way of Latin from the Greek *Lakonikos*, meaning "like a Laconian." A *laconic* person is generally one who expresses much without wasting words, who is terse, to the point, and usually undemonstrative. The traditional *If* story may not be true—Philip of Macedonia *writes* the warning message in another version—but for a military put-down it ranks with General McAuliffe's historic reply to the Germans on being asked to surrender during the Battle of the Bulge—"Nuts!" Another classic concise contender is Punch's famous admonition: "To those about to marry— DON'T." (See also *Spartan.*)

Ladybug, Ladybird, Lady Chapel,

Lady's Mantle "Lady Bennet and her ladies," Samuel Pepys noted in his diary. "Lord! Their mad and bawdy talk did make my heart ake! . . . Their dancing naked, and all the roguish things in the world." That was in 1660, when the word *lady* obviously did not have its present meaning. Originally a *lady* was just "the head farmer's wife," the word deriving from the old English *hlaefdige*, "a woman who kneads bread," but by the seventeenth century, as Pepys observed, a *lady* was a woman of pleasure who made her bread in other ways—you didn't call a *lady* a *lady* then. In *ladybug* the *lady* part is of course associated with the original meaning, the beneficial insect named in honor of "Our Lady," the Virgin Mary. *Ladybugs*, which are bred for use in organic gardening today, are obviously not all female as is sometimes believed. These brightly colored beetles (of the family *Coccinellidae* of the order *Coleoptera*) generally feed on aphids and other insects that are destructive to plants, but several species destroy plants themselves. A *ladybug*, children of all ages still believe, will fly away home if you warn her that her house is on fire and her children will burn. In England the beetles are called *ladybirds*, due not to a British aversion to bugs but to an aversion to the word bug, which is more strongly associated with sodomy there (see *Bugger*). *Ladybird* is also used for *ladybug* in some parts of America; Claudia Taylor Johnson, our former first lady, bears this familiar nickname.

A *Lady's Mantle* (*alchemilla*) is a flowering plant whose large, serrated and many-lobed leaves resemble "the mantle of Our Lady," and a *Lady chapel* is a chapel attached to a large church and dedicated to the Blessed Virgin. The delicate *Lady Fern* (*Athyrium felix-femina*) does not refer to the Virgin Mary, as is commonly believed, taking its name from the legend that possession of its seeds could render a woman invisible.

Lady Godiva Strategically arranging her long golden tresses, Lady Godiva rode through Coventry, relieving herself of her clothes and inhibitions in order to relieve her people of oppressive taxation. According to the traditional story, Lady Godiva (c. 1040–c. 1080) had jokingly agreed to ride naked through the crowded streets at high noon if her husband, Leofric, earl of Mercia and lord of Coventry, and one of the most powerful nobles in England, would lift burdensome taxes he had imposed on the townspeople. At least Leofric *thought* she was joking. To the delight of his twiceblessed tenants, the earl had to keep his promise when his wife took him at his word and kept hers. He removed the exaction almost as soon as she had removed her clothes and displayed herself in the marketplace. The pioneer *Lady Godiva*, a title humorously applied to any undraped woman, was apparently the benefactress of several religious houses in the reign of Edward the Confessor, and founded the Benedictine monastery at Coventry. Her real name was Godgifu, her legendary ride, as famous and more interesting than Paul Revere's, first recorded in *Flores historiarum* by Roger of Wendover (d. 1237), who quoted from an earlier writer. From 1678 until 1836 the patroness of Coventry was honored by an annual procession commemorating her bareback exhibition—usually held on May 31, weather permitting. Godiva is the subject of a number of legends and poems, by Drayton, Leigh Hunt, and Tennyson among others, and since 1949 a bronze statue of her by Sir William Reid Dick has stood in Coventry. For a later version of her side-saddle ride see *Peeping Tom*, who, it seems, lived on the wrong side of the street and saw her.

Laelia These tropical American orchids, comprising about thirty-five species and prized for their showy flowers, may be named for Gaius Laelius, a Roman statesman and general who died about 165 B.C., or for his son Gaius Laelius, a Roman consul nicknamed Sapiens, the wise. Both father and son were soldiers and excellent orators, the father the best friend of Scipio Africanus Major, and the son famous for his friendship with Scipio Africanus Minor. The younger Laelius was also a close friend of Cicero, who writes that he and Scipio used to like to go on holidays to the seaside, "where they became incredibly childish and used to collect shells and pebbles on the beach." Sapiens probably had a hand in writing the plays of Terence, his wide learning admired throughout Rome.

Another candidate English botanist John Lindley may have had in mind when he named *Laelia,* was a vestal virgin of that name, in allusion to the delicacy of the flowers. The vestal virgins, six in number, were daughters of the best Roman families, trained in youth to serve the goddess of hearth and home in her temple in Rome, where they prepared sacrifices and tended a perpetual sacred fire. Their vows included obedience and chastity, and after serving Vesta for thirty years they were allowed to leave the temple and marry, which they seldom did in practice. The virgins were influential, even having the power to pardon criminals, but if they broke the vows of chastity the penalty was a public funeral followed by burial while they were still alive. Needless to say, most remained vestal virgins.

Lambert The son of a poor tailor and largely self-educated, Johann Heinrich Lambert nevertheless managed to win fame as a physicist, philosopher, mathematician and astronomer. The German scientist, though he died of consumption in 1777 when only forty-nine, made important discoveries in many fields. In mathematics Lambert proved the irrationality of *pi* and developed several trigonometry concepts, while in philosophy his *Neues Organon* (1764) pointed out the importance of beginning with experience and using analytical methods to prove or disprove theories. Lambert also made valuable contributions in electrical magnetism, mapmaking and meteorology, several theorems in astronomy bearing his name. It is for his work in physics on the measurement of light intensity and absorption that his name is honored in the dictionaries, the *lambert* being the unit of brightness in the metric system.

Lambert has been used as a synonym for immensity, too. But here the word refers to a fabulously fat English jail-keeper named Daniel Lambert (1770–1809), who weighed 739 pounds when he died, measuring only five foot, eleven inches. Lambert, 102 inches around the waist, was so heavy that his coffin had to be built on wheels. George Meredith

described London as the "Daniel Lambert of cities," and Herbert Spencer used the phrase "a Daniel Lambert of learning," but their countryman wasn't the heaviest of mortals. The accepted record is held by Robert Earl Hughes of Fish Hook, Ill., who died in 1958, aged thirty-two, and at one time weighed 1,069 pounds. Hughes had a rare pituitary gland disorder. Today the champion is American Charles ("Tiny") Kinsey, reported to weigh 777 pounds. A Baltimore woman who died in 1888 holds the female title—at 850 pounds—but then female candidates have always been reluctant to come forth.

Langley In 1896 Samuel Pierpont Langley, already a celebrated physician and astronomer, constructed and flew the first heavier-than-air model plane. This pilotless steam-driven model traveled a distance of 4,200 feet over the Potomac River and though it included no provision for takeoff or landing, convinced many aviation pioneers that powered mechanical flight was possible. The government appropriated $50,000 for the inventor to build a full-size craft, powered by a 50 H.P. gasoline engine, which failed in two 1903 test flights. This subjected Langley to great ridicule, but the fault was in the launching apparatus, the plane being reconstructed and flown successfully in 1914, seven years after his death. Samuel Pierpont Langley (1834–1906) had a rich and varied career in science. Only a high-school graduate, he is remembered as the inventor of the bolometer, still the most sensitive instrument for measuring the heat radiated by stars, and as the head of the Smithsonian Institution from 1887 to 1905. *Langley Field* in Virginia pays tribute to his pioneering aviation work and his accomplishments in physics are honored by the word *Langley,* a measurement unit of solar radiation.

Laodicea, Laodicean, Latakia Every mother should have a boy like Seleucus, founder of the Syrian dynasty. The emperor is said to have named *five* cities after his mother Laodice in about the middle of the third century B.C. This able Macedonian general of Alexander the Great tried hard to build his kingdom in the way that Alexander built his, founding

Greek colonies governed along Persian lines wherever he could. Three of at least five cities Seleucus Nicator named for his mother remain standing today, their names now pronounced *Ladik*, *Ladikiyeh* and *Latakia*. *Latakia*, a seaport of Syria opposite the island of Cyprus, is the most prominent of these, having a population of over 100,000 and chiefly noted now for its well-known *Latakia tobacco*. At one early point in its history *Latakia* was renamed *Julia*, in honor of Julius Caesar, but reverted to its original designation when he passed from the scene.

As for the word *Laodician*—usually meaning someone lukewarm or indifferent in religion or politics—it too derives from the name of a real Laodice. In this case, however, the woman in question is probably not Seleucus' mother, but his grandson's wife. It seems that the grandson, Antiochus II, carried on the family tradition and named yet another Syrian city after *his* wife Laodice. Its ruins can be seen today close to the Gonjele station on the Anatolian railway. Little is known of this *Laodicea's* history, but it was one of the earliest homes of Christianity. Yet the Church of Laodicea grew lazy and indifferent, leading to its chastisement in the Bible: " '*I know of your works: you are neither cold or hot. Would that you were cold or hot! So, because you are lukewarm, and neither cold nor hot, I will spew you out of my mouth. For you say, I am rich, I have prospered, and I need nothing; not knowing that you are wretched, piteable, poor, blind, and naked!*" (*Revelation: 3:15–18*). This Biblical rebuke led to the word *Laodicean* being applied to all people indifferent to religion, the *Laodicean attitude* remaining a major problem to churches today. Ultimately the word came to mean a person unconcerned about politics or even life itself. All for a wife named Laodice, whom Antiochus certainly did not consider to be in the least lukewarm.

Lapageria French Empress Josephine, Napoleon Bonaparte's first wife, was born Marie Josèphe Rose Tascher de la Pagerie. A creole of French extraction, she had been married to Viscount Alexandre de Beauharnais, who was guillotined after the French Revolution, Josephine escaping the blade herself only because of powerful friendships. The empress brought Napoleon much happiness, including two children from her first marriage—Eugene, later viceroy of Italy, and Hortense, who became Queen of Holland —but her numerous love affairs caused him to consider divorce several times. On one occasion, it is said, the glass cracked over the picture of Josephine that Napoleon always carried. The emperor turned pale and declared, "My wife is either sick or unfaithful"—his latter premonition proving true. In any case, Napoleon finally did have his marriage with Josephine annulled in 1809 on the alleged grounds of sterility, marrying Marie Louise of Austria. Josephine lived out her life in retirement at her private retreat, La Malmaison, near Paris, and the emperor continued to consult her on important matters, always having valued her keen mind. She died in 1814, aged fifty-one. An avid botanist as well as an ardent lover (her garden at Malmaison contained the greatest collection of roses in the world), the beautiful Josephine has the monotypic genus *Lapageria*, containing only one species, named for her. This showy Chilean vine of the lily family is among the most attractive climbing vines, its flowers rose colored, trumpet shaped and, unlike Josephine Lapageria, usually solitary. (See also *Napoleon*.)

Larousse The famous reference work series of *Dictionnaires Larousse* commemorates the French grammarian and lexicographer Pierre Athanase Larousse (1817–75). In 1852 Larousse helped found the publishing house that bears his name. He later compiled the fifteen-volume dictionary and encyclopedia *Grand dictionnaire universel du XIX siècle* (1866–76).

Lasthenia Among the students who attended the philosopher Plato's lectures at the Academy in Athens was a woman named Lasthenia, who stole in by disguising herself as a man. Little more is known of her, but centuries later her story inspired the naturalist Cassini to name the plant genus *Lasthenia* for Plato's woman pupil. The small genus contains but three species, two native to California and the other to Chile. Tender annual herbs, the showy flowers are yellow, on long, often nodding, peduncles.

Laura, A

It was the day when the sun's heavy rays
  Grew pale in the pity of his suffering
  Lord
When I fell captive, lady, to the gaze
  Of your fair eyes, fast bound in love's
  strong cord.

Laura of Petrarch's immortal love poems
was no figment of the poet's imagination.
According to tradition, the poet laureate
of Rome wrote his poems for Laura, the
daughter of Audibert de Noves and the
wife of Count Hughes de Sade, an ancestor of the French nobleman who gave us
sadism. Petrarch never revealed the real
Laura's identity, guarding his secret jeal-
ously, but he wrote that he saw her for
the first time in the church of St. Clara
at Avignon on April 6, 1327, and that
this first sight of her inspired him to become a poet. In the eighteenth century
the Abbe de Sade identified her as the
wife of Hughes de Sade, who bore the
old man eleven children before dying of
the plague in 1348 when she was only
forty. But this identification is not certain. It is only known that Laura was a
married woman who accepted Petrarch's
devotion but refused all intimate relations. Their platonic love inspired the
long series of poems that are among the
most beautiful amorous verse in literature, the most famous the sonnet in
praise of their first meeting quoted above.
The Italians call this collection of lyrics
the *Canzoniere* and it is titled *Rime in
Vita e Morte di Madonna Laura*. Petrarch died long after his Laura (whoever she was), in 1374 in his seventieth
year.

Lord Byron put the whole affair in a
more humorous perspective when he
wrote in *Don Juan*: "Think you, if Laura
had been Petrarch's wife, / He would
have written sonnets all his life?"

Laval After the liberation of France,
Pierre Laval was tried for treason, sentenced to death, and executed on October 15, 1945. The French politician,
born in 1883, held many national offices
before becoming premier of the collabo-
rationist Vichy government in 1942. Believing that Germany would win World
War II, he was instrumental in organizing a policy of collaboration with the
Nazis within occupied France. Under
Nazi pressure Laval instituted a rule of
terror, authorizing a French fascist militia and agreeing to send forced labor to
Germany. His name became a hated one,
synonymous with traitor, though he
claimed at his trial that his motives were
patriotic. Laval fled to Spain when France
fell to the Allies, was expelled, and finally
surrendered himself. After his conviction,
he tried to commit suicide, but was saved
for the firing squad. (See also *Petain;
Quisling*.)

Lavaliere, Lavaliere Microphone
Louis XIV, the Sun King, had a voracious
appetite for women as well as food.
Louise Françoise de la Baume Le Blanc,
whom he later made Madame la Duchesse de La Vallière, was only his first
maîtresse en titre or mistress to the king
of France—a semiofficial position which
had been customary since Agnes Sorel,
"the Queen of Beauty," in the thirteenth
century. Louis did not relish his queen,
the Austrian Marie-Thérèse, a good cook
but "an ill-favoured woman who even had
hair between her breasts." So he slyly
took up with his sixteen-year-old sister-in-
law Henrietta of England, who had married his brother Philip of Orléans. There
followed the world's first royal soap opera.
The future Duchesse de La Vallière, the
daughter of an army officer, was the maid
of honor to Henrietta and it was decided
that as a blind she would become Louis's
mistress—this would give Louis all the
excuse he needed to be with Henrietta
and throw his wife off the trail. But the
king and the beautiful maid of honor,
then only about sixteen herself, soon
really fell in love. Louise, an innocent
girl, never asked for anything and it was
only toward the end of their affair in
1667 that Louis made her a duchess,
granting her the estate of Vaujours. Long
before that she had become famous
throughout Europe for her great beauty
and the glamorous fashions she introduced. One of these, called the *lavallière*
in her honor, was a wide fancy necktie
with a large bow. It is still so named in
France, but in England the word was
transferred to the ornamental jeweled
pendant, usually worn on a chain around
the neck, that we know as the *lavaliere*.
Unfortunately, the love story has an unhappy ending. There were seven good

years, but though his mistress bore him two sons and a daughter, the insatiable Louis lost his heart to Madame Montespan. He forced Louise to remain on as his official mistress for another seven years, even making her suffer the indignity of sharing her apartments at the Tuileries with his new mistress. In 1774, at the tender age of thirty, Louise finally retired to a Carmelite convent, where she became celebrated for her piety and may have written the perennially popular devotional book *Reflexions sur la Misericorde de Dieu* (1685). The duchess died in 1710, aged seventy-six. It was probably no consolation to her, but the Sun King's second official mistress suffered an almost identical fate. (See also *Montespan*.)

Today the small television microphone that hangs on a cord from the neck is also called a *lavaliere*, taking its name from the pendant necklace that honors the famous beauty. (See also *Pompadour*.)

Lawrencium While a physics professor at the University of California in 1930, Ernest Orlando Lawrence invented and built the first atom-smashing cyclotron, for which he was awarded the Nobel Prize nine years later. The physicist also played a prominent role in the development of the atomic bomb while director of the radiation laboratory at Berkeley, conducting research into the separation of U-235. Lawrence died in 1958, aged fifty-seven. In 1961 Albert Ghiorso, Almon Lash and Robert Latimer created a new synthetic radioactive element at the Lawrence Radiation Laboratory in Berkeley, naming it after the laboratory dedicated to its former director. *Lawrencium*, its atomic number 103, is believed to be a "dinosaur element" that first formed when the world was born and decayed out of existence within a few weeks.

Lawsonia Linnaeus probably named *Lawsonia inermis*, the mignonette tree and the source of the dye henna, for John Lawson, a traveler in North Carolina said to be burned alive by Indians. Lawson came to America from England in 1700 and traveled about a thousand miles through unexplored territory, recording his observations of native flora and fauna in his *A New Voyage to Carolina* (1709). A founder of Bath and New Bern, N.C.,

he was appointed the state's surveyor general in 1708, but was captured and put to death in the Tuscarora uprising three years later. Whether Linnaeus related red men and death by fire to the red dyestuff taken from the eastern tree's leaves is unknown, though not impossible. At least one authority, however, claims that the Swedish botanist named the plant for a Dr. Isaac Lawson, a Scottish botanical traveler who published an account of a voyage to Carolina in 1709.

Lazar, Lazarist, Lazarone, Lazaretto *Lazar* has almost dropped out of use as a word for a diseased beggar or leper, but *lazarone* still describes a beggar of Naples. Both words are named for Lazarus, the only character in all His parables to whom Christ gave a proper name (see *Dives*). During the Middle Ages *lazar* was a name given to those suffering from leprosy and other diseases, outcasts who were allowed to do nothing but beg. A *lazaretto* or *lazar-house* is a hospital for such persons, taking its name from *lazar* plus (N)*azaretto*, the popular name of a hospital in Venice managed by the Church of Santa Maria di Nazaret. *Lazarone*, from the Italian *lazzarone*, derives directly from the name of another hospital, that of St. Lazarus in Naples, which was a haven for poor vagrants. The Neapolitan *lazarones* once elected a chief called the *Capo Lazzaro* every year and were several centuries ago a strong force in Italian politics.

The name Lazarus comes from the Hebrew *Eleazar*, meaning God-aided, or God will help. Another use of it is in *Lazarist*, or *Lazarian*, a member of the Vincentian Congregation of the Mission, which is chiefly engaged in conducting missions and seminaries. In this case the word comes directly from the priory of St. Lazarus in Paris, a Vincentian center beginning in 1632 and a *lazar house* before that.

Lazarus Strictly speaking a *Lazarus* is someone risen from the dead, but the word is used allusively in many ways. It recalls the brother of Mary and Martha of Bethany, whom Jesus raised from the dead after he had been in his tomb four days. The story is told in *John* 11:38–44: *"Then Jesus, deeply moved again, came to the tomb; it was a cave, and a stone* *lay upon it. Jesus said, 'Take away the stone.' Martha, the sister of the dead man, said to him, 'Lord, by this time there will be an odor, for he has been dead four days.' Jesus said to her, 'Did I not tell you that if you would believe you would see the glory of God?' So they took away the stone. And Jesus lifted up his eyes and said, 'Father, I thank thee that thou hast heard me. . . .' When he had said this, he cried out with a loud voice, 'Lazarus come out.' The dead man came out, his hands and feet bound with bandages, and his face wrapped with a cloth . . ."* One authority notes that "in the fourth century the house and tomb of Lazarus were shown to pilgrims, and the gospel narrative . . . may be based on the story told to first century visitors to Palestine." Incidentally, the Biblical passage cited is from the Revised Standard Version of the Bible, a more scholarly but far less beautiful work than the King James Version. Compare, for example, the King James' "bound head and foot with grave clothes" with the "his hands and feet bound with bandages, and his face wrapped with a cloth" quoted above.

Lazy As Lawrence, St. Lawrence's Tears When the Roman judge demanded that St. Lawrence bring forth the treasures of his church, he came forward with all its poor people. The Romans under Emperor Valerian did not appreciate his philosophy and this deacon to Pope Sixtus II, later St. Sixtus, soon followed his bishop to a martyr's death in 258. St. Lawrence is said to have been burnt alive on a gridiron over a slow fire, and legend has it that he addressed his torturers ironically with the words, "I am roasted enough on this side, turn me round, and eat." Over the years his words have become "turn me around, for this side is quite done," which is supposed to signify that the martyr was too lazy to move in the flames. It is just as likely, however, that the expression *lazy as Lawrence* refers to the heat of St. Lawrence's Day, August 10. In fact, the gridiron speech probably comes from a much older story told by Socrates and others about the Phrygian martyrs.

St. Lawrence is also known as St. Laurentius and St. Lorenzo. Spain's magnificent Escorial was built in honor of the martyr by Philip II, in memory of a battle won on his day. *St. Lawrence's tears,* shooting stars or meteorites that appear annually around August 10, are also named for the saint.

Lazy as Ludlam's Dog This old proverb refers to a dog belonging to a certain Mrs. Ludlam, an English sorceress, tradition tells us, who lived in Surrey near Farnham. Her dog was so lazy that when strangers approached he always lay down or leaned up against a wall to bark, or didn't even bother to bark at all—there are several versions of the tale. A variation on the phrase is *as lazy as David Larence's dog,* or *as lazy as Lawrence's dog.*

Lazy Susan The English call our *Lazy Susan* a dumbwaiter, which the revolving servitor was called in America until relatively recently. It is said that the first use of the term dates back about seventy-five years ago when the device was named after some servant it replaced, Susan being a common name for servants at the time. But the earliest quotation that has been found for *Lazy Susan* is 1934, and it could be the creation of some unheralded advertising copywriter. Therefore, *lazy* may not mean a lazy servant at all, referring instead to a hostess too lazy to pass the snacks around, or to the ease with which guests can rotate the device on the spindle and bring the sections containing different foods directly in front of them. As a dumbwaiter, the servitor, usually with three wine-laden shelves, dates back to the mid-eighteenth century.

Leningrad, Leninism N. Lenin was the pseudonym Vladimir Ilich Ulyanov adopted toward the end of 1901, variants such as V. I. Lenin coming into use a little later as his revolutionary activities in Russia became more prominent. He is thus known in history as Nikolai Lenin or Vladimir Ilich Lenin, his real name being only rarely used. It was the execution of his Populist elder brother Aleksandr for taking part in a plot to assassinate Czar Alexander III that confirmed Lenin in a revolutionary career. He eventually renounced the practice of law and devoted himself to the systematic study of Marx he had begun even before his brother's death. By 1897 Lenin had been exiled to Siberia for his revolutionary activities. He wrote his first book there. A leader in the unsuccessful 1905 Russian Revolution and of the extreme Bolshevik element after the democratic revolution of 1917, Lenin headed the new state when the Bolsheviks emerged victorious and assumed power in Russia. Only fifty-four when he died in 1924, he must still be regarded as one of the most effective political leaders of all time, though not "mankind's greatest genius," as *The Great Soviet Encyclopedia* calls him. But Lenin's name is legendary in the communist world, his body embalmed in a tomb in Moscow's Red Square which has become a shrine to Soviet citizens. The former capital city of *Leningrad*, previously St. Petersburg and Petrograd, was named for him in 1924. *Leninism* refers to the particular communistic principles based upon Marxism propounded by the founder of the modern Soviet state, which are collected in his twenty-two volume life and works. *Leninism's* central point is the dictatorship of the proletariat or working class. (See also *Marxism*; *Stalinism*.)

Leotard, Leotards A baby who has to be hung upside-down from a trapeze bar to stop his crying would suggest to any parent a fledgling star aerialist. Such was the case with Jules Leotard, at least according to his *Memoirs*, a small volume swollen with windy conceit. At any rate, Leotard did become one of France's most famous aerialists in the nineteenth century, perfecting the aerial somersault, among other acrobatics, and starring in Paris and London circuses. But his name is remembered for the *leotard* costume he invented, which is still worn by circus performers. That vanity played a large role as the handmaiden of his invention is witnessed by the plug the performer gave the *leotard* at the end of his *Memoirs*. "Do you want to be adored by the ladies?" he exhorts his male readers. "[Then] put on a more natural garb, which does not hide your best features." So far nobody earthbound has followed his advice. But the *leotard* in the form of *leotards* is more popular today than ever. Originally the costume was a one-piece elastic garment, snug-fitting, low at the neck and sleeveless, but it became a gar-

ment covering the arms as well. Today, though no dictionary has yet noted the distinction, *leotards*, the plural of the word, is used for the pantyhose that little girls wear, really half-tights, and sometimes, though not as often, describes women's pantyhose.

Lesbian, Sapphism, Sapphics Lesbos, a Greek island in the Aegean sea off the west coast of Turkey, was a center of civilization in the 7th and 6th centuries B.C. There Sappho, the most famous poetess of her time, taught the arts of poetry to a select group of young women. The legend has never been proved but the romantic ardor of some of Sappho's lyrical poems probably accounts for the tradition that she and her followers engaged in homosexual love, female homosexuality being named for these *lesbians*, or residents of Lesbos. The word *Lesbian* (with a capital) designates any inhabitant of the island, which is noted for its rich soil as well as its sardine and sponge fisheries. Here Epicurus and Aristotle once lived and the philosopher Theophrastus was born.

Sapphism, from Sappho's name, is a synonym for *lesbianism*. The poetess, according to legend, threw herself into the sea when spurned by the handsome youth Phaon, but the story is generally regarded as pure invention. Sappho was (probably) married and had a son. Her simple passionate verse, characterized by matchless lyricism and vivid use of words, originally formed nine books, only fragments of these extant today. The "Tenth Muse," as she was known, used the four-lined verse form called *sapphics* in her honor, and is in fact noted for her careful control over meter.

Lespedeza Japan or bush clover, sometimes called the hoop-coop plant but widely known as *lespedeza*, is believed to have been brought to America in the early nineteenth century with a cargo of tea unloaded at Charleston or Savannah. The plant became an escape that was first identified at Monticello, Ga., in 1846, this initial collected specimen now preserved at Harvard's Gray Herbarium. A member of the pea family, *lespedeza* has become a very important crop not only for hay and forage but for improving poor soils—it has been shown that corn and cotton crops can be increased 10 to 30 percent by turning under a crop of *lespedeza* previous to their planting. The slender plant grows to a height of about eighteen inches, its leaves divided into three leaflets on many branched stems. The genus *Lespedeza*, however, contains 125 species, of which Japanese clover (*Lespedeza striata*) is only one. Many of these species are native to America and it was to them that the botanist Michaux referred when he named the genus in 1803. *Lespedeza* was named in honor of V. M. de Zespedez, Spanish governor of Florida in 1795, whose name Michaux misread as Lespedez. The Japan clover species of *lespedeza* is supplemented by a number of others, including a Korean species (*Lespedeza stipulacea*), better adapted to northern areas, and *Lespedeza cuneata*, a perennial. In fact, the chief belt of production in this country is planted to *Korean lespedeza*. Only in America is the group used extensively for agricultural purposes, although *lespedeza* plants and shrubs are cultivated as ornamentals throughout the world.

Let George Do It Whenever a particularly difficult task arose, Louis XII was likely to say, "Let Georges do it; he's the man of the age." Satirically intended, the phrase seems to have been invented by the French king and referred to his close friend and advisor, Cardinal Georges d'Amboise (1460–1510). A prodigy who became a bishop when only fourteen, Louis' minister of state was a true Renaissance man. He excelled in everything he did and his interests ranged from literature to science. The phrase eventually became the proverbial *Let George do it*, losing the "s" but immortalizing the cardinal's name more than his magnificent tomb in the Rouen Cathedral.

Levis The word *Levis* has become more popular in the eastern United States recently as a synonym for jeans, denims or dungarees—probably due to the bright-colored styles that Levi Strauss and Company are manufacturing today. The trademarked name has been around since the gold rush days, though, when a pioneer San Francisco overall manufacturer began making them. Levi Strauss reinforced his heavy blue denims with copper rivets at strain points such as the corners of pockets, this innovation making his product especially valuable to miners, who often loaded their pockets with ore samples. Within a few years the pants were widely known throughout the West, where the name *Levis* has always been more common than any other for tight-fitting, heavy blue denims.

The Life of Riley American poet James Whitcomb Riley (1849–1916) has been suggested as a candidate for the source of this metaphor for a joyous life of ease. The Hoosier poet seems to have been rejected for no good reason, but his simple, sentimental poems often concern barefoot boys loafing in the summer and were popular at about the time the phrase came into use. He is certainly as worthy a choice as "The Best in the House is None Too Good for Reilly," a song written by Lawlor and Blake toward the turn of the century that Mencken champions, or "Is That Mr. Reilly?" another song popularized by Pat Rooney of the famous "Dancing Rooneys" in the 1890's. Furthermore, if the saying derived from the poet's name, the change in spelling need not be explained.

Lillian Russell Beautiful and flamboyant Lillian Russell was the toast of the town almost from the night she made her debut at New York's Tony Pastor's Opera House in burlesques of Gilbert & Sullivan comic operas. Only eighteen at the time, the singer and actress was fresh from Clinton, Ia., where she had been born Helen Louise Leonard in 1861. For the next thirty years Lillian Russell's beauty and talent for light opera brought her fame and fortune unsurpassed by any contemporary performer. Success included her own company, a collection of male admirers that has probably never been matched since, and a number of sumptuous apartments and houses, like her summer home in then fashionable Far Rockaway, where she entertained lavishly. Among several things named for her were the *Lillian Russell* dessert, a half cantaloupe filled with a scoop of ice cream, and the town of *Lillian Russell* in central Kansas, which today has a population of about 6,200.

Lincoln, Lincolnian, Lincolniana, Lincolnite It is surprising that only some twenty-five place names in the United States honor our sixteenth president, little more than half those commemorating Jefferson and less than one third named for Andrew Jackson. But this can be explained by early bitterness toward Lincoln in the South. For none of his countrymen, not even Washington, has become a folk hero and giant in American tradition equal to Lincoln, and he is certainly more loved and respected the world over than any other American. His story, from his birth in a log cabin to the Emancipation Proclamation, the immortal Gettysburg Address, and the assassination by John Wilkes Booth, is so widely known in its smallest details that it is, rather than history or myth, a living part of the American legend from generation to generation, making Lincoln a father image to us all, willing and unwilling.

A *Lincolnite* was a supporter of President Lincoln during the Civil War. *Lincolniana* is any material, such as writing, anecdotes or objects, pertaining to Honest Abe, the Rail Splitter or The Great Emancipator, while *Lincolnian* pertains to his character or political principles. *Lincoln's Birthday*, February 12, is a legal holiday in many states, and that it is not a national holiday at this late date is regarded by many as little less than a national disgrace.

Lindbergh Law, Lindy Even today's astronauts returning from the moon have not received the hero worship heaped upon Charles Augustus Lindbergh when he made the first solo flight across the Atlantic on May 20–21, 1927, in his *Spirit of St. Louis*. Lindbergh was awarded the Congressional Medal of Honor for his 33½-hour nonstop flight from New York to Paris, promoted to colonel in the Air Force, and received the French Cross of the Legion of Honor, the English Royal Air Force Cross and the American Distinguished Flying Cross among hundreds of national and international honors. There had never been such adulation and perhaps there never will be again—in June, 1927, alone, it is reported, Lindbergh received 3,500,000 letters, 14,000 parcels and 100,000 telegrams. The Hero, The Lone Eagle, Lucky Lindy, The Flying Fool symbolized

the beginning of a new technical age that in itself made great personal heroism less likely. Lindbergh's unprecedented fame even resulted in the *lindy* or *lindy hop*, a jitterbug dance very popular up until the mid 1950's, being named in his honor. His name made headlines again in 1932 with the tragic kidnapping and killing of his infant son, for which Bruno Richard Hauptmann was found guilty and which led to the *Lindbergh Law*, passed by Congress in 1934, that made all kidnappings across state lines and the use of the mails for ransom communications federal offenses. Lindbergh's popularity only began to fade when he became a prominent isolationist and cofounder of the American First Committee before the outbreak of World War II; nor did the tarnished image regain its luster in the light of his distinguished record as a flier after Pearl Harbor. Still active in public life today at sixty-eight, America's greatest modern hero remains a controversial figure, praised by many and denounced by some. His name, however, more often evokes an indifference that brings him the anonymity he once craved when people in restaurants came up and stared into his mouth to determine what kind of food he was chewing.

The Lone Eagle's family name was changed to Lindbergh by his grandfather Ola Mansson before he emigrated to Minnesota from Sweden in 1859. The old name points out a peculiarity in Swedish nomenclature that no longer exists today. Ola Mansson, like many Swedes, was Mansson simply because his father's first name was Mans, just as his own sons were surnamed Olsson because they were the sons of Ola. Thus the name was a very common one, the primary reason for the change. Secondly, Ola wanted a fresh start in America. He had been a prominent liberal, even radical, member of the Swedish Parliament, and at the time of his migration was in the process of being framed by conservatives for embezzlement while a director of the bank of Sweden. It would be best, he thought, to make a complete break with the past, symbolic for his new life in America, and he chose the less common Swedish name of Lindberg, appending an *h* for added distinction. As it turned out, he was right in all respects. The name Mansson remained one of reproach for many years in the old country, until his essential innocence was established, Ola having been "guilty" of the crime charged only in a trumped-up, technical sense.

Lingua Franca, Pidgin-English, Bêche-de-Mer

Guard: "You-fella you stand fast. You no can walkabout. Suppose you-fella walkabout me kill 'im you long musket."
Translation: "Halt or I'll fire!"

Pidgin English, this example taken from a handbook issued to Pacific troops during World War II, obviously has its faults, but the *lingua franca* has served man well over the past three centuries. It is estimated that thirty to fifty million people speak some variety of pidgin and it ranks at least twentieth among the world's most common tongues.

A *lingua franca* is any hybrid language, a combination of various tongues. Pidgin English and bêche-de-mer, or beach-la mar, are two such trade languages in the Pacific, but the earliest one recorded is *lingua franca* itself, the words Italian for "the Frankish tongue." *Lingua franca* arose along the Mediterranean, a medley or babble of Italian, French, Spanish, Greek, Turkish and Arabic common to many seamen in the ninth century or earlier. A *Frank* was any West European at the time, for the tribe ruled over most of Europe. The language enabled Moslems to conduct business dealings with Europeans and Mediterranean traders still find it very useful in the Levant.

Pidgin English, originally developed by British traders in China, takes its name from the way the Chinese pronounced "business"—"bijin." It combines English and Portuguese—as well as German, Bengali, French and Malayan. There is even a magazine, *Frend Belong Me* (*My Friend*), published in pidgin by the Catholic Mission in New Guinea. Bêche-de-mer, a *lingua franca* known only in the Pacific, is a combination of English and native dialects. The bêche-de-mer was a staple of trade, the natives prizing it for food, and the language takes its name from this sea slug or sea cucumber.

Official: "This man wantchee take you home-side makee wife-pidgin. Can do, no can do?"
Bride: "Can do."
And they lived happily ever after. (See also *Frank; Hobson-Jobson.*)

Linnaean System, Linnaea Linnaeus, the most famous of all naturalists, not only dubbed us *Homo sapiens* but chose the names for far more things than any other person in history, classifying literally thousands of plants, animals and minerals. Carl von Linne—Carolus Linnaeus was the Latin form of his name—showed an early love of flowers that earned him the nickname "the little botanist" when only eight years old. The son of a Lutheran minister who cultivated his interest in nature, he became an assistant professor of botany at Uppsala University, then studied medicine in Holland, where in 1735 he wrote his *Systema naturae*. Linnaeus was only twenty-eight at the time, his masterpiece followed by the *Species plantarium* two years later. These books marked the beginning of a system of scientific nomenclature, taxonomy, that would be elaborated on in over 180 works. The *Linnaean system* the naturalist developed divided the kingdoms of animals, vegetables and minerals into classes, orders, genera, species and varieties, according to various characteristics. It adopted binomial nomenclature, giving two Latin names—genus and species—to each organism. In this two-name system all closely related species bear the same genus name—e.g. *Felis* (Lat. *cat*) *leo* is the lion, and *Felis tigris* is the tiger. The system Linnaeus invented provided scientists with an exact tool for the identification of organisms and is standard today, although many old popular names for plants and animals linger on. Further, it recognized all organisms as part of a grand scheme, a unique concept at the time. Linnaeus continued to practice medicine and headed the botany department at Uppsala, naming thousands of plants that he collected and classifying hundreds more that professional and amateur botanists sent him from all over the world. He named some plants for their characteristics alone, some for prominent people and others for their discoverers, but in every case the designation he applied remains intact. Linnaeus was seventy-one when he died at Uppsala in the cathedral in which he is buried, and his garden at the university, where he grew many of his plants, is still visited by pilgrims from all over the world. Wilfred Blunt's recent *The Compleat Naturalist* is an excellent, sorely needed biography of the man.

Linnaeus himself has the woody ever-green shrub *Linnaea borealis*, a member of the honeysuckle family, named in his honor. His son, called Linnaeus, junior, was an eminent botanist in his own right, naming some twenty-two genera. (See also *Banksia*; *Lobelia*; and other plant names.)

Listerine Practically synonymous to-day for a mouth wash, *Listerine* takes its name, despite his protests, from Joseph Lister, first Baron Lister (1827–1912), famous for founding antiseptic surgery. Basing his methods on Pasteur's theory that bacteria causes infection, Lister in 1865 used a mixture containing carbolic acid as a germicide and invented meth-ods of applying it on wounds and inci-sions, also advocating the sterilizing of all surgical instruments before operations. Such procedures greatly reduced post-operative fatalities from infection. Lord Lister, who became president of the Royal Society, later invented antiseptic, absorbable ligatures and the drainage tube for wounds, the sinus forceps, among other instruments, and perfected numerous operations. He was created a baronet in 1883 and raised to the peerage in 1897 as Baron Lister of Lyme Regis. The eminent surgeon, whose father Jo-seph Jackson Lister is famous for his work in optical science, tried unsuccess-fully to disassociate his name from *Lis-terine* when the product was first mar-keted. He much preferred to see himself commemorated by the *Lister Institute of Preventive Medicine in London*, of which he was a founder.

Lloyd's of London (see A-1)

Lobelia, Lobelia Dortmanna As noted, Linnaeus named over a thousand plants, including hundreds that have be-come household words both to gardeners and almost everyone not an anthophobe or botanophobe, one who fears flowers or plants. The following list of fifty or so Linnaeus-coined plant names barely indi-cates his immense contribution to the language. The well-known genera are: Amaryllis; Anemone; Asparagus; Aster; Azalea; *Begonia*; *Bignonia*; *Camellia*; Canna; Cannabis (marijuana); Capsicum (pepper); Celosia; Clematis; Cumcumis (cucumbers); Cyclamen; Dianthus; Eu-phorbia; Ficus (figs); *Fuchsia*; *Gardenia*; *Gentiana*; Ginkgo; Hibiscus; Ilex (hol-lies); Iris; Jasminium; Juniperus; Kalmia; Lilium; *Lobelia*; *Magnolia*; Orchis (or-chids); Papaver (poppies); *Poinciana*; *Poinsettia*; Portulaca; Prunus (privet); *Quassia*; Rhododendron; Rubus (raspber-ries); Salvia; Smilax (the florist's fern); Spiraea; Taxus (yews); Tulipa; Ulex (gorses); Viola (violets); Wachendorfia (herbs); Xeranthemum (including the best-known of the everlastings, Immor-telli); Yucca; and *Zinnia*.

Many names on this A–Z list are epon-ymous, those italicized treated along with others under separate entries, but Linnaeus honored hundreds more with plant names that cannot conceivably be covered here. Indeed, by labeling species as well as genera, the Swedish botanist sometimes commended two people with the same plant. This is the case with *Lobelia dortmanna*, the water lobelia. Linnaeus named the plant's family *Lo-beliacae* and its genus *Lobelia* after Mat-thias de l'Obel, or Lobel (1538–1616), a distinguished Flemish botanist and physician who lived a century before him. But he called *L. dortmanna*, one of its three hundred species, after an ob-scure druggist named Dortmann whom he met while studying in Holland. Noth-ing is known about Dortmann, but Lobel had been both physician and botanist to England's learned King James I. A na-tive of Lille, he tried to classify plants according to their leaf formations long before Linnaeus and wrote several of the earliest botanical books. The *Lobeliaceae* family commemorating him contains twenty-four genera and over seven hun-dred species, some of which are trees and shrubs, but its *Lobelia* genus consists of about three hundred species of annual or perennial herbs widely grown for their mainly blue, red, yellow, or white flowers. The species *Lobelia inflata* was used by American Indians for Indian tobacco, having a tobaccolike odor, and was also employed as the base for a popular home remedy, though it is considered poisonous in quantity. Another species, *Lobelia syphilitica*, the blue syphilis, was used by the Indians to treat syphilis; it was even introduced into Europe centuries ago for this purpose. (See also *Linnaeus; Syphilis.*)

Lobster Newburg This delectable lobster dish should have blazoned the name of Charles Wenberg, a late-nineteenth-century shipping magnate, across the pages of menus. But he was foolish enough to displease the great restaurateur Lorenzo Delmonico. Wenberg had discovered the dish in South America and on his return described it glowingly to Delmonico's owner. Lorenzo soon instructed his chef to prepare the shelled lobster in its rich sauce of sherry, thick cream and egg yolks, serving the dish to his wealthy patron and naming it *Lobster Wenberg*, in his honor. So it remained on Delmonico's menu for almost a month, until Wenberg, well in his cups, got into a fight in the estimable restaurant's main dining room and was bodily ejected. The next day the dish appeared on an enraged Lorenzo's menu as *Lobster Newburg*, perhaps in honor of the city on the Hudson, which name it retains to this day. Lorenzo's Manhattan restaurants, incidentally, introduced many dishes to America, including Baked Alaska, named for the newly discovered territory, and, believe it or not, a creation called truffled ice-cream that was *de rigueur* for a few years. Lobsters, the better part of *Lobster Newburg*, derive their name from the Latin *locusta*, "a leaping creature." Today a luxury food, they sold for a penny apiece in colonial times and our ancestors often used them for bait. *Homarus Americanus* is the species we usually eat—as distinguished from lobster tails or langoustes, these from clawless spiny lobsters which do not compare in taste. The biggest one ever verified was a 42-pounder caught off Virginia in 1935, but lobstermen tell me they've seen or heard of specimens much larger.

Loganberry California Judge James Harvey Logan (1841–1921), who had been a Missouri schoolteacher before working his way west as the driver of an ox team, developed the *loganberry* in his experimental home orchard at Santa Cruz. Logan, formerly Santa Cruz district attorney, was serving on the superior court bench in 1880 when he raised the new berry from seed, breeding several generations of plants to do so. Though a respected amateur horticulturist, he never adequately explained how the berry was developed. One account claims that the *loganberry* originated "from self-grown seeds of the Aughinbaugh (a wild blackberry) . . . the other parent supposed to be a raspberry of the Red Antwerp type." Other experts believe that it is a variety of the western dewberry, or a hybrid of that species, crossed with the red raspberry. The dispute may never be resolved, but experiments in England have produced a plant similar to the *loganberry* by crossing certain blackberries and red raspberries. In any case, there is no doubt that the purplish-red *boysenberry* is shaped like a blackberry, colored like a raspberry and combines the flavor of both—or that it was first grown by Judge Logan and named for him. Its scientific name is *Rubus loganbaccus* and the trailing blackberrylike plant is grown commercially in large quantities, especially in California, Oregon, Washington and other places having fairly mild winters.

Logan's Lament One branch remained on the centuries-old elm; the tree leafed out in spring, four years ago, but by August the weather and summer drought had taken their toll—the Logan Elm in Circleville, O., one of the nation's most famous landmarks, had finally died, though it still stands lifeless marked by a plaque honoring its name.

It was under this old elm tree that John Logan, a leader of the Mingo Tribe, made his eloquent plea for peace between his tribesmen and the settlers in 1774—*Logan's Lament*—a speech which for generations was memorized and recited in schoolrooms throughout America. But John Logan's real story is far more tragic than either his lament or the legend ever tells. One night in April, 1774, while he was away on a hunting trip, a band of men broke into Logan's cabin, brutally massacring his family. The following morning, upon arriving home, John Logan found the bodies of all the relatives he thought he had in the world. Logan swore to avenge them. Half white himself, his father captured as a child and raised by the Cayugas, John Logan, or Tahgahjute, had been known as a friendly Indian much respected by the Shawnee tribe into which he had married, but now blind hate overcame him. Swearing revenge against the white man, Logan sent a declaration of hostilities to Virginia's Governor Dunsmore—attributing the mass killing to a drunken band led by militia captain Michael Cresap—and when the Shawnee chief Cornstalk supported Logan's declaration, in 1774, the bloody uprising known as Lord Dunsmore's War resulted. Tribes went on the warpath throughout the Ohio valley and before militiamen finally overpowered the Indians at Point Pleasant, hundreds of lives were lost on both sides. Logan was through with war then, had had his revenge, yet so intense was his sorrow that he refused to meet with Governor Dunsmore in a council of peace. Cornstalk, speaking for all the Shawnee, accepted Dunsmore's proposal, but John Logan would not sit with his enemies. Instead, he wrote Dunsmore the following letter—*Logan's Lament:*

"I appeal to any white man to say if ever he entered Logan's cabin hungry and he gave him not meat; if ever he came cold and naked, and he clothed him not. During the course of the last long and bloody war, Logan remained idle in his cabin, an advocate for peace. Such was my love for the whites that my country-men pointed as they passed and said 'Logan is the friend of the White man.' I had even thought to live with you but for the injury of one man—Colonel Cresap who last spring in cold blood and unprovoked, murdered all the relations of Logan, not sparing even my women and children. There runs not a drop of my blood in the veins of any living creature. This called on me for revenge. I have sought it. I have killed many. I have fully glutted my vengence. For my country I rejoyce at the beams of peace. But do not harbor a thought that mine is the joy of fear. Logan never felt fear. He will not turn on his heel to save his life. Who is there to mourn for Logan. Not one."

Logan's Lament was reprinted in newspapers and schoolbooks throughout America, often without the correct historical background, and his words became part of the folklore of many states, although he really read the letter from under the elm in what is now Logan's State Park in Circleville. But Logan's story was more tragic than even his words reveal—for the Indian discovered that his family hadn't been murdered by Captain Cresap at all. Logan learned that a band of marauders led by one Greathouse had really massacred his family and knew that his revenge had no meaning at all, that he had injured those innocent of any crime against him. His death six years later was even more ironic than his life had been. In 1780, after a drunken quarrel, Logan attacked and was killed by another Indian. The other man turned out to be a nephew unknown to him—the last of his once large family.

Lord Haw-Haw Another traitor dishonored by his native tongue. A *Lord Haw-Haw* is especially one who makes propaganda for the enemy. William Joyce (1906–46) earned the sobriquet for his mocking broadcasts from Berlin during World War II. The American-born British Nazi is examined at some length in Rebecca West's brilliant *The Meaning of Treason* (1947). Joyce was captured after the war, adjudged a British subject because he held a passport, and hanged for his crimes. (See also *Tokyo Rose.*)

Louis Heel There is no doubt that France's Louis XIV, called *le Roi Soliel*, the Sun King, because he adopted the rising sun as his personal emblem, was a vain and haughty man who surrounded himself with pomp and ceremony. *Le Grand Monarque* is characterized by the apocryphal remark attributed to him, *L'état, c'est moi*, "the state is I." He is therefore a likely candidate for the inventor of the high *Louis heel*. Because Louis was a short man, the story goes, he ordered his shoemaker to add cork to his shoe heels to make him taller and kept having more and more cork added to them, his loyal court aping the style. The tale is a good one, but probably isn't true. Most likely Louis' grandson Louis XV is responsible for the *Louis heel*, which became the imposing curved French heel on men's shoes that was ultimately copied by women. We could invent another story and say that Louis XV invented the shoe because he became king when only thirteen and wanted to appear older, but Madame Pompadour may have devised the style and named it for him, and La Pompadour became his mistress when he was about thirty. The heel, which is only medium today, once reached such heights that court ladies had to use balancing sticks to navigate. It is interesting to note that high heels have recently become high fashion for men again.

Louisiana, Louisiana Purchase Although the *Louis heel* may not honor Louis XIV, the state of Louisiana definitely does. The Creole or Pelican State was named in 1682 by the French explorer Robert de La Salle, who paid homage to the Sun King by applying the designation to the entire Mississippi Valley. The *Louisiana Purchase*, engineered by President Jefferson because he believed Napoleon might close the Mississippi to United States commerce, brought the one-million square-mile area under American ownership in 1803 for a mere fifteen million dollars. In the history of this country only *Seward's Folly* and, possibly *Manhattan Island* were shrewder real estate deals. The area purchased included part of or all lands for eleven states—Arkansas, Colorado, Iowa, Kansas, Louisiana, Missouri, Montana, Nevada, North Dakota, South Dakota and Wyoming. Mencken notes a child named *Louisiana Purchase* commemorating the event—but then the boy's sister bore the name *Missouri Compromise*. *Louisiana* was admitted as a state in 1812. It still retains much of its early French character, especially in civil law, the division of the state into parishes instead of counties, and architecture such as that in New Orleans' French Quarter.

Louis Styles Four decorative and architectural styles are named after French monarchs reigning when the styles were the vogue:

Louis Treize style, for Louis XIII (1610–13): a period characterized by a gradual transition from the rich free forms of the Renaissance to classicism in both architecture and furniture.

Louis Quatorze style, after Louis XIV (1643–1715): massive baroque designs that emphasized formality and dignity rather than comfort dominated here.

Louis Quinze style, for Louis XV (1750–1774): fantasy, lightness, elegance and comfort are the main themes of this Rococo period, most interior decoration obsessed with a love of curved lines that was almost bizarre.

Louis Seize style, after Louis XVI (1774–1793): here occurred a reaction against the excessive designs of the *Louis Quinze* style, a return to straight lines, and the classic ideal in ornamental details.

All of these styles had one thing in common: they emphasized richness and luxury. Which is why they were swept out with the French Revolution.

Louisville Slugger *Louisville*, the largest city in Kentucky, was named for France's Louis XVI in 1780 in recognition of the assistance he had given America during the Revolutionary War. Home of the proverbial Fort Knox, Kentucky Derby, mint julep, many bourbon distilleries and the only inland United States Coast Guard station, *Louisville* also houses the famous Hillerich & Bradsby's baseball bat factory, where the renowned *Louisville Slugger* has been made since 1884. The bat is of course named after the city named after a king. *Louisville Sluggers* are made from prime white ash lumber, one mature tree needed to make sixty bats, and more than six million are turned out each year. Some 2 percent of the annual production goes to professional ballplayers, these fashioned from specifications noted in a fifty thousand card file covering the bat preferences of ballplayers past and present. Tours of the plant, available every working day, include the "Model Room" where models of historic bats used by the likes of Wee Willie Keeler (he used a 30-ounce model) to Babe Ruth (a 48-ouncer) are displayed. (See also *Spalding*.)

Lounge Longinus, according to the apocryphal gospel of *Nicodemus* (7:8), was the Roman soldier who pierced the crucified Christ's side with a spear. Later, tradition tells us, the soldier became converted to Christianity and in medieval times he was honored as a saint. Contemporary mystery plays may have depicted Longinus, or Longis, as he was also called, as a tall, lazy lout leaning on his spear—at least in the centurion phase of his life. It has been suggested that *to lounge* could have derived from the posture of Longis, *lounges* and *lounge lizards* following after the verb. The theory isn't likely to be confirmed, but *Webster's* and other authorities do give *longis*, the Old French for an awkward, drowsy person, as the source for the word.

Lucullan, Lucullan Feast, Lucullus Will Sup With Lucullus One fabulous banquet the immensely wealthy Roman Lucullus gave cost him well over four thousand dollars, all his "everyday" dinners cost at least five hundred dollars, and the minimum he spent on a meal when dining alone was two hundred dollars. Lucius Licinius Lucullus (ca. 119–57 B.C.), a celebrated Roman general and consul who drove Mithridates' fleet from the Mediterranean among other military successes, had been relieved of his office by Pompey in 67 B.C. But he had amassed a fortune and retired into the elegant leisure for which he has become proverbial, spending huge sums on public displays and his estates. His wardrobe contained some five thousand rich purple robes, Horace tells us, and he lavishly entertained the artists, poets and philosophers with whom he surrounded himself, his *Lucullan feasts* famous throughout Rome. Lucullus introduced the black cherry and other foods to the Romans from Pontus in Asia Minor. The gourmand even had files of menus listed according to cost, serving the most expensive ones to his most important guests, and it is said that on one occasion an unparalleled dinner cost him more than eight thousand dollars. Another time, Plutarch says, he ordered his cook to prepare a particularly magnificent meal and was reminded that he was dining alone that night. "Lucullus will sup tonight with Lucullus," he replied, or "Today Lucullus is host to Lucullus," these sayings now used to indicate a luxurious meal enjoyed by a gourmet who dines alone. The Roman general's military prowess is almost forgotten, but the adjective from his name lives on as a synonym for "gastronomically splendid" and a sumptuous extravagant meal is still called a *Lucullan feast* or *banquet*.

Lucullus was only notably extravagant in a period marked by extravagance—the Roman emperor Heliogabalus, for example, spent ten thousand dollars each for his meals, once imprisoned a cook until he could come up with a better sauce, and fattened his choice conger eels on Christian slaves. Such excesses ultimately made the Romans ripe, or rotten, for the barbarians who swept down from the north in the fourth century. This marked the end of slaves tickling Roman throats with feathers so that they could regurgitate and gorge themselves with the next course, the end of the gorging and regorging cycle, *"vomunt ut edant, edant ut vomant,"* in Seneca's phrase, and the end of the Roman Empire. But the Roman feasts or orgies have often been exaggerated. Writers throw banquet costs like "25,000 sesterces" and "50,000 denarii" around as if they were dollars, which they definitely were not. A sesterce was worth only about two cents, a dinar, eight cents and a gold dinar, two dollars. Also, many dictionaries define a sesterce as "2½ asses" and it has been assumed that the coin was worth "the price of 2½ such animals." *Asses*, however, is in this case merely the plural of *as*, a Roman coin worth less than a penny.

Lucy Stoner A woman who refuses to change her maiden name upon marriage is sometimes dubbed a *Lucy Stoner*. The term recalls American feminist Lucy Stone (1818–93), who should be more of a heroine to today's woman's rights movement than she is. Born near West Brookfield, Mass., Lucy Stone decided as a child to study Greek and Hebrew to determine if the Biblical texts requiring the subjection of women were honestly translated. It took her many years to obtain an education. On graduation from Oberlin, the only college accepting women at the time, she was already twenty-nine, but plunged headlong into the woman suffrage and antislavery causes. Her important work included chairing the first National Woman's Rights Convention, held at Worcester, Mass., in 1850, helping to form the National American Women's Association, of which she was president for three years, and the founding in 1870 of the *Woman's Journal*, the association's official publication for nearly half a century. An eloquent speaker who often swayed antagonistic audiences, Lucy Stone became well-known throughout the United States. In 1855 she married Dr. Henry Brown Blackwell, an antislavery worker, but as a matter of principle refused to change her name, she and her husband issuing a joint protest against the inequalities in the marriage laws. Lucy Stone would never answer to anything but her maiden name all her married life and the *Lucy Stone League* later emulated her, defending the right of all married women to retain their maiden names. This organization attracted a good number of followers who were called *Lucy Stoners*, some of them even persuading their husbands to adopt their maiden names as middle names—i.e., the radio commentator Raymond Gram Swing, his first wife's name having been Betty Gram. Actually, this strategy was nothing new; in fact, the British practice of hyphenated names, dating back centuries, originally began when a man took a wife with too distinguished a name to be usurped by his own. As a result of intermarriage between hyphenated families Britain boasts or is saddled with such unusual surnames as Haldane-Duncan-Mercer-Henderson and Borlase-Warren-Venables-Vernon. Lucy Stone was addressed as Mrs. Lucy Stone in her lifetime but today's feminists might call her *Ms.* Stone—a new form that makes no distinction between a married or unmarried woman, just as *Mr.* tells us nothing about a man's marital status.

Luddite The masked bands of workers who made night raids on English factories (1811–1816) were protesting layoffs, low wages and poor quality goods, all caused by the large-scale introduction of textile machines to replace handicraft. The riots began in Nottingham and spread throughout England, the raiders directing their rage against the machines and systematically destroying them. Led by a "General" or "King Ludd"—named for a probably mythical Ned Ludd, said to have destroyed stocking frames in a Leicestershire factory thirty years earlier —the rioters soon became known as *Lud-dites*. Public opinion supported them and they did not resort to personal violence until one of their bands was shot down by soldiers in 1812. The *Luddites* retaliated by murdering the employer who called in these troops and soon saw repressive legislation introduced against them, despite Lord Byron's eloquent defense in a speech made in the House of Lords. (Byron's poem "Song for the Luddites" was written a few years later but not published until 1830.) King Ludd was probably hanged after a mass trial in 1813, when a number of *Luddites* were executed, but this only led to more widespread destruction of machinery, the raiders better organized now and posting sentinels at the factory gates while they wreaked their destruction inside. Increasing prosperity in the country, combined with even more repressive measures, finally put the *Luddites* down. But not the memory of them. Today a *Luddite* is anyone who fears and would eliminate automation—not only for the unemployment it creates, but for its effect on the quality of life and for the human destruction that the machinery of war might cause. In our rebellion against an impersonal society the word is used much more sympathetically than before. Indeed, some serious observers believe that the *Luddites* were right.

Lumber, Lumberjack, Lumberyard Take some women named "longbeards" because a deity mistook them for men, add twelve hundred years and the first pawnshops, throw in a passel of American pioneers, and you have the complicated recipe for the word *lumber*. How did the *lumber* we use for houses come to be named for long beards and such, how did beards become boards? The story begins with the *Longobardi*, or long beards, a Germanic tribe. Tradition tells us that their name was bestowed upon them when women from the tribe startled Wotan from his sleep, their hair combed full over their faces, the angry god demanding to know the identity of these *longobardi* or "longbearded men" who dared disturb his rest. Be that as it may, Caesar did encounter this Germanic people in one of his campaigns, calling them *Longobardi*. Centuries later, in about 568 A.D., these *Longobardi* invaded Italy, where their name became *Lombardi* in Italian, the tribe settling the Adriatic region now called *Lombardy* after them. The merchants of *Lombardy*, who gradually migrated to the settled area from all parts of Italy, eventually won fame or infamy as bankers, moneylenders and pawnbrokers, there being little distinction between the occupations at the time. Pawnshops were thus called *Lombards* and the crest of the powerful *Lombardy* Medici family, three gold balls, served as the insignia for all such shops. In time, the moneymen and their *Lombards*, or pawnshops, radiated out from Milan and other parts of *Lombardy* to greener pastures. In some places they were given virtual pawnbroking monopolies that lasted for centuries, among these Paris, where they founded the *Rue de Lombards*, and London, where their numerous pawnbroking establishments adorning *Lombard Street* resulted in the naming of that center for impignoration. But *Lombard* came to be pronounced *Lumbard* or *Lumber* in English. *Lombard Street* had its *Lombard shops*, pawnshops, and these had their *Lombard rooms*, storage rooms—all pronounced "lumber," too. Over the years the *Lumber rooms* on the street grew filled with unredeemed pledges on loans—large crates, cumbersome furniture and other odds and ends that are still called *lumber* in England. It is in this sense that the word came to America with the first settlers, meaning any worthless discarded junk that might be found in a cluttered *lumber room*. Here, however, the word *lumber* was put to a new use. There are several explanations for the change, which is recorded as early as 1662. One is that American homesteaders in clearing their land for farming left many discarded trees lying around, this clutter, or *lumber*, later cut or split into the wooden planks we know as *lumber* today. Some of these planks were shipped to England as ballast and British sailors referring to them as "just so much lumber" may have reinforced the word's meaning. Or it may be that the settlers stored logs in out-of-the-way *lumber rooms* for drying before cutting them into what became known as *lumber*. A third possibility is that sawed timber once cluttered or *lumbered up* roads

in certain towns, getting its new name in that way. In any case, the journey from beards to boards was completed.

Lumberjack and *lumberyard* are also American expressions, but the English use neither of them. They still prefer to call cut boards timber. The word *lumber* for to walk clumsily or heavily does not derive from the Longbeards, coming directly from the Middle English verb *lomeren* meaning the same thing.

Lush Near Drury Lane Theatre in London was the Harp Tavern, where a club of hard drinkers called The City of Lushington had been founded in 1750. Lushington's had a chairman, the "Lord Mayor," and four "aldermen," who presided over the wards of Poverty, Lunacy, Suicide and Juniper (the supreme Roman god who presided over all human affairs). The club members, we are told, "were want to turn night into day," and by example their convivial fraternity may have given us another word for a sot or habitual drunk. *Lush*, at least as a generic term for beer or drink, first appeared on the scene in about 1790, long after The City of Lushington's formation, and it could very well be a contraction of the club's name. For in years to come a number of phrases employed the name Lushington. *Alderman Lushington is concerned*, 1810, meant somebody drunk; *to deal with Lushington*, 1820, meant to drink too much, as did *Lushington is his master*, 1825; and by 1840 *a Lushington* meant a drunkard. Even before this a *lush cove* had become a slang term for a drunkard and *lush* itself both a verb for "to drink" and an adjective meaning tipsy. By the end of the last century we finally find *lush* alone being applied to any habitual drunk, as it is to this day.

It is possible that the reverse is true and that The City of Lushington took its name from the *lushes* who formed it in 1750, but there is no record of a word even similar to *lush* specifically describing drunks or their drink before the club's inception. There have been a number of alternate theories. One proposes a well-known London brewmaster named Lushington, and another suggests the Shelta (Irish tinker's jargon) *lush*, "to eat and drink," while a third opts for the standard English *lush*, in the sense of either "wet" or "succulent, full of juice." Perhaps the club itself got its name from one of these sources, particularly the last. But considering The City of Lushington's prominence, the fact that there were no *lush coves* or *Lushingtons* before the club, and the use of "aldermen" in one of the phrases previously quoted, it seems certain that the drinking society on Russell Street strongly influenced the word's formation. One renowned club member was the ill-starred actor Edmond Kean, whose exploits put The City of Lushington in the limelight toward the beginning of the last century. "Seeing him act," Coleridge wrote of Kean, "was like reading Shakespeare by flashes of lightning." But Kean, who had begun his stage career when only fourteen, was "a magnificent uncut gem" whose eccentricities and hard-drinking wasted his talent away and marked him for an early grave. Once he was involved in an adultery suit that almost banished him from the stage; backstage in his dressing room he kept a pet lion someone had given him; he often rode his horse Shylock wildly through the night streets of London. Even the great actor's last performance was in character. While playing Othello to his son Charles' Iago at Covent Garden in 1833, Kean broke down and fell into his son's arms. "O God, I am dying. Speak to them, Charles," were his last words on the stage and the "immortal tragedian," or "horrid little man," died less than two months later, only forty-six. The City of Lushington outlasted him, the club passing out of existence in 1895.

Lycoris Mark Antony is mainly remembered for his fatal romantic entanglement with Cleopatra, and it is often forgotten that he led a riotous life while a youth, having had four wives—Fadia, Antonia, Fulvia and Octavia—before he committed suicide for his Egyptian queen. One of his outside interests was Lycoris, a Roman actress who became his mistress. Centuries later the English botanist Herbert named the six lovely fragrant flowers of the *Lycoris* genus after this beautiful woman. The amaryllis-like *Lycoris* grow from a bulb and are lilac-pink or pink, the flower cluster a loose umbel. Native to China, Japan and Central Asia, they are gen-

erally grown in greenhouses in the United States and England. (See also *Cleopatra*.)

Lynch Our word for extra-legal hanging definitely comes from the name of a man, but just who was the real Judge Lynch? At least a dozen men have been suggested as candidates for the dubious distinction. Scholarly opinion leans toward Virginia's William Lynch, with Virginia magistrate Charles Lynch a strong contender, but the other defendants deserve their day in court.

The earliest challenger for the title is a certain Mayor Lynch of Glasgow; according to a story from the *Pall Mall Gazette* quoted in the New York *Tribune* of January 27, 1881, Mayor Lynch flourished toward the end of the fifteenth century and hanged a criminal with his own hands on one occasion. Another Mayor Lynch, of England, is vaguely mentioned, and then there is Mayor James Fitzstephens Lynch of Galway, Ireland. This last Lynch is said to have sent his son to Spain about 1492 to purchase a cargo of wine. But the young man gambled away all his father's money and bought on credit, the Spanish merchant sending a representative back with him to Ireland so that he'd be sure to collect. While at sea, young Lynch killed and threw the Spaniard overboard. The elder Lynch soon discovered this crime and as town mayor sat in judgment and pronounced the death sentence on his own son. Mayor Lynch must have been insane for "justice," because when his family interceded to save the boy from hanging, he proceeded to hang him from a window of their home.

None of these accounts, if they are true, bothers to explain why the term *lynch* did not come into use until two centuries later, nor do the stories depict *lynchings*, as we know them today. A better choice might be the American John Lynch, a South Carolinian who followed Daniel Boone to Kentucky and was hanged as a horse thief without benefit of trial, or the Judge James Lynch who is said to have imposed brutal sentences in about 1687. But too little is known about these men. The same applies for the theory that *lynch* comes from a Lynch's Creek in South Carolina, where about 1779 a band of "Regulators" met to mete out their particular brand of "justice." One English account even makes the place Lynch Creek in *North Carolina*, ups the date to the Revolution, and says that here "a form of court martial and execution was carried out on the corpse of a Tory who had already been hanged to prevent rescue."

It would be fruitless to mention all the Lynches in history who are merely alluded to as the originators of a practice that is unfortunately not yet purely historical. There are almost endless variations on tales like that of the Irishman hanged by irate neighbors or the American outlaw strung up on a tree somewhere. Either etymologists are very imaginative or the Lynches of this world have had more than their fair share of men on one or another end of a rope.

Up until fairly recently most historians gave Virginia planter and judge Charles Lynch (1736–1796) the doubtful honor of being the first *lyncher*, or rather the first person to be called a *lyncher*. Colonel Lynch, a militia officer who served under General Greene during the Revolution, was a leading citizen of Bedford County and his older brother John founded Lynchburg, Va. (Brother John, incidentally, has also been cited as the eponymous Lynch, complicating matters more.) It seems that the colonel had been a justice of the peace since 1766, and had taken the law into his own hands on a number of occasions. These cases usually involved Tories charged with treason, which, like all felonies, could only be tried at the courts in Williamsburg during the Revolution. Since Williamsburg was some two hundred miles away and the rude roads leading to the capital were controlled by Loyalists, Judge Lynch and three fellow magistrates set up a court, proper in all respects but its jurisdiction, to try treason cases. Judge Lynch became particularly famous in 1780 when he prevented local Tories from seizing ammunition stores for Cornwallis and subsequently tried them as traitors, but neither he nor the other justices ever ordered anyone hanged for the crime of treason. In fact, only in one instance, a case of proven manslaughter—was their sentence ever greater than a fine or flogging. Some-

how Lynch's associate justices—James Callaway, William Preston, and Robert Adams—were never remembered for their part in the extra-legal court. The colonel himself—a Quaker who had established the first public church in Virginia, was a former member of the House of Burgesses, and a delegate to Virginia's constitutional convention in 1776—was brought before the Virginia legislature by Tory sympathizers after the war. The assembly, however, exonerated him of any wrongdoing, terming his actions "justifiable from the imminence of the danger."

Colonel Charles Lynch's name was long accepted as the most likely source for *lynch law* and *lynch* because it was the most obvious one around. But historians began to wonder why someone who had nothing to do with extra-legal hanging or mob action should be held accountable for the word. Then a Captain William Lynch (1742–1820) was discovered. Like Charles Lynch he was a Virginian, a militiaman, and the magistrate of an impromptu court, but his story is far more convincing. Captain William Lynch was brought to light by Edgar Allan Poe in an editorial on *lynching* that he wrote in 1836 when he edited the *Southern Literary Messenger*. Poe claimed that the *lynch law* originated in 1780 when Captain Lynch and his followers organized to rid Pittsylvania County of a band of ruffians threatening the neighborhood. Poe even affixed a compact drawn up by Lynch and his men to the editorial: "Whereas, many of the inhabitants of Pittsylvania . . . have sustained great and intolerable losses by a set of lawless men . . . that . . . have hitherto escaped the civil power with impunity . . . we, the subscribers, being determined to put a stop to the iniquitous practices of those unlawful and abandoned wretches, do enter into the following association . . . upon hearing or having sufficient reason to believe, that any . . . species of villainy (has) been committed within our neighborhood, we will forthwith . . . repair immediately to the person or persons suspected . . . and if they will not desist from their evil practices, we will inflict such corporeal punishment on him or them, as to us shall seem adequate to the crime committed or the damage sustained. . . . In witness whereof we have hereunto set our hands, this 22nd day of September 1780."

There we have the first *lynch law*, down to its exact date. William Lynch's identity was further verified by Richard Venables, an old resident of the county, in the May 1859 issue of *Harper's Magazine*. But without evidence of any actual hanging there was still room for doubt. Finally, additional proof was found in the diary of the famous surveyor Andrew Ellicott, who visited Captain Lynch in 1811 and gained his friendship. William Lynch was then living in a sparsely settled area of South Carolina called Oolenoy Creek, having moved there about ten years after he disbanded his vigilantes in 1788. Ellicott found that Lynch "possessed a strong but uncultivated mind," was "hospitable and generous to an extreme" and "a great stickler for equality and the rights of man as established by law!" The father of twelve described to him how he organized a band for the purpose of punishing crimes without the technical processes of court and police action. The same problems existed in Pittsylvania as confronted Judge Charles Lynch in Bedford County: the proper courts in the Tidewater area were too far away, too difficult to reach, and crimes of violence by both Loyalists and patriots had multiplied during the Revolution. William Lynch related how his *lynch-men*, as they were called, were sworn to secrecy and loyalty to the band. On receiving information accusing someone of a crime, the accused was seized and questioned before a court of sorts. If he did not confess immediately, he was horsewhipped until he did, and efforts were made to make him in-

volve others, who were all given the same treatment. No *legal* means were ever used by the *Lynch-men* to establish guilt or innocence. Ellicott also mentioned the hangings that had been questioned so long. "These punishments were sometimes severe and not infrequently inflicted upon the innocent," he wrote. "Mr. Lynch informed me that he had never in any case given a note for the punishment of death; some however he acknowledged had been actually hanged." But not in the ordinary way: "a horse in part became the executioner . . . the person who it was supposed ought to suffer death was placed on a horse with his hands tied behind him and a rope about his neck which was fastened to the limb of a tree over his head. In this situation the person was left and when the horse in pursuit of food or any other cause moved from his position the unfortunate person was left suspended by the neck—this was called 'aiding the civil authority.'"

At last the mystery was solved, although several major dictionaries still discredit the wrong Judge Lynch. It was not long after William Lynch and his band before vigilantes all over the country were enforcing *Lynch-laws* and being described as *lynchers*. From the time when records were first kept in 1885 to the present there have been forty-five hundred to five thousand lynchings in the United States, though the practice is fortunately very rare today. All named after a man who did not invent the process by any means, but tried to justify it. In fact, the inscription on William Lynch's grave reads: "He followed virtue as his truest guide. . . ." (See also *Dewitt*.)

M

Macabre, Danse Macabre *Macabre*, gruesome, ghastly or grim, comes directly from the *danse macabre* or dance of death, which probably originated with a fourteenth-century German morality play eventually known throughout Europe. Death debates all his victims in this drama, winning his arguments with young and old, rich and poor, wise and foolish —and a weird dance ends the play as he leads his victims off stage. The dance of death survived in many allegorical paintings, sculptures and tapestries, notably the engravings by Hans Holbein (1538), its popularity due to the overpowering awareness of death during the Hundred Years' War and the Black Death, a plague that wiped out two thirds of Europe's population. *La danse macabre* is believed by most scholars to have been suggested by and received its name from the dance of the seven martyred Maccabee brothers recounted in *Maccabees II*, an apocryphal book of the Old Testament. The Medieval Latin *chorea Machabaeorum* became corrupted to *danse macabre* in French, the adjective *macabre* not appearing in English until the end of the nineteenth century. Which suggests a modern preoccupation with the weird and horrible.

In 164 B.C. Judas Maccabeus, "the Hammer," led the Hasmonean clan in a revolt against the laws of Antiochus IV requiring Jews to worship Greek gods, with the result that his guerrilla followers were tortured and killed. But there have been other suggestions for the derivation of *macabre*. The Hebrew *mequaber*, meaning gravedigger or burier, is one strong possibility. According to this theory, a real *danse macabre* may have been performed by commercial gravediggers during the time of the Black Death. Others believe that the word comes from the Arabic *magbarah* ("cemetery") or

from the name of St. Macarius or Macaire, the hermit, who has been identified by some as the figure pointing at the corpses in an early Italian painting by Orcagna called the "Triumph of Death." But the seven tortured Maccabee brothers were prominent figures in the old morality play mentioned and the majority opinion still holds that *macabre* owes its existence to their name.

Macadam, Macadamize, Macadamia, Tarmac Perhaps the smooth, perfectly drained miniature stone roads that John Loudon McAdam (1756–1836) built in his father's garden as a child inspired the first *macadam* roads, but his system seems to have been the improved version of an older French model. McAdam, a Scotsman whose name is also spelt Macadam and MacAdam, emigrated to New York when only fourteen to take a position in his uncle's counting house. He married into the prominent Long Island Nichols family, made a fortune, and lost much of it by supporting the British during the Revolution. Returning to his native heath in 1783, he found the roads around the estate he bought at Ayrshire in terrible condition, as they were throughout the British Isles. Much to the annoyance of many neighbors, McAdam decided to do something about these wretched thoroughfares, on which accidents were commonplace and the average life of a coach horse was only three years. At his own expense the amateur engineer began experimenting in roadbuilding at Ayrshire and then at Falmouth, where he had moved in 1798, his persistent efforts finally getting him appointed as surveyor for all Bristol roads in 1815. McAdam had discovered that an expensive French roadbuilding method invented twenty years before his first experiments offered the best solution to the problem. This scheme consisted of small broken stones spread to a thickness of ten inches over large stones set on edge. The canny Scotsman concluded that the expensive sublayer wasn't usually necessary if good drainage was effected, elaborating on the French method in an essay he published in 1819. The roads he began to build were layers of small, sharp-angled broken stones placed over a drained, gently sloped roadbed, each layer compacted by the traffic that passed over it and water running off into ditches on each side. The durability of these roads depended on the stones' interlocking action and the quality of the cement formed by the stone dust and water, but engineers found that the large stone sublayer was only necessary on poor subsoil, or for roads bearing very heavy loads. McAdam's roads revolutionized transportation, gradually replacing the common dirt road, and in 1827 he was made general surveyor for all highways in England. But his method was improved just as surely as he had improved the French method. Subsequently his stone layers were crushed into the earth with heavy rollers and their surface coated with a bituminous covering, these blacktop roads also called *macadam* or *tarmac* roads. Today concrete highways are poured on a *macadamized* base. The "colossus of roads" was widely honored for his contribution, but there were those like the poet Southey who spoke of "quackadamizing" instead of *macadamizing*, this not so much a reference to the eccentric McAdam as it was a reaction to "progress." Even then a minority felt that nature should not be entombed. Some could already foresee the day when ceremonies would be held not opening a new highway but commemorating the completed paving of the world.

Macadamia, a genus of Australian trees often called the Queensland nut and valued for its edible seeds, is not named for the roadbuilder. It honors a Doctor John Madadam, secretary of the Victoria Philosophical Institute.

Mach I, Mach Number *Mach number* is the ratio of the speed of a body to the speed of sound in air. Almost exclusively used to measure flight speed, it has only become common in the last few decades, increased aircraft speeds having made old M.P.H. measurements too cumbersome. *Mach I*, for instance, is the speed of a plane flying at the speed of sound, 762 miles per hour at sea level, while Mach II is twice the speed of sound. The word derives from the name of German scientist Ernst Mach (1838–1916), who died thirty-one years before Captain Charles Yeager first broke the sound barrier over Edward Air Force Base in Muroc, Cal. (On October 14, 1947 Yeager flew his Bell XS-I rocket plane at Mach 1.015.) Mach's investigations into the supersonic speed of projectiles and the shock waves produced at these speeds, led to both the measurement unit and the *Mach angle*, the angle a shock wave makes with the direction of flight, being named in his honor. But the German professor was a mathematician, philosopher, physiologist and psychologist as well as a physicist and his versatile work profoundly influenced scientific thought. It is said that Mach's criticisms of Newton's system cleared the way for Einstein's theory of relativity.

Machiavellian A politician whose last name is a synonym for political immorality, Niccolò Machiavelli first conceived the idea of conscription or the draft, and his first name was once thought to be the model for Old Nick, or the devil. Not a man to be much loved in an age where honor is given great lip service, but not all that bad. Through his famous book *The Prince*, Niccolò di Bernardo Machiavelli (1469–1527) has become known as the founder of political science. But this remarkable work is remembered mainly for its insistence that while his subjects are bound by conventional moral obligations, a ruler may use any means necessary to maintain power, no matter how unscrupulous. Thus *Machiavellian* has come to mean extremely cynical political scheming, generally brilliant and always characterized by deceit and bad faith. Niccolò Machiavelli lived and plotted shrewdly at the time of the Borgias and Medici in Italy, serving as secretary of the Florentine Republic from 1498–1512. Here Machiavelli laid the foundation for the modern practice of conscription as opposed to mercenary armies. Entrusted with many important diplomatic missions at home and abroad, the statesman gained political insights that have rarely been surpassed. Yet when the Republic was overthrown and the Medici family restored to power, Machiavelli was imprisoned and tortured before being given his freedom. This early *brain trust* was forced to devote himself to a literary life, apparently with no change of heart regarding rulers, for it was *after* his troubles with the Medici that he wrote *Il Principe* (1513). He authored a number of excellent, brilliantly styled works, including two plays and a short novel, but the political treatise is his most famous, a profound study that shows Machiavelli's desire for a united Italy and is much more than a justification for power politics. Despite all the apologies for the diplomat, however, it must be said that his letters reveal him to be reprehensible in many respects. He seemed to have absolutely no sensitivity to ethical considerations, his admiration of Cesare Borgia emphasizing this major failing. The legend of this thin-lipped, sarcastic, hyperactive man gave rise in later years to the theory that his first name was the basis for Old Nick, a synonym for the devil. No one really knows how Old Nick originated, but the *Niccolò* origin is wrong. It stems from Samuel Butler's humorous identification in *Hudibras:*

"Nick Machiavel had ne'er a trick
(Though he gives name to our Old Nick)
But was below the least of these."

Mackintosh Ever since Spanish explorers in the New World tried unsuccessfully to coat their shoes with a white substance that the natives used for waterproofing, man had tried to make waterproof apparel from rubber. But rubber was not even named until 1770, when chemist Joseph Priestley accidentally discovered that the hardened substance could "rub" out pencil marks, but progress in waterproofing did not come until half a century after that. Young James Syme, later to become a famous surgeon, first invented the process for making waterproof fabrics while a student at Edinburgh University in 1823, but the fabric itself was patented a few months later by Scottish chemist Charles Macintosh, who exploited the idea and was really the first person to produce a prac-

tical, waterproof cloth. Macintosh (1766–1843), a Fellow of the Royal Society, had already invented an effective bleaching powder and improved a number of dyes. Finding that rubber could be dissolved by naphtha, he spread the resulting solution on cloth, cementing another layer of cloth to it. Raincoats made from such double-thick fabrics with a middle layer of rubber won popularity overnight, as did numerous waterproof items that Macintosh manufactured at his plant in Glasgow. But the man who revolutionized outdoor living somehow became associated with his raincoat alone, and even this was spelled wrong from the very beginning. Properly, the *mackintosh*, or the *mac*, as it is sometimes called, should be a *macintosh*, although the incorrect spelling prevails. But then this raincoat might even more fairly be called the *Syme coat*.

Madeleine These small, rich, shell-shaped cakes are doubtless the most famous pastry in all literature. They are said to be named for their inventor, Madeleine Paulmier, a nineteenth-century pastry cook of Commeray, France, though André Simon and other gastronomes credit their invention to "one Avice, chief pastry cook to the Prince de Talleyrand." At any rate, Madeleine Paulmier and the anonymous Madeleine, for whom Avice may have named the cakes, both take their given names from Mary Magdalene (see *Maudlin*). It was on a visit to his mother that Marcel Proust was served the scalloped *petite madeleine*, "so richly sensuous under its severe religious folds," whose taste brought back the flood of memories resulting in his eight-volume masterpiece *À la Recherche du Temps Perdu*. One cynic has called Proust's work "the tale of a man who fell in love with a cookie." Proust's fragile *madeleine*, made with flour, butter, sugar and eggs, "the same weight of each," flavored with lemon rind and baked in a small but deep scallop-shaped mold, is no relation to the English sponge bun bearing the same name.

Mae West "Come up and see me some time!" is what the apocryphal soldier, sailor or airman who invented the term *Mae West* is supposed to have said when he tried on his lifejacket and noticed that he bulged prominently where the famous movie star does. Anyway, we do know that the inflatable lifejacket was introduced at the beginning of World War II and named for the world's oldest sex symbol because it "bulged in the right places." Mae West (b. 1892?), whose real age is anybody's guess, is still in fine form and starring in films, a phenomenon of our time at eighty or a few years more or less. Mae West starred on Broadway until the police closed two of her plays, *Sex* and *Pleasure Man*, in 1928, migrating to Hollywood where she won far greater fame as "Diamond Lil," the "Screen's Bad Girl," and the "Siren of the Screen." Her buxom bosom used to be honored in Cockney rhyming slang as *Mae Wests*. Her name, *Webster's* advises, is also given to a twin-turreted tank, a malfunctioning parachute with a *two-lobed* appearance, and a *bulging* sail. At one time a figure-eight-shaped cruller was named for her, too. At least six words or phrases—which is a better record than Pompadour or any other woman. It is said that Mae West acquired the nickname "Baby Vamp" when she played a vamp at a church social when only five and in a stage play the same year, perfecting her famous walk at that time. "I do all of my best work in bed," she once replied when a reporter asked her how she went about writing her memoirs.

Maginot Line Although André Maginot (1877–1932) had barely escaped with his life in World War I when severely wounded during the defense of Verdun, contaminated oysters finally caused his death from typhoid. Decorated with the Cross of the Legion of Honor and the Médaille Militaire, the former sergeant, who had enlisted as a private despite the fact that he was French Undersecretary of War in 1913, returned to government service and eventually became Minister of Defense. Determined that France would never be invaded again, he and his generals proceeded to plan and have a fortified wall built along the eastern border from Switzerland to Belgium, a wall which extended 314 kilometers at two million dollars a mile. The *Maginot line*, complete with self-sufficient forts dug seven floors deep into the earth, was meant to warn against surprise attacks from Germany in Alsace and Lorraine, but only engendered a false sense of security in France that became known as the *Maginot mentality*, even though the wall was never extended to the coast. Maginot's death spared him from seeing it easily by-passed by the Germans in World War II when they entered France through Belgium. The line's impregnability was never tested, but it could easily have been blasted by bombs, battered by tanks, or circumvented by paratroopers if it had been finished. The fault lay not so much with Maginot as with a war-weary country almost wanting to be lulled into a sense of false security. This the *Maginot line*, like the Great Wall of China before it, readily provided. Even now the smaller *Maginot line* fortresses are being sold by the French government. Most have been bought by those with romantic attachments to futile things, for the structures are uninhabitable white elephants with little practical use. Some of the line has already been purchased by the same Germans against whom it was built, as no French law prohibits the sale to foreigners. "It is conceivable," says one French official, "that each of the fortifications could be bought by a different officer of the German General Staff."

Magnolia Like Matthias de l'Obel, for whom Linnaeus named the *lobelia*, Pierre Magnol (1638–1715) was a French physician and botanist who published a book classifying plants. Professor of botany at Montpelier University, Magnol had somehow obtained an education despite the fact that he had been denied entrance to French colleges because he was a Protestant. Through his courses in botany his name became celebrated and Linnaeus honored him further by applying it to the beautiful *magnolia* tree upon devising his own monumental system of classification. The *magnolia* had been introduced into Europe from Japan in about 1709, but wasn't named for the professor until after his death. Linnaeus owed much to Magnol, who originated the system of family classification of plants, and picked a large plant family to honor him—*Magnoliacea*, including ten genera and over one hundred species. The *magnolia* family, native to South Asia and the southeastern United States, contains some of the most beautiful garden shrubs and trees. Its lemon-scented fragrance was once used by the Chinese to season rice. The tree's huge showy flowers, sometimes ten inches across, are commonly white, yellow, rose or purple, appearing with or before the first leaves of spring, and the *magnolia* grows to heights of up to one hundred feet. Leaves of one species, the southern umbrella tree, are often two feet long, and the attractive leaves of *Magnolia grandiflora* are used to fashion funeral wreaths. Mississippi calls itself "The Magnolia State." (See also *Linnaean; Lobelia.*)

Mahabharata, Ramayana The longest poem in the world is the *Mahabharata*, which tells the story of the descendants of the Hindu King Bharata. *Mahabharata* means "the great Bharata," and the poem's 110,000 couplets or 220,000 lines make it four times longer than the Bible and eight times longer than Homer's *Iliad* and *Odyssey* combined. The Indian poet Vyasa contributed greatly to the poem but it is really the combined work of many generations of writers, written between the years 400 B.C. and 150 B.C. Though its main theme is the war between descendants of Kuru and Pandu, it is a vast repository of philosophy and legend. The *Ramayana*, named after the god Rama, is another great Indian epic poem, containing 24,000 stanzas in seven books as we know it today.

Mahernia, Hermannia One of the most unusual of eponymous words, the plant genus *Mahernia* is an anagram of *Hermannia*, another genus to which it is closely allied. Linnaeus must have been in a playful mood when he coined the word from *Hermannia*, which he had also named. In any event, it is the only anagram that is an eponymous word (unless one includes *Mho*, or *Voltairean*—Voltaire, the assumed name of the great French philosopher François Marie Arouet, an anagram of *Arouet le jeune*). Linnaeus named *Hermannia* for Paul Hermann (1646–95), a professor of botany at the University of Leyden, who is surely the only man to be honored by two genera in this odd way. *Hermannia* is a large genus, including some eighty

species of ornamental, greenhouse evergreen shrubs, their flowers usually yellow. The closely related anagram genus, *Mahernia*, includes about thirty species, pretty greenhouse herbs or small undershrubs of which the yellow, fragrant honey-bell (*M. verticillata*) is most notable. Both genera are native to South Africa. (See also *Linnaeus; Lobelia; Mho.*)

Maintenon Born in 1635 in a French prison where her father was being held as a counterfeiter, Françoise D'Aubigné's life seemed to grow no better as she grew older. She married the famous comic poet Paul Scarron while still a girl of sixteen, serving mainly as his nurse until his death in 1660. Several years later she finally got a break of sorts when the king's mistress Madame Montespan interceded with Louis XIV to put her in charge of their illegitimate children. Gradually she supplanted Montespan in the Sun King's esteem and in time he made her the Marquise de Maintenon. Madame Maintenon became Louis' mistress *en titre* when Montespan left the court and was even a great favorite of Queen Marie Thérèse, who died in her arms in 1683. Two years later Louis married his older official mistress in a secret ceremony. Maintenon's influence on court life was considerable, though it has probably been exaggerated as concerns matters of state. A born teacher, she founded the St.-Cyr school for poor girls in Ruil, which is responsible for the famed Cordon Bleu school of cookery. (One of the subjects taught there was cuisine and St.-Cyr eventually became so renowned in this field alone that the *cordon bleu* or blue ribbon awarded to each graduate came to be regarded as the emblem of an accomplished cook.) Madame Maintenon was no slouch as a cook herself, her name remembered for her *Lamb Chops à la Maintenon* and other creations, in addition to being a synonym for a mistress. She died in 1719, four years after Louis. (See also *Lavaliere.*)

Malakoff Malakoff, or Malakhov, a fortified hill overlooking Sevastopol from the east, was the scene of one of the most publicized battles of the Crimean War. After a long siege, the French finally stormed Malakoff and took it on

September 8, 1855. The historic hill is supposed to be named for a drunken Russian sailor who set up a liquor store on the heights after being fired from his job in the Sevastopol shipyards. Houses and finally fortifications were built around him and he ultimately won more fame than most of his more sober contemporaries. At one time a crinoline also honored the man's name and today the reformed drunkard is remembered for *malakoff*, a restricted form of four-handed dominoes, and *malakoff*, a small French cream cheese, which both commemorate the battle fought on his famous hill.

Malpighian His name is not well known outside scientific textbooks, but the Italian physiologist Marcello Malpighi (1628–1694) deserves recognition as the founder of microscopic anatomy, the discoverer of the movement of blood through the capillaries, which completed the theory of circulation formulated by William Harvey, and for his pioneer work in the study of plant and animal tissues. Malpighi, a professor of medicine at Messina University, later served as private physician to Pope Innocent XII. He was one of the first men to use the microscope to study animal and vegetable tissue and the first to attempt an anatomical description of the brain with this instrument. He is commemorated by several words, including the *Malpighiaceae* family of ornamental tropical plants. The technical terms *Malpighian corpuscle*, *Malpighian layer*, *Malpighian tube*, and *Malpighian tuft* recall his important work in anatomy.

Malthusian Malthus is a good old English name identical with Malthouse, Professor Ernest Weekley points out—as is Bacchus, with Backhouse, a certain very British Bacchus, in fact, having been "fined for intoxication, 5 Jan. 1911." Thomas Robert Malthus (1766–1834), an English curate, is the most famous of the clan. Malthus' *An Essay on the Principle of Population as It Affects the Future Improvement of Society* was published in 1798 and his name almost immediately aroused a storm of controversy throughout the world. His essay contained what came to be called the *Malthusian theory*: that population increases faster, geometrically, than the means of subsistence, which increases arithmetically. According to this theory, population would always outstrip food supply unless checked by natural controls such as war, disease or famine. Malthus later revised and refined his pessimistic outlook, including a control that he called moral restraint—late marriage and sexual abstinence. He held specifically that the English poor-law system, with its indiscriminate doles to large families, was self-defeating, though subsequent studies have shown that the great increase in population in England at the time was not caused by an *increased birth rate* among the poor but a *general fall in the death rate*. Most of the economist's predictions haven't been borne out, but his analysis remains correct in many respects and the *Malthusian principle* still operates in parts of the world where the birth rate has not dropped through birth-control practices. A *Malthusian* is one who accepts the pioneer demographer's theory, or an advocate of birth control. It is interesting to note that Charles Darwin was struck by the phrase "struggle for existence" when reading Malthus' *Essay*, the words stimulating him "to find the key to biological change in the process of natural selection." (See also *Darwinian*.)

Mandarin, Mandarin Collar, Mandarin Duck, Mandarin Orange Although irrevocably associated with China, *mandarin* is the version of a Malay word meaning minister of state that early Portuguese settlers gave to Chinese officials in Macao. It became the name for nine ranks of high officials in the Chinese Empire and these officials, in turn, gave the title to a number of things. The *Mandarin* language, for example, was originally the Chinese of official circles, *Mandarin* today being China's standard tongue and spoken by more people (700,-000,000) than any other two languages combined. *Mandarin*, in the lower case, is also used derisively for any pompous official, so many of whom affect mannerisms above their station. *Mandarin duck* and *Mandarin orange*, being superior foods, possibly derive their names by analogy from the sense of superiority implied in the title *Mandarin*. It has been suggested, however, that the orange may take its name from the color of a *Mandarin's* robe. *Mandarin oranges*, a group to which tangerines belong, are loose-skinned fruits that have been cultivated in southeast Asia since ancient times. They were introduced into Europe about 1805 and to the United States thirty-five years later, but are commonly known as tangerines here—this name deriving from Tangier, Morocco, where a variety of *Mandarin orange* is widely cultivated. A *Mandarin duck*, used for the famous Chinese dish, is a crested Asian duck (*Aix galericulata*) with variegated purple, green, chestnut and white plumage, and a *Mandarin collar* is a narrow, standup collar that doesn't quite meet in the front.

Manhattan, Manhattanization The Algonquian Manhattan Indians who sold *Manhattan* island to the Dutch for twenty-four dollars probably got the best of the deal. One statistician figures that if the Indians had invested their twenty-four dollars at the prevailing interest rates, they would now have some thirteen billion dollars—four billion more than all real estate in Manhattan is worth today. But such figuring mainly reflects the bad times New York City is currently experiencing and, despite its problems, the fantastic "jewel of cities" will likely survive, just as it did the Great Fire of 1835 that leveled downtown New York to the ground. *Manhattan*, since 1898, has been the name of New York's central borough and has always been a synonym for the real, though cosmopolitan, New York City itself. From the Manhattan Indians, indirectly, we also have the *Manhattan cocktail*, with whiskey, sweet vermouth and bitters, first mixed about 1890; *Manhattan clam chowder*, made with tomatoes unlike the traditional New England milk clam chowder; and *Manhattan district*, the code name for the project that developed the first atomic bomb. A *Manhattanite* is a resident of the borough of Manhattan, and *Manhattanization* is a new word that seems to have originated only recently. In the 1971 fall elections San Francisco residents were urged to vote for an amendment halting the construction of tall buildings to avoid the *Manhattanization* of San Francisco. The amend-

ment lost, but brings an interesting story to mind that really has no moral to it at all. About 148 years ago there was actually an attempt made to saw Manhattan Island in two because too many tall and heavy buildings were being built near the Battery. To "prevent the tip from breaking off and sinking into the bay," it was proposed that the Island be sawed off near its northern end, rowed into the bay, turned around and attached to firmer ground uptown. Over the two-month period that the project was the talk of the town, hundreds volunteered, huge oars and oarlocks were built, "long-winded" men were recruited to do the underwater sawing, and supplies were finally provided for the workers. But on the appointed day the project's architects, two hoaxers named Lozier and "Uncle John" De Voe, never showed up. They had played one of history's zaniest pranks on the most cosmopolitan of Americans, though they had to wear disguises for a long time after they came out of hiding.

Mansard This type of roof, unlike the conventional $\wedge$ shape, has a double almost vertical slope on each side, the upper part almost flat. *Mansard* refers to the roof and the high room under it, both designed by Nicolas François Mansart (1598–1666), a French architect of the Renaissance who is generally known as François Mansard. The roof he devised allows for high-ceilinged attics and was widely adopted by Victorian architects. Mansard's great Church of Val-de-Grâce, Paris, is said to have influenced Christopher Wren's plan for London's St. Paul's Cathedral. One of the most influential architects of his time, his pure classical designs have been an inspiration to others for centuries. Mansard, the son of a carpenter to the king, was chosen to design the Louvre, but refused to agree that his design could be altered during construction and the Italian Bertini replaced him. His nephew, Jules Hardouin-Mansart, designed the magnificent Hall of Mirrors at the palace of Versailles, the Hôtel des Invalides, better known as Napoleon's Tomb, and the Place Vendôme, among other masterpieces.

Marcel, Marcelling Every hairdresser might wish to have the success Marcel Grateau had with his curling iron. In

1875, when only twenty-three, this Frenchman invented *marcelling*, a process that makes soft, continuous waves in the hair. The *Marcel wave* became so popular with Parisian women and women everywhere that Marcel Grateau made a fortune and was able to retire before turning thirty. He lived a long life of luxury in an elegant chateau he bought and just before his death in 1936, aged eighty-four, France's hairdressers held a week-long celebration honoring him and his contribution to their craft.

Marigold W. Atlee Burpee Co. has long lobbied to make the *marigold* America's national flower, and offers a standing $10,000 prize to anyone who can grow a "pure white" *marigold* variety. Neither endeavor has been successful and although the ubiquitous French and African *marigolds* are not French or African at all, being native to Mexico, the flower does not take its name from the genus generally grown in American gardens. There are several genera whose flowers are called *marigold*, the chief ones being *Tagetes*, which includes the misnamed French and African *marigolds* among about thirty other species, and *Calendula*, a genus that counts the popular *pot marigold* among its twenty species. It was the bright golden *pot marigold* that was found by the early crusaders and brought back to Europe. There it was probably named after the Virgin Mary and the color gold, being called "Mary's gold" or "Marygold" before it became the *marigold*. Linnaeus gave the *pot marigold* its scientific designation, *Calendula officinalis*, but he merely used a name that had been given to the plant centuries before. For the herbalist Gerad remarks that the name *Calendula* was bestowed upon the plant because it supposedly bloomed regularly "in the calends" or first days of almost every month, *calends* meaning the first of the Roman month. The *pot marigold* was once used as a poultice for wounds and is still grown as a flavoring for soups and other dishes. *Calendula officinalis* differs from the so-called French and African species mainly in that its leaves are not strong smelling. But the flowers of the *Tagetes* genus, also herbs, do resemble the *pot marigold*, and early American

settlers gave them the same name. *Tagetes* possibly honors the Etruscan god Tages, but this is not certain. All flowers of the genus are native from North Mexico to the Argentine, which does make the *marigold* an ideal candidate for the national flower.

Among flowers in other genera called *marigolds* are the European *corn marigold*, *Chrysanthemum segetum*, which when dried is often used as hay; the *marsh marigold*, *Caltha palustris*; the *Cape marigolds*, *Dimorphotheca*, which are native to Africa; and the *fig-marigolds*, *Mesembryanthemum*, whose some two thousand species are also found mainly in South Africa. The much cultivated ice plant, whose leaves are sometimes used like spinach, is a species of the last group.

Marijuana *Cannabis sativa* goes by some two hundred names in practically every language throughout the world, including pot, grass, seed, weed, tea, dope, reefers, joints, and Texas tea. But the hemp plant's crushed leaves, flowers and, sometimes, twigs, are best known as *marijuana*. The word comes from the Spanish prenoms *Maria* and *Juana*, translating as *Maryjane*, and no one knows why. Just as no one, Dr. Leary and his detractors to the contrary, really knows whether or not *marijuana* is harmful or not over a long period of time. The Chinese used *Cannabis* at least five thousand years ago and George Washington is said to have grown it at Mount Vernon—for the rope produced from the hemp. Whether pot turns out to be a kind of noose made from hemp remains to be seen. One hundred years ago, according to the National Institute of Mental Health, "extracts of *Cannabis* were as commonly used for medicinal purposes in the United States as aspirin today." But objective observers studying the research available on the subject will wonder how anyone could make a *doctrinaire* statement about its long-range effects, one way or the other.

Marinism Il Cavalier Marino, as the pompous Neapolitan poet Giambattista Marino (1569–1625) was called, headed the *seicento* school of Italian literature, which became noted for its flamboyance and bad taste. Poems like his 45,000-line *Adone* show brilliant mastery of technique but were intended to dazzle the reader at any cost, their extravagance leading to his name becoming a word for any florid, bombastic style, pages full of sound but signifying nothing. Marino, or Marini, had his troubles with censors, too. His satirical works were not appreciated by his satirized patrons and he was forced to leave Italy, taking refuge in Paris for eight years before he could return safely to his homeland. Marino's affectations made him part of a select group that includes the following entry, *marivaudage*, as well as *euphuism*, *gongorism*, and *guevarism*.

Marivaudage Important advances in the development of the novel were made by French writer Pierre Carlet de Chamblain de Marivaux (1688–1763), who is undeserving of his fate at the hands of the dictionaries. *Marivaudage*, however, means an affected overstrained style, as exemplified by the witty bantering of lovers in his two unfinished novels and thirty plays. Marivaux's subtle, graceful works are mostly excellent psychological studies of middle-class psychology and led a contemporary to remark that his characters not only tell each other and the reader everything they have thought, but everything that they would like to persuade themselves that they have thought. *Marivaudage* has also been described as "the metaphysics of love making." The author was much admired in his own time, though not by Voltaire, whose work he criticized, and it is said that Madame Pompadour secretly provided him with a large pension. (See also *Euphuism*; *Gongorism*; *Guevarism*; *Marinism*.)

Marmalade "Mary . . . made a new sort of preserve—called after herself . . . for the cook at her grandmother's chateau of Joinville had made it to tempt her appetite when she was ill; '*Marie est malade*,' he had muttered again and again as he racked his brain to invent something for her; and '*Mariemalade*' they had called it ever since. They ate the bitter orange jam in her honour but preferred honey." Margaret Irwin explains the origin of marmalade this way in her *The Gay Galliard, The Love Story of Mary Queen of Scots*. Another fanciful story tells us that a guest in a noble house in Scotland replied "*Mair, ma Lady*" ("more, my Lady") when asked his opin-

ion of the jam he had sampled and from this the jam came to be called marmalade. Both tales, examples of folk etymology at its best, are charming but untrue. While we generally eat orange *marmalade* today, the word derives from the Greek *melimelon*, or "honey apple," which some ancient gardener succeeded in cultivating by grafting apple scions onto wild quince stock. Somehow the Greek word for the sweet "honey apple" became the Portuguese word for the quince, *marmelo*, which is what they made the first *marmelado* from. Quince *marmalade*, as the British called it, was imported to England by travelers who had enjoyed it in Portugal and by as early as 1524 we read in Henry VIII's *Letters* of "one box of marmalade . . . presented by Hull of Exeter." English housewives of Henry's time soon learned that other fruits, especially oranges, could be substituted for the quinces in the preserve and *marmalade* as we know it today was born.

Martha *St. Martha* is the patron saint of housewives and a *Martha* is a woman somewhat too devoted to her domestic duties. Both references are to the New Testament Martha, the sister of Mary and Lazarus, who unlike Mary was preoccupied with her household duties: "*But Martha was cumbered about with much serving, and came to him, and said, Lord, dost thou not care that my sister hath left me to serve alone? Bid her therefore that she help me. And Jesus answered and said unto her, Martha, Martha, thou art careful and troubled about many things: But one thing is needed: and Mary hath chosen that good part which shall not be taken away from her*" (*Luke* 10:38–42). Though Martha, encumbered with her duties and mildly rebuked by Jesus, represents the active as opposed to the contemplative life, she is later said to have become a missionary in Gaul. St. Martha (her feast day, July 29) is traditionally represented in a plain housedress, a bunch of keys hanging from her belt and a ladle in her hand. The dragon pictured with her is the fearsome Tarasque, which legend tells us she slew at Aix-la-Chapelle while it ravaged Marseilles. Active she certainly was. (See also *Lazarus*.)

St. Martin, St. Martin's Day, St. Martin's Beads, St. Martin's Goose, St. Martin's Summer, All My Eye and Betty Martin, Gossamer, Martin, Martin Drunk, Martinmas The story of this Roman soldier who became converted to Christianity, refused to fight Christians, and was acclaimed Bishop of Tours against his will in about 371, is told under *chapel*, which was originally the sanctuary enshrining his *capella* or cloak. After he became the patron saint of France, St. Martin's name formed the basis for a number of words. His feast day, *Martinmas* (November 11) replaced the Roman Feast of Bacchus, retaining some of its customs, which probably accounts for the fact that he is regarded as the patron saint of bartenders, drunkards, and reformed drunkards as well. The phrase *Martin drunk*, very drunk, also comes from St. Martin's association with this old pagan festival of *vinalia*, which noted the time when wines had reached their prime.

St. Martin's goose was according to legend a bothersome goose that the saint ordered to be killed and served for dinner. Because he died while eating the meal, a *St. Martin's bird* was traditionally sacrificed every *Martinmas* or *St. Martin's Day*.

St. Martin's summer, like *St. Luke's summer* and *All Saints* (or all Hallows) *summer*, is a European term for our *Indian summer*, the weather around November 11 often providing an unseasonable spell of warmth and pleasantness that was called *été de la Saint-Martin* by the French. The halcyon days of *St. Martin's summer* combine with *St. Martin's goose* in a strange way to give us the word *gossamer*. Due to its association with both the geese eaten on *St. Martin's day* and throughout the season, *St. Martin's summer* came to be called goose summer in days past. At this time of the year fine filmy cobwebs are often found floating lazily in the still air and these delicate "goose-summer webs" are the direct ancestors of *gossamer*, which can either be the webs themselves or fabrics like them.

St. Martin's beads also comes from the saint's name, but the cheap, counterfeit jewelry has little to do with St. Martin, originally being fake jewelry that con men sold on the site of the old collegiate church of *St. Martin's le Grand*, since demolished. The same is true of the British expression for nonsense, *all my eye and Betty Martin*. This saying may have originated when a British sailor, looking into a church in an Italian port, heard a beggar praying *"Ah mihi, beate Martine"* ("Ah, grant me, Blessed Martin") and later told his shipmates that this was nonsense that sounded to him like "All my eye and Betty Martin." Most authorities dismiss the theory summarily, especially because *Joe Miller's Jests* included the story, but St. Martin *was* the patron saint of beggars. One etymologist tells us that "no such Latin prayer is to be found in the formulary of the Catholic Church" and another claims to have in his possession "a book of old Italian cosmopolitan life . . . [that] mentions this prayer to St. Francis by beggars." It seems likely that beggars would have recited such a prayer and so the story has some basis in fact, more at least than linguists have been willing to admit. Meanwhile, there is no better identification of "Betty Martin."

St. Martin also gives his name to the small bluish-black swallows called *martins* that begin to migrate southward from France and England at about the time of *St. Martin's Day* and return again in March, the *Martian* month. The *martin* was first called the *martinet* in France. Numerous *martins* occur all over the world, including the American *purple martin*, a bird valuable to farmers because it eats harmful insects and drives away hawks and crows.

Martinet Colonel Martinet, the strict disciplinarian from whose name *martinet* originated, was "accidentally" killed by his own troops while leading an assault at the siege of Duisberg in 1672. Jean Martinet, sometimes called the Marquis de Martinet, had been a lieutenant colonel of the king's regiment of foot and inspector general of infantry in the army of France's Louis XIV. The Grand Monarch, then only twenty-two, and his brilliant nineteen-year-old war minister the Marquis de Louvois had formed a model standing army in 1660, replacing the old system where the state hired entire units for its army—a regiment, for example, being in the employ of its colonel and a company in the pay of its captain. But these old units had to be molded together into an efficient homogeneous group and Colonel Martinet's excellent exacting work with the Sun King's own Royal Regiment made him just the man for the job. As Inspector General, Martinet was assigned the task of designing all drill systems for the new army and training its infantrymen to fight as a unit in battle. His methods, several of them named for him, were later copied by many European countries, for as Voltaire wrote in *Siècle de Louis XIV*, "The exact discipline which was kept up in the army made it appear in a different light from any that had yet been seen." In the process, however, his strict and tedious drills made Martinet's name synonymous with not only sharp military efficiency, but stern spit-and-polish discipline inflicted by a goose-stepping stickler for details, who insists that his men carry out his rigid orders as if they were puppets. Such became the everlasting fame of a man who helped create the first regular army in Europe, his name today applied to excessively severe soldiers and civilians alike.

Martinet later introduced the use of the bayonet in battle tactics and Voltaire confirms the fact that he invented the transportable copper pontoons used by Louis XIV to bridge the Rhine in 1672, a celebrated military operation of the time which another military genius named Napoleon later described as "fourth rate." When he was killed by his own artillery that same year, by then a *maréchal de camp*, Martinet stood at the side of the Swiss captain Soury, both men killed by the same shot. His name had already become so despised in France that this odd circumstance gave rise to the *bon mot* that the battle of Duisberg had "merely cost Louis a martin and a mouse" (*souris* the French for mouse). Only the dictionaries were to be more ungrateful to Martinet than his countrymen. There have been attempts to disassociate the autocratic officer from the word *martinet* but all have proved unsuccessful. Many seem to stem from Professor Weekley's assertion that *martinet*

was "used by Wycherley in 1676, about forty years before Martinet's death," but, as we have seen, Martinet died in 1672. Weekley and others also observe that there is no French use of the word for a disciplinarian—unless you accept the French word *martinet* meaning a kind of cat-o'-nine-tails—but this can be explained in a number of ways. It remains an almost certain fact that the punctilious French taskmaster so impressed Europe with his reorganization of the French infantry that his name became feared and was then made the object of ridicule both at home and abroad. Giving us a word which sounds so appropriate, one writer has observed, that you can almost hear it clicking its heels.

Martingale Residents of the town of Martigues in Provence, France, once wore economical breeches with a strap belt. Some authorities think that these *chausses à la martingale* give us the word for the part of a harness used to keep down a horse's head, as well as part of the rigging of a ship. Other etymologists discount *Martingalo*, an inhabitant of Martigues, and trace the word to the Spanish *almartaga*, a rein or harness. How the reckless *martingale*—a gambling system in which the stakes are doubled or raised even higher after each loss—derived from either the stingy *Martingalos* or a harness is anybody's guess.

Martini, Martini Sandwich H. L. Mencken, the final authority in such matters, traced the *martini* to 1899 and derives the cocktail's name from the Martini and Rossi firm, makers of a popular vermouth, but others say the drink originated with a now forgotten Italian or Spanish bartender named Martini. The dry *martini* is made, according to the classic recipe, by drinking a little vermouth, exhaling into the interior of a cocktail glass and filling it with gin—after you drink it, you'll forget that you forgot the olive. Mencken also mentions the *martini sandwich*, a dry *martini* between two glasses of beer, which he says "is favored by many American linguists." Novices or no, not many American linguists could still claim the title after a few, the tongue so numbed that not much resembling any known language comes out.

Marxian, Marxism, Marxist For the German economist and revolutionary socialist Karl Marx (1818–83). Born into a substantial middle-class milieu, his father and whole family converting from Judaism to Christianity and baptized as Protestants when he was about six years old, Karl Marx never wanted for any material comforts. After taking his doctorate in philosophy at the University of Jenna, however, he engaged in revolutionary activities that led to his expulsion from Prussia. Marx lived in London from then on, supported financially by his friend and collaborator Friedrich Engels. He earned what living he could chiefly as a journalist, even commenting on the U.S. Civil War for the New York *Herald Tribune*. Marx was a founder of the first International Workingmen's Association, but his most important contributions to history were by far the *Communist Manifesto* (1848), which he wrote with Engels, and the enormously influential *Das Kapital* (1867). The dialectical materialism set forth in this last work has come to be known as *Marxism*, and a *Marxist*, depending on one's political inclinations, is either one favoring *Marxian* economic teachings, or one who is economically doctrinaire and extremist. It is *Marxism's* contention that a socialist state and classless society will inevitably arise in every state. Just as dialectical materialism could not be adequately explained in less than Marx's three volumes, the emotions the word Marxist engenders make any brief definition impossible. "A follower of Marx's teachings" will have to do here. (See also *Leninism; Stalinism.*)

Maryland A popular but incorrect belief has it that *Maryland* was named for the Virgin Mary because it was originally settled by Catholics. The "Old Line State" actually bears the name of Henrietta Maria (1609–69), wife of England's King Charles I and daughter of France's Henry IV. Only fourteen when married to Charles by proxy, Henrietta later became very active in the defense of Roman Catholics, urging her husband to relieve his Catholic subjects, as he had promised in their marriage contract, and treat them favorably. Her plots to bring foreign armies into England during the Civil War were partly responsible for her husband's beheading by Cromwell's supporters, and he forced her to take refuge in France until the Restoration. Three of her six children—Charles II, Mary, and James II—became rulers of England.

When *Maryland* was settled under Lord Calvert in 1632 as a haven for persecuted Catholics, Henrietta Maria was a natural selection for its name and in the original Latin charter the area is called *Terra Mariae*. It seems that *Maryland* was to be named for King Charles at first, but he already had the *Carolinas* named after him and suggested *Mariana* as a name honoring his queen. This was rejected by Lord Baltimore because it was the name of a Jesuit who had written against the monarchy and *Terra Mariae* was adopted instead. *Maryland*, one of the original thirteen states, bears the name "Old Line State" because of the bravery of her soldiers—men of the line —during the Revolutionary War.

Masochism, Masochist In *masochism* the individual derives sexual pleasure through having pain inflicted on himself, but, as with its opposite *sadism*, the use of the term has broadened, now including pleasure derived from self-denial and from hardship and suffering in general. The word is taken from the name of Leopold von Sacher-Masoch (1835–95), an Austrian novelist whose characters dwelt lovingly on the sexual pleasure of pain, just as he did. Though *masochistic* behavior is clinically more common among females than males in our essentially male-dominated culture, this novelist's life, as well as his work, clearly reflects three patterns common to *masochism: masochistic* behavior growing out of early incidents in which the experiencing of pain has been associated with sexual excitation and pleasure; *masochism* as a means of increasing sexual pleasure; and *masochistic* sexual behavior as a reaction against sadistic impulses, the repression of which often results in violent, murderous sadistic behavior. Von Sacher-Masoch's early childhood was a terror of bloody, violent tales told him by both his wet nurse Handscha, and his father, a police chief. His mother seems to have figured little in his formative years. At the windows of the elegant edifice that housed this well-to-do, sophisticated and extremely intelligent man was always the trembling, baffled child who had been weaned on tales of cruel, dominating females like the Black Czarina and the concubine Esther; a child whose earliest memories were of brutal, half-savage Galician peasants. Outside, the house was surrounded by flowers, but they were mostly clumps of poisonous aconite and deadly nightshade, a Dr. Rappacini's garden, for the boy grew up in the midst of one of the bloodiest revolutionary periods in history. Leopold received his doctorate in law when only nineteen, but had begun to act out his sexual fantasies even before this. He became the "slave" to a number of mistresses and two wives before he died, even signing one contract with a mistress that read in part: "Herr Leopold von Sacher-Masoch gives his word of honor to Frau Pistor to become her slave and to comply unreservedly . . . Frau Pistor, on her side, promises to wear furs . . . when she is in a cruel mood. . . ." Furs so fascinated him that they became prominent in his most widely read novel, *Venus in Furs*, and his first marriage was marked by a private ceremony in which he wore white tie and tails and his bride took her vows in a long fur coat. *Venus* not only described *masochism* fully but went far in explaining the pathetic life of a man who could only be satisfied by birches, studded whips and betrayals by the women he loved. A prolific, talented novelist who had published several scholarly histories and had once been a professional actor, Sacher-Masoch became a leading literary figure of his time. But he finally suffered a complete breakdown before turning fifty, his second wife committing him to an asylum after he tried to kill her on several occasions. In a fitting ending to his bizarre life, his wife officially announced that he had died, even mourning him, ten years before his actual death in confinement. The pre-Freudian psychiatrist Richard Kraft-Ebing probably first used his name to describe his ailment, the word *masochism* first recorded in 1893. (See also *Sadism*.)

Mason-Dixon Line Although *Dixie* wasn't named for the *Mason-Dixon line*, the latter term has come to be used as a figure of speech for an imaginary dividing line between the north and the south. The *Mason-Dixon line* has an interesting history. Originally the 244-mile boundary line set between Pennsylvania and Maryland in 1763–67 by English surveyors Charles Mason and Jeremiah Dixon, it was extended six years later to include the southern boundary of Pennsylvania and Virginia. The line had been established by English courts to settle a territorial dispute between the Pennsylvania Penns and the Calverts of Maryland, but the use of *Mason-Dixon line* in Congressional debates during the Missouri Compromise (1819–20) gave the expression wide currency as a dividing line between free and slave states. After the Civil War the term was retained as the boundary between North and South, more as a demarcation line of customs and philosophy than geography. Its existence probably did influence the popularity of the word *Dixie*.

Mason Jar With the renewed interest in vegetable gardening and fresh, healthy foods that are raised for taste and not looks, the *mason jar* is coming into prominence again. The widemouthed glass jars are used for home preserves put up for use when the vegetable gardening season is over. *Mason jars* are made with either glass or metal screw tops. They were named for their inventor, New Yorker John Mason, who patented them in 1857.

Mata Hari Is the most famous of modern spies and courtesans a myth? Behind the patina of the pseudonym Mata Hari is a rather prosaic Dutch name. Margaretha Geertruida Zelle (1876–1917) used Mata Hari as both her stage name and *nom de guerre* when she chose to become a spy for the Germans before World War I. Acclaimed throughout Europe for her interpretations of naked Indonesian dances, she met many men in high places, including German officials in Berlin who recruited her as a spy in 1907. During World War I, her dancing was the rage of Paris and she became intimate with top Allied officers who confided military secrets to her. Mata Hari, who literally slept with hundreds, thrived in the deceit of spies active in Paris, but she was eventually betrayed to the French secret service by another German agent,

Captain Walter Wilhelm Canaris, later to become head of the German secret service in World War II. Her trial was the most publicized of the many espionage trials held during the war and her name became synonymous for a glamorous female spy and femme fatale. Mata Hari was convicted by a French court-martial and executed by a firing squad.

There is some dispute as to both Mata Hari's alleged charms and her effectiveness as an agent. Allen Dulles, who should know all about secret operatives, male and female, does not include her in his anthology of great spies. The former head of the C.I.A. writes: "I do not find greatness . . . in her motives nor her methods, nor, as far as history records, in her achievements. It is doubtful that the information she elicited from her admirers was worth the paper it was written on. I do not doubt what she might have achieved under able guidance. She was, after all, primarily a free-lancer. The drama of her execution is chiefly responsible for her being remembered. She became a victim of wartime spy hysteria, and the pressure on the French authorities in 1917 to set an example. . . . I have left out Mata Hari because she was not much of a spy. . . ." But it has become fashionable to debunk this modern-day *Delilah*. Anyone taking the trouble to go to the records will find that the French claim that she cost them fifty thousand lives is an understatement rather than an exaggeration. Mata Hari truly had shorn a hundred Samsons in her time and her naked dance was in reality a dance of death. Her lovers included prime ministers, crown princes, heads of states—all of whom paid at least $7,500 a night for her favors, as she boasted without exaggeration, and on the day of her execution at least four plots were brewing to save her from the firing squad. One particularly absurd or typically French scheme called for her to wear only a fur coat on the morning of her execution. As soon as the rifles were raised, she would throw open her fur and, *certainment*, no red blooded male would be able to fire upon her glorious nakedness.

Mata Hari's name means "Eye of the Dawn" and was the pseudonym she adopted when she left her cruel, drunken roué of a husband and began her career as a dancer. She had learned her Indonesian dances in Bali, where her spouse Captain McLeod was stationed with the Dutch Colonial Army, but told her audiences that she had been born "in the south of India . . . the child of a family within the sacred caste of Brahma." Her sensuous *baya* temple dances, performed in the nude, obviously attracted the right people and Mata's animal beauty was still hers when she died at forty. Incidentally, the beautiful daughter of the "Red Dancer of the Thousand Veils" became a spy, too. Daughter Banta, in fact, advised an apathetic United States, to no avail, that communist forces would invade South Korea. She was later shot as a spy like her mother.

Maudlin, Maudle, Magdalene Christ freed Mary Magdalene of evil spirits and her name in the form of *Magdalene* has become a synonym for a repentant or reformed prostitute. However, in classical paintings and old folk plays, based on the Bible stories relating to her, Mary was often shown with eyes red and swollen, disheveled and weeping endlessly for her sins. Her name—pronounced *maudlin*, just as Oxford's Magdalene College is pronounced today—was applied by the British with their mistrust of easy emotion, to the excessive, tearful sentimentality that is often associated with drunkenness. In fact, the fifth stage of drunkenness in Thomas Nashe's analysis of intoxication presents us with the "maudlin drunk," and *maudle*, to talk in a drunken way, comes from this use of the word. But it should be added that Biblical scholars cannot agree on the identity of Mary Magdalene. The Mary of Magdala who was the first witness to the Resurrection may not have been the Mary who washed Christ's feet with her tears, wiped them with "the hairs of her head," and whom Christ forgave because "she loved much." Legend, however, combines the three Marys figuring in Christ's ministry into one. (See also *Madeleine*.)

Mauser Another rifle in our arsenal of eponymous weapons. The *Mauser* is rightfully associated with the German Army, which used the original and improvements on it for many years following its introduction in 1871. Its inventors were Peter Paul Mauser (1838–1914) and his older brother Wilhelm (1834–82), the younger Mauser also inventing the *Mauser magazine rifle* in 1897.

Mausoleum Queen Artemisia of Caria, it is said, was so grief-stricken when her husband King Mausolus died in 353 B.C. that she collected his ashes and mixed a portion of them with her daily drink until she died of her inconsolable sorrow two years later. But she had ordered a sepulchral monument erected to her husband's memory in the Carian capital of Halicarnassus that became one of the Seven Wonders of the World. Built on a base of about 230 by 250 feet and towering over 100 feet, the tomb of Mausolos (or more correctly Maussollus) wasn't completed until after her own death, in 350 B.C. Caria, located in what is now southwest Turkey, attracted the greatest Greek architects to work on the vast white marble edifice, which was richly decorated with the sculpture of Scopas and Praxiteles and included statues of Mausolus and his Queen. Nothing quite like this ornate super-tomb had ever been seen before and the Greeks called it a *Mausoleion* after the dead king—*Mausoleum*, the Latin form of this word, becoming our *mausoleum*. The imposing structure stood for almost eighteen hundred years before it crumbled in an earthquake in 1375. The Crusaders who occupied Halicarnassus in the fifteenth century used much of its marble to build a castle, but in 1859 Sir Charles Newton brought some of the structure's remains, including the statue of Mausolus, to the British Museum. Whether King Mausolus deserved all this fuss is debatable. Actually a crafty Persian satrap who virtually ruled Caria for twenty-four years, he is noted mainly for deviously extending his rule over neighboring Greek cities. By fomenting the revolt of Rhodes, Cos and Chios against the Athenian Confederacy in 357 B.C., he not only added these states to his dynasty but weakened Athens so that it was unable to effectively resist Philip of Macedon of *philippic* fame. Today *mausoleum* means any great and gloomy structure—be it bed, room or building—as well as

a large and stately sepulcher. Among the famous mausoleums standing today are the *Taj Mahal*, Napoleon's under the *Dome des Invalides* in Paris, Grant's Tomb on New York's Riverside Drive, and Lenin's in Moscow's Red Square.

Maverick Texas lawyer Samuel Augustus Maverick (1803–70) reluctantly became a rancher in 1845 when he acquired a herd of cattle in payment for a debt. Maverick, a hero who was imprisoned twice in the war for independence from Mexico and a signer of the Texas Declaration of Independence, eventually moved his cattle to the Conquistar Ranch on the Matagorda Peninsula fifty miles from San Antonio. But he was too involved in other activities to prove much of a rancher. When in 1855 he sold out to A. Toutant de Beauregard, their contract included all the unbranded cattle on the ranch. Since careless hired hands had failed to brand many of Maverick's calves, Beauregard's cowboys claimed every unbanded animal they came upon as a *Maverick*. So, apparently, did some of Maverick's neighbors. Though Sam Maverick never owned another cow, his name soon meant any unbranded stock, and later any person who holds himself apart from the herd, a nonconformist. Maverick, whose adventures would make a book in themselves, was elected to the Texas legislature after the state was annexed to the United States, became one of the largest landowners of his day, and left his property to his wife and five of his ten surviving children. The story that he branded neighbors' cattle as his own is untrue, as is the tale that his descendant Congressman Maury Maverick first used *maverick* in its political sense in 1936 when he organized a group of insurgent congressional "mavericks" who did not accept any party leadership. The word had been similarly used since at least 1886. Maury Maverick was *maverick* enough to invent the word *gobbledygook* in the 1940's, however, in an effort to deflate the egos of Capitol Hill windbags by aptly describing their meaningless rhetoric. His autobiography (1937) is entitled *A Maverick American*.

Mavericking, by the way, caused many a cattle war in the old West when cattlemen stopped merely collecting strays on the great plains and began cutting un-branded cows out of one another's herds. They even resorted to *mavericking* young calves still following their mothers, such calves traditionally regarded as being of the mother's brand until they quit her.

Maxim Gun, Maxim Silencer, Max-imite Sir Hiram Stevens Maxim, inven-tor of the first automatic machine gun, also invented a better mousetrap, an auto-matic fire sprinkler, a gas meter, a de-layed-action fuse, a smokeless powder, a heavier-than-air airplane, an inhalator for bronchitis and sundry other items. The world did beat a path to his door, for his arms company merged with the Vickers firm in 1896 to become the giant Vick-ers Armstrong Ltd. and he was knighted for his accomplishments. Sir Hiram (1840–1916) was born in Maine, but be-came a naturalized British subject in 1881, after serving as chief engineer for America's first electric power company. The *Maxim machine gun*, invented in 1883, is a single-barreled, recoil-operated weapon that fires some ten rounds a sec-ond, the first modern machine gun in that the recoil from one cartridge was used to both expel the empty shells and reload the weapon. It was modified by the *Maxim-Nordenfelt*.

The Maxims were a unique and re-sourceful family. Brother Hudson Maxim, who remained an American, invented and manufactured the high explosive *maximite* used in explosive powders, among numerous inventions, and formu-lated an atomic theory very similar to that held by scientists today. He later sold his factory to the E. I. Dupont Com-pany, remaining with them as a consult-ing engineer, and the town of *Maxim*, N.J. was named for him. But what has turned out to be the greatest of the Maxim inventions is the *Maxim silencer* devised by Hiram's son Hiram Percy Maxim (1869–1936), who also remained an American and who invented the *Maxim automobile* as well. *Maxim si-lencers* were weapon attachments origi-nally developed only to make the ex-plosion of firearms practically noiseless. But they were soon perfected to eliminate noise from many modern machines. Thanks to the silencer, noise pollution is much less than it would be, the inven-tion prolonging lives rather than making it easier to take them.

Maxwell, Maxwell's Equations, Max-well's Law For no logical reason, the brilliant Scottish physicist James Clerk Maxwell (1831–79) was better known in his lifetime than he is today. Despite his relatively brief career, Maxwell ranks as one of the greatest theoretical physicists of all time. His most important work was in the field of electricity, where he ad-vanced the theory that light and elec-tricity might be the same in their ulti-mate nature, and his theory of electro-magnetism, published in 1873 in his *Treatise on Electricity and Magnetism*, has been called "one of the most splen-did monuments ever raised by the genius of a single individual." Maxwell began his scientific career when a boy of fifteen. After teaching at Scottish colleges, he was appointed the first professor of ex-perimental physics at Cambridge, direct-ing the organization of the renowned Cavendish Laboratory. *Maxwell's law* and *Maxwell's equations* arise from his elec-tromagnetic theory, but he is more widely honored by the *maxwell*, the unit of magnetic flux named in his honor.

Mayonnaise *Portus Magonis* in Mi-norca was named after the conqueror Hannibal's brother, General Mago, some-time in the early second century. Even-tually the capital of the Mediterranean Baleric island became known as Port Mahon and Port Mahon gave its name to *mayonnaise*. The story is that the Duc de Richelieu attacked the island and drove out the British for a while in 1756. But Richelieu—noted for his love of de-licious food and delectable women, as exemplified by his naked dinner parties back in France—was ravenously hungry after the battle. The Frenchman stormed the nearest kitchen ashore, tossed all the food he could find into one pot, and blended it all together. This possibly apoc-ryphal tale got back to Paris, where chefs concocted a dressing of blended-together ingredients that they named *Mahonnaise* in honor of his victory at Port Mahon.

McCarthyism Here is one word whose exact origins are recorded. *McCar-thyism* was coined by author Max Lerner and introduced for the first time in his newspaper column on April 5, 1950. The word notes the witch-hunting practices, ignoring civil liberties, that his critics accused Senator Joseph McCarthy (1909–57) of using and inspiring during the "Red" scare in the early 1950's. The Wisconsin senator, a great patriot to his supporters, first charged the Democratic administration with allowing Communist infiltration of the State Department. After taking on other governmental departments, he finally met his match when he attacked the army for alleged security lapses. The army, in turn, accused him of seeking special privileges and while McCarthy was acquitted by the Senate of this charge, he was censured by a vote of 67–22 for his insolent behavior toward Senate committees. The *McCarthy hearings* were televised and his countenance and repeated "Point of order, Mr. Chairman, point of order" became familiar throughout America. His low tactics ruined the lives of a number of innocent people. A host of other eponymous *isms* have arisen since the senator's time, including *Castroism, Fidelism, Birchism,* etc.

McCoy, The Real McCoy "Kid McCoy" happened to hear a barroom braggart claim that he could lick any of the McCoys around—any time, any place. The Kid, then at the top of his boxing division, promptly delivered his Sunday punch in person. When the challenger came to, he qualified his statement by saying that he had only meant that he could beat any of the other fighters around using the Kid's name, not "the real McCoy" himself. Another version, which also takes place in a saloon, has a heckler sneer that if the Kid was the real McCoy he'd put up his dukes and prove it. McCoy does so and the heckler, rubbing his jaw from his seat in the sawdust, exclaims "That's the real McCoy, all right."

But there have been numerous explanations for the origin of *the real McCoy,* the genuine, the real thing. Bill McCoy, a rum-runner during Prohibition whose stuff was always "real good," is one candidate, and the housewife in an Irish ballad of the 1880's who keeps proclaiming she is the real McCoy has also been nominated. Then we have the theory

that uncut dope from the island of Macao became "the real Macao," finally "the real McCoy" to addicts. And the guess that the phrase has to do with the high quality of a Scottish wool, "the Real Mackay." Partridge feels "almost certainly" that the term referred to the excellent whiskey imported to this country by A. M. MacKay of Glasgow at the turn of the century, and this may be the answer, for the slang word *McCoy* did refer to good whiskey (1908) before it was used in the complete phrase. Partridge advances this theory in several works. In *From Sanskrit to Brazil* (1950) he ties several theories perhaps too neatly together by stating that *the real MacKay* was later "transformed to the real McCoy, first under the impact of the hero worship that, in the late 1890's, accrued to boxer Kid McCoy and then under that which, in the early 1920's, accrued, at least in New York State, to bootlegger Bill McCoy."

Another explanation is that advertisements of Kid McCoy's fights proclaimed that the real McCoy, and not some imitation, would appear. The fabulous Kid McCoy won the welterweight title in 1896, but outgrew his class; he is ranked by *Ring Magazine* as the greatest light heavyweight of all time, though he never held this title, and I suggest that the use of his name may have been further strengthened by the ring exploits of one Al McCoy, who held the middleweight title from 1914–17. Certainly there were a lot of McCoys around in the early days of boxing among the myriad Mysterious Billy Smiths, Dixie Kids, Honey Mellodys and Philadelphia Jack O'Briens. But which McCoy is *the real McCoy* remains open to debate.

McGuffey's Reader, McGuffey Reader More than 123,000,000 copies of *McGuffey's readers* have been sold since they were first published in 1836, and as many as 30,000 copies were sold as recently as 1960. The school readers, noted for their moral lessons and selections from great English writers, have had a profound effect on the shaping of the American mind. They were the work of educator and linguist William Holmes McGuffey (1800–1873). McGuffey, reared on the Ohio frontier, was possessed of a phenomenal memory that enabled him to become a teacher when only thirteen. After he graduated from Washington and Jefferson College in 1826, he became in turn a professor of languages at Miami University, O. and president of both Cincinnati College and Ohio University. He later served as a professor at Woodward College, Cincinnati, and the University of Virginia, and was a founder of the Ohio public school system. The educator's initial book was published under the title *McGuffey's First Eclectic Reader*. Five more were to follow—the Fourth Reader selling for twenty-seven cents—the last being issued in 1857. These schoolbooks were constantly revised and passed through edition after edition, almost universally used in the United States for two generations and the most widely circulated American book of the past three centuries. Only by the 1920's did they begin to drastically taper off in sales, after being the core of most grammar school curricula for about a century. A memorial to McGuffey stands at his birthplace in West Finley, Pa. *Old Favorites from the McGuffey Readers* (1936) gives familiar examples of his work.

McIntosh Like many fruit varieties, the *McIntosh* apple was discovered accidentally. It is named after John McIntosh, an Ontario farmer, who found the late red apple in 1796 while clearing woodland in Dunclas County and was so impressed by it that he began to cultivate the variety. Today the *Early McIntosh*, one of the best early red apples, bears the same name, as does the *Sweet McIntosh*, regarded by many as the sweetest of all red varieties. The original *McIntosh* is still grown, however, a self-sterile type with whitish-yellow flesh and a superb though slightly acid taste. *McIntosh* account for some 10 percent of apples grown in this country, but they constitute about 75 percent of the New England harvest and 50 percent of the New York State crop. Most connoisseurs rate them superior in taste to the Red and Golden Delicious apples that have become the dominant American varieties.

Medicean The immensely wealthy Florentine banker Giovanni Medici (1360–1429) founded Italy's powerful Medici family. Giovanni's son Cosimo is believed to have been the prototype for Machiavelli's political treatise, *The Prince*, and his grandson, Lorenzo the Magnificent, was an outstanding Renaissance figure. The Medicis ruled in Florence from the fifteenth to the eighteenth centuries, their influence felt throughout Italy, especially due to the fact that three Popes—Leo X, Leo XI, and Clement VII—came from their ranks. Catherine de Medici, Lorenzo's daughter, became queen of France, as did Marie de Medici. A genealogical table of the Medici would yield a score of figures who greatly influenced their times, but the family did so much, both good and evil—ranging from patronage of the arts to political poisonings and tortures—that their name came to mean a variety of things. *Medicean*, then, is simply "pertaining to the Medici," its meaning depending on the way it is used, or to which Medici it refers. (See also *Borgia, Machiavellian*.)

Melba Toast, Peach Melba *Melba toast*, according to the traditional story, originated as several pieces of burnt toast served to the Australian opera star Dame Nellie Melba at the Savoy in London. The prima donna had been on a diet, ordered toast, and enjoyed the crisp, crunchy, overtoasted slices that were served to her by mistake. The maître d' named them in her honor and put *melba toast* on the menu. Whether the story is true or not, thin crispy *melba toast* honors Dame Nellie, as does the peach, ice-cream and raspberry-sauce dessert, *peach melba*, that the French chef Escoffier concocted for her. Nellie Melba was the stage name adapted from the city of *Melbourne* by Helen Porter Mitchell (1861–1931), who became a Dame of the British Empire in 1918. The world-famous soprano made her debut in *Rigoletto* in Brussels (1887) and went on to star at London's Covent Gardens, the Paris Opera, La Scala and New York's Metropolitan among numerous opera houses. Unlike many opera stars, Nellie Melba did not study singing until she was over twenty-one years old, although she had previously been trained as a pianist. Few equaled her before or since in pure vocalization and unsurpassed agility, her lyric soprano having bell-like clarity.

It is said, however, that she nearly ruined her voice in 1896 when she sang Brunnehilde in Siegfried. The celebrated singer retired in 1926, becoming President of the Melbourne conservatoire.

Mendelevium Every attempt to classify the elements had failed before Dmitri Ivanovich Mendeleyev (1834–1907) invented his system in 1869–71. The Russian chemist's *Periodic Law of the Chemical Elements* arranged the elements in order of increasing atomic weight, which made it easy to check the now commonplace tables of vertical columns, and left spaces into which undiscovered elements would probably fit. His law was fully accepted when elements later discovered agreed with his predictions. Many valuable discoveries can be traced to this brilliant broad formulation and its stimulating effect on the sciences. Mendeleyev— his name is also spelled Mendeleeff, Mendelejeff, and Mendelyeev—taught organic chemistry at the University of St. Petersburg. Known as one of the greatest teachers of his time, his *Principles of Chemistry* (1869) was a standard textbook. Deeply involved in research that developed Russia's petroleum industry, the scientist also served as manager of the Office of Standard Weights and Measures, introducing the metric system into his country in 1899. The artificially produced radioactive element *mendelevium* was named in Mendeleyev's honor in 1955 when four American scientists— Glenn Seaborg, Bernard Harvey, Gregory Choppin, and S. G. Thompson—formed it in the laboratory by bombarding the element *einsteinium* with alpha particles.

Mendelism, Mendelian *Mendelism* is the theory of heredity formulated by the Austrian Augustinian abbot and botanist Gregor Johann Mendel (1822–84). Mendel's painstakingly careful experiments, crossing different strains of peas in his monastery garden at Brunn, led to *Mendel's law*, reported in 1865, stating that characteristics of the parents of crossbred offspring reappear in successive generations in certain proportions and according to fixed laws. His *Mendelian laws* were neglected until long after his death, when Hugo De Vries and others independently rediscovered his findings in about 1900. They soon became the foundation for the modern study of heredity. Mendel was not uneducated as is sometimes inferred, having studied natural science at the University of Vienna 1851–1853.

Mercator's Projection Gerardus Mercator, his name the Latinized form of Gerhard Kremer, devised *Mercator's projection* in 1568. His famous cylindrical chart gave all meridians as straight lines at right angles to the parallels of latitude, and is the basis of map making today. Mercator, born in 1512, was a Flemish geographer and mathematician whose accurate maps and globes freed geographers from "the tyranny of Ptolemy," the earlier astronomer and geographer having underestimated the earth's size. The father of modern cartography, Mercator revolutionized map making and navigation and died in 1594 in Duisburg, Germany. He had fled there many years before to escape charges of heresy and there he did his most important work.

Mercerize A mercer is a dealer in textiles, but the old word has nothing to do with the method for treating cotton textiles called *mercerization*. The process was invented by John Mercer (1791– 1866), an English calico printer who discovered it in 1850. *Mercerizing* involves treating material under tension with a caustic soda solution and then acid to neutralize the alkali used. This shrinks, strengthens and gives a permanent silky luster to the yarn or fabric, also making it easier to dye. Mercer's method wasn't widely successful until long after he died, the breakthrough coming in 1895 when the 25 percent shrinkage was virtually eliminated by treating the material under tension, the one factor he had overlooked. The inventor had named his process "sodaizing," but the hundreds of millions of yards of material and thread annually produced by the method are called *mercerized* in tribute to his pioneering work. Mercer was elected to the Royal Society late in his life for his process and other scientific discoveries, including the development of a number of dyes. He was a self-educated man, not having learned to read until he was ten or so, and then becoming regularly employed in a cotton mill, teaching himself chemistry from an old book he had found while browsing through a bookstall.

Merry Andrew Henry VIII's personal physician Dr. Andrew Borde or Boorde (c. 1490–1549) has been regarded by some as the original *Merry Andrew*, at least since Thomas Hearne designated him so in the preface to his *Benedictine Abbas Petroburgensis* in 1735. Borde did have a reputation for a salacious wit and a bedside manner that mixed facetiousness with healing, but to call the eccentric doctor a buffoon or clown would be stretching the evidence too far. He did not author a contemporary joke book, as is sometimes alleged, but he was a man known for his vast learning as well as his reputation for enjoying a good joke. The *Oxford English Dictionary* notes Hearne's statement, and like most authorities, dismisses it, claiming that the author based his identification on little evidence or even intrinsic probability. The expression did arise in Borde's time, but probably from the generic name for menservants or serving men, "Andrew" commonly bestowed on servants in those days. The first *Merry Andrew* was most likely such a servant, the cognomen later being applied to any conjuror's assistant who engaged in buffoonery to help make the magician's hands quicker than the eye.

Mesmerism, Mesmerize Franz Anton Mesmer doesn't entirely deserve his centuries-old reputation as a charlatan. Though he wasn't aware of the fact, Dr. Mesmer was one of the first to treat patients by hypnosis, and his motives generally seem to have been beyond reproach. Unaware of his hypnotic powers, the Austrian physician first believed that his medical successes were due to a method he had devised in which he stroked patients with magnets. Mesmer even kept a little magnet in a sack around his neck and "magnetized" everything in sight at his offices in Vienna, from the tableware to the trees in the garden. His cures for ailments ranging from gout to paralysis made him respected enough to be elected to Bavaria's Academy of Sciences, but the success of another practitioner who effected cures by manipulation alone made him abandon his magnets. Forced to leave Austria on its ac-

count, Mesmer introduced his new "animal magnetism" to Paris in 1778. He knew that he was the "animal" involved in the process, but believed his "magnetism" to be other worldly, not hypnotic. In any event, his spectacular method became the "in" thing, enjoying the vogue that various group therapy methods enjoy today. Mesmer made himself a fortune, prominent Frenchmen like Lafayette, Marie Antoinette and Montesquieu either supporting him or flocking to his lavish Place Vendôme quarters, where he conducted rituals that did cure some people. Garbed in the flowing, brightly colored robes of an astrologer and waving a magic wand, Mesmer would arrange his patients in a circle, have them join hands in the dimly lit room and then pass from one to another, fixing his eyes upon, touching and speaking to each in turn while soft music played in the background. Apparently he never did understand that the supernatural had nothing to do with his success, that his hypnotic powers accomplished this. Many reputable physicians supported his claims, but when Louis XVI appointed a scientific commission— which included Benjamin Franklin—to investigate his practice, Mesmer fell into disfavor, the investigators' report labeling him a charlatan and impostor. A man born before his time, the unknowing hypnotist died in obscurity in Switzerland in 1815, aged eighty-two. Freud and others would profit from his work, but he would mainly be remembered as a quack occult healer. *Mesmerism*—first named and identified by his pupil Puységur—was used for hypnotism before the latter word was coined, but today is employed mostly in the sense of to spellbind, to enthrall by some mysterious power, in fact, to sway a group or an individual by some strange animal or personal magnetism.

Message to Garcia Elbert Hubbard's *Essay on Silence*, published in 1898, and containing nothing but blank pages, indicates that he was ahead of his time. We have since had an *e*-less novel, written with the *e* key on the author's typewriter tied down; *Great International Paper Airplane Books*; executive coloring books; books with double, triple and quadruple endings; and even an epic called *One Million*, by Hendrik Hertzberg, which consists of exactly one million dots pocking precisely two hundred pages, marginal notes on each page noting an important statistic relating to the number of dots thereon—i.e., there are 867,564 Indonesian Boy Scouts, or 198 Siberian tigers still roam Siberia. But nothing has approached the purity of Hubbard's perennial avant-garde vision. The author, who went down with the *Lusitania*, was not above the platitudinously arty story, either. In fact, Hubbard's inspirational essay, "A Message to Garcia," first published in his magazine *The Philistine* in March, 1900, remained required reading in most elementary school English classes until about twenty years ago and "so poignantly appealed to industrial magnates that they distributed countless copies to promote greater efficiency among their employees." Sample: "It is not book learning young men need, nor instruction about this and that, but a stiffening of the vertebrae which will cause them to be loyal to a trust, to act promptly, concentrate their energies, do a thing—'carry a message to Garcia.' " Hubbard's essay dramatized the true adventure of Lieutenant Andrew Summers Rowan, United States Bureau of Naval Intelligence, who during the Spanish-American War was sent by the chief of staff to communicate with General Calixto Garcia, leader of the Cuban insurgent forces. No one knew just where the elusive Garcia might be, but Rowan made his way through the Spanish blockade in a small boat, landing near Turquino Peak on April 24, 1898, contacted local patriots who directed him to Garcia far inland, and returned to Washington with information regarding the insurgent forces. The brave and resourceful Rowan became a hero, but Hubbard transformed him into an almost Arthurian figure and it was his essay that made *to carry a message to Garcia* a byword. For better or worse, "do a thing," as Hubbard advised, has largely been replaced by "do *your* thing."

Messalina, Messaline The notoriously cruel, greedy and venal Valeria Messalina managed to cuckold her weak-minded husband Emperor Claudius I so many times that even in corrupt Rome her name became proverbial for a lascivious, unfaithful woman. One of the profligate empress' favorite tricks was to make love to men and learn of their real estate holdings, later condemn them to death for treason, and then confiscate their property. But she went too far when she eliminated the freedman Polybius. Shortly afterward, in her husband's absence, the empress forced her current lover, a handsome youth named Gaius Silius, to divorce his wife and marry her in a public ceremony. The freedman Narcissus, alarmed at Polybius' fate, took this opportunity to inform Claudius of her treachery and he ordered his third wife put to death. She was either killed in the gardens of Lucullus, which she had obtained by confiscation, or forced to commit suicide there with her paramour. She was only twenty-six when she died in 48 A.D.

Recent historical research indicates that Messalina might have been divorced by Claudius and that her marriage to the senator Silius could have been part of a plot to oust the emperor from the throne. This would go far in explaining Claudius' unparalleled stupidity and Messalina's brazenly foolish public marriage. In any case, her conduct justifies the use of her name. No one knows why, but the fabric *messaline*, a thin, soft silk with a tweed or satin weave, also pays the empress homage.

Messerschmitt, Dornier, Focke-Wulfe, Heinkel, Junkers

They come like brazen birds on wing,
Each one a proud, rapacious thing.
The poet, Walter N. Sinkinson, referred to *Dorniers, Junkers, Heinkels* and *Messerschmitts* in his *The Battle of Britain* (1940), but the last-named eponymous plane was the most famous German fighter of World War II and the main support of the *Luftwaffe*. The aircraft, technically the ME-109 and ME-110 pursuit planes, were designed by German aircraft engineer and manufacturer Wilhelm or Willy Messerschmitt (b. 1898). Messerschmitt built his first plane when he was eighteen and owned his own factory by 1923, his early experience in gliding leading to his interest in power driven

aircraft. Besides the renowned fighter he built a remarkable twin jet, the ME-262. The inventor had been awarded the Lilienthal prize for aviation research in 1937, but was declared a minor offender in the postwar trials of Nazis.

Many German planes were named after their designers or builders. The *Junkers* bomber, designed by Hugo Junkers (1859–1935), was the first all-metal plane to perform satisfactorily; the *Heinkel* bomber commemorates manufacturer Ernst Heinkel (b. 1888); the *Dornier* bomber takes the name of Claude Dornier (b. 1884), its designer and manufacturer; and the *Focke-Wulfe* fighter was principally designed by Heinrich Focke (b. 1890).

Methuselah *As old as Methuselah*, incredibly old, refers to the grandfather of Noah, who the Bible tells us lived until 959 before he perished in the year of the Deluge. The patriarch is the oldest person mentioned in the scriptures and is the son of Enoch, descended from Seth, son of Adam. This primeval ancestor of mankind is mentioned in *Luke* 3:37 as well as *Genesis*. To recap Methuselah's longevity, and virility, which followed an heredity pattern: "*When Enoch had lived sixty-five years, he became the father of Methuselah. Enoch walked with God after the birth of Methuselah three hundred years. . . . When Methuselah had lived a hundred and eighty-seven years, he became the father of Lamech. Methuselah lived after the birth of Lamech seven hundred and eighty-two years, and had other sons and daughters. Thus all the days of Methuselah were nine hundred and sixty-nine years; and he died*" (*Genesis* 5:21–28). The oldest "irrefutably authenticated" human life known to science was lived by French-Canadian Pierre Joubert, who died on November 16, 1814 when 113 years and 124 days of age. The title of oldest father probably goes to the Reverend James E. Smith of Carbondale, Ill., whose thirty-six-year-old wife gave birth to twins on March 16, 1950, just four months before he turned one hundred.

Mho I think it is safe to make the earthshaking claim that this is the only word deriving from a man's name spelled backwards. This unusual crossword puzzle and Scrabble word means just the opposite of the *ohm*, being the electrical unit of conduction while the *ohm* is the electrical unit of resistance. The inverted word, whose plural is *mhos*, was coined by Lord Kelvin and of course honors physicist Georg Simon Ohm just as the *ohm* does. In fact, the *mho* is often called a *reciprocal ohm*. For another eponymous anagram see *Mahernia*.

Micah Rood's Apples Here's a story to tell about any apple with streaks of red running through the white flesh. It seems that a jewelry peddler visited Micah Rood's farm at Franklin, Penn., one spring day in 1693. The peddler was found murdered under an apple tree in Rood's orchard shortly afterwards; his jewelry never was recovered and the farmer never was convicted of the crime. According to legend, though, all the apples on the tree that autumn had streaks of blood inside. Micah Rood died soon after seeing them, the "damned" spots or streaks called "Micah Rood's curse" from that day on.

Michigan (see *States*)

Mickey Finn When someone slips a powdered drug or purgative into a drink to render its drinker unconscious or otherwise helpless, he has concocted a *Mickey Finn* or *Mickey*. The term seems to have originated in Chicago in the late nineteenth century and has been attributed to an underworld figure named Mickey Finn, remembered for his sleight of hand but nothing else. Possibly, *Mickey Finn* derives from some unknown bartender named Mickey, whose potent mixes quickly finished his formerly bellicose patrons, but one guess is as good as another here. The original *Mickey Finn* is said to have been a laxative commonly used for horses.

Mickey Mouse "Mouse, Mickey," as at least one scholarly index lists him, deserves a place in our gallery of eponyms along with *Bucephalus*, *Jumbo*, *Moby Dick* and the several other animals endowed with humanlike characteristics that have made their names proverbial. The anthropomorphic mouse, doubtless the most famous rodent and perhaps the most celebrated animal in all history, was certainly based on a real mouse and his/her name has made for a score of words. So, at the risk of being called misanthropic, let us forthwith embark upon our first biography of a mouse—we have already included here biographies of far less appealing subjects.

For the sake of convenience we'll call Mickey "him," though the original may have been a female. Mickey Mouse (b. 1923) was born *Mortimer* Mouse somewhere in the walls of the garage that served as Walt Disney's Laugh O'Gram studio in Kansas City, Mo. He appears to have come from a family of ten, though no accurate description of his ancestors is available. To those who question his reality, we submit abundant testimony that he did exist. "The mouse came to offer consolation during periods of despondency," writes one Disney biographer. "Some say, even, that he trespassed on the master's drawing board, cleaning his whiskers with unconcern or hitching up his imaginary trousers." Disney's daughter confirms this: "Several stories have been told about Father's having had a mouse who lived on his desk during his Newman Laugh O'Gram days in Kansas City. The thought back of this tale is that that mouse had given Father a special fondness for mice. 'Unlike most of the stories that have been printed,' Father told me, 'that one is true. I do have a special feeling for mice. Mice gathered in my wastebasket when I worked late at night. I lifted them out and kept them in little cages on my desk. One of them was my particular friend. Then before I left Kansas City I carefully carried him out into a field and let him go!' "

From another source we learn that fellow artists had wanted to eliminate the marauding mice plaguing the Laugh O'Gram office and decided to set a mousetrap. Disney forbade this, devising a harmless trap to catch ten of the mice and fashioning them a roomy cage from a wire wastepaper basket. The mouse he named Mortimer became so tame that he freed it at nights when he worked alone, letting it frisk atop his drawing board. But he had to release all his pets when he left Kansas City for Hollywood in August, 1923. It was a sad occasion. Often he had brought two lunches to the office, one for himself and the other

for his mice, and at a time in his life when he more than once literally had to scrounge stale bread for his dinner. Carrying the cage to an empty lot he let the mice go: "Nine mice skittered off into the weeds, but the tenth stayed put. It was Mortimer, watching him with bright eyes. Walt stamped his foot and shouted. The mouse took fright and ran. "I walked away," Walt would recall later, "feeling such a cur."

There we have all the existing facts on the mouse's real life. But we can speculate that he was about three months of age when Disney caught him in April, 1923, six months or so old when Walt let him go free, and judging by the average 1½ year life span of micekind, lived until August, 1924—unless famine, feline or other bad fortune befell him. He could have had as few as nine brothers and sisters, but then again the common house mouse bears five to eight litters a year, so the family probably was much larger, say fifty siblings. As for his physical statistics, the mouse was probably a little smaller than the average full-grown *Mus musculus*, which attains 2½–3 inches in length. His heart, however, though weighing only the usual 1.15 grams, was decidedly larger in another way, inspiring Disney to the greatness he achieved.

No one before had ever created a mouse anything like Disney's. The idea came almost five years after he let Mortimer go—on March 16, 1928, aboard a train carrying the cartoonist from New York to Hollywood, when Disney dreamed of his all but forgotten pet. Mortimer was actually put on paper for the first time on the next day, somewhere between Toluca, Ill. and La Junta, Colo. Walt at first drew him with ruffled hair like Lindbergh's—for his first cartoon, *Plane Crazy*, was to parody the great flier, who had just flown across the Atlantic. But the red velvet pants with red buttons, the black dots for eyes, pear-shaped body, pencil limbs, big, yellow shoes, and three-fingered hands in white gloves were already all there. So was a tail, which the rodent was to lose in the future. Mortimer Mouse was the name the artist proposed, but his wife disagreed and he came up with Mickey

Mouse instead. It was both a second life, a reincarnation for the pet mouse long in his grave and a new birth for Disney, who was even to become the mouse's squeaky voice when sound films were made by Mickey. "I fathered him when he was called Mortimer Mouse," the artist once told reporters, "and he was my first born and the means by which I ultimately achieved all the other things I ever did—from Snow White to Disneyland."

Disney produced both *Plane Crazy* and *Galloping Gaucho* before he was able to sell Mickey Mouse in the black-and-white talkie, *Steamboat Willie*, the world's first animated sound cartoon. With its appearance in 1928 the Mouse became an overnight sensation. Mickey won fame enough to satisfy the most ambitious man. In France he was called *Michel Souris*; in Italy, *Topolino*; in Japan, *Miki Kuchi*; in Spain, *Miguel Ratoncito*; in Latin America, *El Raton Miguelto*; in Sweden, *Muse Pigg*; in Germany, *Michael Mouse*; and in Russia, *Mikki Maus*. By 1931, Mickey Mouse clubs had a membership of over one million, the mouse appeared in twenty foreign newspapers, was enshrined in Madame Toussard's Wax Museum, and *Film Daily* estimated that over 100,000 people a day saw him on the screen. Mary Pickford, America's sweetheart, announced that Mickey was *her* sweetheart, and Mohamet Zahin Kahn, potentate of Hyderbad, called him the leading American hero in India.

Today the Mouse's name adorns thousands of things, having appeared on some five thousand commercial items alone. *Mickey Mouse* was the password chosen by intelligence officers in planning the greatest invasion in the history of warfare—Normandy, 1944. *Mickey Mouse diagrams* were maps made for plotting positions of convoys and bombarding forces at Normandy. The special insulated boots issued to combat troops in Korea were called *Mickey Mouse boots*, and *Mickey Mouse discipline* was used and is still applied to childish rear-echelon inspections and the like, though stronger terms have been more popular. The expression *Mickey Mouse* means, among other things, anything that is trite or commercially slick in character, such as *Mickey Mouse music*. All in honor of a real mouse who died almost half a century ago, a mouse reborn to revitalize fantasy in our time and to take his unassailable place in the pantheon of world folk heroes.

Midas, Midas Touch Just as the word Pharaoh was bestowed upon all Egyptian rulers, Midas was the title of the kings of Phrygie an ancient kingdom in what is now central Turkey. Historical records reveal a Phrygian king named Midas who lived in the eighth century B.C., but the King Midas who became the basis for the Midas legends has never been positively identified. In legend King Midas is the father of Gordius (see *Gordian knot*). Several tales are told of him in Greek mythology, the most famous of these making his name proverbial. This story had King Midas befriending Silenus, the Greek god of wine and fertility, a jolly old man, often drunk but gifted with great powers of song and prophecy. Midas led Silenus to Dionysus, his pupil and boon companion, and this grateful god of fertility and wine rewarded him by promising to fulfill any wish he might make. King Midas told Dionysus that he wished everything he touched would turn to gold and his wish was granted. But Midas got much more than he bargained for—even his food and drink turned to gold, and he nearly starved to death. The greedy king's appetite for gold decreased and he asked the god to take his gift away. Dionysus commanded him to bathe in the Pactolus River, which washed him clean of his cursed power and has ever since then had gold-bearing sands.

From this original moral tale, on which there have been many embellishments, we have *the Midas touch*, referring to anyone who somehow effortlessly makes money from every project he undertakes. The real King Midas must have been an unlikeable character, for none of the legends about him do him much honor except in noting his repentance. In another Greek myth Midas judged a flute-playing contest between Apollo and Pan (or, in a different version, Marsyas). He indiscreetly declared Pan the winner and Apollo angrily gave him the ears of an ass. Midas concealed his new ears under his cap, but obviously couldn't fool his barber, who discovered them while giving him a trim. This wise man, anxious to relieve himself of his secret but afraid to tell anyone, dug a hole in the ground, whispered his secret into it and filled in the hole—an admirable practice. However, the resourceful Apollo was not to be foiled—reeds grew out of the hole and whenever the wind blew through them, they whispered, "King Midas has the ears of an ass."

A third Greek legend, little told, says that Midas caught the god Silenus by mixing wine with the waters of a spring and making him drink. "Teach me your wisdom," the king implored, but it appears that Silenus could only tell him that it was "happiest for a man not to be born at all and, failing that, to die as soon as possible." Whether Midas took his advice is not recorded, but there is mention of a king Midas in history who became disgusted with the raiders invading his kingdom and "drank bull's blood and died." (See also *Croesus*.)

Milliner Milan, Italy, was one of the great fashion centers of the world in the early sixteenth century, setting styles for all Europe. Milan bonnets, Milan gloves, Milan point lace, Milan ribbons, Milan needles, and even Milan jewelry were among the many items imported to England from the Paris of its day. Small shopkeepers who sold these imported articles, only some of them merchants from Milan, were naturally named *Milaners*, but the English pronounced and spelled the word *Milliners*, which eventually lost its capital. The small shops, run primarily by men at first, did often specialize in making and selling ladies' hats, but the use of *milliner* exclusively for a designer or seller of women's headgear is fairly recent. Up until a century ago, the designation included a seller of any of the female finery mentioned above. As Shakespeare writes in *A Winter's Tale*, "No milliner can fit *his* customers with gloves."

Minnie Ball French Army Captain Claude Étienne Minié (1814–79) invented the *minnie* or *minié ball* bullet that became famous around the world and was extensively used in the Ameri-

can Civil War. Minié's invention came in 1849, designed for the *Minié rifle* but more importantly something of a final answer in the search for an ideal bullet. The *Minnie ball* had a flat base, a cylindrical body, and a head like a pointed arch. The elongated bullet, one of the first of its shape, was more accurate and could be loaded faster than any shell before it. Experts thought it to be the ultimate in ballistic ingenuity and it was certainly the first step in the development of the modern bullet. With it a soldier could fire *two* aimed shots a minute!

Missouri (see *States*)

Mithridatize, Eupatorium Mithridates VI trusted no one. Coming to the throne when only eleven, this king of Pontus, an area in Asia Minor along the Black Sea, eventually murdered his mother, his sons, and the sister he had married in order to retain power, and once killed all his concubines to prevent his harem from falling into enemy hands. But Mithridates really earned his title of Eupator, "the Great." Subduing Asiatic Greece, he succeeded in driving his hated enemies the Romans from Asia, ordering a wholesale massacre of those remaining. On invading European Greece, however, he was defeated and though he won the Second Mithridatic War (83 B.C.) when the Romans attempted to conquer Pontus, he was ultimately defeated by Pompey in 66 B.C. after his own troops, led by his own son, rose up and revolted against him. An implacable enemy of Rome, Mithridates, or Mithradates, is endowed with heroic qualities by ancient writers. Supposedly a courageous warrior of giant size, strength and speed of foot, he is said to have possessed a remarkable mind that enabled him to master twenty-two languages and made him the center of cultural life in his kingdom. A renowned collector of art works and natural science curiosities, he presided over a court noted for its Greek men of letters, but that he loved the sensual life equally well is evidenced by the fact that he awarded prizes to both the greatest poets and the greatest eaters in his kingdom. Mithridates the Great came to an ironic end. All his days he had guarded himself against poisoning by accustoming his body to small amounts of poison, rendering himself immune by gradually increasing these daily doses. Then, weary of his son's treachery, he decided to commit suicide and found that he had *mithridatized* himself far too well. No poison in any amount worked, for he had total immunity. He had to have a mercenary or slave stab him to death.

Such is the story, anyway, that the credulous Pliny the Elder tells us about Mithridates, King of Pontus (120–63 B.C.), betrayed by a son as treacherous as his father, betrayed by the very poisons he himself had so often used to kill. A *mithridate* is the antidote to all poisons that Pliny claims Mithridates had developed. It contained seventy-two ingredients, none of them given by the historian. The last ingredient, however, was *to be taken with a grain of salt*, Pliny says, and it is from his acceptance and presentation of Mithridates' story that the phrase probably originates. In earlier times many *mithridates* were offered by pharmacists as universal antidotes. Today they have been dismissed from a scientific standpoint, but some individuals still try to *mithridatize* themselves from poisons.

The botanical genus *Eupatorum*, comprising over five hundred species of chiefly tropical American herbs, is also named for Eupator, King Mithridates VI of Pontus. He is said to have used it or some related plant for healing.

Moby Dick Mocha Dick, the stout gentleman of the latitudes, the prodigious terror whale of the Pacific, the redoubtable white sperm whale that fought and won a hundred sea battles against overwhelming odds; such was the reputation in the extravagant language of the time of the whale Herman Melville immortalized as *Moby Dick*.

There is no doubt about it—Mocha Dick was a real whale. Dick was probably first fought in 1819, the year Melville was born, and he was still terrorizing whalemen when the author was writing *Moby Dick* in 1850. So renowned was the leviathan that whenever whalers gammed, "Any news from Mocha Dick?" was a standard greeting. Boats and even ships were shattered by his immense flukes or ground to pieces in the crush of his powerful jaws. One report has him measuring out longer than a whaler—110 feet, his girth 57 feet, his jaw alone 25½ feet long. If we accept all contemporary accounts, he wrecked seven ships, destroyed some twenty boats and killed at least thirty men. Truly a *greater* whale than Moby Dick in his physical prowess.

Melville probably first read about Mocha Dick in a piece by Jeremiah N. Reynolds in the May 1839 *Knickerbocker Magazine*; undoubtedly though, he heard of him long before in the forecastles of ships he sailed. Reynolds told how Dick was sighted toward the coast of Chile close aboard the conical peak of Mocha Island from which the white whale took his name, how, after two encounters, Dick was finally captured, his back crusted with white shells and barnacles, and more than twenty harpoons rusted with age removed from him. But according to later accounts, Mocha Dick was fought again. Reynolds' story may have been correct *except* for the killing of the white whale, or it may be that other whales were later mistaken for him, but his name is mentioned in the logs of at least seven more ships, including an account of how he defeated not one but three whalers.

The last mention in history of Mocha Dick is dated August, 1859, when off the Brazilian banks he is said to have been taken by a Swedish whaler. Measuring 110 feet in length, he weighed more than a ton for each swimming foot. The whale that Melville and others believed caused the 1819 *Essex* sinking, which formed the basis for *Moby Dick*, was captured without much of a struggle. The Swedish whaler's log discloses that he was dying of old age, blind in his right eye, his head a mass of scars, eight teeth broken off and the others all worn down. But no one would ever remember him this way. He had already become legend when Herman Melville wrote *Moby Dick* in 1850—Melville changing his prenom to *Moby* probably to suggest his amazing *mobility* and to avoid association with the color "mocha." Melville had made Dick something more than a whale. Mocha Dick, in the words of one writer, "had been absolved of mortality . . . readers of *Moby Dick* know that he swims the world unconquered, that he is ubiquitous in time and place."

Mohammedanism, If the Mountain Will Not Come to Mohammed Mohammed (or Muhammad, or Mahomet), "the praiseworthy," was the title given to the founder of the Moslem religion, his original name having been Kotham or Halabi. The prophet of the Arabs was born after his father's death in about 570 A.D. and grew up as an orphan in Mecca, dying in Medina in 632. A camel driver at twenty-five, he married his employer, a rich widow fifteen years his senior, who became the first of his ten wives. Mohammed was forty when he felt he had been called to be a prophet and began receiving messages he believed were from God, messages God commanded him to relay to his countrymen. He called the monotheistic religion he preached Islam, not *Mohammedanism*, its keystone being that "There is no God but Allah and Mohammed is his prophet." Mohammed's converts were very few at first, his teachings met with jeers. His flight from Mecca to Medina in 622 with a mere 150 believers is traditionally called the Hegira. Later the prophet of the sword invaded Mecca with ten thousand followers and established an empire, Islam now embracing some twenty-five million people. The religion's Bible is the Koran, which is said to have been communicated to Mohammed by the angel Gabriel, and Mecca remains a place of holy pilgrimage to believers.

If the mountain will not come to Mohammed, Mohammed must go to the mountain is a saying that arises from the time when Mohammed brought his message to the Arabs and they demanded miraculous proof of his claims. He ordered Mt. Safa to move and when it failed to do so, explained that God had been merciful—for if the mountain had moved it would have fallen on and destroyed them all. Mohammed then went to the mountain to give thanks to God. The proverb is used to indicate that it is wise to bow before the inevitable after failing to get one's way.

Mohicans, Last of the Mohicans Contrary to James Fenimore Cooper's famous story, we have not yet seen the last of the Mohicans. Cooper adopted

the name of the Algonquian-speaking confederacy of tribes for the second of his "Leatherstocking Tales," and his title *The Last of the Mohicans* became an expression still used to indicate the last of any group with a certain identity or beliefs. But the Mohicans—at least mixed-blood remnants of the confederacy —still survive near Norwich, Conn. and Stockbridge, Mass. The Mohicans or Mahicans were a powerful group in the past, occupying both banks of the upper Hudson in New York, while another branch, the Mohigans, lived in eastern Connecticut. War with the Mohawks and white settlement pushed them out of these areas—Dutch guns supplied to their enemies hastening their dispersal— and they almost entirely lost their identity. At last count they numbered about eight hundred. In Massachusetts they are part of the so-called Stockbridge Indians.

Mohocks, Mohawks, Hiawatha The Mohawk Indians were one of the smallest tribes of the Iroquois League of Five Nations, but were probably the most fierce and aggressive. In fact, *Mohawk* comes from *Mohawauuk*, "man-eaters," a name given the tribe by their enemies the Narragansett. They formerly lived along the Mohawk River in New York State from Schenectady to Utica. The Mohawks sided with the British during the Revolution, but the British did not honor their name in English, *Mohawk* or *Mohock* being used as early as 1711 to indicate "one of a class of aristocratic ruffians who infected the streets of London." These *Mohocks* were said to have mauled passers-by "in the same cruel manner which the Mohawks . . . were supposed to do," being in Swift's words: "A race of rakes . . . that play the devil about the town every night, slit people's noses, and beat them." The word, which even became a verb, *to mohock*, is now only of historical interest—there being no more *mohocks* to overturn coaches on trash heaps and roll people down hills in tubs, nor coaches or tubs for that matter. The real Mohawks number about one thousand today, living mostly on reservations in Ontario, Canada. A settlement in Brooklyn, N.Y., supplies New York with its ablest high structural steelworkers, men fearless of heights who have worked on every major skyscraper construction in the city.

Longfellow derived the name *Hiawatha* for his poem from a Mohawk statesman living in about 1570 who helped form the League of Five Nations, or at least from the name of his clan, *Haienhwatha.*

Molly Of the many tropical fish kept in millions of home aquariums only guppies are more popular than *mollies,* but few enthusiasts know that the fish takes its feminine name from a man. Count Nicolas François Mollien (1758–1850) wasn't a tropical fish collector—the hobby only dates back to about 1860—but a French financial genius who served several governments. Mollien was often consulted by Napoleon, who unfortunately refused to accept his advice against instituting his ill-fated "continental system." The tropical fresh-water fish genus *Mollienesia* was irregularly named in Mollien's honor and since then all *mollies* with their female nickname bear this man's abbreviated surname. *Mollies,* which give birth to live young, appear in a wide variety of forms and colors, a relatively recent introduction being the all black *molly.* (See also *Guppy.*)

Molotov Cocktail, Molotov Breadbasket This "cocktail for Molotov" was so named by the Finns when fighting the Russians in 1940. It is a gasoline-filled bottle with a slow burning wick that is ignited before the crude incendiary is thrown, the bottle bursting and the ignited gasoline spreading when it hits a tank or other objective. Vyacheslav Mikhailovich Molotov (b. 1890) was Soviet premier at the time the Finns derisively named the "cocktail" after him. He had only the year before negotiated the infamous Russo-German nonaggression pact, which is sometimes called the *Molotov-Ribbentrop pact* but is best known as the Pact of Steel. Molotov, a communist from his early youth, changed his name from Skriabin to escape the Czarist police. He rose quickly in the party hierarchy, serving in many capacities. In 1940 the city of Perm was renamed *Molotov* in his honor, but the wily diplomat later fell into disfavor, being sharply attacked by Krushchev at the 22nd Party Congress in 1961, and was expelled from the Communist party in 1964. During World War II, *Molotov breadbasket* was slang for a canister of incendiaries that showered bombs over a wide area.

Mona Lisa Smile It is said that Leonardo Da Vinci worked over a period of four years on his celebrated portrait of Madonna Lisa, wife of the Florentine gentleman Francesco Giocondo. The portrait, one of the most beautiful and finished in the world, was completed in 1506 and is most famous for the enigmatic smile that the sitter wears, which has generally been regarded as subtly sensual, a smile of feminine mystery expressing some secret pleasure or emotion. But the mysterious smile has been the subject of extensive imaginative speculations, those of the critic Walter Pater in 1873 perhaps the best known. Leonardo himself had music played during Madonna Lisa's sittings for the portrait so that the strange rapt expression would not fade from her face. The painting was sold to Francis I for four thousand gold florins and has remained one of the glories of the Louvre ever since, except for a brief period when it was stolen and brought back to Italy. The *Mona Lisa smile* is often called the *Giaconda smile* and the enigmatic lady's husband is sometimes identified as Zanobi del Giocondo, of Naples instead of Florence. Madonna Lisa's portrait is probably the most familiar in the world and has even made her the subject of a modern-day popular song, *Mona Lisa,* originally recorded by the late Nat "King" Cole. The *Mona* of *Mona Lisa* is simply short for Madonna or Milady.

Mondrian The nonobjective paintings of Dutch artist Pieter Cornelis Mondrian, or Piet Mondrian (1872–1944) have had a tremendous influence on twentieth-century design and architecture as well as painting. His abstract geometric designs, such as *Broadway Boogie Woogie,* which hangs in New York's Museum of Modern Art, are concerned with the geometric order underlying nature. Mondrian's dislike of curved lines and use of only primary colors developed, starting in about 1910, when he came under the sway of the French cubists; he is regarded as one of the purest nonobjective painters. The artist's work influenced the German Bauhaus school movement, which insisted on modern, functional design in industry, architecture, and interior decoration. In the mid sixties, various *Mondrian fashions* in women's suits and dresses were named after his style, the connection often tenuous.

Monkey, Monkey Wrench One would think that the *monkey wrench* is so named because it's "monkeywise" or because the wrench's sliding jaws reminded someone of a monkey's chewing apparatus. This may be the case, but there is some reason to believe that the tool was named after its inventor. One source suggests that this mechanical wizard was London blacksmith Charles Moncke, but the British do not commonly call the tool a *monkey wrench*, using the term adjustable spanner wrench, or spanner, so this theory is suspect. A more likely explanation turned up some years ago in a collection of undated clippings on word origins collected by a Boston doctor. One article from the *Boston Transcript*, appearing in the winter of 1932–33, attributed the wrench's invention to a Yankee mechanic by the name of Monk employed by Bemis & Call of Springfield, Mass. Monk supposedly invented the movable jaw for a wrench in 1856 and although it was given a special name at first, workers in his shop were soon calling it *Monk's wrench*, finally jokingly turning this into *monkey wrench*. The tale has not been confirmed, but the 1856 date coincides with the first use of the word in the *Oxford English Dictionary* (1858), making the theory plausible. None of the big dictionaries make an attempt to trace the word's origin, not even to say that the wrench resembles a monkey's jaw, just as a crane resembles a crane's neck.

As for the word *monkey*, it may derive from a proper name, too. In one Low German version of the *Reynard the Fox* animal tale, published in about 1480, *Moneke* is the son of Martin the Ape. *Moneke* either took his name from the German surname *Moneke*, which has many variants, or from the Italian *monna*, a female ape. It is certain that the name for *monkey* persisted due to the popularity of *Reynard the Fox* and the little *moneke* that the tale included.

Monroe Doctrine, Monrovia The *Monroe Doctrine* was promulgated in President James Monroe's annual message to Congress on December 2, 1823. It said in effect that the United States would keep out of Europe, would not even spread democratic propaganda, but that European countries must not molest New World governments or set up colonies in the New World. Madison had been influenced by the 1812 war with England, a Russian attempt to ban foreign vessels off Alaska, and the threat that the Holy Alliance might help Spain to reconquer her revolted colonies. The oldest and best-known principle of American foreign policy has been variously interpreted over the years—often encouraging isolationism—and has been used to great advantage. Few other policies have been so vehemently praised and condemned. Abrogated in both World Wars, it was recently applied again with the establishment of Communist regimes in Guatemala and Cuba. Monroe's Secretary of State John Quincy Adams deserves much of the credit for the *Monroe Doctrine*, but the president took the responsibility for it and it rightly bears his name. James Monroe (1758–1831), fifth president of the United States, served two terms, from 1817–25. Though not considered one of the great presidents, Monroe, who had been wounded during the Revolution and studied law under his friend Jefferson, presided over an administration in the period known as the "era of good feelings." His terms in office are particularly noted for the acquisition of Florida (1819), the Missouri Compromise (1820), and the addition of five new states to the Union. Monroe spent so much of his own money in his long public service that he found himself in serious financial straits after he retired from the presidency. In 1826 Congress awarded him thirty thousand dollars for reimbursement of his expenses.

Monrovia, the seaport capital of Liberia, was named for President Monroe in 1822 when the American Colonization Society founded it as a haven for ex-slaves from the United States. Mencken quotes a Liberian diplomat who says that the descendants of these American slaves, now Liberia's ruling class, "prefer to be called . . . *Monrovian Liberians* to distinguish themselves from the natives of the hinterland, who are generally called by their tribal names."

Montespan Another of Louis XIV's favorites whose name became synonymous for a mistress. Françoise Athénaïs de Pardaillan, the Marquise de Montespan, was the daughter of a nobleman, Gabriel de Rochechouart, duc de Montmart. While serving as maid of honor to Louis's Queen Marie-Thérèse in 1663 she married the Marquis de Montespan. The Sun King's first mistress La Vallière introduced Madame Montespan to him and she eventually regretted this, for the beautiful and brilliant woman replaced her in the king's affections. La Vallière was cruelly discarded and Montespan became Louis's mistress, bearing him seven children, in addition to the two she bore her husband, all of whom were later legitimized by the crown. In the end, however, Montespan lost out to Madame Maintenon, her companion and the governess of her children, suffering the same fate as her predecessor. But she did not give up so easily. When Louis's affections showed signs of ebbing and he turned to Madame Maintenon in about 1673, Montespan tried resorting to magic, consulting the infamous sorceress La Voison. She even tried to poison the Sun King's food, but Louis had such fond memories of her that the affair was hushed up. In 1691, she retired to a convent with a large pension from the king. She died sixteen years later, aged sixty-six. (See also *Lavaliere; Maintenon; DuBarry; Pompadour.*)

Morgan Horse Justin Morgan is the only American horse ever to sire a distinctive breed of horses. A bay stallion foaled in about 1793, he belonged to Vermonter Justin Morgan (1747–98). The horse bearing this schoolteacher's name was probably a blend of thoroughbred and Arabian with other elements, fairly small at fourteen hands high and eight hundred pounds. Morgan, an aspiring musician, bought his colt in Massachusetts, naming him Figure and training him so well that he won races against much larger thoroughbreds. Eventually, Figure came to be called after his master. After his owner died, Justin Morgan

was bought and sold many times in the twenty-eight years he lived. One of those unusual horses whose dominant traits persist despite centuries of interbreeding, his individual characteristics remain essentially unchanged in the *Morgan* breed of horses he sired. *Morgans* are still compact, virile horses noted for their intelligence, docility and longevity, many of them active when thirty years of age or more. Heavy-shouldered, with a short neck but delicate head, they are noted for their airy carriage and naturally pure gait and speed, long being the favorite breed for American trotters until the Hambletonian strain replaced them. But *Morgans* were far more than trotters; size considered, experts contend they were never equaled as all-purpose horses, "in harness or under saddle, on the farm or the road, the racetrack or the tanbark." Once the most famous of all light horses in America, the variety is used less and less each year, its breeding now supervised by the government. Justin Morgan's ancestors are still often bay colored, but can be black and chestnut, too. Their height remains about the same as their founder's, from fourteen to fifteen hands, but their weight ranges somewhat higher —from eight hundred to over one thousand pounds. (See also *Bucephalus; Byerly Turk.*)

Morris Chair Something of a complete Renaissance man was English poet, artist, and pamphleteer William Morris (1834–96). His collected works fill twenty-four volumes and it would take a good many volumes to do justice to his full life. In addition to his poetry and art, Morris found time to help establish England's Socialist party and can be counted an architect, interior decorator, master craftsman, novelist, translator, editor, publisher and printer as well. In 1861 he founded a company to reform Victorian tastes by producing wallpaper, furniture, stained glass, metalware, and other decorations. This began the arts and crafts movement in England, which emphasized naturalness and purity of color in objects produced by hand and was inspired by a passion for beauty. Morris and Company incorporated what its founder thought best in medieval society—the essential equality of the designer—craftsman and his closeness to his product, a factor many critics of industrial society contend is wanting today. Among the furniture made by the company was the *Morris chair,* a large easy chair with an adjustable back and removable cushions which came to be used more in America than in England. Morris also became noted for his Kelmscott Press where he designed the Golden, Troy and Chaucer type faces. The *William Morris Society* in London honors the memory and work of this multitalented man.

Morris Dance The *Morris dance,* originally a "Moorish dance," derived from the ancient military dances of the Moors. Introduced into England from Spain by John of Gaunt in about 1350, its name in French was *danse mauresque* and in Flemish *mooriske dans.* But the dance, which used the tabor as an accompaniment, eventually assumed a very British flavor. It was usually performed by groups of five men and a boy—the five miming Robin Hood, Little John, Friar Tuck, Allan-a-Dale and other characters from the Robin Hood stories, while the boy played Maid Marion. Generally danced on May Day and in various processions and pageants, the fantastic spectacular was banned by the Puritans but was later revived. It has been revived recently with the renewed interest in folk dancing.

Morse Code "What hath God wrought?" were the famous first words sent in *Morse Code* by its inventor on May 24, 1844. Samuel Finley Breese Morse (1791–1872) had begun experimenting with his electric telegraph twelve years earlier, when well over forty, Congress later granting the penniless inventor thirty thousand dollars to build the experimental line from Washington to Baltimore over which he sent his historic message. The *Morse Code* he invented in conjunction with his telegraph was first called the *Morse alphabet* and is of course a system of dots and dashes representing letters, figures and punctuation, the dash in the system equaling three times the length of the dot in time. Morse didn't start out as a scientist. After graduation from Yale, he studied in England and began a career in art,

earning a reputation as a portrait painter, one of the founders of the National Academy of Design, and professor of painting and sculpture at New York University. Though his interest in electricity began during his college days, he was unaware that a number of telegraphs had been independently invented before his, notably Joseph Henry's electromagnetic telegraph in 1830. Morse was forced to defend his invention in various patent suits, but emerged a victorious and very wealthy man. He later introduced the *daguerreotype* into America and experimented with submarine cable telegraphy.

Mosaic, Mosaic Code, Moses Boat, Moses' Cradle, Moses' Rod The two words *mosaic,* a design or picture made from small pieces of stone or other material, and *Mosaic,* referring to the prophet Moses, are unrelated. In fact, the Jewish and Mohammedan interpretation of the Ten Commandments Moses brought down from Mt. Sinai hold that the second commandment forbids the making of any likeness of anything, so the capital letter in *Mosaic* is an important one. The word for the design *mosaic* comes to us via French and Latin from the Greek *Mousa* ("a Muse"), *mosaic* work being associated with the Muses in ancient Greece.

A *Moses' cradle* is a shallow wicker bassinet, its name deriving from the hiding of the child Moses by his mother in a basket made of bulrushes when the oppressed Israelites were ordered to kill all their male children (*Exodus* 2:1–5). Pharaoh's daughter found the child, named him Moses, "Because I drew him out of the water," and let his mother nurse him. When a young man, Moses, who grew up in the splendor of the court, killed an Egyptian oppressing a Jew and fled into the wilderness, but at the age of eighty was called by God, through a voice from a burning bush, to return to Egypt and free the Hebrews. Pharaoh refused God's demand until ten plagues were sent and Moses then led his people to Mt. Sinai. For forty years after he led them through the wilderness, drawing up the religious and ethical rules known as the *Mosaic code* during this time. The first five books of the Bible, the Hebrew Torah or the Pentateuch, are regarded as

Moses' work. After viewing Canaan from Mt. Nebo, he died alone at 120, his people compelled to wander in the wilderness until one generation had passed away because they had rebelled against crossing into the Promised Land.

Moses' rod is a divining rod, named for the rod with which Moses smote the rock at Horeb to bring forth water (*Exodus* 17:5–6). The broad, flat-bottomed *Moses boat*, formerly used for transferring cargo in the West Indies, may also be named for Moses but more likely takes its name from the famous eighteenth century Massachusetts boatwright Moses Lowell.

Mosey *Webster's*, Mencken and other authorities suggest that the Spanish *vamos*, "let's go," became *vamoose* in American, which begot the slang word *mosey*, to stroll or saunter about leisurely. But it is possible, one theory holds, that the word takes its name "from the slouching manner of wandering Jewish peddlers in the West, many of whom were called Moses or Mose or Mosey." The first explanation seems too complicated and the second takes too much for granted, but nothing better has been offered.

Mother Carey's Chickens, Mother Carey's Goose "It is certain that one of the crew must die and be thrown overboard to become a Mother Carey chicken to replace the one that has been destroyed." So writes Captain Frederick Marryat in *Poor Jack* (1840) in relating the superstition that storm petrels should never be killed. All petrels are regarded as the protectors of sailors, but how they got the name *Mother Carey's chickens* is a mystery. No Mother Carey has been found, many etymologists upholding Brewer's theory that the words are a corruption of the Latin *Mater Cara* (Dear Mother), another name for the Virgin Mary. Brewer claims, "The French call these birds *oiseaux de Notre Dame* or *aves Sanctae Mariae*," but it should be pointed out that this has never been confirmed. In the absence of evidence, Weekley's conclusion in *The Romance of Words* seems best: "*Mother Carey's chicken*, probably a nautical corruption of some old Spanish or Italian name; but, in spite of ingenious guesses, this lady's

genealogy remains as obscure as that of Davy Jones or the Jolly Roger."

Mother Carey's goose is the large "great black petrel or fulmar of the Pacific," and when *Mother Carey is plucking her goose*, it is snowing. (See also *Parrot, Peter; Petrel.*)

Mother Shipton For a female *Nostradamus*. Mother Shipton is a legendary figure in English literature who is supposed to have foretold the death of Cromwell and the great London fire of 1666, among other accurate predictions. According to the *Life of Mother Shipton*, written by Richard Head in 1667, more than a century after her death, her real name was Ursula Shipton and she lived in Knaresborough, Yorkshire from 1488–1561. Born Ursula Southill or Southiel, her peasant mother was regarded as a witch by villagers and Ursula appears to have been so ugly that she was called the Devil's child, though not so ugly as to prevent a builder named Tobias Shipton from marrying her. Virtually nothing is known about her life, all the "facts" at best traditions, but Mother Shipton's prophecies, like Mother Nixon's, had a phenomenal hold on the minds of rural folk until as late as 1881. In that year the rumor that she had predicted the end of the world caused people to flee their homes and pray in the fields and churches all night. It developed that this prediction, along with others foretelling the coming of the steam engine, telegraph, telephone and other modern inventions, arose out of a forgery of the early *Life* by Charles Hindley, in which he added many predictions. Hindley had confessed to the forgery in 1873, but not too many people had heard about his confession.

Muller Our murderer wore a low-crowned felt hat pulled down over his face in an attempt to disguise himself. But his scheme didn't work. Mr. Muller was arrested and convicted of murder, the publicity attending his hat making it more famous than the killer himself. Not only was Muller the prototype for countless real and fictional villains with large-brimmed hats pulled down over their eyes, but his name meant a deerstalker hat in England from about 1855 to 1885, a *muller* probably being the only hat in history that was named for a murderer.

Mulligan, Mulligan Stew When you're allowed to take a *Mulligan* in golf —a free shot not counted against the score after your first one goes bad— you're not emulating some duffer of days gone by. *Mulligan* probably comes from the brand name of a once popular sauce that was standard in barrooms. This potent seasoning of water and hot pepper seeds was sometimes mixed with beer and jokers swore that it ate out your liver, stomach and finally your *heart*—just what happens when you accept too many *mulligans* on the golf course.

Mulligan stew is made of meat and vegetables—whatever is available or can be begged or stolen. It is an American term, honoring an Irishman whose first name has been lost but who must have made a tasty Irish stew. *Mulligan*, popular among American tramps, is also called slumgullion or slum, the term coming into use during the American gold rush when slumgullion was originally the muddy residue remaining after sluicing gravel.

Mumbo Jumbo *Mama Dyumbo*, the explorer Mungo Park tells us in his *Travels in the Interior of Africa*, was the spirit or god protecting the villages of the Khassonke, a Mandingo African tribe on the Senegal. The words literally mean "ancestor with a pompom," or wearing a tuft on his hat. *Mama Dyumbo* was actually more a ploy used by crafty husbands to silence their noisy wives. He was called upon when one of a man's wives talked too much, causing dissension in his house. The husband or a confederate disguised himself as *Mama Dyumbo* and seized the troublemaker, frightening her with his mask, tufted headdress, and the hideous noises he made. He would then tie the offender to a tree and "whip her silent" amid the jeers of onlookers. Mungo Park called the bogy employed in this ritual *Mandingo*, but he became known as *Mumbo Jumbo*, a corruption of *Mama Dyumbo*. Because the god bewildered offending women *mumbo jumbo* came to mean confusing talk, nonsense, and meaningless ceremony, or even technical jargon that could be put into plain English. The *Mumbo Jumbo* custom recalls the ducking-stool procedure employed by our ancestors.

Munchausen, Munchausen Syndrome Baron Munchausen once shot a stag with a cherry stone and afterwards found the stag with a cherry tree growing out of its head. At least so Rudolph Erich Raspe wrote in his *Baron Munchausen's Narrative of his Marvellous Travels and Campaigns in Russia* (1785). Raspe was a German librarian who fled to England to escape the consequences of a jewel theft he had committed and wrote the very successful book to restore his resources. But he did base his character and many of his adventures on an actual Karl Friedrich Hieronymus, Freiherr von Münchausen (1720–97), a German officer who served in the Russian cavalry against the Turks and was known to grossly exaggerate his experiences. Raspe probably became acquainted with Baron Munchausen after the officer retired to his estates at Gottinger in 1760 and amused himself by matter-of-factly telling his friends his preposterous tales of his prowess as a sportsman and soldier. Thanks to Raspe's further exaggerations of his escapades in his one-shilling book, and many additions afterward in editions fathered by other authors, the real baron's name soon meant both a fantastic liar and a marvelous, classic lie. There is even a word *munchausenize*, meaning to tell a tale like Munchausen's and so great is the baron's fame that in 1936 the city of Bodenwerder, his birthplace, established a museum in his house. Doctors sometimes call a feigned illness the *Munchausen syndrome*.

Murcott Honey Orange (See *Temple orange*)

Murphy, Murphy Bed A *murphy* is a confidence game, originating in America, in which the victim is let in on "a good thing" and asked to put up evidence of his good faith in the form of cash. When he supplies the required amount, the con man pleads that he must leave somewhere quickly on business, but will return shortly, depositing the envelope containing the cash with his victim. Only when the mark opens the envelope later does he realize that paper cut to size has been substituted for his money. There are endless variations on the game, including the trick where a prostitute collects from a customer first and then goes out the back door. No one has identified the Murphy who first used this ruse to *murphy* someone. The same holds true for the *murphy* that is an Irish or white potato, named so because Murphy is a very common Irish name and potatoes, the English believed, were the staple food of the Irish diet. *Donovan* is also used by the English as slang for a white potato.

Murphy bed, on the other hand, can be positively identified. It is the space-saving bed, which can be folded or swung into a closet or cabinet, and is named after American inventor William Lawrence Murphy (1876–1950).

Musa The banana tree, really a giant herb whose collection of fruits or "fingers" forms the familiar banana "hand," was given the scientific name *Musa* by Linnaeus in honor of Antonio Musa, personal physician to Augustus, the first emperor of Rome (see *August*). Linnaeus writes that he honored Dr. Musa with both the genus *Musa*, comprising eighteen species, and the family *Musaceae*, containing five genera and 150 species. *Musa sapientum*, the most common banana tree species, takes its second name from the Latin word for "wise men," in reference to the sages of old who reposed in its shade and ate of its fruit. The banana is one of the oldest fruits known to man and among the first to be cultivated, our word *banana* of later African origin. As previously mentioned, the Koran says that the forbidden fruit was a banana, not an apple. Together with the plantain, a *Musa* species commonly called the cooking banana, the fruit is a staple foodstuff throughout the world. The most common eating variety today is the Cavendish (*Musa cavendishi*), a dwarf plant less resistant to disease and wind damage that was discovered in southern China in 1829 and named either for its discoverer or developer.

Mutt and Jeff We use this expression frequently to compare two friends or a loving couple, one short and one tall. The term is from the comic strip *Mutt and Jeff* created by Henry Conway (Bud) Fisher in 1907, but the little guy is named after former heavyweight champion James J. Jeffries. It happened when artist Fisher had Augustus Mutt, the tall, chinless member of the duo, visit a sanitarium in an early strip; there Mutt met a pleasant little inmate who fancied himself the boxing-great Jim Jeffries. Mutt dubbed him Jeff for this reason. Jeffries (1875–1953) was one of the few heavyweight champions to retire undefeated, but as Joe Louis was KO'd when he made a comeback so was Jeffries—by Jack Johnson in 1910.

Not many comic strip characters are known to be based on real persons, but quite a few have contributed words to the language. As fictional characters they are outside the scope of this book, but include: *Jeep*, a little animal in *Thimble Theatre* that became the word for the army vehicle; *Goon*, a strange creature in the same strip whose name is now a synonym for a strong-arm racketeer; and a host of characters like *Maggie* and *Jiggs*, *Popeye*, *Little Orphan Annie*, *Tarzan*, and *Dick Tracy* whose names are used to describe various characteristics.

N

Nabokov's Pug Just to indicate the thousands of specialized eponymous words that can't be included here, we might mention the butterfly *Nabokov's Pug*. It is named for the Russian-born author and lepidopterist Vladimir Nabokov (b. 1899), who, most specifically, discovered *Eupithecia nabokovi* McDonough "on a picture window of [publisher] James Laughlin's Alta Lodge in Utah" in 1943. We haven't attempted to trace *McDonough*. The prose stylist, author of *Mary, Invitation to a Beheading, Lolita, Pale Fire*, and many other novels, emigrated from Russia shortly after the Revolution, residing in the United States and Europe. Once a Harvard research fellow in lepidoptera, a number of his discoveries are named for him. "Butterfly" itself, incidentally, may be a *Spoonerism* for "flutter-by."

Namby-Pamby

Timely blossom, infant fair,
Fondling of a happy pair,
Every morn, and every night
Their solicitous delight,
Sleeping, waking, still at ease
Pleasing without skill to please.
Little gossip, blithe and hale,
Tattling many a broken tale.

Ambrose Philips (c. 1675–1749), a sample of his seven-syllabled lines on children quoted above, had the bad luck to accidentally tread on Alexander Pope, easily the most venomous and malicious of the great English poets. Politics and envy had more to do with his misfortune than insipid versifying, for Philips was a Whig and Pope a Tory, and in 1713 the Whig *Guardian* praised the Whig pastoral poet as the only worthy successor of Spenser. This inane criticism enraged "the Wasp of Twickenham" and initiated a quarrel between the two poets that Samuel Johnson described as a "perpetual reciprocation of malevolence." Pope was particularly incensed because *his* pastorals had appeared along with Philips' in *Tonson's Miscellanies* (1709) —he thought it obvious that he, if anyone, was Spenser's successor. The articles praising Philips in the *Guardian* implied a comparison with Pope's pastorals, being subtle veiled revenge on him because he had dedicated his poem *Windsor Forest* to Tory secretary for war George Granville. So Pope ingeniously submitted an anonymous article to the periodical that ostensibly attacked his own poems. In it, as Dr. Johnson observed in *The Lives of the Poets*, he drew a "comparison of Philips' performance with his own, in which, with an unexampled and unequalled artifice of irony, though he himself always has the advantage, he gives the preference to Philips." Pope ridiculed the *Guardian's* principles and disposed of Ambrose's pretentions in one bold stroke, but Philips was not to be deterred. Pope's rival continued to turn out his pastorals and even indited a few pieces to political powers like Sir Robert Walpole: "*Votary to public zeal, / Minister of England's weal / Have you leisure for a song, / Tripping lightly o'er the tongue, / Soft and sweet in every measure, / Tell me, Walpole, have you leisure?*" Such slavish deference won him coveted political appointments in Ireland, including a seat in Parliament there and a judgeship, not to mention Pope's further enmity. "Lo, Ambrose Philips is preferred for Wit," Pope sneered, and Ambrose in turn denounced him as an enemy of the government. But it was Philips' juvenile poems that did him most harm. He wrote several simple sentimental little poems (1725–26) for the infant children of his friends Lord John Carteret and Daniel Pulteney, including his *To Mistress Charlotte Pulteney*, quoted above. These adulatory verses were addressed "to all ages and characters, from Walpole steerer of the realm, to Miss Pulteney in the nursery," and if any further inspiration was necessary, may have inspired Pope to criticize Ambrose, among others, in his essay, "Martinus Scriblerus . . . or the Art of Sinking in Poetry" (1727). Pope scoffed that the verses were "little flams on Miss Carteret" and soon Pope's friend poet and composer Henry Carey joined in the fray. Carey, rumored author of the words and music of the British anthem *God Save the King*, satirized Ambrose in the same book that included his popular song, "Sally in our Alley," parodying Philips' juvenile poems and writing: "So the nurses get by heart Namby-pamby's little verses." The author of *Chrononhotonthologos*, a burlesque which he characterized as "the Most Tragical Tragedy that was ever Tragedized by any Company of Tragedians," even entitled his parody of Philips' *Namby-Pamby*, taking the *amby* in each word from the diminutive of Ambrose and the alliterative *P* in the last word from *Philips*. Pope, ready for the kill, seized upon the contemptuous nickname and included it in the edition of his enormously popular poem *The Dunciad* that appeared in 1733. The phrase immediately caught the public fancy and much to his distress, Ambrose Philips saw his name come to mean not only feeble, insipidly sentimental writing, but a wishy-washy, weakly indecisive person as well.

Philips wasn't really as bad as all that. In collaboration with his friend Swift he wrote *The Distrest Mother* (1712), a play taken from Racine, and certain of his poems have been included by anthologists as excellent examples of Augustan poetry, formal yet impassioned. As for his verses for children, several critics find them charmingly sentimental rather than saccharine or sickeningly sentimental, and Dr. Johnson, among others, says they are his pleasantest work. Some of Philips' poems are indeed flies in the amber of English verse, as one writer claims, but the man owes his enduring ignominy more to the almost unparalleled age of literary and political intrigue in which he lived and the childish love of intrigue and fame that characterized its great poet

Alexander Pope. Not bad at all are poems like Philips' *The First Pastoral*:

The flowers anew, returning seasons bring!
But beauty faded has no second spring. . . .

Yet the unlucky poet is remembered by the word taken from Carey's poem about him:

Namby-Pamby's doubly mild,
Once a man and twice a child . . .
Now he pumps his little wits
All by little tiny bits.

Nap, Napoleon, Code Napoleon, Napoleon Boots, Napoleon Brandy, Napoleonic, Napoleonic Wars, Napoleonize At seventeen, Napoleon Bonaparte proposed marriage to the illegitimate daughter of Louis XV and was turned down because he had "no future." His life, of course, is legend now, the "Man of Destiny," despite his glaring defects, one of the immortals, having changed the course of history in the comparatively short fifteen-year period during which he held sway. Well known is the small but imposing "Little Corporal"—his head so big when he was a child that he couldn't keep his balance. Even mannerisms like the hand inside the shirt are still remembered and joked about today. Hated and feared by some, loved and idolized by others—it is said that his troops burned the flags that he had kissed when he bade them farewell, and ate the ashes—the emperor's name is honored by words and expressions ranging from the *Code Napoleon* to *Napoleon brandy*. *Napoleonic* means resembling Napoleon I, the *Napoleonic Wars* those wars he waged principally against England, Prussia, Austria and Russia (1796–1815), and to *Napoleonize* is to govern or rule like Bonaparte. The emperor is also remembered by *Napoleon boots*, the French name for *Wellingtons*, which were similar to the top boots Napoleon wore; the *Napoleon*, a French twenty-franc gold piece commemorating him; and his name is a synonym for a master strategist and tactician. The *Code Napoleon* was the codification of laws Napoleon began which came to govern all countries under French rule and was the model for the state of Louisiana. But *napoleon pastries* were not named for him. A traditional story says he carried *napoleons* in his breast pocket when retreating from Moscow, a tale that persists despite the fact that *napoleon* in this case is simply a corruption of *Napolitain,* the pastries first made by Neopolitans in Italy.

Six years after his defeat in 1815 at Waterloo, Napoleon died of cancer at the age of fifty-two while imprisoned on the island of St. Helena. His body was brought back to Paris and enshrined in the Invalides in 1840. The emperor's nephew Napoleon III also figures prominently in history, several words bearing his name, too. The card game *Nap* recalls both emperors, being named for Napoleon III but using terms like *Wellington* and *Blucher* that recall his uncle's famous campaigns. (See also *Bonaparte Gull; Imperial Mustache; Lapageria.*)

Nasmyth Crater, Nasmyth's Membrane So many places on the moon are named for people that the satellite sometimes seems like a dumping ground for scientists who want to honor their worthy but often obscure favorites. The crater in the third quadrant of the moon called *Nasmyth* is an example, though its eponym is most deserving. It pays tribute to James Nasmyth (1808–90), a Scottish engineer who invented the steam hammer independently of Watt. Nasmyth, the son of artist Alexander Nasmyth, perfected a number of devices, including the *Nasmyth steam arm,* a planing machine. His hobby was astronomy and he wrote *The Moon Considered as a Planet, a World and a Satellite* with James Carpenter in 1874. Nasmyth advanced the theory that moon craters were caused by volcanic forces. His own crater is fifty-three miles in diameter.

Nasmyth's membrane, probably honoring a scientist of that name, is the anatomical term for the cutaneous covering of the teeth of a foetus—literally the skin of our teeth.

Nations Named After People Following is an incomplete but representative selection of nations named after individuals or groups of people that are not given under separate entries:

Belgium: the name honors the ancient Celtic settlers, the Belgae.

Bulgaria: named for the Turkic speaking Bulgars, who conquered the Slavs in the seventh century.

Burma: after the Burmese, a Mongoloid tribe from Tibet.

Finland: for the Finns, a tribe that had pushed out the earlier Lapps by the eighth century.

Liechtenstein: a principality created in 1719 by uniting the barony of Schellenburg and the county of Vaduz, both of which had been purchased by the Austrian family of Liechtenstein.

Philippines: the Spanish took control of the islands in 1571 and named them for Philip II of Spain.

San Marino: reputedly the world's oldest republic, San Marino is said to have been founded in the fourth century A.D. by Marinus, a Christian stonecutter who was later canonized as Saint Marinus or San Marino.

Saudi Arabia: named for the Arabian Saud family, the political unit dating from the eighteenth century.

Singapore: owned originally by the Sultan of Johore, who ceded it to the British in 1824.

Somalia: for the Somalis, a blend of Asian and African peoples.

Swaziland: named after the Swazi tribe, who settled there in 1820.

Sweden: for the Suiones, a native tribe that became dominant by the sixth century.

Thailand: after the Thai people, who moved southward from China in the eleventh century.

(See also *Cities; Pancake, Pa.; States.*)

Ned Kelly, As Game As Ned Kelly It cost nearly half a million dollars to finally capture Australia's Kelly gang, even though the band was only four in number. Ned Kelly (1854–80), the son of a transported Belfast convict and a convicted horse thief himself, took to the hills with his brother Daniel when the latter was charged with horse stealing. Joined by two other desperados, the brothers held up towns and robbed banks for two years until the police finally caught up with them. Ned Kelly became something of a folk hero and the great deprivations he suffered led to the phrase *as game as Ned Kelly.* When the gang was traced at last to a wooden shanty hideout, police riddled it with bullets, burned the shack down and found Ned Kelly alive and dressed in a suit of armor. He was tried, convicted and hanged for his crimes. Ned's colorful career was treated in the biography *The Last of the Bushrangers* (1892) by F. A. Hare.

Negus History tells us little about Colonel Francis Negus except that he lived in Queen Anne's reign and concocted the first *negus* known to be devised by man. A *negus* is brewed by mixing wine, usually port or sherry, with hot water, sugar, lemon juice and spices like nutmeg. Walpole and other writers have praised the hot drink, which warms a body up but can be perilously potent. Colonel Negus died in 1732 and ten years later people were commonly calling his bequest by his name.

Nelly Bly American journalist Elizabeth Cochrane Seaman (1867–1922) adopted the pen name Nelly Bly from a song by Stephen Foster. She is said to have taken it when an editor insisted that she use a pseudonym and an office boy happened to walk by whistling the tune. One of the first female reporters, Nelly Bly began her career when only eighteen. Her forte became exposés, such as her account in *Ten Days in a Madhouse* (1887) of the horrible conditions on New York's Blackwell's Island, where she was an inmate for ten days after feigning insanity. In 1889 the New York *World* sponsored her famous trip around the globe, which she completed in record time of seventy-two days, six hours and eleven minutes and which brought her international fame far exceeding that of any woman of her day. Flowers, trains and race horses were named for Nelly Bly and songs were written in her honor. Nelly later married millionaire manufacturer Robert L. Seaman, who at seventy-two was forty-four years her senior. When Seaman died, she became one of the country's leading women industrialists, but mismanagement forced her into bankruptcy. Though she went back to reporting, she found that her days of wine and roses were over. There were only memories left like the lines from the operetta *The Black Hussar:*

I wonder when they'll send a girl
To travel round the sky,
Read the answers in the stars,
They wait for Nelly Bly.

Nelson, Nelson's Blood The earliest wrestlers must have employed some form of the many variations on the full nelson, for scenes on the walls of the Egyptian tombs of Beni Hasan dating from 3000 B.C. or earlier depict practically all the wrestling holds and falls known today. But the term did not come into use until the nineteenth century, named either for some celebrated grappler who favored the pressure hold, or for *Nelson*, a town in Lancashire, England, once famous for its wrestling matches. The town of *Nelson* changed its name from Marston in the nineteenth century, calling itself after the *Lord Nelson Inn* there, which in turn honored Britain's greatest naval hero. So if the town *Nelson* is responsible for the hold, the hold can also be said to honor the great Horatio.

Lord Nelson's name definitely gives us the British slang expression *Nelson's blood*, or rum. Nelson was killed at the battle of Trafalgar in 1805 by a sniper firing from the top of the French ship *Redoubtable* and his body was brought back to England to be buried in St. Paul's Cathedral. The fabled hero, who had lost an eye in one sea battle and an arm in another, became the subject of many legends, including one claiming that his body was brought home pickled in rum. Needless to say, it wasn't long before British sailors were calling rum *Nelson's blood.*

Nero, Nero Antico, Nero's Crown Cruel, vindictive, dissolute, profligate, treacherous, tyrannical, murderous—it would take a far longer string of adjectives to describe Nero, the last of the Caesars. *Nero* means a bloody-minded tyrant for good reason. Among the Roman emperor's countless victims were the rightful heir to the throne, Britannicus—he poisoned him; his own mother Agrippina—he had her killed by his soldiers after failing to drown her in a specially constructed boat designed to fall to pieces in the water; his first wife Octavia; his pregnant second wife Poppaea—he is said to have kicked her to death; the son of his benefactor Lucan; and a woman who refused to marry him. Nero may well have set fire to Rome in 64 A.D. because he wanted to see what Troy looked like when it burned, although there is no trustworthy proof for the story. And that *Nero fiddled while Rome burned* is essentially true, though he probably sang and played the harp, not the fiddle, while regarding the spectacle with cynical detachment. The tyrant rebuilt Rome, including a grandiose "Golden House" for himself, blamed the blaze on the Christians and persecuted them with such fury that they regarded him as an Antichrist. (He is now believed to be the fantastic beast called 666 in *Revelation* 13:11–18.) St. Paul and St. Peter are said to have been among the martyred victims of the emperor's persecution. Nero, who was adopted into the family of Caesars by his stepfather Claudius (later poisoned by his mother), thought himself a great artist and seems to have had some talent for poetry, painting and singing. "What an artist dies in me!" were his last words. Fortunately, these came when he was only thirty-one, in 68 A.D., before he had a chance to do any more damage to man or property. The spindle-shanked, pot-bellied despot somehow found the courage to cut his throat when the Praetorian guard revolted against him and he heard that the Roman Senate had decreed his death. The memory of Nero Claudius Caesar Drusus Germanicus, born Lucius Domitius Ahenobarbus, was publicly execrated when he died.

Nero is also remembered by *nero antico*, a black marble found in the Roman ruins and later used for ornamental purposes; in *Neronize*, to rule, oppress or make depraved in the manner of Nero; and by *Nero's crown*, the grape jasmine. The word *colosseum* also owes something to him. An eleven-foot-high statue, or *colossus*, of him by Zenodorus stood near where the emperor Vespasian built the huge amphitheater called the Colosseum, the amphitheater taking its name from Nero's *colossus* and giving its name to *colosseum*.

Nestor There may have been a real King Nestor behind the character the poet Homer describes both in the *Iliad* and the *Odyssey*. Nestor, in Homeric legend, was the youngest of Neleus' twelve sons and the King of Pylos in Greece. At about seventy, he was the oldest and most experienced of the Greek chieftains besieging Troy, being represented as a wise and indulgent prince who lived so long that he ruled over three generations of subjects. Nestor counseled moderation among the quarreling Greek leaders. Full of wise advice and stories of his exploits in days gone by, his wisdom was revered, much sought after despite his prolixness. But the fact that Nestor talked too much was redeemed by the fact that he had a lot to talk about. He had been, for example, the only person spared when Hercules took Pylos. His name is frequently used today to describe a wise old man and *Nestor* does not imply that said sage is garrulous.

New Jersey Though it doesn't look like it at first glance, the state's name is another that has to be credited to the Caesars. *New Jersey* was named after *Jersey*, the largest of England's Channel Islands, in honor of Sir George Carteret, who had been governor of the Isle of Jersey and successfully defended it against Cromwell's forces. In 1664 Charles II had granted all lands between the Delaware River and Connecticut to his brother, the Duke of York, who in turn granted the *New Jersey* portion to Carteret and Lord Berkeley. England's Isle of *Jersey* (a corruption of *Caesaria*) had been named for the Caesars when the Romans added it to their possessions, and so *New Jersey* also bears the immortal name. The relationship can be best seen in *New Jersey's* official Latin name, *Nova Caesaria*.

New Jersey was first sighted in 1524 by Giovanni da Verrazano, for whom the *Verrazano Bridge* is named, but settlement began only after Henry Hudson's voyage in 1609. The state, once called "the cockpit of the Union" because so many important battles were fought there during the Revolution, is better known as the Garden State. (See also *Jersey; Caesar.*)

Newtonian Sir Isaac Newton (1642–1727) is perhaps the greatest figure in the history of science, yet he was essentially as modest and unassuming as Galileo before him and Einstein after him. "If I have seen a little farther than others," he once said, "it is because I have stood on the shoulders of giants." Newton's life and work are only being fully assessed by scholars today with the recent publication of his complete papers, but these will not likely diminish his reputation. Only the barest outline of his momentous discoveries can be attempted here, but they include the law of universal gravitation and the basic laws of motion, differential calculus, and important theories of light and color. The English philosopher and mathematician's name is recorded in many scientific words and expressions. A *Newton*, for example, is in physics a standard unit of force. *Newton's law of gravitation* and *Newton's law of motion* are laws in physics, while *Newtonian fluid* is a term used in hydrodynamics, and *Newton's method* a mathematical expression. There is also a reflecting *Newtonian telescope* and *Newton's rings* is a term used in optics. *Newtonian* generally means "pertaining to or arising from the theory of the universe propounded by Newton" and in this sense his name is most widely used. Everyone knows the story of the apple falling on Newton's head, Voltaire having first told the tale that the scientist began pondering the question of gravitation when he saw an apple fall in his garden. Less familiar, and perhaps even less reliable, is the story of his little dog Diamond. It seems that Diamond upset a candle on his master's papers one winter morning, setting on fire and destroying the results of many years' experiments. But Newton didn't turn the dog out in the cold. "Oh, Diamond, Diamond, thou little knowest the mischief done!" he is said to have exclaimed, sitting down at his desk and beginning all over. As for his modest opinion of himself, from Brewster's *Memoirs of Newton:* "I do not know what I may appear to the world, but to myself I seem to have been only a boy playing on the sea-shore, and diverting myself in now and then finding a smoother pebble or a prettier shell than ordinary, whilst the great ocean of truth lay all undiscovered before me."

New York As noted previously, James, Duke of York and Albany, was granted the patent to all lands between the Delaware River and Connecticut in 1664 by his older brother, King Charles II. The Duke of York gave the New Jersey portion away but held on to what was then the Dutch colony of New Netherland. York became the patron of Colonel Richard Nicholls, who that same year set sail for the New World with four ships and thirty soldiers, captured New Amsterdam from the Dutch governor Peter Stuyvesant and named both the city of New Amsterdam and the colony of New Netherland after the duke.

New York's capital, Albany, is also named for the Duke of York and Albany. The scene of fully a third of the battles fought during the Revolution, *New York State* was admitted to the union in 1788. George Washington was inaugurated in *New York City* the following year, the city serving as the country's capital from 1785–1790. The Empire State is *New York's* popular name, in reference to the belief that *New York* is the leading state of the Union—*New York* the Empire State of America just as Rome was that of the Roman Empire.

Nicotine $C_5H_4NC_4H_7NCH_3$, as the *nicotine* staining my writing fingers is scientifically described, is named for Jean Nicot, Lord of Villemain (c. 1530–1600), French ambassador in Lisbon in 1560 when Portuguese explorers were first bringing back tobacco seeds from the new continent of America. Nicot was given a tobacco plant from Florida, cultivated what is said to be the first tobacco raised in Europe and sent the fruits of his harvest to France's Queen Mother Catherine de Medici and other notables. After introducing what Catherine called the ambassador's powder (snuff) into France, the enterprising ambassador proceeded to grow a tobacco crop that he brought back to Paris and built a tidy fortune on. The "American powder" became so popular that the tobacco plant itself was called *nicotiana* after Nicot and Linnaeus later officially named the whole *Nicotiana* genus of the nightshade family in his honor, this group including the tobacco plant most commonly cultivated today, the species *Nicotiana rustica*. *Nicotine*, the oily liquid found in tobacco leaves, wasn't so named until 1819, when it was first isolated. Though not truly addictive, it is one of the most physiologically active drugs known, producing most of the observed effects of smoking. The alkaloid is poisonous to bugs as well as humans, used as an insecticide in agriculture.

M. Nicot's namesake was as controversial in his own time as it is today, the dispute over smoking raging strong even then. One old story tells of Sir Walter Raleigh's servant dousing him with a bucket of water when he saw him smoking. Others mention rulers who condemned to death and impaled all persons found indulging, and a Russian czar who decreed that the noses be cut off all smokers. The Jesuits recommended excommunication for the offense and the Swiss senate went so far as to include "Thou shalt not smoke" in one of the Ten Commandments. But enough people were already "addicted" and tobacco tax revenues already high enough to insure Jean Nicot's affluence. He could finally afford to turn his attentions to the articles he liked to write on the subject of philology and completed the earliest French dictionary, published posthumously in 1600. There is no record of the cause of his death that same year.

Nietzschean The philosophy of Friedrich Wilhelm Nietzsche, much distorted by the Nazis and other "supermen," did however champion the "morals of master men," especially in the philosopher's famous four-part work *Thus Spake Zarathustra* (1883–91). The son of a German pastor, Nietzsche was acidly antagonistic to humble and compassionate Christianity—a slave morality born of resentment, he thought. The philosopher denied the values of beauty, truth and goodness and asserted that man is perfectible through the will to power. Nietzsche did not claim that the Germans were a master race, as Nazi propagandists insisted, his doctrine of the *Übermensch*, or dominant men above good or evil, applying to no particular nationality. *Übermensch*, incidentally, means "overman" or "beyondman" in German, not "superman." George Bernard Shaw coined the latter word from Nietzsche's term when he wrote *Man and Superman* in 1903. Nietzsche, rejected and reviled by his contemporaries,

died insane in 1891, eleven years after suffering a physical and mental collapse that prevented him from doing more work. He was fifty-six years old. It is interesting to note that the philosopher criticized anti-Semitism and many other tendencies that led to Nazism. Few other men have had so strong an influence on twentieth-century thought.

Nightingale Florence Nightingale, the first and greatest of war nurses, is generally considered to be the founder of modern nursing. Born in the Italian city for which she was named, "the Lady with the Lamp" spent her childhood in England. At seventeen, she is said to have heard the voice of God calling her to service and several years afterwards she decided that she was meant to be a nurse. Despite the objections of her wealthy parents, she embarked upon a career in public health, in spite of the fact that nursing at the time was a disreputable profession filled with drunken prostitutes and worse. World fame came to her when she and thirty-eight other nurses offered their services to the British army in the Crimean War (1854), taking over a badly run military hospital in what is now Scutari and reducing the death rate from 42 percent to 2 percent. Overcoming the initial suspicion of the troops, sometimes working as long as twenty hours a day, she became venerated as the Lady with the Lamp because she unfailingly made rounds of the wards each night to check on her patients. Returning to England on a special man-of-war sent by the government, she refused all public honors for her work, but used a fifty-thousand-pound fund raised in recognition of her services to establish the Nightingale training school for nurses at St. Thomas's Hospital in July, 1860. This date marked the beginning of modern, scientific nursing. Despite her poor health, Florence Nightingale remained England's leading authority on public, private and military nursing and sanitation almost all her life, her work in public health international in scope. The first woman to be awarded the British Order of Merit (1907), she received many honors in her lifetime, among the least of which was the single-piece hospital jacket named after her. It was her wish that she not be interred with honors in Westminster Abbey. When the Lady with the Lamp died on August 13, 1910, aged ninety. she was buried in the family plot in a small country churchyard in Hampshire, the service private except for the six British soldiers who carried her coffin to the grave.

Nimrod Unlike most other names mentioned in *Genesis*, Nimrod is that of an individual. In the Bible Nimrod is the son of Cush and the founder of Babel. He may have been an Assyrian king who built the city of Nineveh, the capital of the Assyrian empire. According to scripture, Nimrod was "a mighty hunter before the Lord" (*Genesis* 10:8–10), and historians tell us that the Assyrian kings were noted for their prowess in hunting. Aramaic translations of the Old Testament say "that mighty hunter before the Lord" means sinful hunting of the sons of men, which accounts for Pope's and Milton's description of Nimrod as "a mighty hunter, and his prey was man." But a *Nimrod* is more generally the nickname for a great, daring and skillful hunter, or even sportsman. There is a legend that the real Nimrod's tomb is in Damascus and that rain never falls upon it.

Nobelium "The day when two army corps will be able to destroy each other in one second," Alfred Nobel predicted, "all civilized nations will recoil away from war in horror and disband their armies." The Swedish inventor of dynamite proved to be wrong in his prophecy, which may have been a rationalization for his invention, but the $9,200,000 he left in his will to set up the *Nobel Prize Foundation* has greatly aided the cause of peace. *Nobel Prizes* are awarded to persons, irrespective of nationality, who have done outstanding work in the five fields Nobel considered most important to the benefit of mankind: Physics, Chemistry, Medicine and Physiology, Literature, and Peace. The prizes, given in Stockholm and Oslo on December tenth of each year in which awards are made, consist of about forty thousand dollars, a diploma and a gold medal. The first ceremony was held in 1901.

Alfred Bernhard Nobel, who suffered ill health all his life—"[My] miserable existence should have been terminated at birth by a humane doctor"—died in 1896, aged sixty-three. He was a lonely, brooding man, well aware of the military uses of his inventions, and guilt probably partly accounted for his humanitarian actions. But his invention of dynamite, a safe explosive, was undertaken to save lives, his experiments beginning when his younger brother was killed in the family munitions factory by an explosion of highly unstable nitroglycerin. Nobel created dynamite in 1867 by combining nitroglycerin with the inert powder kieselguhr. He invented blasting gelatin in 1875 and the first smokeless powder, ballistite, three years later. These inventions were revolutionary at the time, the inventor setting up factories to manufacture his explosives in many countries and making an immense fortune.

Nobel is also commemorated by *nobelium*, an artificially produced radioactive element discovered in 1957 by an international team of scientists from the United States, Britain and Sweden. *Nobelium* was specifically named after the *Nobel Institute* where it was first produced.

Norfolk Howard On June 26, 1862, Joshua Bug of Norfolk ran an ad in the London *Times* announcing that he would henceforth be known as Norfolk Howard, this being one of England's most aristocratic names. His countrymen soon foiled the poor man's grandiose plans, however, adopting *Norfolk Howard* as a slang synonym for bedbug. The unfortunate Mr. Bug had made his metamorphosis "to avoid the opinion of baseness," as one writer puts it, but changed into something worse, falling prey to the British sense of humor so many say doesn't exist. Ironically enough, *bug* means warrior or hero in old English.

Other notable name changes in history include C. J. Crook to C. J. Noble; W. Jones, unaccountably changed to W. Smith in 1798; and Antoni Przybsy, changed to Clinton Przybsy in Detroit in 1940. An interesting one I have never seen recorded is that of a largely neglected avant-garde artist in New York's Greenwich Village. Fred Mowlugubgub changed his name from a more prosaic specimen, claiming that in choosing his new patronym he honored a drowned ancestor (*gub, gub*). The pope who began the custom of pope's taking a new name on accession was Cardinal Grugno in 1009. The cardinal had a good reason for adopting the name Sergius IV, Grugno meaning swinesnout.

North Carolina, South Carolina Both states really honor three kings—deriving from the Latin *Carolus*, meaning Charles. Originally dedicated to France's Charles XI in the sixteenth century, the territory now comprising *North* and *South Carolina* was next named for England's Charles I. Charles I granted the patent for the *Carolinas* to Sir Robert Heath in 1629, Heath calling the territory *Carolana* in his honor. This it remained until 1663, when Charles II granted a new patent and the colony was called *Carolina* in *his* honor.

Roanoke Island, off what is now the coast of *North Carolina*, marked the site of the first English settlement in the New World (1585) and was the birthplace of the first English child born in America, Virginia Dare (b. August 18, 1587). *North Carolina's* popular name is the Tar Heel State, while *South Carolina* is commonly called the Palmetto State. Both were among the original thirteen states admitted to the Union, *South Carolina* the first to secede from the Union shortly before the Civil War and *North Carolina* the last.

There is a story that says John Wilmot, Earl of Rochester, wrote the following rhyme on the bedchamber door of Charles II:

Here lies a great and mighty king,
Whose promise none relies on;
He never said a foolish thing,
Nor ever did a wise one.

To which Charles replied: "This is very true—for my words are my own, and my actions are my ministers'."

Nosey Parker Matthew Parker, who became Archbishop of Canterbury in 1559, acquired a reputation for poking his nose into other people's business. Actually, he was an intelligent, if somewhat overzealous, churchman of marked Protestant persuasion who introduced many administrative and ceremonial reforms into the Anglican church. His reputation is largely undeserved, but Catholics and Puritans alike resented his good works, taking advantage of his rather long nose and dubbing him *Nosey Parker*, which has meant an unduly inquisitive person ever since. Parker had been chaplain to Anne Boleyn and Henry VIII before becoming archbishop. A scholar of some note, he died in 1575, aged seventy-one.

The above, at least, is the most popular folk-etymology for *Nosey Parker*. But other candidates have been proposed. Richard Parker, leader of the Sheerness Mutiny in 1797, is one strong contender. This Parker poked his nose so deeply into what the military thought their exclusive bailiwick that he wound up hanged from the yardarm of H.M.S. *Sandwich* on July thirtieth of that year.

Nostradamus The *Centuries* of Nostradamus, a book of rhymed prophecies, was published in 1555. The French doctor and astrologer gained a reputation as a seer when some of his predictions came true and as a result won an appointment as personal physician to Charles IX. His real name was Michel de Nostredame, his book, divided into centuries, drawn from the whole body of medieval prophetic literature. Nostradamus was sixty-three when he died in 1566. The Papal Court condemned his prophecies in 1781, but they have enjoyed wide attention since on a number of occasions, one generation or another applying them to contemporary situations. Detractors claim that the prophecies are so ambiguously worded that they could mean anything, and when *Nostradamus* is used for a seer or prophet it is generally employed in a contemptuous sense. (See also *Mother Shipton*.)

O

Obsidian *Obsidian* is a glasslike rock of volcanic origin formed by the rapid cooling of lava on the earth's surface. Usually it is a bright, glossy black, but some examples are gray, green, brown or red, ranging from opaque to translucent. Usually sharpedged, the rock was often used for arrows and other weapons by the ancients. Pliny the Elder tells us in his *Natural History* that *obsidian* was named for its discoverer Obsius, who first found it in Ethiopia. In early editions of his work Pliny's *obsianus* for the mineral was misprinted as *obsidianus*, this explaining the mysterious "d" in the word. If Pliny is right, *obsidian* is probably the earliest mineral honoring its discoverer.

Occam's Razor *Occam's razor*, the philosophic principle of economy or parsimony, holds that universal essences should not be unnecessarily multiplied, which means simply that a scientific explanation should contain only those elements absolutely necessary, that all superfluous facts must be eliminated. The axiom is named for William of Occam (c. 1280–1349), an English philosopher and Franciscan who dissected every question as with a razor. Occam was a pupil of Duns Scotus (see *Dunce*). The Invincible Doctor, as he was called, so formidable was he in debate, opposed Pope John XXII over a question of monastic poverty, which led to his imprisonment and excommunication. He later joined emperor Louis of Bavaria and the Franciscans in their opposition to Pope John, continuing to teach his nominalist doctrines. Occam became general of the Franciscan order and his philosophy helped pave the way for pragmatic Renaissance science. He and his followers held that the existence of God and immortality are not capable of philosophical proof and must be accepted on faith alone. His name comes from the town of Ockham in Surrey, where he was probably born, and he is sometimes called William Ockham.

Oersted The Danish physicist and chemist Hans Christian Oersted (1777–1851) founded the science of electromagnetism when he discovered that direct electric current causes a magnetic needle to take a position at right angles to the wire carrying it. This basic fact of electromagnetic induction was the starting point for all future work in the field. Unlike many scientific discoveries, the Copenhagen professor's attracted immediate and widespread attention when he published a Latin monograph describing it in July 1820, about a year after his discovery. In 1825 Oersted added to his laurels by becoming the first experimenter to isolate aluminum. The scientist's name in Danish is actually Orsted, but this has become anglicized to Oersted. The *oersted* honoring him is a unit of magnetic field intensity and his name has also been given to a walled plain in the first quadrant of the face of the moon.

O. Henry Ending O. Henry was the penname of American writer William Sydney Porter. Born in North Carolina, Porter went to Texas as a young man to seek his fortune. After trying several occupations, including journalism, he became a bank teller in Houston, where he was indicted for embezzlement in 1896. Only a small sum had been involved, Porter's crime more one of mismanagement than theft, but he fled the country to South America. When he returned to his dying wife several years later, he was imprisoned, serving a three-year sentence. It was in prison that the author began writing and selling the stories which would make him famous, adopting the pseudonym O. Henry to conceal his real identity. On his release in 1902 he journeyed to New York to pursue a literary career. An immensely prolific author, O. Henry's tales are characterized by ironic, surprise endings, "twists" or "snappers" often dependent upon coincidence but always ingenious. Only forty-eight when he died in 1910, "the American Maupassant" published at least fifteen books of short stories, including such perennial favorites as the "Gift of the Magi" and "The Furnished Room"; his O. *Henry endings* long served as the model for popular magazine fiction. O. Henry suffered from hypoglycemia, or hyperinsulinism, the opposite of diabetes, his classic summary of the condition being "I was born eight drinks below par." The author's famous last words, quoting a popular song, were "Turn up the lights, I don't want to go home in the dark."

Ohm, Ohm's Law Unlike his contemporary Oersted, German scientist Georg Simon Ohm (1787–1854) was so poorly treated by fellow scientists that he protested by resigning his post as professor of mathematics at the Jesuits' college in Cologne. In 1827 the physicist had published a pamphlet including what is now known as *Ohm's Law*. His study of electric currents eventually became the basic law of current electricity, but was coldly received at the time. Ohm may have thought of becoming a locksmith like several generations of his family before him, but despite his humiliations he hung in there. About ten years later, the importance of his work began to be realized and in 1841 he was awarded the Copley medal of the British Royal Society. It is said that none of Ohm's work before or after his pamphlet is of the first order, this perhaps a reason for his initial rejection. He does appear to have been something of a scientific politician, having sent copies of his first book to all the monarchs of Germany in order to obtain his first teaching position. It was in 1893 that the International Electrical Congress adopted his name for the *ohm*, a unit of electrical resistance. For the *ohm's* unusual antonym see *mho*.

O.K. Most word authorities believe that *O.K.* comes from the nickname of Martin Van Buren (1782–1862), who rose from potboy in a tavern to president of the United States. A colorful character (as vice-president he presided over the Senate with dueling pistols on his desk), Van Buren was elected president in 1836. He became an eponym, however, during the campaign of 1840, when he ran for re-election in a tight race against "Tippecanoe and Tyler, too," General William Henry Harrison, legendary hero who fought against the Indians at Tippecanoe, and Virginian John Tyler.

The election of 1840 had brought with it the first modern political campaign—mostly to President Van Buren's disadvantage. One popular advertising stunt was "to keep the ball rolling" for Harrison: ten foot "victory-balls," made of tin and leather and imprinted with the candidate's name, were rolled from city to city for as far as three hundred miles. Harrison's followers, trying to identify Van Buren with the aristocracy, christened the general the "log cabin and hard cider candidate," and tagged Van Buren "Little Van the Used Up Man," "King Martin the First," "The Enchanter," "The Red Fox," "The Kinderhook Fox," the "Little Magician," and several other of the derogatory nicknames he had earned over the years. But "Old Kinderhook," a title bestowed upon the president from the name of his birthplace in Kinderhook, N.Y., sounded better to his supporters, better even than "the Sage, Magician, or Wizard of Kinderhook." In order to stem the tide somewhat a group in New York formed the Democratic O.K. Club, taking their initials from "Old Kinderhook." These mystifying initials, appealing to man's love of being on the inside of events, became a sort of rallying cry for the Democrats, one contemporary newspaper account reporting how "about 500 stout, strapping men" of the O.K. Club marched to break up a rival Whig meeting where "they passed the word O.K. . . . from mouth to mouth, a cheer was given, and they rushed into the hall like a torrent." The mysterious battle cry spread rapidly and soon acquired the meaning "all right, all correct," probably because "Old Kinderhook" or O.K. was all right, all correct to his supporters. But neither mystification, ruffians nor new words did Van Buren any good, for voters remembered the Panic of 1837 and he was defeated in his bid for re-election. Not that victory was any blessing to Harrison; the old general contracted pneumonia on the day of his inauguration and died shortly thereafter.

Scores of interesting theories had been offered on the origin of O.K. before Columbia Professor Allen Walker Read supposedly laid the ghost to rest with his *Saturday Review* article (July 19, 1941), tracing the word to the President who was *O.K.* Most etymologists accept Read's explanation, but fail to mention that he has made an important qualification. Read has established an earlier date than the campaign of 1840 for the first use of O.K. He has shown that the expression was used in the Boston *Morning Post*, March 23, 1839, in the same sense —all correct—by editor Charles Gordon Greene, but claims that the word got a second *independent* start in the 1840 campaign and really owes its popularity to Old Kinderhook's candidacy. No earlier reliable date than Read's for the use of O.K. has been found, and so the matter is apparently settled for all time— although another scholar has recently come up with an entirely different explanation that etymologists are still debating. It will prove difficult, however, to take the vogue for O.K. away from President Van Buren. And the word honoring his name is undoubtedly the best known of American expressions. International in use and what H. L. Mencken calls "the most shining and successful Americanism ever invented," O.K. does service as almost any part of speech. Surprisingly, the effort to give it an antonym (*nokay*) has failed, but the expression A-O.K. has gained currency from the space flights, and the older *oke-doke*, from an abbreviation of one of its forms, *okey*, is still commonly heard in everyday speech. O.K. is used more often than *salud* in Spain, has displaced the English *right-o*, is spelled *O-ke* in the Djabo dialect of Liberia. The most universally used of all human words in any language since World War II, it is inscribed everywhere, from the town of *Okay*, Okla., to the pieces of equipment marked with *O.K.s* that are no doubt on the moon. But the useful little word may become even smaller and more useful. To this writer it sounds like *k* with more frequency every year and perhaps someday that will be the spelling.

Okies Overplanting and overgrazing combined with the drought and dust storms to make Oklahoma a part of the Dust Bowl in the depression days of the 1930's. Many tenant farmers were forced to leave their arid farms and go west, mostly to California, in seeking employment as migrant laborers. These Oklahoma migrants were called *Okies*, as were refugees from Texas and other Dust Bowl states. Their plight is the theme of John Steinbeck's novel *The Grapes of Wrath* (1939).

Oklahoma (see *States*)

Oliver, Oliver's Skull Oliver Cromwell's name "fairly stank" to the Royalists (see *Cromwell*), which is why they dubbed their chamber pots *Oliver's skulls*. The term was popular slang in England from 1690 to 1820 and puts Cromwell in the select company of the relatively small handful of people who have been discommoded by commodes. On the other hand, Cromwell's *supporters* so admired the way he hammered at the Royalists that the *oliver*, a small smith's hammer, was probably named after him. Whether the British underworld term *oliver* for the full moon is a compliment or an insult is uncertain, but it definitely arises from the fact that Oliver Cromwell led the *Roundheads*. (See also *Crapper; Fontange; Furphy; Sacheverell; Twiss*.)

Onanism "*Then Judah said to Onan, 'Go in to your brother's wife, and perform the duty of a brother-in-law to her, and raise up offspring for your brother.' But Onan knew that the offspring would not be his; so when he went in to his brother's wife he spilled the semen on the ground, lest he should give offspring to his brother. And what he did was displeasing in the sight of the Lord, and he slew him also.*" This passage from the Revised Standard Version of the Bible (*Genesis* 38:8–11) shows what scholars have long told us, that Onan was not a habitual masturbator as the word *onanism* suggests. It is not even clear from the Biblical passage whether Onan's one such mentioned act was masturbation or *coitus interruptus*, and many Biblical scholars tell us that his real sin was not *onanism* but his refusal to take the childless Tamar to bed, get her with child and rear their offspring as the son of his dead brother in accordance with the law of the levirate marriage. Psychiatrists, of course, regard anything but excessive masturbation as normal. Theologians range in their opinions from fire and brimstone condemnation to the paraphrase of Gertrude Stein made by a respected liberal clergyman, William Graham Cole, that "an orgasm is an orgasm is an orgasm."

One for Ripley "Believe It or Not!" first appeared in book form in 1928, when the newspaper syndicated cartoon feature was already an American and international favorite bringing its creator fame and riches. California-born cartoonist Robert Leroy Ripley (1893–1949) traveled widely to collect bits of odd information for his series, books and radio program, but much of the material was library researched. His name became as well known as "Believe It or Not" itself, the phrase *One for Ripley* used to describe any strange, almost unbelievable fact or happening. Ripley's series is still run in newspapers today, along with a host of imitators. There was a Ripley "Odditorium" at the Chicago World's Fair of 1933–34 and today there are "Believe It or Not" wax museums in seven locations throughout the United States and England. The famous one on Broadway in New York closed its doors late in 1971. The series has pointed out some interesting word facts. For example, the surname Johnson is so common in Minnesota that one local office seeker didn't bother to offer a platform or campaign—by merely announcing that his name was Johnson he polled 44,029 votes out of 151,686 cast. *One for Ripley.*

Oregon (see *States*)

Orrery All planetariums can trace their ancestry to the first *orrery*, invented in about 1700 by George Graham. This complicated mechanical device showed the movements of the planets and satellites around the sun by means of rotating and revolving balls. Graham sent his model to instrument maker John Rowley, who made a copy that he presented to his patron Charles Boyle (1676–1731), fourth earl of Orrery, the apparatus

named in the earl's honor. Orrery, who used the device to educate his children, was a noted patron of science and one of his ancestors was the physicist Robert Boyle. But the British author and soldier is satirized in Swift's famous *Battle of the Books* (1697) for his trivial quarrel with Richard Bentley over modern and ancient scholarship.

Oscar, Wildean Hollywood's gold-plated Oscars remained nameless four years after the Academy of Motion Picture Arts and Sciences first gave the awards in 1927. Called simply The Statuette, the ten-inch-high trophy was designed by Cedric Gibbons, each weighing about seven pounds, bronze on the inside, and originally costing about one hundred dollars. The statuette quickly became a symbol of film fame, but it wasn't until 1931 that it got a name. At that time Mrs. Margaret Herrick reported to work as librarian of the Academy and when shown one of the trophies, observed, "He reminds me of my Uncle Oscar." As fate would have it, a newspaper columnist happened to be in the room when she made her remark and he soon reported to his readers that "Employees of the Academy have affectionately dubbed their famous statuette 'Oscar.'" The name stuck and Mrs. Herrick's uncle won immortality. Uncle Oscar was in reality Oscar Pierce, a wealthy Texan from a pioneer family who had made his fortune in wheat and fruit and migrated to California, where he could now bask in glory as well as the sun. The *Oscars* honoring him are today given annually in twenty-three categories, the seven most widely known being best motion picture, best leading actor and actress, best supporting actor and actress, best direction, and best screenplay. Cedric Gibbons, the Oscar's designer, received six *Oscars* for best art director.

Another famous Oscar is the Australian Oscar Asche (1872–1936), a musical comedy star who made a tidy fortune on the stage and whose full name became Australian rhyming slang for cash. *Oscar Asche* for cash was eventually shortened to *Oscar*, making him the only man whose prenom means money in a generic sense. A third Oscar to make the dictionaries is the British writer and wit Oscar Wilde (1854–1900). His much publicized affairs and trial made his first name a British slang expression for a homosexual, *to Oscar*, *Oscarizing* and *Oscar-Wilding*, in fact, meaning active homosexuality.

Wilde is also represented by *Wildean*, referring to his razor-sharp wit. In this respect he was probably even greater than George Bernard Shaw (see *Shavian wit*). Once Wilde told a customs inspector that he had nothing to declare but his genius; another time he remarked to some proud chamber of commerce types that Niagara Falls "would be more spectacular if it flowed the other way." But Wilde could be put down, too. When he confided to James Whistler that he wished he had made a certain clever remark, the artist replied, "You will, Oscar, you will." It wasn't long before Wilde got even though. "As for borrowing Mr. Whistler's ideas . . ." he soon wrote, "the only thoroughly original ideas I have ever heard him express have had reference to his own superiority as a painter over painters greater than himself."

Oslerize   To kill all men over forty was commonly thought to be the plan of Canadian-born Sir William Osler (1849–1919). Professor Osler taught at McGill University, the University of Pennsylvania, and Johns Hopkins, later becoming a regius professor at Oxford. One of the most influential teachers and clinicians of his time, he founded the *Quarterly Journal of Medicine* and his renowned textbook *Principles and Practices of Medicine* (1891) has gone into a score of editions. Osler also made valuable researches into diseases of the spleen and blood, among many maladies, was an eminent medical historian, and served as curator of the Bodleian library. The physician enraged more than half of the population when a plan of his was interpreted as meaning that all men over forty should be put to death as useless. Sir William's scheme actually provided for retirement at sixty on a generous pension, but the misconception prevailed and from 1905 on *to oslerize* meant just the opposite of "life begins at forty." This prospect makes the present-day

maxim "don't trust anyone over thirty" seem kindly. Osler's frequently misquoted statement had been made at an address at Johns Hopkins University in February, 1905. What he really referred to was: "The uselessness of men above sixty years of age, and the incalculable benefit it would be in commercial, political and in professional life if, as a matter of course, men stopped work at sixty." It is interesting to note that Dr. Osler made some of his most valuable scientific contributions *after* he turned sixty, his date for compulsory retirement.

Ottoman, Osmanli   Osman I (1259–1326) would not appreciate the fact that many readers are resting their feet on him, or his namesake, while reading this. But the *ottoman*, a stuffed footstool more often called a hassock, its Old English designation, is definitely named for him. Osman, sometimes called Othman, led his Moslem followers farther west from Asia Minor in the late thirteenth century to found the *Ottoman Empire*, principally what we know as Turkey today. Tales of this great empire, which lasted until its dissolution in 1918, excited the imagination of Europeans and toward the end of the eighteenth century merchants saw that there was a ready market in Europe for items of eastern luxury, for the carpets, pillows and divans of delight that people imagined sultans lounged upon in their luxurious harems. These included a small, backless couch for two that the French called the *ottoman* because they imported it from the *Ottoman Empire*, ignoring its Turkish name. The couch or divan eventually became both the overstuffed English *ottoman sofa*, acquiring a back in the process, and, in a much smaller form, the *ottoman footstool*. Sultan Osman I would undoubtedly be prouder that the Turks call themselves *Osmanli* in his honor. (See also *Turk*.)

Oysters Kirkpatrick   *Oysters Rockefeller's* closest rival was named in honor of James C. Kirkpatrick, manager of San Francisco's Palace Hotel in the late nineteenth century. *Oysters Kirkpatrick* shares its fame with Green Goddess dressing and Strawberries Romanoff, also invented in the Palace's kitchen. The

Palace Hotel, born during the Gold Rush, destroyed in the fire and rebuilt to become one of America's greatest eating places, offers the following simple original recipe for the delectable dish: "Open oysters on deep shell, put in oven for about 3 or 4 minutes until oysters shrink. Pour off the liquor, then add small strip of bacon and cover with catsup and place in very hot oven for about 5 or 6 minutes (according to oven) until glazed to a nice golden brown." (See also *Rockefeller*.)

Ozarks The *Ozark mountains* in Missouri, Arkansas and Oklahoma, ranging up to 2,300 miles high, cover an area of 50,000 square miles, noted more for their beautiful scenery and mineral springs, which make them a resort area, than their rich deposits of lead and zinc. The *Ozarks* are named for a local band of Quapaw Indians that resided in the Missouri and Arkansas region of the mountains. "The French were in the habit of shortening the long Indian names by using only their first syllables," an article in the St. Louis *Globe-Democrat* explains. "There are frequent references in their records to hunting or trading expeditions 'aux Kans,' or 'aux Os,' or 'aux Arcs,' meaning 'up into' the territory of the Kansas, Osage, or Arkansas tribes." This *aux Arcs* seems to be the more likely explanation for *Ozarks*, although the local Arkansas band may have been named from the French *aux Arcs* meaning "with bows," which could also have been corrupted to *Ozarks* and later applied to the mountains where the Indians lived. Missouri was once called the "Ozark State." The *Ozarkian language* is the dialect of *Ozark* mountaineers, including many old English and Scottish expressions.

P

Pamphlet *Pamphilus, seu de Amore* was the title of an erotic love poem of the twelfth century, nothing known about its author Pamphilus except his name in the title. No more than a few pages in length, the Latin verses became very popular during the Middle Ages, the best-known love poem of its time. Just as the small book containing *Aesop's Fables* came to be familiarly called *Esopet* in French, the little poem became known as *Pamphilet*, the English spelling this *Pamflet*, and eventually *Pamphlet*. By the fourteenth century any small booklet was called a *pamphlet* and within another three hundred years the word had acquired its sense of "a small polemical brochure," the transition completed from sensuous love poem to political tract. Generally, a *pamphlet* is defined as a paper-bound or unbound booklet of less than one hundred pages. *Pamphleteers* employed them especially well during the eighteenth century, notable practitioners including Milton, Burke, Defoe and Swift.

Pancake, Pa., and Other Eponymous Places Fully half of the states, not to mention the District of Columbia, are named after famous men or Indian tribes that once inhabited the areas. These are found under the appropriate entries, as are the names of other important or interesting places, but there is no room here to include the wealth of small towns, hamlets, mountains, molehills, rivers and brooks that bear people's names. Some are unusual to say the least. Pancake, Pa., for example, honors not some breakfast food dynasty, as you might think, but early settler George Pancake. Contrary to all expectations, Conifer, Colo., is named for roadhouse keeper George Conifer, not a tree, and Famous Hills, still unrecorded in most atlases, was never famous, taking its name from one L. G. Famous. Then there is Mesmerizer Creek, Tex., honoring a settler on its banks who tried to domesticate the American bison by hypnosis, and Elmira, N.Y., named, legend tells us, for a little girl whose mother called her home so frequently and stridently that fellow citizens immortalized her. For these and many more fascinating stories, consult George R. Stewart's *American Place-Names* (Oxford), a new dictionary that complements his excellent *Names on the Land*.

Pants, Panties, Pantywaist Poor St. Pantaleone, who should be hailed for his virtue and courage, is usually remembered only by men's *pants*, ladies' *panties* and a word meaning sissy. St. Pantaleone, tradition tells us, came from Nicomedia in Asia Minor, his name meaning, depending on the original spelling, either "all lion" or "all compassionate." He was both of these. A Christian doctor and personal physician to Emperor Galerius Maximianus, San Pantaleone treated the poor without charge. The fame of the "Holy Moneyless One" probably inspired other jealous physicians to report him to Maximianus' co-ruler the Emperor Diocletian, who was then busily occupied persecuting Christians. Condemned to death in 305, San Pantaleone miraculously survived six attempts to kill him—his hapless executioners trying liquid lead, burning, drowning, wild beasts, the wheel and the sword before finally beheading him successfully. The Greek saint's story was a favorite one in Venice, where he became both the patron saint of doctors and a martyr especially revered by the Venetians, his name all the more popular because so many boys were baptized in his honor. Probably for this reason, and because it was comical to call a foolish character all lion, the saint's name attached itself to the buffoon in the fifteenth century Italian *commedia dell' arte*. The "amorous" Pantaleone was always played by an emaciated bespectacled old man wearing slippers, one-piece, skintight breeches, and stockings that bloused out above the knees. Strolling bands of players performed variations of the comedy featuring the "seedy, needy" dotard throughout Europe and both his name and the name of the trousers he wore became *pantaloon* in England by the late 1600's. In time *pantaloons* was used as a designation for trousers in general, the word shortened to *pants* when a new style, tight fitting from the thighs to the ankle, was introduced to America in the early eighteenth century. *Pants* persisted in America, ever after applied to all changes in styles and always preferred by most Americans to the *trousers* purists have insisted upon. The word *pants* is even used for women's undergarments, though its more feminine form *panties* generally describes these.

What with the miniskirts and tights popular today, women are wearing a costume very similar in silhouette to that of the stage pantaloon of the fifteenth century. As for *pantywaist*, a sissy or effeminate boy, it goes back to the 1890's, deriving from the name of a sleeveless underwaist that a little girl's *panties* were attached to, but which boys were sometimes made to wear. Which made the brave St. Pantaleone's humiliation as complete as theirs.

Pap Test Women should be more familiar with this simple, painless test, which can detect cancer of the womb in its early stages, enabling it to be treated before it is too late. Best known as the *Pap test*, although the more accurate *Papanicolaou's stain* and *Pap smear* are also used, the procedure involves no more than the insertion of a small wooden spatula into the vagina to remove fluid mixed with uterine cells. This fluid is then dyed, spread on a glass slide and examined under the microscope. Few people know that Greek-born American physician George Nicholas Papanicolaou (1883–1962) invented the *Pap test*, his rather difficult name corrupted to the shortened form and obscuring the fame he so richly deserves. *Pap smears* can be taken of respiratory, digestive and genitourinary secretions, too, cancer detected by examining the normally shed cells from these areas.

Pariah The Indian class called the *Paraiyar* in Tamil are not outcasts at all. The *Paraiyar* were forced into menial positions with the Aryan invasion some two thousand years before Christ and form one of the lower castes in southern India, but, although they are regarded as "untouchables" by the Brahmans, they are not the lowest Hindu caste. Their name derives from *parai*, a large drum, for their duty was to beat the drum at certain religious festivals. Eventually the *Paraiyars* became field workers in the Tamil country of Madras; however, when the British came to India they employed most of their household servants from that class, whose name they corrupted to *Pariah*. Believing that they were the lowest caste or had no caste at all, many British and other Europeans began to use *pariah* as a word for the lowest of the low, an utter social outcast among his own kind—unjustly degrading the *Paraiyars* in language just as their countrymen degraded them in life.

Parkinson's and Other Laws "Work expands to fill the time allotted to it, or, conversely, the amount of work completed is in inverse proportion to the number of people employed." So proclaims the serio-comic *Parkinson's Law* formulated by British author and educator C. Northcote Parkinson. Parkinson's is only one of a number of similar maxims popular today. In the *Peter Principle*, for example, Dr. Lawrence J. Peter and Raymond Hull conclude that "In a hierarchy, every employee tends to rise to the level of his incompetence." *Frankel's Law*, set forth by Columbia Professor Charles Frankel in *High on Foggy Bottom*, advises that "Whatever happens in government could have happened differently and it would usually have been better if it had." The trend seems to have begun with the anonymous *Murphy's Law*, in which the sage writes that "If anything can go wrong, it will."

Parrot, Parakeet, Poll Parrot It may be that *parrot* derives from the name of the apostle Peter "because he talked a lot," but there is as yet no proof of this.

The colorful bird with bent beak was first found in Africa and Madagascar, and since it could imitate the human voice, it is reasonable to assume that it was therefore given a man's name. But these are only ingenious guesses. Some etymologists think that parrot comes directly from *Pierrot*, little Peter, the French word for the house sparrow, others that it came into the language as *Perrot* or *Parrot*, a Middle English diminutive of the French *Pierre* for Peter. In any event, there seems to be a connection with the apostle Peter discussed under *Peters* and *Petrel*. The same holds true for *parakeet*, which may come from one or a confusion of three words—French, Spanish and Italian—that can be traced to Peter. If *parrot* does derive from the man's name, as it almost certainly must in one way or another, then the extension *Poll parrot*, as Weekley points out, "is a kind of hermaphrodite," a Poll(y) Peter. All the confusion exists because *parrot* is not recorded in English before 1525, when it was first used in John Skelton's poem *Speke, Parrot*. "Parrot is my name, a bird of Paradise," Skelton begins. His *parrot* describes itself—"my beke bent, my little wanton eye, my feathers fresh as is the emerald green"—but fails *to parrot* its name's ancestry, which must still be listed as specifically unknown.

Parson Brown Orange (see *Temple orange*)

Parthian Shot, Parting Shot When you get in the best last word in an argument, a *parting shot*, you are shooting a *Parthian shaft* or *Parthian arrow*. The expressions refer to the Parthian soldiers of antiquity, who were famed as mounted archers. Located in what is now northwest Iran, Parthia was founded in 250 B.C. Ruled by Scythian nomads, the country became a world power due to the military skill of her warriors, crushing the Romans under Crassus in 53 B.C. and defeating Mark Antony seventeen years later when he attempted to invade Iran. The Parthians were deadly archers who fought on horseback, training their slaves to serve as infantry. These mail-clad horsemen would customarily ride furiously to the attack, pour a shower of arrows on their enemies and then evade any closer action by rapid flight, withdrawing according to plan and firing their shafts backwards from their horses while galloping away. *Parthian glance*, for a very keen backward glance, became proverbial, as did *Parthian arrow*, or *shaft*, or *shot*, the last by extension giving us our expression *parting shot*.

Pasquinade The first *pasquinades*, witty lampoons or satires, especially those posted in a public place, were hung upon an ancient statue unearthed in Rome in 1501 and re-erected at the corner of his palace near the Piazza Navona by Cardinal Caraffa. The multilated old statue, possibly a likeness of Ajax, Menelaus, or some unknown gladiator, was dubbed Pasquino or Pasquillo—either because that had been the name of the Roman gladiator represented or more probably because it stood opposite quarters where a sharp-witted, scandal-loving old man named Pasquino had lived. Pasquino, variously described as a barber, tailor, cobbler and schoolteacher, had died some years previously. But it became customary on St. Mark's Day to salute and mockingly ask advice from the statue named for the caustic old man, such requests being posted on the statue after a while. These written Latin verses soon took the form of barbed political, religious and personal satires, often upon the Pope, which were called *pasquinate*, a book of such squibs collected and published in 1509. The lampoons, really a kind of graffiti first written on paper, reached their height of popularity when another statue called Marforio—the figure of a recumbent river god thought to be Mars—was unearthed at the other end of Rome and people began to affix replies to the *pasquinate* all over him. The fame of the *pasquinate* spread throughout Europe and in England a *pasquinata* became a *pasquinade*.

Pasteurize, Pasteur Treatment, Pasteur Institute We remember Louis Pasteur for the germ-free *pasteurized* milk that we drink in safety today, but often forget that his well-known discovery arose out of experiments with France's national beverage—wine. In the 1850's the immortal French chemist first discovered that certain bacteria caused rapid "artificial" fermentation of wine, then that fermentation could be prevented if the wine was exposed to high temperatures—which led to the method whereby milk and other foods could be sterilized by heating and rapid cooling. A mediocre chemistry student, just as Einstein was in math, Pasteur made many brilliant discoveries in his field. This compulsive worker—"I would feel that I had been stealing if I were to spend a single day without working,"—proved that the spontaneous generation theory of germs was a myth, his most revolutionary scientific contribution. Pasteur also saved France's silk industry by discovering microbe-caused disease in silkworms, identified the staphylococcus and streptococcus microbes, and developed the anthrax vaccine. The *Pasteur treatment* honors his cure for rabies, which has reduced the death rate from hydrophobia to less than one percent. The dramatic story of Pasteur developing his rabies vaccine and testing it successfully on nine-year-old Joseph Meister, who had been bitten by a mad dog, attracted great public interest at the time. Pasteur suffered a stroke in 1868 that left him a very sick man over the greater part of his working life, most of his discoveries made despite the infirmities he struggled against. He died in 1895, aged seventy-three. The Pasteur Institute, in Paris, founded in 1888, carries on his work, having developed many vaccines and drugs.

Patagonian In his essay "The Greatest Living Author" published in 1959 Karl Shapiro describes Henry Miller as "a talker, a street corner gabbler, a prophet, and a Patagonian." The word in this sense means a gigantic specimen of his kind, humankind, a great soul, an immense figure in his field. Today *Patagonian* generally refers to "a native of Patagonia," but the word was in frequent literary use up until the beginning of the twentieth century and, as in the poet's praise, is still effectively used today. *Patagonia* is a regional name applied to extreme southern South America, specifically the area south of the Colorado River in Argentina, which, incidentally, includes part of the Argentinian province *Eva Peron* (once La Pampa) named for the wife of the former dictator. The original inhabitants, now virtually extinct, were the *Tehuelches*, whom the Spanish called "the *Patagonian* giants" when they attempted settlements in southern South America in the sixteenth century. Early travelers had described these natives as being almost giants and they were named *Patagonians* from the Spanish *patagon*, a large, clumsy foot.

Paul Bunyan *Paul Bunyan* may have been patterned on a French-Canadian lumberjack known only as Bon Jean. Bon Jean must have been quite a man even to be the prototype for the giant lumberjack and American folk hero. *Paul Bunyan*, as many books collecting Bunyan tales tell us, created the Grand Canyon by dragging his pick behind him, had a blue ox named Babe measuring in height forty-two axe handles, a giant griddle greased by men who skated on it with sides of bacon strapped to their feet, invented the double-bitted axe and logged on the Big Onion River in the Pacific Northwest, where it was so cold that cuss words froze in the air and didn't thaw out until the next Fourth of July. . . . Bon Jean, at least, must have been able to stir his hot coffee with his thumb.

Paul Jones Dance "Sir, I have not yet begun to fight," is the reply traditionally ascribed to John Paul Jones when British Captain Richard Pearson of the *Serapis* demanded that he surrender the sinking *Bon Homme Richard*. Jones won the celebrated Revolutionary War sea battle off Scarborough, England, boarding the *Serapis* after a 3½-hour struggle by moonlight, the casualties so great on each side that neither captain ever issued a complete casualty list. The intrepid seaman came to be regarded as America's greatest naval hero and founder of the American naval tradition, but his genius wasn't much appreciated in his own time.

The naval hero's real name was John Paul, not John Paul Jones. Born near Kirkcudbright, Scotland, John Paul went to sea when only twelve, serving as first mate aboard a slaver and even having some experience ashore as an actor before receiving his first command in 1770. It was then that his troubles began. A ship's carpenter he had had flogged for laziness died, this resulting in a murder charge. Released on bail, John Paul purchased a ship in the West Indies in order to hunt for evidence proving his innocence, but in 1773, killed the ringleader of a mutinous crew. To avoid trial he fled to America and changed his name to John Paul Jones, receiving a commission as a senior lieutenant in the new Continental navy under this name in 1775. His naval genius soon resulted in a promotion to captain and command of the new *Ranger*, whose daring raids off England were climaxed with the capture of the British warship *Drake*, the first ever to surrender to an American vessel. But political machinations, which plagued him and obscured his fame all his life, forced Jones to relinquish command of *Ranger*, and it was on the old rebuilt merchantman named *Bon Homme Richard* in honor of Benjamin Franklin and his *Poor Richard's Almanac* that he fought his most famous battle. It is little known that Jones became a rear admiral in the Russian navy after the Revolutionary War. Here again political intrigue and scandal prevented his recognition, his victories against the Turks credited to others and his name dishonored when he was falsely accused of a criminal assault on a young girl.

John Paul Jones died in Paris in 1792 when only fifty-five, a broken and embittered man. Buried in an unmarked grave in the St. Louis cemetery for Protestants, it was more than a century before his remains were brought back to America to be enshrined in a crypt in the naval chapel at Annapolis. Jones had greatly enjoyed dancing in his youth. The *Paul Jones dance*, a popular square dance, featuring promenades and numerous changes of partners, was named for him during the Revolution, one of the few honors accorded his name at the time.

Peeping Tom According to a later version of the original story, *Lady Godiva* had but one admirer when she rode raw through the streets of Coventry. The earlier story has *everyone* in town feasting their eyes on Godiva, but here the plot thickens. Our later version says that a more cunning Lady Godiva issued a proclamation ordering all persons to stay indoors and shutter their windows. In this way she could ride naked through Coventry as her husband dared her to, Lord Leofric would remit the town's oppressive taxes as his part of the bargain, and she could remain modest as well. But *enter stage left* Peeping Tom, the unfortunate town tailor, or butcher. We say "stage left" because Peeping Tom must have lived on the left-hand side of Hertford Street—assuming that Lady Godiva rode sidesaddle—and add "unfortunate" because he happened to reside there. At any rate, Peeping Tom peeped, ruined Lady Godiva's plan, and was struck blind for his peeping—cruel and unusual punishment for merely being human and living in a strategic location. It is said that in future commemorative festivals honoring Lady Godiva a bust of Peeping Tom was placed on the sill of the window where he allegedly looked out, but this may have been an image of St. George. In some accounts of his story Peeping Tom is killed by the irate townspeople and in still others Godiva is turned invisible before he can view her embarrassment of riches. History now regards him as a synonym for a voyeur.

Pennsylvania, Harrisburg *Silvania* is the Latin for woodland, and *Pennsylvania*, formed on the analogy of Transylvania (that home of monsters and werewolves in fiction), means "Penn's woodland." The name does not honor the Quaker William Penn, as is generally believed, but his father, Admiral Sir William Penn (1621–70). Admiral Penn, a naval hero who helped frame the first code of tactics for the British navy, had been imprisoned in the Tower in 1655 for political reasons still unknown and the author Samuel Pepys speaks bitingly of him in his diary. The crown, however, had become indebted to the admiral, Penn having loaned Charles II sixteen thousand pounds. On June 24, 1680, the younger Penn petitioned Charles for repayment of this debt, asking for a 300 by 160 mile "tract of land in America north of Maryland, bounded on the east by the Delaware, on the west limited as Maryland [limited by New Jersey], northward as far as plantable ["three degrees northward"]." The tract was to become a colony for Protestant Quakers suffering religious persecution and Charles repaid his debt with a charter. Penn's account tells us that he suggested the names Sylvania and New Wales. When Charles II added the "Penn" in honor of his father, he strongly objected—Quakers being opposed to such use of personal names—but failed to get the name changed even though he went so far as to attempt bribing the royal secretary. It seems that the king had to have his little joke. In Penn's own words: ". . . nor could twenty guineas move the under secretary to vary the name; for I feared lest it should be looked upon as a vanity in me and not as a respect in the King . . . to my father, whom he often mentions with praise."

Although fully one third of his company died of smallpox, Penn landed with sixty-six others at New Castle, Del., on October 27, 1682, to begin his "Holy Experiment." The devout Quaker proceeded to launch an experiment in religious tolerance that can be equated with the American dream, establishing Philadelphia, "the city of brotherly love," on the banks of the Delaware and making his colony a haven for the dissident and persecuted from all over Europe. Breadbasket of the colonies during the Revolution, the site of many decisive battles of both the Revolutionary and Civil Wars, *Pennsylvania* ranks second to no state in its importance in American history. Here the Declaration of Independence was signed and the Constitution drafted at Philadelphia's Independence Hall, here are the hallowed battlegrounds of Valley Forge and Gettysburg. The state has been the home of many great Americans, including Benjamin Franklin, Robert Morris and Haym Salomon.

Philadelphia served as America's capital from 1790–1800. *Pennsylvania's* capital since 1812 has been *Harrisburg*, named after trader John Harris, first settler in the area in about 1715. Attracted to the site because it was an easy place to ford the Susquehanna, Harris operated a ferry in the vicinity, the settlement known as *Harris's Ferry* until his son laid out a town and named it *Harrisburg* in 1785.

Peritas If any dog ever had a city named after him, it was Alexander the Great's favorite, Peritas. Tradition has it that Alexander so loved this mongrel that he founded an ancient city called *Peritas* after it died, naming the city in his pet's honor. The tale is not unlikely, considering that Alexander named another city after his horse. (See *Bucephalus*.)

Pernod Absinthe was generally made from various spices of wormwood, *Artemisia absinthium*, the plant so named because it had been dedicated to Artemesia, Greek goddess of the hunt and moon. Long prized for its reputed aphrodisiac powers by the French, the liqueur is 70–80 percent alcohol, but the oil of wormwood in it can cause blindness, insanity and even death. For this reason absinthe was banned in Switzerland in 1908, in the United States four years later and outlawed by France in 1915. *Pernod*, a greenish-colored, licorice-flavored liquor named for its French manufacturer, quickly took its place. *Pernod* does not get a person drunk as quickly as absinthe, being 40–50 percent alcohol, but, except for the anise used to replace the banned oil of wormwood, it contains all the same ingredients. Though it unleashes the libido by rendering the eye less critical and the will less obdurate, there is no proof that it is more an aphrodisiac than any other liquor. Too much, as Shakespeare said of sack, certainly will "increaseth the desire but taketh away from the performance."

Pétain Henri Philippe Pétain, at a cost of 350,000 dead, halted the German advance at Verdun in World War I under the famous slogan "They shall not pass!" Acclaimed a hero and made commander-in-chief of the French armies, "the savior of Verdun" became associated with extreme rightist political elements in later years. In World War II, when eighty-four, Marshall Pétain was appointed chief of staff of the Vichy government, collaborating with the Nazis and turning France into an authoritarian state. After the war he was found guilty of treason and sentenced to death. President de Gaulle, his former aide, commuted this to life imprisonment. Pétain, his name long a synonym for traitor, died in 1951, aged ninety-five. Senility may account in part for Pétain's actions and after 1942 he was largely a figurehead, replaced by *Laval*. (See also *Quisling*.)

Peter, Peterboat, Peterman, Peter's Pence, Peter's Grass, Peterward, Camphor It is not often that the exact origin of a first name is recorded, especially a common one like Peter, but the fact remains that every Peter ever born derives his given name from St. Peter. Peter was the name Christ gave the "Prince of the Apostles," this apparently the first time the name was ever used. "Thou art Peter," Christ tells his disciple, "and upon this rock I will build my church and the gates of hell will not prevail against it (*Matthew* 16:15–19)." This is the authority on which the papacy is based, and Christ uses the nickname Peter just after addressing his disciple by his proper name Simon Bar-jona, Simon the son of Jonah. Simon's new name, meaning stone, though translated as rock, is *Cephas* in Aramaic, but *Petros* in Greek and *Petrus* in Latin, both latter words giving us the name *Peter*, as well as *Pierre*, *Pietro*, *Pedro* and other national variations.

Peter was a fisherman of Galilee. He denied knowing Christ three times during His trial, but later repented. Tradition tells us that he was crucified in 67 A.D., head down at his request because he said he was not worthy to suffer the same death as Jesus, and his tomb is under the high altar of St. Peter's in Rome. Many words and expressions derive from his name, Partridge alone devoting a page or so to them in his *Dictionary of Slang*. The patron saint of fishermen and many other occupations connected with the sea gives us the standard English *peterman* for a fisherman and *peterboat* for a fishing boat with stem and stern alike, as well as *peter*, the underworld slang for a safe (as firm as a rock) and *peterman* for a safe-cracker. *Peter's Pence* was an annual tax of one penny originally paid by each householder to the papal see. Abolished by Henry VIII, the tax is paid on a voluntary basis by some Catholics to the representative of St. Peter in Rome— *Peter's Pence boxes* are, in fact, still found in Catholic churches and the contributions, no longer pennies, yield a sub-stantial income each year. Among plants, *Peterwort* was a name for the cowslip, and *Peter grass* for wild thyme, this last becoming *camphor* from the French words for it, *herbe de Saint Pierre*— which was corrupted to *samphire* and then *camphor* in English. *St. Peter's fingers* are the fingers of a thief, because they picked money from the mouth of a fish (see *John Dory*), but *rob Peter to pay Paul* remains of unknown origin. The same has to be said of the expression to *peter out*, though it arose in American mining camps in the 1850's and may have something to do with the fact that veins of ore *petered* or turned into stone. Several of the numerous other words deriving from Peter are discussed under *Mother Carey's Chickens*, *Parrot* and *Petrel*.

Peter Pan Peter Pan, the boy who refuses to grow up, has been familiar to readers and theatergoers for several generations and we now use his name to describe a person who retains in mature years the naturalness of spirit and charm associated with childhood, or one who absolutely refuses to escape from the comfortable irresponsible stage of childhood. British dramatist and novelist Sir James M. Barrie introduced his immortal character on the stage in the play *Peter Pan* (1904), although the fantastic whimsical world of Peter Pan had previously been presented in his *The Little White Bird* (1902). Peter Pan, a poetical pantomime, as it has been called, charmed audiences from the night it first appeared. Peter has since been played by many great stars, ranging from Maude Adams to Mary Martin, and a statue of him stands in Kensington Gardens, London. Barrie, who described his business as "playing hide and seek with angels," named Peter for one of his nephews, for whom he wrote the story, giving the character his last name from the god Pan, goat-footed god of forests, meadows, flocks and shepherds. Wendy, Peter's girl friend, also comes from a real name. This was Barrie's own nickname, bestowed upon him by the daughter of his friend, poet W. E. Henley. Little Margaret Henley called him Friendly, then Friendly-wendy, and this ultimately became Wendy, the name he dubbed his character. It has been said of Barrie's plays that some petered out altogether and others panned out very well. His *Peter Pan* made the use of both Wendy and Peter popular as given names in England, Peter having fallen out of favor at the time of the Reformation. (See also *Admirable Crichton; Alice in Wonderland*.)

Petrel, Leach's Petrel, Stormy Petrel, Wilson's Petrel Because they feed on surface-swimming organisms — small shrimp and squid—*petrels* fly close to the water with erratic fluttering wing motions. In stormy weather the bird seems to be patting the waves with one foot and then the other, as though it were walking on water. For this reason, as William Dampier noted in 1703, "seamen give them the name of Petrels, in allusion to Saint Peter's walking upon the Lake of Gennersareth" to join Jesus (*Matthew* 14:28). *Petrel* was either first spelled *pitteral* in English, from the Latin Petrillus (little Peter), or *peterel*, which would make it a diminutive of the English Peter. The common *petrel* is a small, sooty-black bird about the size of a sparrow with white markings, its scientific name *Procellariidae pelagicius*. But *petrels* actually came from three avian families: *Hydrobates, Procellariidae* and *Oceanitidae. Hydrobates pelagicius* is one of various species called the *stormy petrel* or *Mother Carey's chicken*, and is believed to be a harbinger of bad weather, figuring in a number of superstitions. In *Poor Jack*, for instance, Captain Marryat writes that the birds were thought to be the souls of drowned and shipwrecked sailors "come to warn us of the approaching storm." Therefore *stormy petrel* or *petrel* is used figuratively to describe someone whose coming indicates trouble, or one who delights in discord or controversy. Other important Atlantic forms are *Leach's* or the fork-tailed *petrel* (*Oceanodroma leucorrhoa*), a pearly gray species with white undersides named for nineteenth-century British naturalist William Elford Leach, and *Wilson's petrel* (*Oceanites oceanicus*), a bird common to the American side of the Atlantic that is named for American ornithologist Alexander Wilson (1766–1813). (See also *Mother Carey's Chickens; Parrot; Peter*.)

Petrie Dish German scientist Julius Richard Petrie invented this thin glass or plastic dish with a loose cover commonly used in laboratories today. The shallow dish named for the bacteriologist, who died in 1921, is generally employed in making bacteria cultures. Petrie was an assistant of the great German scientist Robert Koch when he devised his dishes in 1887. Koch—the first scientist to introduce a rationalized system of bacteria culturing—had previously grown bacteria in a gel on flat glass slides, his assistant substituting the shallow glass dishes with covers that have been used ever since.

Pharisee, Pharisaical The Pharisees were a strict, ascetic Jewish sect arising in the second century whose name in Hebrew means apart (from the crowd), separated (from the rest of mankind). Although their strict observances of tradition were greatly responsible for the survival of Judaism after the end of the Jewish state, this sect the basis of orthodox Judaism, the Pharisees' tendency to look upon themselves as holier than others led to the opprobrious New Testament sense of the word, which gives us our modern definition of a *Pharisee* as "a self-righteous, hypocritical person." The Pharisees opposed Christ's relationship with publicans and sinners. The Talmud describes ten classes of this sect, whose members refused to associate with others. These include the "Immovables," who stood like statues for hours while praying; the "Bleeders," who put thorns in their trousers so that their legs would be pricked as they walked; and the "Mortars," who wore mortars, or caps, which covered their eyes so that their meditations wouldn't be disturbed by the sight of passersby.

Philadelphia Lawyer One story has it that Alexander Hamilton, former attorney general of Philadelphia, was the first *Philadelphia lawyer*. Hamilton, it is said, successfully defended New York printer John Peter Zenger against charges of libel in 1735, the Zenger trial establishing the right of freedom of the press in America, observers noting that it took a *Philadelphia lawyer* to get the printer off. Unfortunately, the story hasn't been proved, nor have half a dozen variations on it, including the theory that the words come from a New England saying that *any three Philadelphia lawyers are a match for the devil.* The first recorded use of the term is in 1788 in the form of "it would puzzle a Philadelphia lawyer," and the phrase was being used in *London* at that time. The unexplained expression means both a very clever lawyer, well versed in the fine points of the law, and, rarely, a lawyer who indulges in unethical practices. *It would puzzle a dozen Philadelphia lawyers* was recorded in 1803.

Philander Our word for a male flirt who makes love without serious intentions comes from the name given to lovers in various medieval romances, but certain marsupial animals also bear the name *Philander* and these are named for the Dutch naturalist Kornelius Philander de Bruyn. *Philanders,* whose males may or may not be philanderers, include the small wallaby (*Macropus brunnii*), first described by de Bruyn in about 1700; the Australian bandicoot (*Perameles lagotes*); and the South American opossum (*Didelphys philander*). Curiously, the name Philander comes from the Greek *philandros,* a lover of men or mankind.

Philippic Incomparable orator that he was, Demosthenes' eloquent words could not triumph over the military might of Philip of Macedon (382–336 B.C.). Eventually, Philip II, father of Alexander the Great, defeated the Athenians, imposing a very generous peace settlement on them so that he could employ them as allies in his future plans for conquest. But Demosthenes had made such brilliant denunciatory orations against Philip over a period of seven years that these speeches are still known in history as *Philippics.* The *Philippics* were specifically a series of three passionate invectives against the Macedonian monarch's plan to weld Athens into his kingdom and comprised a great defense of Athenian liberty, taking their name from the object of their fire. In the *First Philippic,* delivered in 351 B.C., Demosthenes tells his countrymen that after six years something should be done

about the menace of Philip; he compares Athens to an amateur boxer fighting a skilled professional—helpless hands have only followed blows that a trained eye would have taught them to counter. The *Second Philippic* in 344 replies to a complaint of Philip II that he has been termed a tyrant by Demosthenes. "If Philip is the friend of Greece," Demosthenes says, "we are doing wrong. If he is the enemy of Greece, we are doing right. Which is he? I hold him to be our enemy, because everything that he has hitherto done has benefited himself and hurt us." The *Third Philippic,* which came in 341, is generally considered the greatest. At last Demosthenes so alarms Athens, telling of Philip's conquests thus far, that the citizens finally take some concrete action, diverting festival monies into funds for the military. This was, however, too little too late and Philip defeated the Athenians in 338, completing his conquest of Greece. The greatest military genius of his time was assassinated by a young Macedonian, Pausanias, while attending his daughter's wedding two years later, the killing probably ordered by his first wife Olympias, who had long since left him out of jealousy for the six other wives he had. The man who Demosthenes compared to a black cloud hanging over Greece was only forty-five when he died, and never had a chance to carry out his plans for the conquest of Persia. But he left behind an army that enabled his son Alexander the Great to change the face of the world. Surviving him, too, were the words *Philippic,* describing Demosthenes' speeches against him and Cicero's eloquent orations against Mark Antony, and *philippic,* referring to bitter, biting speech that censures anyone. (See also *Alexander; Appeal from Philip Drunk to Philip Sober; Demosthenes.*)

Philistine The original *Philistines* made their home in Philistia on the southwest coast of Palestine. These barbarians were Israel's worst enemy, even capturing the sacred ark at one time, until Saul and David, the first Israelite kings, decisively defeated them in battle. They were considered a crude, avaricious people but their name did not come into the language until centuries later, in

1689. At that time a town-and-gown battle in the German university city of Jena had resulted in the death of several people, and a local preacher gave a sermon on the values of education to the ignorant townspeople, choosing as his text "The Philistines be upon thee . . ." from *Judges* 16. The German word for *Philistine* was *Philister* and students began calling ignorant townspeople opposed to education by this name. Almost two centuries later, in 1869, English poet and critic Matthew Arnold used the German slang in his book *Culture and Anarchy*, translating it from *Philister* to *Philistine* and giving the word its present meaning. Wrote Arnold: "The people who believe most that our greatness and welfare are proved by our being very rich, are just the very people whom we call Philistines." Since then *Philistine* has meant a materialistic, uncultured person.

Phryne *Phryne* is a synonym for a prostitute, and a rather complimentary one considering its source. It refers to the Athenian courtesan Phryne, who lived and loved memorably in the fourth century B.C. There was a gold statue of Phryne at Delphi dedicated by her admirers. Her real name was Mnesarite, but the hetaera was commonly called Phryne, "toad," because of her smooth complexion. Born in Boeotia (see *Boeotian*), the country girl made good at her trade in Athens, where her beauty earned her a fortune so great that she once offered to rebuild the walls of Thebes if the words "Destroyed by Alexander restored by Phryne the courtesan" were inscribed upon them. (There were no takers.) That her body was the most beautiful of her time, or any other, is illustrated by Praxiteles' statue of Aphrodite of Cnidus, which she is said to have posed for. During a festival of Poseidon at Eleusis, Phryne took off her clothes, let down her hair, and in full view of the crowd stepped into the sea, inspiring Apelles to paint his great Aphrodite Cenadyomene, for which she modeled. But there is no better story about Phryne than that of her trial for impurity. One of her lovers, the great orator Hyperides, defended her. Just when it seemed that she would lose her case—and her life was at stake—Hy-

perides pulled the courtroom stunt of all time. Ripping open her robe, he exposed her breasts to the jury, who agreed with him that something so good could not be all bad and let our Phryne go free.

Pickle A sour pickle is the last thing anyone would expect to be named after a man, but at least one source claims that the word pickle derives from the name of a William Beukel or Beukelz, a fourteenth-century Dutchman who supposedly pickled the first fish, inventing the *process* by which we shrink and sour our cucumbers. But this pickled herring theory may be a red herring. All the big dictionaries follow the *Oxford English Dictionary's* lead in tracing pickle to the medieval Dutch word *pekel*, whose origin is ultimately unknown. Beukel does seem very similar to *pekel*, though.

Piker Settlers who migrated to California from Missouri's Pike County during the gold rush in 1849 were called *Pikers*, or *pikies*, their name coming to mean lazy good-for-nothings because they created such an unfavorable impression. This is one explanation for *piker*, another being that the word derives from the name of Colonel Zebulon M. Pike, who during the War of 1812 headed a poorly armed regiment that drilled with pikes instead of bayonets. In either case the word derives from Colonel Pike's name, as *Pike County*, Missouri, was named in his honor. A third theory holds that the older English word *pike*, deriving from *turnpike* in about 1838 and meaning tramp or vagrant, combined with *Pikers* to give us *piker*, which is first recorded in its present sense of poor sport or cheapskate in 1901. For more on old Z. M. Pike see *Pikes Peak or Bust* below.

Pikes Peak or Bust At 14,110 feet *Pikes Peak* is not America's highest mountain, but it is hard to think of another whose name is better known. The Colorado landmark was discovered by Zebulon Montgomery Pike in 1806 while he was exploring the headwaters of the Arkansas River. Pike had been chosen to map the northern part of the Louisiana Purchase (see *Jefferson*) and his reports that the area was a desert discouraged expansion there. He sighted the mountain in 1806, initially calling it Blue Mountain, but his badly equipped party failed to reach the summit. Nevertheless, the peak was given his name in years to come.

Pike was accused of complicity in the plot of Aaron Burr and James Wilkerson to detach western territory from the United States, but the secretary of war exonerated him. The American explorer and army officer seems to be irrevocably associated with rocks. He was killed during the War of 1812 at the early age of thirty-four while storming the British garrison at York (now Toronto), Canada. Colonel Pike had been leading his troops into the garrison on April 27, 1813, when the retreating British set fire to their powder magazine, which exploded and unloosed a piece of rock that fell right on his head. His father, Captain Zebulon Pike, in whose company he had trained, lived long after his unfortunate son, the old hero of the Revolution dying in 1834 at the age of eighty-three.

Pikes Peak became a guidepost for traders in the early nineteenth century and by the time of the California gold rush of 1849 Indians in the area had begun to tell of gold deposits on the mountain. Thousands of people headed west to answer the call, "Pikes Peak or Bust." Farmers who had deserted their farms, merchants who had closed their shops and tradesmen who had left their jobs streamed West by wagon or on horseback, some even walking, pushing their belongings in wheelbarrows and carrying picks and shovels on their shoulders. A settlement was established on the banks of Cherry Creek where Denver is today. Many did "bust" for gold wasn't found high in the hills until 1860, a year after the height of the Colorado gold rush. The fortunes made from the pockets of gold deposits found in the soft quartz and sandy fillings of what was called "pay dirt" established Colorado as the successor to California in gold mining, but crime, violence, hardship and death proved to be the common lot of the prospector, most returning home bitterly disappointed. Today *Pikes Peak* is a famous tourist attraction, whose summit can be reached by a highway, a cog railroad, or up trails on rented burros. Some still say the words *Pikes Peak or Bust* as they make the journey, but not with

the same sense of elation going up or grim sense of desolation coming down. (See also *Piker*.)

Pilgrim Fathers, Pilgrims The story of the 102 Pilgrims who founded Plymouth Colony is too well known to bear repeating here, except to say that these *Pilgrim Fathers* landed on Plymouth Rock instead of in Virginia, as planned, because bad weather had kept them too long at sea and they had run out of beer among other supplies. Plimoth Plantation in Plymouth, Mass., is a recreation of the second permanent settlement in America as it appeared in 1627, seven years after the *Pilgrims* landed. The word *pilgrim* means a wanderer, a traveler, a person who journeys a long distance to a sacred place. It has an interesting history, coming from the Latin *peregrinus*, meaning a stranger. This came into English as *pelegrin* in about 1200, but dissimilation, slothful pronunciation over the years, eventually made *pilgrim* out of *pelegrin*. Thus the *Pilgrim Fathers*, a proverbially industrious group, take their name from a lazy man's word.

Pinchbeck, Pinchbeck Napoleon Christopher Pinchbeck (1670–1732) died the same year that he introduced the *pinchbeck* alloy of 15 percent zinc and 85 percent copper that he had invented. Mr. Pinchbeck used the gold-colored alloy for the imitation gold watches and jewelry he sold in his shop on London's Fleet Street. A watchmaker and ingenious toy maker famous for his mechanical singing birds and "Astronomico-Musical Clocks" showing the movements of the planets and stars, he hailed from Pinchbeck in Lincolnshire, from which his surname derives. Pinchbeck did not live to see *pinchbeck* become another word for false or counterfeit, a cheap imitation. The term probably caught on because its first syllable suggests "cheap," which the alloy was, compared to gold, but whatever the reason, the word has survived. Anything spurious but resembling the genuine article is called *pinchbeck*, Thackeray even describing ladies' golden tresses as such in his *Virgin*. Later a *pinchbeck Napoleon* became almost a cliché in describing a Hitler or Mussolini or anyone with pretensions to

Napoleon's greatness without his abilities. (See also *Prince Rupert*.)

Pinkerton When he came to America from Glasgow in 1842, Allen Pinkerton opened a cooper's shop in West Dundee, Ill., his shop becoming a station in the underground railroad smuggling slaves north. Later he captured a ring of counterfeiters, this leading to his appointment in 1850 as the first city detective on Chicago's police force—a one-man detective squad. In Chicago Pinkerton also organized a detective agency to capture railway thieves, which became Pinkerton's National Detective Agency in 1852. But he achieved national prominence in February, 1861, upon foiling a plot to assassinate President-elect Lincoln when his train stopped in Baltimore on the way to his inauguration in Washington. Pinkerton's operatives had infiltrated a Baltimore secret society headed by a barber named Fernandina, who had brandished a long, glittering knife before one meeting and exclaimed, "This hireling Lincoln shall never, never be president. . . . I am ready to die for the rights of the South and to crush out the abolitionists." The society had purportedly drawn red ballots to determine Lincoln's assassin and Pinkerton's warning, coupled with others, persuaded the president-elect to go along with a plan the detective hatched to insure his safety. Lincoln, disguised as an invalid and traveling with a woman detective, took an earlier train than anticipated and reached Washington without incident. He did not, however, wear the long military cloak and Scotch plaid hat that cartoonists drew in caricaturing his journey, simply donning an old overcoat and an uncharacteristic soft wool hat that a friend had happened to give him. Pinkerton's part in the plan earned him the position of Union espionage and counterespionage agent. Working under the pseudonym Major E. J. Allan, he organized a system of obtaining military information behind enemy lines, the federal secret service developing from this organization. Soon he became even better known with his arrest of the thieves responsible for the $700,000 Adams Express Company robbery in 1866, and the breaking up of the Molly Maguires, a secret society terrorizing coal-mine operators in Pennsylvania. In the latter case one of his detectives had again infiltrated an organization, James McParlan posing as a Molly Maguire from 1873–1876, and obtaining the evidence that convicted the terrorists. Pinkerton wrote four books that helped popularize his name: *The Molly Maguires and the Detectives* (1877); *Criminal Reminiscences and Detective Sketches* (1879); *The Spy of the Rebellion* (1883); and *Thirty Years A Detective* (1884). He died in 1884, aged sixty-five, but his sons Robert and William continued the agency. It is from this period on that Pinkerton's was chiefly engaged by industry as spies and strikebreakers, earning the bitter condemnation of labor, especially for the methods it employed in suppressing the Homestead Strike in 1892. A *Pinkerton* or *Pinkerton man* came to mean either a private detective, or, in the opinion of many working men, something lower than a *fink* (q.v.). In 1937 the agency was subjected to a Congressional investigation during industrial disputes over the recognition of unions. *Pinkerton* remains something of a synonym for an American Sherlock Holmes, though the word is not commonly used anymore. Scottish dialect, ironically, gives the nickname *Pinkerton* to "a person of small intelligence."

Pitman

> *In memori ov*
> MERI PITMAN,
>   *Weif ov Mr. Eizak Pitman,*
> *Fonetik Printer, ov this Site.*
> *Deid 19 Agust 1857 edjed 64*
>   *'Preper tu mit thei God'*
>   EMOS 4, 12.

So reads the phonetic epitaph Sir Isaac Pitman, author and inventor of *Stenographic Soundhand*, wrote for his wife Mary. Pitman devised his system in 1837, basing his simpler phonetic shorthand on an earlier method invented by Samuel Taylor. The former clerk and schoolteacher lived to see almost universal acceptance of his invention, which his brother Benn helped popularize in the United States when he emigrated here in 1852 and established the Phonographic Institute in Cincinnati. Isaac

Pitman, a former Sunday School superintendent, devoted his life to spelling reform and improving his method for shorthand based on phonetics, issuing many works from his own publishing house. The phonographer died in 1897, aged eighty-four, but even at that time the simpler *Gregg system* was replacing *Pitman*, which had already become synonymous with shorthand. *Gregg*, based on ordinary, written script, did not require the intricate forms and shadings of distinctive sounds that made *Pitman* so difficult to master. (See also *Tironian notes*.)

Platonic, Platonic Love, Platonics, Platonic Year, Platonism The familiar phrase *platonic love* comes from the Latin *amor Platonicus*, but did not originally mean spiritual or intellectual love between members of the opposite sex as it does today. Such love, devoid of anything sexual, was first described by Plato, generally considered the greatest philosopher of all time, in his *Symposium*, where he tells of the pure love of Socrates for young men, a purity unusual in its day. Later, in about 1626 in England, the phrase was applied to similar love between man and woman, the word often heard today in phrases like *a harmless platonic relationship*. *Platonics* is the talk between *platonic lovers*, whereas *Platonism* is connected with the idealistic philosophy of Plato, the basic theme of his twenty-five dialogues being his theory of knowledge: that man must understand the nature of all things, including himself, in order to function properly and live happily. Plato (c. 427–347 B.C.) founded his famous school, the Academy, after his master Socrates' death, teaching philosophy, mathematics, logic, and government. His philosophy, best known in his *Apology*, *Crito*, *Phaedo*, *Republic*, and *Laws*, is the basis for most Western idealist thought, but not much is known about the philosopher. Plato, originally called Aristocles, was probably born of good family in Athens and had won fame as both a poet and athlete before studying some eight years with Socrates beginning when he was a youth of twenty. After Socrates died, he traveled widely and seems to have been captured and sold into slavery for a time. Curi-

ously, despite preoccupation with political theory at the celebrated Academy, he was comparatively inactive in political affairs. The pupil of Socrates and teacher of Aristotle died when about eighty, while attending a wedding feast in Athens.

The *Platonic year* or *cycle* is the 25,800 or so years that ancient astronomers believed elapsed before the heavenly bodies went through all their possible movements and returned to their former positions. (See also *Aristotle; Socrates*.)

Plimsoll Mark, Plimsolls "Coffinships," sailors called the overloaded, undermanned, unseaworthy vessels that greedy owners sent to sea before Samuel Plimsoll, "the Sailors' Friend," appeared on the scene. Merchants generally profited handsomely even if such ships went down, for they were invariably overinsured, and the only ones who stood to lose were the hapless crews aboard them. That is, until Samuel Plimsoll (1824–98), a brewery manager turned London coal dealer, made the British seaman's cause his own. Shortly after being elected to Parliament from Derby in 1868, Plimsoll had tried to pass a bill improving the situation and his failure prompted him to write a book, *Our Seamen*, which he published four years later. *Our Seamen* was largely a collection of dramatic stories about the hard lot of British sailors that its crusading author had obtained second hand while haunting the waterfront to educate himself in maritime affairs. Though he was sued for libel by certain ship owners and forced to apologize in Parliament for revealing privileged information, Plimsoll's book accomplished its purpose. Its condemnation of ship owners and underwriters incensed the British people, enlisting their support. A royal commission was appointed in Parliament to investigate the murderous maritime situation and a reform bill introduced. However, when Disraeli announced that the bill would be dropped in 1875, Plimsoll rose to his feet, shook his fist in the speaker's face and shouted that his fellow house members were "villains." Again he was forced to apologize, yet due almost solely to his efforts reform was in the air. The following year saw passage of the Merchant Shipping Act, providing for strict inspection of all vessels, this followed by a number of similar maritime acts, one of them bearing Plimsoll's name. The *Plimsoll mark* or *line*, adopted in 1876, was named in honor of the reformer's suggestion that every vessel have a load line, a mark that indicates the limit to which a ship may be loaded. Located amidships on both sides of the ship, it is a circle with a horizontal line drawn through it showing the water level at maximum permitted loading. This innovation reformed shipping all over the globe, making Plimsoll's name world famous, although today American merchant ships use what are known as A.B.S. marks (for the American Bureau of Shipping), four lines amidships that show maximum loading conditions in fresh water and salt water during summer and winter. As for "the Sailors' Friend," Plimsoll was re-elected to Parliament in 1880, but resigned to become president of the Sailor's and Fireman's Union. He continued to agitate for further maritime reform and later visited America in an effort to change the bitter tone of American history books toward England, his mission successful in many respects. His name is also remembered by *plimsolls*, rubber-soled cloth shoes or sneakers with the rubber extending about halfway up the shoe, the line between cloth and rubber somewhat resembling a *Plimsoll mark*.

Poinciana The tropical *royal poinciana* with its brilliant long-clawed scarlet or yellow-striped flowers is probably the most striking of all cultivated trees. Popular in Florida and California as well as its native Madagascar, the broad-headed tree grows from twenty to forty feet high and is sometimes called the *Delonix* (Greek for long claw) and the *peacock flower*. *Poinciana regia*, as well as the entire Poinciana genus, containing several showy plants of the pea family, was named by Linnaeus in honor of M. de Poinci, a seventeenth-century governor of the French West Indies, where the tree is also much grown and admired. Another more descriptive name for the tree is *flame-of-the-forest*.

Poinsettia This bright red flower, a symbol of Yuletide, could not have been named for a more fiery personality. Joel Roberts Poinsett (1779–1851) had much of the Christmas spirit in him, too, at least a great love for the oppressed and a romantic revolutionary desire to better their lives. Poinsett, whose rich father indulged his brilliant but sickly son, was born in Charleston, S.C., but educated in Europe, where he dropped out of both medical and law courses and devoted himself to travel for seven years. His poor health did not prevent the young man from meeting Napoleon, Metternich, Queen Louise of Prussia, and even the czar, who sent him on an official tour of southern Russia from which only Poinsett and two others came back alive. After he returned to the United States, Poinsett was sent to South America by President Madison in 1809 to investigate countries struggling for independence. But he did much more than investigate. Officially the consul to Buenos Aires, Chile and Peru, he made himself, strictly on his own, a kind of ambassador of revolution. His support of Chilean revolutionaries inspired the British to call him "the most suspicious character" representing the United States in South America, "a scourge of the American continent" who was "contaminating the whole population." Finally, he was declared *persona non grata* and when the War of 1812 broke out between the United States and Great Britain, he managed to make his way back home. Poinsett served as a member of the South Carolina legislature and as a Congressman for a number of years, but found himself more in his own element again when appointed the first American minister to Mexico in 1825. Here his revolutionary ardor was so excessive that it lasted only four years, his recall demanded first by the regime that he helped overthrow and then by the republican regime that replaced it. By this time Poinsett was a familiar public figure and when he sent specimens of the large, fiery flowers that we know so well back to this country, they were inevitably named after him. Poinsett hadn't discovered the plant, of course, and it had even been introduced to the United States before him, his popularity alone accounting for the honor. The ousted ambassador went on to become Van Buren's secretary of war, and a Union leader during the Civil War, despite his southern origins. The *Poinciana* genus commemorating him is now considered part of the genus *Euphorbia*, but the gorgeously colored Mexican species, its tapering scarlet bracts so ineluctably part of Christmas, is still called the *poinsettia*. In England it is known as the *Mexican flame-leaf*.

Polack, Polka, Polka Dot, Polka Mazurka, Polonaise, Polska At least four dances have been named for the Poles by other countries, and the most popular of them, the *polka*, is not even Polish in origin. *Polka* simply means a Polish woman, just as *Polak*, which gives us the slang expression *Polack*, means a Polish man. Either the Czechs called the Bohemian dance *pulka* ("half"), because of its short half steps and this word became corrupted to *polka*, or they named it as a tribute to Polish womankind. At any rate, the lively dance—three steps and a hop in double time—took Europe and America by storm after it was introduced about 1830. The *polka* craze resulted in many fashionable garments and designs being named after the dance, these including a close-fitting knitted jacket called the *polka*, and even the American dress fabric with a *polka dot* pattern introduced in 1880 or so. *Polka dot* may have been inspired by the hopping around characteristic of the *polka*. Its use was originally confined to the uniform, evenly spaced dots in the material, but the words *polka dot* or *polka dotted* are widely applied today.

A dance named after the Poles that *did* originate in Poland is the slow, three-quarter-time *polonaise*. The French named this eighteenth-century dance, calling it *polonais*, which again is a feminine form for Polish. The dance led to many famous *polonaises* for the piano, the browned butter-and-breadcrumb sauce called the *polonaise*, and a *polonaise dress* with bodice and a skirt that opened from the waist down.

The *mazurka* or *mazurka polka*, is another native Polish dance, this named by the Russians, whose word *mazourka* meant "a dance of the Mazurs," natives of the region in southeastern Poland where the *mazurka* originated.

Finally, there is the *polska*, popular when the Swedish and Polish kingdoms were united in 1587. The Swedish word for Polish is *Polska* and hence the name for this dance.

Pompadour, Poissonades, Pompadour Green Madame Pompadour, born Jeanne Antoinette Poisson, is probably history's most famous mistress or courtesan. In fact, La Pompadour, who became *maîtresse en titre* to Louis XV when twenty-seven years old, had been educated with great expense to be a royal mistress. Raised from an early age by her mother's lover, a wealthy financier who took her from her poor parents, her future had been prophesied when she was only nine by an old fortuneteller, whom Pompadour later pensioned for the accuracy of her prediction. An extremely beautiful girl, she was trained by the best teachers of her day in art, literature, singing, dancing and all the social graces. Her benefactor finally gave her a large dowry and married her to his nephew Charles Guillaume Lenormant d'Etoiles, a French nobleman himself. But after she intrigued to meet Louis XV at a masked ball in 1744, and captivated him, she promptly left her devoted husband of three years. Louis bought her the estate of Pompadour within a few years and made her the Marquis and later Duchesse de Pompadour. For almost two decades she was the king's mistress and constant companion, gathering about her all the greats of France, most of whom, like Voltaire, genuinely admired her beauty and intellect. She wielded great power at Versailles but did not exercise it with anything like the abandon that early historians suggested. Disliked by the public because she had bettered her position and by the nobility because she was considered an upstart, La Pompadour was subject to much malicious rumor, including the anonymous little poems and epigrams called *Poissonades* that became popular. But she proved to be a kind, generous and talented woman once she had entrenched herself with the monarch. Surrounding herself with beautiful objects was her passion and she was the undisputed leader of Parisian fashions, causing many styles and costumes to be attributed to her. The most famous historically is the *pompadour hair style*, which was at first worn in loose rolls around the face but swept upward high above the forehead in the next century and came to be a style worn by men as well as women. The woman's dress called a *pompadour*, cut square and low in the neck, is also named for her. So is an American bird; the colors *pompadour green* and *pompadour*, a claret purple; and various fabrics with a bright-hued design of small flowers or bouquets. Her name is best known, however, as a synonym for a mistress. Pompadour died in 1764, when only forty-three, her poor health made the worse by the many miscarriages she had suffered trying unsuccessfully to bear Louis a child. It is said that even on her deathbed she painted her face for the king, who promptly took up with *Madame Du-Barry*.

Porterhouse Steak Martin Morrison's Porterhouse in New York City introduced the *porterhouse steak* about 1814, according to the *Dictionary of Americanisms*, the steak named after Morrison's little tavern. The tender steak taken from the loin next to the sirloin is an even more succulent cut than its neighbor, but has a lot of waste. In England, there is generally no distinction between it and sirloin. A porterhouse was a tavern serving the dark brown beer or ale called porter, once favored by porters and other laborers.

Portland Vase (see *Wedgwood*)

Portuguese Man-of-War *Physalia pelagica* was derisively named the *Portuguese man-of-war* by the English in the eighteenth century, when the once powerful Portuguese navy had gone into a state of decline. The designation is a strange one, for small as it is the *Portuguese man-of-war* can be deadly. Actually not an individual animal, but a colony of highly specialized polyps, it has tentacles up to fifty feet long which discharge a toxic substance that has painfully stung, paralyzed and even killed swimmers coming into contact with them. With its red saillike crest it does resemble a little ship, but either afloat or beached it

should be more an object inspiring respect than ridicule.

Praline The Maréchal du Plessis-Praslin, César de Choiseul, got heartburn from eating almonds but couldn't resist them, one story goes. So his servant suggested that he have his chef brown the almonds in boiling sugar to make them more digestible and *voilà!*—the *praline*. But another story says that sugar-coated *praline* candy was named for Praslin when he had his cook prepare something special for King Louis XIV, the field marshal's dinner guest one night. More likely, *pralines* were invented by Praslin's man as one of the many culinary triumphs that all chefs vied with each other to produce in the seventeenth century. At first they were called *Praslins* and in time the spelling was altered to *Pralines*. On the American frontier *pralines* were made with roast corn and it was in Creole Louisiana that locally available pecans and brown sugar were substituted for almonds and white sugar to give us the creamy candy we know today. The Comte du Plessis-Praslin, who put down a revolt of the nobles in 1649 and may have served Louis *pralines*, became Louis XIV's minister of state in 1652 and was later rewarded with the title of duke for which he had politicked so long. He died in 1675, aged seventy-seven, a silver tray of *pralines* or *praslins* no doubt at his side.

Prince Albert Coat, Albert Chain, Lake Albert Queen Victoria married Albert Francis Charles Augustus Emmanuel, Prince of Saxe-Coburg-Gotha in 1840, despite many objections, loved him deeply, and mourned him in seclusion many years after his untimely death in 1861, aged forty-two. A man of great character and culture, the royal consort was much loved by British people, one token of their esteem shown by the heavy gold watch chain presented to him by the jewelers of Birmingham in 1849. The prince consort wore this watch chain from one pocket to a button of the waistcoat, setting a fashion named the *Albert chain* or *albert* in his honor. Also named for Albert are *Lake Albert* or *Lake Albert Nyanza* in central Africa, discovered by Samuel Baker in 1864, and, oddly enough, the *alberts* or rags that Australian tramps wear in place of socks.

The Prince Albert, a long double-breasted frock coat, is named for the royal consort's eldest son, Albert Edward, Prince of Wales (1841–1910), who became Edward VII, King of England in 1901. Prince Albert often wore the formal overcoat at afternoon functions. Widely traveled, he visited Canada and the United States in 1860, the city of *Prince Albert* in central Saskatchewan, Canada, as well as *Prince Albert National Park* there later named in his honor. Ephemeral fashions, ranging from shoes to hats, were called after this society leader, not to mention many commercial products, notably a pipe tobacco. Children used to call up the corner store to ask if they had Prince Albert in a can (adding "then let him out"), and probably still do.

Prince Rupert, Prince Rupert's Drops, Prince Rupert's Metal, Rupert's Land General of the Royalist armies against Cromwell during the Civil War, admiral of the British navy in the Dutch Wars, Prince Rupert (1619–82), grandson of England's James I, was a multitalented military man also strongly interested in art and science. One of the earliest mezzotinters, his *Head of St. John the Baptist* justly famous, he experimented with guns, shot and gunpowder. Prince Rupert invented the modified brass called *Prince Rupert's metal*, the alloy resembling gold and consisting of 60 to 80 percent copper and 15 to 40 percent zinc. *Prince Rupert's drops*, which he also devised, are toys made by dropping molten glass into water, the glass forming small tadpoles which explode into dust if their tails are nipped off. The port of *Prince Rupert* in British Columbia bears the prince's name also, *Rupert's Land*, once the name for all the land in Canada which drained into Hudson Bay, Prince Rupert having been the first governor of the Hudson's Bay Company when it was formed in 1670. (See also *Pinchbeck*.)

Prussian, Prussianize, Prussian Blue, Prussiate, Prussic Acid Since the Franco-Prussian War of 1870, when Prussia's militarism came into full flower, *Prussian* has been a synonym for arrogant, overbearing, cruel, and excessively military. This militaristic spirit was a major cause of both World Wars. *Prussianize*, to make *Prussian* in character and organization, also refers to the Prussian army. *Prussian blue*, however, has nothing to do with the military, merely having been discovered by the Prussian chemist Diesbach in 1704. It is a color ranging from moderate to deep greenish blue used in painting and fabric printing. A *prussiate* is a ferricyanide or ferrocyanide, which the color was made from, while *prussic acid*, hydrocyanic acid, is made from *Prussian blue*. *Prussian blue* is sometimes called *Berlin blue* for its place of discovery.

Ptolemaic System Before Copernicus scientists believed that the earth was the stationary center of the universe, philosophy affected accordingly in the snug, smug and complacent little world where the sun, planets and stars moved benignly around us. This theory, the *Ptolemaic system*, was essentially that of Ptolemy, an Alexandrine astronomer who lived from about 100 to 170 A.D. Claudius Ptolemaeus took his name from the Ptolemaic dynasty of Egypt, which reigned from the late fourth to the first century B.C., his famous work the *Almagest*, thirteen books compiling his own and other astronomical findings, setting forth the *Ptolemaic theory*. Nothing reliable is known about the great astronomer, geographer and mathematician aside from his work, which included his famous *Geography*. His *Ptolemaic system* remained virtually unchanged and unchallenged until the heliocentric system advocated by Copernicus and Kepler replaced it in the sixteenth century. Today it is known that the sun is actually 332,000 times more massive than the earth.

Puget Sound (see *Vancouver*)

Pulitzer Prize Hungarian-born Joseph Pulitzer was persuaded to emigrate to America by an agent who recruited him for the Union Army in 1864. After serving until his discharge a year later, he settled in St. Louis, where he founded the St. Louis *Post-Dispatch* in 1878. But when his chief editorial aide, Col. John A. Cockerell, shot and killed lawyer Col. Alonzo Slayback during a bitter political quarrel, Pulitzer left his paper and moved to New York, where he founded the New York *World* in 1883. A liberal, crusading newspaper, the *World* did much to raise the standards of American journalism, employing many of the greatest reporters and columnists of the day. Absorbed by the Scripps-Howard chain in 1931, it was eventually "merged" out of existence. When Pulitzer died in 1911, aged sixty-four, his will provided a fund to Columbia University, where he had established and endowed the school of journalism, the fund used since 1917 to give annual monetary awards for writing. Prizes in journalism are one thousand dollars each for local, national and international reporting, editorial writing, news photography, cartooning, and meritorious public service performed by an individual newspaper. There are also six prizes of five hundred dollars for fiction, nonfiction, drama, history, biography and poetry, as well as a prize of five hundred dollars for music, first awarded in 1943, and four traveling scholarships. A *Pulitzer Prize* is commonly called a *Pulitzer*.

Pullman President Lincoln's assassination made the Pullman sleeping car a reality. George Mortimer Pullman (1831–97), a cabinetmaker, had experimented building much-needed railway sleeping cars just before the Civil War, but couldn't sell his idea, even though he had made a successful test run with two converted coaches on the Chicago and Alton Railroad. In 1863, after working as a storekeeper in a Colorado mining town and perhaps digging for gold in his spare time, he invested twenty thousand dollars, every penny he had, in a luxurious sleeping car called the Pioneer that he and his friend Ben Field built on the site of the present-day Chicago Union Station. But the Pioneer, unfortunately, was too wide to pass through existing stations and too high to pass under bridges. For two years it lay on a siding, a well-appointed waste—until President Lincoln was assassinated in 1865. Every area through which Lincoln's black-creped funeral train passed brought out its finest equipment, and Illinois, the rail-splitter's birthplace, could be no exception. The Pullman Pioneer was the best that the state had and Illinois spared

no expense in promptly cutting down station platforms and raising bridges so that the luxurious car could join the presidential funeral train in its run from Chicago to Springfield. The funeral party traveling in the Pioneer was greatly impressed by the car, especially General Grant, who later requested the *Pullman* for a trip from Detroit to Chicago. As a result, the Michigan Central cleared the line for the big car and other railroads around the country began to follow suit. Pullman soon went into partnership with Andrew Carnegie in the Pullman Palace Car Company, his sleeping, dining and club cars, and the services he provided for them, eventually making him a multimillionaire. The magnate then built a model town called Pullman, a community now part of Chicago's South Side, to provide housing for his employees, but the courts forced him to sell all the property when the twelve thousand inhabitants sued him, charging that their rents and utility charges were much higher than those of the surrounding area. Pullman's name fell deeper into disrepute when his firm's grossly unfair labor practices caused the Pullman strike of 1894, which resulted in bloody riots and at least twelve deaths. In a 1947 antitrust suit, the Supreme Court ordered his company sold to a railroad syndicate, but sleeping cars are still called *Pullmans* on all trains in this country.

Pumpernickel *Webster's* derives *pumpernickel*, a coarse, dark rye bread, from the German *pumpern* ("to pass wind") and *Nickel* ("a goblin"), an interesting story in itself, inferring that *pumpernickel* made one "pass wind like the devil." But another theory claims that the bread takes its name from Napoleon's horse. When in Germany, Napoleon's groom was supposedly offered a slice and indignantly refused it, saying that it was fit only for the Emperor's horse, Nickel. "*C'est du pain pour Nickel*," he protested ("It is bread for Nickel"), and *pain pour Nickel* stuck as the name for the bread. (See also *Bucephalus*.)

Puritan, Puritanical, Puritanism The *Puritans* were originally members of a mid-sixteenth-century Protestant reformation group that wanted to rid the English Church of all traces of Roman Catholicism. Their name means "pure of heart" and a *Puritan* was first defined as "an advanced reformer in the Anglican Church." In time their theology became *Calvinist,* however, many of them driven into exile with the accession of James I in England. Emigrating to America, they comprised the bulk of the population of Plymouth Colony, Massachusetts, and Connecticut. Noted for industry and intellectual intensity, among other fine qualities, they were even more noticeable for their strict morality and absolute reliance on Scripture. It was these latter qualities, often carried to fantastic extremes, that made *puritan* become a word for a narrow-minded, excessively religious person blind to the beauty around him.

Pussyfoot In its meaning of crafty, cunning, or moving in a cautious manner, *to pussyfoot* refers to the way cats can walk stealthily by drawing in their claws and walking on the pads of their feet. Theodore Roosevelt either coined or popularized the word about 1905. But as an historical term for an advocate of prohibition, *pussyfoot* derives from the nickname of William Eugene "Pussyfoot" Johnson (1862–1945), a crusading American do-gooder. This prohibition lecturer was so named "because of his catlike policies in pursuing lawbreakers in the Indian Territory," according to *Who's Who in America,* having been chief special officer in the United States Indian service from 1908–11 and obtaining 4,400 convictions in that time. "Pussyfoot" Johnson's efforts were instrumental in securing the passage of Prohibition in 1919. When he came to England that year in support of the cause, however, he found more drinking men than *pussyfooters* around. He was, in fact, blinded by a stone thrown by some irate lush in a crowd he was addressing at London's Essex Hall.

Pygmy We take our word *Pygmy* for a very short person from the various tribes of equatorial Africa whose average height for males is about four feet, eleven inches and whose females average about four feet, four inches. The body proportions of the *Pygmies* are normal and these dwellers in inaccessible forest regions are either dwarf varieties of local populations or surviving remnants of early mankind. The name *Pygmy* was given to the natives by the Greeks after early travelers to southern Egypt brought back tales of a race of dwarfs along the upper Nile who were so small that they had to use axes to cut down cornstalks and were in constant danger of being attacked and eaten by cranes. Impressed by these greatly exaggerated stories, Greek writers invented the word *Pugmaioi* to describe the natives, basing their name on the length-measure *pugmë*—the length of a man's arm from his elbow to the knuckles, or about thirteen inches. Everyone believed that the *Pugmaioi* were no taller than this and their name became *Pygmaeus* in Latin, giving us our *pygmy.*

Pyrrhic Victory "One more such victory and we are lost," King Pyrrhus is supposed to have said after the battle of Asculum, in which he defeated the Romans at tragic cost. Pyrrhus lost the flower of his army that day in 279 B.C. He had come to Italy with twenty-five thousand troops two years before when Tarentum asked him to help organize resistance against the Romans. But after Asculum and several other battles, he returned to his kingdom of Epirus in northwest Greece with only eight thousand men. Other versions of his immortal words are, "One more victory and I am undone," and, "Another such victory and I must return to Epirus alone." In any case, his name is remembered by *Pyrrhic victory,* a victory in which the losses are so ruinous that it is no victory at all. The great warrior, a second cousin of Alexander the Great, never did live to revive Alexander's empire as he had hoped. He died in 272 B.C., aged forty-six, during a night skirmish in a street in Argos—fatally struck by a tile that fell from a roof. Every war has its *Pyrrhic victor.* There is a saying that the first named in any war always loses—the examples given being the Spanish-American War, the Russo-Japanese War, the Vietnam War, and both World Wars. (See also *Cadmean victory.*)

Q

Quai D'Orsay (see *D'Orsay Pump*)
Quaker, Quaker Bonnet, Quaker Gun, Quaker Ladies, Quakerly, Quaker Meeting After so many *Pyrrhic victories*, the *Quakers*, who oppose war, slavery, and any form of man's inhumanity to man, are a refreshing change. The religious group was founded by George Fox in 1650 as the Society of Friends, but readily accepted the name *Quakers* derisively bestowed upon them because they bade people to "quake and tremble at the word of the Lord." George Fox claimed that he had spoken these words when being arraigned before Justice Bennet of Derby in 1650 and that the Judge sneeringly called him a *quaker*, but there are earlier references to the term. In one London letter dated October 14, 1647, for example, the writer observes, "I hear of a secte of woemen (they are at Southworke) come from beyond sea, called *Quakers*, and these swell, shiver and shake. . . ." It could well be, then, that the name derives from the trembling of Friends under the stress of religious emotion, which once caused them to "quake, and howl, and foam with their mouths." Despite intense persecution, the beliefs of the *Quakers* persisted and spread through England and America (see *Pennsylvania*). The *Quakers*, incidentally, forsook the use of *you* because it was at the time the second-person pronoun employed when addressing superiors. The *thou* they chose in preference to *you* was used in the seventeenth century to address familiars or inferiors, affirming to them the equality of mankind.

A number of words derive from the *Quakers'* name. A *Quaker gun* is a wooden dummy gun used for drills or as camouflage on ships and forts, an allusion to the *Quakers'* opposition to war. A *Quaker meeting* is a meeting of the Friends at which all members except those moved to speak remain silent. *Quakerly* means in the manner of the Quakers; *Quaker bonnets* are plain, close-fitting ones; and *Quaker-ladies* are bluets, any of various species of *Houstonia*, a plant having flowers of a blue color like the *Quaker* dress. Philadelphia is called the *Quaker city*; John Greenleaf Whittier (1807–92) the American *Quaker poet*; Bernard Barton (1784–1849) the British *Quaker poet*; and *Quakertown* is a city in Pennsylvania.

Quassia, Quassim The Negro slave Graman Quassi gives his name to this genus of small trees. Quassi discovered the medicinal value of the bark and heartwood of a group of tropical trees common to the Dutch colony of Surinam in the South American Guianas. Using the drug he extracted to treat his fellow natives, he "came to be almost worshipped by some" and when his discovery was communicated to Linnaeus by C. G. Dahlberg in 1730, the botanist named the genus of trees in the slave's honor. Quassia's name probably comes from the Ashanti dialect word *Kwasi*, which means boy born on Sunday (*Kwasida*). The drug he discovered is known as *Surinam quassi* today, being effective against intestinal worms, as a tonic, and as an insecticide. The drug's chief constituent is the bitter *quassin*, which is extracted from the nearly white wood in minute quantities. *Surinam quassi*, obtained from the *Quassia amara*, has been replaced to a great extent by *Jamaica quassi*, which is extracted from the larger *Picrasma excelsa* tree. The *Quassia tree* is also called the bitterwood.

Queen Anne's Lace, Queen Anne's Bounty, Queen Anne's Fan, Queen Anne Is Dead, Queen Anne Style, Queen Anne's War According to folklore, the wild carrot (*Daucus Carota*) was named for Anne of Bohemia, who married England's Richard II in 1382. A ward of the queen, it seems, chose this herb's delicate flower as a tatting pattern. The little girl came to Anne's attention when she was found innocent of a childish prank and the queen discovered her pattern, which she liked so much that she gave the child permission to name it after her. *Queen Anne's lace* was later transferred to the wild carrot's flower and then to the herb itself. The plant used to be valued as a diuretic and stimulant, its relative the cultivated carrot botanically named *Daucus Carota sativa*.

Queen Anne style is an architectural style that flourished in seventeenth-century England and was named for James II's daughter, who reigned from 1702 to 1714. The style included many gabled, red-brick houses, and inlaid upholstered furniture with a greater emphasis on comfort. This Queen Anne's name is remembered by many phrases. *Queen Anne's War* (1702–13) was the American counterpart of the War of the Spanish Succession, the British and French struggling in the New World for colonial and commercial supremacy. *Queen Anne's bounty* is a perpetual fund originated by Her Majesty for augmenting the incomes of the clergy and the building of parsonages. *Queen Anne is dead* is British slang for "That's stale news; tell me something I don't know"; and a *Queen Anne's fan* is made by putting your thumb to your nose and spreading your fingers.

Queensberry Rules Boxing gloves had been introduced to England by champion Jack Broughton in the eighteenth century and the father of British boxing also drew up the first boxing rules, under which gentlemen like the poet Lord Byron learned to box scientifically from teachers like "Gentleman" John Jackson. "And men unpracticed in exchanging knocks / Must go to Jackson ere they dare to box," Byron wrote, but much was still to be desired for the art of hitting without getting hit. Bareknuckle fighting had caused many deaths and injuries under the London Prize Ring Rules, for brutality was the byword in the ring. It remained for boxing enthusiast John Sholto Douglas, the eighth Marquis of Queensberry (1844–1900), to put the sport on a more humane basis.

Douglas joined with lightweight boxer John Graham Chambers, who had formed an amateur boxing club that encouraged the wearing of boxing gloves, to draw up a code of twelve rules to govern all boxing matches. These instituted many modern features, including the use of gloves, a limited number of three-minute rounds, the ten-second count for a knockout, and the outlawing of gouging and wrestling. Promulgated in 1867, the same year that Queensberry presented cups for British amateur champions to encourage their acceptance, the *Queensberry Rules*, as they came to be called, were generally accepted by 1875 and standard by 1889. American James J. ("Gentleman Jim") Corbett is generally considered the first recognized world's heavyweight champion under the rules, which are the basis for all world boxing procedures and still govern all contests in Great Britain.

The *Queensberry rules* are now a synonym often used allusively for "fair play in any sport—or elsewhere." The marquis was of the Scottish House of Douglas, its members long associated with sports in England, especially "Old Q," the fourth duke of Queensberry, a patron of the turf notorious for his romantic escapades and dissolute life. John Douglas had served in the British army and navy before formulating his famous rules and sat in the House of Lords from 1872–80. He is also remembered for his insulting letter to Oscar Wilde objecting to the writer's friendship with his son, Lord Alfred Douglas. Wilde sued him for libel but, although he dropped the suit, the letter revealed information that led to the poet's conviction for "immoral conduct" later in 1895. (See *Oscar*.)

Quisling, Quisle Of the men and women whose names have become synonyms for traitor (see *Benedict Arnold, Bolo, Laval, Pétain, Lord Haw Haw, Tokyo Rose*) only Vidkun Quisling's has shed its capital letter in the dictionaries. A *quisling* is universal for a traitorous puppet of the enemy and was one of the most quickly adopted of modern additions to the language, even inspiring the little-used verb *quisle*, which means "to betray one's country." Major Vidkun Quisling (1887–1945) earned his rank in the Norwegian Army, having served as military attaché in Russia and Finland. An ardent fascist, he formed the National Unity Party shortly after Hitler came to power in 1933, but never attracted more than a minuscule following, most Norwegians considering him mentally unbalanced. Then the Nazis invaded Norway on April 8–9, 1940, and the ridiculous lunatic of the right came into power. Quisling had met with Hitler in Berlin three days before, confiding strategic information to the Fuehrer when told that Norway's occupation was imminent. The morning of the invasion he went on Nazi-controlled radio to countermand King Haakon's order for full mobilization of the army. Haakon and his government barely escaped to England, and Quisling, who had no official authority at all, was appointed premier. Public reaction forced him to resign a week later, but Hitler insisted that he be reinstated the following September. Quisling had no administrative talents and proved an embarrassment to the Nazis on many occasions. Brutally suppressing all opposition, the minister-president assumed King Haakon's chair in the palace and drove around in the bulletproof limousine presented him by Hitler. He surrounded himself with luxuries, occupying a bombproof, 46-room villa on an island near Oslo, where the walls were hung with priceless paintings from the national museum and he ate from gold dishes. So paranoid did he become that 150 bodyguards accompanied him at all times and every scrap of food he ate was sampled by someone else first, but this did not prevent him from becoming one of history's greatest megalomaniacs. He gave himself authority to make any document legal, issued postage stamps bearing his portrait, ordered pictures of himself hung everywhere. Norwegians came to despise Quisling and his S.S. organization, the Hird, like no other countryman before him and long before the war ended his name was a synonym for a puppet traitor. After the Germans surrendered in Norway, he was charged with treason, theft, and murder, specifically the deaths of one thousand Jews, whom he had ordered deported, and a hundred other countrymen. Found guilty on all counts, Quisling was shot by a firing squad on October 24, 1945, Norway changing its longstanding law against capital punishment for this purpose.

Quisqualis Like *Mahernia*, the name of the plant genus *Quisqualis* is another joke played by the pioneer botanist Linnaeus. *Quisqualis*, the genus containing a few woody vines from Malaya and the Philippines, is today grown in southern Florida for its showy pink or red flowers. When Linnaeus examined the plant, he did not know how to classify it or for whom he could name it. He therefore called the genus *Quisqualis* which in Latin means, literally, who or what for. Although *Quisqualis* (kwis-kwal-is) is not eponymous, it clearly shows that the naming process is not always so serious a matter; it might even be called an anonymous eponymous word, or a word in want of an eponym.

R

Rabelaisian Broad, coarse exhuberant humor and sharp satire mark the *Rabelaisian* spirit or style. The word honors the prodigious French humanist and humorist François Rabelais (c. 1490–1553), who "drank deep as any man," of life as well as wine. Rabelais, whose voracious appetites would have sufficed for any two ordinary men, started out as a Benedictine monk, later turning physician, but his immortality rests on his ribald writing, a paean to the good life—love, drink, food—a satire on the bigotry and blindness of church, state and pedant. Gross and noble at the same time, marked by vast scholarship, his masterpieces are *Pantagruel* (1533) and *Gargantua* (1535). The last book, though Gargantua had been a figure in French folklore, gives us the word *gargantuan*—enormous, gigantic—from the giant prince of prodigious appetite who was eleven months in the womb, as an infant needed the milk of 17,913 cows, combed his hair with a 900-foot-long comb, once ate six pilgrims in a salad, and lived several centuries. Pantagruel, Gargantua's son, is just as famous and classic a character. Rabelais, incomparably virile and vivacious, knows no counterpart in any contemporary literature, ranking with Aristophanes. He rejoiced in it all, from copulation to corruption. "Ring down the curtain, the farce is over . . . I go to seek the great perhaps," are said to be his last words. "Let her rip!" (*Vogue la galére*), "The appetite grows by eating," and "Do what thou wilt" were his bywords.

Rachel Discovered singing for pennies in the streets by the famous voice teacher Alexandre Choron, Élisa Felix, the daughter of poor Parisian peddlers, was trained for the stage and made her debut at the Comédie Française just before her seventeenth birthday. Élisa took the stage name Rachel, her genius as a tragic actress, especially in the plays of Racine and Corneille, acclaimed throughout Europe. Rachel the immortal ranks second only to Sarah Bernhardt among French actresses. While at the height of her fame in such roles as Phèdre in Racine's play of that name, the fawncolored *Rachel face powder*, sometimes called *rachel* for short, was named in her honor by a Parisian cosmetic specialist. On a visit to America Rachel contracted tuberculosis, which led to her death three years later in 1858. She was only thirty-eight, her tragic last illness and death the theme of a poem by Matthew Arnold.

Raffles, Raffles Hotel, Rafflesia, Stapelia Naming the genus *Rafflesia* after English administrator Sir Thomas Stamford Bingley Raffles (1781–1826) could be interpreted as a compliment or an insult. On the one hand, the species *Rafflesia arnoldi* has the largest single flower known to man—its bloom measuring up to six feet in diameter, three quarters of an inch thick and attaining a weight of fifteen pounds. On the other hand, this same bowl-shaped, mottled orange-brown and white flower is commonly called the stinking corpse lily. A parasite that grows on the roots of vines in its Malaysian habitat, only the plant's bloom is visible above ground, the rest a fungus growing beneath it, and its smell of decaying flesh attracts the carrion-flies that pollinate it. On balance it seems that Sir Stamford would have been better off if he had only had the world famous *Raffles Hotel* in Singapore named for him, but since he discovered the plant genus, he really had no one to blame but himself—he should have kept quiet about it. Raffles gained no gratitude from the British powers that were, either. An able colonial administrator in the East Indies, he did much to suppress the slave trade, was conspicuous for his liberal treatment of his subjects, zealously collected much historical and zoological information, and secured the transfer of Singapore to the East India company in 1819. But he was censured for freeing slaves and after his death his wife had to pay the costs of his mission to found Singapore.

The Zoological Society of London was established by Raffles, who served as its first president. He shares his niche in the dictionaries with one other man who did not come out smelling like a rose. Dutch physician J. B. Stapel (d. 1636) is also remembered by a carrion flower; the large flowers of the cactuslike *Stapelia* genus, containing some hundred species, having a very unpleasant, fetid odor. Native to South Africa, a few of these curiously marked species—variously colored and sometimes marbled or barred—are grown in the greenhouse for their flowers.

Raffles for a gentleman burglar comes from the name of a suave character created by Australian writer Ernest W. Hornung in a collection of stories published in 1899.

Raglan "I say, bring back my arm— the ring my wife gave me is on the finger!" Lord Raglan is supposed to have said something to this effect immediately after field surgeons cut off his badly wounded sword arm at the Battle of Waterloo. In any event, Fitzroy James Henry Somerset (1788–1855), first Baron Raglan, was renowned for his courage. Raglan served as aide-de-camp and secretary to the Duke of Wellington, whose niece he married, succeeding him on his death as commander of all British forces. During the Crimean War, Raglan was a familiar figure on the battlefields, dressed in his *raglan* overcoat, a loose-fitting coat with sleeves extending to the neck. The *raglan* had been named for him at about this time and today the loose *raglan sleeve* is a popular woman's fashion. If anyone ever had the unprepared "two-o'clock in the morning courage" Napoleon found so rare among men, it was this commander. He always rode far ahead of his troops in the field and on one occasion found himself facing Russian cavalry with no one behind him. Raglan simply sat there calmly on his

horse until the enemy turned and left, believing he could be nobody important. Unfortunately, the modest, unassuming hero was not a strategist of the first order. Although Queen Victoria promoted him to field marshal in 1854 for his victory at Inkerman, his orders at Balaclava were in great part responsible for the disastrous charge of the Light Brigade (see *Cardigan*) and his tactical mistakes were numerous. He did not, however, deserve the bitter invective hurled at him for his conduct of the unpopular war. But General Raglan was a convenient scapegoat. He died soon after the siege of Sevastopol, in which fifteen hundred British troops were lost and his men blamed him for the rout. No one knows the cause of his death, his doctors claiming that he died of a broken heart, the official report citing cholera.

Reaumur Another thermometer and temperature scale still in use in many European countries and named after its inventor. René Antoine Ferchault de Réaumur (1683–1757) invented the Réaumur thermometer and the thermal scale (0°–80°) on which it is based. Like the *Celsius scale* it was considered by some to be an improvement on Fahrenheit's invention seventeen years earlier in 1714. Réaumur has been called "the Pliny of the eighteenth century." Both a physicist and naturalist, his versatility involved him in researches ranging from the expansion of fluids and gasses to an exhaustive study of insects. The fluid under glass in his thermometer, unlike Fahrenheit's, was four-fifths alcohol and one-fifth water. (See also *Fahrenheit*.)

Rhodesia, Rhodesian Man, Rhodesian Ridgeback, Rhodes Scholarship Poor health, which plagued him all his life, forced empire builder Cecil John Rhodes to leave England and Oxford for Africa in 1870. There he joined the rush to the Kimberley diamond fields and by 1888 had established De Beers Consolidated Mines, dominating both the diamond mine area and later the Transvaal gold mines. His huge fortune facilitated his entrance into politics and he served as prime minister of the Cape Colony 1890–1896. It was Rhodes' desire from his youth to see the world governed by the British. When the British government failed to take action, he formed a private company to occupy and develop the territory of *Rhodesia* in 1889, *Rhodesia* named for him five years later. (The British protectorate *Northern Rhodesia* became the republic of Zambia in 1964, but self-governing *Southern Rhodesia* still bears his name.) Rhodes was ruined politically by his participation in the Jameson Raid to seize the Transvaal from the Boers in December 1895 and resigned as Cape Colony prime minister. Censored by Parliament, he devoted the rest of his life to the development of *Rhodesia*, dying in 1902, aged forty-nine. His last words are said to have been, "So little done, so much to do."

The "Empire Builder" had returned to Oxford several times in the course of his brief life—once being sent back to Africa under a virtual death sentence, the doctor noting privately that he had only six months to live. He finally earned his degree at the university and his will left an endowment of six million pounds for the famed *Rhodes Scholarship* that bears his name. Some two hundred *Rhodes Scholarships* are granted each year for students from the British colonies, dominions, the United States and Germany to finish their education at Oxford, recipients chosen on the basis of scholarship, character, leadership and athletic ability.

The *Rhodesian ridgeback* is a large dog developed by Boer farmers in what is now *Rhodesia*. Often called the African lion dog, it was developed from crosses of terriers, great Danes, greyhounds, bloodhounds, mastiffs and many other breeds with a half-wild Hottentot hunting dog that has a ridge of forward-growing hair on its back. *Rhodesian man* is a late Pleistocene primitive man whose remains were found in *Northern Rhodesia*.

Cecil Rhodes was much eulogized and much maligned in his lifetime. Mark Twain represented the anti-Rhodes school. "I admire him," Twain once commented, "I frankly confess it; and when his time comes I shall buy a piece of rope for a keepsake."

Rigadoon There is no Señor Mambo or Mademoiselle Twist, but there apparently once lived a Monsieur Rigadoon— a M. Rigaud, anyway. The *rigadoon* does sound Scottish, indeed the Scottish song *Mally Lee* tells about it: "A *Prince came out frae 'mang them a', wi' garter at his knee, / And danced a stately rigadoon wi' bonnie Mally Lee.*" But the lively dance —which resembles the twist in that the two dancers do their pirouetting at a distance from one another—is decidedly Provençal in origin. It is named for Marseilles dancing master Rigaud, who invented it in the late seventeenth century, the English *rigadoon* being *rigaudon* in French.

Ritzy There are *Ritz Hotels* and *Ritz Hotels* throughout the world, all of them trying to cash in on the name of the original *Ritzes* in Paris and London, and many of them none too *ritzy*. César Ritz (1850–1918), Swiss restaurateur and hotel manager, built his first *Ritz* in Paris in 1898. By hiring the master chef Georges Auguste Escoffier and adopting such practices as sleeping in every room at least once in order to test the quality of its mattresses, this perfectionist made his hotel at 15 Place Vendôme the greatest of *la belle époque* and himself the greatest hotelier in the history of the western world. (The hotel is still run by a Ritz, his son Charles, and the famous *Ritz* bar where Hemingway and Fitzgerald held court is still manned by the same bartender, Bertin.) Impressed by his success in attracting notables to this elegant Parisian hotel, as well as his management of the Savoy in London, a group of investors financed César Ritz in the construction of the palatial London *Ritz*. Opened in 1906, on Piccadilly, it constituted the last word in elegant, sumptuous luxury. *Ritzes* opened up in New York and other cities, *ritzy* or *like the Ritz* quickly becoming American slang for anything lavish and costly. The word can mean vulgarly ostentatious, too, *to put on the ritz* meaning putting on the dog or showing off, and *to ritz* a person meaning to behave *ritzily* or superciliously toward him. But it can be safely said that César Ritz, the thirteenth child of a peasant couple, lived to see his name become the most elegant four-letter word in the language.

Robert's Rules *Robert's Rules of Order*, the last word in parliamentary procedure, was originally published as the *Pocket Manual of Rules of Order for Deliberative Assemblies*—a cumbersome title for a little book. Written in 1876, the manual has had surprisingly few revisions, revised once in 1915 and again in 1943. Its author Henry Martyn Robert (1837–1923) was an American military engineer responsible for the defenses of Washington, Philadelphia and the New England coast. He worked on improvement of our rivers, harbors and coasts until 1901, when he retired as a brigadier general and chief of the Army Engineers.

Robin Hood, Robin Hood's Barn Robin Hood, chivalrous defender of the poor and oppressed, may have been based on the Earl of Huntington, Robert Fitz-Ooth, an outlawed twelfth-century English nobleman (b. ca. 1160) who harassed England's Norman invaders. According to this popular theory, *Fitz* taken away from *Fitzooth* leaves us with *ooth*, the *th* in this changing to *d* and yielding *Robert Ood*—not too far removed from *Robin Hood*. Both the bow and arrow of Robin Hood and the site of his grave are at Kirklees Hall in Yorkshire, where Robert Fitzooth, legend says, was bled to death by a treacherous nun in 1247. But there are abundant theories and places claiming Robin Hood as their own. The legendary outlaw is likely a composite of numerous stories about many early English heroes.

Places and plants named for Robin Hood abound all over Britain. *To go all around Robin Hood's Barn* means to wander in a roundabout way, to arrive at the right conclusion in this manner. Robin Hood, of course, had no barn, living in Sherwood Forest, and trying to get around a barn that wasn't there was an apt description for early travelers lost in the woods.

Rockefeller, Rich as Rockefeller, Rockefeller Center, Oysters Rockefeller *Rich as Rockefeller* refers to the family fortune amassed by John Davison Rockefeller (1839–1937). The oil refinery that became the Standard Oil Company made Rockefeller a billionaire before it was dissolved by Supreme Court decision in 1911, when the largest trust of its kind in the world. Variations on the phrase above include *he's a regular Rockefeller*, and *Rockefeller* itself is the American equivalent of *Croesus*. John D. may have given only dimes to beggars, but his philanthropies included the founding of the University of Chicago, the *Rockefeller Institute for Medical Research* (1901) and the *Rockefeller Foundation* (1913) for worldwide humanitarian purposes—in all worth about half a billion dollars. John D. Rockefeller, Jr. built New York's *Rockefeller Center*, Radio City completed in 1940. *Oysters Rockefeller*, the bivalves broiled with a puree of spinach, other vegetables and seasonings on a bed of rock salt, probably originated in 1899 at Antoine's, the famous New Orleans restaurant. The first customer to taste the fabulous dish is supposed to have said, "It's as rich as Rockefeller," the name appearing on the menu shortly afterward.

Roentgen Ray The first Nobel Prize in physics was awarded to German scientist Wilhelm Konrad von Roentgen (Röntgen) in 1901 for his discovery of the X-ray six years earlier. Roentgen called his largely accidental discovery the X-ray because he was at first unable to fathom the nature of this shortwave ray; it was an unknown quantity to him and he borrowed the symbol from algebra for it. The physicist, a professor at Munich the last twenty or so years of his life, did much valuable work in thermology, mechanics and electricity, most of it overshadowed by his great discovery. He died in 1923, aged seventy-eight. X-rays are sometimes called *roentgen rays* in his honor today, and the fluoroscope the *roentgenoscope*. To *roentgenize* is to X-ray someone or something, which is done by *roentgenologists*, who take *roentgenograms*, or photographs made with X-rays. But the use of Roentgen's name does not end here by any means. A *roentgen* is a measurement unit of radiation, and a *roentgenometer* is an instrument used for measuring X-ray intensity. *Roentgenotherapy* is radiology, or the treatment of disease by means of X-rays. Finally, *roentgenopaque* means not permitting the passage of X-rays, while *roentgenoparent* means visible by means of X-rays. Ten words in all—without including *roentgenograph,* an obsolete synonym for *roentgenogram.*

Roland for an Oliver Roland and Oliver were two evenly matched knights of Charlemagne who once engaged in a combat on an island in the Rhine that lasted five full days. Every time Roland got in a resounding whack, Oliver replied in kind and the contest to determine who was the better warrior ended in a draw. Roland, Charlemagne's nephew, and the intrepid Oliver became devoted friends. Both brave knights were killed by the Arabs in 778 A.D., in an ambush at Roncevaux in the Pyrenees, though one legend tells us that Oliver accidentally killed Roland after receiving a fatal wound from the enemy. The long epic poem *Chanson de Roland* of the eleventh century tells how Roland and Charlemagne's paladins died and how the king of the Franks avenged them. Many great deeds are credited to the two knights, so many that *a Roland for an Oliver* can mean an exchange of tall tales as well as blow for a blow, tit for tat, or an effective retort.

Roman Alphabet, Romance Fireworks, animals, love, flowers, even a characteristic nose are among the many things called *Roman* because of their association with the ancient Romans. These include the words and expressions:

Roman alphabet: the Latin alphabet, deriving from the Etruscan, which has since been adopted with additions and modifications by many countries, including England and France.

Roman architecture: a massive much-ornamented style of architecture based on Greek models and making use of the semicircular Roman arch.

Romance: the word deriving from the Latin *Romanice scribere,* to write in the *Roman* vernacular, as distinguished from literary Latin. The *Romance languages,* French, Italian, Spanish, etc., are derived from vernacular Latin. The old French adverb *romany,* for *Romanice,* became a noun meaning a tale told in verse about some hero of chivalry, this becoming *romance* in English.

Roman bird: the eagle, which was the ensign of the Roman legion.

Roman brick: a long, thin, yellow-brown face brick, its length about eight times its thickness.

Roman candles: first made or used by the Romans, fireworks that shower sparks and shoot balls of fire from an upright tube.

Roman holiday: "bread and circuses," a public spectacle marked by onlookers pleasuring in the brutal, barbaric display, just as the Romans obtained their enjoyment at the expense of the doomed gladiators who fought in the arenas. Byron invented the phrase in his poem "The Dying Gaul"—"Butcher'd to make a Roman holiday."

Roman mile: a unit of length the ancient Romans used, about 1,620 yards.

Roman nettle: Urtica pilulifera, an herb of southern Europe with heart-shaped leaves.

Roman nose: one with a prominent high bridge, such as those commonly seen on busts of Roman emperors.

Roman notation clock: a tall-case clock with Roman numerals.

Roman numerals: the I, II, III, etc., that are usually written in capitals and are used in place of the more common Arabic numbers for special purposes, such as the dates on buildings or the hours on clocks.

Roman peace: peace imposed and maintained as the Romans did, by armed force.

Roman punch: lemon-water ices flavored with various liquors.

Roman ride: when a trick rider stands astride a pair of horses, he is performing the *Roman ride* that the Romans perfected in their arenas.

Roman rings: the hanging rings used by acrobats and gymnasts.

Roman type: ordinary type with upright letters, based on letters used in old Roman manuscripts and inscriptions.

When in Rome do as the Romans do was St. Ambrose's advice to St. Augustine when the latter consulted him as to the proper day of the week on which to fast.

Romeo, Romeo and Juliet Not much is known about Romeo and Juliet, but they were real lovers who lived in Verona, Italy, and died for each other in the year 1303. The Capulets and Montagues were among the inhabitants of the town at that time and as in Shakespeare's play, Romeo and Juliet were victims of their parents' senseless rivalry. Their story was told in many versions before the Bard of Avon wrote of his "star-crossed lovers." The tale can be traced to Masuccio's *Novelle* (1476) and even before that to *Ephesiaca* by the pseudonymous third- or fourth-century writer Xenophon of Ephesus. Shakespeare found the tale in Arthur Brooke's poem *The Tragical Historye of Romeus and Juliet, containing a rare example of love constancie . . .* (1562). *Romeo* alone means a male "lover" today and has a derisive ring, but *Romeo and Juliet* still means a pair of youthful, often helpless, lovers.

Rorschach Test Popularly known as the ink-blot test, this widely used psychological diagnostic technique was invented in 1921 by Swiss psychiatrist Hermann Rorschach (1884–1922). The *Rorschach test* consists of a series of ten standardized ink blot designs that the subject observes, relating what he sees by free association to a trained tester. The way the ambiguous colored blots are perceived often reflects the interpreter's personality and emotional conflicts. Though it has been used since 1921, the validity of the *Rorschach* is not universally accepted, but it has often proved helpful to psychologists in diagnosis.

Roscian Roman actor Quintus Gallus Roscius (c. 126–62 B.C.) was born a slave but became the greatest performer of his time. Excelling in comedy roles, he was so esteemed that the golden-tongued orator Cicero took lessons from him and became his friend, the two often competing to see who could better express an idea or emotion. Roscius, in fact, wrote a treatise comparing acting and oratory. In an age when actors were held in contempt his grace and eloquence were praised in poems, Sulla awarded him the gold ring signifying equestrian rank, and he amassed a great fortune, retiring from the stage when still a young man. Over two thousand years have passed and his name is still a synonym for eminence or perfection in acting. *Roscian* means pertaining to or involving actors, and when we say someone gave a *Roscian*

performance, we mean one of outstanding skill.

Roscoe, Roscoelite A *roscoe* is underworld slang for a gun. In his *Dictionary of the Underworld* Eric Partridge suggests that the name derives from either the inventor or manufacturer of a *Roscoe* revolver. Several major dictionaries tentatively accept this derivation, but it has not been confirmed.

Roscoelite has to do with the underground, not the underworld. It is a brown variety of the mineral muscovite named for English scientist Sir Henry Enfield Roscoe (1833–1915), who is best known for his work in chemistry and his isolation of the metal vanadium.

Roystonea It isn't often that someone's entire name, first and last, is taken for a word, but that is just what happened with General Roy Stone, a nineteenth-century American engineer in Puerto Rico who had the *Roystonea*, or royal palm, named after him. The genus *Roystonea* is well known, including six species of palms. Often used as an ornamental to line avenues in tropical America, its beautiful crest dominates every landscape where it grows, and every portion from its roots to its crown serves some useful purpose. Some of these feather palms species grow to over one hundred feet high and the *Roystonea regia* species is widely planted in southern Florida. Florida's Palm Beach, the wealthy resort where twenty-five thousand millionaires are said to be resident in season, became a palm-fringed paradise when a cargo of coconuts washed ashore from a shipwreck in 1879, and early residents planted the nuts along the once desolate beach.

Rube, Rube Goldberg As a political cartoonist the late Reuben Lucius ("Rube") Goldberg won two Pulitzer Prizes, yet he was best known for his syndicated comic strips. Goldberg began as a cartoonist in San Francisco but came to New York in 1907, where he created the comic strip *Boob McNutt* and the series *Foolish Questions*, among others. His diagrammed panels showing preposterously complicated "logical" machinery which performed childishly simple tasks seemed to some like a parody of this mechanized world. In any event, these weird and wonderful contraptions won him lasting fame, exhibitions in conservative museums, and made his name synonymous with any complicated, wildly impractical invention or scheme. In his last years the artist turned his talents to sculpture that can only be described as unique. He died in 1970, aged eighty-seven.

The American slang *Rube*, for a hick, comes from the prenom *Reuben*, but no one has ventured to guess from what actual *Rube* American circus workers took the name.

Rudbeckia Under *Adam's apple* we mentioned the Swedish professor who tried to prove that the site of the Garden of Eden was located in the Land of the Midnight Sun. The professor, Olof Rudbeck (1630–1702), also claimed in his book *Atlantikan* that Sweden had been the locale of Plato's Atlantis. But he was otherwise a fine scientist, discovering the lymphatic system and making various botanical contributions. Linnaeus so admired the Rudbeck family that he named the North American coneflower after both Professor Rudbeck and his son, the junior Professor Rudbeck a contemporary of Linnaeus. The *Rudbeckia* genus, some twenty-five species, includes the popular black-eyed Susan and golden glow. Plants in the genus are herbs, usually having yellow rays, and can be annual or perennial.

Rumford Stove, Rumford Medal Before Benjamin Thompson, Count Rumford (1753–1814), invented his "kitchen range" most housewives prepared meals over open fireplaces. But the *Rumford stove* was among the least of the count's accomplishments. Rumford led a remarkable life. The Massachusetts-born physicist, statesman, soldier and philanthropist fought for the British during the Revolution, leaving his wife, a wealthy widow fourteen years his senior, and a baby daughter in New Hampshire. After serving as British under-secretary of state, and being elected to the Royal Society, he entered the Bavarian civil and military service in 1783. Here he effected numerous reforms, including a reorganization of the army and education of the poor. It is said that in one day he had twenty-six hundred beggars arrested and sent to a Munich workhouse he had planned, where they were taught to support themselves. It was in this workhouse that the *Rumford stove* was invented, the wood- or coal-burning range proving so efficient that Rumford was commissioned to build similar cast-iron models for many aristocrats of the day.

Made a count of the Holy Roman Empire in 1791 by the Elector of Bavaria (after having been knighted earlier by George III), Rumford chose his title from Rumford, N.H. (today Concord), the town where his wife was born and doubtless the only American town that has had a count adopt its name. Count Rumford's marvelous range was adapted by manufacturers in America in a wide variety of shapes and sizes. His work on the source of heat had led him to the invention and in 1798 he presented a paper to the Royal Society containing his theory that heat was not a natural substance but was produced by the motion of particles. A close friend of Napoleon and Lafayette, Rumford took the wealthy widow of the celebrated French chemist Lavoisier as his wife in 1804, his first wife having died twelve years before. It would be impossible to recount here the many contributions of this neglected genius, but they included experiments with gunpowder and firearms, a system of naval signaling, studies of nutrition, work on light leading to an oil lamp that remained standard until the introduction of kerosene, and sociological reforms in Bavaria, England and Ireland incorporating his principle that it is necessary to make poor or unfortunate people happy before they can be made virtuous, which ran counter to the thought of his day. Rumford can be said to be the first scientist to conceive that technological advances are made by first undertaking pure research and then applying the results to practical problems. A philanthropist who gave large sums of money to encourage research, he established the *Rumford medal* of the Royal Society and founded England's Royal Institution (1799). The *Rumford medal* of the American Academy of Arts and Sciences and the *Rumford professorship* at Harvard University were also established by him.

S

Sacheverell Not many preachers or politicians have been put down as properly as Dr. Henry Sacheverell (c. 1674–1724). "Famous for blowing the coals of dissention," the English clergyman had both "the blower of a stove" and a chamberpot named *sacheverells* after him. The naming was undoubtedly done by Whigs, whom Sacheverell had violently attacked in 1709 in two sermons, especially lashing out against the government's toleration of dissenters. Charged with seditious libel, the extreme Tory was suspended from preaching for three years. But his trial brought about the downfall of the Whigs and he was rewarded with the important rectory of St. Andrew's immediately after his sentence expired. It remained for the dictionaries to take revenge for the Whigs. (See also *Crapper; Fontange; Furphy; Oliver's Skull; Twiss*.)

Saddler of Bawtry *Like the saddler of Bawtry, who was hanged for leaving his liquor.* This Yorkshire proverb describes someone too much in a hurry. It seems that the real saddler of Bawtry was on his way to the gallows and adamantly refused to stop with his guards for a last drink, as was the custom in York in the eighteenth century. Passing the tavern by, he hurried to the gallows, where Jack Ketch quickly accommodated him. His pardon from the king arrived only a few minutes later.

Sadism Physically, at least, Count Donatien Alphonse François de Sade seems to have been one of the beautiful people, a handsome little man—five feet two, eyes of blue, but oh what those five feet could do, as a masochist might describe him. Actually, various descriptions of the miniature aristocrat exist. One writer gives him "blue eyes and blonde well kept hair," another "a delicate pale face from which two great black eyes glared," a third tells us that he was "of such startling beauty that even in his early youth all the ladies that saw him stood stock still in rapt admiration." Unfortunately, there is no authentic portrait of de Sade, but one might expect the probable descendant of the *Laura* (q.v.) made famous in Petrarch's immortal love poems four centuries before to present a striking appearance. In any case, this scion of high nobility was reared by his grandmother and his uncle, a literary man who prepared him for the College Louis le Grand, which numbered among its other notable graduates that one-man Gestapo, Maximilien de Robespierre. School was followed by considerable active service in the army, beginning when he was only fourteen, and from there de Sade seems to have emerged a full-blown "fanatic of vice," the Philosopher of Vice and *professeur de crime* that Michelet and Taine called him. When it happened, how it happened, would stymie a panel composed of Freud, Jung, Job and the living Buddha. De Sade's upbringing was a factor, as were the licentious times in which he lived, his long years in prison, and perhaps there was even an organic problem. There is simply not enough reliable information available about de Sade—all his voluminous diaries were burned—and to try and make biography from a writer's fiction is fruitless. We know that de Sade married Renée-Pelagie de Montreuil for her money, trading his title for her half-million-dollar dowry. The count, who always encouraged people to call him Marquis, then embarked on a life of scandalous debauchery marked by habitual infidelity and sexual perversions. These included the notorious Rosa Keller affair, in which he whipped and tortured a Parisian prostitute, and what is sometimes called the Marseilles Scandal, an orgy in which he was accused of sodomy, torture, and poisoning participants with chocolate covered bonbons containing powdered "Spanish fly." His mother-in-law, embittered about his treatment of her daughter, did her best to get him convicted on this last charge. De Sade had been in jail previously but for the Marseilles scandal—and though the charges were ultimately proved untrue in great part—he was sentenced to death. He fled to Italy. On returning to Paris three years later, he found a none too comfortable jail cell waiting for him. Though the authorities dropped the death penalty, de Sade from 1777 on would spend all but thirteen of his remaining thirty-seven years in prisons or in the lunatic asylum at Charenton. While imprisoned he began writing the novels and plays that give his name to the language. The *120 Days of Sodom* (1785), in which six hundred variations of the sex instinct are listed, *Justine, or Good Conduct Well Chastised* (1790) and *The Story of Juliette, or Vice Amply Rewarded* (1792), are among his works replete with myriad descriptions of sexual cruelty. Never able or willing to reform, de Sade died in 1814, aged seventy-four, while still at Charenton, where he wrote and directed fashionable plays performed by the inmates, many of whom he corrupted in the process. Sometimes his insights were deep and remarkable, but his was in the main the disordered, deranged mind reflected in his life and licentious work. *Sadism*, the derivation of satisfaction or pleasure from the infliction of pain on others, can be sexual in nature or stem from a variety of motives, including frustration or feelings of inferiority. De Sade's life indicates that many such causes molded his twisted personality. His final testament read in part: "The ground over my grave should be sprinkled with acorns so that all traces of my grave shall disappear so that, as I hope, this reminder of my existence may be wiped from the memory of mankind."

Salisbury Steak, Hamburger *Hamburger* literally signifies an inhabitant of Hamburg, the great German seaport, the *Hamburg steak* originating there, but *Salisbury steak*, a *hamburger* without a bun, derives from the name of a nine-

teenth-century English physician, Dr. James H. Salisbury. *Salisbury steak*, as every veteran knows, is really something more, or less, than a *hamburger*. The "steak" part makes it look good on menus, but today it is usually either well-done *hamburgers*, or ground beef, eggs, milk and bread crumbs cooked in patties and drowned in a gooey gravy.

Salisbury steak started out as well-done hamburger alone. In 1888 Dr. Salisbury advised his patients to eat well-cooked ground beef three times a day, with hot water before and after each feast. This diet, the health faddist claimed over the laughter of his colleagues, would either cure or relieve pulmonary tuberculosis, hardening of the arteries, gout, colitis, asthma, bronchitis, rheumatism, and pernicious anemia.

During World War I and again in World War II, efforts were made to drive German loan words like *hamburger* out of the language, a *hamburger steak* becoming a *Salisbury steak* and a *hamburger* a *liberty sandwich*. These efforts by superpatriots didn't succeed. One suspects that *Salisbury steak* only survived because it made an excellent euphemism for hamburger. Certainly practically no one eats ground beef and hot water for health reasons anymore. (See also *Graham Bread*; *Tartar*.)

Sally Lunn Sally Lunn used to cry out her wares in the streets of the then fashionable English resort city of Bath toward the end of the eighteenth century. Her basket was filled with slightly sweetened tea biscuits, which are still called *Sally Lunns*, although a number of cakes and breads also bear the name today. It took an enterprising baker and musician by the name of Dalmer to make Sally Lunn's buns universally known. Dalmer bought her recipe, built some portable ovens mounted on wheelbarrows to deliver *Sally Lunns* fresh, and even wrote a song about them. The song made the name a catchword that was still popular when nearly a century later a Gilbert and Sullivan character in *The Sorcerer* sang about "the gay Sally Lunn."

Salmagundi The origin of the word is really unknown. A *salmagundi*, any mixture or miscellany, began as a mishmash of minced veal, chicken or turkey, anchovies or pickled herring, and onions served with lemon juice and oil. One theory has it that the word comes from *salame condite*, Italian for "pickled meat," another that it derives from the name of a lady-in-waiting to Marie de Médicis, wife of France's Henri IV. Marie is supposed to have invented the eclectic dish, or made it *de rigueur* at least, and named it after Madame or Mademoiselle Salmagundi, her lady-in-waiting. Later the word was used by Washington Irving for a series of twenty periodical pamphlets he and two other writers published, 1807–08. *Salmagundi; or the Whim-Whams and Opinions of Launcelot Langstaff, Esq. and others,* consisted of satirical essays and poems on New York society and politics, generally satirizing "mobocratic" and "logocratic" Jeffersonian democracy. But the "magazine" also took on such diverse topics as women's clothing, music and theater. Its apt name made the word *salmagundi* fashionable, especially when a second set of papers appeared about ten years later. *Salmagundi* is still sometimes served as a salad and a New York club of noted writers and artists also uses the name today. It was in the *Salmagundi Papers* that Irving first applied the name Gotham to New York City.

Salmonella, Salmonellosis Salmon have no connection with *Salmonella* or *Salmonellosis*. The latter is a very common form of food poisoning that can result in death and is caused by bacteria of the *Salmonella* genus, comprising some fifteen hundred species. The *Salmonella* genus was first identified by nineteenth-century American pathologist and veterinarian Daniel Elmer Salmon, who died in 1915. There are often outbreaks of *salmonellosis*, which is usually caused by infected and insufficiently cooked beef, pork, poultry and eggs, as well as food, drink or equipment contaminated by the excreta of infected animals. Almost all animals are hospitable to the rod-shaped bacteria causing the acute gastroenteritis in humans, and food poisonings caused by them are almost as common as those caused by staphylococci. One of Berton Roueche's excellent medical detective stories, the

"Santa Claus Culture," in the *New Yorker* (9/14/71), deals with a curious outbreak caused by *S. cubana,* a *salmonella* species. Incidentally, there *is* a "salmon disease" dogs and other animals get from eating salmon infested with cysts of flukes—it has nothing to do with *salmonellosis. Salmonella,* some experts fear, could become an "Andromeda Strain." It seems that generations of livestock raised for human consumption have been fed miracle drugs for so long that they have developed races of bacteria that are immune to the germ-killing properties of antibiotics. These *salmonella* could be passed on to the consumer, infecting humans in epidemic proportions with a *salmonellosis* antibiotics would be powerless against. The theory is highly controversial, but the F.D.A. considers it likely enough to be conducting extensive investigations at this writing.

Samarskite, Samarium Russian engineer Colonel M. von Samarski became one of the few men to have an element named after him through an unusual set of circumstances. In 1857 a glasslike, velvet-black mineral was discovered in Russia and named *samarskite* in honor of this mine official. Twenty-two years later the scientist Lecoq de Boisbaudran found by means of the spectroscope that *samarskite* contained a new element. He named this *samarium,* after the mineral in which he discovered it. Thus the little-known engineer was commemorated, indirectly, in a way usually reserved for the great. *Samarium* belongs to the rare-earth group and has little commercial importance, though it is used as a catalyst and in the ceramics industry. In about 1901 another element was discovered in *samarskite,* this called *europium,* after the continent.

Sambo Few black men would agree that *Sambo* is a pet name or a nickname for a Negro as it is often defined—almost all would call the term disparaging and offensive, if pausing to explain. Apparently of American origin, the term was introduced via the slave trade. The word, some believe, derives from the Kongo *nzambu,* monkey, which became *zambo,* bowlegged, in Spanish. An alternate choice is the Foulah *sambo,* uncle. But possibly the word doesn't have an offensive origin at all. It may be that *Sambo* simply comes from the name of a West African tribe called the *Samboses*, mentioned in European literature as early as 1564. By the way, the resourceful hero in the children's story, "Little Black Sambo," is an East Indian.

Sam Browne Belt Born in India, Sir Samuel Browne, V.C. (1824–1901) served most of his military career there with the British Army. Awarded the Victoria Cross and knighted for putting down the Indian Mutiny, a rebellion among native troops, he was promoted to general in 1888. Sometime during his long military career Browne invented the belt that bears his name. Designed originally as a sword belt that would support the weight of a sword smartly without sagging from the hips, it consisted of a belt with two auxiliary straps attached, the straps crossing over each shoulder. Later modified to one strap crossing from the left hip over the left shoulder —swords were worn on the left side— the *Sam Browne belt* became compulsory dress for all British officers and was widely adopted by armies throughout the world. It was declared optional in 1939, but is still seen today, especially as part of drill, band and cadet uniforms.

Sam Hill If someone could locate any historical record of a Col. Samuel Hill of Guilford, Conn., we might find the origin of the phrase *go like Sam Hill* or *run like Sam Hill*. Edwin V. Mitchell makes mention of the man in the *Encyclopedia of American Politics* (1946)— it seems that Colonel Hill perpetually ran for office—but no other evidence of his existence can be found. Since no one knows *who in the Sam Hill* he was, Sam Hill must remain "a personified euphemism our Puritan ancestors used for 'hell.' "

Samoyed *Samoyeds* are working dogs resembling the chow, but their gentleness and intelligence make them highly valued pets. The dog takes its name from the Samoyed people, a nomadic race of Mongols living in northwest Siberia who number only seven thousand or so and are gradually becoming extinct. The strong, heavy-coated *samoyeds*, usually white or cream colored, were developed for pulling sleds, hunting and herding

reindeer. Their masters are an interesting people who domesticate the reindeer and use it for riding as well as milking. The Samoyeds eat carnivorous animals, including the wolf, build their homes with stones, and make their graves of boxes left in the tundra, among other strange customs. The *samoyed husky* happens to be the most widely traveled of all dogs, one having gone along for the space ride in 1957 aboard the Russian Sputnik II, which attained an altitude of 1,050 miles. In Russia the breed is called *laika*.

Samson Just as Delilah's name symbolizes treachery, Samson's symbolizes strength. The Biblical Samson at one time or another "tore the lion asunder as one tears a kid"; "caught three hundred foxes" and tied them tail to tail, putting a torch between each tail and turning them loose to burn the grain fields and olive orchards of the Philistines; slew a thousand men with the jawbone of an ass like a number of orators after him; and performed various other prodigious feats as recorded in *Judges* 13–17. Samson's Achilles heel was not so much his hair as his weakness for Philistine women, and he met his match in Delilah, who cut off his long locks, in which his strength or soul resided. After his betrayal by Delilah to the Philistines, Samson's eyes were gouged out and he was brought down to Gaza. Eyeless in Gaza, he performed his last heroic deed when the Philistines tried making sport of him, pulling down the temple of Dagon on his tormentors and himself, "the dead whom he slew at his death . . . more than those whom he had slain during his life." Samson's name has been used for weight lifters and strongmen since at least May 28, 1741, when Thomas Topham was called the British Samson. On that date, it is said, Topham effortlessly lifted 1,836 pounds over his head. (See also *Delilah*.)

Sandwich At 5 A.M. on August 6, 1762, John Montagu, fourth earl of Sandwich, looked up from the gaming table and decided that he was hungry. The earl, an inveterate gambler in the midst of one of his famous round-the-clock sessions, wouldn't dare leave his cards for a meal and ordered his man to bring him some cold, thick-sliced roast beef between two pieces of toasted bread. Thus the first *sandwich* as we know it today was born. The Romans had a similar repast called *offula* before this and it is said that the refreshment was first invented when in about 100 B.C. Hillel ate bitter herb and unleavened bread as part of the Jewish Passover meal, symbolizing man's triumph over life's ills. But the modern *sandwich*, certainly our most convenient quick lunch or snack and possibly our main source of nourishment in this frenetic age, definitely evolves from those mighty gambling sessions, some lasting forty-eight hours and more, in which the industrious earl passionately participated. Those few authorities who say that the earl was at the *writing* table, or out on a long day's hunt and not at any table at all, only dampen a good story and are probably not correct. At any rate, the *sandwich* was named for Lord Sandwich and within eight years after the above date the term was recorded by visiting Frenchman Pierre Grosley in his *Londres* as the term for such a snack.

Gambling was only one of John Montagu's lesser vices, but the earl has as many complimentary words honoring him as any politician, another example being the beautiful *Sandwich Islands* (Hawaii) that Captain James Cook named after him because he headed the British admiralty during the American Revolution and outfitted the great explorer's ships. Lord Sandwich deserves no such glory and wasn't accorded it in his own lifetime. Sandwich became an earl when only eleven, was educated at all the right schools—Eton and Cambridge—but he did very little that was right. His administration as first lord of the Admiralty was notoriously mismanaged, many public charges were made against him for graft, bribery, and general incompetence—and the result of the American Revolution might have been different if he hadn't been on hand to sabotage the British navy. Lord Howe, among many officers, refused to accept a command under Sandwich, but his unpopularity dates back long before the revolt of the colonies. After a promising start in politics, his party fell from power and the bored earl dedicated himself to

a life of lechery. In an age studded with libertines, Lord Sandwich shone brightest. Under a *nom de débauche* he became a member of the notorious Hell-Fire Club, infamous for its wild orgies and black masses, but soon fell out with his friend the great wit John Wilkes, M.P. and Lord Mayor of London, one of the club's founders. Wilkes had dressed a black baboon with horns and hoops and let him loose while Sandwich was invoking the devil during a black mass, the earl's embarrassment exceeding even his initial fright, when he ran out of the chapel shouting, "Spare me, gracious Devil. I am as yet but half a sinner. I have never been as wicked as I intended!" The two became bitter enemies, but when Sandwich sought revenge before the House of Lords by reading Wilkes' indecent "Essay on Woman," a parody (now lost) on Pope's "Essay on Man," the strategy backfired. On that same day John Gay's *Beggar's Opera* happened to be playing in London and Sandwich became identified in the public's mind with the play's villain, the "despicable cad" who betrays the hero, his nickname remaining *Jemmy Twitcher* ever after.

Sandwich also knew notoriety for the sixteen-year-old mistress he took. Margaret or Marth Reay—a "commoner" he educated at the best schools in Paris—bore him five children in the some twenty years they lived together. She was killed by a rejected suitor in 1779, making her paramour's private life a matter of public controversy just when he was having his worst troubles with the Admiralty. In 1882 the earl left the navy when his party fell from power but the scandals associated with him plagued him the rest of his life. He died ten years later, aged seventy-four, an embittered man who never realized how history would honor him. Only one celebrated riposte mars his popular historical reputation. Though attributed to a number of people, the most famous political put down in history probably made Lord Sandwich its victim. It appears that the earl had verbally attacked his arch enemy Wilkes, shouting, "You, Wilkes, will either die on the gallows or from syphilis!" The great wit Wilkes simply turned, tapped his snuff-box, and looked Sandwich square in the eye. "That depends, my Lord," he said, matter-of-factly, "on whether I embrace your principles or your mistress."

Santa Claus Yes, Virginia, there was a Santa Claus, a real one—probably. The custom of giving presents at Christmas is based on the legend that St. Nicholas—a bishop of Myra in Asia Minor during the fourth century—gave secret dowries to three sisters who could not have been married otherwise and would have been sold into prostitution if it hadn't been for his generosity. Nicholas, the story goes, was out walking one night when he heard the three sisters crying behind their curtained window. On being told that their poor father could find no husbands for them and had to sell them to a brothel, our Santa Claus dug into his coat and threw three bags of gold to them, saving the girls and disappearing into the night before their father could thank him. A twist on the tale has the bishop turning three brass balls into the bags of gold, which is appropriate for the patron saint of pawnbrokers.

St. Nicholas is also the patron saint of the Russian Orthodox Church, Greece, Sicily, Aberdeen, scholars, travelers, sailors, thieves, and children, among other groups. Little is known about him except the various legends linking him to those enjoying his patronage. Sometimes he is called St. Nicholas of Bari, or St. Nicholas the Wonderful. It is believed that he was tortured and imprisoned for his faith under the emperor Diocletian and that he may have participated in the Council of Nicaea (325). St. Nicholas probably died about 350, his reputed relics stolen from Myra by Italian merchants in the eleventh century and now enshrined at Bari in Apulia. The good saint is always saving someone in legend. Once he even restored to life three little boys who had been slaughtered and pickled to be used for bacon! Yet despite the lack of historical facts about him, he is no doubt the basis for our Santa Claus. The eve of his feast day, December 6, is a children's holiday when gifts are given in the Netherlands and elsewhere, the custom calling for someone to dress up as St. Nicholas and present gifts. The English who settled in New York borrowed both the saint and this custom from the earlier Dutch settlers, moving his day to Christmas, their own gift giving day, and corrupting his name from the Dutch dialect from *Sint Klaas* to *Santa Claus*.

Gradually, the tall, sad-eyed St. Nicholas of sixteen hundred years ago was transformed into the plump, jolly Santa that we know today. Sometimes he is still called St. Nicholas, as in Clement Moore's poem, "The Night Before Christmas," which was originally titled "A Visit from St. Nicholas." Few of the beliefs children have about him—from North Pole to red-nosed reindeer—have anything at all to do with this bishop from what is now Turkey. But the custom of hanging Christmas stockings does stem from a story that he cast gold pieces down the chimney of the cottage of the three poor sisters he saved from the brothel, the gold landing in stockings they had hung there to dry.

"Yes, Virginia, there is a Santa Claus," was the title of a much-reprinted editorial on the spirit of Christmas that appeared in the New York *Sun* on September 21, 1897. A famous "real life" portrait of Santa Claus, or St. Nicholas, by Bicci de Lorenzo can be seen in New York's Metropolitan Museum.

Sapphism, Sapphics (see *Lesbian*)

Sarah Bernhardt, Sally Bee "The divine Sarah," as Oscar Wilde called her, is regarded by many as the greatest actress of all time. Born Rosine Bernhard, the daughter of Jewish parents who converted to Catholicism, she was brought up in a convent until she entered the Paris Conservatoire at thirteen. After making her debut at the Comédie-Française in 1862, she played internationally, winning her great fame in tragic roles largely because of her "voice of gold" and magnetic personality. Probably the tallest, thinnest woman ever to star on the stage (Arthur "Bugs" Baer once wrote that "An empty cab drove up, and Sarah Bernhardt got out") her nickname *Sally Bee* became the nickname for any tall, lean woman. Sarah's great talents enabled her to play almost equally well in English as in French, and she toured America, among many other countries.

The queen of the French stage even performed the title role in *Hamlet* successfully and the loss of a leg in an accident late in her career did not diminish her talent or activity at all. "Energy creates energy," she once said in explaining her remarkable vitality. "It is by spending oneself that one becomes rich." Sarah Bernhardt made two motion pictures in 1912, *Queen Elizabeth* and *La Dame aux Camélias*, these remaining as evidence of the incomparable talent that makes her name a synonym for a great actress. She died in 1923 aged seventy-nine, but had prepared herself for death long before then. During her adolescence, Sarah had conquered a morbid fear of death by persuading her mother to buy her a silk-lined rosewood coffin, which she kept in her bedroom for the rest of her life and often slept in, she said, "to get used to her final resting place."

Sardanapalian, Sardanapian

I was the king, and while I lived on
*   earth,*
And saw the bright rays of the genial sun,
I ate, and drank, and loved; and knew
*   full well*
The time that men do live on earth was
*   brief*
And liable to many sudden changes,
Reverses and calamities. Now others
Will have the enjoyment of luxuries
Which I do leave behind me. For these
*   reasons,*
I have never ceased one single day from
*   pleasure.*

Thus read the epitaph the Assyrian king Ashurbanipal reputedly left beside his burial mound in Ninevah. Ashurbanipal was probably the prototype of Sardanapalus, the semilegendary king of Greek fable whose name has become a synonym for effeminate luxury. King Ashurbanipal lived in the seventh century B.C., the Greeks calling him Sardanapalus because his real name was a difficult one for them to pronounce. It is hard to separate fable from fact concerning Sardanapalus, but he does not deserve the designation "effeminate." Rather he appears to have been a shrewd military strategist and bloodthirsty tyrant who reigned for over forty years beginning in 668 B.C., conquering Babylon, parts of Egypt, the Medes and the Persians. But as he grew older, Sardanapalus surrounded himself with luxuries, his philosophy, it is said, summed up in a monument he had erected in the city of Anchiale, its inscription reading: "Sardanapalus the king. . . . In one day built Anchiale and Tarsus. Eat, drink and love, the rest's not worth this!" The epicure retired to his magnificent palace filled with tempera paintings, woven carpets and furniture inlaid with gold. Locked up with his wives and concubines, he devoted himself to sensual pleasures and became obsessed with gluttony, establishing what were the world's first cookery contests with his prizes of up to a thousand gold pieces for the creators of delectable new recipes. Sardanapalus became a patron of the arts and a scholar, his library of over thirty thousand clay tablets now in the British museum, but he refused to see his ministers or have anything to do with affairs of state. So the legend goes, anyway. Finally, the Medes, led by Arbaces, rose up against him, figuring the corrupt king an easy mark. Sardanapalus, spurred on by his favorite concubine, Myrna, won three battles against them but was ultimately defeated two years later. Legend has it that he and Myrna built a funeral pyre and leaped into the flames together with all his wives, or that Sardanapalus turned his luxurious palace into his funeral pyre, which burned for fifteen days. Actually, this was the fate into which the real Sardanapalus, Ashurbanipal, frightened his rebellious half-brother Shamash-Shumukin in 648 B.C., during the siege of Babylon. At any rate, King Ashurbanipal, whose real life only faintly resembles the Sardanapalus of the Greeks, died about 626 B.C. We only know for certain that the virile king, last of the great Assyrian monarchs, was depicted as effeminately hedonistic by Greek writers under the name Sardanapalus and that he became proverbial for the extreme of luxury. Lord Byron helped this misconception along with his poem *Sardanapalus* (1821) in which he writes: "*And femininely meanth furiously / Because all passions in excess are female.*"

Sardonic, Risus Sardonicus A *sardonic* person might be called a dead one, inside and out. The ancient Greeks believed that the *sardonē* (*herba Sardonia* in Latin), a poisonous plant native to Sardinia that gave the island its name, was so deadly that anyone unlucky or foolish enough to eat it would immediately succumb to its effects. Victims were said to literally die laughing, going into convulsions, their final contorted expressions after these death throes resembling bitter, scornful grins. The Greeks called their last bitter appearance of laughter *Sardonios gelos*, "Sardinian laughter," *Sardo* being their name for the island. *Sardonios gelos* became the French *rire sardonique*, this resulting in our *sardonic laughter* and *sardonic*, laughter or humor characterized by bitter or scornful derision. Whether the folklore is true or not remains unknown, but there is a real plant called the *herba Sardonia*. Named after the ancient city of Lydia in Asia Minor, the acrid plant does cause involuntary contortions of the facial nerves when tasted, these resembling a painful or bitter smile.

The medical term *risus sardonicus* is still used to describe the peculiar grin seen on the face of a corpse after deaths caused by tetanus and other diseases, an acute spasm of the facial muscles responsible for the bitter "smile."

Sauce Mornay French Protestant leader Philippe de Mornay (1549–1623) invented *Sauce Mornay* for his King Henry IV. Made with fish broth, the white sauce is enriched with Parmesan and Gruyère cheese and butter. Popularly known as the Protestant Pope, Mornay was Henry's right-hand man until the king converted to Catholicism and the Seigneur Duplessis-Mornay fell out of favor. After Henry's assassination, Louis XIII finally retired Mornay as governor of Saumur because of his opposition to the government's rapprochement with Catholic Spain. Mornay's spiritual writings and organizing abilities strongly influenced the development of a Protestant party in France. Henry IV, incidentally, originated the saying "a chicken in every pot" as a synonym for prosperity three hundred years before Herbert Hoover used it.

Sauce Robert This mouth-watering French sauce, which took hours to prepare in its original form, has been credited to Robert Vinot, an early seventeenth-century sauce maker of whom nothing else is known. But Rabelais described the sauce earlier and it could not have been invented by Vinot, although he may have improved it and given it his name. Still in use today, the ancient sauce is made with white wine, beef gravy, onion, mustard, butter and salt.

Saxophone While working in his father's renowned musical instrument workshop in Brussels, 1840–44, Antoine Joseph Sax invented a series of valved brass wind instruments with a new tone quality. These he named the *sax-horn* (which his father Charles actually invented and he improved upon); the *saxophone*; the *saxtromba*; and the *sax-tuba*. Antoine Joseph, often called Adolphe, left his ten brothers and sisters in Brussels and journeyed to Paris to make his fortune with his inventions. Sax made many influential friends among musicians, including Hector Berlioz, and they helped him to borrow money for a workshop and to promote his innovative instruments. The most important of his inventions proved to be the *saxophone*, although he thought of it as merely a bass instrument, unaware of its true potential. He demonstrated the *saxophone* in public on February 3, 1844, at a concert featuring a piece Berlioz wrote for his instruments, the *saxophone* unfinished and held together with string and wax, but winning great favor nevertheless. Sax later won the monopoly for supplying French army bands with musical instruments when a band furnished with his inventions defeated another using the then standard horns, oboes and bassoons. The inventor received many awards in his lifetime, but poor business sense prevented him from making the fortune he set out to make. He died in 1894, aged eighty, just before the *saxophone* or *sax* became of great importance in modern bands.

Scavenger's Daughter More subtle methods of torture have generally replaced this vicious device among modern states. The infamous *scavenger's daughter* consisted of wide iron hoops or manacles on which screws were tightened until the victim's head was clamped so tightly to his knees that blood was literally forced from his nose and ears, and sometimes from his hands and feet. The instrument had been invented by Sir William Skeffington or Skevington, lieutenant of the Tower in London during the reign of Henry VIII. First known as *Skeffington's gyres* or *irons*, it came to be jocularly called the *scavenger's daughter*, which both insulted the inventor and was more descriptive, feeding on dying flesh as it did. The terrible rack, invented by the duke of Essex, constable of the Tower in 1447, had earlier been called *Exeter's daughter*, so there was a precedent to go on in the naming. Such tortures were only permitted twice by the *courts* in recorded English history, but they were often employed.

Schick Test, Schick Razor While a professor of pediatrics at the University of Vienna in 1913, Dr. Béla Schick devised the famed *Schick test*, a skin test to determine susceptibility to diphtheria. His test consists of injecting diphtheria toxin into a person's skin, the skin becoming red and swollen if the person is not immune. Dr. Schick, born in Hungary, immigrated to the United States in 1923, becoming a naturalized citizen six years later. A pediatrician for many years at New York's Mt. Sinai Hospital, he did important work on allergies, wrote several books on child care, and helped found the American Academy of Pediatrics. He died in 1967, aged ninety.

Although it is a trade name and not generic anymore, the *Schick razor* deserves mention, its inventor, Jacob Schick, devising the first electric razor in 1928.

Schillerlocken A German fish dish named after the hair of a poet. *Schillerlocken* is curled chips of smoked fish commemorating the curly locks of the poet Schiller. Johann Christoph Friedrich von Schiller (1759–1805) was one of the founders of modern German literature, only Goethe overshadowing him in his time. Forced to become a doctor, while serving in military school against his wishes, Schiller finally rebelled and lived as a fugitive for a time. A poet, dramatist, historian and philosopher, many of his ballads became German favorites as well. Schiller was an idealist who hated tyranny in any form and his

philosophy influenced Einstein and Schweitzer among other famous Germans. The trilogy *Wallenstein* (1775), and *William Tell* (1804) are two of his masterworks and his renowned *Ode To Joy* (1785) was used by Beethoven in the chorale finale to his Ninth Symphony. Schiller often inspired himself to write by smelling a drawerful of rotten apples. A great favorite of the German people, the wide popularity of his works led to the affectionate word made from his name and *locken* (curl).

Schlemiehl, Schlemihl Nothing ever turns out right for the awkward and unlucky *schlemiehl*. The word, by now common American slang, comes from the Yiddish *shelumiel*, one who is worthless, which is said to derive from the name of the first Shelumiel mentioned in the Bible. Shelumiel appears four times in the Book of *Numbers* as the son of Zurishaddai and the leader of the tribe of Simeon. Nothing is said about him except that he is the leader of 59,300 people and makes an appropriate offering for the dedication of the altar at the Lord's command, but it has been suggested that Shelumiel lost in battle all the time while the other tribal leaders were victorious. Be that as it may, the word *schlemiehl* got a boost from the allegorical tale *Peter Schlemihls Wunderbare Geschichte* (*The Wonderful Story of Peter Schlemihl*) written by the German botanist and poet Adelbert von Chamisso in 1814. In the story the impecunious Peter Schlemihl makes a foolish bargain with the devil, selling his shadow for a never-empty purse and finding himself an outcast from human society because he has no shadow anymore. Through this story, which was translated into many languages and virtually became legend, *schlemihl* came to mean anyone making a foolish bargain, both living a life of its own and reinforcing the meaning of the earlier *schlemiehl*.

Scotch "If a body could just find oot the exac' proper proportion and quantity that ought to be drunk every day, and keep to that, I verily vow that he might leeve forever, without dying at a', and that doctors and kirkyards would go oot of fashion."

These were the words of a pioneer

sage of Dufftown, Scotland, on the benefits of *Scotch* whisky, which has a base of malted barley and was first made by the Scotch in Scotland. There seems no end to words prefixed with Scotch or Scotland. *Scotland Yard*, famous in the annals of crime and fiction, stands on the site of an ancient palace used by the Scottish kings when they came to London once a year to pay homage to the English sovereign. *Scotty* is short for the little *Scottish terrier* so popular as a pet. The national name Scotch is used to describe many things, often referring to the penuriousness traditionally attributed to the Scottish, *scotch* itself sometimes meaning tightfisted. Some examples follow:

Scotch Blackface: a breed of mountain sheep with black face and long wool.

Scotch bonnets: Marasmius oreades, the fairy ring mushroom.

Scotch broom: Cytisus scoparius, the broom plant.

Scotch broth: a thick broth made from mutton, barley, and vegetables.

Scotch cap: a round, brimless cap ornamented with two streamers.

Scotch coffee: "hot water flavored with burnt biscuit."

Scotch collups: a dish of steak and onions.

Scotch crocus: the common garden bulb *Crocus biflorus* with purple-striped flowers.

Scotch gray: a variety of both potato and buckwheat.

Scotch heather: Calluna vulgaris, the heath plant of the Scottish moors.

Scotch hands: paddles for shaping butter.

Scotch mist: both a combination of fog and drizzle and a cocktail made with *Scotch* poured over crushed ice.

Scotch pine: the handsome evergreen *Pinus sylvestris.*

Scotch pint: a two-quart bottle.

Scotch plaid: the checkered pattern copied from the tartan type cloth worn as a national costume in Scotland.

Scotch rose: the pink-, white- or yellow-flowered *Rosa spinossima* of Eurasia.

Scotch sixpence: a threepence.

Scotch tape: the trademarked cellophane tape; the word is also used as a verb.

Scotch thistle: the national emblem of Scotland, the thistle variety *Onopordom acanthium.*

Scotch woodcock: scrambled eggs served on toast spread with anchovy paste.

To play the Scotch organ: to put money in a cash register.

Additionally, the *schottische,* a dance similar to the polka, comes from a mispronunciation, probably French, of "Scottish dance." The expression *Scot-free,* the verb *to scotch,* or put an end to, and the game *hopscotch* have no connection with the Scotch, deriving from different words.

Scrimshaw   Sailors on long voyages in whaling days would often spend their spare time carefully carving whalebone, shells and ivory into decorative and useful objects, ranging from clothespins to elaborate canes and jewelry boxes. This intricate work was called *scrimshaw,* a word whose origins are rather vague. *Webster's* traces *scrimshaw* to the French *escrimer,* to fight with a sword, in the sense "to make flourishes," while others suggest *scrimshank,* English military slang for "to evade duty, be a shirker." Just as many authorities believe the word comes from the proper name Scrimshaw, referring to some once illustrious sailor-carver noted for his craftsmanship. But our Scrimshaw, if he did exist, hasn't been identified. *Scrimshaw* work was also called *scrimshander* and today it can mean any good piece of mechanical work.

Septuagint   Seventy-two men give their "name" to this word. Tradition has it that Ptolemy II, who reigned from 285 to 247 B.C., had the laws of the Jews translated into Greek by seventy-two scholars, six from each of the twelve Jewish tribes, in a period of seventy-two days on the island of Pharos. The translation became the earliest Greek version of the Old Testament, later erroneously named the *Septuagint* from the Latin *septuaginta,* which means seventy, not seventy-two. Scholars believe that the translation was made in Alexandria at this time, but not at Ptolemy's request, not by seventy-two Jewish scholars, and not in seventy-two days. Nevertheless, the fable about "the seventy" is responsible for the word. The tradition, however, only applies to the Pentateuch, the other books of the Old Testament translated later. *Septuagint* is often printed as the Roman numeral LXX.

Sequoia, Sequoia National Park, General Sherman Sequoia, Howard Libby Redwood, Metasequoia The largest and tallest living things on earth, the giant *sequoias* of California and Oregon, are named for the exalted Indian leader Sequoyah, who invented the Cherokee syllabary, which not only made a whole people literate practically overnight but formed the basis for many Indian languages. Sequoyah (also Sequoya, or Sikwayi) was born about 1770, the son of a white trader named Nathaniel Gist, his mother related to the great king Oconostota. Though he used the name George Guess, he had few contacts with whites, working as a silversmith and trader in Georgia's Cherokee country until a hunting accident left him lame. With more time on his hands now, Sequoyah turned his attention to the "talking leaves" or written pages of the white man and set out to discover this secret for his own people. Over a period of twelve years, ridiculed by family and friends, he listened to the speech of those around him, finally completing a table of characters representing all eighty-six sounds in the Cherokee spoken language. His system, which he devised by taking letters of the alphabet from an English spelling book and making them into a series of symbols, was adopted by the Cherokee council in 1821, one story claiming that Sequoyah's little daughter won over the council chiefs by reading aloud a message that they had secretly instructed her father to write down. Thousands of Indians would learn to read and write thanks to Sequoyah's "catching a wild animal and taming it," in his own words. He joined the Arkansas Cherokee the following year and in 1828 moved with them to Oklahoma after helping to negotiate in Washington for more extensive lands. Here he devoted himself to his alphabet and the study of common elements in Indian languages, translating parts of the Bible into Cherokee and starting a weekly newspaper. Sequoyah was also instrumental in avoiding bloodshed and forming the Cherokee Nation when in 1839 the federal government heartlessly drove other Cherokees to Oklahoma from their ancestral homes in Alabama and Tennessee. He is believed to have died somewhere in Mexico in about 1843 while searching for a lost band of Cherokees who were rumored to have moved there at about the time of his birth in 1770. It is said that he and his party of horsemen did ultimately find their lost brothers and taught them to read and write.

Sequoyah, legendary in his own time among Indians and whites, is the only man ever to invent an entire alphabet adopted by a people. Not long after his death, in 1847, the botanist Endlicher gave the name *Sequoia sempervirens* to the redwood tree, and it is generally assumed, though not definitely known, that he had the great Cherokee leader in mind. There are three types of *sequoias*, all members of the pine family. The redwood mentioned, native to the coast of Calfornia and a few miles into Oregon, is probably the tallest tree in the world, and towering above all other redwoods is the specimen called the Howard Libbey or Tall Tree growing along Redwood Creek in California's Redwood National Park. Standing 367.8′ tall, the Tall Tree may be the tallest tree of all time, although there are unconfirmed reports that an Australian eucalyptus felled in 1868 reached 464 feet. It was first named the Howard Libbey after the president of the Arcata Redwood Company, on whose land it was located until Congress established the park.

Another *sequoia* type is *Sequoia gigantia*, which grows on the western slopes of California's Sierra Nevada. These are generally called *giant sequoias* or big trees, not redwoods. They are not as tall as their relatives but are the *largest* plants on earth. Greatest among them is the 272.4′ tall *General Sherman sequoia* in California's *Sequoia National Park*, this largest of all living things popularly named for General William Tecumseh Sherman (1820–91), ablest Union cavalry leader of the Civil War and leader of the devastating march through Georgia that dealt the Confederacy a blow from which it never recovered. It would take at least seventeen men, arms outstretched, to encircle this 101.6′-wide tree, which contains enough timber to make 35 five-room houses. From its beginnings as a minuscule seed nearly forty centuries ago the massive *General Sherman* increased in weight over 125,000 millionfold and in combined height and girth dwarfs any other plant. The *General Sherman*, 3,000 years old, is also one of the oldest of living things, but a bristlecone pine in California's Inyo National Forest holds the record here, tree *Methuselah* having endured for over 4,600 years on the wind-swept slopes of the White Mountains—since 2600 B.C.

The third *sequoia* is the dawn redwood or living fossil, *metasequoia glyptostroboides*. Only discovered growing in China in 1946, these trees are reputedly the ancestors of all *sequoias* and their fossil remains date back 30–50 million years. The dawn redwood is now grown in the United States and has thus far reached heights of up to 35 feet, closely resembling other redwoods but more similar to our Southern cypress. Incidentally, it is little known that some *sequoias* have been grown successfully in the east—including one at Rochester, N.Y., that reached a height of over 50 feet. *The Forest Giant* by Adrian Le Corbeau, translated by T. E. Lawrence, Lawrence of Arabia, is a beautifully written appreciation of the giant *sequoia*.

Seward's Folly, Seward's Icebox, Seward Peninsula, Bering Sea After having been wounded by John Wilkes Booth's fellow conspirator Lewis Powell at the same time that Abraham Lincoln was assassinated, William Henry Seward recovered and remained in the cabinet of Lincoln's successor Andrew Johnson as secretary of state. A vigorous opponent of slavery—he had originated the well-known phrases "there is a higher law than our constitution" and "irrepressible conflict," the last expressing the state of the nation until it became all slave or all free—Seward nevertheless backed Johnson's conciliatory policy toward the South during Reconstruction. Seward, a lawyer, had handled both the Trent Affair and the Alabama Claims with great skill under Lincoln, but his most important work in Johnson's administration was the purchase of Alaska from Russia in 1867. Very few had the foresight to appreciate Seward's $7,200,000 acquisition at the time and because Alaska was purchased almost solely due to his determination, although others had made overtures toward buying it before the Civil War, it was widely called *Seward's folly* or *Seward's icebox*. William Henry Seward died in 1872, aged seventy-one, but the famous nicknames were used long after his death, even when fortunes were being made in Alaskan gold and fur. Alaska, from the Aleut *A-la-as-ka*, "the great country," became the forty-ninth American state in 1959. The largest, least populated state is of course worth thousands of times its original purchase price of less than two cents an acre—the $900 million bid for Alaskan oil leases in 1969 far exceeding it alone. The *Seward Peninsula* in West Alaska on the *Bering Strait* also bears the statesman's name, and *Bering Strait* and *Bering Sea* honors Captain Vitus Bering, a Dane who in exploring for Russia in 1741 is believed to have been the first white man to visit Alaska. William Seward had proposed the purchase of the Virgin Islands when Alaska was bought, but public opposition to his "icebox wasteland" made this impossible and the Virgin Islands of the United States were not acquired from Denmark until 1917—for $25,000,000.

Shakespearian *Shakespearian* means much more than "pertaining to the work of English author William Shakespeare." The word has come to represent profound universal magistry and vision in writing, among a veritable dictionary of superlatives. Little is really known about the personal life of the world's greatest poet and dramatist. Shakespeare was born in 1564 at Stratford-on-Avon of substantial middle class parents, his father an alderman, and received a solid grammar school education, well above the standards for the times. There is evidence that the Sweet Swan of Avon, as Ben Johnson called him, left Stratford for London to avoid a charge of poaching. He probably acted in the earl of Leicester's company and by 1592 had achieved fame as a dramatist and actor. By this time Shakespeare had acquired property and lived like a gentleman with his wife Anne Hathaway, whom he had married ten years previously, and with their children Susanna and the twins Hammet and Judith. Shakespeare was one of the few writers in his day to win fame and wealth. The Bard of Avon died on his own birthday in 1616, aged fifty-two, in Stratford, where he had retired five years before. Countless stories and speculations surround the dramatist's life, ranging from the spelling of his name—the plentiful variations including Shakspeare, Shakspear, and Shakspere—to the alleged infidelity of his wife, the identity of the "dark lady" of the sonnets, and the fantastic theory that Bacon actually wrote his plays. Most of these are familiar, but none has been proved. It is not even certain that Shakespeare wrote the famous epitaph on his gravestone at Holy Trinity Church in Stratford: GOOD FREND FOR IESUS SAKE FORBEARE / TO DIGG THE DUST ENCLOSED HERE! / BLESTE BE YE MAN THAT SPARES THES STONES, / AND CURST BE HE THAT MOUES MY BONES.

Shakespeare's plays and poems have appropriately evoked even more comment. Thirty-seven plays in all have been attributed in whole or part to him, beginning possibly with *Love's Labour's Lost* in 1588 to *Henry VIII* in 1613. The names of almost all the plays are well known—*The Taming of the Shrew, Romeo and Juliet, A Midsummer Night's Dream, The Merchant of Venice, Julius Caesar, Hamlet, King Lear, Macbeth,* etc., and it would be impossible to even try to show here in how many ways the 814,780 words in his plays or the 1,277 speaking characters he created have enriched English—the irrepressible Falstaff and all Shakespeare's characters coming so alive in the dramas that they stepped off the stage and into the language forever. Despite his "borrowings," his assimilative temperament, despite his "lack of education" the "myriad minded" Shakespeare remains "great above rule," "not for an age but for all time," "not England's poet but the world's."

A seventeenth-century joke about Shakespeare from the diary of John Manningham is worth recording: "Upon a time when Burbage played Richard III there was a citizen grew so far in liking him, that before she went from the play she appointed him to come that night unto her by the name of Richard III. Shakespeare, overhearing their conversation, went before, was entertained and at his game ere Burbage came. Then, message being brought that Richard III was at the door, Shakespeare caused return to be made that William the Conqueror was before Richard the Third!"

Shavian Wit Few are the humans who have the talent or will to impose their own names on the language, but George Bernard Shaw, no ordinary mortal, did just that. Shaw did not like the way "Shawian" sounded and so Latinized his name to *Shavius* and coined the word *Shavian* from it. *Shavian*, meaning characteristic of the work or style of George Bernard Shaw, soon bred the phrases *Shavian wit* or *Shavian humor*, referring to the dramatist's brilliant written or impromptu lines. Shaw, who began as a music reviewer and novelist, should be an inspiration to every fledgling author, for he earned exactly six pounds ($20) in his first *nine years* of writing. He went on to write *Arms and the Man* (1898), *Man and Superman* (1903), and *Pygmalion* (1912), among many far-famed plays, his work marked by large social themes and brilliant rhetoric that is often found in their controversial prefaces. But the personal life of this self-confessed genius became almost as famous as his plays. Shaw's *Fabian* socialism, his vegetarianism, his phonetic spelling reform ideas, and not least of all, his love affairs, fascinated the public right up until his death in 1950, aged ninety-four. The cantankerous iconoclast was probably too brilliant for the good of his plays, but their rich humor and mastery of dialogue make up for his inability to create living characters. As for the *Shavian* wit, Shaw was as celebrated for it in real life as in his plays. The portly author G. W. Chesterton, for example, once thought he had scored when he told the stringy Shaw, "Looking at you, one would think there was a famine in England." But not after Shaw replied, "Looking at you, one would think you caused it." Then there was the time Shaw received an invitation from a celebrity hunter reading: "Lady Blank will be home Thursday between four and six." He returned the card with the message "Mr. Bernard Shaw likewise" written underneath. Or take his advice to William Douglas Home: "Go on writing plays, my boy. One of these days a London producer will go into his office, and say to his secretary, 'Is there a play from Shaw this morning?' and when she says 'No,' he will say, 'Well, then we'll have to start on the rubbish.' And that's your chance, my boy." But for all his wit, the bearded Irishman could be bested. He was an immense target. "Bernard Shaw had discovered himself and gave ungrudgingly of his discovery to the world," wrote Saki (H. H. Munroe). "Shaw isn't prominent enough to have enemies and none of his friends like him," Oscar Wilde quipped. The actress Cornelia Otis Skinner got the best of Shaw in the following exchange of telegrams after a revival of *Candida*—Shaw: *Excellent. Greatest.* Skinner: *Undeserving such praise.* Shaw: *I meant the play.* Skinner: *So did I.* And even Mrs. Shaw occasionally bested the master. "Isn't it true, my dear, that male judgment is superior to female judgment?" Shaw once asked his wife. "Of course, dear," she replied. "After all, you married me and I you." (See also *Oscar*.)

Sheraton Style Only Thomas Chippendale has been more widely acclaimed than Thomas Sheraton (1751–1806) as a furniture designer. Unlike many of his predecessors, Sheraton was not a cabinetmaker and there is no record that he ever had a shop of his own or worked with his own hands building furniture. In fact, only one piece—a glass-fronted bookcase stamped with his initials—is known to have belonged to him. Sheraton's fame comes principally from his *The Cabinet-Maker and Upholsterer's Drawing Book* (1791), which introduced designs noted for simplicity and grace combined with utility. This book, followed by a cabinetmaking dictionary (1802) and an unfinished encyclopedia (1804), was intended for London cabinetmakers and the chairs and other pieces drawn in its pages strongly influenced many designers to adopt the *Sheraton style*, which was based on rectangular shapes, preferring straight lines to curves. One of the first professional designers,

Sheraton was born into poverty and lived in extreme poverty all his years, barely eking out a living by teaching drawing. His early work, owing much to Robert Adam and others, is highly valued today, but his style in later years is said to be marred by excessive ornamentation. Woods capable of taking a high polish appealed to Sheraton, particularly satinwood, and he created many original pieces, including the first mirrors attached to a bureau, and furniture with dual functions, such as a library table that concealed a step ladder. These so-called "harlequin pieces" even included an *ottoman* with built-in heating urns "so that the seat may be kept in a proper temperature in cold weather."

Sherry Via an indirect route, *sherry* is another word that derives from *Caesar's* name. *Sherry* is made in *Jerez de la Frontera*, Spain, for which it was named, and *Jerez*, in turn, commemorates Julius Caesar, having originally been called *Xeres*, this an adaptation of the Latin *urbs Caesaris*, "the town of Caesar." Sixteenth-century Spaniards pronounced *Jerez* something like *sherris*, which the English adopted and changed to *sherry* because they believed *sherris* was a plural form. Shakespeare wrote "a good *sherris*-sack hath a twofold operation in it" in *2 Henry IV*, but today the false singular is always used.

Jerez is still famous for its vineyards and manufacture of *sherry*, the native wine so rich in organic ethers that it rivals cognac in this respect. A peculiar thing happens in Jerez when the wine ferments. Over some barrels a delicate scum called a *flor* forms and this *sherry* will always be pale golden and dry, while barrels with no *flor* turn deep brown, mellower and sweeter. Dry *sherries* are called *finos* and sweet ones *oloroso*, or fragrant. *Finos* aged many years are known as *amontilladoes*, and *finos* aged on the seacoast in casks become so dry that they are called *manzanilla*.

It is said that when Sir Francis Drake burned the port of Cadiz in 1587, he seized twenty-five hundred butts of *sherry* from nearby Jerez. Drake called the wine *sack*, according to the old folk story, but the dockers unloading the barrels noted the letters XERES (for

Jerez) on them and became the first to use the word *zherry* or *sherry*.

Shill, Shillibeer London's first buses were introduced from Paris by George Shillibeer (1797–1866) on July 4, 1829. His omnibuses, coaches carrying twenty-two passengers and pulled by three horses, immediately caught on in London and were being called buses within three years. Apparently, Shillibeer later went into the undertaking business, or at least a combined hearse and mourning coach was named the *shillibeer* after him. The word *shill*, for a swindler's assistant, a "booster" hired to entice customers, may also derive from his name, especially considering that *shills* were and are still used to pack tourist buses in order to lure customers aboard. Shillibeer's connection with buses makes him a likely candidate, but there have been other suggestions. One is some notorious *shill*, probably a circus or carnival employee, surnamed Shillibeer. Another possibility is the American humorist Benjamin Penhallow Shillaber (1814–90), who printed Mark Twain's first work in his *The Carpet Bag*, a weekly important in developing the new school of American humor. In 1847 Shilliber created the character Mrs. Partington, which he used in a number of books, beginning with his *Life and Saying of Mrs. Partington* (1854). Critics charged Shilliber with lifting his character from English politician and author Sydney Smith. The American admitted that he took the name from Smith's allusion to the legendary Dame Partington, who had tried to sweep the flooding Atlantic Ocean out of her cottage and whom Smith had compared in an 1831 speech with the opposition of the House of Lords to reform (see *Dame Partington*). Although Shillaber denied using anything more than the Partington name for his gossiping Yankee Mrs. Malaprop, his own name came into some disrepute and may have become the basis for *shillaber* and then *shill*. As a matter of fact, Mark Twain owes far more to Shilliber's Mrs. Partington for Tom Sawyer's Aunt Polly than Shilliber owes to Smith for Mrs. Partington.

Shimose What word did Masashika Shimonose Kogakubachi give us? Masashika Shimonose Kogakubachi got his name in the dictionaries when in 1914 he invented an explosive made of picric acid. *Shimose powder*, or *shimose*, was used against the Russians in the Russo-Japanese war and proved highly effective. Its chief constituent, picric acid, is an intensely bitter and poisonous yellow crystalline acid used as a painkiller for burns and for dyeing as well as for dying. In France a powder to fill shells was made from it in 1886 and called *melenite*, while in England experiments in the town of Lydd two years later resulted in the explosive *lyddite*. All were names for essentially the same explosive, but *shimose* was the first to be extensively tested in war. Under whatever name you choose to call it, the first modern shell powder—it replaced black powder—has probably caused as much intentional death and destruction as any invention, still being one of the most common military explosives. Perhaps Masashika Shimonose Kogakubachi would rather have had it called by its scientific name of trinitrotoluene.

Shortia *Shortia* is definitely a *"low-growing"* genus of evergreen herbs, "comprising *only two* species," but that is not the reason for its name. The genus honors Dr. Charles W. Short (1794–1863), a Kentucky botanist. Native to the mountains of the Carolinas and Japan, the flowers are well adapted for use in the rock garden, the American species sometimes advertised as "Oconee Bells" and the Japanese, "Nippon Bells." The plants have beautiful white bell- or heart-shaped flowers, solitary and nodding on long stalks. They are more often called *Shortia*, or *coltsfoot*, than by their "Bell" names.

Shrapnel *Shrapnel's shell* or *shrapnel's shot*, as it was first called, was the brainchild of Henry Shrapnel, a British artillery officer who held the rank of second lieutenant and had only turned twenty-three when he began work on his deadly contrivance in 1783. Shrapnel had joined the army at the age of eighteen and served in Gibraltar, the West Indies and Flanders under the duke of York. He devoted all his spare time and money to developing his invention, the *shrapnel shell* consisting of a spherical projectile filled with lead musket balls and a small charge of black powder that was set off by a time fuse, exploding the shell in midair and scattering the shot in an ever-widening sheaf over a large area. This antipersonnel weapon, which laid low everyone in its path, was finally adopted in 1803 due to Shrapnel's persistent efforts and he was promoted to regimental lieutenant colonel the following year. The British first used *shrapnel* when they seized part of Surinam from the Dutch and established British Guiana in South America. But its most important test came eleven years later in 1815 when it was employed during the Peninsula War by Wellington's forces and helped to defeat Napoleon at Waterloo. By this time Shrapnel was an inspector of artillery and working at the royal arsenal at Woolrich, where he began to develop other weapons, including improved howitzers and mortars. Shrapnel's shot had already become known as *shrapnel*, and over the years added velocity would be imparted by a larger powder charge embodied in the missile, enabling the bullets now used in place of shot to cover an area 250 by 200 yards. Although the shell itself wasn't used during World War II, the term *shrapnel* is still applied loosely to shell fragments from any high explosive, whether artillery, bomb, or mine. Henry Shrapnel, who had been promoted to lieutenant general in 1837, died five years later, aged eighty-one. He had never been paid a cent for his important invention and the government refused even to compensate him for the several thousand pounds of his own money that he had spent in developing the weapon.

Shyster A lawyer named Scheuster who practiced law in New York around the middle of the nineteenth century may be the source of the word *shyster*. *Shyster* is an American slang term for a shady, disreputable lawyer and its first recorded use in 1846 coincides with Scheuster's notorious career. At any rate, Professor H. B. Woolf and others list the New York advocate as a possible source. Shakespeare's moneylender Shylock has also been suggested, as has a racetrack form of the word *shy*, i.e., to be shy money when betting. Most authorities,

trace *shyster* to the German *Scheisse*, excrement, possibly through the word *shicir*, "a worthless person," but councilor Scheuster is just as good a choice, probably better.

Siamese Twins, Siamese Cat, Siamese Fish, Siamoise P. T. Barnum coined the name *Siamese twins* for Chang and Eng Bunker, the Siam-born Chinese joined twins who had appeared as the "Chinese Double-Boys" before he brought them to America to star in his museum and circus. Their name soon became generic, describing all twins joined at birth by musculofibrous tissue, either side by side or back to back. Siamese twins probably arise by the almost complete separation of a single egg into two parts, human identical twins representing an extreme of the same process—a complete separation. Always the same sex, one usually left-handed and the other right-handed, such twins make common use of one or more parts of their bodies and the organs of one twin are usually a mirror image of those of the other—the heart of one, for example, being normally placed and that of the other in inverse position, what is known scientifically as *situs-inversus*. Siamese twins can easily be severed at birth where the union is superficial, but deeply united pairs like Chang and Eng seldom survive and only a few have lived joined together.

Chang and Eng Bunker were born in Bangesau, Siam, on April 15, 1811, and were discovered at Mekong when they were sixteen. Their bodies were joined by a ligament between the xiphoid cartilages, a short tubular band uniting them at the chest through which their circulatory systems communicated. After Barnum brought the world-renowned "Chinese Double-Boys" to America, he had considerable trouble with them, claiming that they were the only show business people he couldn't get along with. But then Chang and Eng hated everybody, even each other, Barnum said. At any rate, the two often quarreled with the impresario over his methods and only exhibited when they needed the money. In April, 1846, they married two English sisters, Sarah and Adelaide Yates, fathering twenty-two children between them—Chang, ten and Eng, twelve—

according to the records. They finally settled with their families on a farm in New Hampshire where they died on January 17, 1874, within two or three hours of each other, but the surviving twin did not die of a broken heart as the story goes—fatal illness in one *Siamese twin* dooms the other unless they can be separated, which was impossible in Chang and Eng's case. The Siamese Twins, as they were billed, gave their name to all others so born after them and the term is also used to describe inseparable friends. Doubles of many kinds are called *Siamese,* such as the *Siamese pipes* with two openings almost at ground level outside some buildings— fire engines using these to pump water into a building for its standpipes and sprinkler system.

Siamoise is simply short for *couche Siamoise,* Siamese birth. But *Siamese cat* and *Siamese fighting fish* have nothing to do with Chang and Eng except that they too come from Siam, the former name of Thailand. The short-haired, blue-eyed *Siamese cat,* with fawn-colored body and darker tail and face, may have originated in the seventeenth century from matings of the sacred Burmese cats with Annamite cats. *Siamese fighting fish, Beta splendens,* are long-finned, brilliantly colored labyrinth fish, noted for their pugnacity, these qualities bred into them over centuries. (See also *Barnum; Jenny Lind; Jumbo.*)

Sideburns, Burnside Carbine, Burnside Hat   On Ambrose Burnside's first wedding day his wife-to-be took one last look at him and responded with a resounding "No!" when the minister asked her if she took this man to be her lawful wedded husband. Whether this had anything to do with the doubtlessly abrasive whiskers Burnside wore, if indeed he wore any at the time, remains unknown to history, but the story does show how unusual situations simply "happened" to the luckless soldier. Not only did the wrong things happen, but General Ambrose Everett Burnside, who later married another bride successfully, had a flair for doing the daring, innovative thing in war as well as fashion, another quality that kept his photographs in the papers and his countenance in the pub-

lic's mind. Burnside started off on the wrong foot from the moment he entered the military. After serving as a tailor's apprentice in his native Liberty, Ind., he had been appointed a cadet at West Point, graduating low in his class and excelling more in extracurricular singing and cooking than in military tactics. Following a tour with the cavalry in the West, he resigned from the army in 1853 to set up the Bristol Rifle Works in Rhode Island where he manufactured the breechloading *Burnside carbine* of his invention. Things went badly for him, as usual, his business failing despite his new type rifle's success, but not so badly as they would after he re-entered the army at the outbreak of the Civil War. Burnside's expedition to the North Carolina coast in 1862, resulting in the capture of Roanoke Island, New Bern, Beaufort and Fort Macon, won him the rank of major general and much acclaim. Yet when he took command of the Army of the Potomac later that year, he proved to be a distinct failure both as a leader and a strategist, his plan to capture Fredericksburg by crossing the river resulting in a slaughter so bloody that a special truce had to be called to bury the 100,000 Union dead—making Fredericksburg long known as Burnside's Slaughter Penn. Victories would come later for the general, but they would somehow never rival his spectacular setbacks, as, for example, the much-publicized "Mud March" when Burnside marched his men out of camp near Fredericksburg and had to march them directly back again due to a heavy rainstorm that made maneuvers impossible. Relieved of his command early in 1863, the unlucky general was next officially reprimanded by President Lincoln when while heading the Department of the Ohio, he "court-martialed" ex-Congressman Clement Vallandigham for an antiwar political speech and closed the Chicago *Tribune* when that paper protested. Finally, Burnside was transferred back to the Ninth Corps he had originally commanded when he enlisted (Burnside's Peripatetic Geography Class, as it was called because it traveled so widely on foot), only to face a final spectacular defeat at the battle of Petersburgh in 1864.

Again it was a daring scheme that caused his downfall. Burnside approved a plan to dig a tunnel under the Confederate lines, fill it with high explosives and attack at the moment the charges were set off. Sad to say, the tunnel was built, the attack made, and the attack repulsed. General Burnside was relieved of his command by a court of inquiry, in fact, nearly drummed out of the army.

All of Burnside's failures hinged on *ifs*. *If* engineers had built pontoon bridges in time for his Fredericksburg attack, he might not have been routed. *If* it hadn't unexpectedly rained, his "Mud March" wouldn't have come about. *If* he had been allowed to use the crack black troops he wanted to at Petersburgh instead of an untrained white regiment, his attack there might have been successful. Perhaps these *ifs* account for the fact that he remained so popular, for he went on to be elected as governor of Rhode Island for three terms, 1866–69, and United States senator for two terms, from 1875 until his death in 1881, aged fifty-seven. But his winning personality and patriotic spirit probably played a more important role in his political triumphs. From the constant publicity given him, the flamboyant *Burnside hat* that he wore in the field came to be called after the big bluff and hearty general, as were the *burnside whiskers* or *burnsides* he affected. Innovative as ever, he had chosen to wear the hair on his face in a new way, shaving his chin smooth below a full mustache and big muttonchops or sidebar whiskers. Thousands imitated him and his *burnsides*, because they were only on the sides of the face, were soon called *sideburns*, this reversal of Burnside's name having nothing to do with his *military reversals*, though that might have been appropriate. The word *sidebars* probably also influenced the inversion, but, whatever the case, Burnside's name became one of the best known eponymous words. Though the general's whiskers have long since gone out of style, *sideburns* are even more popular today than they were in his time, the word now applied to any continuation of hair down the side of a man's face.

Silhouette Madame Pompadour had her friend Étienne de Silhouette appointed France's controller general in 1759, but was probably disappointed with the results. Silhouette, then fifty and noted as a translator of Pope and the author of several studies on national finance, proceeded to try and get France back on her feet after the bankruptcy brought about by the Seven Years' War, not to mention the luxury-loving court where La Pompadour set the life style and spent more than anyone else. The new minister started out well enough, raising a seventy-two-million-livres loan, but he soon placed restrictions on the spending of Louis XV himself, proposed a land tax on the estates of nobles, and ordered a cut in government pensions. This naturally angered the nobles, who often found ways to circumvent Silhouette's reforms, and the minister trotted out plans to levy an income tax, triple the poll tax on bachelors, institute a luxury tax, and levy a stringent sales tax. People generally thought such reforms cheap, capricious and petty, resenting the sacrifices demanded, and when financiers boycotted his treasury operations Silhouette was forced to resign less than nine months after he took office. In the meantime, his parsimonious regulations had inspired the phrase *à la silhouette*, "according to Silhouette" or "on the cheap." Pants without pockets—and who needed pockets with such confiscatory taxes— were said to be made *à la silhouette*, as were snuffboxes constructed with wood, and coats that were required to be fashioned without folds. The term was also applied to shadow portraits made by tracing the outline of a profile and filling it in with black, or cutting the outline out of black paper. These were called portraits *à la silhouette*, cheap portraits according to Silhouette, and soon became known simply as *silhouettes*. Monsieur Silhouette did not invent the drawings—shadow portraits were made by the cavemen—they just happened to be the rage of Paris at the time. Other versions of *silhouette's* origin, however, claim that M. Silhouette's hobby was making the shadow portraits, that he decorated the walls of his chateau at Bry-sur-marne with them, and that he advocated their use to save money on portraits. *À la silhouette* could also refer to the minister's brief term of office, or to his attempts to reduce French finance to its simplest form, but no matter how the phrase resulting in the word specifically came about, it has some connection with what were regarded as his niggardly regulations that cut expenses to the bone until they became shadows of their original selves. *Silhouettes* were long popular as an inexpensive substitute for portraits and were the hobby of many greats, including Goethe. Photographs have since replaced them, but today Étienne Silhouette's name is applied to any outline of a shadow, giving him the dubious honor of being our most insubstantial eponymous personality.

Simenon A *Simenon* is a serious psychological novel of about fifty thousand words written by author Georges Simenon—and written in a rather unique way. Simenon gets a complete medical examination before he begins one of these critically praised short novels. He then literally locks himself in a room and working from the barest of notes, allows himself seven days to write each book and three days to revise. *Simenons* are distinct from the author's popular Inspector Maigret stories, which are highly respected in the mystery field. Born in Liége, Belgium, on February 13, 1903, the prolific but not prolix Simenon has authored some five hundred novels since he began writing at the age of nineteen, many of these admittedly pot boilers or breadwinners turned out under a score of pseudonyms. This does not make him the most fecund of authors. Lope de Vega, for example, wrote over eighteen hundred plays alone, not to mention his other works; American author Charles Hamilton (Frank Richards), the creator of Billy Bunter, produced a lifetime total of seventy-two million words, grinding out eighty thousand words a week at his peak; and contemporary British mystery writer John Creasy's output dwarfs Simenon's. But Simenon's critical acclaim, at least for his *Simenons*, far exceeds that given any modern prolific writer, André Gide having called him "perhaps the greatest French novelist in French literature to-

day." Simenon lived in America for a long period, now resides in Switzerland.

Simony There is a legend that Simon Magus the magician tried to prove his divinity in a dispute with Peter and Paul before the emperor Nero. He attempted to fly up to heaven after jumping out a high window, succeeded in defying the laws of gravity for a few moments, and then found himself cast down to earth by the prayers of the disciples. Simon, who lived in the first century in Samaria, was a skillful magician, his last name, in fact, meaning sorcerer. The story of his conversion to Christianity is told in the Bible (*Acts* 8:9–24). But the passage instructs us that Simon's conversion was made only so that he could obtain the new powers of sorcery that he thought the apostles possessed: "*Now when Simon saw that the Spirit was given through the laying on of the apostles' hands, he offered them money, saying, 'Give me also this power, that anyone on whom I lay my hands may receive the Holy Spirit.' But Peter said to him, 'Your silver perish with you, because you thought you could obtain the gift of God with money! You have neither part nor lot in this matter, for your heart is not right before God.'*" Simon's name, in the form of *simony*, has since then been a synonym for traffic in sacred things, such as the buying and selling of church offices, a *simoniac* one who practices simony. Not much is known of Simon after he was reproached by Peter, but it is believed that he founded a rival religion, a Gnostic sect combining elements of Christianity and paganism, traveling with a former prostitute named Helen and winning a number of disciples called *Simonians*. The traditional belief is that the wily magician died trying to prove his divinity when he attempted to imitate the resurrection of Christ. Simon, it seems, allowed himself to be buried alive, mistakenly believing that he would rise on the third day.

Slave, Slav The word *slave* originated long after Athens in the Periclean Age had twice as many *slaves* as freemen, even after Rome had become the great *slave* empire. *Slave* derives from the name of a tribe living in what is now Poland and other areas of eastern Europe. Their name meant "glory" or "noble, illustrious" in their own tongue, but about 6 A.D. this entire people was conquered by warlike German tribes from the west and either forced to serve their conquerors or sold into bondage to the Romans and Greeks. To the Romans their name was *Sclavus,* which became the Medieval Latin *sclavus,* a Slav captive, this term of contempt applied to any bondsman or servile person. *Sclavus* became *esclave* in French and came into English as *sclave,* retaining the *c* until about the sixteenth century, when *slave* was first used. The word *Slav,* for the race of people in eastern Europe, comes from the same source, the proud "noble" tribe whose name underwent a complete metamorphosis.

Slide, Kelly, Slide; Kelly Pool; Kelly Green; Kelly Hat; Kelly *Kelly pool,* where a player draws a number and tries to pocket the ball bearing it, is a corruption of *Keely pool,* origin unknown. *Kelly green,* a strong yellow-green, is so called because the color is associated with the Irish and Kelly is a common Irish name, and the *kelly hat,* a stiff derby or straw skimmer, is associated with the numerous stage Irishmen named Kelly who wore such hats when vaudeville was in flower. None of these terms can be traced to any particular Hibernian, but the word *kelly* for the topsoil that must be lifted before the clay used in making bricks can be removed may come from the name of baseball star Michael J. Kelly (1857–1894), who played for Chicago and Boston. "King" Kelly, born in Troy, New York, was called the Ten Thousand Dollar Beauty because he signed for that sum one year, an incredible amount of money for a ballplayer at the time. In 1889 a song was written about Kelly exhorting him to *slide, Kelly, slide,* an expression which in itself has become proverbial. Since a lot of dirt is removed when someone slides into a base, especially someone like hustling Mike Kelly, it was natural for laborers to use the name of the song's hero for the topsoil they removed. As Dizzy Dean would have put it, when Kelly slud, he slud hard. However, if Kelly didn't become famous for his slide *before* the song was written, the word *kelly* must come

from another source. It was used before 1884 and some authorities suggest that it is a corruption of *callow,* an English word meaning the same.

Smart Aleck If there ever lived a real "smart Aleck," an Alexander so much of an obnoxiously conceited know-it-all that his name became proverbial, no record of him exists. The term can be traced back to about the 1860's and is still frequently used for a wise guy today. The original *smart aleck* may have been at least clever enough to cover up all traces of his identity.

Smith & Wesson, Equalizer American inventors Daniel B. Wesson and Horace Smith founded the *Smith and Wesson Arms Company* at Springfield, Mass., three years after they invented the first firearm magazine in 1854. Their *Smith & Wesson* pistols replaced the *Colt* to a large extent and have been famous ever since. In fact, the term *equalizer* for a gun may come indirectly from their names. It is said that the term derives from a remark made by Chicago gangster Tim Smith, who died in a gangland killing on June 26, 1928. "Smith and Wesson made all men equal," this Smith is supposed to have said. Tim was no relation to the manufacturer, just a good customer.

Smithsonian Institution, Smithsonite Despite the fact that he neither had visited nor known anyone living in America, British chemist James Smithson (1765?–1829) left over $508,000 in American money, the whole of his estate, "to the United States of America to found at Washington under the name of the Smithsonian Institution an establishment for the increase and diffusion of knowledge among men." The money was actually willed to his nephew with the stipulation that the above condition apply if the nephew died without children—which he did in 1835. Smithson, the illegitimate son of Sir Hugh Smithson and Elizabeth Macie, made many valuable analyses of minerals and *smithsonite,* an important zinc ore, is also named in his honor. Congress took ten years debating whether or not to accept his bequest, finally accepting largely through the efforts of John Quincy Adams. The museum was founded in

1846. Numerous bequests have been received since and the *Smithsonian* today is the largest organization of its kind in the world. An agency of the government that maintains art galleries and a zoo as well as numerous museums, conducting scientific explorations and investigations in many fields, the *Smithsonian* is an excellent example of a "living museum" that hasn't failed to change with the times. (See also *Henry*.)

Smooch, Smouch *Smooch*, to kiss or pet, to make love, is of unknown origin. It may, however, have something to do with *smouch*, to pilfer, perhaps referring to "stolen kisses" originally. *Smouch*, a favorite of Mark Twain's, probably comes from the derogatory Dutch *Smous*, "a German Jew," this word possibly formed from the proper name Moses. Meaning to obtain illicitly by cheating or swindling, the word is another example of prejudice in language—if the story is true. (See also *Hobsonize*.)

Soapy Sam

If I were a cassowary
On the plains of Timbuctoo,
I would eat a missionary,
Cassock, band, and hymn-book too.

This much printed verse is often attributed to the first *Soapy Sam*, Samuel Wilberforce, Bishop of Oxford and later Winchester, a nonconformist and controversial clergyman if ever there was one. Wilberforce, son of the great antislavery leader William Wilberforce, tried to steer a middle course between High Church and Low Church factions in England. Although a devout man in his personal life, this position forced him to develop a suave, unctuous manner of speaking, persuasive but versatile and expedient almost to a fault. By 1860 he had earned the nickname *Soapy Sam*, which has since been applied to any slippery, unctuous speaker who can talk his way out of anything. The coining was perhaps given an assist by the initials S.O.A.P. of the floral decorations above the stall where he preached—these standing for the names Sam Oxon and Alfred Port. Once someone asked him about the nickname and he assured his questioner that he was called *Soapy Sam*, "Because I am often in hot water and always come

out with clean hands." Bishop Wilberforce died in 1873, aged sixty-eight. Either the English were poor riders or had spirited mounts, for like a disproportionate number of his countrymen—Sir Robert Peel of the *Bobbies* and Lord Cardigan in these pages—"Soapy Sam" died after being thrown from his horse.

Socrates Cup of Hemlock, Socratic Irony, Socratic Method By feigning ignorance, Socrates led his audience into traps, easily defeating them in argument, this pretended ignorance since known as *Socratic irony*. The great Greek philosopher also developed the inductive *Socratic method*, conducting a cross-examination by questions and answers carefully designed to impart knowledge, or to evoke knowledge from those who may have believed they were unknowing. Socrates was born about 470 B.C., the child of a sculptor and a midwife. After receiving a good education and completing a tour of military service in which he was distinguished for his bravery, he devoted his life to the investigation of virtue, justice and purity. Refusing the comforts of life, Socrates ate only simple foods and owned only one garment. His profound spiritual influence led him to be called the philosopher who "brought down philosophy from the heavens to earth" and he liked to call himself "the midwife of men's thoughts," but he left behind no writings and his work is known primarily through the *Dialogues* of Plato. Condemned to death by the Athenian government in 399 B.C. for neglecting the old gods, introducing new ones and corrupting youth, he was forced to commit suicide by drinking hemlock, *Socrates cup of hemlock*. "The hour of departure has arrived," he said at the last, "and we go our separate ways—I to die, and you to live. Which is the better, God only knows." (See also *Xanthippe*.)

Sodomite, Sodomy Sodom and Gomorrah, the twin sin cities of the Plain in the Bible, have long represented male and female vice respectively—a *Gomorrhean*, in fact, meaning a *lesbian* in sixteenth-century England. A *sodomite* is one who practices *sodomy*, "unnatural intercourse with a human or animal," such homosexual practices attributed to Sodom's male inhabitants. The story of

Sodom and Gomorrah is told in *Genesis* 18–19, their history ending when *"the Lord rained . . . brimstone and fire from . . . out of heaven, and he overthrew those cities, and all the plain, and all the inhabitants of the cities. . . ."* Old Testament scholars believe the story is a mythological attempt to account for the destruction of a city once located near the Dead Sea.

Solecism An error in grammar, the use of words, or even a breach of etiquette, is called a *solecism*. Soli, or Soloi, was an ancient Greek colony in the province of Cilicia, Asia Minor, far removed from Athens. Colonists who settled there developed a dialect of their own that Athenian purists considered barbarous and uncouth, leading them to coin the word *soloikos* as a slang term for ignorant speech. From *soloikos* came the Greek noun *soloikismos*, "speaking incorrectly," like an inhabitant of Soloi, which through the Latin *soloecismus* made its entrance into English as *solecism*. In years to come Yankee colonists would be criticized in much the same way by Englishmen, but the label *Americanism* has always been accepted with pride by Americans. Soloi, located in what is now Turkey, was an important prosperous port in the time of Alexander the Great. When Pompey rebuilt the city after it was destroyed by Tigranes in the Mithridatic War, he named it *Pompeiopolis*. Little of Soli's ruins remain today, but *solecism*, originally slang itself, endures in all modern European languages as a remembrance of the way its citizens "ruined" Greek.

Solomon, Solomonic, Solomon's Ring, Solomon's Seal Solomon, the son of David and Bath-sheba, ruled over Israel for some forty years, noted for his wisdom and wealth. The latter and perhaps the former are witnessed by the seven hundred wives and three hundred concubines he kept in great splendor. His wisdom is shown by the tale of the baby he proposed to divide in two. By suggesting this, Solomon determined the child's rightful mother—the false claimant accepting his proposal and the real mother asking that the child be given to her rival rather than be killed. His reign was a great one marked by peace and eco-

nomic and literary development, Solomon himself having the Song of Songs and the books of *Ecclesiastes* and *Proverbs* attributed to him. Yet there was a religious decline and increasing social injustice in the king's time, the northern tribes revolting upon his death in about 933 B.C. Solomon left Israel saddled with taxes and dissension, but his name remains a synonym for wisdom, the Bible referring to him as "wiser than all men . . . his fame . . . in all nations round about." *The wisdom of Solomon* is sometimes expressed by the phrase *to have Solomon's ring*, referring to a legendary ring he wore which told him all he wanted to know. *Solomon's seal* (*Polygonatum multiflorum*) is a plant with hanging greenish-white flowers whose rootstock bears scars of the previous year's stem growth, these scars somewhat resembling seals, while *solomonic* is an adjective only rarely used to describe *the wisdom of Solomon*.

Solon, Seven Wise Men "I grow old ever learning many things," wrote the sage Solon in the often quoted line. The wise statesman and lawgiver lived some eighty-two years before he left Athens in about 558 B.C. and died, according to tradition, while wandering somewhere in the east. One of the Seven Sages of Greece, his motto was "Know thyself." Solon initiated many legal and social reforms, including a new constitution for Athens that revived the popular assembly at a time when tension between the rich and poor had reached the breaking point. The lawgiver, who can also be called the first Attic poet, gained his knowledge of economics from his wide experience as a trader in foreign commerce, his economic reforms including the annulling of all mortgages and debts. His love poems and patriotic verse were well known, but the proverbial remark, "Call no man happy till he is dead," was probably not his, though traditionally attributed to him. Elected archon, officer of the state, in 594 B.C. Solon's reforms laid the foundations for Athenian democracy. His name has come to mean any lawmaker, not necessarily a wise one, *solon* often used because it takes up less space in headlines and newspaper stories than representative or congressman. The other six wise men of Greece were Thales of Miletus, Bias of Priene, Chilo of Sparta, Cleobulus of Lindos, Pittacus of Mitylene, and Periander of Corinth.

Sophism, Sophist, Sophistry, Sophomore The Sophists were not really a school of philosophers, but individual teachers who toured the cities of Greece in the mid fifth century teaching rhetoric and other subjects. They did, however, share common beliefs. Far less idealistic than the Socratic school, they prepared their pupils for public life, placing little store in "truth for truth's sake" and accepting money for their teaching, being what might be called pragmatists today. Although their name derived from *sophos*, the Greek word for wise, it was a contemptuous term among their contemporaries. Because they taught the art of persuasion to young men eager for political careers and the methods they taught were often unscrupulous and overingenious, a *sophist* became someone who tries to mislead people with clever arguments, one who tries to "make the worse seem the better reason." *Sophism* is now used to mean a plausible but fallacious argument, and false, specious reasoning is called *sophistry*. The word has thus had almost a complete reversal in meaning since the time when the wise men of Greece were called *sophists*—before the Sophists came on the scene. The word *sophomore*, a second-year college student, probably comes from *sophom*, an obsolete form of *sophism*, plus the suffix *or*.

Soubise Charles de Rohan, Prince de Soubise, may have created the superbly simple sauce that bears his name, but it is more likely that it was created and named in his honor by his major-domo, the great chef Marin. Marshal Soubise (1715–87), a famous gourmet who was the grandson of the princess de Soubise, one of Louis XIV's mistresses, became marshal of France in 1758 through the influence of Madame Pompadour, Louis XV's mistress. The prince did like to cook as much as he liked making love and war, but his chef Marin was among the greatest of eighteenth-century culinary artists, his cookbook *Les Dons de Comus* (*Gifts From the Kitchen*) appearing in 1739 and intended to brighten the tables of the bourgeoisie, enabling "even third-class persons to dine with grace." A *soubise* is a brown or white sauce containing strained or pureed onions and served with meat; it is made by blending onions simmered tender in butter with a creamy *Bechamel sauce* and rubbing this through a fine sieve. Toward the end of the eighteenth century a popular cravat was called the *soubise*, too, probably because the prince wore a similar one.

Sousaphone "The Stars and Stripes Forever," "The Washington Post," "Semper Fidelis," "Hands Across the Sea," "Liberty Bell," "High School Cadets"—John Philip Sousa composed over one hundred such popular marches, inspiring an English magazine to dub him The March King, a title that remained with the bandmaster throughout his long career. Sousa, the son of Portuguese refugees, began conducting theater orchestras when only nineteen. He became bandmaster of the U.S. Marine Corps band in 1882, his father having played there before him, and formed his famous Sousa's Band ten years later. His band toured the world, bringing him great renown, and he composed numerous comic operas, suites, songs and orchestral music in addition to his marches. Sousa died in 1932 aged seventy-eight. Besides greatly improving the quality of band music, he invented the *sousaphone*, a large circular tuba standing fifty-two inches high and weighing some twenty-six pounds, with a flaring adjustable bell, adjustable mouth piece, and a full, rich sonorous tone. The story of the most popular bandmaster who ever lived is told in his autobiography *Marching Along* (1928).

South Carolina (see *North Carolina*)

Spalding, Spaldeen Alfred Goodwill Spalding (1850–1915) deserves his place in baseball's Hall of Fame as much as any man. He may not be "The Father of Baseball," but is certainly "Father of the Baseball," and it was only when he came upon the scene with his uniform manufacturing methods that what had been a chaotic minor sport was fashioned into the national pastime. Lively balls were once so rubbery that baseball scores like 201–11 were not uncommon, and others so dead that the phrase "fell with a dull thud" found its way into the language. The former Chicago manager did not invent the hard ball when he founded his company in 1880, but the rigid manufacturing standards he maintained made it possible for the newly formed National League of Professional Baseball to survive. Today, both major league balls (*Reach* for the National League) are made in the Spalding plant in Chicopee, Mass. by a staff that includes a sewing circle of some three hundred New England ladies, each of whom daily laces some ten thousand stitches into the horsehide-covered, rubber-cored balls—more motions than most major league pitchers make in a season. About fifteen thousand balls—each core wound with eleven hundred feet of yarn—are turned out every day, all measuring up to the strict tolerances specified in the official rule book. Such careful preparations over the years have made the *Spalding* trademark synonymous for a baseball. Other sporting equipment manufactured by the firm includes a red rubber ball called the *Spaldeen* which has been known by that name to several generations of American youngsters. (See also *Louisville Slugger*.)

Spaniel Shakespeare has Antony speak of the "hearts that spaniel'd me at heels, to whom I gave their wishes." *Spaniel* can be a verb and adjective, "a symbol of affectionate humility," as well as a noun. The dog's name simply means "Spanish dog," deriving from the old French *chien épagneul*, which was shortened to *espagnol*, Spanish, and then *spaniel* in English. The spaniel was either a breed developed in Spain, or the dog reminded Europeans of the Spaniards, who were regarded as submissive and fawning during the Middle Ages. Neither the Spaniards nor the dog are servile, but the breed's silky hair and soft, soulful eyes may have suggested the appearance of the Spaniards. There is no hard evidence for this, however. The *cocker spaniel* gets his first name from the way he cocks his long, drooping ears, or possibly because he was trained to retrieve woodcock.

Spanish The French call a louse an *Espagnol*—a Spaniard—and a flea an *Espagnole*—a Spanish woman. There is no apparent reason for the differences in gender, the louse and flea merely a part of the never-ending war between nations with words as weapons. The Spanish haven't suffered the casualties the Dutch and other nationalities have borne, but their escutcheon is not unstained, as can be seen in some of the following words and phrases:

Spanish bayonet: several species of yucca from tropical America, where the Spanish once ruled supreme, these plants having narrow bayonetlike leaves.

Spanish beard or *moss:* the southern United States black moss, *Tillandsia usneoides*, which hangs down from the branches of trees.

Spanish bluebell: the bulbous herb *Scilla hispanica* of Spain and Portugal.

Spanish broom: a spiny shrub, *Genista hispanica*, of southern Europe.

Spanish cedar: the typical American timber tree, *Cedrela odorata*, whose mahoganylike wood is valued for making furniture and is widely used for cigar boxes.

Spanish chestnut: *Castarea sativa*, the sweet or edible chestnut of southern Europe.

Spanish dagger: *Yucca gloriosa*, the stemless plant of southeastern America with sharp-pointed leaves over two feet long.

Spanish fly: the blister beetles, *Lytta vesicatoria*, used to make this dangerous reputed aphrodisiac are abundant in Spain; cantharides, or *Spanish fly*, is medicinally a diuretic and skin irritant.

Spanish flu: the devastating respiratory infection that spread throughout the world in 1917–18 was called *Spanish influenza* or *Spanish flu*; the Spaniards were not responsible for the pandemic disease and *influenza* itself is an Italian word.

Other *Spanish* words include *Spanish button*, knapweed; the *Spanish foot* carved on furniture legs; the high *Spanish heel* on women's shoes; *Spanish iris*; *Spanish mackerel*; *Spanish omelet, onion,* and *rice*; and the *Spanish pointer dog*.

Spartan Either come back with it or on it, the proverbial Spartan mother tells her only son when she hands him the shield he is to carry into battle. The inhabitants of ancient Sparta, the Greek city state noted for its military excellence if little else, were forced to be courageous, frugal and sternly disciplined almost to a fault. Life there seems to have been equal to one long term of military service without leave from the barracks and battlefields, for women as well as men. Weak children were discarded and the survivors subjected to an ascetic discipline without luxuries or even comforts. Spartan virtues, which can easily become vices, give us the terms *Spartan fare*, a frugal diet; *Spartan courage*, that of one who can unflinchingly bear pain or face danger; and *Spartan simplicity*, the barest necessities of life. The Spartans, made great militarily by their stern *Spartan discipline*, defeated Athens in the Peloponnesian War (404 B.C.) and became dominant in Greece. After Philip of Macedon defeated them in 338 B.C., they rapidly declined in importance. But then Sparta wasn't ever a great place to live, or even to visit. (See also *Laconic*.)

Spencer, Spencer Rifle, Spencer Wig

Two noble earls, whom if I quote,
Some folks might call me sinner;
The one invented half a coat,
The other half a dinner.

The "half a dinner" referred to in the old rhyme is the *sandwich*, named after the earl of Sandwich. The "half a coat" is the *spencer*, a close-fitting outside jacket reaching just below the waist that was popular in the late eighteenth and early nineteenth centuries. The *spencer* was named for George John Spencer, the second Earl of Spencer (1758–1834), who wore such a coat at a time when tailed outer garments were "proper." According to one story, Lord Spencer won a bet that he could set a new style just by appearing in the streets wearing any kind of garment, the *spencer* resulting from this wager. While England's lord of the admiralty, Spencer selected Nelson to command the fleet that won the historic battle of the Nile; he served as home secretary in 1806. The short, close-fitting woman's bodice called the *spencer* derives its name from a Mr. Knight Spencer, who apparently designed it about 1803; and the *spencer wig* is most likely named after the third earl of Sutherland, Charles Spencer (1674–1722). The *Spen-*

cer rifle, a breechloading carbine that was the favorite arm of Union cavalrymen during the Civil War, was invented by C. M. Spencer (1833–1922). On the frontier it was largely supplanted by the simpler *Henry*, which developed into the *Winchester*.

Spencerian, Spencerian Penmanship, Spencerian Script, Spenserian, Spenserian Stanza Even as recently as twenty-five years ago penmanship remained an important subject in American grammar schools. But the increased use of the typewriter has made all the penmanship exercises almost obsolete. In those days of yesterday, when a fine hand was a great social asset and absolutely essential in conducting a business, one of the first American styles of calligraphy was that developed by Platt Rogers Spencer (1800–64), a system based on precise slanted strokes marked with flourishes at the end of words. Spencer taught classes in a log cabin on his Geneva, N.Y., farm and lectured at various business schools and academies. His *Spencerian style*, popularized by a series of textbooks he wrote, greatly influenced early nineteenth-century American calligraphy, so much so that today the term *Spencerian script* is used by collectors to describe the handwriting of his period and beyond.

Spencerian also refers to the thought of English philosopher Herbert Spencer (1820–1903), especially his attempt to unify all knowledge through the single principle of evolution, his "synthetic philosophy." *Spenserian* means pertaining to the work of the great English poet Edmund Spenser (c. 1552–99), the *Spenserian stanza* the meter in which he wrote his *The Faerie Queene*.

Spinet Only in this century has *spinet* been used in this country to describe a small, upright piano. Invented about 1500 by Venetian musical instrument manufacturer Giovanni Spinetti, the *spinet* was at first similar to the clavicord. Having one keyboard, one string to each note, and up until the middle of the eighteenth century, no attached legs, the small instrument had often been called the virginal. In England today *spinet* still designates all small keyboard instruments with one string to a note that are plucked by a quill or plectrum of leather. The *spinet* may also be named from the Italian *spina*, a thorn, in reference to the quill points on the instrument, the naming probably influenced by both *Spinetti* and *spena*. At any rate, the historical information available on the etymology is scanty. In fact, the only reference to the inventor is found in a rare old book entitled *Conclusione nel suona dell' organo, di Adriano Banchieri*, published in Bologna in 1608. Its author states that: "Spinetta (the spinet) was thus named from the inventor of that oblong form, who was one Maestro Giovanni Spinetti, a Venetian; and I have seen one of those instruments . . . within which was the inscription—Joannes Spinetvs Venetvs fecit, A.D. 1503."

Spode Ware "Josiah Spode produced a better porcelain than any that had yet been made in England," wrote Alexandre Brogniart, director of the French plant producing the famous Sèvres ware. "He endeavoured to equal the soft porcelain of Sèvres, which his paste closely resembled. He introduced, or at any rate perfected, the use of calcined bones in the body of the ware." Brogniart was referring to English potter Josiah Spode (1754–1827), who developed his formula of bone ash and feldspar at Stoke-on-Trent in 1799. England's leading chinaware manufacturers all adopted Spode's formula to produce the durable, fine bone china much esteemed ever since as *Spode-ware* or *spode*. (See also *Wedgwood*.)

Spoonerism The Reverend William Archibald Spooner, dean and later warden of New College, Oxford, was a learned man, but not spell woken, or well spoken, that is. "We all know what it is to have a half-warmed fish inside us," he once told an audience, meaning to say "half-formed wish." On another occasion he advised his congregation that the next hymn would be "Kinkering Congs Their Titles Take," instead of "Conquering Kings Their Titles Take," and he is said to have explained to listeners one time that "the Lord is a shoving leopard." Spooner's slips occurred both in church, where he once remarked to a lady, "Mardon me Padom,

this pie is occupied, allow me to sew you to another sheet," and told a nervous bridegroom that "it is kisstomery to cuss the bride," and in his classes, where he chided one student with, "You hissed my mystery lecture," and dismissed another with, "You have deliberately tasted two worms and can leave Oxford by the town drain!" Other mistakes attributed to him are "The cat popped on its drawers," for "the cat dropped on its paws"; "one swell foop," for "one fell swoop"; "sporn rim hectacles," for "horn rim spectacles"; "a well-boiled icicle," for "a well-oiled bicycle"; "selling smalts," for "smelling salts"; "tons of soil," for "sons of toil"; "blushing crow," for "crushing blow"; "Is the bean dizzy?" for "Is the dean busy?" and "the Assissination of Sassero," for a Roman history lecture on "the Assassination of Cicero." Spooner lived eighty-six years, and committed many *spoonerisms* in public, too. "When the boys come back from France, we'll have the hags flung out!" the canon told a gathering of patriots during World War I, and Queen Victoria once became "our queer old dean," instead of "our dear old Queen." Nobody knows how many of these *spoonerisms* were really made by Spooner, but they were among the many attributed to him. Spooner was an albino, his metathetical troubles probably due to nervousness and poor eyesight resulting from his condition. The scientific name for his speech affliction is metathesis, the accidental transposition of letters or syllables in the words of a sentence, the process known long before Spooner made it so popular that his slips of the tongue and eye were widely imitated. Some of the best *spoonerisms* therefore aren't really *spoonerisms* at all, being carefully devised and far from accidental.

Spruce, Spruce Up Courtiers in the reign of England's Henry VIII affected the dress of Prussian noblemen, those *hautest* of the *haut* who wore such fashionable attire as broad-brimmed hats with bright feathers, silver chains around their necks, satin cloaks and red velvet doublets. Anything from Prussia had been called *Pruce* during the Middle Ages, but by the sixteenth century an *s* had somehow been added to the word and courtiers who dressed as elegantly as the Prussian nobleman were said to be appareled in *spruce* fashion. *Spruce* soon meant a smart, neat or dapper appearance, as is reflected in the phrase *to spruce up*. The neat, trim form of the *spruce tree* may have suggested its name, too, but it more likely derives from the belief that the *spruce* was first grown in Prussia. (See also *Prussian*.)

St. Bernard Men crossed the Alps between Switzerland and Italy centuries before St. Bernard de Menthon (923–1008) founded the shelter now called the Hospice of the Great St. Bernard. But the house of refuge he built in 982 made it much easier for travelers to make pilgrimages to Rome through the Mons Jovis pass, 8,111 feet above sea level and covered with snow ten months of the year. St. Bernard, a wealthy French nobleman who renounced his fortune to become a man of God, was canonized in 1681. Perhaps two hundred years before this the monks at his hospice had begun breeding the great dogs that are named after him and training them to track down and rescue travelers lost in blizzards and avalanches. The breed is said to be a cross between a bulldog and a Pyrenean shepherd dog, or a Molossian hound, and once had long hair believed to result from matings with the Newfoundland dog. The long hair was found to be a handicap in the snow, however, a smooth-haired variety developed in relatively recent times. *St. Bernards* are still trained by the monks of the alpine hospice. Measuring up to about six feet long, they are capable of carrying a man and are bred for intelligence and docility as well as strength. The breed happens to be the world's heaviest dog, one specimen having reached a weight of 246 pounds. Numerous individuals have been honored as heroes, including the famous Barry whose statue is in the St. Bernard Hospice. Barry saved the lives of forty travelers in ten years of heroic service. In one rescue he found a small boy unconscious in the snow, warmed the child with his breath and licked his hands and face, rousing him from his deadly sleep. Then the dog managed to make the boy understand by movement and nudging that he wanted him to climb on his back carrying him to safety.

St. Boniface's Cup, Boniface Anyone who wants an excuse for an extra drink from time to time might do well to revive the custom of *St. Boniface's cup*. The expression derives from an indulgence granted by Pope Boniface VI or Pope Boniface I to anyone who drank to his good health. A *St. Boniface's cup* was long an excuse for another one of the same.

The phrase is not related to *boniface*, for an innkeeper, which we owe to the convivial landlord of that name in the comedy *The Beaux' Stratagem* (1707) by Irish playwright George Farquhar.

St. Elmo's Fire " 'Look aloft,' cried Starbuck. 'The corpusants! the corpusants!' All the yard-arms were tipped with a pallid fire; and touched at each tri-pointed lightning-rod-end with those tapering white flames, each of the three tall masts was silently burning in that sulphurous air, like three gigantic wax tapers before an altar." Melville's description of corposants in *Moby Dick* reveals the superstitious awe with which mariners regarded these luminous discharges of electricity that extend into the atmosphere from projecting objects. Corposants, the word deriving from the Italian *corpo santo*, holy body, are better known nautically as *St. Elmo's fire*, and were believed by sailors to be a portent of bad weather. St. Erasmus, the patron saint of Neapolitan sailors, was a fourth-century Italian bishop whose name became corrupted to St. Elmo. An Italian legend tells us that he had been rescued from drowning by a sailor and as a reward promised to ever after display a warning light for mariners whenever a storm was approaching. *St. Elmo's fire* does not involve enough discharge of electricity to be considered dangerous. The jets of fire are also seen on the wings and props of aircraft, mountain tops, church steeples, on the horns of cattle and blades of grass, and even around the heads of people, where it is said that they merely cause a tingling sensation. In ancient times *St. Elmo's fire* has been called *Castor and Pollux*, for the twin sons of Jupiter and Leda in Roman mythology. A single burst of fire was called an *Helena*, for the twin's sister, an *Helena* said to be a warning that the worst of a storm was yet to come, while two lights, *Castor and Pollux*, supposedly meant that the worst had passed. This has given rise to the theory that *St. Elmo* may be a corruption of *Helena* instead of *St. Erasmus*. Still another suggestion is that *St. Elmo* is a corruption of *St. Anselm* of Lucca.

St. Swithin's Day

St. Swithin's day if thou doest rain
For forty days it will remain;
St. Swithin's day if thou be fair
For forty days twill rain na mair—
These doggerel lines contain a well-known weather myth popular as early as the twelfth century. The legend claims that St. Swithin or Swithun, a ninth-century bishop of Winchester and counselor to King Egbert, had been buried in the churchyard outside the north wall of Winchester minster, where the "sweet rains of heaven might fall upon him as he wished and he be trodden under foot by those who entered the church." A century after his death it was decided that he should be canonized for miraculous cures he performed and his remains were to be reburied within the cathedral. The day was set, but as a miraculous sign of Bishop Swithin's displeasure, it began to rain on that day and rained for forty days and forty nights, causing the monks to abandon their plans. The date selected for the Bishop's reinterment was July 15, 971, and July 15 has ever since been generally regarded as *St. Swithin's Day*. Due to calendar changes, however, the real day could just as well be December 2, April 3, June 8, June 19 or July 4—depending on which scholar calculates the date. St. Swithin may have worked miracles, but it is also possible that he was never made a saint. Several saints in other countries have been associated with similar legends, including St. Gervais in France and St. Godeliève in Flanders.

Stakhanovite, Stakhanovism Soviet coal miner Aleksei Stakhanov is said to have voluntarily increased his production in 1935 by the use of more rational working techniques and teamwork, he and his seven men having increased their output sevenfold in the mines in the Donets Basin, producing 102 tons of coal in one shift when the norm was seven tons. This voluntary efficiency system, called *Stakhanovism* or the *Stakhanovite Movement* in the miner's honor, was strongly encouraged by the Soviet government to speed up completion of the current Five-Year Plan and did much to accomplish this national objective. *Stakhanovite* workers were rewarded with higher pay, bonuses and other incentives, and while *Stakhanovism* was nothing new, its success in the Soviet Union made the word widely known throughout the world. Oddly enough, the system is a kind of private enterprise. It has been criticized outside the U.S.S.R. as little more than a version of the speed-up system unions have long fought against, but this is not true if the *Stakhanovism* was voluntary. Some authorities say that Stakhanov increased his work output on instructions from the Communist Party under artificially created conditions. In any case, the movement, which established a new record of 225 tons of coal in one shift, gradually lapsed beginning in about 1940. Aleksei Grigorevich Stakhanov, born in 1905, was last reported to be working for the U.S.S.R. Ministry of Coal Industries, having made the great leap forward from worker to commissar. He holds many awards, including the Order of Lenin.

Stalinism, Stalingrad, De-Stalinization Iosif Vissarionovich Dzhugashvili (1879–1953) took the name Joseph Stalin after joining the Russian revolutionary movement in 1896. Stalin, which means "made of steel," was to become in the form of *Stalinism* a synonym for ruthless dictatorship rarely equaled in any other time or place. There is no doubt that the Soviet leader transformed his country into a great modern military and industrial power after succeeding Lenin. But no nation ever paid a higher price for such "progress." Ten million kulaks, wealthy peasants, were exterminated in order to make Stalin's collective farms a success; another ten million people were eliminated in the Great Purge that lasted from 1934 to 1938; no one knows how many more millions were killed in the continual vengeful, fearful purge that seemed at times to be this paranoid's sole reason for living. Yet the secrecy with which he surrounded himself and his part in these campaigns of terror allowed Stalin to become almost a god to the Soviet people. School days began with a hymn of praise to him; he settled literary questions, scientific questions, was regarded as infallible in every field of knowledge. This all came to an end at the twentieth party congress, three years after his death, when Nikita Khrushchev exposed Stalin's inhuman crimes and a campaign of *de-Stalinization* began. By 1961 Stalin's body had been removed from the mausoleum in Red Square and every factory, mountain, street and city in the U.S.S.R. named after him had been renamed—even the city of *Stalingrad* (now Volgograd), which had been dedicated to him in 1925 because forces under his command drove out the White Armies during the Civil War. *Stalingrad* will always be known historically for the great battle that proved to be the turning point in World War II, but Stalin's name is best remembered for the terror *Stalinism* inspired.

Stapelia (see *Raffles*)

States Named for Indian Tribes Besides those thirteen states and the District of Columbia honoring famous people, all noted under separate entries, twelve states are probably named for Indian tribes:

Alabama: for an Indian tribe of the Creek confederacy called the Alibamu, their name meaning "I clear the thicket."

Arkansas: from an Algonquin name of the friendly Quapaw Indians, the Akansea; Marquette visited them in 1673.

Illinois: see *Illinois.*

Indiana: the name denotes that the state was the domain of Indians.

Iowa: from a name of the Sioux tribe, the Ioways or Aiouez, meaning "sleepy ones"; the tribe, however, didn't consider themselves lazy, calling themselves the Pahoja, "gray snow."

Kansas: from the name of a Sioux tribe meaning "People of the South Wind."

Michigan: from *Michigama*, both the name of an Indian tribe and a place, translating as "Great Water."

Missouri: after the name of a Sioux tribe.

Oklahoma: from the Choctaw word for "red people," the Indians who lived there.

Oregon: possibly from the Spanish *oregones*, meaning "big-eared men" and referring to an Indian tribe.

Texas: from a Caddo Indian word meaning "friends" (written *texas, texias, tejas, teyas*) and applied to the Caddos by the Spanish in eastern Texas.

Utah: from the fierce, proud tribe called Ute Indians; in 1850 the area encompassing present-day Utah was constituted Utah Territory, the colorful Mormon name for it, *Deseret*, or "honeybee," discarded when rejected by Congress.

From 1784 to 1788 Tennessee was called the State of Franklin, or Frankland, in honor of Benjamin Franklin. (See also *Columbus; Delaware; Georgia; Illinois; Louisiana; Maine; Maryland; New Jersey; New York; North Carolina; Pennsylvania; South Carolina; Virginia; West Virginia.*)

Sten Gun This British light machine gun of World War II is an unusual blend of the first initials of its two inventors' names, Sheppard and Turpin, plus the first two letters of the name of their country, England. The *Sten gun* or *sten* is not extremely accurate, but is easy to operate, can be fired from the shoulder, weighing only eight pounds, and fires rapidly at the rate of 550 rounds per minute, making it an effective short-range weapon. Mass-produced mainly from stamped parts, the inexpensive *sten* should really be classed as a submachine gun, like the American *Thompson*, or *Tommy gun*, and the German *Schmeisser*, or burp gun.

Stentor, Stentorian, Stentorphone In the *Iliad* Homer tells the story of Stentor, a Grecian herald of the Trojan War who faced the enemy to dictate terms and had "a voice of bronze . . . as loud as that of fifty men together." One suspects that the legendary herald was based on some top sergeant of old, although Greek legend claims that Stentor finally met his match in Hermes, herald of the gods, dying as a result of a contest with him. At any rate, real or not, his name became proverbial in Greece for loud-voiced, and gives us the English word *stentorian*, meaning extremely loud. There is both a howling monkey and a trumpet-shaped protozoan genus of the class Ciliata called a *stentor*, and the *stentorphone* is an electrical speaker for magnifying sound. (See also *Hector; Nestor; Thersitical*.)

Stetson Poor health forced John Batterson Stetson to travel west at the time of the Civil War and the trip must have done him good, if his longevity indicates anything, for he died in 1906, aged seventy-six. While out West it occurred to Stetson that no one was manufacturing hats suited to the practical needs of the Western cowboy, and on his return to Philadelphia in 1865 he went into the hat business, specializing in Western-style headgear. The wide-brimmed, ten-gallon felt hats he manufactured immediately became popular with cowboys and have been called *Stetsons* or *John B.s* ever since. In 1885 Stetson formed the John B. Stetson Company which is today one of the world's largest hat manufacturers. John B. Stetson University at De Land, Fla., formerly De Land University, was named for him in 1889 out of gratitude for his generous donations.

Strad, Stradivarius Recently the *Lady Blunt Stradivarius* (1721) was auctioned off at Sotheby's in London for $200,000, the highest price ever paid for a musical instrument. Nor is this violin considered to be the finest violin made by Antonio Stradivari, that honor usually accorded to the Messiah or the *Alard Stradivarius*. Amazingly, some six hundred of the eleven hundred or so violins, violas and cellos made by Stradivari from 1666 to 1737 still survive today, half of them in the United States, a tribute to the master craftsman's genius that surpasses any words. Only the barest essentials are known about the supreme Italian violin maker. Born at Cremona in north Italy in 1644, he was an apprentice of the distinguished craftsman Nicolo Amati, but he soon developed his own methods, in 1684 opening a shop where his sons Francesco and Omobono worked with him. Stradivari was famous in his own time, his commissions including instruments for England's James II and Spain's Charles III. He died in 1737, aged ninety-three, and to this day his secrets of success have not been discovered. No one knows why *Strads* sound better than modern instruments, whether this is due to the aging of the violins, the way the F-holes were cut, or the soft-textured, orange to red varnish whose formula apparently went to the grave with their designer. Although scientists claim there is no appreciable difference between a good modern instrument and a Cremonese, professional violinists, almost to a man, believe something is wrong with their hearing, and the great violinists have generally owned two such violins, which are alternated to lessen the abuse daily concert work inflicts on an instrument. Stradivari's workmanship brought the violin to perfection in his greatest period from 1700 to 1725, his instruments possessing a combination of sweetness and power that is unequaled. Violins like that selling for $200,000 today originally sold for about $20, having increased ten thousand times in value over the past two centuries.

Sword of Damocles "Uneasy lies the head that wears a crown." Both Cicero and Horace tell the story of the flatterer Damocles, a fifth-century court follower of Dionysius I (405–367 B.C.), the Elder of Syracuse. Damocles annoyed Dionysius with his constant references to the ruler's great power and consequent happiness. Deciding to teach the sycophant the real perils of power, he invited Damocles to a magnificent banquet, surrounding him with luxuries that only a king could afford. Damocles enjoyed the feast until he happened to glance up and see a sharp sword suspended by a single hair pointing directly at his head, after which he lay there cowering, afraid to eat, speak or move. The lesson was that there are always threats of danger, fears and worries that prevent the powerful from fully enjoying their power, and the *sword of Damocles* has become a symbol of these fears. The phrase also gives us our expression *to hang by a thin thread*, to be subject to imminent danger.

Sybarite One ancient Sybarite, legend says, complained to his host that he could not sleep at night because there was a rose petal under his body. Inhabitants of the Greek colony of Sybaris on the Gulf of Tarantum in southern Italy, the Sybarites were noted among the Greeks for their love of luxury and sensuousness, and to some extent for their effeminacy and wantonness, all qualities associated with the word *sybarite* today. The fertile land in Sybaris, founded in the sixth century B.C., made luxurious living possible, but too many pleasures weakened the people. The neighboring Crotons, assisting the Troezenians, whom the Greeks had earlier ejected from the city, destroyed Sybaris in 510 B.C., diverting the river Crathis to cover its ruins. It is said that the Sybarites had trained their horses to dance to pipes and that Crotons played pipes as they marched upon them, creating such disorder among their rivals that they easily won the battle. The city of Thurii was later built on or near the site of Sybaris.

Syphilis A full-scale epidemic of this venereal disease apparently first broke out in the Old World at the Siege of Naples during the Italian Wars (1495), although it had been noted in Europe long before Columbus. The plague became known under many names as it spread over the continent (see *French sickness*), but the word *syphilis* itself derives from the name of a character in a 1530 poem by Girolamo Fracastro called *Syphilis sive Morbus Gallicus*, "Syphilis or the French Disease." In Fracastoro's New World fable Syphilis was a blasphemous shepherd who so enraged the Sun God that he struck him with a new disease: *"He first wore buboes dreadful to the sight, / First felt strange pains and sleepless past the night; / From him the malady received its name."* Fracastoro could have derived his character's name from the Italian for "a native of *Sypheum* (now Montato) in Southern Italy," though the personal name more likely is from the Greek *suphilos*, "lover of pigs," or swineherd. In any case, the disease wasn't contracted among natives in the New World. In fact, the symptoms of syphilis may have been described by Thucydides as far back as 430 B.C. as "the plague of Piraeus." Over the ages its victims have included Herod, Julius Caesar, three popes, Henry VIII, Ivan the Terrible, Keats, Schubert, Goya and Goethe. Tragically, syphilis until only recently has been hidden in dark corners, and is still something of a "Mrs. Grundy's disease." It is on the increase in the United States and throughout the world along with all venereal diseases.

T

Tabby, Tabby Cat Prince Attab, the great grandson of Omeyza, famed in Arab legend, lived in a quarter of old Baghdad named *Attabiya* in his honor. Here a striped silk taffeta material was woven, the streaked fabric called *Attabi* by the Arabs after the quarter, *Attabi* eventually transformed to *tabis* in French during the Middle Ages and translated in English as *tabby cloth*. *Tabby* became a verb for "to stripe" soon after, and by 1695 the word was used to describe a brownish dark-striped or brindled *tabby cat* whose markings resembled the material. Old maids were also called *tabbies* and this may have been because they often kept *tabby cats* and shared their careful habits, but the word for a spinster is more likely a pet form of *Tabitha*, a name common among elderly women at the time. Besides becoming a cloth, a cat, and possibly an old maid, Prince Attab's name may have been used for the "falsies" that flat-chested girls wore in the eighteenth century, though these *tabbies* may have been suggested by *tabs*.

Taj Mahal Shah Jahan built the magnificent *Taj Mahal* to commemorate his favorite wife, Mumtaz Mahall, whose title was Taj Mahal, Crown of the Palace. The mausoleum near Agra, India, was begun by the Turkish or Persian architect Ustad Isa three years after Mumtaz died in 1632 and completed by about 1650, nearly twenty years later. The royal lovers are buried in a vault beneath the floor in the octagonal tomb chamber, surrounded by what many consider to be the finest example of romantic architecture in the world. If any structure proves that beauty can be the sole function of a building, it is this magnificently spectacular edifice, which is actually more a sculpture than architecture. The great tomb, the luxurious gardens, even the four 133 foot-high minarets at the great tomb's corners, were all built for beauty alone. The tomb itself, 186 feet square, rises with its towering dome to 210 feet, four smaller domes at the corners and a two-storied gallery surrounding it. Built at a cost of some fifteen million dollars, the white marble exterior is inlaid with semiprecious stones arranged in Arabic inscriptions and designs. No other building in the world uses marble to such marvelous effect. Viewed by moonlight, the *Taj Mahal* seems unearthly and in rainy seasons the famous Rajput marble turns a cloudy gray, as if soaked in tears. The "exquisite elegy in stone" is reflected in an oblong pool lined with dark cypresses. Every detail seems perfect, "those who designed like Titians finished like jewelers," making this tribute to a Moslem princess the most beautiful building in the world. (See also *Mausoleum*.)

Tammany, Tweed Ring *Tammany Hall* hasn't the power it once did, thanks to its fairly recent defeats by various reform groups, but for over 150 years the machine held sway over New York City politics under such bosses as William Tweed, Richard Croker and Carmine DeSapio. *Tammany's* unsavory association with machine politics dates back to the late eighteenth century, but *Tammany* clubs thrived in this country long before this, mostly as patriotic Revolutionary War organizations that ridiculed Tory groups like the Society of St. George. The clubs were named for Tammanend or Tammenund, a Delaware Indian chief said to have welcomed William Penn and signed with him the Treaty of Shakamaxon calling for friendly relations. Tammanend (sometimes his name is given as Taminy or Tammany) may have negotiated with Penn for the land that became Pennsylvania and may have been George Washington's friend, as is claimed, but little is really known about him except that his name means "affable." The colonists jocularly canonized this friendly Indian chieftain as St. Tammany and adopted his name for their patriotic societies. These gradually died out, but not before one William Mooney had formed a *Tammany Society* in New York in 1789. Based on pseudo-Indian forms, its officials even taking Indian titles, the club fell into the hands of Aaron Burr in 1798, Burr having used it in his political dispute with Alexander Hamilton. At this time the *Sons of St. Tammany* split into two factions, one becoming a social club and purchasing a meeting place called "The Hall" in which it rented space to its political half. The political twin prevailed, however, and still survives today. *Tammany No. I*, as it was first called, certainly has had many affable men among its members through the years, one of the secrets of its successes, but that is where the resemblance between *Tammany Hall* and the Indian chieftain ends. Ironically, *Tammany* gained much power, thanks to Thomas Jefferson, one of our most idealistic presidents. *Tammany* had supported him during the election of 1800 and Jefferson threw much patronage to the society when he took office. By the *Jacksonian* era the club became one of the strongest Democratic political organizations in America. Thomas Nast created the famous symbol of the *Tammany tiger* in his cartoons attacking the machine in the 1870's, when the corrupt *Tweed Ring* was fleecing the city of over $100 million. It has remained one of the best known political symbols, along with the Republican elephant and Democratic donkey, these also created by Nast. Thanks to Nast, the Indian chief whose name had originally symbolized democracy versus aristocracy had finally come to stand for complete corruption.

Tantony, St. Anthony's Fire The smallest pig in a litter, one that is traditionally believed to follow its master anywhere, is called a *Tantony pig* after St. Anthony, long the patron saint of swineherds. St. Anthony probably had nothing to do with pigs, other than citing an "unclean demon" as one of the temptations he resisted, but he is often represented in art with a pig by his side. In the Middle Ages, when the pig began to lose its reputation as an unclean demon, it was popularly supposed that the animal was dedicated to the saint. St. Anthony, born in the year 251 in upper Egypt, defeated many "assaults by the devil," including temptations such as "gross and obscene imaginings" of beautiful, naked women that Lucifer sent to "harass him night and day," this particular temptation a favorite theme of medieval art. When his parents died, St. Anthony gave his considerable inheritance to the poor, going to live in solitude for the great part of his life, and he is considered to be the first of the fraternity of ascetics who dwelt in the deserts. He is said to have died at 105. The *Tantony bell*, a small hand bell or church bell, is also named for him, referring to the bell often depicted around his staff or the neck of his pig. The *Tantony crutch*, "a peculiarly Egyptian T-shaped form of the cross," comes from his name, too, possibly "an indication of the saint's great age . . . or [in] reference to his constant use of the cross in his conflict with evil spirits." *St. Anthony's fire*, erysipelas, is so named because the saint is said to have saved those who prayed to him from the pestilential "sacred fire" during an eleventh-century epidemic of the disease. Erysipelas is an infectious disease caused by a streptococcus and characterized by a spreading deep red inflammation of the skin.

Tartar, Tartar Sauce, Steak Tartare, Tatterdemalion Bloodthirsty about their meals as well as their conquests, the nomadic Tartars liked their meat raw, or almost always so—sometimes they placed a hunk of meat under the saddle and cooked it by friction during hours of riding. At any rate, in medieval times traveling Hamburg merchants learned about a recipe for scraped raw meat seasoned with salt, pepper and onion juice and named it *Tartar steak* or *steak Tartare* in their honor. This was the first hamburger, remaining so until some anonymous Hamburger shaped *steak Tartare* into patties and cooked them. *Tartar sauce*, a mayonnaise containing diced pickles, onions, olives, capers and green herbs, takes its name from *Tartar steak*, which was often seasoned with similar ingredients.

The Tartars were chiefly Mongolian and Turkish tribes who overran Asia and much of eastern Europe during the Middle Ages. Originally known as the Ta-Ta Mongols—the correct, Persian spelling of their name is *Tatar*—these fierce warriors were led by Genghis Khan and massacred everyone who opposed them, leaving complete devastation in their path. Their name came to mean "savage," there being one old legend that said a Tartar would bite the hand of anyone holding him and devour anyone who let him loose. A violent-tempered, savage person, or a shrewish woman, is still called a *tartar*, and the expression *to catch a Tartar* means to deal with someone or something unexpectedly powerful or troublesome. *Tatterdemalion* may also derive from the Tartars or Tatars, who became mere wandering gypsies or *tatterdemalions* after their fiendish days of glory, but this word is probably at the very least influenced by a Scandinavian word meaning rags or shreds of cloth. The name change from Tatar to Tartar during the Middle Ages was influenced by the fact that *Tartarus* was the Latin word for Hell, and the Tartars made life hell on earth for Europeans of the time. Their supremacy extended, at one time or another, from China to as far west as Poland—but supremacy could not last long for a people who actually ate books to acquire the knowledge therein. Though the old loosely knit kingdom of *Tatary* is gone, the *Tatar Republic* is today an autonomous state of the Soviet Union. (See also *Frank*.)

Tawdry Anglo-Saxon Princess Aethelthryth seems to have spent her married life trying to preserve her chastity. Daughter of the king of East Anglia, she protected her virginity through two unwanted marriages that her father had arranged for political reasons, keeping the promise she had made as a girl that she would dedicate her life to God. Aethelthryth escaped from her persistent second husband and founded a monastery on the island of Ely, which her first husband had left her, and ruled over it until her death in 679. The pious princess carried but one sin on her conscience: in her youth she had loved wearing golden chains and necklaces, and she believed that the cancer of the throat that she died of had been caused by this worldly vanity. In Norman times Aethelthryth's name was shortened to Audrey and she was finally canonized as St. Audrey. It became the custom to hold fairs on the isle of Ely on St. Audrey's Day, October 17, and the souvenirs sold at these fairs included lace scarves and golden necklaces that were called *St. Audrey's laces*. This merchandise, at first treasured articles, declined in quality until it became known as cheap and showy. Shouted by hucksters as *St. Audrey's lace*, it was soon clipped in speech to *Sin t'Audrey lace* and eventually *tawdry lace*. All the gaudy, worthless objects like it were sold as *tawdry*, too, and by the eighteenth century the word had come to mean anything cheap and tasteless, "showy, tinsel stuff." *Tawdry*, like *Tantony*, offers an excellent example of aphesis, the lopping off of first syllables from words, one of the many "phonetic accidents" Professor Weekley explains so well in his *The Romance of Words*.

Teddy Bear A Brooklyn candy store owner named Morris Michtom fashioned the first *teddy bear* out of brown plush in 1902 and named it after President Theodore Roosevelt. Michtom, who went on to make a fortune in *teddy bears*, had been inspired by a cartoon by Washington *Post* cartoonist Clifford K. Berryman called "Drawing the Line in Mississippi" that had been reprinted in newspapers throughout America. Berryman's cartoon was based on a news story about an expedition "Teddy" Roosevelt made to hunt bears near the Little Sunflower River in Mississippi and showed Roosevelt with his back turned on a helpless bear. Gallant Teddy, it had been reported, refused to kill and even set free a small brown bear that his obliging hosts had stunned and tied to a tree for him to shoot. True or not, the story did Roosevelt no harm and enhanced his reputation as a conservationist. Later Roosevelt presented a few bears to the Bronx Zoo, the *teddy bear* still associated with him in 1911, when he received an honorary degree at Cambridge, England, and students lowered a large teddy bear onto his head from the ceiling while he stood on the platform.

Some sixty million *teddy bears* have been manufactured since the first one, which Michtom presented to Roosevelt's grandson a few years ago and is now in the *Smithsonian*. Probably the most famous and profitable *teddy bear* of all is Winnie the Pooh, the creation of English author A. A. Milne. Christopher Robin's bear, now fifty, is enshrined in a glass case in the offices of Milne's American publisher. Arctophiles, bear and teddy bear lovers, will enjoy English actor Peter Bull's *The Teddy Bear Book*, which tells of *teddies* that have been kept by their sometimes distinguished owners for sixty years and more.

Although Theodore Roosevelt died in 1919, when only sixty, he crammed more action into his lifetime than any two people. Surely our most energetic president, he was celebrated for his Spanish-American War "Rough Riders"—who, incidentally, fought their most noted battle on foot—his big-game hunting, trust busting, and his colorful use of language. Among the words he coined or revived were *muckraker, square deal, weasel word, nature faker, mollycoddle, big stick* and *lunatic fringe*. One member of the lunatic fringe, John Schrank, tried to assassinate Roosevelt in 1912. The bullet struck the folded manuscript of a speech he was carrying in his breast pocket and failed to do fatal damage. The intrepid Teddy refused to be treated for his wound until after he had delivered his speech with the bullet hole in it.

Teddy Boys, Teddy Girls, Edwardian London's rebellious *Teddy boys* and *Teddy girls* are well-dressed teenagers whose attire often conceals their ferocity. They take their name from the *Edwardian* styles they prefer, especially the boys' tightly fitted trousers and jackets. *Edwardian* in this case refers to the styles popular in the reign of England's Edward VII, Queen Victoria's son, who ruled from 1901–1910. The opulent styles of the period reflect the self-satisfaction prevalent before World War I and perhaps indicate a rebellious desire on the part of the *Teddy boys* to return to better days. (See also *Albert; Mohock*.)

Temple Orange, Murcott Honey, Parson Brown Thousands of varieties of fruits are named after their developers and the orange is no exception. The best-known eponymous orange variety is the *Temple*, named after its early propagator Floridian William Chase Temple. Others include the *Murcott Honey* orange, named for Florida grower Charles Murcott Smith, and the *Parson Brown*, which honors Nathan L. Brown, a Florida clergyman. All of these varieties are natural hybrids that were nursed along by their discoverers. Oranges are one of the oldest known fruits, the word deriving from the Arabian *naranj*, and today the United States is by far their largest producer, growing some twenty-five billion a year. An orange's color, incidentally, has nothing to do with its ripeness. Oranges turn orange only as a result of cold weather, which breaks down a membrane protecting their green chlorophyll. This is the reason why summer oranges are often dyed and stamped with those familiar words, "color added."

Thersitical, Thersitian Among the loudest, most foulmouthed men of all time was Thersites, an officer in the Greek army at the siege of Troy. The ugly, deformed Thersites, whose name means "the Audacious," liked nothing better than arguing, we are told in the *Iliad*, his mean temper sparing no one, be he humble or great. Greek legend tells us that he reviled even Achilles—laughing at his grief over the death of Penthesilia, the queen of the Amazons—and that Achilles promptly kayoed him permanently with one blow to the jaw. Thanks largely to Shakespeare's treatment of the scurrilous Thersites in *Troilus and Cressida*, we have the adjective *thersitical*, "loudmouthed and foulmouthed." *Thersitian*, meaning the same, is less used. (See also *Hector; Nestor; Stentor*.)

Thespian

Thespian, the first professor of our art
At country wakes sang ballads from a cart.
                                        Dryden

A *thespian* is an actor and as an adjective the word means "pertaining to tragedy or dramatic art." Both words pay tribute to the first professional actor. According to legend, Thespis was a Greek poet of the latter sixth century B.C. who recited his poems at festivals of the gods around the country; he is even said to have invented tragedy and to have created the first dialogue spoken on the stage in the form of exchanges between himself as an actor reading his poems and responses by a chorus. Thespis is probably a semi-legendary figure, his name possibly an assumed one. The popular story that he went around Attica in a cart in which his plays were acted is of doubtful authenticity, but may be partly true. (See also *Roscian*.)

Throgmorton Street What Wall Street is to America, Throgmorton Street is to England—the center of the financial or business world. The stock exchange is located on this narrow London street, which was named for Sir Nicholas Throckmorton or Throgmorton (1515–71), who served Queen Elizabeth as a soldier and ambassador to France and Scotland. The diplomat was given to intrigue, however, and also served two stretches in the Tower, once for alleged complicity in the Wyatt Rebellion in 1554 and again in 1569 for a plot to marry Mary, Queen of Scots, to the duke of Norfolk. Throckmorton's daughter Elizabeth became the bride of Sir Walter Raleigh. (See also *Downing Street; Quai d'Orsay*.)

Thugs One of the original "Thugs," a vicious little man named Buhram, confessed after his capture that he had strangled 931 persons to death: Buhram belonged to an Indian sect of religious fanatics called the *P'hansigars*, "noose operators," whom the British euphemistically called Thugs, from a Sanskrit word (*sthaga*) meaning rogue or cheater. The sect dates back to at least the thirteenth century and supposedly honored Kali the Hindu goddess of destruction with their murders and thievery. Thugs would worm their way into the confidence of travelers, or would follow a wealthy victim for weeks sometimes before finding him in a lonely place and slipping a rope or cloth noose around his neck. The dead man—dead before he hit the ground—would then be buried in accord with the sect's religious beliefs and a portion of the money or goods stolen assigned to devotion of the goddess. The murders were done according to an elaborate ritual, including the consecration of the pickaxe used for the burial, and the group was as well organized as the syndicate today, even speaking a secret language, Ramasi, and bribing government officials for protection. The British eliminated the Thugs in India in the 1830's when they hanged 412 and sentenced another 2,844 to life imprisonment, but the name of the band lives after them. *Thug*, an ugly word, is still used for ugly criminal types from tough guys to assassins, and *thuggee* is sometimes heard for the crime of strangulation the Thugs perfected.

Tiffany, Tiffany Glass, Tiffany Setting, Tiffany Lamp Shades Tiffany and Company, the famous jewelry firm in New York City, was founded by Charles Lewis Tiffany (1812–1902). Tiffany opened his "fancy goods" shop in 1837 with John B. Young, becoming Tiffany & Co. sixteen years later. During the Civil War the firm turned out swords and other war supplies, but was noted for its manufacture of gold and silver jewelry, the improvement of silverware design, and the importation of historic gems and jewelry from Europe. Branches were soon opened in London and Geneva, Charles Tiffany winning fame as the inventor of the *Tiffany setting*, as in a ring where prongs hold the stone in place. His son, Louis Comfort Tiffany (1848–1933), became an artist and art patron, remembered chiefly for his invention of *Tiffany glass* in 1890. Trademarked as *Favrile glass*, the iridescent art glass was made by the Tiffany Furnaces, which Louis established at Corona, N.Y. There glass for mosaics and windows, vases, and the *Tiffany lamp shades* so popular today were manufactured. Before he died, the younger Tiffany also founded and endowed the *Louis Comfort Tiffany Foundation* for art students at Oyster Bay, N.Y. The gauze fabric *Tiffany* has nothing to do with either father or son, taking its name from the Latin *theophania*, "the manifestation of God to man," because it was once worn on *Epiphany* or Twelfth Night celebrations.

Tight as Dick's Hatband The phrase refers to the fact that the crown was too tight or dangerous to be worn by a certain king of England. The particular king's identity is unknown, but one popular theory suggests Oliver Cromwell's son Richard, often called Tumbledown Dick, who was nominated by his father to succeed him but served only for seven months, beginning in September, 1658, because he received no support from the army. Another candidate is King Richard III, who assumed the throne in 1483, denouncing the rightful claims of his two young nephews. Long regarded as an evil king who ordered the "accidental deaths" of his nephews, Richard is said to have been uncomfortable wearing a crown bought with blood. He was killed by the earl of Richmond at the Battle of Bosworth Field in 1485. In recent times his historical reputation has improved considerably.

Timothy Grass, Herd's Grass *Timothy* is another, more popular name for *herd's grass*, both designations referring to meadow cat's-tail grass, *Phleum pratense*, which is native to Eurasia and is widely cultivated in the United States for hay. The species was probably brought to America by early settlers. Then, about 1770, one John Herd supposedly found the perennial grass with its spiked or panicled head growing wild near his New Hampshire farm, the grass receiving his name when he began cultivating it shortly thereafter. Timothy Hanson or Hanso gave his prenom to the same grass when he quit his New York farm in 1720 and moved to Maryland, or possibly Carolina, introducing *Phleum pratense* seed there. *Timothy's seed* became *timothy grass* when it grew and this was finally shortened to *timothy*.

Tinker to Evers to Chance Still synonymous with a routine double play in baseball, *Tinker to Evers to Chance* refers to the Chicago Cub infield combination of Joe Tinker, shortstop, Johnny Evers at second base, and Frank Chance at first. It was over half a century ago that this smooth trio completed many a double play on ground balls hit to Joe Tinker. They starred for the National

League Cubs starting in 1902 and all three are now enshrined in Baseball's Hall of Fame at Cooperstown, New York —Tinker with a .264 lifetime batting average, the second lowest of any batter in the Hall of Fame; Evers with an average of .270; and Chance with .297—far better fielders than hitters.

Tironian Notes, Tironian Sign Marcus Tullius Tiro, the man who invented the & sign, or ampersand, introduced it as part of the first system of shorthand of which there is any record. A learned Roman freedman and amanuensis to Cicero, Tiro invented *Tironian notes* about 63 b.c. in order to take down his friend's fluent dictation. Though a rudimentary system, Tiro's shorthand saw wide use in Europe for almost a thousand years, outlasting the Roman empire. The & sign, sometimes called the *Tironian sign* in Tiro's honor, was a contraction for the Latin *et* or "and." Taught in Roman schools and used to record speeches made in the senate, Tiro's system was based on the orthographical principle and made abundant use of initials. Tiro also wrote a lost life of Cicero, a number of the great orator's speeches, and even some of Cicero's letters to Tiro! (See also *Gregg; Pitman.*)

Titian Tiziano Vecellio, or Vecelli, whose name is anglicized as Titian, began his training as an artist in 1486 when nine years old and did not stop painting until his death of the plague ninety years later when he was approaching one hundred. The greatest artist of the Venetian school, Titian trained under Gentile and Giovani Bellini. He produced hundreds of paintings during his unusually long and prolific career, including portraits and religious and mythological works, all noted for their magnificent use of color and design rather than for his drawing. "That man would have no equal if art had done as much for him as nature," Michelangelo said of Titian, adding it was a pity "that in Venice they don't learn to draw well," but Titian's drawing was competent at the very least. In his many paintings the artist often depicted a model with shades of bright golden-auburn hair, and rendered the color so beautifully that the lustrous bronze has since been called *Titian hair*, or simply *Titian*. One tradition claims that Titian's auburn-haired model was his daughter Lavinia, whom he did paint several times. (See also *Alice Blue; Van Dyke*.)

Tokyo Rose, Axis Sally *Lord Haw Haw, Axis Sally and Tokyo Rose* were the best known Axis radio propagandists of World War II. Of the triumverate only Tokyo Rose worked for the Japanese and "she" was actually a number of women, her name bestowed upon her by American G.I.'s in the Pacific. Iva Togori D'Aquino and Ruth Hayakawa, both Americans of Japanese descent, were mainly responsible for the radio programs beamed from Tokyo. Their sweet, seductive voices and the sentimental music they played were designed to promote homesickness, but more often than not were good for a laugh. Mrs. D'Aquino was sentenced to ten years in prison for treason in 1949, and was paroled in 1956. Mildred E. (Axis Sally) Gillars was convicted of treason by a Federal jury the same year, receiving a ten-to-thirty-year sentence but winning a parole in 1961.

Tom Collins Many sources tell us that the *Tom Collins*—that refreshing, tall drink made with gin (or vermouth), lemon (or lime), sugar, and soda water—honors its bartender-creator. Yet no one has been able to establish who Tom Collins was, where he came from, or when he first mixed the drink. Variations on the *Tom Collins* include the John Collins (whiskey) and the Marimba Collins (rum). The *Tom Collins* is claimed by many, but the lack of evidence indicates that its real creator didn't mix well, at least socially. The best prospect is probably John Collins, a nineteenth-century bartender at London's Limmer Hotel who did not devise but was famous for his gin-slings—a tall gin and lemon drink that resembles the *Tom Collins*.

Tommygun The infamous "chopper," so often hidden in violin cases, in gangster movies, takes its name from the patronym of one of its inventors, American army officer John T. Thompson (1860–1940). Thompson and Navy Commander John N. Blish invented the .45 caliber portable automatic weapon during World War I and much improved it in later years. Gangsters and reporters popularized the nickname *tommygun* in the Prohibition era along with colorful expressions like torpedo, triggerman, bathtub gin, hideout, hijacker, to muscle in, and to take for a ride. Although *tommygun* originally identified the *Thompson machine gun*, with its pistol grip and shoulder stock, the term is now used to describe any similar lightweight weapon with a drum-type magazine. The *Thompson* was developed too late to be of use in World War I—when an estimated 80 percent of casualties were caused by heavy machine gun fire—but like the British *sten gun* was employed by Allied troops in World War II. Because of their short barrels, about thirty inches, most submachine guns are relatively inaccurate except at close range. They weigh from six to twelve pounds and hold twenty to fifty shots.

Tontine Mystery novelists have made good use of the *tontine*, an early form of life insurance devised by Italian banker Lorenzo Tonti (1635–1690) and introduced by him into France in 1653. Under the system a number of people subscribe to the *tontine*, the annuity increasing in value to the survivors as each subscriber dies. Finally, the last surviving member takes all—which makes the *tontine* particularly suitable for a murder mystery. When the *tontine* was first introduced, the fund reverted to the state after the death of the last subscriber. The original system came to be used by many governments to raise money, France, for example, floating over a million livres in these life annuities, and England raising 300,000 pounds in 1765.

Torquemada More than 100,000 cases were tried and 2,000 people executed under the administration of Tomás de Torquemada (c. 1420–98) after the Pope appointed him Spanish Grand Inquisitor in 1483. The harsh rules Torquemada devised and strictly enforced for the Inquisition, including the use of torture as a means of obtaining information, made the inquisitor-general's name a synonym for a cruel persecutor or torturer. Torquemada particularly distrusted the *Maranos* and *Moriscos*, Jewish and Moorish converts to Catholicism, many of whom he felt were insincere, and he was partly responsible for the royal decree in 1492 which expelled 200,000 unconverted Jews from Spain. The Spanish Dominican had been prior of the Convent of Santa Cruz, a post he held until his death, and confessor to Queen Isabella and King Ferdinand before assuming his powerful office. Inquisitors who succeeded this man exceeded him in cruelty, but he set the pattern for them to follow in dealing with heretics, most of whom were burned at the stake. One story, probably exaggerated, says that the hated grand inquisitor never traveled anywhere unless guarded by 250 armed retainers and 50 horsemen.

Tournedos, Tournedos à la Rossini *Tournedos* are small, round thick pieces of beef, served with a number of sauces and garnished. The Italian composer Gioacchino Antonio Rossini (1792–1868), best known for his *Barber of Seville* (1816), is said to have invented the dish when he conceived *Tournedos à la Rossini* at the height of his popularity. According to the old tale, Rossini was dining at the Café Anglais in Paris. Tired of the beef dishes on the menu, he gave instructions for his meat to be prepared in a different way.

"Never would I dare to offer such a thing—it is unpresentable!" the *maître d'hôtel* protested.

"Well then, arrange not to let it be seen!" the composer countered.

Ever after, we are told, *tournedos* were to be served not before the eyes, but behind the diner's back. Hence the name in French: *tourne le dos* ("turn one's back").

There is no doubt, anyway, that *Tournedos Rossini* are named in the composer's honor: succulent slices of fried fillet of beef set on fried bread, capped with foie gras, crowned with truffles and coated with Périgueux sauce. One of the richest, most expensive dishes in the world.

Trojan Horse, a Regular Trojan, to Work Like a Trojan Inhabitants of Troia, an ancient city in what is now Turkey that came to be called *Troja* in Medieval Latin, the Trojans were a courageous, industrious people. Legend tells us they labored energetically and cheer-

fully at even the most arduous tasks. Hence the expressions *to work like a Trojan* and *a regular Trojan* for hard work done without complaint and a high-spirited, industrious worker. Troy, as we call Troia today, is said to have been located where Hissarlik, Turkey, now stands. Here the Greeks waged the Trojan War about 12 B.C. in an effort to claim their Queen Helen, who had been abducted by Paris, the son of the King of Troy. At least so the classical writers claim. The war, probably fought for the control of trade, lasted for some ten years before Troy fell in about 1184, the last year of the siege recorded by Homer in the *Iliad* and the burning of Troy described by Virgil in the *Aeneid*. Troy finally fell, Virgil writes, when the proverbial *Trojan horse* was left in the city overnight. The Trojans believed the giant horse to be a gift to the gods, but its hollow insides were filled with Greek soldiers who slipped out in the dark and opened Troy's gates to their comrades. Since then the phrase *Trojan horse* has been used for any deceptive scheme.

Trugen Stroke John Arthur Trudgen (1852–1902), an outstanding British amateur swimmer, introduced the *Trugen* or *Trugen stroke* in 1893 after seeing it used in South America. The stroke, employing a double overarm motion and a scissors kick, is regarded as the first successful above-water arm action widely used in swimming. Trudgen popularized the idea of minimizing resistance by bringing the arms out of the water, which paved the way for the reception of the now common Australian crawl adopted from South Sea natives. The stroke was sometimes called the *Trudgeon*, another misspelling of the swimmer's name.

Turk, To Round Cape Turk, Young Turk A cruel, brutal and domineering man is sometimes called a *Turk*, or an *unspeakable Turk*, such qualities ascribed to the Turks from early times. The word *Turk* itself is Arabic or Persian for a native of Turkey. *Turk*, uncapitalized, can also mean one of a breed of Turkish horses similar to the Arabian horse, the destructive plum curculio insect, and a scimitar. *To round Cape Turk* is an expression meaning "to regard women only as instruments of pleasure," and a *Young Turk* is an insurgent within any group, such as a political party, supporting progressive policies. The latter phrase derives from the Turkish reform party that dominated Turkish politics 1908–18. Many modern European methods were introduced by these *Young Turks*, who succeeded in making Turkey a republic.

Turpinite Used in making shells, *turpinite* was for a short time the most powerful explosive in the world, and like the atom bomb inspired the false hope that its terrible effects would end war for all time. The French inventor Turpin concocted *turpinite* about 1894, about six years after he had invented the explosive *lyddite*, which is named after Lydd, England, the town where its preliminary tests were made. *Turpinite*, said to be tested among sheep with devastating results, inspired fear even among French troops. (See also *Nobel*; *Shimose*.)

Tutania British manufacturer William Tutin, who had a plant in Birmingham in about 1770, may have been as patriotic as the inventors of the *sten gun*, who named their invention from their initials plus the *En* of England. Tutin manufactured a silvery white alloy of tin, antimony and copper which he probably named after himself and four letters from Brit*annia*. Possibly someone else fashioned the odd word, however, and the coining of *Tutania* was probably influenced by *tutenag*, a crude zinc.

Typefaces Named for Printers Numerous typefaces for printing have been named for their designers. Several of the most famous are:

Baskerville: named for Englishman John Baskerville, who died in 1775; Baskerville is said to have manufactured all the tools of his trade, including his own inks.

Bodoni: Italian printer Giambattista Bodoni (1740–1813), the son of a printer, produced many works over his long career that are considered classics today.

Caslon: named after Englishman William Caslon (1692–1766), one of London's leading printers.

Gill: for British sculptor and type designer Eric Gill (1882–1940).

Plantin: famous for his excellent craftsmanship in his own lifetime, Christophe Plantin, who died in 1549 when he was only 35, is now honored by the Musée Plantin in Antwerp, which was the site of his famous printing house.

Tweedledum and Tweedledee

Some say compared to Bononcine
That mynheer Handel's but a ninny;
Others aver that he to Handel
Is scarcely fit to hold a candle.
Strange all this difference should be
'Twixt Tweedledum and Tweedledee.

The epigram, variously attributed to John Byrom, Pope and Swift, first used the words *Tweedledum* and *Tweedledee*, which has since described two people or groups identical in looks, opinions or certain characteristics. The nicknames were given to German-born English musician George Handel or Haendel and the musician G. B. Buononcini when a rivalry sprang up between the two while Handel served as director of the Royal Academy of Music in 1725. The words suggested the contrast between high and low pitched musical instruments. English aristocrats, except for a few nobles like the Prince of Wales, sided with Buononcini, who is little known today and left no work nearly as popular as Handel's *Messiah*. Tweedledum and Tweedledee were made more famous as the twins in Lewis Carroll's *Through the Looking Glass* (1872).

Twiss Here the Irish had the last word, as is often the case. Author Richard Twiss (1747–1821) may have thought he had put the natives down when he published his uncomplimentary *Tour in Ireland* in 1775, but he hadn't counted on the Irish wit. They promptly began to manufacture a chamber pot called the *Twiss*, but didn't let it go at that. On the bottom of the chamber pot was a portrait of Richard Twiss, the picture captioned thus:

Let everyone ——
On lying Dick Twiss.

For our continuing twilight serial of people who have been execrated by chamber pots see *crapper, fontange, furphy, Oliver's skull,* and *Sacheverell.*

U

Uncle Sam Samuel Wilson, though known as jolly, genial and generous, wasn't called Uncle Sam only because he was a friendly avuncular sort of man. The man some say was the original *Uncle Sam* happened to be the nephew of army contractor Elbert Anderson, who owned a store or slaughterhouse on the Hudson River in Troy, N.Y., and had a contract to supply the army with salt pork and beef during the war of 1812. Uncle Sam, a former bricklayer, and *his* uncle Ebenezer worked as army inspectors and had occasion to inspect the meat Elbert Anderson packed in barrels with the initials *E.A.—U.S.* stamped on them. According to a popular version of the story, one soldier asked another what the initials U.S. (United States) meant and his companion jokingly replied that they stood for Elbert Anderson's Uncle Sam. Some respected scholars dispute the story, but no better explanation has been offered for how *Uncle Sam* became associated with the army and eventually replaced the earlier *Brother Jonathan* as a symbol of the United States government. In any case, there was a real Uncle Sam. Samuel Wilson was born in Menotomy (now Arlington), Mass., in 1766 and died at the ripe old age of eighty-eight in Troy, where he lies buried in the Oakwood Cemetery next to his wife Betsy. The preceding account of the origin of *Uncle Sam* was widely accepted during Wilson's lifetime, the major objections coming from historian Albert Matthews, who claimed that the name evolved from the initials U.S. stamped on government property, *the* Uncle Sam possibly being the official who saw to it that these markings were made. The term's first recorded use was in the Troy *Post* of September 7, 1813, which would speak well for the Sam Wilson theory except that the story says the words derive from the initials on government wagons. Regardless of its origin, the term caught on quickly and lasted. *Uncle Sam* first appeared in cartoons in 1830, but he was clean shaven and wore a robe rather than trousers until Lincoln's day, when he acquired his goatee and his present attire. His costume was based on that pictured in cartoons of the comic Yankee character Major Jack Downing created by humorist Seba Smith, the first American homespun philosopher. Today *Uncle Sam* is best known by the ubiquitous "I Want You" posters the armed forces have used for recruiting purposes. In a recent development, Walter Botts, the model who posed for these posters, was declared ineligible for a veteran's pension—by *Uncle Sam*.

Urginea Ben Urgin, not a man but an Arabian tribe in Algeria, gives its name to the genus *Urginea*, comprising about seventy-five species belonging to the lily family and native to the Mediterranean, the East Indies and South Africa. The bulbs of *U. maritenia*, the only species found in the Mediterranean, are known in medicine as squills. Generally gathered for their drug properties, they are used in Sicily for making whiskey. These bulbs often weigh up to four pounds and yield a fluid once considered valuable medically as an expectorant, a diuretic and for its digitalislike action on the heart. The first specimen of *Urginea* was found in the territory of the Ben Urgin tribe and named by the German botanist Steinheil.

Utah (see *States*)

V

Valentine, Valentine Bun, Valentining There were at least two St. Valentines, legend tells us, both Christian martyrs who were put to death on the same day, one an Italian priest and physician and the other the bishop of Terni. Butler's *Lives of the Saints* recounts the priest's story, which is almost identical to the bishop's: "Valentine was a holy priest in Rome, who . . . assisted the martyrs in the persecution under Claudius the Goth. He was apprehended and sent by the emperor to the prefect of Rome who, on finding all his promises to make him renounce his faith ineffectual, commanded him to be beaten with clubs, and afterwards to be beheaded, which was executed on February 14, about the year 270." Little else is known about this St. Valentine except that he restored the sight of his jailer's daughter, and only his or the bishop's name day has anything to do with the romantic traditions of *Valentine's Day*. February 14 had been associated with the mating of birds in ancient times, making *St. Valentine's Day*, which accidentally fell on this date, an excellent choice for a day for lovers, the day also being fairly close to spring, when, as Tennyson wrote, "a young man's fancy lightly turns to thoughts of love." It became the custom to draw lots for sweethearts or *valentines* for the ensuing year on *St. Valentine's Day*, this practice probably deriving from a similar Roman custom said to be taken from either the feast of Lupercalia, the Feast of Februata, or the day honoring the goddess Juno, all of which fell around *St. Valentine's Day*. By the end of the eighteenth century the exchange of gloves and other gifts that accompanied the drawing of lots became the exchange of letters, which were sometimes secret and often humorous or insulting. These letters evolved into the *valentines* that we know today, some twenty million such cards sent in England alone in 1967. In olden times English children celebrated *Valentine's Day* much as Halloween is celebrated in America today, going begging or *valentining* from door to door, where they were often given *Valentine buns*, sweet buns made for the occasion.

Valentino To say silent screen star Rudolph Valentino was a sex symbol is putting it mildly. Italian born Rodolpho d'Antonguolla came to the United States in 1913 and after working as a gardener, a cabaret dancer-gigolo, and then a bit player in Hollywood, he zoomed to stardom under his stage name in *The Four Horsemen of the Apocalypse* (1921), which was followed by hits like *The Sheik, Blood and Sand, Monsieur Beaucaire*, and *The Son of the Sheik*. Valentino became the embodiment of romance and sex to women all over the world, his name still a synonym for a handsome lover. Women had always been attracted to Valentino—it is said that he left Italy to escape an enraged husband, and when he came to New York he was arrested when police found him in the apartment of a woman suspected of extorting money from fun-seeking businessmen. But after his movie successes, Valentino became an object of worship to thousands of females. Women ripped his clothes off him in the streets for souvenirs, exposed their bodies to him, climbed uninvited into his bed. The crowds were unbelievable wherever he went—once when he took a stroll aboard the *Leviathan* so many women rushed to his side that the captain feared the danger of a disastrous list. The antics of individuals were even more unbelievable— one woman broke her leg climbing into his dressing room, others gladly paid his valet twenty dollars for a vial of his used bath water. Yet despite his dark good looks, this star of stars was a timorous lover, a superstitious man who tried to bolster his sexual powers with aphrodisiacs and magic amulets, who always preferred food to women and found his neurotic, clamorous admirers completely undesirable. Valentino died of peritonitis caused by a bleeding ulcer, when only thirty-one years old. Over 50,000 people, overwhelmingly women, attended his funeral in New York in 1926 and even today admirers come to mourn at his crypt in the Los Angeles cemetery where he is buried. Some 250 women have claimed publicly that the "Sheik" fathered their love children, many of whom were born years after Valentino's death.

Vancouver, Vancouveria, Vancouver Island, Puget Sound *Vancouver*, the largest city and chief port in British Columbia, *Vancouver Island*, the largest island off the west coast of North America, and the city of *Vancouver, Wash.* are all named for English navigator and explorer George Vancouver (1757–98). Captain Vancouver, who had sailed with Cook on his second and third voyages, explored and surveyed the northwest coast of America aboard *Discovery* in 1792, *Vancouver Island*, which he circumnavigated, named in his honor at the time. *Vancouver, Wash.* was named directly from *Fort Vancouver*, founded by the Hudson Bay Company in 1825, and *Vancouver, B.C.*, honored the explorer when it was incorporated in 1886. *Puget Sound* is named for Vancouver's lieutenant Peter Puget, who helped the captain's brother finish his book, *A Voyage of Discovery to the North Pacific Ocean and Round the World* (1798) when Vancouver died prematurely, only about forty years old. *Vancouveria*, a small genus of low-growing evergreen shrubs belonging to the barberry family, also remembers the explorer, the shrubs native to northwestern America.

Vandal, Vandalism In the year 455 A.D. the Vandals, all eighty thousand of them, were led by their King Genseric into Rome, which they captured easily and sacked thoroughly, loading their ships with plunder and sailing off to new conquests. The savage Teutonic tribe finished off the Holy Roman Empire before falling from power almost a century later, after persecuting Christians and extorting their sacred treasures. The Vandals did not destroy many precious cultural objects when they sacked Rome and it is probably from their later behavior that the word *vandalism* derives, meaning as it does willful wanton destruction of property, especially works of art. It is interesting to note that a French churchman first used the word *vandalisme* in this sense at the end of the eighteenth century. The name Vandal literally means "the Wanderers." Before they sacked Rome the tribes had wandered across the Rhine to France, Spain and Africa, making conquests all the while.

Vandyke When only nineteen, Flemish artist Sir Anthony Van Dyck became Rubens' assistant and pupil. One of twelve children of a wealthy silk merchant, the artist had shown great talent from his early youth and learned much from his Flemish master. Later he went to England where he married a Scotswoman and was knighted by Charles I, becoming one of the most noted portrait and religious painters of his day. Vandyke, as his name was spelled by the English, lived a life of luxury, keeping numerous mistresses, and had to paint prolifically to maintain his life style. He is known to have done at least 350 portraits in England alone and overwork is often cited as the reason for his early death—he died in 1641, forty-two years old. Vandyke turned out masterpieces on a kind of assembly-line basis. He trained assistants to paint a sitter's clothes, used special models for the hands, in the painting of which he excelled, and would never allot more than an hour at a time to a sitting. Among his notable works are portraits of King Charles and Henrietta Maria, his queen. Vandyke invariably depicted noblemen attired in wide collars adorned with V-shaped points forming an edging or border, and his subjects often wore sharp V-shaped beards similar to his own. The large points on these *Vandyke capes* or *collars* were called *vandykes*, the verb to *vandyke* meaning to adorn a collar with such points, and the characteristic beards were and are still known as *vandykes*. Although there are only about forty authentic Van Dyck portraits in existence, some two thousand forgeries are said to be distributed around the world.

Varnish (see *Berenice's Hair*)

Vauxhall It is very rare for an English word to be adopted in Russian as anything more than a slang expression. But that is just what happened with the *Vauxhall* railroad depot in London, which became the Russian *voksal*, their generic word for railroad station. The London depot was named for the *Vauxhall district* in London, which contained the famous *Vauxhall gardens*, a popular pleasure resort from 1661 till 1859. The gardens, in turn, took their name from Falkes or Fulkes de Breante, who was lord of a manor called *Falkes Hall* on the site in the early thirteenth century. Pepys mentions the public gardens, which soon came to be called *Vauxhall*, and Thackeray described them later before the gardens were closed and the site built over. From manor to garden to district to depot to Russian word—many stops along the line, but so it is that the communists, who would not consciously pay homage to royalty, honor an early Norman knight.

Vernier, Vernier Calipher, Vernier Compass, Vernier Engine A *vernier* is any small, auxiliary movable scale attached to another graduated instrument. It is often attached to the transit, sextant, quadrant and barometer for very accurate measurements. French mathematician Pierre Vernier (1580–1637) invented the scale, describing it in a treatise he wrote in 1631. Vernier was commandant of the castle in his native town of Ornans in Burgandy and later served the king of Spain as a counselor. His invention estimates the nearest tenth of the smallest division on the scale it is attached to. It was originally an improvement on a scale called the *nonius*, invented by the Portuguese scientist Nunez, and proved to be a milestone in the techniques of precise measurement. The *vernier caliper*, the *vernier compass*, both incorporating *verniers*, and the *vernier engine*, a small rocket engine that corrects the heading and velocity of a long-range missile, also bear the French inventor's name.

Victoria, Victoria Cross, Victorian Myriad things have been named after England's Queen Victoria, who reigned an amazing sixty-three years, from 1837–1901. A plum, a cloth, a large water lily, and a pigeon all bear the name *victoria*, as does the low carriage for two with a folding top and an elevated driver's seat that was designed in France and named in her honor. *Victoria* is also the capital of both British Columbia and Hong Kong and a state in Australia; there is a *Lake Victoria* in Uganda, Africa; the *Great Victorian Desert* in Australia; a *Mount Victoria* in New Guinea; a *Victoria Falls* between Zambia and Southern Rhodesia; a *Victoria Island* in the Arctic Ocean; and *Victoria Land*, a region in Antarctica. Then we have *Victoria Day*, May 25, a Canadian national holiday; the *Victorian box*, a tree; the *victorine*, a ladies' fur tippet; and the *Victoria cross*, a military decoration first awarded "for valor" by Victoria in 1856. And that isn't nearly a complete list. *Victorian* means of, or pertaining to, the queen or the period of her reign and adds a score of terms, such as *Victorian sideboard*, to the total. *Victorian* alone often refers to the smugness and prudery characteristic of the period, especially concerning sex. But Victoria's reign was on the whole a great one, marked by an extension of the franchise and by important achievements in science and the arts. Her long rule saw the beginning of the industrial revolution and an expansion of Britain's colonial empire that brought great prosperity to England. She lived in seclusion after the death of her husband Albert in 1861—more than half of her reign as a widow. The queen was much loved by her subjects. She died in 1901, aged eighty-two, her casket carried from the Isle of Wight between twin rows of warships and escorted by a military procession to London. (See also *Albert*.)

Virginia, West Virginia That gallant of gallants Sir Walter Raleigh suggested that *Virginia* be named after England's Elizabeth I, the Virgin Queen, when in 1584 he founded his colony there, probably on what is now Roanoke Island. (The island, which is in North Carolina, was originally part of the great area from Florida to Newfoundland that *Virginia* encompassed.) *Virginia*, the Old Dominion state, was the site of the first permament English settlement, at Jamestown in 1607, and the scene of the British surrender in the American Revolution at Yorktown. Called the Mother of Presidents, the state sent Washington, Jefferson, Monroe, Madison, Tyler, William Henry Harrison, Taylor, and Wilson to the White House, and is renowned for many historic shrines. As to the state's exact naming, one writer tells us that "Queen Elizabeth graciously accorded the privileges proposed by Raleigh, giving to this new land a name in honour of her maiden state, and it was called Virginia. Raleigh was knighted for his service and given the title of 'Lord and Governor of Virginia.'" Another source adds, "The glowing description given by the adventurers, on their return, of the beauty of the country, the fertility of the soil, and pleasantness of the climate, delighted the queen, and induced her to name the country of which she had taken possession, Virginia, in commemoration of her unmarried life."

West Virginia is composed of forty western mountain counties that seceded from Virginia at the outbreak of the Civil War, these counties voting not to secede from the Union and forming their own state government. After rejecting New Virginia, Kanawha and Alleghany, the new state settled on West Virginia for a name, an ironic choice as Virginia extends ninety-five miles farther west than it does. West Virginia had considered seceding from Virginia several times, due to unequal taxation and representation, and the Civil War provided an excellent excuse. Its constitution was amended to abolish slavery and President Lincoln proclaimed West Virginia the thirty-fifth state in 1862, justifying his action as a war measure. Called the Panhandle State, it has an odd outline, leading to the saying that it's "a good state for the shape it's in."

Volt, Voltaic Pile Count Alessandro Giuseppi Antonio Anastasio Volta invented Volta's pile or the voltaic pile in 1800, this the first electric battery or device for producing a continuous electric current. Volta, the son of an Italian Jesuit priest who left the order to marry, was something of a prodigy as a child. His brilliance triumphed over poverty and by the time he turned twenty-seven he had invented the electrophorus, a simple electrostatic device, had made a number of important experiments with electricity, and had become professor of physics at the University of Pavia. Even before he began his experiments with his famous pile, the widely traveled Volta was elected to England's Royal Society, for he had become internationally famous in his controversy with Galvani over the source of electricity. In 1791 Volta became the first foreigner to receive the Royal Society's Copley Medal. Volta's voltaic pile consisted of zinc and silver plates stacked alternately with moist pads and touched with a conductor to produce an electric force. He also invented an electric condenser and devised the electrochemical series. Before his death in 1827, aged eighty-two, the scientist had reaped honors in almost every country in Europe, had statues erected to him and kings contending for his presence. Napoleon, who once visited his classroom to praise him, made Volta a member of France's National Institute and a count and senator from the Kingdom of Lombardy in 1801. It is said that Bonaparte so admired the great pioneer that he once crossed out the last three letters from the phrase "Au grand Voltaire" inscribed on a wall of the National Institute library. The old story may not be true, but it shows how highly the scientist was regarded in his time. Today the unit of electrical force called the volt sings electrically of his fame. (See also Galvanize.)

Voodoo The Waldensians, followers of Peter Waldo or Valdo (d. 1217), were accused of sorcery and given the name Vaudois by the French. French missionaries later remembered these "heretics" when they encountered the witch doctors who preached black magic in the West Indies. They called the native witch doctors Vaudois and the name was soon applied to any witchcraft similar to the magic spells they cast, Vaudois eventually corrupted to voodoo. This is the view of Ernest Weekley and other respected etymologists on the origin of voodoo, however, the *Oxford English Dictionary* and a majority of authorities believe the word derives from the African *vodun,* a form of the Ashanti *obosum,* "a guardian spirit or fetish." Today the West African religion is practiced in its best integrated form in the villages of Haiti, *voodoo* having been brought to the New World by slaves as early as the 1600's.

W

Washington *Washington* is the most popular place name in the United States, recorded in the nation's capital, Washington, D.C., the state of *Washington*, at least twenty-nine counties, and numerous towns. *Washington State*, the only state named for an American, was admitted to the union on February 22, 1889, appropriately on *George Washington's birthday*, which is, of course, a national holiday. Other words honoring the "Father of his country," "first in war, first in peace, first in the hearts of his countrymen," are *the bird of Washington* (the American eagle), *the American Fabius* (see *Fabian tactics*), *Washingtonia* (a California palm tree), the *Washington thorn*, the *Washington lily*, and *Washington pie*. A *George Washington*, for an honest person, derives from the famous cherry tree story apparently invented by M. L. (Parson) Weems in his biography of the first president written about 1800. George Washington (1732–99) is the one American political figure Americans have nothing but praise for; in fact, all the legends about him have almost made him unreal. Mention should also be made of *Mount Washington*, the highest peak in the northeast, Virginia's *Washington and Lee University*, and the *Washington National Monument* dedicated in 1885 in the capital. Incidentally, after leading American forces in the Revolution, and serving two terms as president, Washington served briefly as commander in chief of the army in 1798 when war with France seemed imminent.

Wasserman Test Many medical tests, including the *Pap test* for cancer and the *Schick test* for diphtheria, are named for the physicians who devised them. The *Wasserman test* was invented in 1906 by August von Wasserman (1866–1925), a German physician and bac-

teriologist. This laboratory blood test for the diagnosis of syphilis, also known as the cardiolipin test, has been perfected to the point where it is 99 percent effective on normal persons. The test is based on the presence of antibodies in the blood. In most cases a positive *Wasserman* reveals that the patient has syphilis, although vaccination procedures and several diseases, such as leprosy, also produce a positive *Wasserman*. August von Wasserman, who began his career as a physician in Strasbourg, won international fame for his discovery. He became director of Berlin's Kaiser Wilhelm Institute in 1913 and contributed to many medical journals, doing important research in cell structure, germ isolation, antitoxins, cancer, and tuberculosis. His test is especially valuable because it can diagnose syphilis even when symptoms of the disease are not observable. (See also *Syphilis*.)

Watt, Kilowatt There is probably no truth in the charming old tale that James Watt watched his mother's teakettle whistling when a child and many years later invented the steam engine as a result. Watt, born in Scotland of poor parents, did, however, get off to an early start in his scientific endeavors. After completing a seven-year apprenticeship as an instrument maker in only one year, he found a position as mathematical instrument maker to the University of Glasgow. In 1765 the inquisitive Scotsman launched into a study of steam when a model of Thomas Neucomen's steam engine was brought to him to repair. He soon invented the first economical steam engine, which was initially used only for pumps in mines but eventually brought steam power to industry on a large scale. Watt devoted his life to perfecting and producing his new engine, manufacturing it with Matthew Boulton of Birmingham. Among his minor inventions were a clothes dryer, and manuscript and sculpture copying machines, but he was too shortsighted, or jealous of his patent, to encourage work on any improvements of his engine, or on either the revolutionary steam locomotive or automobile. In pure science Watt discovered the composition of water and he and Boulton coined the term horsepower. He died in 1819, aged eighty-three. Toward the end of the century the International Electrical Congress named the *watt*, the unit of electrical power—736 *watts* equal to about one horsepower—in the inventor's honor. His name is also remembered by the *kilowatt*, one thousand watts; the *kilowatt hour*, a measurement by which electricity is sold; the *watt-hour* meter, which measures *kilowatts*; the *watt-meter*, an instrument for measuring a power load; and the *watt-second*, a unit of work. *Wattage* is power measured in *watts*, and *wattless* is an electrical term meaning without *watts* or power.

Weber, Weberian Apparatus, Weber's Law The *weber* is the practical unit of magnetic flux, named after German physicist Wilhelm Eduard Weber (1804–91). While a professor at the University of Gottingen, Weber worked with Karl Gauss (see *gauss*) on terrestrial magnetism, devised an electromagnetic telegraph, and did valuable research on electrical measurements—the *coulomb*, in fact, once known as the *weber*. A politically committed teacher, he was dismissed from the university for protesting the king's suspension of the constitution. Weber's two brothers were also noted scientists. Wilhelm Eduard collaborated with his younger brother Eduard in 1833 on a study of human locomotion. With his elder brother Ernest he wrote a well-known book on wave motion published in 1825. This same Ernest Heinrich Weber (1795–1878), a physiologist and early psychophysical investigator, is the author of *Weber's law*, a mathematical formulation showing that the increase in stimulus necessary in producing an increased sensation depends on the strength of the preceding stimulus. The *Weberian apparatus*, small bones connecting the inner ear with the air bladder in certain fishes, honors Ernest, too. The unusually

smooth teamwork between the brothers also produced the discovery of the inhibitory power of the eye's vagus nerve —this collaborative research made by Ernest and Eduard.

Webster's Noah Webster's name has become a synonym for a dictionary since he published his *Compendious Dictionary of the English Language* in 1806 and his larger *An American Dictionary of the English Language* twenty-two years later. But the "father of American lexicography" was a man of widespread interests, publishing many diverse books over his long career. These included his famous *Blue-Backed Speller*, in use since 1783; *Sketches of American Policy* (1785), on history and politics; *Dissertations on the English Language* (1789), advocating spelling reform; and A *Brief History of Epidemic and Pestilential Diseases* (1799). Webster also found time to edit *The American Magazine* and the newspaper *The Minerva*. Beginning in 1806, he lived on the income from his speller— which sold at the rate of over one million copies a year—while he took the twenty-two years needed to complete his monumental dictionary. *Webster's*, as it came to be called—it is now published as *Webster's Dictionary* by Merriam—introduced many "Americanisms," 12,000 new words that had never been included in any dictionary. Its sales of 300,000 annually helped standardize American pronunciation and simplify spelling. Webster's major fault seems to have been his prudery, the norm in those days. In 1833 he published a *bowdlerized* edition of the Bible, removing "offensive words" that might make young ladies "reluctant to attend Bible classes." "Breast" was substituted for "teat," "to nourish" for "to give suck," "peculiar members" for "stones" (testicles), and so on. This hardly fits in with the legend about him being caught kissing the chambermaid. "Why Noah, I'm *surprised!*" his wife is supposed to have said. "Madame," Webster replied, most correctly, "*You* are astonished; *I* am surprised."

Wedgwood, Wedgwood Scale, Portland Vase, Queen's Ware Despite the fact that a childhood illness had caused the amputation of his right leg, barring him from using the potter's wheel, Josiah

Wedgwood (1730–95) became the greatest craftsman of his time, practically founding the English pottery industry and revolutionizing standards for ceramic manufacture. Poor and uneducated, Wedgwood began his career in his family's small pottery shop. So well did he learn that he founded a firm in Staffordshire, where he made a wide variety of ceramic ware. Wedgwood's most famous inventions were jasper ware, a mat-surfaced stoneware; *Queen's ware*, a glazed, cream-colored household ware named after Queen Charlotte; vases and other articles of black composition known as basalt or Egyptian ware; and the *Wedgwood scale*, the scale of degrees, as shown on the pyrometer, to measure pottery kiln temperatures. In 1769 he built a factory called Etruria that eventually grew into a village, naming his plant for ancient Etrusca because it was believed at the time that Greek vases had been made there. *Wedgwood ware* is still manufactured by the potter's descendants, though the factory is presently in Barlaston. Wedgwood created dinner services for Catherine the Great and many notable figures, and he collaborated with John Flaxman on a number of fine designs that are now in museums.

There is an interesting story about the ubiquitous blue and white vases that Wedgwood made. These he copied from the famous *Portland Vase* that Sir William Hamilton, husband of Nelson's great love, purchased with a collection of Grecian vases when he served as ambassador to Naples. Hamilton sold the blue and white glass vase to the duchess of Portland, for whom it is named, and Wedgwood copied it after she donated it to the British Museum in 1784. What nobody realized was that the *Portland Vase* wasn't a Greek vase at all, but a heavy-handed Roman imitation from the time of Augustus, what we might call kitsch today. The Wedgwood firm has made a fortune with the popular blue-and-white line, but far more fascinating is the story of how poet John Keats wrote his immortal *Ode on a Grecian Urn* about a Grecian vase that never existed. It seems that Keats had seen a Wedgwood imitation of the Roman imitation of a Greek vase, this inspiring him to

write so beautifully: "Thou still unravished bride of quietness, / Thou foster-child of Silence and slow Time . . ." and to end his great poem with " 'Beauty is truth, truth beauty,—that is all / Ye know on earth and all ye need to know.' "

Weigela, Weigelia, Diervilla The long-popular *Weigela* genus of the honeysuckle family, containing some twelve species, is named for German physician C. E. Weigel (1748–1831). *Weigela*, sometimes spelled *weigelia*, is often grouped with the *Diervilla* genus, the bush honeysuckle, but its bushes have larger, much showier flowers than the latter. *Diervilla* itself is named for a Dr. Dierville, a French surgeon in Canada. Native to Asia, the *weigela* bush is easily cultivated in America and Europe, its funnel-shaped flowers usually rose pink but varying in color from white to dark crimson.

Wellington Napoleon's greatest adversary fares as well in the dictionaries as he did on the battlefield. Arthur Wellesley, the first duke of Wellington, who began his army career in India and was knighted for his victories there, drove the French from Spain during the Peninsular War and completely crushed Napoleon at Waterloo in 1815. One of England's greatest soldiers, "the Iron Duke" served as prime minister from 1828–30 and in 1842 was made commander in chief of the British armed forces for life. About the only blemish on his record was his aristocratic opposition to parliamentary reform, which caused his ministry to fall. Wellington died in 1852, an idolized old man of eighty-three, and it is said that even death "came to him in its gentlest form." A number of hats, coats and trousers were named after the great soldier, as were two types of boots: the full *Wellington riding boots*, which were tight-fitting and came up slightly over the knee, and the *half-Wellington*, which came halfway up the calf, having a boot made of patent leather and a top of softer material. One probably apocryphal story says that Queen Victoria once asked the duke the name of the boots he was wearing. When he replied that they were called *Wellington's*, she remarked, "Impossible! There could not be *a pair* of Wellington's!" The capital of New Zealand is also named for Wellington, as well as the *Wellingtonia,* a New Zealand sequoia, and a term in the card game *Nap* (see *Napoleon*). The duke took his title from the town of Wellington in England, where a statue of him stands today.

Welsh, Welsher, Welsh Rabbit, Walnut England's native Celts were called *wealhs,* "foreigners"—by the invading Saxons of all people—and driven off into the western hills. *Wealhs* became *Welsh* in time and these inhabitants of Wales suffered almost as much abuse at the hands and tongues of the English as did the Scotch or Irish. Their traditional enemies used *Welsh* to signify anything poor, such as a *Welsh comb,* the fingers, a *Welsh carpet,* a painted floor, and *Welsh rabbit,* melted seasoned cheese poured over buttered toast.

To welsh or renege on a bet is another contemptuous English reference to the Welsh. The most common explanation is that there were thought to be a great many crooked Welsh bookmakers at the racetracks in the nineteenth century, *Welshers* or *welshers* who did not pay when they lost. Names of individual bookmakers, such as a Mr. Bob Welch, have also been suggested, but with no positive proof or identification.

Walnut, an ancient word, comes from the Anglo-Saxon *wealhhnutu,* meaning "the foreign or Welsh nut." Kinder terms using the *Welsh* prefix include three breeds of dogs—the *Welsh corgi, springer spaniel,* and *terrier;* the *Welsh poppy* with its pale yellow flowers; and the small sturdy *Welsh pony* originally raised in Wales.

West Virginia (see *Virginia*)

Whig The Whiggamores were a group of insurgents from west Scotland who marched on Edinburgh in 1648, their expedition called the "Whiggamore raid." Their name's origin is unknown—though *whig* meant both a country bumpkin and a mare—but these Presbyterians supported Cromwell's imprisonment of Charles I and demanded that their parliament stand against the king. Other, wealthier Presbyterians, who de-

tested the monarch's attempts to bring Scotland into the Church of England, but wanted no harm to come to his person, strongly supported Charles and even tried to rescue him, the Wiggamore raid a reaction by their more militant brethren. The word Whiggamore was shortened to *Whig* in time and became the name for the English political party opposed to the royalist Tories. Today the *Whig* party has been displaced by Labor and the Tories by the Conservatives in England. In the United States the *Whigs* were a political party formed in opposition to the Democrats in 1834, the party lasting until 1855 when the Republicans took its place. (See also *Cromwell.*)

Williamson Like the gypsies of old, "the terrible Williamsons" have fleeced so many people in recent years that their name has become a generic term for itinerant hustlers. An inbred clan of gyp artists numbering about two thousand, the family descends from Robert Logan Williamson, who emigrated from Scotland to Brooklyn in the 1890's and soon imported his relatives. Today the wandering clan makes its headquarters and major burial grounds in Cincinnati, a crossroads city, or at least it meets there once a year in the spring to bury their dead, exchange notes and renew friendships. There is not a nonviolent hustler's trick unknown to the Williamsons', from resurfacing a homeowner's driveway with crankcase oil—and departing with the payment across the county line before the next rain washes the "blacktop" away—to an attractive Williamson woman selling her "dead mother's valuable Irish linen" door to door in order to "buy milk" for a baby conveniently bawling in her arms. If arrested, a Williamson often jumps bail and simply chalks the cost up as an operating expense. Their mobility makes it difficult to catch up with members of the clan, and they do so well at their trade that their traditional annual meetings just before Memorial Day are marked by an orgy of spending on Cadillacs, new trailers, clothes, and blue chip stocks—generally paid for with crisp hundred-dollar bills. Security at their funerals is tight and admittance can be gained only by reciting a password in a Scottish brogue. The clan, which has eight or ten family names, such as McDonald, Stewart and Reid, uses only a limited number of common given names, like John and Jean and George, making things even more difficult for the police. Exotic nicknames are not unknown, however, two former family leaders being Isaac "Two Thumbs" and Jennie "Black Queen" Williamson, whose sons were dubbed Gopher, Goose Neck and Texas. In some respects the Williamsons have changed over the years. Today their children do not go uneducated as they did in the past, and the clan doesn't only bury their dead in the spring anymore—they used to hold their dead bodies in storage until they could meet in Cincinnati. But they are still the itinerant hustlers they were almost a century ago, hustlers whose numbers and ploys have proliferated. "You try to keep the public aware," says a Better Business Bureau official of the clan, "but there's always somebody else to fool."

Winchester The Model 73 Winchester rifle, made in 1873, is the prototype for all the famous *Winchester* models now extensively used for hunting. The first *Winchester*, however, was made in 1866. Oliver F. Winchester (1810–1880) manufactured the rifle at his plant in New Haven, Conn., the weapon based on a number of patents the industrialist had acquired from different inventors. This early repeater became generic for any repeating rifle and was widely used on the frontier. The *Winchester*, a lever-action rifle with a tubular magazine in the forestock, became the standard repeating rifle mechanism, the Winchester Arms Company, which still operates today, a unique eminence in its field for many years. Predecessor to the early *Winchester* was the *Henry* repeating rifle mentioned previously and the *Henry's* precursor was the *Spencer*.

Wisteria, Wistaria An error made by Thomas Nuttal, curator of Harvard's Botanical Garden, led to the accepted misspelling of this beautiful flowering plant—*wisteria* being the common spelling today even though *wistaria* is correct. "Wisteria . . ." Nuttal wrote in his *Genera North American Plants II* (1818), "In memory of Casper Wistar, M.D. late professor of Anatomy in the University of Pennsylvania." Nuttal, who named the plant after Wistar, had meant to write "Wistaria," but his slip of pen was perpetuated by later writers and *wisteria* has become accepted. All attempts to remedy the situation have failed, even Joshua Logan's play, *The Wistaria Trees*, in which the author purposely spelled the word with an *a* in order to influence its proper spelling. A Philadelphia Quaker, Caspar Wistar taught "anatomy, midwifery, and surgery" at what was then the College of Pennsylvania. The son of a noted colonial glassmaker, Dr. Wistar wrote America's first anatomy textbook, succeeded Jefferson as head of the American Philosophical Society, and his home became the Sunday afternoon meeting place of many notable Philadelphians. Wistar included among his accomplishments "the first scientific description of the ethmoid bone, posterior portion," whatever and wherever that may be. His anatomical collections became part of Philadelphia's *Wistar Institute of Anatomy and Biology*, endowed by his great-nephew Issaac Jones Wistar (1827–1905), a self-made railroad millionaire with an adventurous past as a trapper, gold miner, western lawman and much-wounded general during the Civil War. The good doctor was only fifty-seven when he died in 1818, the same year in which Nuttal honored him but spelled his name wrong. The *Wisteria* genus includes seven species native to Japan, China and eastern North America. A climbing woody vine of the pea family, the plant blooms profusely in the late spring, its flowers hanging in clusters up to three feet long and either lilac-purple, violet, violet-blue, white or pink in color. Old gnarled *wisteria* often reach to the top of houses and are a sight to behold when flowering. If you are ever in the vicinity of Sierra Madre, Cal. in the late springtime, go out of your way to see the giant Chinese *wisteria* near the Los Angeles State and County Arboretum. During its five-week blooming period this giant Chinese species becomes a vast field filled with over one and a half million blossoms, the largest flowering plant in the world. Planted in 1892 the fabulous vine covers almost an acre, has branches surpassing 500 feet in length and weighs over 252 tons. You won't be alone—more than thirty thousand people come to see it every year. (See also *Sequoia*.)

X

Xanthippe Legend has made Socrates' wife Xanthippe the classic shrew and her name has become proverbial for a quarrelsome, nagging, shrewish wife or woman. In *The Taming of the Shrew* Shakespeare writes: "*Be she as foul as was Florentius' love, / As old as Sibyl, and as curst and shrewd / As Socrates' Xanthippe, or a worse, / She moves me not.*" The gossips in Athens talked much of Xanthippe's terrible temper and she may have literally driven Socrates out into the open and his marketplace discussions. But then Socrates may have been a difficult husband, and by most accounts is said to have been unusually ugly and uncouth in appearance. Xenophon writes that Xanthippe's sterling qualities were recognized by the philosopher, and various historians, including Zeller in his *Vorträge and Abhandlungen* (1875), argue that she has been much maligned, that Socrates was so unconventional as to tax the patience of any woman, as indeed would any man convinced that he has a religious mission on earth. (See also *Socrates*.)

Y

Yale, Yale Blue, Yale Lock *Yale University*, ranking after Harvard and William and Mary as the third oldest institution of higher education in the United States, is named for English merchant Elihu Yale (1649–1721). Founded in 1701 as the Collegiate School of Saybrook, Conn., the school was named Yale College at its 1718 Commencement, held in the first college building at New Haven. It became a university in 1887. *Yale* might have been called Mather University, for Cotton Mather suggested naming it so in return for his financial support, but Elihu Yale won out when he donated a cargo of gifts, books and various goods that brought about 562 pounds when sold. Yale had been born in Boston in 1649, but returned with his family to England three years later. He served with the British East India Company, and as governor of Fort St. George in India until scandals in his administration led to his removal in 1692.

Yale blue, a reddish blue, takes its name from the university colors. It is the royal blue of the Egyptian Rameses dynasty, also called Rameses. *Yale lock* has no connection with the school. American inventor Linnus Yale (1821–68) invented numerous locks including the key type with a revolving barrel that bears his name. Linnus founded a company to manufacture locks at Stamford, Conn., the same year that he died. Although *Yale* is a trademark, it is often applied generically to any lock with a revolving barrel.

Yankee The source of this word has long been disputed and its origin is really uncertain. Candidates, among many, have included a slave named Yankee offered for sale in 1725, a Dutch sea captain named Yanky, the Yankaw Indians, the Dutch name *Janke* ("Johnny") which they applied to the English, and an Indian mispronunciation (*Yengees*) of the word English. The most popular explanation is that *Yankee* comes from *Jan Kees*, a Flemish and German nickname for the Dutch that the English used to signify "John Cheese," and contemptuously applied to the Dutch in the New World. But why was the nickname transferred to the English themselves? At any rate, ironically transferred or not, *Yankee* described a New Englander by the middle eighteenth century and was used by the British to designate an American during the Revolution, the most notable example found in the derisive song *Yankee Doodle*. Nowadays the British still use the word for an American, southerners use it for northerners, and northerners use it for New Englanders, who are usually proud of the designation.

Yarborough Little is known about Charles Anderson Worsley, the second earl of Yarborough, aside from the fact that he was a knowledgeable card player and made himself a small fortune giving 1,000 to 1 odds that his bridge-playing companions would not be dealt hands containing no cards higher than a nine. The odds were with the English lord, for the chances of drawing such a thirteen-card hand are actually 1,827 to 1 against. Yarborough, born in the early nineteenth century, died in 1897, an old and probably rich man. Since his wagers, a *Yarborough* has been any hand in whist or bridge with no card higher than a nine, although the term also means a hand in which there are no trumps. Yarborough is a parish in England and the earls of Yarborough are descended from Sir William Pelham, Lord Justice of Ireland and soldier under Queen Elizabeth.

The odds against a bridge suit distribution of 13-0-0-0 are about 158,755,357,-992 to 1.

Yegg A *yegg* can mean a safecracker, an itinerant burglar, a thief, or an insignificant criminal. The most common explanation has the word deriving from the surname of John Yegg, a late nineteenth-century American safe-blower whose life remains a blank. The word first appeared in print as *yegg-men*, tramps, in 1901. Other suggestions for its source are the German *jäger*, meaning hunter; *yekk*, a Chinese dialect word used in San Francisco's Chinatown that means beggar; and the Scottish and English dialect *yark* or *yek*, to break.

Youngberry The *youngberry* is generally considered to be a hybrid variety of dewberry, which, in turn, is simply an early ripening prostrate form of blackberry. The large, dark purple sweet fruit has the high aroma and flavor of the *loganberry* and native blackberry. The *youngberry* was developed by Louisiana horticulturist B. M. Young about 1900 by crossing a southern dewberry and trailing blackberry, or several varieties of blackberries. Its long, trailing canes are generally trained on wires. Popular in the home garden, the berry is extensively planted in the American southwest, south, Pacific northwest and California. (See also *Boysenberry*; *Loganberry*.)

Z

Zaluzania, Zaluzianskya Polish physician Adam Zaluziansky von Zaluzian probably didn't expect that his long tongue twister of a name would be given to anything, yet it became the scientific designation for not one but two plant genera. *Zaluzianskya* (often spelt with an "ie" ending) is the beautifully fragrant night-blooming phlox, the genus embracing about forty South African species. While all such nocturnal flowers may bloom daytimes, on overcast days or toward evening, their finest flowering and greatest fragrance comes long after sunset. The Prague doctor, who published an important herbal, *Methodus Herbariae* (1602), has his last name honored by the genus *Zaluzania*, comprising about seven species of small shrubs with white or yellow flowers that are mainly grown in the greenhouse outside their native Mexico. Strangely enough, despite their long, scientific designations, neither genus seems to be known by any popular common name.

Zenadia Bird (see *Bonaparte gull*)

Zeppelin After a career as a soldier that included a volunteer stint with the Union army during the Civil War, the intrepid German adventurer Count Ferdinand von Zeppelin retired from the German army with the rank of general and devoted himself to the development of dirigible airships. Zeppelin, inspired by a balloon ascent he made in St. Paul, Minn., built and flew his first rigid airship in 1900 when sixty-two years old, the initial flight lasting twenty minutes. But he had to build and test four *Luftschiff Zeppelins* in all before convincing the German government that his invention was militarily sound. *Zeppelins* came to be used extensively by the Germans in World War I, some eighty-eight of them constructed by their inventor at his factory in Friedrichshafen. Neverthe-less, they didn't work out. Although they attained speeds of up to thirty-six miles per hour and were used to bomb Paris and London, the airships ultimately proved too unwieldly in combat. Count Zeppelin died in 1917, aged seventy-nine, *zeppelin* being used by then to mean any dirigible. The brave old man was spared the pain of seeing his invention involved in a number of tragic accidents. The *zeppelin* never became the great air carrier he hoped it would be and was obsolete by the end of World War II.

Zinnia Youth-and-old-age, the *zinnia* species *elegans* is called and anyone who has seen how profusely the annual flower blooms and how quickly it succumbs to the first frost will appreciate the folk name. The same applies to all the *zinnia* genus, which Linnaeus named for Johann Gottfried Zinn, whose life was as bright and brief as his namesake's. Zinn, a German botanist and physician, who was a professor of medicine at Gottingen, died in 1759 when barely thirty-two. In 1753 he had published what is said to be the first book on the anatomy of the eye. There are about fifteen species of the *zinnia*, which is the state flower of Indiana. Most modern tall forms, with flowers in many colors, come from the Mexican *Zinnia elegans*, introduced in 1886 and growing to heights of about three feet. Another explanation for *elegans'* youth-and-old-age nickname may be the stiff hairs on the stem or the coarse plant itself, in contrast to the warm flowers, or the plant's tendency to develop the powdery mildew disease when poorly cultivated. But the spring-frost analogy is nicer.

Zoysia Grass For some odd reason none of the major dictionaries include *Zoysia grass*, which is commonly planted today, especially for play areas and for lawns in the Deep South. The popular grass, generally planted by bits of rootstock called *Zoysia plugs,* is named for Austrian botanist Karl von Zois. There are only four species of the creeping grass. *Zoysia* takes a lot of wear and tear, forming a dense, tough turf, but has one major drawback—it turns a haylike color in the late fall and is among the slowest of grasses to green up again in the spring. Some zealous *zoysia* lawn keepers give nature a tender, loving hand by painting their grass with green latex and other preparations in the off-seasons. Yet another reason why anyone reincarnated in this part of the world wouldn't do badly if he came back as a lawn.

Zwinglian, Zyrian Few readers will come in contact with the word *Zwinglian,* which means of or pertaining to Huldreich Zwingli or his doctrines. Huldreich, or Ulrich Zwingli (1484–1531), a Swiss Protestant reformer, served as chaplain and standard bearer to troops fighting against Catholic sections of Switzerland that did not accept the official recognition of the Reformation. He was killed at the battle of Kappel. Zwingli's views were close to Luther's, except for his purely symbolic interpretation of the Lord's Supper, which estranged the two men and made a united Protestantism impossible. Frankly, *Zwinglian* is included primarily because it is the last human word in any major dictionary—unless we include *Zyrian,* which is a Uralic language spoken by the Komi, a Finnic people of Northeast European Russia who were formerly known as the *Zyrians.*

ADDENDUM
Other Eponyms

Space permits here only a sampling of the thousands of additional eponymous words on hand, but too numerous to be included in the main list. Almost all unfamiliar scientific eponyms (minerals, inventions, laws, etc., named after scientists) had to be omitted here, as did most words referring to the reigns of royalty (i.e., *Carolean, Caroline, Edwardian*), and numerous purely historical expressions or words pertaining exclusively to the works of writers, artists and philosophers (such as *Addisonian, Rembrandt-esque,* and *Hegelian*). However, a very large representative selection of these and other eponyms are to be found in the preceding alphabetized entries and even more can be located under general headings like *Cities, Nations, States* and entries treating national groups such as *Dutch, Irish,* etc. Flower names are extensively covered in the main body of the book, but a fascinating work could be done on them alone. Most good horticultural encyclopedias note some eponyms among plants, but the writer suggests that gardening enthusiasts track down the following interesting handful among hundreds: *Abelia; Bloomeria; Boltonia; Buddleia; Clintonia; Deutzia; Dieffenbachia; Edgeworthia; Fittonia; Hosta; Juanulloa; Kalmia; Libertia; Murraya; Nicandra; Oliveranthus; Parrotia; Robinia; Samuela; Sinningia* (not named for a sinner, incidentally); *Stranvaesia; Tillandsia; Wyethia;* and *Zenobia.* The words included in this appendix were chosen, like the main entries, on the basis of their importance, uniqueness, frequency of use today, and as further examples of the wide range of occupations and characters represented by "human words." Needless to say, the selection had to be arbitrary and only brief definitions are possible herein. The author would welcome any additions or corrections for future editions of the work, in which it is hoped there will be space for an even fuller selection.

Agag—to walk like (softly)—Biblical King Agag (I *Samuel* 15:32)

Ahnfelt's seaweed—Swedish botanist N. Ahnfelt (1801–37)

Algorism—decimal system—Jafer Mohammed Ibn-Musa, 9th century Arab mathematician called *al-Kowarazmi*, "the man of Kwarazm"

Amati—violin—16th–17th century Italian violinmaker family

Anacreontic—amatory—6th century Greek poet Anacreon

Anselmo—yellow color—artist Giorgio Anselmi (1723–97)

Anthony Eden—hat—former British Prime Minister Anthony Eden

Appian way—Roman highway begun in 312 B.C. by Appius Claudius Caecus

Aristarchus—a severe but fair critic—3rd century Greek astronomer, Aristarchus

Armstrong—high trumpet note—jazz-great Louis "Satchmo" Armstrong (1900–71)

Assassin—11th century Mohammedan order of Assassins—*its* name from the Arabic *hashshasin*, "eaters of hashish or hemp"

Baddeley cake—British theatre tradition—actor Robert Baddeley (1732–94)

Balboa—Panamanian monetary unit —explorer Vasco Nuñez de Balboa (1475–1517)

Baldwin apple—first grown by American officer Loammi Baldwin (1740–1807)

Ballyhoo—possibly for the boisterous villagers of Ballyhoo, County Cork

Barabbas—robber freed from cross instead of Christ (*Matthew* 27:15–16)

Barcelona—Spanish city founded by Hamilcar Barca, ca. 230 B.C.

Baud—telegraphy term—French inventor Jean Baudot (1845–1903)

Bayard—an honorable man—Pierre Terrail (1473?–1524), Seigneur de Bayard, "*Chevalier sans peur et sans reproche*"

Belmont Stakes—part of racing's Triple Crown—named for Belmont Park, N.Y., which bears the name of millionaire August Belmont

Bertha—lace cape worn over lowcut dresses—Charlemagne's mother, Queen Bertha, famed for her modesty

Biddy—Irish maid—from common Irish name Bridgett, as is "Old Biddy"

Biedermeier cabinet—named for imaginary 19th century German writer who was in reality *several* writers

Bircher—member of ultra-conservative John Birch Society—said to be named for the last American soldier to be killed in W.W. II

Bismarckian—aggressive diplomacy or politics—German statesman Otto von Bismarck (1815–98); *Bismarck herring* also "honors" him

Blackburnian warbler—named for 18th century English birdwatcher Mrs. Hugh Blackburn

Boanerges—a loud noisy orator or preacher—for the sons of Zebedes, whom Christ named *Boanerges*, "the sons of thunder" (*Mark* 3:17)

Boolean algebra—for George Boole (1815–64), English mathematician

Bradshaw—British railway guide—printer George Bradshaw (1803–53)

Bragg's Law—physics—Sir William Henry Bragg (1862–1942) and his son Sir William Lawrence Bragg (b. 1890)

Braidism — hypnotism — Scotsman James Braid (c. 1795–1860)

Brasher doubloon—gold coin—N.Y. goldsmith Ephraim Brasher or Brashear

Brigham tea—medicinal tea named for Mormon founder, Brigham Young

Buchmanism—post W.W. I. "moral re-armament" philosophy—Englishman Frank Buchman (b. 1878)

Burley tobacco—apparently from a proper name

Caldecott award—annual U.S. award for best juvenile book—for Randolph Caldecott (1846–86), English illustrator

Capone—1920's criminal's name became synonymous for a mobster and cheap cigar

Cappuccino—espresso coffee, steamed milk, and whipped cream—named after the Capuchin monks, who may have invented it

Carley float—life-saving device invented (1899) by American, Horace Carley

Carthaginian peace—a destructive peace settlement like the severe Punic War treaties the Romans imposed on the Carthaginians

Carver chair—after John Carver, *owner* of one of these 17th century chairs

Castroism, Fidelism—Communism of Cuban revolutionary Fidel Castro (b. 1927)

Chalybean—of steel—for the Chalybes, ancient people of Asia Minor

Cheval-de-frise—spiked portable military obstacle—literally "the horse of Frisia," first used by the Frisians

Cimmerian—very dark—for the Cimmerian nomads of the 7th century, who also gave their name to the *Crimea*

Cincinnatus—someone like the simple and loyal Cincinnatus, ancient Roman statesman and savior of his country

Clarke's gazelle—possibly for English soldier George S. Clarke (1848–1933)

Claude glass—colored mirror for receiving a reflected landscape—French landscape artist Claude Lorrain (1600–82)

Clausewitz—a formidable strategist—German military author Karl von Clausewitz (1780–1831)

Cochise—pertaining to S.E. Arizona Indian culture—named after Cochise County, Arizona, which honors the Apache leader Cochise (1815–74)

Code of Hammurabi—one of the first legal codes, instituted in the 20th century B.C. by Babylonian ruler Hammurabi

Coke upon Littleton—suggesting the subtleties of law—for legal experts Edward Coke (1552–1634) and Thomas Littleton (1407–81)

Congreve—match—inventor Sir William Congreve (1772–1828)

Cordoba—Nicaraguan monetary unit —Spanish explorer Francisco de Cordoba (c. 1475–1526)

Corfam—a leather substitute—a trademark coined by a computer

Cretan—a liar—for the ancient Cretans, noted for their mendacity

Crockford—British clerical directory —after one compiled by a John Crockford in 1865

Cudbear—18th century Scotch chemist Dr. *Cuthbert* Gordon made the violet coloring made from lichens, coining its name from his own

Cutter number—system used in libraries supplementing the *Dewey Decimal system*—invented by Boston librarian Charles A. Cutter

Cyrenaic—philosophy of pleasure as the chief end of life—philosopher Aristippus of Cyrene (?435–356 B.C.)

Cyrillic—script derived from Greek uncial letters—said to be invented by St. Cyril, "Apostle of the Slavs" (A.D. 827–869)

Dear John letter—no one has identified the original jilted John

Delsarte method—improvement of musical and dramatic expression by bodily attitudes and gestures, named for its devisor French musician François Delsarte (1811–71)

Deweyan—pertaining to the educational philosophy of U.S. educator John Dewey (1859–1952)

Dogwood—the tree got its name not from any dog, but because its juices were used as a flea remedy

Doppler effect, radar—Austrian physicist C. J. Doppler (1803–53)

Doran — electronic — *Do*(ppler) + *ran*(ge) (see *Doppler*)

Dorcas—a model housewife—from the Biblical Dorcas (*Acts* 9:36, 39)

Drago Doctrine—doctrine that European nations cannot collect debts from American countries by armed force—for Argentine statesman Luis Drago (1859–1921); see *Monroe Doctrine*

Dreyfusard—any defender of French army officer Alfred Dreyfus (1859–1935), convicted of treason in 1894 and acquitted in 1906

Eddie—annual award made since 1941 by the American Cinema Editors for the best editing of films—after the common nickname

Edgar—statuette honoring writers given yearly by the Mystery Writers of America—named for Edgar Allan Poe

Edsel—a car manufactured by the Ford Motor Co. and since subjected to much ridicule—named for Edsel Ford, who to his greater fame also has the *Edsel Ford Range* in Antarctica named after him

Elgin marbles—famous classical works taken from Athens by Lord Elgin (1766–1841) and purchased by Britain in 1816

Elijah's cup—wine set aside for Elijah at Jewish Seder meal

Emmy—the National Academy of Television Arts and Sciences had no one specifically in mind on naming this award, simply emulating the *Oscar*

Engels' law—the percentage of income spent on food decreases as income increases—for economist Ernst Engels (1821–96)

Ermine—fur—the old world weasel was named in Latin *Armenius mūs*, "the Armenian rat"

Eustachian tube—auditory canal— Italian anatomist Bartolommeo Eustachio (1524?–1574)

Fabergé—fine gold, enamel ware— 19th–20th century Russian artist Fabergé

Fallopian tubes—Italian anatomist Gabriello Fallopio (1523–62)

Fenian—secret Irish revolutionary society established in 1858—from the Fiann, old Irish militia named for a traditional Irish hero

Flaminian—relating to Roman censor Gaius Flaminius, or the public works constructed while he held office

Fleur-de-luce—France's emblem— "flower of Louis" of France's Louis VII

Foliatum—beauty cream made from spikenard—named for the Roman Folia who first prepared it

Fulbright—a scholarship grant provided under the U.S. Congress Fulbright Act (1946) introduced by Senator James William Fulbright (b. 1905)

Gadsden Purchase—1853 purchase of land now in New Mexico for $10 million from Mexico, treaty negotiated by U.S. diplomat James Gadsden (1788–1858)

Galilean telescope—Italian scientist Galileo Galilei (1564–1642)

Gallium — element — Latin *gallus* (cock) is the translation of *Coq* from name of 19th century French chemist *Lecoq* de Boisbaudran

Gandhian, Gandhiism, Gandhi cap— pertaining to Indian religious leader and reformer Mohandas Gandhi (1869–1948)

Gaullism, Gaullist—the political principles and followers of French General Charles De Gaulle (1890–1971)

Gay-Lussac's Law—French chemist Joseph P. Gay-Lussac (1778–1850), who also has a street in the Latin Quarter named for him

Geika—small reptile—Scottish geologist Sir Archibald Geikie (1835–1924)

Geordie—miners' safety lamp—for its 19th century inventor George Stephenson; see also *Davy lamp*

Germane—a variation of *German* (q.v.)

Gibeonite—a drudge—for the Gibeonites described in *Joshua* 19:27

Goliath crane—heavy-duty gantry crane named after the Biblical Goliath slain by David (1 *Samuel* 17:48–51)

Grahamize—severely edit—British Home Secretary James Graham (1792–1861)

Grammy—award made by the National Academy of Recording Arts & Sciences—the name taken from "gramophone"

Grimthorpe—to restore a building— English architect Sir Edmund Beckett, 1st Baron Grimthorpe (1816–1905)

Grolier binding—ornate bookbinding honoring bibliophile Jean Grolier de Servières (1479–1565), French Treasurer-General

Guarneri—violin—Italian Guarneri family, 17th–18th centuries

Guggenheim—grant in aid given by the foundation established by American philanthropist Daniel Guggenheim (1856–1930)

Guggenheim—word game—after the proper name, perhaps from above

Guyot—flat-topped submarine mountain or seamount named after American geologist Arnold Guyot (1807–84)

Hadassah—benevolent Jewish women's organization—from the Hebrew name of Queen Esther (*Esther* 2:7)

Hadrian's Wall—defensive wall in Britain built by Roman Emperor Hadrian (A.D. 76–138)

Hampden, Village Hampden—defender of popular liberties—Englishman John Hampden (1594–1643)

Harrison red—a brilliant red perhaps named after American artist B. Harrison (d. 1929)

Harris Poll—public opinion survey originated by contemporary pollster Lou Harris

Hatch Act—1939 and 1940 Congressional Acts regulating campaign expenditures, etc., sponsored by Congressman Carl A. Hatch (b. 1889)

Hellenic—pertaining to the ancient Greeks—from the name of King Hellen, ancestor of the Hellenes

Hick—unsophisticated provincial person—from Hick, a familiar form of the prenom Richard

Hickey—a device or gadget (also dohickey); a pimple; a mark on the neck from a passionate kiss—perhaps from the surname Hickey

Hicks yew—a hybrid yew (*Taxus media hicksi*) developed by the Hicks nurseries in Westbury, New York

Hillel Foundation—organization for Jewish college students named after Palestinian philosopher Hillel (c. 60 B.C.– A.D. 9?)

Hindenburg line—German W.W. I fortification on French-Belgium border honoring Field Marshal Paul von Hindenburg (1847–1934)

Ho Chi Minh Trail—jungle war trail from N. Vietnam through Laos and Cambodia named for N. Vietnam leader Ho Chi Minh (d. 1970)

Hooker's green—color named for English artist W. Hooker (d. 1832)

Hooper rating—radio rating of listeners tuned in to a specific show—Claude E. Hooper (d. 1954), American statistician

Impeyan—pheasant—Lady Impey and Sir Elijah Impey (1732–1809)

Jack Rose—cocktail of apple brandy, lime juice and grenadine—French nobleman and general J. N. Jacqueminot (1787–1865)

Jacobin—political radical—after radical party active during French Revolution

Jacobite—partisan of England's James II overthrown in 1688, or the Stuarts—from Latinized form of James' name

J. B. King—similar to *Kilroy* (q.v.)—said to be for a millionaire turned hobo who first chalked graffiti on boxcars, many of which he *owned*

Jenny, Jennet—female ass—from the name of a Berber tribe, *Zanatch*

Jiminy—mild exclamation of surprise—possibly from the Latin *Jesu Domine*, Lord Jesus, as is euphemistic *Jeez*; and *Jesuit*

John—Slang for bathroom—special use of proper name

Johnny Appleseed—a planter, even ecologist—for John Chapman, the partly mythical "Johnny Appleseed" (1774–1845), rich plantsman

Josephine's Lily—honors Napoleon's empress Josephine (see *Lapageria*)

Justinian Code—Roman law codified under Emperor Justinian I (A.D. 483–565)

Kenny method—polio treatment—Australian nurse "Sister" Elizabeth Kenny (1886–1952)

Keynesian—economic theories of British economist John Maynard Keynes (1883–1946)

Klaxon horn—from the Klaxon Company, musical instrument manufacturers

Knoop scale—hardness scale, like *Brinell*—for American chemist F. Knoop

Kunyite—a gem—American jewelry expert George F. Kuny (1856–1932)

Lafayette—the butterfish, various hats, buckles, etc.—French Marquis de Lafayette (1757–1834)

Lamarckian—pertaining to the theory of organic evolution of French naturalist Jean Lamarck (1744–1829)

Laurite—mineral—named by its finder German chemist F. Wohler (1800–82) for a Mrs. Laura Joy

Liebfraumilch—from the German *Liebfrauenstift*, convent of the Virgin (in Worms where the white wine was first made), *milch* being the German for milk

Liebig—meat extract—named for inventor Baron Justus von Liebig (1803–73)

Limousine—originally any closed car—its name from a *hood* worn by *Limousins* of the French province of Limousin

Lindley Murray—an able grammarian—for "the father of English grammar" (1745–1826)

Lippes loop—an S-shaped plastic intra-uterine device to prevent conception—invented by American physician Jack Lippes

Logie—imitation stage jewelry—named for a David Logie in about 1869

Lulu—a beauty, a remarkable thing—after the proper name Louise

Lutheran—pertaining to the works of German theologian Martin Luther (1483–1546) or the Lutheran church

Lycurgus—severe lawmaker—honors Spartan lawyer Lycurgus, 9th century B.C.

Lysenkoism—much derided genetic doctrine supported by Stalin—named after Soviet scientist Trofim Lysenko (b. 1898)

Magpie—Mag, nickname of Margaret, + *pie*

Malamute—after the Malamutes, the Eskimo tribe that bred the dogs

Manichean—adherent of religious system of the early Persian prophet Manes

Mann Act—1910 law outlawing transporting women across state lines for immoral purposes—named for N.Y. Congressman Mann

Mannerheim Line—Finnish fortification along Russian-Finnish border before the Finno-Russian War—named for Baron von Mannerheim

Marconigram—Italian inventor Marchese Marconi (1874–1937)

Marian—of or pertaining to the Virgin Mary; or to various rulers such as Mary Tudor of England, or Mary, Queen of Scots

Marionette — puppet — from the French *Marionette*, little Marie or Mary

Maronite—member of the religious sect founded by 4th century monk St. Maron, from which may come, indirectly, the Italian *Marone!*

Marshall Plan—broad European Recovery Plan aiding Europe after W.W. II—proposed by General George C. Marshall (1880–1959), U.S. Secretary of State (1947–49)

Mau Mau—a terrorist—for the revolutionary Kenya society composed chiefly of Kikuyus, active in the 1950's

Maumet—a doll or other figure representing a human—after Mahommet, Mohammed, his image believed to be an object of worship

Mazarini—rich dark blue—for French cardinal Jules Mazarin (1602–61)

Meglip—a color vehicle for artists—possibly honoring a manufacturer named McGilp

Meker burner—similar to but hotter than the *Bunsen Burner*—named for 20th century chemist George Meker

Mengel module—tradename—interchangeable basic units of furniture manufactured by the Mengel Co. in 1946

Mergenthaler—linotype—named for Ottmar Mergenthaler (1854–99), its German-born U.S. inventor

MIG—Russian-built fighter, especially the MIG-15, named after designers *Mi*(koyan) and G(urevich)

Minniebush—not because it is a small shrub but because it's named for Scottish botanist Archibald Menzies (1754–1842)

Möbius strip, transformation—mathematics—German mathematician August Möbius (1790–1868)

Mohole—a hole bored through the earth's crust for geological study—Yugoslavia geologist A. *Mo*(horovicic) + *hole*

Mohorovicic discontinuity—geology (see above)

Montessori system—educational system for young children named for Italian educator Maria Montessori (1870–1952)

Montgolfier—balloon—honors Jacques Montgolfier (1745–99) and Joseph (1740–1810), inventor of the first practical balloon

Moog synthesizer—computer-like musical instrument—for its contemporary inventor Robert Moog

Mumetal—alloy—short for *Muntz metal* named for 19th century English manufacturer G. F. Muntz

Nasserism — pan-Arabism — Egyptian leader Gamal Abdel Nasser (1918–1971)

Nattier blue—soft blue—French painter Jean Nattier (1685–1766)

Nehru jacket—for Indian Prime Minister Jawaharlal Nehru (1889–1964)

Neroli oil—made from orange tree flowers—after *Neroli* Italian title of Anne Marie de la Tremoille, 17th century French princess

Nesselrode—preserved fruits and nuts used over desserts—invented by the chef of Russian Count Karl Nesselrode (1780–1862)

Nielson method—artificial respiration—after Holger Nielson its 20th century Danish inventor

Nielson rating—T.V. audience rating poll named for its devisor

Ninon—silk fabric—French modiste Ninon de L'Enclos (1620–1705)

Noisette—rose variety—after American plantsman Noisette, ca. 1816

Norman—after the 10th century Northmen or Scandinavians who conquered Normandy

Obie—Off-Broadway play award given by the *Village Voice*, "Off Broadway" suggesting "Obie"

Ordovician—geological time period—named for the ancient British tribe the Ordovices of Northern Wales

Otto—an early bicycle named for its inventor in about 1877

Paisleyism—recent movement led by Ulster clergyman Ian Paisley opposing cooperation with the Republic of Ireland

Parrot guns—American inventor Robert Parrot (1804–77)

Pavlovian—conditioned reflex—Russian physiologist Ivan Pavlov (1849–1936)

Peekskill Mts.—named for N.Y.'s Peeks Kill creek, in turn named for trader Jan Peek in 1665 (see *Pancake, Pa.*)

Perique—tobacco—from the nickname of its developer, Louisiana tobacco grower Pierre Chenet

Peronist—a follower of former Argentine dictator Juan Peron (b. 1895)

Perse—deep shade of blue or purple—from the Latin *Persicus*, Persian

Pressenda—violin—Italian craftsman Johannes Pressenda (1777–1854)

Priscian's head, to break—to break a grammatical rule—Priscian, 4th–5th century A.D. Latin grammarian

Proustian—pertaining to the writing of French novelist Marcel Proust (1871–1922); complex, obsessed with the past

Rachmanism—the practice of driving out low-paying tenants by harassment in the manner of British landlord Peter Rachmann

Rasputin—a spellbinding advisor—after Grigori Rasputin, peasant monk influential at the court of Russia's Czar Nicholas II

Remington rifle, typewriter—American manufacturer Eliphalet Remington (1793–1861) and family

Reuben—cartoonist of the year award made by the National Cartoonist Society —named for no particular Reuben so far as is known

Rhonddaed—lost—David Alfred Thomas (1856–1918), Lord Rhondda

Rob Roy — cocktail — nickname of Scottish outlaw Robert Macgregor

Roget—a thesaurus—English lexicographer Dr. Peter Mark Roget (1779–1869)

R.O.K.—a South Korean soldier—from Republic of Korea (called "Roks")

Roué—a rake—from the French *rouer*, "to break on the wheel," but the name first applied to companions of the Duc d'Orléans, ca. 1720

Sabin—sound absorption unit—American physicist W. C. Sabine (1868–1919)

Sacco-Vanzetti pencils—these are manufactured in Russia; originally they were named Hammer pencils for the American brothers who set up the first Soviet pencil factory in the 1920's, but the controversial U.S. trial and execution of Nicola Sacco and Bartolomeo Vanzetti in 1927 made far better propaganda, the two capitalists losing out to the two anarchists

Sadomasochism—disturbed personality condition—a combination of *sadism* and *masochism*, which are named for Count D. A. F. de Sade and L. von Sacher Masoch

Salk vaccine—polio—American scientist Dr. James E. Salk (b. 1914)

Sandwich coin—a coin with a core of one metal sandwiched between layers of another (see *Sandwich*)

Schuman plan—the plan for the European Coal and Steel Community proposed by French politician Robert Schuman (1886–1963) in 1950

Seashore test—psychological test of musical ability—American psychologist Carl Seashore (1866–1949)

Shamus—detective, policeman—anglicized form of the Irish *Seamus*, James

Sherman Antitrust Act—U.S. diplomat John Sherman (1823–1900)

Silurian—geological time period—for the ancient British Silures tribe

Singer—sewing machine—American inventor Isaac Singer (1811–75)

Siwash—Alaskan dog—for a northern Pacific Indian tribe

Skinner box—psychology—American psychologist B. F. Skinner (b. 1904)

Smersh—a contraction of the Russian N.K.D.V. *Smyrt Shpionaus* (Death to Spies), a top counterintelligence operation

Somerset—special padded saddle—for Lord Fitzroy Somerset (see *Raglan*)

Sorbonne—seat of the faculties of arts and letters of the University of Paris, founded as a theological college by Robert de Sorbon, 1257

Souvenir de Madame Salati-Mongellaz, Archduchesse Marie Immaculate—probably the longest named and most flattering of roses honoring people

Sproat—a specialized fishhook—19th century English angler W. H. Sproat

Stanislavski Method—acting—Russian actor and director Konstantin Stanislavski (1863–1938)

Stanley Cup—one of many hockey trophies named after their donators

Stovaine—anaesthetic—for its early 20th century French discoverer named *Fourneau* + coc*aine*; *Four* translated from French is *stove* in English, thus *stovaine*

Swartout—an embezzler—American embezzler Samuel Swartout, who absconded with one million dollars in 1838

Swiftean—satirical—English writer Jonathan Swift (1667–1745)

Tannhäuser—the opera takes its name from a 13th century German poet

Tasmanian devil—marsupial native to Tasmania, which was named for its discoverer Abel Tasman (1603–59)

Teepee project—monitoring system detecting nuclear explosions and rocket launchings, derived from Thaler's Project, which is named for Office of Naval Research scientist William J. Thaler

Therblig—a term used in time and modern study, the word an anagram of the name of American engineer F. B. Gilbreth (1868–1924) of *Cheaper By The Dozen* fame

Titoism—a form of nationalistic communism associated with Marshal Tito

(b. 1891), president of Yugoslavia since 1953

Tony—annual award for stage production and performances—from the nickname of Antoinette Perry (1888–1946), U.S. actor and producer

Tortoni—ice cream—likely for a 19th century Italian caterer in Paris

Townsend plan—U.S. pension plan proposed in 1934 by American reformer Francis Townsend (1867–1960); never passed

Trotskyism—form of communism advocated by Russian revolutionary Leon Trotsky (1879–1940)

Tuckermanity—extreme literary conventionality—American author Henry Theodore Tuckerman (1813–71)

Tupperism—trite moralistic philosophy—English preacher Martin Tupper (1810–89)

Turle knot—angling—19th century English angler Major W. G. Turle

Uncle Tom—a servile Negro—for the character in *Uncle Tom's Cabin*, said to be based on a real person

Vansittartism—doctrine advocating strong repression of Germany advocated by Sir Robert Gilbert, British 1st Baron Vansittart (1881–1957)

Verrazano-Narrows Bridge—the longest center span in the world, connecting Brooklyn and Staten Island in New York —honors Italian explorer Giovanni da Verrazano (c. 1480–1527?)

Very lights—signal flares—American inventor Edward Very (1847–1907)

Volsteadism—the policy of prohibition from the Volstead Act implementing the 18th amendment to the Constitution forbidding the sale of alcoholic beverages— introduced in 1919 by Congressman Andrew Joseph Volstead (1860–1946)

Walker Cup—golf trophy named for its donator, as are the *Curtis* and *Ryder* cups

Wankel—properly pronounced "Vankel"—rotary internal combustion engine invented by contemporary German Dr.

Felix Wankel, who sold certain rights to G.M. alone for $50 million

Watusi—frug-like dance—after the African people of Rwanda and Burundi

Whatman—artists' paper—18th century English manufacturer James Whatman

Widow—slang for champagne—for the French firm *Veuve* Cliquot

Woolworth's—5 & 10¢ stores—American merchant Frank Woolworth (1852–1919)

Xavierian—pertaining to Spanish Jesuit St. Francis Xavier (1506–52)

Yahoo—perhaps, before Swift coined it, "a degraded E. African tribe cited by early travelers," or "after the Cariban tribe the *Yahos*"

Zany—from the Venetian Italian *zanni*, for John

Ziegfeld—a great showman—U.S. impresario Florenz Ziegfeld (1867–1932)

Zolaesque—realistic literature—French author Émile Zola (1840–1902)

Zoroastrianism—Iranian religion said to be founded by 6th century Persian religious teacher Zoroaster

Zouave—woman's jacket—for Algerian Zouave tribe

Zulu—angling fly, hat—for African Zulu tribe

Additionally, like some in the main list and addendum, the following and numerous other words derive from common names or specific eponyms of unknown origin: Billyclub; Billygoat; Blackeyed Susan; Blue Funk; Bobwhite; Collie (Colin); Dandy; Davit (Davy); Dickey; Dobbin; Doll; Donkey; Floozy; Goblet; Goblin; Harlequin; Hillbilly; Humpty-Dumpty; Jackass; Jacket; Jay; Jimmy (burglar's tool); John Doe; Jolly Roger; Katydid; Mallard; Mollycoddle; Muggins; Ninny; Paddy Wagon; Rabbit; Tin Lizzie; Tommyrot; Sissy; Sweet William; Whippoorwill.

BIBLIOGRAPHY

It would be both impractical and of little interest to the general reader to list all the books, pamphlets, magazines and newspaper articles I have consulted over the many years spent in preparing this work. These include obvious sources ranging from *Who's Who*, the *New York Times' Index* and *Webster's Biographical Dictionary* to specialized dictionaries in the many fields covered and of course, biographies of the eponyms included. Rather, I have attempted to give a representative selection of the works and to provide the basic tools for those readers interested in delving deeper into the fascinating study of word lore. By using the word list following, for example, and checking out specific words in the appropriate sources, the investigator will find a wealth of little-known tales as fascinating to track down and more rewarding than the solution to any detective story. The *sine qua non* of this or any other English etymology still has to be the great ten-volume *Oxford English Dictionary*, which just this year became available in a *complete* one-volume edi-

tion. Almost indispensable, too, are *Webster's New International* and the *Random House Dictionary*, Eric Partridge's *Dictionary of Slang . . .* and Mitford Mathew's *Dictionary of Americanisms*. Embarking from these points, the student can next consult any or all of the listed reference works and go on from there to encyclopedias, biographies and even diaries and papers of the individuals concerned—or, in the case of contemporary figures, check them out in such reference works as *Who's Who*, the *New York Times' Index*, *The Reader's Guide to Periodical Literature* and *Current Biography*. Books of particular value are marked with asterisks, but a final note of caution must be sounded. No derivation should be accepted without confirming it first in several places—even when cited by the cautious *O.E.D.* Many of the works given in the large bibliography following are good in the main, yet err in numerous instances; others are almost invariably wrong, but uniquely arrive at the truth in enough cases to make them more than worthwhile.

Adams, James T. *Dictionary of American History*. 7 vols. New York: Charles Scribner's Sons, 1940.

American Heritage Dictionary of the English Language. New York: American Heritage Publishing Co., Inc., 1969.

Andrews, Edmond. *A History of Scientific English*. New York: R. R. Smith, 1947.

Aresty, Ester. *The Delectable Past*. New York: Simon & Schuster, Inc., 1964.

Asbury, Herbert. *Gangs of New York*. New York: Alfred A. Knopf, Inc., 1928.

—— *Sucker's Progress*. New York: Dodd & Co., 1938.

Asimov, Isaac. *Biographical Encyclopedia of Science and Technology*. New York: Doubleday & Company, Inc., 1964.

Audubon, John James. *The Birds of North America*. New York: The Macmillan Company, 1937.

Barrère, A. *Argot and Slang*. London: Whittaker & Co., 1887.

*Bartlett, John R. *Dictionary of Americanisms*. Boston: Little, Brown & Company, 1848, 1859, 1877.

Bartlett, John, ed. 13th edition. *Familiar Quotations*. Boston: Little, Brown & Company, 1955.

Bates, Marston. *Gluttons and Libertines*. New York: Random House, Inc., 1967.

*Berrey, Lester V. and Melvin Van Den Bark. *The American Thesaurus of*

Slang. New York: Thomas Y. Crowell Company, 1962.

Bloomfield, Leonard. *Language.* New York: Henry Holt & Co., 1933.

Bodmer, Frederick. *The Loom of Language.* New York: W. W. Norton & Company, Inc., 1944.

*Bombaugh, C. C. *Oddities and Curiosities of Words and Language.* Edited by Martin Gardner. New York: Dover Publications, Inc., 1961.

*Brewer, E. Cobham. A *Dictionary of Miracles.* Philadelphia: J. B. Lippincott Co., 1934.

*Brewer E. Cobham. *Dictionary of Phrase and Fable.* New York: Harper & Row, Publishers, 1964.

*——— *The Historic Note Book.* Philadelphia: J. B. Lippincott Co., 1891.

Bridgewater, William and Elizabeth J. Sherwood. *The Columbia Encyclopedia.* New York: Columbia University Press, 1950.

*Brown, Ivor. *A Word in Your Ear.* New York: E. P. Dutton & Co., Inc., 1963.

*——— *I Give You My Word.* New York: E. P. Dutton & Co., Inc., 1964.

*——— *Just Another Word.* New York: E. P. Dutton & Co., Inc., 1963.

*——— *Say the Word.* New York: E. P. Dutton & Co., Inc., 1964.

——— *Words in Our Time.* London: Jonathan Cape, 1958.

Butler's Lives of the Saints (revised). London: Burns & Oates, 1956.

Cambridge Modern History, The. 13 vols. Cambridge: Cambridge University Press, 1902–12.

*Chambers, Robert. *The Book of Days.* Philadelphia: J. B. Lippincott Co., 1899.

Crispo, Dorothy. *The Story of Our Fruits and Vegetables.* New York: Dorex House, 1968.

Diary of Samuel Pepys. Edited by Henry Wheatley. New York: Random House, Inc., 1954.

Dictionary of American Biography. 20 vols. New York: Charles Scribner's Sons, 1928–37. Supplement One, 1944; Supplement Two, 1958.

*Edwards, Gillian. *Uncumber and Pantaloon.* New York: E. P. Dutton & Co., Inc., 1969.

*Ernst, Margaret S. *More About Words.* New York: Alfred A. Knopf, Inc., 1964.

Evans, Bergen and Cornelia Evans. *A Dictionary of Contemporary American Usage.* New York: Random House, Inc., 1957.

*Evans, Bergen. *Comfortable Words.* New York: Random House, Inc., 1962.

*Farmer, John S. *Americanisms Old and New.* London: T. Poulter, 1889.

*Farmer, John S. and W. E. Henley. *Slang and Its Analogues.* 7 vols., New Hyde Park, N.Y.: University Press, 1966.

Farrow, Edward S. *Dictionary of Military Terms.* New York: Thomas Y. Crowell Company, 1918.

*Franklyn, Julian. *A Dictionary of Nicknames.* New York: British Book Centre, 1962.

Frazer, Sir James. *The Golden Bough.* 3rd ed. London: The Macmillan Company, 1951.

*Funk, Charles Earle. *A Hog on Ice.* New York: Harper & Brothers, 1948.

*———. *Heavens to Betsy! and Other Curious Sayings.* New York: Harper & Brothers, 1955.

*———. *Thereby Hangs a Tale.* New York: Harper & Row, Publishers, 1950.

*——— and Charles Earle Funk, Jr. *Horsefeathers and Other Curious Words.* New York: Harper & Brothers, 1958.

Funk, Wilfred. *Word Origins and Their Romantic Stories.* New York: Funk & Wagnalls, Inc., 1950.

Gardner, Martin. *Fads and Fallacies.* New York: Dover Publications, Inc., 1957.

Garrison, Webb. *What's in a Word?* New York: Abingdon Press, 1965.

———. *Why You Say It.* New York: Abingdon Press, 1955.

Goldberg, Isaac. *The Wonder of Words.* New York: Frederick Ungar Publishing Co., Inc., 1957.

*Goldin, Hyman E. *Dictionary of American Underworld Lingo.* New York: Twayne Publishers, Inc., 1950.

*Granville, Wilfred. *A Dictionary of Sailors' Slang.* London: Andre Deutsch, 1962.

Grolier Universal Encyclopedia. 1965 edition.

Groom, Bernard. *A Short History of English Words*. New York: The Macmillan Company, 1934.

*Grose, Francis (ed. Eric Partridge). *A Classical Dictionary of the Vulgar Tongue*. London: Routledge and Kegan Paul, 1963.

Guy, Christian. *An Illustrated History of French Cuisine*. New York: Bramhall House, 1944.

*Hargrove, Basil. *Origins and Meanings of Popular Phrases and Names*. Philadelphia: J. B. Lippincott Co., 1925.

Hart, James D., ed. *The Oxford Companion to American Literature*. New York: Oxford University Press, 1956.

Harvey, Sir Paul. *The Oxford Companion to Classical Literature*. Oxford: Clarendon Press, 1955.

———. ed., *The Oxford Companion to English Literature*. Oxford: Clarendon Press, 1955.

Hayakawa, S. I. *Language in Thought and Action*. New York: Harcourt Brace Jovanovich, Inc., 1949.

Haywood, Charles F. *Yankee Dictionary*. Lynn, Mass.: Jackson & Phillips, Inc., 1963.

*Holt, Alfred H. *Phrase and Word Origins*. New York: Dover Publications, Inc., 1961.

*Hunt, Cecil. *Word Origins, The Romance of Language*. New York: Philosophical Library, 1949.

Jennings, Gary. *Personalities of Language*. New York: Thomas Y. Crowell Company, 1965.

Johnson, Wendell. *People in Quandaries*. New York: Harper & Brothers, 1946.

Ketchum, Alton. *Uncle Sam, The Man and the Legend*. New York: Harper & Bros., 1959.

Kirk-Othmer. *Encyclopedia of Chemical Technology*. New York: John Wiley & Sons, Inc., 1963.

Lehner, Ernst and Johanna Ernst. *Folkways and Odysseys of Food and Medicinal Plants*. New York: Tudor Publishing Co., 1962.

Lyons, Albert. *Plant Names*. Detroit: Nelson, Bater & Company, 1907.

*Mathews, Mitford M., ed. *Dictionary of Americanisms*. Chicago: University of Chicago Press, 1951.

McWhirter, Norris and Ross McWhirter. *Guinness Book of World Records*. New York: Bantum Books, Inc., 1964.

*Mencken, H. L. *The American Language*. 3 vols. New York: Alfred A. Knopf, Inc., 1936–48.

Menke, Frank G., ed. *New Encyclopedia of Sports*. New York: A. S. Barnes & Co., Inc., 1963.

*Migliorini, Bruno. *Dal Nome Propio al Nome Comune*. Geneva: L. S. Olshki, 1927.

Montagne, Prosper. *Larousse Gastronomique*. New York: Crown Publishers, Inc., 1961.

Morris, Richard B., ed. *Encyclopedia of American History*. New York: Harper & Bros., 1953.

*Morris, William and Mary Morris. *Dictionary of Word and Phrase Origins*. 3 vols. New York: Harper & Row, Publishers, 1962.

New York Times Encyclopedic Almanac, 1970 & 1971.

*Nicholson, George, ed. *The Illustrated Dictionary of Gardening*. 4 vols. Mass., U.S.A., n.d. (ca. 1890).

Ogg, Oscar. *The 26 Letters*. New York: Thomas Y. Crowell Company, 1948.

Oliver, Raymond. *Gastronomy of France*. Cleveland: World Publishing Company, 1967.

*Onions, C. T. *The Oxford Dictionary of English Etymology*. London: Oxford University Press, 1966.

Oxford Dictionary of Quotations. London: Oxford University Press, 1954.

Oxford English Dictionary. 10 vols. London: Oxford University Press, 1888–1935.

*Partridge, Eric. *A Dictionary of Slang and Unconventional English*. New York: The Macmillan Company, 1961.

*———. *A Dictionary of the Underworld*. New York: The Macmillan Company, 1961.

———. *Dictionary of Clichés*. New York: The Macmillan Company, 1950.

*———. *From Sanskrit to Brazil*. London: Hamish Hamilton, 1952.

*———. *Name into Word*. London: Routledge and Kegan Paul, 1949.

*———. *Origins*. London: Routledge and Kegan Paul, 1958.

*Payton, Geoffrey. *Webster's Dictionary of Proper Names*. New York: World Publishing Company, 1971.

Pei, Mario. *All About Language.* Philadelphia: J. B. Lippincott Co., 1954.

*Pyles, Thomas. *Words and Ways of American English.* New York: Random House, Inc., 1952.

Radford, Edwin and M. A. M. Radford, eds. *Encyclopedia of Superstitions.* New York: Philosophical Library, 1945.

*Radford, Edwin. *Unusual Words and How They Came About.* New York: Philosophical Library, 1946.

*Reisner, Robert. *Graffiti.* New York: Cowles Book Co., Inc., 1971.

Roback, Aaron A. *Dictionary of International Slurs.* Cambridge, Mass.: Sci-Art, 1944.

Sabin, Robert, ed. *The International Cyclopedia of Music and Musicians.* New York: Dodd, Mead & Co., 1964.

*Shankle, George Earlie. *American Nicknames.* New York: Wilson, 1955.

*Shipley, Joseph T. *Dictionary of Word Origins.* New York: Littlefield, Adams & Company, 1967.

Simon, André. *A Concise Encyclopedia of Gastronomy.* New York: Harcourt Brace Jovanovich, Inc., 1946.

*Skeat, Walter W. *An Etymological Dictionary of the English Language* (revised). London: Oxford University Press, 1963.

Sledd, J. H. and Kolb, G. J. *Dr. Johnson's Dictionary.* Chicago: University of Chicago Press, 1955.

Smith, Elsdon C. *American Surnames.* Philadelphia: Chilton Book Company, 1969.

———. *Dictionary of American Family Names.* New York: Harper & Bros., 1956.

Sorel, Nancy Caldwell. *Word People.* New York: American Heritage Press, 1970.

Stevenson, Burton, ed. *Home Book of Quotations* (revised). New York: Dodd, Mead & Co., 1947.

*——— *The Home Book of Proverbs, Maxims, and Familiar Phrases.* New York: The Macmillan Company, 1948.

*Steward, George R. *American Place Names.* New York: Oxford University Press, 1971.

———. *Names on the Land.* Boston: Houghton, Mifflin Company, 1958.

Summer, William G. *Folkways . . .*

New York: Ginn and Company, 1906.

Taylor, Isaac. *Words and Places.* London: Dent, 1911.

Taylor, Norman, ed. *Taylor's Encyclopedia of Gardening.* Boston: Houghton Mifflin Company, 1961.

The Century Dictionary and Cyclopedia. New York: The Century Co., 1911.

The Encyclopedia Americana, 1957 edition.

The Encyclopedia Britannica, 1957 edition.

The Holy Bible. Revised Standard Version. New York: American Bible Society, 1952.

The 1971 World Almanac and Book of Facts.

The Random House Dictionary of the English Language. New York: Random House, Inc., 1966.

Wallis, Charles L. *Stories on Stone. A Book of American Epitaphs.* New York: Oxford University Press, 1954.

Wason, Betty. *Cooks, Gluttons and Gourmets.* New York: Doubleday & Company, Inc., 1962.

Webster's New Twentieth Century Dictionary, Unabridged. 2nd ed. New York: World Publishing Company, 1966.

*Weekley, Ernest. *Concise Etymological Dictionary of Modern English.* New York: E. P. Dutton & Co., Inc., 1924.

*———. *Romance of Names.* London: J. Murray, 1922.

*———. *Surnames.* London: J. Murray, 1917.

*———. *The Romance of Words.* New York: Dover Publications, Inc., 1961.

*Wentworth, Harold and Stuart Berg Flexner. *Dictionary of American Slang.* New York: Thomas Y. Crowell Company, 1960.

*Weseen, Maurice H., ed. *Dictionary of American Slang.* New York: Thomas Y. Crowell Company, 1934.

Who's Who in the U.S.S.R. New York: Scarecrow Press, Inc., 1966.

Wolcott, Imogene. *New England Yankee Cookbook.* New York: Coward-McCann, Inc., 1939.

Woodham-Smith, Cecil. *The Reason Why.* London: Constable, 1955.

THE AUTHOR

Robert Hendrickson, who was born and has lived all his life on Long Island, had through background and education been preparing to write *Human Words* for many years before the actual writing began. He is that rarest of all human animals, the self-employed writer. In fact, he has always made his living by the pen.

He graduated cum laude from Adelphi University with an A.B. degree in history and was awarded a Ford Foundation Fellowship for his M.A. in education. He has written for most of the important newspapers and magazines, including *The New York Times, Saturday Review, Sports Illustrated, The Saturday Evening Post, North American Review, New England Review, True, Redbook, Playbill* and many others.

Mr. Hendrickson and his wife and five children live in Far Rockaway, New York, and soon after publication of *Human Words* there will be a sixth.